THE KINGFISHER
CHILDREN's
ENCYCLOPEDIA

KINGFISHER
a Houghton Mifflin Company imprint
222 Berkeley Street
Boston, Massachusetts 02116
www.houghtonmifflinbooks.com

First published in 1998
This updated edition published in 2004
10 9 8 7 6 5 4 3 2

2TR/0305/CNC/("UV)NEW/128MA

LIBRARY OF CONGRESS CATALOGING-IN-PUBLICATION DATA
The Kingfisher children's encyclopedia / edited by
Sarah Allen.—1st ed.
p. cm.
Summary: Presents alphabetically arranged
entries on a variety of topics.
1. Children's encyclopedias and dictionaries. [1. Encyclopedias
and dictionaries.] I. Allen, Sarah.
AG5.K56 1998
031—dc21 97-47595
CIP AC

ISBN 0-7534-5767-9
ISBN 978-07534-5767-2
Printed in China

The web sites listed in this book are correct at the time of going to print. However,
due to the ever-changing nature of the Internet, web site addresses and content
can change. Web sites can contain links that are unsuitable for children. The publisher
cannot be held responsible for changes in web site addresses or content or for
information obtained through third-party web sites. We strongly advise that
Internet searches are supervised by an adult.

THE KINGFISHER
CHILDREN's
ENCYCLOPEDIA

KINGFISHER

BOSTON

Editorial Director
Jennifer Justice

U.S. Consultant
William E. Shapiro

U.S. Editor
Aimee Johnson

Managing Editor
Sarah Allen

Editorial team
Trevor Anderson, Max Benato, Jane Birch, Harry Boteler, Anne Davies,
Caitlin Doyle (new edition), Rebecca Fry, Tracey Kelly, Sarah Kovandzich,
Elizabeth Longley, Miren Lopategui, Rupert Matthews, Jayne Miller,
Susan Scharpf, Vicky Weber (new edition), Brian Williams

Creative Director
Val Pidgeon

Art Director
Mike Davis

Art Editor
David Noon

Design team
Liz Black, Pete Byrne, John Jamieson,
Ruth Levy, Emma Skidmore, Nina Tara

DTP Operator
Primrose Burton

Picture Research
Veneta Bullen, Davina Bullen,
Sophie Mortimer, Yannick Yago

Maps
Hardlines

Contributors & Consultants
Sue Aldridge, Sarah Angliss, Max Benato, Martyn Bramwell,
Enid Broderick, Tim Brown, David Burnie, Catherine Halcrow,
Jack Challoner, Michael Chinery, Maria Constantino, Chris Cooper,
Sophie Cooper, Alan Cowsill, Jeff Daniel, David Darling, Dougal Dixon,
John Farndon, Sue Gordon, John Graham, Ian Graham, Catherine Headlam,
Lesley Hill, Caroline Juler, Anne Kay, Robin Kerrod, J.C. Levy, Keith Lye,
Tim Madge, David Marshall, Bob McCabe, Iain Nicolson, Steve Parker,
Jane Parker, John Paton, Malcolm Porter, Sue Reid, Meg Sanders, Philip Steele,
Richard Tames, John Tipler, Ian Westwell, Brian Williams

INTRODUCTION

The word *encyclopedia* comes from the Greek for "all-round education," and *The Kingfisher Children's Encyclopedia* provides just that, in a way that is both accessible and stimulating.

This comprehensive encyclopedia covers everything from ancient history to up-to-the-minute developments in technology; from animal and plant life on Earth to plans for the next millennium in outer space. Geography, natural history, religion, the human body—all the topics that children explore at home and at school are included here.

We have rejected the "sound bite" approach to children's reference in favor of more in-depth coverage, which makes this encyclopedia perfect for project work and homework assignments. At the same time, the text is broken up into manageable paragraphs, suitable for both confident readers and younger browsers. Colorful photographs and superb illustrations and maps not only enhance the text, but also encourage readers to find out more for themselves.

Easy access is the key to this encyclopedia. Major subject areas, such as ELECTRICITY, have been arranged alphabetically, but the encyclopedia also has a comprehensive index so readers can refer quickly to related topics such as CIRCUITS and SWITCHES.

The encyclopedia has been written and checked by a team of specialist authors and consultants, and produced by a team of editors and designers with years of experience in children's reference. We are confident that it is a book in which children, and parents, can put their trust.

The Editors

HOW TO USE THIS ENCYCLOPEDIA

This book is fun and easy to use. All the entries are arranged alphabetically and provide information on two levels—quick reference and in-depth knowledge. The features explained in the guide below will help you get the most from your encyclopedia.

Eye-catching color photographs bring subjects to life

Main headings always appear in the top left-hand corner of the page for quick reference

All entries begin with a concise definition of the subject

Headings divide the text into self-contained sections

Authoritative text is approachable and packed with facts

Text can be read section by section or as a complete article

Colorful identification panels expand on the main topic by highlighting specific subjects

ARCHITECTURE

Architecture is the art of designing buildings and other structures so that they are soundly built, pleasing to look at, and suitable for their purpose.

The classical style uses flat beams, columns, and sculpture.

The style of architecture used for a building depends on the materials available, the architect's ideas, and what the building is going to be used for.

ARCHITECTS AT WORK
As well as needing to know a building's purpose, an architect must know the space allocated and how much money can be spent. Detailed models and drawings are produced for the builders, showing every part of the building and how it is to be constructed. These plans include practical features, such as heating and lighting systems, and pipe work for plumbing.

The Romans built aqueducts with curved arches and thick walls.

WESTERN STYLES
Western architecture began in Greece around 500 B.C. with the classical style. Pillars were built to precise mathematical patterns, such as those in the Parthenon, in Athens, built 447–438 B.C. From about 200 B.C., the Romans used curved arches and domes to make bridges and aqueducts.

Japanese castles have upturned roof edges and contrasting colors.

MEDIEVAL IDEAS
During the Middle Ages, the pointed arches and colorful stained glass of the Gothic style began to appear, especially

▲ Today's architects use modern materials to create startling new designs. Disney World's EPCOT Center in Florida is a geodesic dome. These are strong, lightweight domes with no internal supports or straight walls. They are constructed from ready-made sections.

in churches. Like the classical styles of the Romans and Greeks, the Gothic style has been used by many architects since then.

MODERN MATERIALS
Since the mid-1800s, inventions such as heating and lighting, and new building materials such as steel, plastic, and reinforced concrete, have revolutionized architecture. Steel-framed skyscrapers were first developed in the United States after the invention of the elevator in 1854. Modern architecture is often characterized by a combination of borrowed ideas with the newest materials and techniques.

India's Taj Mahal features domes and minarets typical of Islamic architecture.

HIGH-TECH BUILDINGS
The Sydney Opera House in Australia uses high-tech materials such as glass, concrete, and ceramics in its structure. Complex calculations were used to work out whether the materials would take the weight of its unusual component parts. Modern architects begin with a series of drawings, and use computers to calculate weights and forces. Then building begins.

The shells posed huge engineering problems—continuous glass surfaces enclose a steel structure

The white roofs were designed to look like boat sails in the harbor

Glass walls and tall office buildings dominate modern architecture.

Enlarged details focus on
distinctive elements and
provide further definition

Special picture features
complement the main text by
providing additional information

Running heads make
subjects easy to find

GOTHIC ARCHITECTURE

Chartres Cathedral in France was built between 1194 and
1260. It is a leading example of the Gothic style, which European
architects began using around 1150. The weight of the building
is carried by pillars and buttresses. This makes the structure
appear as delicate as possible. The architects used models
to test their designs before building in stone and wood.

Concise, informative
captions clarify
illustrations and
photographs

The wooden
spire is covered
with lead to
prevent it from
rotting

GIVING SUPPORT
Rows of delicately
decorated columns
and arches support
the upper walls.

The weight of
pinnacles adds
stability to the
corners

Stone vaulting,
or arched
ceiling, supports
the roof

The roof is made of
wood and copper

Chartres has
nearly 200
stained-glass
windows

Complex diagrams
are fully labeled for
easy comprehension

Beautifully detailed
artwork encourages
children to find
out more

Side aisles are
located under the
flying buttress

FLYING BUTTRESS
A flying buttress
allows architects
to build thin walls
with large windows.
The flying buttress
supports the roof
and arches, so that
the wall does not
need to be very thick.

Foundations use
as much stone as
the building

Vertical buttresses draw
the eye upward

FAST FACTS

• The Ancient Greeks
knew that straight lines
look bent from a distance,
so their temple pillars
lean slightly inward and
bulge a little at the top

• The first earthquake-
proof buildings were built
by the Inca. They carved
massive blocks of stone
to fit together perfectly.
In an earthquake, the
huge interlocking stones
jumped up, then just
settled back into place

Fact boxes contain
key dates, essential
data, and extra
information

SEE ALSO

Bridge, Construction,
Design, Greece (Ancient),
Seven Wonders of the
World, Skyscraper

Cross-reference boxes
guide the reader to
related articles and
subject areas

▲ Example of Aboriginal bark painting by the artist Milpurrur, Arnhemland, Northern Territory, Australia.

ABORIGINE

The term "aboriginal" is used to describe the native inhabitants of any country. The original people of Australia have come to be known as Aborigines.

The Aborigines arrived in Australia from Southeast Asia. They lived in nomadic groups, traveling around their territories, hunting with spears and boomerangs, fishing from canoes, and gathering fruits and vegetables. They had no written language, but passed on valuable knowledge by word of mouth and in song.

▶ A songman, accompanied by a didgeridoo player, tells stories through songs and poetry.

▲ These pieces of bark arc painted with clan signs of the Napaljarri people of the Northern Territory. Originally, there were about 500 Aboriginal clans, each with its own territory and complex language.

EUROPEAN SETTLERS

When the British settled in Australia in the late 1700s, there were more than 300,000 Aborigines. Many were killed by the settlers or driven off their land. By the mid-1900s, the Aboriginal population had dropped to around 45,000. Today, it has risen again to more than 250,000, and since the 1960s, the government has begun to recognize Aboriginal land claims.

THE ABORIGINAL WAY OF LIFE

The Aborigines traditionally lived out in the open or in shelters made from branches and bark. They wore little apart from body paint, ornaments, and waistbands, or coats made from kangaroo skin. Small numbers of Aborigines remain in the Outback (interior), living in the same way as their ancestors, but most have moved to towns and cities.

ART AND MUSIC

Aboriginal art mainly portrays religious beliefs in paintings on cave walls and on bark, or in poetry and songs. Today, some Aboriginal artists live by selling paintings made with earth pigments and charcoal. Aboriginal music is played on a didgeridoo (a long wooden pipe) and two clapping sticks, which are traditionally boomerangs.

▶ Witchetty grubs are the large, white larvae of the goat moth. The grubs are high in protein and are traditionally regarded as a great delicacy by Aborigines.

DREAMTIME

Rituals play an important role in Aboriginal beliefs, and body painting is a part of many rituals. Their beliefs are centered on the land and include an idea of eternity called Dreamtime—a world with no beginning and no end. Through Dreamtime, the ancestors—spirits that shaped mountains, rivers, plants, animals, and people—can be contacted.

SEE ALSO

Australia

AFRICA

Africa is the second largest continent and covers about one fifth of the Earth's land area. It includes 53 countries, six of which are islands.

▲ The Tuareg are a nomadic people who inhabit a large area of the Sahara Desert. Some still travel the desert with camel trains laden with goods such as dates and salt.

KEY FACTS

- **Area:** 11,819,340 sq. mi.
- **Population:** 841,628,000
- **Number of countries:** 53
- **Largest country:** Sudan (917,400 sq. mi.)
- **Smallest country:** Seychelles (176 sq. mi.)
- **Highest point:** Mount Kilimanjaro (19,340 ft.)
- **Largest lake:** Lake Victoria (26,200 sq. mi.)
- **Longest river:** Nile (4,135 mi.)

▼ Chobe National Park in Botswana is home to herds of elephants and impala. Many African countries have set aside large stretches of land as wildlife reserves.

The world's hottest continent, Africa has rain forests and tree-scattered grasslands (known as savanna), which are inhabited by a huge variety of wild animals. A third of Africa is covered by the Sahara, the largest desert on Earth.

HIGHS AND LOWS

Much of Africa is made up of plateaus (flat areas of land high above sea level). The plateau in East Africa is broken up by two extinct volcanoes—Mount Kenya and Tanzania's Mount Kilimanjaro—and the Great Rift Valley. The Rift is a long crack in the Earth's crust that runs from Mozambique through East Africa, the Red Sea, and into southwestern Asia. Elongated lakes have formed in the valley. Africa's natural features include the Nile, the longest river in the world, and Lake Tanganyika, the world's longest lake, which stretches for 420 mi. (676km).

HOT AND DRY

Because Africa lies across the equator, most of the continent gets extremely hot. The world's highest temperature in the shade was recorded in Libya in 1932 at 136°F (58°C). The land around the tropics, each side of the equator, is starved of rain and more than half of Africa's land has less than 20 in. (500mm) of rain per year.

RAIN FORESTS AND SAVANNA

In some regions, particularly around the equator in western and central Africa, rainfall is high and large rain forests grow. Monrovia, the capital of Liberia, averages 200 in. (5,140mm) of rain per year. Between the rain forests and the deserts are vast areas of tropical savanna. They are prone to drought, with a mixture of rainy and dry seasons.

MEDITERRANEAN SEA

RED SEA

ATLANTIC OCEAN

INDIAN OCEAN

N

miles
0   500
0   500
km

Countries and features labeled on map: MOROCCO, TUNISIA, ALGERIA, LIBYA, EGYPT, SAHARA DESERT, Nile, CAPE VERDE, MAURITANIA, MALI, NIGER, CHAD, SUDAN, ERITREA, SENEGAL, Niger, GUINEA, BURKINA FASO, Volta, NIGERIA, ETHIOPIA, IVORY COAST, LIBERIA, CAMEROON, CENTRAL AFRICAN REPUBLIC, SOMALIA, SÃO TOMÉ AND PRÍNCIPE, GABON, CONGO, Zaire (Congo), UGANDA, Mt. Kenya, KENYA, DEMOCRATIC REPUBLIC OF CONGO, Kasai, Lake Victoria, Lake Tanganyika, Mt. Kilimanjaro, GREAT RIFT VALLEY, TANZANIA, SEYCHELLES, COMOROS, ANGOLA, ZAMBIA, MOZAMBIQUE, MADAGASCAR, Zambezi, ZIMBABWE, NAMIB DESERT, NAMIBIA, BOTSWANA, KALAHARI DESERT, SOUTH AFRICA, Orange

THE ANIMAL KINGDOM

Gorillas, chimpanzees, monkeys, leopards, chameleons, and tropical birds live in Africa's rain forests; crocodiles and hippopotamuses wallow in the savanna's lakes and rivers. Antelope, giraffes, wildebeest, and zebras graze on the savanna alongside fierce predators, including lions and cheetahs. But this wildlife is threatened because people are destroying the animals' natural habitats. Many areas are now protected as national parks.

VEGETABLE AND MINERAL

Tea, cocoa, cotton, bananas, coffee, peanuts, rubber, and sugar are among the many crops grown in Africa. Mahogany and walnut wood are harvested from the rain forests. Minerals such as diamonds, gold, bauxite (aluminum ore), iron ore, and copper are mined for export. Oil is exported from Gabon, Libya, and Nigeria.

PEOPLE AND LANGUAGES

Many Africans live in tribal villages with their own cultures. Over 1,000 languages are spoken south of the Sahara alone. Country borders take little account of tribal differences, and in one country there may be many tribal groupings. ▶

KEY TO MAP

1 GAMBIA
2 GUINEA-BISSAU
3 SIERRA LEONE
4 GHANA
5 TOGO
6 BENIN
7 EQUATORIAL GUINEA
8 LESOTHO
9 SWAZILAND
10 MALAWI
11 BURUNDI
12 RWANDA
13 DJIBOUTI
14 MAURITIUS
15 WESTERN SAHARA (occupied by Morocco)

◀ The Korup National Park in Cameroon is one of Africa's densest rain-forest areas.

▲ The people of Tahoua in Niger build reed huts from locally available materials. Huts like these are typical of the Sahel region, an area of dry grassland on the edge of the Sahara.

RELIGIOUS BELIEFS

The people who live in northern Africa are mostly Arabs and Berbers who speak Arabic and follow Islam. The countries in southern Africa are largely populated by black Africans. Although most are Muslims or Christians, ancient local traditions still flourish, and more than a quarter of Africa's people follow local beliefs.

THE EARLY DAYS

Many scientists believe Africa is the continent where human beings first evolved, about two to four million years ago, but little is known about this very early history. Around 10,000 years ago, the Sahara had a moist climate, and many people lived there hunting animals, gathering plants for food, and later raising crops and herding cattle.

ANCIENT EGYPT AND ISLAM

In about 3100 B.C., Ancient Egypt—one of the world's greatest early civilizations— was formed out of Upper and Lower Egypt in northern Africa. It thrived on the fertile banks of the Nile until, in 30 B.C., it became part of the Roman Empire. In the A.D. 600s, the Arabs conquered northern Africa and converted the people of Egypt and its neighbors to Islam.

GREAT KINGDOMS

For centuries, people outside Africa knew little about the continent south of the Sahara. Between 1100 and 1500, Arabs trading for gold, ivory, and slaves brought back news of great empires

◄ The Masai people of East Africa are one of many tribal groups that live in Africa. A nomadic people, they raise cattle and hunt wild animals.

▲ The snakes coming out of the nostrils of this 18th-century Benin bronze head represent the belief that those with magical powers could release snakes to destroy their enemies.

in West Africa such as Ghana, Mali, Benin, Songhai, and Kanem. Kingdoms such as Benin, which was founded around A.D. 900, produced beautiful bronze sculptures that are highly prized today. Many of the sculptures symbolize the magical aspects of the obas (kings) of Benin. Kingdoms also arose in the south, such as the huge stone city of Great Zimbabwe. News of Africa's wealth attracted great curiosity among Europeans.

CONQUERING A CONTINENT

Portuguese explorers were the first Europeans to map the coasts of Africa. In 1498, the explorer Vasco da Gama rounded the tip of southern Africa, the Cape of Good Hope, on a journey that led him to discover a new route to India. Others later sailed on to East Africa. The Portuguese were also the first Europeans to export slaves from West Africa, a trade that continued until the 1800s.

EUROPEAN INFLUENCE

The Dutch took over many Portuguese trading posts during the 1600s. In 1652, they founded a settlement at Cape Town,

◄ About two thirds of Africa's people live in villages. In some areas, the markets are full of fresh produce, but in others, drought, poverty, and civil war have led to food shortages and widespread famine.

which became part of South Africa. By the late 1800s, almost all of Africa was ruled by European powers.

INDEPENDENCE
Colonial rule continued in Africa until the 1950s, when the colonies began to gain their independence. By the early 1970s, most countries were independent, but economic problems have led to instability in many areas. The Organization of African Unity (OAU), set up in 1963, aims to promote economic, political, and cultural cooperation across the continent.

▲ Harare, named after the African chief Neharawe, is the capital of Zimbabwe in southern Africa. It is a modern city, with tall skyscrapers and tree-lined streets.

A HARD WAY OF LIFE
Two thirds of the world's poorest countries are in Africa. Most Africans live in villages and farm the land. Poverty, disease, and war in many areas mean that people often do not reach old age. The average age a person in Sierra Leone, Uganda, or Malawi can expect to live is 45 years.

BUSY CITIES
Although most Africans live in villages, the continent has some large, bustling cities. Cairo, the capital of Egypt, is the largest, with a population of 6,800,000. Other important cities have grown up around ports, such as Cape Town in South Africa, Casablanca in Morocco, and Algiers in Algeria.

TIME OF EQUALITY
One of the most important events in Africa's history took place in 1994, when South Africa became a democracy under the leadership of Nelson Mandela. This finally ended apartheid, the official policy that separated people of different races from the whites. Since 1948, this policy had given whites power, while denying people of other colors basic rights in education, at work, and in everyday life.

▲ Soccer is one of a number of areas in which African countries are increasing their world presence. England's Liverpool Football Club paid $16 million for Senegal's El Hadji Diouf in 2002.

SEE ALSO
Civil war, Continent, Egypt, Egypt (Ancient), Empire, Explorer, Grassland, Kenya, Nigeria, Roman Empire, Slavery, South Africa, Sudan

AIRCRAFT

An aircraft is a machine that can fly through the air.
Airplanes, helicopters, gliders, airships, and balloons
are all different types of aircraft.

KEY DATES

1903 Orville and Wilbur Wright make first powered, controlled flight in their aircraft *Flyer 1*

1937 British engineer Frank Whittle designs jet engine. In 1939, the Heinkel He 178 is first jet plane

1939 American engineer Igor Sikorsky designs first modern helicopter

1947 In the United States, the rocket-powered Bell X-1 is first aircraft to fly at supersonic speed

1950s The first jet airliners, the DeHavilland Comet and Boeing 707, enter service

1970 The Boeing 747 "jumbo jet" enters service

1976 Concorde starts its supersonic service

The Wright brothers' *Flyer 1* made the first controlled, powered flight in 1903. It covered 118 ft.

The first aircraft were balloons and airships, which relied on lighter-than-air gases to keep them up. Sir George Cayley in Britain and Otto Lilienthal in Germany flew the first gliders in the 1800s. But it was the invention of the gasoline engine in the 1880s that led to powered flights in heavier-than-air craft, such as helicopters and airplanes.

A gas burner heats the air inside a hot-air balloon to make it rise. It can only go where the wind takes it.

EARLY AIRPLANES
Airplanes are aircraft with fixed wings that provide the upward force known as lift, engines to provide thrust, and hinged control surfaces for steering. Airplanes were developed at the start of the 1900s and were originally built with wood and canvas to make them light.

Like all gliders, the Delphin SF-34 uses air currents to stay airborno. Long, thin wings give maximum lift.

WHAT KEEPS A PLANE UP?
An airplane's wings hold it up as it flies. They have a curved upper surface and a flat lower surface. Air travels more slowly across the bottom of the wing than the top, creating an upward push.

PROPELLER VERSUS JET
All early airplanes had small piston engines that drove propellers. As the propeller turned, it pulled the aircraft forward. Most modern, large airplanes are powered by jet engines. These burn fuel and air to produce a stream of exhaust gases that thrusts the airplane forward. Jets provide more power, but are costly to maintain.

THE FUSELAGE
The main body of a plane is called the fuselage. It contains the crew, passengers, cargo, and equipment. The front of the fuselage houses the cockpit where the pilot sits, and at the rear is the tailplane, made up of a vertical fin and two small wings.

Helicopters, such as the Robinson R-22, can hover in midair and fly in any any direction.

Short wings

Piston engine

Propeller

◀ This Cessna monoplane (single-winged airplane) is a light aircraft that can carry up to three passengers. Short, straight wings provide good lift at moderate speeds. The piston engine turns the propeller that supplies the power to produce lift.

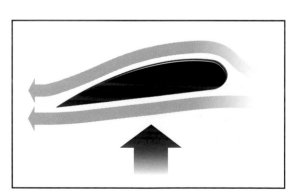

A wing is an airfoil, with a curved top and a flat underneath. Air travels farther and faster over the top of the wing than the bottom when the plane is in the air. As a result, air pressure is higher beneath the airfoil than above. This sucks the wing up, creating lift.

THE JET AIRLINER

Long-distance travel has been made cheap and reliable by jet airliners. The first wide-bodied jet was the Boeing 747, or jumbo jet. It can carry up to 560 passengers over 4,900 mi. (8,000km). Hundreds of 747s have been produced in nine different versions. Swept-back wings cut down air resistance, or drag, at high speeds. This reduces lift, however, so airliners need long runways and high speeds to take off and land. All new airplanes now have to meet strict environmental and safety rules.

Low-speed aileron

"Black box" records flight details

Rudder

Wing flaps used for takeoff and landing

Tail fin

Lever to lower landing gear (wheels)

Elevator

Parking brake

High-speed aileron

"False horizon" tells the pilot if the aircraft is flying level

Tailplane

Engine thrust levers

Fuselage

Skin of aircraft made of aluminum alloy

Passenger toilets

Wingtip fin reduces air resistance

Radar equipment

Cockpit

Cargo hold

Passenger seats

Engines

Fuel tanks located inside wings

FLY-BY-WIRE

Large flaps on the back edge of the wings increase lift and reduce speed for landing, while ailerons, elevators, and the rudder change direction. These are usually controlled by the pilot, but some modern aircraft use a system called "fly-by-wire," whereby the flaps and ailerons are adjusted with the help of computers.

FLYING AND FLOATING

Airplanes come in many forms. Jet airliners fly all around the world, while small airplanes, called light aircraft, ferry people, mail, and supplies over short distances. Some planes have floats instead of wheels to land on water. Military planes hold radar, cameras, and bombs. Biplanes (airplanes with double wings) are used by display teams and as crop dusters because they can fly slowly and make sharp turns.

Propelled by rocket engines, the supersonic X-15 holds the world air speed record at 4,520 mph, set in 1967.

Concorde is the world's only supersonic passenger airplane. Its cruising speed is about 1,350 mph.

The Harrier jump jet uses the downward thrust of its engines to rise straight up without needing a runway.

▶ The B-2 Stealth Bomber has flat, slablike panels made of special materials. These scatter beams from enemy radar, making the craft almost undetectable. Special paint also absorbs radar waves.

SEE ALSO
Airport, Balloon and airship, Engine, Helicopter, Transportation, Warfare

AIRPORT

Airports are places that airline passengers pass through and where freight is handled. They are also where aircraft are refueled, repaired, and maintained.

◄ Air traffic controllers are positioned high above the airport in the control tower. They use radar to track each plane on their screens and computers to plan flight paths. They radio their instructions to the pilots.

The biggest airports are like small cities with tens of thousands of people working in them 24 hours a day. Domestic airports handle passengers flying within the same country. People flying to or from another country go through international airports. Specialist services here include passport control, immigration, and customs.

ON ARRIVAL

All passengers arriving on international flights go through customs to make sure that they are not bringing anything illegal, such as drugs, into the country. Customs officers can stop and search anyone they think might be carrying illegal goods. They also check for goods on which travelers should pay tax.

KEEPING SAFE

Security at airports has become a high priority since the 1960s, as the number of terrorist attacks on planes has increased.

All passengers boarding a flight must go through a metal detector while their hand baggage is put through an X-ray machine. This is to make sure that they are not carrying any weapons or explosives onto the aircraft. International travelers also use passports to prove their identity.

CONTROLLING AIR TRAFFIC

Aircraft landing and taking off have to comply with air traffic control to make sure they do not collide, either on the ground or in the air. At very large airports, the area under air traffic control extends for hundreds of miles horizontally and thousands of feet vertically in all directions. Aircraft circle above the airport waiting for permission to land.

Aircraft taking off use a different runway from aircraft landing

ON LANDING

Airplanes land on runways and then taxi (move slowly) to a gate. Here, the doors of the aircraft can be opened safely. Passengers leave the aircraft with their hand baggage and either walk or are driven by bus to the main terminal buildings.

Control tower staff direct air traffic in the air and on the ground

Passenger terminal

Air bridges connect aircraft to the terminal gate

Aircraft are refueled between flights

Baggage and cargo are taken from the hold to the terminal

Service vehicles are used for carrying freight

SEE ALSO

Aircraft

ALLIGATOR AND CROCODILE

Alligators and crocodiles are large, scaly reptiles with powerful jaws. They live on the banks of rivers and in swamps, feeding on fish, mammals, turtles, and birds.

An alligator's lower teeth are not visible when its jaws are shut.

The fourth tooth on the lower jaw of a crocodile sticks out.

Closely related to alligators, caimans feed on fish and other prey.

The gavial has a long, thin, tooth-lined snout and feeds mainly on fish.

Alligators and crocodiles are some of the largest living reptiles on the planet—the biggest crocodiles can grow to around 23 ft. (7m) and weigh over 2,400 lb. (1,120kg). Alligators are usually smaller, and can be distinguished from crocodiles because they have a broader, flatter snout and their teeth are hidden when their jaws are closed. Caimans and gavials, alligators, and crocodiles belong to a group called crocodilians.

STRONG JAWS
Like crocodiles, alligators float with only the tip of their snout and their eyes protruding, waiting to pounce on prey. Although crocodiles have been known to attack humans, alligators rarely do so, even though their jaws are strong enough to crack the bones of an animal such as a pig. Alligators eat a wide variety of animals. Young ones feed on insects, crayfish, frogs, and minnows, while the diet of an adult may include waterbirds, turtles, and small mammals, including the occasional dog.

◀ A crocodile pounces on a wildebeest, seizing it in its strong jaws and spinning it around in the water.

ALLIGATOR HOLES
During the winter, alligators stay in the water to keep warm, burying themselves in mud or in holes they have made with their bodies. In times of drought, these holes are often the only places where water can still be found, and they are used as a refuge by alligators and other aquatic animals until the rain returns.

ENDANGERED CREATURES
There are 12 species of crocodile, but only 2 of alligator: the American alligator of the southeastern United States and the Chinese alligator of the Chang (Yangtze) River. All crocodilians are hunted for their skin and meat. Their habitats are also threatened; the American alligator was protected by law from 1969 to 1987.

DEVOTED PARENTS
Alligators lay between 30 and 80 eggs in a concealed nest. After incubating for 60 days in the heat of the sun, the young make high-pitched yelps from inside the eggs. The mother then scrapes away the sand and waits until the young hatch out to carry them to the water in her mouth. She watches over them in their first year.

Bones and scales act like armor

The fourth tooth of the lower jaw fits into a pocket in the upper jaw

SEE ALSO
Africa, Animal, Reptile, Swamp and marsh, United States of America

AMPHIBIAN

Amphibians are cold-blooded animals that are able to live both in water and on land. Most start life breathing through gills, but later develop lungs.

▲ The extraordinary Mexican axolotl salamander usually spends its life as a tadpole, breathing through gills.

Like many frogs, the European common frog has smooth, moist skin and long legs for jumping.

Like many toads, the European common toad has dry, lumpy skin and walks rather than leaps.

The long-tailed salamander's bright color helps it warn off predators.

Newts, such as this smooth newt, are salamanders that spend long periods in water.

Caecilians have no legs and live underground. They are found only in tropical areas, and many are blind.

Frogs, toads, salamanders, newts, and caecilians are all types of amphibian. They are cold-blooded creatures that rely on their surroundings for warmth, and are found in most parts of the world. Adult amphibians usually have soft, thin, moist skin that absorbs oxygen from the air, helping them to breathe. But some frogs and toads have thick, warty skin to help them survive in drier conditions.

JELLIED EGGS
The way amphibians breed and develop is unique in the animal kingdom. Females lay their jelly-covered eggs, called spawn, in water. These hatch into tadpoles, which develop limbs and lungs so that they can live on dry land. Some amphibians need only a small amount of water in which to lay their eggs. The tree frog lays its eggs on moist leaves and the male midwife toad carries the female's eggs on its back legs, dipping them into pools of water. The Australian gastric (stomach)-brooding frog swallows her eggs. Once they develop into froglets, they hop out of her mouth.

BIG EATERS
All amphibians are hunters. Many use their bulging eyes to track fast-moving prey, swallowing it whole. Small frogs and salamanders eat insects and tiny fish. Large toads gulp down mice and birds. They usually sit and wait, or crawl toward their prey, before lunging with mouth open. Some frogs and salamanders have a long, sticky-tipped tongue attached to the front of their mouth, which they can flick out to grab insects.

LEAPING FROGS AND TOADS
Over 80 percent of all amphibians are frogs and toads, known as anurans. They have long, five-toed back legs for leaping and shorter, four-toed front legs used to cushion the landing. There is no scientific difference between frogs and toads, but anurans with smooth, moist skin that usually jump are called frogs, and those that waddle and have drier, lumpy skin are called toads.

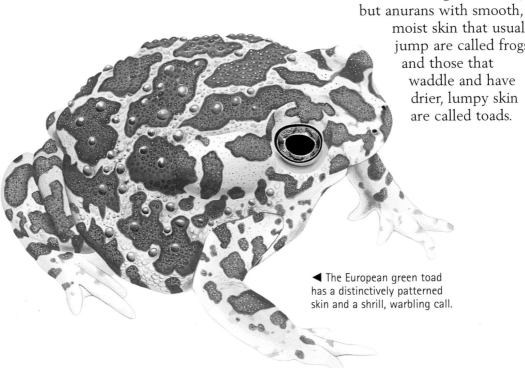

◄ The European green toad has a distinctively patterned skin and a shrill, warbling call.

THE GLANDS
Pores that hold the salamander's poison can be found across its back and on the sides of its head.

THE POISON
When the fire salamander is attacked by a predator, poison oozes out of the pores in its skin.

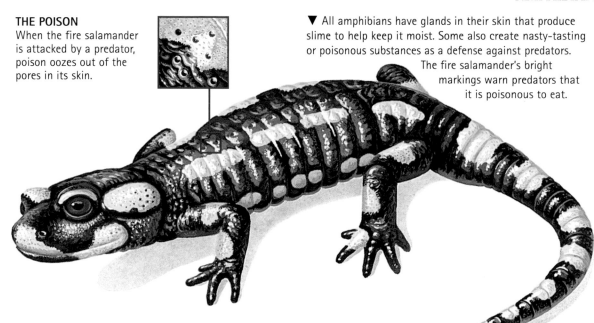

▼ All amphibians have glands in their skin that produce slime to help keep it moist. Some also create nasty-tasting or poisonous substances as a defense against predators. The fire salamander's bright markings warn predators that it is poisonous to eat.

SALAMANDERS AND CAECILIANS

Newts and salamanders (urodelans) have short limbs and long tails. Salamanders in Europe and North America that spend long periods in water are called newts. Most salamanders breathe with lungs and through their skin, although some have no lungs. Caecilians (apodans) are the third and smallest group of amphibians. They are wormlike, with blunt snouts for tunneling, tiny eyes, and wide mouths. They hunt mainly at night.

▼ The spectacled salamander has a bright red tail that it curls along its back when alarmed.

THE AMPHIBIAN LIFE CYCLE

When frogs mate, the male usually sits on the female's back for up to three days. As soon as the female lays her eggs in the water, the male releases sperm to fertilize them. The eggs hatch into tadpoles, which eventually metamorphose (change) into froglets (young frogs) and leave the water for life on land.

1 The female frog lays her eggs, or spawn, in large masses in a pond or stream. The eggs are protected by a special jelly.

2 The larvae, or tadpoles, develop inside the eggs. About a week later, the tadpoles hatch out and attach themselves to plants.

3 The tadpoles breathe through feathery gills and start to swim at about three days of age. They feed on waterweeds and algae in the water.

4 The tadpoles slowly turn into frogs, developing limbs and lungs so that they can live on land. Their tails are absorbed into their bodies.

5 Fully grown, the young frogs leave the water. They feed on small insects and will not reproduce themselves until they are a year old.

SEE ALSO
Animal, Frog and toad, Hibernation

ANIMAL

Animals are multicellular living creatures that can move, eat food, sense their surroundings, and reproduce, usually by mating with a partner.

The rotifer is one of the smallest animals—seen only through a microscope.

The octopus is a type of mollusk, a group that also includes snails and squid.

The angelfish is just one of 20,000 different species of fish.

The shield bug belongs to the largest group—insects, with over a million species.

The peacock is one of 9,000 species of bird, most of which can fly.

The rabbit is a mammal. Its young are fed on milk produced by the mother.

More than a million kinds of animal live on Earth, and many more are discovered each year. Every animal is unique, but there are common features that set creatures in the animal kingdom apart from other living beings such as plants, fungi, and single-celled organisms.

THE MATING GAME
Like all living creatures, animals must reproduce. Most do this by mating with a partner. It is usually the female that chooses a mate, so many males are brightly colored or use elaborate courtship rituals to attract a suitable partner.

BILLIONS OF TINY CELLS
All adult animals are multicellular, which means they are made up of more than one cell. Some animals, such as rotifers and hydras (aquatic animals), have just a few dozen cells, but large animals, such as humans, are much more complex and can have up to 50 billion cells.

▲ The galago, or bush baby, is a nocturnal animal, so it comes out at night to feed. Huge, round eyes, a good sense of smell, and an excellent sense of hearing are essential for hunting prey at night.

FOOD FOR LIVING
Unlike plants, animals cannot make their own food—they must eat ready-made plant or animal food. Most have some sort of mouth, but the way in which the food is broken down inside their body varies. Birds have no teeth, so the food is ground by stones in their stomach. Snakes swallow prey alive and whole, digesting it slowly with strong juices. The tapeworm has no mouth, but lives in another animal's intestines, soaking up digested food through its skin.

MOTHERLY LOVE
Many animals go to great lengths to keep their young alive. For example, the female scorpion, best known for her sting, is a very caring mother. She carries her newborn young on her back for up to 12 days, until they can fend for themselves.

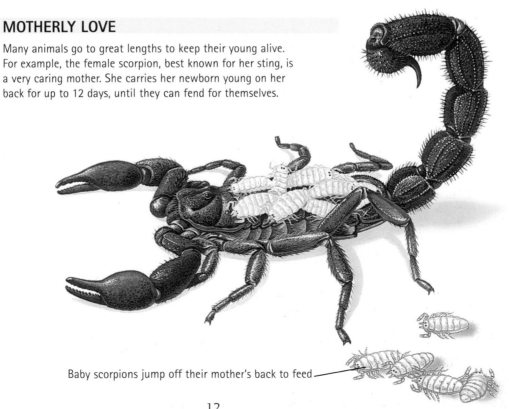

Baby scorpions jump off their mother's back to feed

NERVES AND SENSES

All animals sense their surroundings with a set of nerves and sense organs that are adapted to suit the way they live. For example, many night hunters have whiskers to find their way in the dark, and some snakes have infrared sensors to "see" the body heat of their prey. Sharks can smell blood in the water many miles away and home in on it accurately, while migrating animals, such as gray whales, have an extra sense that allows them to travel great distances without getting lost.

ON THE MOVE

All animals, from the slowest snail to the fastest gazelle, move, usually by using an efficient set of muscles. The way they move varies: some crawl or walk, some slither, while others hop or run—in the case of crabs, sideways. Even a drifting jellyfish pulsates to move itself up or down in the water. This ability to move has allowed some species to spread all over the world. Some animals, such as sponges and corals, can only move when young, and remain in one place as adults. ▶

The golden lion tamarin is a rare monkey, another type of mammal.

THE FASTEST ANIMAL

Predatory animals use many methods to catch their food. Some use stealth, others use camouflage, but the cheetah's strategy is speed. It is the fastest animal on four legs, reaching speeds of 70 mph (110kph) in mid-chase. Its favorite food is the young antelope that graze on the African savanna. But a cheetah's stamina is poor—if it does not catch the antelope in the first few hundred yards, the prey usually gets away.

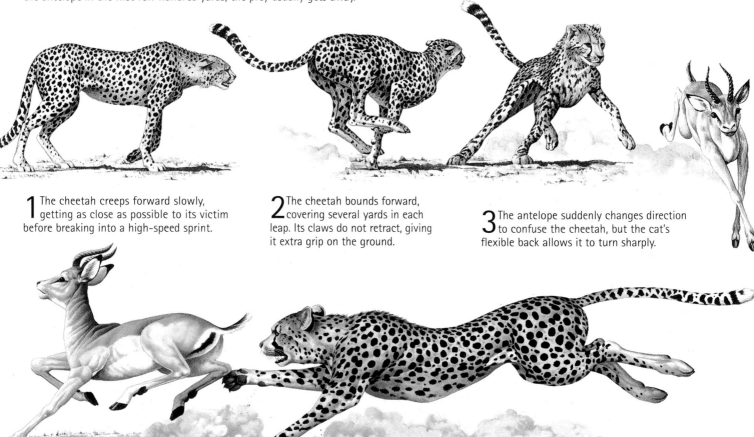

1 The cheetah creeps forward slowly, getting as close as possible to its victim before breaking into a high-speed sprint.

2 The cheetah bounds forward, covering several yards in each leap. Its claws do not retract, giving it extra grip on the ground.

3 The antelope suddenly changes direction to confuse the cheetah, but the cat's flexible back allows it to turn sharply.

4 The gap closes. The cheetah swipes with strong paws at the antelope's legs to knock it off balance and bring it down, before killing it with a bite.

A QUESTION OF CLASS

Zoologists divide the animal kingdom into about 30 major groups, or phyla (the largest of which are shown in this chart). Each group, or phylum, can be further divided into subphyla, classes (shown), then orders, families, genuses, and species (not shown). Animals from different species cannot breed together, except in rare circumstances.

INVERTEBRATES
(animals without backbones)

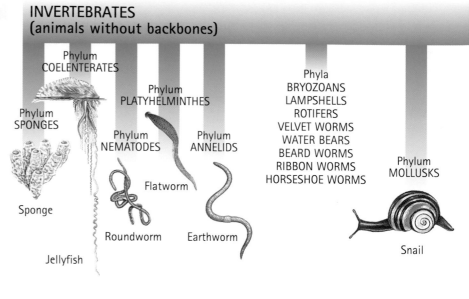

Phylum
COELENTERATES

Phylum
PLATYHELMINTHES

Phylum
SPONGES

Phylum
NEMATODES

Phylum
ANNELIDS

Phyla
BRYOZOANS
LAMPSHELLS
ROTIFERS
VELVET WORMS
WATER BEARS
BEARD WORMS
RIBBON WORMS
HORSESHOE WORMS

Phylum
MOLLUSKS

Sponge

Flatworm

Roundworm

Earthworm

Snail

Jellyfish

▲ The marbled polecat belongs to a family of carnivores (meat-eating mammals) that includes weasels, badgers, otters, and skunks. All of these animals have short legs and long, flexible bodies.

FAMILY GATHERINGS

Zoologists classify, or group, animals by their common features. For example, all insects have six legs, all birds have feathers, and all mammal mothers feed their young on milk from their own bodies. The grouping of animals in this way is known as taxonomy. It helps zoologists to work out when animals first appeared on Earth, how they have changed through time, and which creatures are closely related.

WITH BACKBONES

All animals can be divided into two main groups: those with backbones, called vertebrates, and those without backbones, called

invertebrates. Vertebrates include fish, amphibians, reptiles, birds, and mammals. All other animals are invertebrates.

THE MYSTERIOUS BARNACLE

It can be difficult for zoologists to tell if some creatures are animals at all. For example, an acorn barnacle attached to a rock on the seashore does not even look alive, let alone animal-like. By studying its life cycle, zoologists discovered that before the barnacle attaches itself to a rock, it looks like a young shrimp. This proved that barnacles are crustaceans, along with crabs and lobsters.

▲ Acorn barnacles

WHO IS RELATED TO WHOM?

Scientists study the genetic makeup of animals compared to other animals to reveal who is related to whom. For many years zoologists argued over whether red pandas were related to bears, raccoons, or

► The anteater is an edentate. This is an order of mammal with few or no teeth. Other members of the group include sloths, which are herbivores (plant-eaters) and armadillos. The anteater is an insectivore (insect-eater), living solely on ants and termites, which it sniffs out with its snout and licks up with its long, sticky tongue. Its powerful front claws are used for digging.

Phylum
ARTHROPODS

Class
MYRIAPODS

Class
CRUSTACEANS

Class
ARACHNIDS

Class
INSECTS

Crab

Spider

Centipede

Butterfly

Phylum
ECHINODERMS

Starfish

Phylum
CHORDATES

Subphylum
VERTEBRATES (animals with backbones)

Subphylum
PROTOCHORDATES

Class
CHONDRICHTHYANS

Class
AMPHIBIANS

Class
BIRDS

Class
MAMMALS
(including
humans)

Class
FISH

Frog

Eagle

Sea squirt

Class
REPTILES

Parrotfish

Crocodile

Great white shark

mongooses. Genetic studies finally revealed that red pandas belong to the raccoon family. In another study, the kiwi, thought to be one species of bird, was shown to have two species—they look very similar, but cannot breed together.

DEEP-SEA TREASURES

In the 1970s, when scientists sent deep-sea equipment down to new depths, over 200 new animal types were discovered living around deep-sea hydrothermal vents (jets of hot, mineral-rich water spurting out from the sea floor). Transparent fish, two-yard-long tube worms, plate-sized clams, and blind white crabs were among the amazing finds.

SPECIES UNDER THREAT

Many animals in the world are now rare or nearly extinct. Once an animal species has

died out, it is lost forever, which is why zoos have breeding programs for threatened species. There may be more than five million animal species still waiting to be discovered by science. These too are under threat as many natural areas, especially the tropical rain forests and coral reefs, are destroyed or polluted.

▶ The giraffe is the tallest animal. It is a mammal and grows up to 18 ft. (5.5m) tall. It lives in Africa and eats thorny acacia leaves, which it strips from the branches with its 20 in. (50cm)-long tongue.

▲ Some animals, called detritivores, help to recycle other animals' waste products. The dung beetle eats animal dung. Some species eat the dung where they find it, while others dig a hole and bury it to eat later.

AMAZING ANIMAL FACTS

• Insects are the most numerous animals on Earth. It is estimated that for every human there are 200 million insects

• The largest animal to have lived on Earth is the blue whale. Belonging to the order of mammals called cetaceans, blue whales can grow to over 100 ft. (30m) in length

• The fastest animal is the peregrine falcon. It can swoop at up to 220 mph (350kph)

• Unlike most animals, the sponge can regrow its entire body from a tiny fragment of itself

• The giant squid has the largest eye of any animal that has ever lived: 15 in. (40cm) in diameter, ten times the size of a human eye

SEE ALSO

Amphibian, Bird, Conservation, Crab, Evolution, Fish, Insect, Mammal, Microorganism, Reptile, Worm, Zoology

ANTARCTICA

Antarctica is the fifth largest continent. It surrounds the South Pole, and 98 percent of it lies buried beneath a thick sheet of ice.

▲ Norwegian explorer Roald Amundsen was first to reach the South Pole on December 14, 1911.

KEY FACTS

• **Area:** 5,405,442 sq. mi.

• **Population:** no permanent population

• **Number of countries:** none, although some countries claim sections of the continent

• **Highest point:** Vinson Massif (16,865 ft.)

• **Largest ice shelf:** Ross (74,000–80,309 sq. mi.)

• **Position of South Pole:** 767 mi. from the nearest coastline

Only a few mountains and barren, rocky areas show above the ice that hides Antarctica. The thickness of the polar ice sheet makes Antarctica the highest continent—and also the windiest. It is largely a frozen desert, with snowfall near the Pole equivalent to less than 6 in. (150mm) of water per year. The world's coldest air temperature, –128.6°F (–89.2°C), was recorded there.

FIRE AND ICE
A string of mountains cuts across the icy mass. On their eastern side, near the coast, the ice sheet reaches depths of 15,750 ft. (4,800m). Ross Island, to the west, holds the active volcano Mount Erebus. Ice flows down to the coast as glaciers and spreads out as huge ice shelves over the sea. When the ice becomes too heavy, parts break away to form enormous, flat-topped icebergs up to 200 ft. (60m) high and many miles long.

FUR AND FEATHERS
Antarctica has few land animals because, even in the summer, most of the continent is covered with ice. The animals live mainly in the air or sea and have thick fur,

◄ Two emperor penguins with their chick. To withstand the winter cold, emperors have very dense feathers and large fat reserves. They also huddle together in groups of up to 5,000 birds to keep warm.

feathers, or blubber (fat) to keep them warm. The ocean is home to many types of krill (tiny shrimplike creatures), squid, fish, seals, whales, and eight types of penguin. Antarctic birds include the predatory skua and large-winged albatross.

STUDIES ON ICE
Antarctica has a temporary population of up to 10,000 scientists from 18 countries. Their interests vary from space research to microbiology, and all must abide by the Antarctic Treaty. This agreement bans the mining of valuable mineral resources buried beneath the ice, and prevents any military or industrial activities on the continent. Up to 10,000 tourists also visit Antarctica each year during the summer.

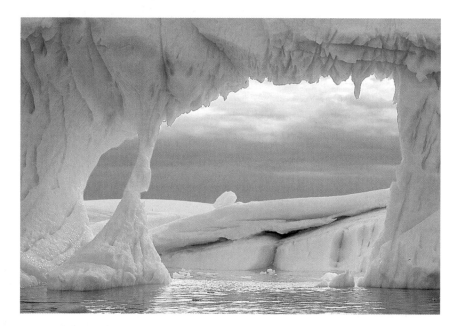

◄ Icebergs break away from the ice shelves that surround Antarctica. The ice builds up in layers over thousands of years.

SEE ALSO
Animal, Bird, Climate, Conservation, Desert, Explorer, Glacier

ARCHAEOLOGY

Archaeology is the study of the remains of the past that people have left behind them, such as objects and buildings. Often remains are buried or sunken.

CHINA'S BURIED ARMY

In 1974, thousands of life-size clay soldiers were found near the tomb of Shi Huangdi, the first emperor of the Qin Dynasty in China who died in 210 B.C. They were part of a massive burial complex built to protect the emperor in the afterlife.

1 Archaeologists use computerized equipment to find buried objects.

2 The site is divided into a grid with string. Squares are excavated one by one. Topsoil is removed with diggers and trowels.

3 Finds are cleaned by carefully brushing away soil. Each find is recorded and numbered before it is removed.

4 The position of an object can reveal important information.

5 Objects are carefully examined before being restored and preserved. They can then be put on display.

By studying objects from the past, such as buildings, pottery, weapons, and bones, archaeologists can learn about vanished civilizations. Archaeology can take us back to a time before people began writing, more than 5,000 years ago.

CLUES TO THE PAST

To know where to dig, archaeologists often start from a small clue such as a coin or a fragment of pottery. Many archaeologists now work on rescue digs—recording a site before it is destroyed, usually by being built on. Aerial photography and scanners reveal what is under the ground.

SORTING THE FINDS

Finds are sorted by type and age. For objects up to 50,000 years old, a technique called radiocarbon dating is used. This measures the remaining carbon content. X rays can show up faded details on pottery, and tests on bones can reveal the illnesses people suffered from. Wood objects can be dated by dendrochronology—a technique that compares the tree rings.

LOST CITIES

Sites may be as small as a grave or as large as an entire city. The ancient city of Troy, for example, was uncovered in Turkey by German archaeologist Heinrich Schliemann in 1870, after years of searching. Many sites, however, are discovered by accident. The Indus Valley civilization in Asia, which was destroyed in about 1700 B.C., was found by chance in the 1920s by railroad workers.

▲ An Egyptian mummy, or preserved body, from about 600 B.C. Remains like this reveal a lot about the lives of ancient people.

◄ A Minoan vase from about 1500 B.C., found on the island of Crete. Distinctive styles in art and pottery allow archaeologists to identify different groups of people.

SEE ALSO

Aztec, Babylon, China, Egypt (Ancient), Greece (Ancient), Roman Empire

ARCHITECTURE

Architecture is the art of designing buildings and other structures so that they are soundly built, pleasing to look at, and suitable for their purpose.

The classical style uses flat beams, columns, and sculpture.

The Romans built aqueducts with curved arches and thick walls.

Japanese castles have upturned roof edges and contrasting colors.

India's Taj Mahal features domes and minarets typical of Islamic architecture.

Glass walls and tall office buildings dominate modern architecture.

The style of architecture used for a building depends on the materials available, the architect's ideas, and what the building is going to be used for.

ARCHITECTS AT WORK
As well as needing to know a building's purpose, an architect must know the space allocated and how much money can be spent. Detailed models and drawings are produced for the builders, showing every part of the building and how it is to be constructed. These plans include practical features, such as heating and lighting systems, and pipe work for plumbing.

WESTERN STYLES
Western architecture began in Greece around 500 B.C. with the classical style. Pillars were built to precise mathematical patterns, such as those in the Parthenon, in Athens, built 447–438 B.C. From about 200 B.C., the Romans used curved arches and domes to make bridges and aqueducts.

MEDIEVAL IDEAS
During the Middle Ages, the pointed arches and colorful stained glass of the Gothic style began to appear, especially

▲ Today's architects use modern materials to create startling new designs. Disney World's EPCOT Center in Florida is a geodesic dome. These are strong, lightweight domes with no internal supports or straight walls. They are constructed from ready-made sections.

in churches. Like the classical styles of the Romans and Greeks, the Gothic style has been used by many architects since then.

MODERN MATERIALS
Since the mid-1800s, inventions such as heating and lighting, and new building materials such as steel, plastic, and reinforced concrete, have revolutionized architecture. Steel-framed skyscrapers were first developed in the United States after the invention of the elevator in 1854. Modern architecture is often characterized by a combination of borrowed ideas with the newest materials and techniques.

HIGH-TECH BUILDINGS
The Sydney Opera House in Australia uses high-tech materials such as glass, concrete, and ceramics in its structure. Complex calculations were used to work out whether the materials would take the weight of its unusual component parts. Modern architects begin with a series of drawings, and use computers to calculate weights and forces. Then building begins.

The shells posed huge engineering problems— continuous glass surfaces enclose a steel structure

The white roofs were designed to look like boat sails in the harbor

The wooden spire is covered with lead to prevent it from rotting

GIVING SUPPORT
Rows of delicately decorated columns and arches support the upper walls.

The weight of pinnacles adds stability to the corners

GOTHIC ARCHITECTURE

Chartres Cathedral in France was built between 1194 and 1260. It is a leading example of the Gothic style, which European architects began using around 1150. The weight of the building is carried by pillars and buttresses. This makes the structure appear as delicate as possible. The architects used models to test their designs before building in stone and wood.

Stone vaulting, or arched ceiling, supports the roof

The roof is made of wood and copper

Chartres has nearly 200 stained-glass windows

Side aisles are located under the flying buttress

FLYING BUTTRESS
A flying buttress allows architects to build thin walls with large windows. The flying buttress supports the roof and arches, so that the wall does not need to be very thick.

Foundations use as much stone as the building

Vertical buttresses draw the eye upward

FAST FACTS

• The Ancient Greeks knew that straight lines look bent from a distance, so their temple pillars lean slightly inward and bulge a little at the top

• The first earthquake-proof buildings were built by the Inca. They carved massive blocks of stone to fit together perfectly. In an earthquake, the huge interlocking stones jumped up, then just settled back into place

SEE ALSO

Bridge, Construction, Design, Greece (Ancient), Seven Wonders of the World, Skyscraper

ARCTIC

The Arctic is the area within the Arctic Circle—an imaginary line around the northern part of the globe with the North Pole at its center.

The Arctic is made up of the frozen Arctic Ocean, the surrounding seas and small islands, and the northern parts of Canada, Alaska, Russia, Finland, Sweden, Norway, and Greenland.

LAND OF THE MIDNIGHT SUN

Temperatures creep above freezing point for only about four months of the year. There are some days during the summer when areas near the North Pole are in constant daylight because the sun never sets. This is why the Arctic is sometimes known as the Land of the Midnight Sun.

TUNDRA LIFE

Treeless plains, or tundra, cover the land. In the summer, these plains are home to animals such as reindeer, lemmings, musk oxen, and Arctic hares, which graze on scrubby plants and shrubs. Migratory birds, such as the Arctic tern, return from winter homes to breed in the short warm season.

▲ Arctic hares live on the tundra. In summer, their fur is brown. They grow white coats in the winter.

THE DARK OF WINTER

Wintertime in the Arctic is cold, dark, and long. For a short time the sun does not come above the horizon at all. The ocean is frozen and the tundra snow-covered, with only a few mosses and lichens growing. Most animals and birds migrate south until summer returns. Polar bears thrive in these harsh conditions, hunting seals and catching fish in the icy water.

▼ An airplane arrives with supplies for the store at Savissivik, Greenland. Aircraft are a vital link for scattered settlements around the Arctic.

PEOPLE IN THE ARCTIC

A number of different people live in the Arctic, including the Inuit of Greenland, Canada, and northeast Asia and the Sami (Lapps) of Scandinavia. Those on the coast live by hunting and fishing. Those living inland hunt wild caribou or, like the Nenet tribe from Siberia in northern Russia (below), herd reindeer for a living.

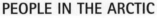

SEE ALSO

Animal, Asia, Canada, Climate, Magnetism, Migration, North America, Ocean and sea, Russia and the Baltic States, United States of America

ARGENTINA

Bordered by the Andes Mountains to the west, Argentina is the second largest country in South America and the eighth largest in the world.

Area: 1,056,600 sq. mi.
Population: 37,812,817
Capital: Buenos Aires
Language: Spanish
Currency: Argentinian peso

Argentina has two warm and rainy regions in the north: the Gran Chaco and Mesopotamia. The central areas are made up of a fertile, grassy plain called the Pampas, while Patagonia in the south is largely desert. In the far south is the cold and windswept land of Tierra del Fuego.

UNIQUE WILDLIFE
Jaguars, monkeys, and tapirs are found in rain forests in the north. Patagonia is home to unique animals such as the pudu, a tiny deer, and rhea, a flightless ostrich-like bird.

TOWN DWELLERS
Most Argentinians are of European descent, with *mestizos* (people of mixed European and American Indian descent) making up about 15 percent. Skilled cowboys, known as *gauchos*, herd cattle across the plains. However, almost 90 percent of the population lives in cities and towns. Many people work in meat-packing industries and in factories using farm products, including wool and hides.

SPANISH TREASURE SEEKERS
Spanish explorers reached Argentina in 1516. They were looking for treasure and they named the country after *argentum*, the Latin word for "silver." European

▲ Cacti flourish in the warm, dry air of the plateaus (flat areas of land high above sea level) in the Andes Mountains. Many species of cactus grow across Argentina.

▲ Argentina's capital, Buenos Aires, whose name means "favorable winds," is one of the world's great ports.

settlers arrived soon afterward and became rich by farming the fertile land.

MODERN TIMES
In 1816, Argentina declared independence after almost 300 years of Spanish rule. Since the 1930s, the country has faced many problems, including harsh military rule and high unemployment. In 1982, Argentina invaded the Falkland Islands, a British dependency, but was defeated. Elections in 1983 ended military rule.

◀ *Gauchos* work on the huge cattle ranches of the pampas. They are regarded as folklore heroes.

SEE ALSO
Grassland, South America

ART

Art can be any creative work used to portray images and to express feelings—from drawing, painting, and sculpture to architecture and computer graphics.

Japanese silk-screen prints, like this one from the 1800s, greatly influenced Western art in the 1900s.

Native American art, such as this mask carved around 1850, combines geometric styles with strong colors.

This pot by Clarice Cliff is typical of the 1930s' art deco style, with its bold lines, colors, and shape.

The first examples of art were cave paintings and images carved out of stone, the oldest of which were made about 40,000 years ago. Most early art was dedicated to gods, because religion and worship were important influences, but over the centuries new styles of art have evolved.

CLASSICAL STYLE

It was during the Renaissance, about 1300–1600, that the word "artist" was first used. Before that, painters were thought of merely as skilled craftsworkers. Renaissance means rebirth, and artists such as Michelangelo and Leonardo da Vinci took their ideas from the classical lines of the Ancient Greeks and Romans.

PAINTING FROM LIFE

The Renaissance artists were the first to use live models. By using light and shade, these artists gave their images depth, resulting in a three-dimensional appearance on the canvas. They also began to use perspective to indicate whether objects were near or far.

STRONG FEELINGS

In the late 1500s, art started to become more personal. Scientific advances made people question their religious beliefs, and this was reflected in the art of the baroque

▲ René Magritte's *The False Mirror* (1928) is typical of his work, which often put together two ordinary images to produce something dreamlike and surreal.

movement. Caravaggio's *The Death of a Virgin* was rejected by the priest who commissioned it, because it showed the Virgin Mary as an old woman. Artists like Rubens created paintings—many large-scale—full of passion and drama.

EVERYDAY LIFE

During the 1600s, artists began to paint everyday life and ordinary people. Before then, only important people and grand themes were thought to be worth painting. Rembrandt van Rijn seemed to reveal the sitter's character, and William Hogarth's work commented on social conditions.

▶ Jeweler Carl Fabergé (1846–1920) was famous for the jewel-encrusted eggs he made for the czars of Russia.

▲ This scene, *The Creation of Adam*, is on the ceiling of the Sistine Chapel, Rome. It is one of nine scenes from the Old Testament painted by Michelangelo between 1508 and 1512.

▲ The vibrant, rapid strokes of Edgar Degas's *Dancer Fastening Her Pump* (1880s) capture a sense of movement.

◄ *As I Opened Fire* (1964) by Roy Lichtenstein, who was a leading exponent of pop art. This used mass-produced imagery to create a powerful impact.

Pablo Picasso tried to see subjects from many different angles as in his *Little Girl with Hoop* (1919).

CAPTURING SUNLIGHT
By the 1700s and 1800s, many artists were trying out new methods and ideas. In the late 1800s, the French impressionists, such as Claude Monet and Edgar Degas, became more spontaneous, daubing their canvases with bold strokes of color to try and capture the fleeting effects of light.

THE SHOCK OF THE NEW
During the early 1900s, artists experimented in radical new ways. Cubists, such as Pablo Picasso and Georges Braque, began to show images as though they were seen from several sides at once, and opened the door for other forms of abstract art. Surrealists, such as René Magritte and Salvador Dali, used dreams to explore hidden feelings, painting unlikely objects together in surprising situations.

Photography gained a new status as an art form, with haunting images of landscapes or witty and innovative surrealist images. Artists today continue to discover new styles and materials, including video and multimedia techniques, as well as taking inspiration from traditional folk art.

EASTERN ART
In some cultures, artistic styles have changed little over thousands of years. Chinese art has been very influential, with its accurately observed landscapes executed with simple brush strokes on silk and paper.

DECORATIVE ARTS
Distinctive styles can also be seen in the decorative arts—in ceramics, textiles, and metalwork. Art deco of the 1930s, for example, took art into every aspect of life.

Man Ray started a trend for surreal photography as in this image entitled *The Violin* (1925).

▲ *Marriage à la Mode* (1743) by William Hogarth was a series of scenes criticizing manners.

◄ Duane Hanson's life-size fiberglass work *Old Couple on a Bench* (1994) is an example of realism in the 1990s.

SEE ALSO

Architecture, Color, Design, Music, Paint and dye, Photography, Renaissance, Sculpture

ASIA

Asia is the largest continent. It covers 30 percent of the Earth's land area and has a bigger population than all the other continents put together.

▲ A dragon boat festival in Taiwan. At the end of the race, the winning team raises its oars. Boats are an important means of transportation along Asia's wide rivers.

KEY FACTS

- **Area:** 12,387,960 sq. mi.
- **Population:** 3,785,470,000
- **Number of countries:** 48
- **Largest country:** Russia, 75 percent of which (4,944,600 sq. mi.) is in Asia
- **Smallest country:** Maldives (116 sq. mi.)
- **Highest point:** Mount Everest (29,028 ft.)
- **Largest lake:** Caspian Sea (143,630 sq. mi.)
- **Longest river:** Chang (Yangtze) (3,906 mi.)

The immense size of Asia means it has a huge variety of environments and weather conditions. Its natural habitats include dense tropical forests, fertile plains, arctic regions, and deserts—both hot and cold. The world's ten highest mountains are found in Asia, as well as the lowest point on land: the shores of the Dead Sea, at 1,289 ft. (393m) below sea level.

NATURAL BORDERS

Asia is separated from Europe by the Ural Mountains in the northwest and from North America by the Bering Strait, a strip of water only 56 mi. (90km) wide, in the northeast. The Red Sea and the Suez Canal divide Asia from Africa in the southwest.

EXTREMES OF TEMPERATURE

Northern Asia is cold and often desolate, with few plants to support people or animals. Noril'sk in northern Russia is the coldest city in the world, with average temperatures of 12.4°F (–10.9°C). In contrast, Tirunelveli in India has average temperatures of 82.4°F (29°C).

WET AND DRY

Ten of the worst floods of the last century occurred in Asia—in China, Bangladesh, and India. The monsoon winds from the Indian Ocean bring heavy rain to much of southern and eastern Asia. Vast areas of central Asia, on the other hand, have very little rain, and deserts such as the Gobi dominate the landscape.

DANGER ZONE

Because Asia lies on faults in the Earth's crust, many Asian countries, especially Japan, have experienced devastating earthquakes. The coasts of eastern and Southeast Asia are also prone to typhoons—violent storms that come from the China Sea.

▲ The snow leopard is found in some of the most remote areas of central Asia. Its pale, spotted coat allows it to blend in with its surroundings.

▶ The yak is used in the mountainous regions of Tibet (a region of China since 1950) as a source of food, milk, and clothing, and for carrying goods.

KEY TO MAP
1 CYPRUS
2 SYRIA
3 LEBANON
4 ISRAEL
5 JORDAN
6 UNITED ARAB EMIRATES
7 QATAR
8 BAHRAIN
9 KUWAIT
10 ARMENIA
11 GEORGIA
12 AZERBAIJAN
13 TURKMENISTAN
14 UZBEKISTAN
15 TAJIKISTAN
16 KYRGYZSTAN
17 AFGHANISTAN
18 NEPAL
19 BHUTAN
20 BANGLADESH
21 MYANMAR (BURMA)
22 THAILAND
23 LAOS
24 CAMBODIA
25 VIETNAM
26 SINGAPORE
27 BRUNEI

▲ Terraces are cut in the hillsides in the Philippines to provide land for growing rice and other crops.

ENDANGERED ANIMALS

Thousands of animal species live in Asia, especially in the tropical south and southeast. But the effect of people clearing the land for farming and hunting animals for their skins has been to put several species in danger of extinction, including the giant panda, the orangutan, the tiger, and the snow leopard.

THE LAND PROVIDES

Rice is the main crop of warm, wet southern Asia, while wheat, barley, and millet grow in the colder, drier north. Spices such as pepper and cloves have been a source of wealth for India, Sri Lanka, and Indonesia for centuries. Other major crops include tea, tobacco, cotton, sugar, coffee, cocoa, jute, and fruit. Forests cover a third of Russia's land in Asia, and 20 percent of the rest of the continent.

NATURAL RESOURCES

Raw materials are among Asia's most important exports. Asia provides more than half of the world's tin. Coal, gas, aluminum, and other metals needed for manufacturing are exported worldwide. The continent includes the five countries with the largest oil reserves: Saudi Arabia, Iraq, Kuwait, the United Arab Emirates, and Iran.

WAY OF LIFE

In the desert areas of Saudi Arabia and Iran, and the steppes (dry, grassy, treeless plains) of Mongolia and neighboring ▶

25

countries, there are many nomadic (wandering) tribes. These nomads live by herding camels, goats, sheep, and horses. Farming is the most common occupation for the people of many Asian countries, including China, India, and Indonesia.

CROWDED CITIES
In Asia, only one person in five lives in a city, compared to three out of four in Europe and the United States. But Asian cities, such as Tokyo, Kolkata (Calcutta), and Bangkok, house populations that are among the largest in the world.

BIG BUSINESS
Industry is a major employer in countries such as Japan, South Korea, and Taiwan, and it is becoming increasingly important in Thailand and Malaysia. Other areas such as Singapore and Hong Kong have become important financial centers. Fishing and forestry, as well as manufacturing, are important industries in many Asian countries. Japan is the

▲ Mongolians have traditionally survived off the infertile land of central Asia by herding cattle. Bactrian (two-humped) camels are used as beasts of burden.

▼ San'a, the capital of Yemen, is one of the most beautiful Islamic cities. Handmade goods, such as cloth, leatherware, glassware, and pottery, are sold in its bazaars.

▲ China is the world's largest rice producer. Rice is grown in wet regions south of the Chang River.

world's largest manufacturer of cars and televisions, and shipbuilding is important in both Japan and Taiwan. China has one of the world's fastest-growing economies.

CRADLE OF CIVILIZATION
Asia was the birthplace of some of the world's most ancient civilizations, including Mesopotamia (in modern-day Iraq), China, and the Indus Valley (in modern-day Pakistan). These areas had large cities and were ruled by a small governing class of priests, officials, and warriors. Their rich cultures attracted both trade and conquering armies.

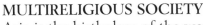

▲ Followers of Buddhism worship outside a temple in Yangon (Rangoon), the capital of Myanmar (Burma). About 85 percent of Myanmar's population is Buddhist.

GAINING INDEPENDENCE

Colonial rule continued until the 1900s, when many of the colonies won their freedom, and created independent nations such as India and Jordan. In other countries, such as the former Soviet Union and China, communism took a firm hold. Since the break-up of the Soviet Union in 1991, republics such as Kazakhstan and Tajikistan have become independent nations once more. The establishment of new industries and government investment have helped to improve the economies of many of the Asian countries.

MULTIRELIGIOUS SOCIETY

Asia is the birthplace of the world's major religions. Buddhism and Hinduism were spread from India by merchants and missionaries. Islam was carried from Asia to Europe and Africa by conquering armies such as the Mongols in the 1100s. Judaism and Christianity were exported from Asia during the Roman period. Today, all of these religions still thrive in Asia, but it is Hinduism that has the most followers.

GLITTERING EMPIRES

By the 1500s, the Ottoman Empire in the Middle East, the Safavid Empire in Iran, the Mogul Empire in India, and the Ming Dynasty in China were the richest and most powerful states in the world. They had grown rich on exports such as silk, spices, ceramics, and jewels. But these riches attracted European explorers.

▲ Trade routes, known as the Silk Road, were used to carry goods between Asia and Europe from 1000 B.C. until the 1400s. Luxury items, such as the Ming vase shown here, as well as silks and spices, were carried through Pakistan, Tajikistan, Uzbekistan, and Kazakhstan to the Middle East, from where they were taken by boat to Europe.

COLONIAL RULE

From the beginning of the 1800s, much of Asia was colonized by European powers, whose steamships and modern weapons gave them superior mobility and firepower. The colonists transformed large areas of Asia into plantations for growing tea, coffee, cotton, and rubber for export to Europe.

▲ A holiday in Uzbekistan brings out dancers in brightly colored costumes. This Asian republic exports silk and ranks third among world cotton producers.

SEE ALSO

China, Communism, Crop, Earthquake, Empire, Indian subcontinent, Indonesia, Japan, Mesopotamia, Middle East, Religion, Russia and the Baltic States, Southeast Asia

ASTRONAUT

Astronauts are people who are specially trained to work in space. They often spend weeks or months carrying out research on a space station or spacecraft.

▲ Astronauts train for long periods in a giant water tank, known as the Neutral Buoyancy Simulator, in order to prepare for the work they will do on space walks. These astronauts are training for repair work on a satellite.

Experiments carried out by astronauts help to discover what exists in space and how conditions in space affect life on Earth. Since the first human space journey was made in 1961, astronauts have walked on the Moon and lived in orbit.

On April 12, 1961, Yuri Gagarin of the U.S.S.R. became the first man in space on board *Vostok 1*.

JOBS IN SPACE
Work aboard a spacecraft includes maintaining the equipment, conducting scientific experiments, and launching and repairing satellites. To fly a spacecraft, an astronaut must be trained as a military pilot; mission specialists are highly qualified engineers or scientists.

Valentina Tereshkova from the U.S.S.R. became the first woman in space on June 16, 1963 on board *Vostok 6*.

CRUSHING FORCES
Astronauts must be prepared for the unusual conditions found in space. First, they are trained to survive the g-forces (crushing forces of take off) which make the body seem up to six times heavier than usual. To get used to the lack of gravity in space, astronauts train in giant

Apollo 11 astronaut Neil Armstrong of the U.S.A. was the first to walk on the Moon, on July 21, 1969.

water tanks and high-altitude aircraft, which provide a sense of weightlessness.

SPACE SICKNESS
Over 40 percent of astronauts suffer from space sickness for the first few days, because weightlessness affects their sense of balance. Gradually, a lack of gravity also reduces the number of red cells carrying oxygen in the astronauts' blood, causing tiredness.

ASTRO-GYMS
Astronauts can grow about 2 in. (5cm) in space due to the lack of gravity, and their heart, muscles, and bones weaken. These

FAST FACTS

• Russian astronauts are called cosmonauts

• In 1957, the U.S.S.R. sent the first animal into space, a dog named Laika. Her capsule could not return to Earth and she died in space

• The longest period spent in space is 437 days. It was achieved by Russian cosmonaut Vareriy Poliyakov in 1995

• Over 400 people have now traveled in space

▲ Scientific experiments are carried out in space to observe the effects of the lack of gravity on such things as fungi and plants.

◄ Everything in the spacecraft, including the astronauts, floats around the cabin unless it is secured.

Space tools are specially adapted from tools used on Earth

The space suit has as many as 15 separate layers

The astronaut communicates using a microphone and headphones

A video camera films the mission

The backpack includes a radio and enough oxygen for several hours

Heated or cooled water is pumped through tubes in the suit to keep the body's temperature constant

The astronaut is anchored to a cranelike arm so he or she does not float off into space

EMUS AND RESCUE BALLS

An EMU (Extravehicular Mobility Unit) space suit (above) protects the astronaut from radiation when working outside the spacecraft. A special Rescue Ball (below) has been designed to move astronauts between craft in an emergency.

changes can be controlled with a special diet and by carrying out a regular exercise routine in a gym aboard the spacecraft.

THE OUTER LIMITS

Spacecraft are constantly bombarded with radiation particles that would normally be blocked by the Earth's atmosphere. Each astronaut carries an instrument to measure his or her exposure to radiation. The recommended limit in a lifetime is 100 rads (units of radiation). This restricts the amount of time an astronaut can spend in space and could jeopardize plans for long-distance missions to Mars or

more remote planets, which would take two or more years to reach.

NO DAYS AND NIGHTS

Temperature in space can change from extremes of –328°F (–200°C) to more than 212°F (100°C) when the craft is in the full glare of the Sun. It is important to maintain a steady temperature in the spacecraft, and this is done in the same way as in an air-conditioned office on Earth. There is no day or night in space, but astronauts keep to a routine that imitates the cycle on Earth so that they know when to sleep and when to work.

SEE ALSO

Gravity, Planet, Rocket, Satellite, Spacecraft, Space exploration

ASTRONOMY

Astronomy is the scientific study of objects in space, such as planets, stars, comets, and black holes, using equipment such as telescopes and space probes.

Nicolaus Copernicus discovered that the planets orbit the Sun.

Johannes Kepler claimed that the planets move in elliptical (oval) orbits.

Galileo Galilei was the first astronomer to use a telescope.

Isaac Newton described how gravity affects cosmic objects.

Early civilizations watched the stars and planets to predict the coming of the seasons. But it was the Ancient Greeks who first studied them as a science. The word astronomy comes from two Greek words meaning "star laws."

COPERNICUS TO EINSTEIN

Modern astronomy began with Nicolaus Copernicus, who realized that the Sun, not the Earth, was at the center of our solar system. His ideas were published in 1543, the year he died. Galileo Galilei used his newly invented telescope in 1610 to help prove those ideas. In 1667, Isaac Newton put forward his laws of gravity, which explained how objects move in space.

THE KECK OBSERVATORY

Observatories are special buildings used to study the skies. The Keck at Mauna Kea, Hawaii, is one of the highest in the world. At the top of an extinct volcano, it is 13,770 ft. (4,200m) above sea level and has two telescopes in twinned domes that track the stars like binoculars.

▲ Our galaxy seen through a telescope.

▶ An X-ray picture of our galaxy. The central red and yellow area may be a black hole.

Albert Einstein published a theory of gravity in 1915, which led to ideas like the Big Bang and black holes.

SIGNALS TO THE PLANETS

Modern astronomers can calculate Earth's distance from other planets in our solar system by bouncing radar signals off the planets' surfaces and timing how long they take to return to Earth. The distance to faraway stars can be worked out from their brightness and by using a method called parallax (see diagram far right).

The temperature of the dome is kept near freezing to stop the glass from warping

A ladder leads to an outside observation platform

Second mirror

The main mirror is made up of 36 small mirrors, working together as one

Underground control rooms are between the two domes

A third mirror is angled to reflect light to a camera or spectroscope

Microsensors and pistons align each mirror as the dome rotates

Radio antenna

▶ The Hubble Space Telescope was placed in orbit by a space shuttle in 1990. It can detect objects 50 times fainter than telescopes on Earth can, and has revolutionized our view of the universe, revealing previously unseen stars and galaxies.

Second mirror

Solar panel

(7.9 ft./240cm) Main Mirror

Cameras and other scientific recording equipment

Edmond Halley predicted that the comet of 1682 would return in 1758.

Albert Einstein created important theories about space and time.

LIGHT YEARS AWAY

The nearest star to our Sun is Proxima Centauri, more than 26 million million miles away. Star distances are measured in light years (light travels almost 6 million million miles in one year). Proxima Centauri is 4.26 light years away, which means its light takes four years and three months to reach Earth.

SECRETS OF STARLIGHT

The temperature and chemical makeup of objects in space are revealed by the radiation that they give off. This radiation includes light, radio waves, microwaves, infrared, ultraviolet, X rays, and gamma rays. Astronomers use optical and radio telescopes as well as spectroscopes (radiation detectors), set up in observatories, to study cosmic radiation.

PLANETARY PROBES

Sending unmanned spacecraft to the planets is now the most technically challenging area of astronomy. The spacecraft are launched aboard rockets and either land on the planet or send

down a probe that transmits information back to Earth. In 1997, a probe entered Jupiter's clouds and, in the same year, the first remote-controlled, robotic probe landed and roamed around on the surface of Mars. Saturn and her moons will be visited in 2004 by the *Cassini* spacecraft. It will orbit the planet for four years and release a probe into the dense atmosphere of Saturn's largest moon, Titan.

◀ In 1997, a probe from the *Galileo* spacecraft plunged into Jupiter's gas clouds. It sent back photographs and chemical data to Earth for over an hour before being destroyed.

KEY DATES

3000 B.C. First known records of astronomy made by the Babylonians

125 B.C. Hipparchus groups the stars according to their brightness

1543 Nicolaus Copernicus proposes that the Earth orbits the Sun

1600 Johannes Kepler discovers that the planets orbit the Sun in ellipses

1781 William Herschel discovers Uranus

1846 Neptune discovered

1908 Giant and dwarf stars first noted

1930 Clyde Tombaugh discovers Pluto

1938 Radio waves from space detected

1955 250-ft. (76-m) radio telescope built at Jodrell Bank, England

1997 Probe enters Jupiter's atmosphere to collect data; the *Sojourner* probe lands on Mars

PARALLAX

The distances of nearby stars can be calculated by plotting their positions at different times of the year, and then applying a simple geometric equation. The bigger the parallax angle, the closer the star.

Where the star seems to be on January 1

Where the star seems to be on July 1

Real position of star

Parallax angle

Sun

Position of Earth on July 1

Position of Earth on January 1

SEE ALSO

Black hole, Constellation, Galaxy, Gravity, Solar system, Space exploration, Star, Telescope

ATMOSPHERE

The atmosphere is an envelope of gases surrounding the Earth. It shields us from the Sun and contains the air we breathe. Without it life would not exist.

▲ In the atmosphere above the Arctic and Antarctic, colliding particles from the Sun create flickering bands of light known as auroras.

◀ A false-color satellite image of the atmosphere above Antarctica, showing the hole in the ozone layer (center). The hole forms each spring, mixing in with the rest of the stratosphere in summer.

The gases that form the atmosphere are held in place around the Earth by gravity. They can be divided into four layers: the troposphere, stratosphere, ionosphere, and exosphere. Each contains a mixture of gases, which gets thinner the farther away the layer is from the Earth.

THE WEATHER ZONE
The lowest and densest layer is the troposphere, which extends about 8 mi. (13km) above the Earth's surface. It contains 78 percent nitrogen, 20 percent oxygen, and small amounts of other gases and is where life exists, clouds form, and where most of Earth's weather occurs.

OZONE LAYER
Above the troposphere, up to about 30 mi. (50km), is the stratosphere. This is where jet planes usually fly, and near its top is the ozone layer, which absorbs most of the Sun's harmful ultraviolet radiation.

Holes in the ozone layer have been linked to industrial chemicals, such as the CFCs that used to be used in spray cans, fire extinguishers, and refrigerators.

HIGH-ENERGY RAYS
Above the stratosphere is the ionosphere. In this layer, the Sun's rays break up some gas atoms into charged particles, or ions. Temperatures in the upper ionosphere (which is called the thermosphere) can reach 3,600°F (2,000°C).

MERGING INTO SPACE
Above 310 mi. (500km) the ionosphere merges into the exosphere, which stretches up to a height of several thousand miles. Any gas molecules found here are on their way out toward space.

EVOLVING ATMOSPHERE

The atmosphere is constantly evolving. At first it was made up of high levels of carbon dioxide. Oxygen appeared about 1,800 million years ago, but advanced life was possible only after the ozone layer formed.

Satellite

Space shuttle

Aurora

Meteor shower

Weather balloon

Concorde

Hole in ozone layer

Harmful ultraviolet rays from the Sun reach the Earth's surface through holes in the ozone layer

Exosphere

Upper ionosphere (thermosphere)

Lower ionosphere (mesosphere)

Stratosphere

Troposphere

SEE ALSO
Climate, Conservation, Earth, Gravity, Pollution, Sun, Weather

ATOM AND MOLECULE

Atoms are the basic building blocks of everything around us, from plants and animals to planets and stars. A molecule is two or more atoms joined together.

Every substance in the universe is made of atoms. An atom is the smallest part of any substance that can exist on its own—it is less than ten billionths of a yard in diameter. The period at the end of this sentence contains billions of atoms.

EMPTY SPACE
Most of an atom is made up of empty space, but at its center is a tiny nucleus. If an atom were scaled up to the size of a football field, the nucleus would be no bigger than a peppercorn.

THE NUCLEUS
The nucleus is the densest part of the atom and usually contains an equal amount of smaller, subatomic particles called protons and neutrons. Electrons are even lighter subatomic particles that whirl around the nucleus in all different directions at the speed of light.

▶ A polymer is a compound with large molecules made from thousands of smaller molecules joined together in a long chain. Rubber and plastic are polymers.

FORMING BONDS
Some substances consist of molecules that are formed from only one type of atom, and these are called elements. But when different types of atoms join to make molecules, they form compounds. A water molecule is a compound of one oxygen atom and two hydrogen atoms.

SOLID, LIQUID, OR GAS?
Water is a liquid, which means its molecules can move around (flow), whereas the molecules in a solid such as wood are fixed together in a definite pattern. Gas molecules buzz around randomly, filling all the available space.

Crystals form regular shapes as their atoms are arranged in set patterns.

Pencil lead is soft because its atoms slide easily over each other.

Diamonds are very hard because their atoms are in a rigid framework.

DNA, the basis of life, consists of two strands of molecules in coils.

INSIDE AN ATOM
The nucleus of every atom consists of particles called protons and neutrons (except for the hydrogen atom, which has no neutrons). Other particles, called electrons, flit around the nucleus in a random motion, making billions of trips in a millionth of a second.

Nucleus consisting of protons and neutrons

Electron orbit

Electron

SEE ALSO
Chemistry, Electricity, Energy, Genetics, Heat, Nuclear power, Solid, liquid, and gas

AUSTRALIA

Australia is the sixth largest country in the world, covering about four percent of the Earth's surface. It is also the smallest, flattest, and driest continent.

Area: 2,941,300 sq. mi.
Population: 19,546,792
Capital: Canberra
Language: English
Currency: Australian dollar

KEY FACTS

- **Number of states:** 6 (Western Australia, South Australia, Queensland, New South Wales, Victoria, and Tasmania)
- **Number of territories:** 2 (Northern Territory and the Australian Capital Territory)
- **Highest point:** Mount Kosciuszko (7,316 ft.)
- **Longest permanent river:** Murray (1,200 mi.)
- **Largest lake:** Eyre (3,700 sq. mi.)

Australia is often referred to as Down Under because it lies below the equator, in the Earth's Southern Hemisphere. It is both a country and a continent.

THE GREAT DIVIDING RANGE

With the exception of a few mountain ranges, Australia is low and flat. The mountains of the Great Dividing Range run down the coast of Queensland and New South Wales. Fertile plateaus (flat areas of land high above sea level) lie along the top, where dense forests once grew. Today, many of the forests have been cleared for cities and farms.

SUNSHINE AND MONSOONS

The weather is cool and wet in the southernmost parts of the country, but most of Australia is hot or warm all year round. There are just two seasons in the far north: wet and dry. The wet season, from November to April, is hot and humid, with monsoon rains that turn huge areas of land into lakes.

▲ Rain forests on the northeast coast of Queensland, where the climate is wettest, are now national parks.

THE OUTBACK

The country's vast central region, which the Australians call the Outback, is hot and dry and mostly a desert—the second largest in the world. The temperature at Alice Springs, in central Australia, is often over 100°F (38°C). The rest of the interior is made up of land covered in coarse grass, low shrubs and trees, and provides grazing for cattle and sheep.

LIFE-BRINGING WATER

The many billabongs (waterholes) and rivers in the Outback are dry most of the year, and the parched plants sometimes catch fire. There are occasional heavy rains, however, when the buried seeds of flowering plants come to life and the riverbeds fill with water. The Australian

▼ Uluru (Ayers Rock) is a huge outcrop of sandstone sacred to the Aborigines.

TIMOR SEA

ARAFURA SEA

CORAL SEA

PACIFIC OCEAN

INDIAN OCEAN

● Darwin

Victoria

Mitchell

Great Barrier Reef

NORTHERN TERRITORY

GREAT SANDY DESERT

Hamersley Range

AUSTRALIA

Great Dividing Range

Lake McLeod

GIBSON DESERT

Macdonnell Ranges

● Alice Springs

SIMPSON DESERT

Ayers Rock (Uluru)

WESTERN AUSTRALIA

SOUTH AUSTRALIA

QUEENSLAND

● Brisbane

Lake Eyre

GREAT VICTORIA DESERT

Lake Everard

Lake Torrens

Lake Gairdner

Darling

NEW SOUTH WALES

Great Dividing Range

● Perth

Great Australian Bight

Murray

Lachlan

Murrumbidgee

● Sydney

● Adelaide

Canberra ■

AUSTRALIAN CAPITAL TERRITORY

VICTORIA

▲ Mt. Kosciuszko

● Melbourne

TASMAN SEA

TASMANIA

● Hobart

miles
0 ——— 500
0 ——— 500
km

N

lungfish has adapted to this climate by developing both gills and lungs.

A LAND ON ITS OWN

Australia has been isolated from any other landmass since about 65 million years ago, when it split from Antarctica. About 130 million years ago, Australia and Antarctica were both part of a great southern continent. Many species of animal that are unique to Australia evolved during this time. These include marsupials (pouched mammals), such as kangaroos, koalas, and wombats, as well as two unusual egg-laying mammals, the duck-billed platypus and the echidna (also known as the spiny anteater).

AUSTRALIA'S EXPORTS

Australia's farms produce wheat, beef, mutton, and wool, as well as wine made from grapes grown in the south. Australia is rich in minerals, such as coal, gold, iron ore, bauxite (aluminum ore), uranium, diamonds, and opals. Minerals and farm products are the country's main exports, with manufactured goods representing about 20 percent. Australia's factories ▶

▲ The kookaburra is often seen in parks and gardens. Its strange call, like a chuckling laugh, led to the name "laughing jackass."

◀ The Great Barrier Reef is a chain of more than 2,500 small reefs and coral islands. It stretches for 1,250 mi. (2,010km) along the northeast coast.

▲ New South Wales and Western Australia produce more than half of Australia's wool.

▼ Sydney is Australia's oldest and largest city, with a population of about 3,770,000. The city is built around a huge natural bay, jutting out into which is the world-famous Sydney Opera House.

State. The cattle live and breed until it is time for market, when the rancher rounds them up, often using a helicopter.

SCHOOL ON THE AIRWAVES

People living on sheep stations and cattle runs are often hundreds of miles from the nearest town. They must rely on flying doctors, who arrive by light aircraft, for medical help. Children in the Outback send and receive schoolwork by mail and listen to lessons broadcast on the radio. They can communicate with their teachers via two-way radios.

produce goods such as cars and trucks, textiles, chemicals, and household goods. Australia also has a movie industry, which is rapidly expanding.

SHEEP STATIONS

Most of the Outback is too dry to grow crops, but vast sheep farms, called sheep stations, cover thousands of acres. Huge cattle ranches are known as cattle runs, a few of which are the size of New York

IN THE BIG CITIES

Eighty percent of people in Australia live in cities, where most of the jobs are to be found. The largest cities—Sydney, Melbourne, and Brisbane—lie on the south and east coasts. In Sydney, the population of more than 3.5 million enjoys the attractions of city life, including the world-famous Sydney Opera House, as well as the beach. Bondi Beach lies about 5 mi. (8km) south of the center and attracts many swimmers and surfers.

▲ A favorite pastime in coastal cities is surfboat racing. Lifeguards give demonstrations of their skills at festivals.

THE AUSTRALIAN GOLD RUSH
In 1851, many more people dashed to Australia seeking their fortune after news that gold had been found in New South Wales and Victoria. Melbourne, the capital of Victoria, soon became a wealthy city and Australia's population more than doubled. In 1854, gold miners at the Eureka Stockade rebelled against their colonial rulers, hastening reform and self-government.

FIRST INHABITANTS
Australia's first, or aboriginal, inhabitants arrived about 50,000 years ago from Southeast Asia. They lived off the land, hunting animals, gathering plants, and fishing, for thousands of years, until European settlers destroyed their way of life in the 1700s.

CAPTAIN COOK LANDS
The Dutch were the first Europeans to explore the coast in the 1600s, but they never established any settlements. The first Europeans to settle in Australia were the British. In 1770, Captain James Cook reached the east coast of Australia and immediately claimed it for Britain, calling it New South Wales.

AUSTRALIA—THE NATION
In 1901, Australia became a nation. The colonies became states and united as the Commonwealth of Australia. During World War I, Australian troops helped the British; in World War II they defended their country against Japanese invasion. People from many countries migrated to Australia after both wars, and the population rose from five million in 1918 to over 19 million today. One out of four Australians comes from a family where English is not the first language. Increasingly, Australia looks to Asia and Pacific countries for trade links, especially to Japan.

▲ Cattle ranches, or runs, can be thousands of miles in size. Farmers use motorcycles and helicopters to round up huge herds of livestock.

CONVICTS ARRIVE
The first British fleet landed at Botany Bay in January 1788, with soldiers, convicts, and the colony's first governor, Arthur Phillip. The first settlement, named Sydney, was set up nearby, and as more free settlers arrived, other farming settlements grew up around the coast.

◀ Tasmania has a cooler, wetter climate than the Australian mainland. Much of the island is unpopulated and covered in thick forest.

◀ Britain sent many thousands of convicts to Australia between 1788 and 1853 under a system called transportation. The early years in prison settlements were harsh.

SEE ALSO
Aborigine, Architecture, Continent, Explorer, Gold, Kangaroo, Platypus

AZTEC

The Aztecs were members of one of the last great native civilizations of the Americas. They created a large empire in Mexico during the 1400s.

Quetzalcóatl (meaning plumed serpent) was one of the main Aztec gods.

This ceremonial mask was made from precious stones on a human skull.

The Aztecs' rise to power began in the 1300s, when they built the city of Tenochtitlán on an island where Mexico City now stands. They began to create their great empire by conquering nearby cities, largely to the south and east.

THE PEOPLE

The Aztec ruler was an emperor who relied on a warrior class to defend and expand the empire. Next in importance were the priests. Ordinary people were farmers, traders, craftsworkers, and slaves. Food was farmed on floating gardens (called *chinampas*) on Lake Texcoco, which surrounded Tenochtitlán. Indian corn, vegetables, and cotton were grown; turkeys and dogs were kept for meat. The Aztecs were among the first to use cocoa beans

▶ The Aztecs used two calendars: this solar one, divided into 18 months, and a sacred one.

to make a chocolate drink, and the words "tomato" and "avocado" come from the Aztec language.

TEMPLES OF DOOM

The main religious building was the Great Temple at Tenochtitlán, a stone pyramid with sacrificial altars at the top. Each ruler built a larger, more impressive temple on the same site. It was rebuilt six times.

CONQUERED BY A LEGEND

The Aztec Empire was at its height when Montezuma II became emperor in 1502 and built a vast palace. Under his rule, the empire stretched across Mexico from the east to the west. In 1519, a small force of Spanish soldiers and bounty hunters, led by Hernán Cortés, arrived in Mexico. Many Aztecs, including Montezuma, believed Cortés was the legendary god Quetzalcóatl, and at first welcomed the Spaniards. By 1521, Cortés's army had completely destroyed Tenochtitlán, and Cortés was made governor of Mexico.

HUMAN SACRIFICE

Religion was very important to the Aztecs. They worshiped many gods—of war, rain, sun, and wind—and carried out human sacrifices to win the favor of their gods. Captives taken in battle were killed by the priests. They cut out the still-living hearts using ceremonial knives made of very sharp stone. The blood was used to bathe statues of the gods.

Stone knives were used to cut out the heart

Feathers from the quetzal bird were used for headdresses

SEE ALSO
Mexico

BABYLON

Babylon was a large and wealthy city beside the Euphrates River in modern Iraq. It was founded around 2300 B.C. and flourished for 2,000 years.

▼ These standard Babylonian weights were used in ancient markets.

The city of Babylon was famous for its power, beauty, and magnificent buildings. The name Babylon means "gate of god," and it was a great religious center.

PYRAMID TOWERS
The city was dominated by its pyramid-shaped temple towers called *ziggurats*, made from sun-dried bricks. Around the city was a great wall, and canals fed water from the river to fields outside the city for growing grain, vegetables, and fruit.

WEALTH OF KNOWLEDGE
The Babylonians were skilled in science, mathematics, and astronomy. They divided the circle into 360 degrees and the hour into 60 minutes, and grouped numbers into tens. They studied the Sun and stars in order to predict the future, and they used a form of writing, called cuneiform, scratched with pointed reeds in soft clay.

RIGHTS FOR CHILDREN
Babylon's rulers had military, religious, and legal powers. One of their greatest leaders was Hammurabi, who ruled from 1792 B.C. to 1750 B.C. He drew up a set of laws, the oldest surviving in the world, that protected women, children, and slaves. The Code of Hammurabi was carved on a black pillar, which is now in the Louvre Museum in Paris, France.

RISE AND FALL OF BABYLON
After Hammurabi, the Babylonians were ruled by Assyrians until a new empire arose under Nebuchadrezzar II in 605 B.C. Under his rule, Babylon was fortified and many fine buildings were built. After he died, in 562 B.C., Babylon collapsed into civil war. It fell to the Persians in 539 B.C., and was conquered in 331 B.C. by the Greeks, led by Alexander the Great.

▲ Hammurabi's army conquered neighboring cities to form a large, strong empire.

GRAND ENTRANCE
Babylon's narrow streets were crowded with traders who entered through one of eight gates in the double city walls. The grand Ishtar Gate, named after a fertility goddess, was the main entrance. It was covered with blue tiles and decorated with figures of bulls and dragons.

The Ishtar Gate stood 39 ft. (12m) high

The city wall was so wide that a chariot could be driven along it

Babylon's Hanging Gardens were built by Nebuchadrezzar to please his wife

SEE ALSO
Law, Mesopotamia, Seven Wonders of the World, Weights and measures

BALLOON AND AIRSHIP

Balloons and airships are aircraft that use gas, which is lighter than air, to fly. They consist of a gas-filled bag, or envelope, with a basket or cabin underneath.

The gas in a balloon or airship is lighter than the surrounding air, and so it lifts the aircraft off the ground, like a bubble floating upward in water. Airships have engines and equipment for steering; hot-air balloons drift with the wind.

▶ Modern hot-air balloons are twice as tall as a house. They are made of nylon and carry up to five people.

In 1783, the Montgolfier brothers built the first-ever passenger hot-air balloon from paper and linen.

Count Ferdinand von Zeppelin set up the first airship service in 1910. They could fly at 60 mph.

Richard Branson's 1997 round-the-world balloon had a pressurized cabin to protect the passengers.

Like airplanes, modern airships are steered with joysticks, which move fins on the tail.

LIGHT GAS

The weight that a balloon or an airship can carry depends on the gas used. Hydrogen provides the most lift, but it catches on fire very easily. Today, airships usually use helium because it is safer. Balloons are most often filled with nothing more than hot air. They have a burner that reheats the

CHANGING COURSE

Hot-air ballooning is a popular sport. A burner heats the air inside the balloon. This takes the balloon up, because hot air is lighter than cold air. To come down, the pilot pulls a rip cord which opens a vent in the bag to let hot air escape.

air whenever the balloon starts falling. Hot air expands, making it lighter, or less dense, than cold air, so the balloon rises.

FLYING AN AIRSHIP

The first airships were rigid with a huge hull, or body, made out of a frame covered with a skin. These were no longer built after 35 people died on the *Hindenburg* in 1937 when the hydrogen gas caught on fire. Today's airships are nonrigid and are made from a gas bag stretched into shape by the gas inside pressing against it. They are powered by engines and are used for advertising, pleasure trips, and as television camera platforms at major sporting events.

The envelope is made of a thin, leakproof polyester fabric

A side vent is used to change course

The deflation port is opened with a rip cord

The skirt shields the burner from the wind

A cylinder of propane gas supplies the burner

THE BURNER
Propane gas is fed to the burner through tubes. It is ignited to heat the air in the bag. Deciding when to use the burner calls for skilled judgment, especially when the balloon is coming down to land.

SEE ALSO
Atmosphere, Solid, liquid, and gas, Transportation

BAT

Bats are the only mammals that are capable of true flight. Most are nocturnal (active at night). They live all over the world, except at sea and in polar regions.

The big brown bat of North America gives birth to twins. Other bats have only one baby.

Kitti's hog-nosed bat from Thailand is the world's smallest mammal. It was first recorded in 1974.

Free-tailed bats have a tail that extends beyond the wing membrane. These bats can fly high and fast.

Horseshoe bats have circular flaps of skin around the nose to direct sound while hunting.

The Rodrigues fruit bat lives on an island in the Indian Ocean. Its forest home has now almost gone.

A clawed thumb is used for scrambling up rocks inside caves

Large ears help the bat to hear the returning echoes

Bats use their tails to brake or change direction in flight

Sound waves bounce off the moth and back to the bat

With their large wings of leathery, lightweight skin held stretched out by very long finger bones, bats are the only mammals that can truly fly. There are so many different species of bat that, added together, they make up almost a quarter of the whole mammal group.

A MAMMAL WITH WINGS
Apart from its wings, the bat has the typical features of a mammal. It has a furry body, warm blood, and its young are fed on their mother's milk. When resting, the bat wraps its wings around its body and hangs upside down by its claws in a roost, such as a cave, a hollow tree, high up in a roof, or down in a cellar.

GROUPS OF BATS
Bats are divided into two main groups according to their size. Fruit bats are large bats, often called flying foxes because they have a face that looks like a fox. Most live in tropical forests and eat leaves and fruit. Other bats, called microbats, are much smaller and eat insects, which they hunt in flight. Microbats look like winged mice.

ECHOLOCATION
Most bats can see in the dark, but the microbat also uses echolocation to find its way around. It makes very high-pitched (ultrasonic) squeaks—as many as 500 per second. The sound waves from these squeaks "hit" objects or prey in front of the bat, making an echo return. The bat can tell from these echoes exactly where the prey is.

Some bats are specialist feeders. The fishing bat of South America grabs fish in its long claws. Vampire bats, from South and Central America, feed on the blood of cattle and horses, but rarely of humans.

KEEPING WARM
Bats in colder climates hibernate in the winter by clustering in cool, dry places. Others, such as the Mexican free-tailed bat, migrate. Most bats give birth to one offspring a year, early in the warm season. The young cluster together in nursery roosts while the parents go off to feed.

PROTECTED BY LAW
Many bat species are threatened because their habitats have been destroyed by people building roads and houses. Bats are also often treated as pests. Fruit bats especially are accused of destroying crops and damaging trees. In many countries, bats are now protected by wildlife laws.

> ### SEE ALSO
> Conservation, Hibernation, Mammal, Migration, Radar and sonar, Seed and pollination

BEAR

Bears are large, strong mammals with stocky bodies, thick fur, and big claws. There are seven species, living mainly in Europe, Asia, and North America.

Sloth bears love honey so much they are also known as honey bears.

The spectacled bear is the only bear that lives in South America.

The American black bear lives in remote areas and feeds on almost anything.

There are several types of brown bear. The Kodiak is the world's largest bear.

Meat is the main source of food for most bears. They are classified as carnivores (meat-eaters), but bears will eat just about anything and are particularly fond of fruit, nuts, fish, and honey. They use their strong sense of smell to track down food, because their small eyes have only poor vision.

LIVING IN A DEN
Bears spend most of the year alone, but come together to mate or to scavenge on the bodies of dead animals. In regions with cold winters, most bears spend long periods asleep in dens, which can be caves, tree stumps, or holes under rocks. This is not true hibernation since they often wake up. It is during this time that the cubs are born—usually two every second year. The female polar bear gives birth to her cubs in a snow den.

COLOR AND MARKINGS
The seven species of bear include the polar bear, white-coated for camouflage in the snow, and two black bears, the

▲ Bears use their front feet for digging, hunting, and climbing. Their claws may grow up to 5 in. (12cm) long.

American and the Asian. The sloth bear hangs from forest trees in India and Sri Lanka. South America's spectacled bear gets its name from white markings around its eyes; the Malayan or sun bear has a sun-shaped patch on its chest. Brown bears include the grizzly and Kodiak.

IN DANGER
Bears have almost no predators—except for humans, who hunt and kill them for their fur, teeth, or claws. Largely peaceful, bears will defend themselves and their cubs fiercely only if under attack. Wildlife conservation groups are fighting to protect the remaining bear population from human cruelty and destruction.

AS WHITE AS SNOW

The polar bear lives among the treeless tundra and cold seas of northern polar regions. It is white-coated for snow camouflage and can grow to over 2,200 lb. (1,000kg). Thick, water-repellent fur allows the bear to swim in icy seas, where it hunts seals, fish, walruses, and small whales. Polar bears are known to ambush seals by lying in wait at breathing holes in the pack ice.

SEE ALSO
Animal, Arctic, Forest, Hibernation, Mammal

BICYCLE AND MOTORCYCLE

Bicycles, which rely on pedal power, are the most energy-efficient form of transportation. Motorcycles are based on the bicycle design, but are powered by an engine.

▶ Off-road motorcycles are strong for rough terrain and jumping obstacles.

The dandyhorse, built in 1817 by Karl von Drais, had no pedals and was pushed along by foot.

The penny farthing, produced in 1870, had solid tires and a step to help the rider climb on.

Bicycle design has changed little since the 1880s, when the chain-driven rear wheel and air-filled tires arrived.

Early motorcycles, such as this one built by Gottlieb Daimler in 1885, were slow and uncomfortable to ride.

The first bicycle with pedals appeared in the 1860s, when Frenchman Pierre Lallement introduced the velocipede. Twenty years later, the German Gottlieb Daimler fitted a gasoline engine to a bicycle and made the first motorcycle.

MODERN BICYCLES

All modern bicycles have the same basic design. The front wheel, connected to the handlebars, steers the bike, while the back wheel drives it. Today's bicycles can be divided into three categories: touring, racing, and mountain bikes. They are built for speed and strength from tough, yet lightweight materials, including aluminum and carbon fiber. The number of gears on a bicycle ranges from 3 to 21, and tires can be very thin to reduce friction or extra wide to absorb shocks from rough, uneven ground as on cross-country bikes.

ENGINE POWER

Motorcycles have either a four-stroke engine like a car, or a simpler two-stroke engine. The smallest are just 50cc (cubic centimeters) in size; the most powerful can be over 1,100cc. Scooters and mopeds are the smallest motorcycles. Most have electronic ignition and up to five gear speeds.

RACING MOTORCYCLES

Motorcycle racing is an international sport and includes motocross (dirt-track racing), enduros (endurance racing), and speed racing. The fastest models can have 18 gear ratios and reach speeds of 155 mph.

BICYCLE GEARS

Gears make it easier to cycle. If the cyclist selects a low gear, a device called a derailleur moves the chain onto the largest sprocket on the rear wheel. This allows the back wheel to turn with less pedaling, making it easier (but slower) to go uphill. Selecting a high gear to go downhill has the opposite effect.

Bike frame

Direction of chain movement

Front chain wheels

Direction of foot stroke

Rear wheel sprockets

Pedal

Chain

Rear wheel

Rear derailleur

SEE ALSO

Engine, Sports, Transportation

BIG BANG THEORY

The Big Bang is the term used to describe a huge explosion that scientists believe happened about 15 billion years ago, creating our universe.

Matter, energy, space, and time are all thought to have been created in a fraction of a second 15 billion years ago, when there was a colossal explosion called the Big Bang that created tremendous heat.

PEA-SIZE UNIVERSE
Nobody knows what caused the Big Bang, since we cannot look back to a time before it. But just after the event, the universe is believed to have been a knot of tightly packed particles only about the size of a pea. Its temperature was ten thousand trillion, trillion degrees Celsius.

COSMIC COOLING
From that moment on, the universe began to expand and cool. First, hydrogen and helium (the two most common atoms in the universe) were created. Over the next billion years, the first stars and galaxies formed, gathered together by the force of gravity. Finally planets began to form.

MICROWAVES IN SPACE
A discovery made in 1965 seems to support the Big Bang theory. A steady glow of microwave radiation comes from every direction in space. Scientists believe that this is the cooled remains of the fireball in which the universe was formed.

SPEEDING GALAXIES
Scientists have also found that, apart from a few nearby galaxies, everything in space is racing away from us. This suggests that all matter and energy in the universe were once concentrated at a single point, just before the Big Bang. The universe may expand forever, or it may eventually stop expanding and collapse inward.

▲ A microwave map of our galaxy, showing radiation ripples thought to be left over like an afterglow of the Big Bang.

FAST FACTS
- Most of the helium nuclei in the universe today were made in the first 15 minutes after the Big Bang
- The Oscillating Universe theory says that the universe will eventually contract. When all of the matter collides, a new Big Bang will be triggered

THE UNIVERSE IS BORN

In the first split second after the Big Bang, matter was created in the heat of the newborn universe. As it cooled down, a dense fog of atoms, made up of protons, neutrons, and electrons, appeared.

5 One billion years later: gravity pulls matter together to form galaxies.

6 15 billion years later: the ever-expanding universe that we see today.

4 300,000 years later: electrons begin to orbit the nuclei to form atoms. The universe fills with light.

3 Three minutes later: protons and neutrons combine to form hydrogen and helium nuclei.

2 A fraction of a second later: the temperature begins to drop. Protons and neutrons form.

1 The Big Bang takes place.

SEE ALSO
Atom and molecule, Energy, Galaxy, Planet, Solar system, Star, Universe, Wavelength

BIRD

Birds are warm-blooded, egg-laying vertebrates (animals with backbones). They have wings, and are the only animals with feathers.

The large beak of the toucan is useful for plucking fruit from trees.

An avocet's long, slender bill probes for shellfish in soft mud.

The eagle uses its hooked beak to tear meat into chunks.

A swift gathers insects in its wide beak while flying.

There are about 8,800 different kinds of bird. They are found all over the world, even on polar ice caps. Only a few birds cannot fly at all. These include the long-legged, fast-running ostrich of Africa, the rhea of South America, the emu of Australia, and penguins in the Southern Hemisphere, which use their flipperlike wings to "fly" through water.

HOLLOW BONES

A bird is designed for lightness. Its bones are thin and hollow, and its beak is toothless. In the front limb, the upper-arm and forearm bones are long. The wrist, hand, and three finger bones are joined together to support the feathers.

BIRD SENSE

Birds have excellent eyesight and good hearing, but their sense of smell is less developed. A bird's feeding habits vary with habitat and species. Some, such as the parrot, are nut-eaters; others, such

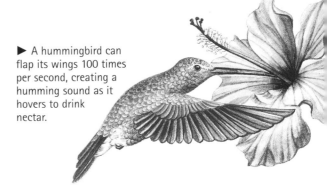

► A hummingbird can flap its wings 100 times per second, creating a humming sound as it hovers to drink nectar.

as the snipe, feast on worms. Some birds like to scavenge dead bodies. The raven has a reputation as an evil bird because in medieval times it pecked at the dead bodies of executed criminals.

CHEWING STONE

Since they have no teeth to chew with, seed-eating birds grind food in the gizzard, a muscular stomach part. Digestion is aided by pieces of stone and grit that they have swallowed for this purpose. ►

THE FLAMINGO'S BEAK AND DIET

The shape of a bird's beak depends on what it eats. The flamingo strains its food from mud and water, so its long beak contains a filter of little hooks to trap tiny plants and crustaceans (shellfish). It is the shellfish that give the flamingo its bright pink color. If the flamingo doesn't eat them, its feathers turn grayish white.

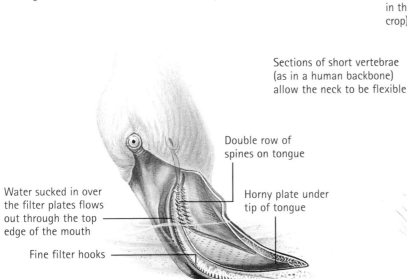

Water sucked in over the filter plates flows out through the top edge of the mouth

Fine filter hooks

Double row of spines on tongue

Horny plate under tip of tongue

Wing bones

Intestines

Gizzard

Proventriculus (part of stomach)

Pectoralis major (chest muscle)

Trachea (windpipe)

A baglike section in the gullet (the crop) stores food

Sections of short vertebrae (as in a human backbone) allow the neck to be flexible

Long legs allow the flamingo to wade deeper than other birds

Webbed feet help it to walk on soft mud

NESTS

Birds' nests vary widely, from the bare cliff ledge of the guillemot to the stick-and-twig pile of an eagle's aerie.

Swallows build nests of mud high up on cliffs or on the sides of buildings.

The Indian tailorbird builds its nest by sewing leaves together with spider silk.

A plover lays its eggs on shingle—their only protection is camouflage.

Some ducks, grebes, and other waterbirds build floating nests.

The ovenbird builds an oven-shaped nest of mud on a branch or fence post.

FEATHERS

Birds have three types of feathers. Fluffy down feathers near the body keep the bird warm. Contour feathers give the body a streamlined shape. Flight feathers, on the wings, have barbs that form smooth, flat surfaces.

Down feather

Contour feather

Flight feather

COLORS AND BREEDING

The colors of a bird's feathers usually help to conceal, or camouflage, it in its natural habitat. Most birds molt (shed) their old feathers and grow new ones each year. This molting may be linked to breeding, as some male birds, such as the bird-of-paradise and peacock, grow colorful feathers to attract mates. The females, however, tend to be drab in color so that they are hidden from predators while sitting on the nest.

COURTING COUPLES

As the spring or mating season arrives, a male and female pair up to mate. Most birds court with a variety of calls and displays. Some males give gifts of food such as insects to the females. Usually the males show off their colors and skills in flight and on perches, or try to outsing and outdance rivals. Grebes perform a very elaborate dance that involves crouching, head wagging, and swaying.

LAYING EGGS

Most bird pairs breed alone, but some, such as rooks or puffins, breed in large groups called colonies. The female lays hard-shelled eggs and sits on them to keep them warm until they are ready to hatch. This process is called incubation. The number of eggs laid in one clutch varies— a kiwi lays a single egg, while a North American bobwhite can lay up to 25. Eggs can take at least ten days to hatch; albatross eggs take the longest, up to 70 days.

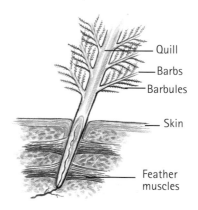

Quill

Barbs

Barbules

Skin

Feather muscles

MICROSCOPIC HOOKS

Each feather is made of keratin (found in the hair and nails of humans) and has a long, stiff shaft, or quill, with side parts called barbs, linked by tiny hooklike barbules.

MATCH-MAKING

Larger, long-lived birds, such as gannets, storks, cranes, and albatrosses, often return to the same nest site and the same partner each year. The male ostrich, however, courts several females, which all lay eggs in one nest. He then guards all the eggs (there may be up to 30) and—when they hatch—the chicks.

▲ Male birds-of-paradise have beautiful feathers. They show off their plumes in a dance to attract a mate.

HOW A BIRD FLIES

The goose, like other birds in flight, lowers its wings using its strong pectoral (chest) muscles. The wings push the air down and back, thrusting the bird up and forward in the air. The wing and tail feathers can be twisted and fanned to help the goose maneuver as it flies.

1 The powerful downstroke lifts the bird upward.

2 Legs and tail are in line with body to keep the bird streamlined as it flies.

3 The upstroke is less powerful. Feathers are twisted, letting air through.

4 The tail is used for steering and for braking.

MOVING HOUSE

Birds are warm-blooded. Their average body temperature is 105.9°F (41°C)—slightly hotter than humans'. This means they can stay active in cold weather but they need food, so many species leave colder climates and migrate to warmer places somewhere else in the world.

BETWEEN CONTINENTS

Birds such as geese and waders fly from the Arctic to Europe, Asia, and North America. Birds from Europe, like swifts and bee-eaters, fly south to Africa and India. The Arctic tern is the greatest migrator of all birds, flying an amazing 9,320 mi. (15,000km) to the Antarctic.

FAST FACTS

• A large bird such as a swan has about 25,000 feathers, whereas a tiny hummingbird has 1,000

• The world's largest bird, the ostrich, is too heavy to fly. The largest flying bird is the Kori bustard, weighing 40 lb. (18kg)

• The pitohui of New Guinea is the only bird that is poisonous

FEEDING THE CHICKS

The crow belongs to the group known as perching birds, which is the largest of the 28 bird groups. Its toes are designed for gripping, as crows build their nests in trees or on the sides of cliffs. The chicks are often born blind and helpless, and the parents feed them until they are ready to leave the nest.

The bones are thin and hollow, so that birds are very light

The inside of the chick's mouth is bright red to attract its parent's attention

Like all birds, the crow has thousands of feathers

These two-week-old chicks have soft, downy feathers, and their eyes are now open

SEE ALSO

Animal, Eagle, Migration, Prehistoric animal, Zoology

BLACK DEATH

The Black Death was a disease that struck Asia, Europe, and North Africa during the 1300s. It killed over one third of the people living there.

Fleas passed on the bubonic plague when they bit people.

The fleas lived on black rats, which thrived in the tightly packed houses.

Medieval artists often portrayed the Black Death as a murderous skeleton.

More people were killed by the Black Death in the late 1340s than by any other disease in history. Milder outbreaks of the disease, also called the bubonic plague, continued for about 300 years.

DEADLY SYMPTOMS

The name Black Death came from the blood spots that turned black under the skin. Some victims died within hours. Only about five percent of people who caught the disease survived. Fleas from diseased rats spread the plague by biting humans. It was also possible to catch the plague from an infected person.

THE PLAGUE SPREADS

The Black Death began in central Asia in about 1339, and in 1347 Italian soldiers brought it back from the Crimea, on the Black Sea. It spread rapidly through North Africa and Europe, where rats and fleas thrived in conditions of poor hygiene. As people fled the disease-infested cities, the Black Death spread with them.

▲ The Black Death swept through Europe from Asia in 1347, reaching its peak in 1349. Only a few areas, such as Belgium and eastern Germany, were unaffected.

A TERRIBLE PUNISHMENT

The appearance of the Black Death was a horrible mystery. Many saw it as God's punishment; some whipped themselves in public and prayed to be saved. Doctors did not know what caused the disease and so had no idea how to treat it. Many believed cats and dogs spread the plague, so they killed them. The true carriers, black rats, only increased. Today, cases of plague would be cured by antibiotics.

DEVASTATED POPULATIONS

Many doctors and priests died looking after the sick, leaving few educated people alive. Because so few workers survived after the worst of the plague was over, those remaining demanded higher wages instead of simply working to pay rent for land. The economy became based on money, as it is today.

"BRING OUT YOUR DEAD!"

During an outbreak of the plague, people tried to control the disease. Infected houses were marked with a cross to warn visitors. Prisoners or volunteers patrolled the streets with wheelbarrows, calling for people to bring out the bodies of the dead. The bodies were then taken to large plague pits outside the town and quickly buried.

SEE ALSO
Asia, Disease, Medicine, Middle Ages

BLACK HOLE

A black hole is a region of space where the pull of gravity is so strong that nothing can escape from it, not even light.

Nearby star

INVISIBLE FORCE

When a black hole lies close to another star, its immense gravity sucks particles or gas away from the star. These are pulled into a gassy spiral, called an accretion disk. The gas inside the disk is heated to millions of degrees Celsius and gives off X rays. It is these powerful, flickering X rays that reveal the presence of a black hole.

Black hole

Particles, gas, and matter spiral downward

Scientists believe that a black hole forms after a massive, heavy star has exploded at the end of its life. The outer parts are hurled into space, but the core of the dead star, with no light and heat left to support it, shrinks very quickly.

DEAD STARS

The gravity of a dead star is thought to pull all the material left behind inward, squeezing it tighter to make it smaller and extremely compact. A tiny black hole, the size of a period, could hold enough matter to make a mountain. Vast black holes, thought to exist at the center of galaxies, may contain as much matter as tens of millions of stars.

COSMIC VACUUM

Black holes are invisible—they can only be tracked down by their effect on a nearby object. They tug matter away

from the surface of a star, like a vacuum cleaner. This debris enters a whirlpool, which spins around the black hole before disappearing inside, like water going down a giant drain.

THROUGH A WORMHOLE

Some black holes may be the entrances to strange tunnels through space and time known as wormholes. It has been suggested that a spacecraft could travel along a wormhole and reappear in a different part of the universe.

▲ A black hole is shaped like a funnel. Objects are pulled into the funnel and, once inside, never escape.

◀ This ultraviolet image shows galaxy M77. Its center is thought to be a black hole with the mass of several million suns.

SEE ALSO

Astronomy, Big Bang theory, Constellation, Galaxy, Gravity, Star

BLOOD

Blood is a vital liquid that is pumped through arteries and veins around the body by the heart. Blood carries oxygen, nutrients, hormones, and waste products.

◄ Chemicals in the blood form a net over a wound. The net traps red blood cells, platelets, and white blood cells (shown in yellow) to form a clot.

Most animals have a bloodlike fluid. It is red in most vertebrates (animals with backbones), but can be different colors in other animals. Lobsters have blue blood, snails have gray blood, some insects have green blood, and a worm's blood is colorless.

KARL LANDSTEINER
This Austrian-born pathologist (1868–1943) discovered blood groups, making blood transfusions safe for the first time.

BLOOD PLASMA
Just over half (55 percent) of human blood is a pale yellow liquid called plasma. This contains hundreds of substances, including nutrients, sugars, salts, minerals, hormones, and chemicals.

OXYGEN CARRIERS
About 45 percent of blood is made up of blood cells and platelets. The vast majority of blood cells are small, red, and doughnut-shaped. They are made inside the bones and released into the blood, where they carry oxygen around the body. When red cells have plenty of oxygen, as in most arteries, they are bright red. When low in oxygen, as in most veins, they are dark red.

FAST FACTS
• An average human has 11 pt. (5l) of blood

• A blood spot the size of a pinhead contains about 5 million red cells, 10,000 white cells, and 250,000 platelets

• Anemia is a lack of oxygen in the blood

DEFENDING THE BODY
Less than one percent of blood is made up of white blood cells and platelets. There are several types of white blood cell, all of which defend the body. Some fight invading bacteria and viruses by bombarding them with chemicals. Others surround invaders and eat them.

CLOTTING AND HEALING
Platelets are cell fragments that help wounds to heal. They gather around a cut and release chemicals to slow blood loss and form a clot. This stops the blood flow and seals the wound, stopping germs from getting in while new skin grows.

BLOOD GROUPS
There are several different types of human blood, including A, B, AB, and O. The blood group depends on the chemicals that the white blood cells produce. If a person needs a blood transfusion, the right group must be given because some chemicals do not mix. The wrong chemicals may clot with the existing blood and make the illness worse or even cause death.

Outer layers of vein wall

Muscle

Inner layers of vein wall

White blood cell that makes chemicals to fight disease

White blood cell that eats dying and dead germs

Red blood cell

BLOOD IN A VEIN

Blood is carried toward the heart by veins and away from the heart by arteries. Red blood cells returning to the lungs from the heart are dark red in color because they are no longer carrying oxygen. All blood contains plasma, platelets, red blood cells, and several types of white blood cells.

Valve to stop blood flowing the wrong way

Platelets help blood to clot

White blood cell that attacks invaders

SEE ALSO
Cell, Disease, Heart and circulatory system, Immune system, Medicine

BOAT

Boats are small watercraft powered by oars, sails, or an engine. They are smaller than ships— usually no more than about 65 ft. (20m) long.

Boats in Ancient Egypt were made by tying reed bundles together.

A coracle is a round boat made of animal skin stretched over a frame.

A junk is a traditional Chinese boat and is still in use today.

A catamaran is a sailboat with two hulls arranged side by side.

A paddle wheeler's engine turns a huge paddle wheel to drive the boat forward.

Small, powerful tugboats are used to tow much larger vessels into port.

▶ A sailboat can travel in almost any direction, but at different rates. Sailing with the wind behind the boat (running) is not the fastest. Sailing across the wind (reaching) is faster. To sail into the wind a boat must tack, or zigzag, at an angle of 45° to the wind direction with the sails drawn in as close as possible.

Close-hauled

Reach

Broad reach

Wind direction

Run

With the wind

Across the wind

Into the wind

POWERED BY THE WIND

The skill in sailing lies in positioning the sail so that it catches the wind most efficiently. Sails are adjusted by a sheet (rope). Sideways movement is reduced by the centerboard (keel) reaching far down into the water. The boat is steered using the tiller to adjust the position of the rudder (a board attached to the back of the boat).

Mast

Mainsheet

Sail

Tiller

Window

Centerboard

Rudder

Working boats are used for fishing, transporting goods and people, and moving ships in harbors. Yachts, motorboats, sailboats, and canoes are all used for racing and for fun.

HOLLOWED-OUT TRUNKS

The first boats were built in prehistoric times, when people hollowed out tree trunks to make dugouts. Boats such as Inuit kayaks were made from animal skins, and the Ancient Egyptians made their boats from bundles of reed.

DESIGNED FOR THE JOB

A boat's design depends on its use. A lifeboat must be built to travel long distances quickly and to cope with rough seas. A small motorboat must be tough enough to withstand the pounding of the waves as well as its own engine vibrations.

PARTS OF A BOAT

The keel runs along the base of a boat. It keeps it stable and provides a framework from which to build up the boat. The hull, or outer shell, can be made of wood, but plastic and fiberglass are tougher and cheaper. The bow, or front of the boat, cuts through the water and pushes it to the sides so that the hull can glide smoothly.

ON THE MOVE

Rowboats are moved by muscle power, using oars which have a wide blade at one end. The paddles of some canoes have blades at each end and this makes it much easier to steer in fast-moving rapids. Sailboats, or yachts, use sails to catch the wind and drive them through the water. Most working boats and some sports boats are powered by an engine. This makes a propeller spin in the water, moving the boat forward.

▲ Small, light motorboats rise out of the water when they travel at speed.

SEE ALSO
Egypt, Engine, Fishing industry, Ship, Transportation, Wind power

BRAIN AND NERVOUS SYSTEM

The brain is the body's control center, responsible for action, thought, memory, behavior, and emotion. It is linked to the body by the nervous system.

Fish have simple brains, with areas that process smell extending forward to the tip of the nose.

Snakes have brains with large sight areas, showing the importance of sight for hunting.

Birds have brains with large movement centers which control the complex movements used in flight.

Cats, like other mammals, have brains with large cerebrums for complex and adaptable behavior.

The average adult human brain weighs about 3.1 lb. (1.4kg). It is a large grayish-colored organ. The brain is made up of tiny cells that send electrical messages to the body along a network of nerves known as the nervous system.

IN THREE PARTS
All vertebrates (animals with backbones) have a brain that can be divided into three main areas: brain stem, cerebellum, and cerebrum. The brain stem and cerebellum keep the body functioning. The cerebrum deals with thought, memory, and sensation.

THE BRAIN STEM
The brain stem is at the bottom of the brain, where it joins the spinal cord (the bundle of nerves linking the brain to the body). The stem controls the body's automatic processes, such as heartbeat, breathing, body temperature, blood pressure, digestion, and getting rid of waste.

THE CEREBELLUM
The cerebellum lies at the back of the brain. When movement instructions come from the cerebrum, the cerebellum analyzes the instructions. It then sends signals to the muscles to make smooth and coordinated movements. The cerebellum also controls posture and balance.

THE CEREBRUM
About 90 percent of the human brain is taken up by the cerebrum—the center of all thought. It is split into two halves, called cerebral hemispheres, which contain gray matter and white matter. Gray matter lies on the surface and is made up of nerve cell bodies, which create messages. The inner white matter is packed with nerve fibers carrying the messages to the body.

CEREBRAL CENTERS
The human cerebrum looks the same all over, but different areas carry out special functions. One area receives and processes nerve signals from the eyes. Another is for touch, processing nerve signals from the skin. Just in front of this is the motor

FAST FACTS

- About 1.9 pt. (0.85l) of blood pass through the brain every minute

- Brain activity uses one fifth of the body's energy supply

- The longest nerve, the sciatic, runs from the base of the spine to the knee. Nerve signals can travel at up to 250 mph (400kph)

- Meningitis is the inflammation of the meninges. Encephalitis is inflammation of the brain

HOW NERVE CELLS PASS ON MESSAGES

The brain and nervous system are made of microscopic nerve cells called neurons. Each nerve cell has two parts: a spiderlike cell body and a long nerve fiber. The cell body receives signals from other nerve cells and passes these along its fiber, like a tiny telephone wire, to yet more nerve cells, until the message reaches its final destination.

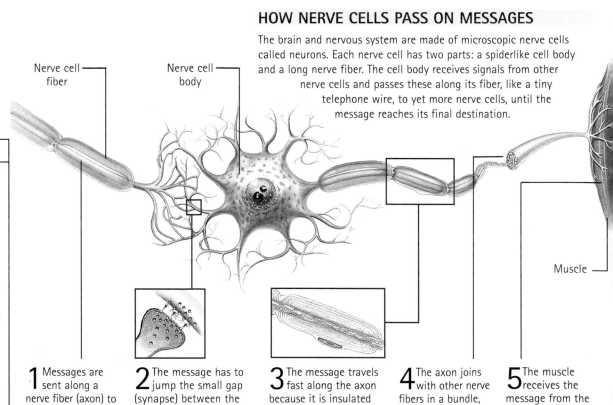

Nerve cell fiber

Nerve cell body

Muscle

1 Messages are sent along a nerve fiber (axon) to another nerve cell.

2 The message has to jump the small gap (synapse) between two nerve cells.

3 The message travels fast along the axon because it is insulated with a sheath of myelin.

4 The axon joins with other nerve fibers in a bundle, creating a pathway.

5 The muscle receives the message from the brain to move.

THE BRAIN AND SKULL

The brain is protected by a bony skull, three thin layers of membrane, called meninges, and a pool of fluid. The two sides of the cerebrum (the cerebral hemispheres) are joined by the corpus callosum. The left side of the brain usually controls logic, and the right side is more active in creative pursuits.

The hypothalamus is the site of emotion and instinct

The pituitary gland controls the hormones

Bony skull

Fluid

Meninges

Cerebrum

Corpus callosum

Cerebellum

Thought and consciousness

Skilled movement

Touch

Speech

Hearing

Sight

Brain stem

Cerebellum

Spinal cord

center, which sends nerve signals to the muscles. There are also areas for hearing, taste, speech, and other body processes. Consciousness and thought are believed to originate at the front of the cerebrum.

CROSSING THE DIVIDE

Nerve signals arriving or leaving one side of the brain cross over to affect the opposite side of the body, so signals from the body's right side go to the brain's left hemisphere and vice versa. The two sides are joined by a strip of nerve fibers, the corpus callosum.

INSTINCTS AND EMOTIONS

Basic instincts, such as hunger, thirst, and sleep, as well as strong emotions, such as

fear, anger, and joy, come from the hypothalamus, which lies at the top of the brain stem. Dangling beneath it is the pituitary, a pea-size gland that controls the body's hormones (chemical messages).

THOUGHTS AND MEMORIES

The human brain contains 100 billion nerve cells and is far more complex than the most advanced supercomputer. One thought or memory involves millions of nerve signals, flashing around billions of brain cells, along trillions of pathways. An electroencephalogram (EEG) records these electrical nerve signals.

A NETWORK OF NERVES

The brain is linked to a branching network of nerves by the spinal cord. Sensory nerves bring information from the senses to the brain. Motor nerves carry signals from the brain to the muscles. The brain and spinal column make up the central nervous system. The nerves in the rest of the body make up the peripheral nervous system.

Nerve fibers (axons)

Vertebra

Three protective membranes

Bundles of nerves going to the body

▲ The spinal cord runs through a tunnel formed by vertebrae in the spine. Its nerves are surrounded by protective membranes.

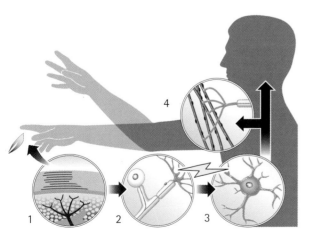

▲ A reflex is an automatic response. The flame's heat stimulates pain sensors in the finger (1) that send a signal to the spinal cord (2). The signal passes to a motor nerve (3), which makes muscles contract (4), pulling away the hand. Signals also pass to the brain, which registers pain.

SEE ALSO

Cell, Gland, Hearing, Human body, Sight, Taste and smell, Touch

BRAZIL

Brazil is the largest country in South America, covering almost half the continent. It is also South America's richest and most heavily populated country.

Area: 3,265,100 sq. mi.
Population: 176 million
Capital: Brasília
Language: Portuguese
Currency: Real

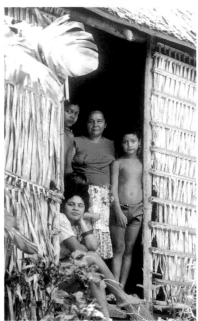

◀ Many families living in the heart of the Amazon rain forest still build their houses out of bamboo.

Two thirds of Brazil is covered by the Amazon River basin, which contains the world's largest rain forest. Some 3,900 mi. (6,276km) long, the Amazon flows across the northwest of the country and carries about a fifth of the world's river water.

ON THE EQUATOR
Brazil is warm all year round, with temperatures rarely dropping below 68°F (20°C), because the equator lies across the north of the country. Rainfall is highest inland, with more than 11 in. (280mm) of rain falling in January, the wettest month.

LIFE IN THE RAIN FOREST
The Amazon rain forest is a dense and steamy region, with at least 40,000 kinds of plants and thousands of different insects, exotic birds, and wild animals including macaws, monkeys, jaguars, sloths, armadillos, piranha fish, and anacondas. But the wildlife and the way of life of the small groups of Indians who inhabit the rain forest are under threat because of the number of trees being cut down. Efforts to protect the rain forest—an area of global environmental importance—are now being made. Farming, logging, and mining all threaten the region.

▲ São Paulo, Brazil's largest city, is ringed by shanty towns called *favelas*. Poverty is a serious problem for Brazil's rapidly growing population.

FARMING THE LAND
Most of Brazil's wealth comes from crops grown in mountainous areas. Coffee is the country's largest export—Brazil produces about a fifth of the world's supply. Other exports include orange juice, soybeans, rice, sugarcane, and cotton. Valuable timber, such as mahogany, as well as nuts, rubber, and medicines are harvested in the forests.

INDUSTRY AND MINING
Factories around the major cities make cars, aircraft, cement, and chemicals. Brazil's vast mineral wealth includes iron, lead, copper, magnesium, uranium, gold, and diamonds. Most of Brazil's power is hydroelectric, from projects such as the Itaipu Dam on the Paraná River at the Paraguay border.

▶ Sugarloaf Mountain overlooks the beautiful natural harbor of Rio de Janeiro, once the capital of Brazil. The mountain gets its name from the days when sugar was sold in pyramidlike, solid blocks.

miles
0   500
0   500
km

N

VENEZUELA

GUYANA

SURINAM

FRENCH GUIANA (FRANCE)

COLOMBIA

Rio Negro

Manaus

Amazon

Bélem

São Luís

Fortaleza

Tapajos

B R A Z I L

Paranaíba

Recife

SERTÃO

PERU

Purus

Madeira

Xingu

Araguaia

Tocantins

São Francisco

BOLIVIA

PLATEAU OF MATO GROSSO

Salvador

Brasília

BRAZILIAN HIGHLANDS

ATLANTIC OCEAN

PARAGUAY

Paraná

Belo Horizonte

Rio de Janeiro

São Paulo

ARGENTINA

URUGUAY

▲ Each year, huge areas of forest are cleared for their timber and to make way for cattle ranches and roads. If this continues at the current rate, in 100 years there may be no rain forest at all left in Brazil.

WHERE PEOPLE LIVE

As many as 80 percent of Brazilians live in cities on the Atlantic coast and in the south. The best farming and mining areas, as well as the two biggest cities—São Paulo and Rio de Janeiro—are found there.

CULTURAL MIX

About 75 percent of Brazilians are of European origin, many with Portuguese ancestry. The rest are of mixed Indian, European, and African descent. Ancient settlers reached Brazil thousands of years ago; the Portuguese arrived in the 1500s, bringing African slaves with them. Brazil declared its independence from Portugal in 1822.

BRAZIL TODAY

Brazil is now a country of 27 states, each with its own local government. The country's capital, Brasilia, was built in the 1950s on the Central Plains to encourage development in inland areas of the country. Since the 1950s, Brazil's economic status in the world has grown, but at the expense of many of its natural resources. One third of Brazilians are under 15 years old, and the population is set to double before the middle of this century. It is important that the country continues its economic growth if its population is to be housed, educated, and employed.

▲ The Brazilian carnival lasts for five days just before Lent. It is especially spectacular in Rio de Janeiro.

SEE ALSO

Conservation, Rain forest, South America, Sports

55

BRIDGE

Bridges are structures that are built to allow people, animals, or vehicles to cross rivers, canals, canyons, railroads, or roads.

Most bridges are fixed, but some are movable—all are designed to withstand the effects of traffic, floods, high winds, earthquakes, and temperature changes. The main types of fixed bridges in use today are truss, arch, suspension, and cantilever.

STRAIGHT ACROSS

The earliest bridges were simply logs or large, flat stones laid across a river. Truss or girder bridges take this idea further. They have a flat deck, sometimes supported by piers (pillars), and can span gaps of almost 1,000 ft. (300m). A cantilever bridge is a type of truss bridge with two halves balanced on piers and joined by a short span in the middle.

ARCH BRIDGES

Because of its curved shape, the arch bridge can reach farther than the truss bridge. Its supports at either end are called abutments. They take the strain of the outward thrust created by the weight of the arch. The Romans were the first to build arch bridges, using bricks or stone.

BRIDGES IN SUSPENSION

Suspension bridges can cover very long distances where piers cannot be used, perhaps because the river is too deep. The traffic deck is suspended

Cable anchored to the bank

Towers made of concrete and metal

Suspension cable
Hanger cable

745 ft. (227m)-high tower

98 ft. (30m)-deep pier

HOW BRIDGES WORK

Bridges are designed to withstand huge forces (shown by the arrows in the diagrams below). They must be strong enough to carry their own weight, as well as that of the people and vehicles that use them. Bridges must also withstand the strong vibrations set up by high winds.

In an arch bridge, the downward pressure (load) is pushed out toward the foundations on each bank.

In a cantilever bridge, the load on the central span is balanced equally over each supporting pier.

In a suspension bridge, curving cables transfer the bulk of the load to anchored points on each bank.

In a cable-stayed bridge, the load is balanced equally over one or more central supports.

→ Load   → Support   → Tension   → Compression

from towers by steel cables. A modern version of this is the cable-stayed bridge, which does not need the heavy anchorages required to stabilize a suspension bridge.

MOVABLE BRIDGES

Some bridges are built to move so large ships can pass through them. Drawbridges lift up by splitting in the middle or at one end, swing bridges turn sideways, and lift bridges have a central section that can be raised. Deck sections can also be floated on pontoons to create temporary bridges.

◀ The 8,981 ft. (2,737m)-long Golden Gate suspension bridge in San Francisco hangs from two 3 ft. (1m)-thick suspension cables, each made of 27,450 wires.

SEE ALSO

Architecture, Construction, Industrial Revolution, Iron and steel

BUDDHISM

Buddhism is a religion that was first practiced in Asia about 2,500 years ago. Today, it is estimated that there are around 350 million Buddhists across the globe.

▲ The Wheel of Life symbolizes the process of change and rebirth. When we reach Nirvana, the process stops and we come off the wheel.

Buddhism was founded in northeast India by a prince called Siddhartha Gautama. Born around 563 B.C., he left his home at the age of 29 to lead a life of meditation and preaching. He became a great religious teacher before his death in about 483 B.C.

▲ A young Thai Buddhist, in traditional orange robes, sits contemplating under a tree. Buddhists believe that meditation plays a vital role in the path to enlightenment.

THE ENLIGHTENED ONE
While sitting under a fig tree, Gautama entered a peaceful state of mind called enlightenment—Nirvana ("absence of sorrow"). He taught others how to reach this state, and gained the title Buddha— "Enlightened One." The Buddhist religion spread from India to China, Japan, and other parts of Asia.

REBIRTH
Buddhists believe in reincarnation—being reborn until Nirvana is reached. The form of each new life, or reincarnation, depends on how the being behaved during previous lives. A human might have been an animal in the last life; a male might have been a female. This is known as their karma.

FOUR NOBLE TRUTHS
Buddha's teachings are based on the Four Noble Truths. These state that all suffering is caused by attachment to the material world. Buddhists believe

▲ A Buddhist monastery in Tibet. Buddhism was introduced into Tibet in A.D. 749. Tibetan monks are called lamas. The chief lamas are the Dalai Lama and the Panchen Lama.

that they will be free of these attachments, and therefore of suffering, if they follow the Eightfold Path. This consists of eight steps involving wisdom, understanding, morality, and meditation.

TYPES OF BUDDHISM
There are two main types of Buddhism: Theravada is common in Southeast Asia and teaches that Buddha was an ordinary human being who achieved enlightenment; Mahayana is popular in northern Asia and claims that Buddha was the divine spirit in human form. A branch of Mahayana, called Zen Buddhism, was established in Japan in the 1100s.

◄ Many images of Buddha show him sitting serenely, legs crossed in the lotus position. The image reminds followers of Buddha's goodness and helps them to meditate

EIGHTFOLD PATH TO ENLIGHTENMENT
- Right views
- Right thought and intention
- Right speech, plain and truthful
- Right action, including never taking a life
- Right occupation, harming no one
- Right effort, always persevering
- Right awareness of the past, present, and future
- Right contemplation or meditation

SEE ALSO
Asia, Japan, Religion

BUTTERFLY AND MOTH

Butterflies and moths are flying insects with two pairs of wings, which are often brightly colored. They hatch as caterpillars and change into butterflies or moths as adults.

The turquoise blue has been hunted almost to extinction by collectors for its beautiful wings.

A peacock butterfly's eye spots may help it scare off small birds when it suddenly opens its wings.

The white admiral is a woodland butterfly. Its caterpillar is covered with protective spines.

Swallowtails are large and colorful butterflies, found in North Africa, Europe, and across Asia.

The large white is a very common butterfly. Its caterpillars feed in groups, often on cabbage plants.

There are more than 170,000 kinds of butterflies and moths in the world. They form the group of insects known as Lepidoptera, which means "scale-wing." Their wings are covered with thousands of tiny scales that give the wings their colorful appearance.

COLORFUL BUTTERFLIES
Most butterflies fly by day and have brightly colored wings that close together over their backs when they are resting. They have a slim body and thin antennae (feelers) with clubbed tips, which are used to detect smells. The monarch, cabbage white, tortoiseshell, and peacock are all types of butterfly.

DULL MOTHS
Most moths are dull in color, fly at night, have feathery or hairy antennae and a stout and hairy body. At rest, a moth holds its wings open. A moth's forewing is often linked to its hindwing on each side by tiny hairs that act like hooks. The hawk moth, ermine, eggar, and tussock are all types of

◄ The back part of the hawkmoth caterpillar looks like a viper in order to deceive any predators into leaving it alone.

▲ Tropical birdwing butterflies, such as the Rajah Brooke, can have a wingspan of 12 inches.

moth. The scarlet tiger and burnet are examples of moths that are brightly colored and fly by day.

SENSING THE WORLD
An adult butterfly or moth sees well with its large eyes. Its sensitive antennae pick up the scents of flowers and fruits and can detect the smell of a mate. Most species of butterfly or moth feed on flower nectar, which is sucked up by a long, strawlike mouth called a proboscis.

EGG TO CATERPILLAR
After mating, female butterflies and moths lay their eggs on or near the plant that their caterpillars like to eat. The brimstone butterfly likes buckthorn, while the green oak tortrix moth chooses oak leaves. Some species will feed only on one type of plant.

LIVING TO EAT
Butterfly and moth eggs hatch into soft-skinned, wingless larvae called caterpillars. Their job is to eat—a large group of caterpillars can destroy crops within a few weeks. A caterpillar sheds its skin (molts) four or five times as it feeds and grows. Despite having a variety of devices to protect themselves from predators, such as sharp spines that secrete a stinging fluid, few caterpillars manage to escape their attackers and reach adulthood. Others are brightly colored as a warning.

◄ This peppered moth is a pale, speckled gray in color to camouflage it against lichen on tree bark.

LIFE SPAN

Most butterflies and nearly all moths live for just one breeding season or year. A few, such as peacock and monarch butterflies, survive the winter as adults. Their main predators are birds by day and bats at night. The breeding season is usually in the spring or summer, although tropical species can breed at any time of the year.

ALL CHANGE

When they are ready to become adults, caterpillars enter a pupal stage (chrysalis). Many moth caterpillars spin cocoons of silk. Butterfly caterpillars grow a hard skin. Inside these cases, they gradually change. After a few weeks, or the following spring, the chrysalis splits and the adult winged insect (imago) emerges.

Like all hawkmoths, the privet hawkmoth is a fast flyer. Its caterpillars have a curved horn at the end.

CATERPILLAR TO BUTTERFLY

The monarch butterfly lays its eggs on a milkweed plant. A week later, a single caterpillar emerges from each egg. First it eats its egg case, then it feeds on the plant. Once fully grown, the caterpillar becomes a chrysalis (pupa). Inside, it metamorphoses (changes form) before emerging as a butterfly. The whole cycle from egg to adult takes about five weeks.

1 The female monarch lays a cluster of eggs on the leaves of a milkweed plant.

2 Each tiny caterpillar (larva) hatches and starts to eat. It grows very quickly.

3 When fully grown, the caterpillar spins a silken thread and firmly attaches itself to a twig.

4 The caterpillar sheds its striped skin, revealing a chrysalis (pupa). It now looks still and lifeless.

5 Inside the chrysalis a new body slowly begins to form. Finally, the skin splits and an adult butterfly emerges.

6 The butterfly clings to the twig of the milkweed plant, letting its new wings hang down to help force blood into them.

7 When the wings have dried and hardened, metamorphosis is complete and the adult monarch butterfly can fly away.

SEE ALSO

Animal, Flower, Insect

CANADA

Canada is the second largest country in the world. It lies at the top of the continent of North America and a large percentage of its area lies within the Arctic Circle.

Area: 3,560,200 sq. mi.
Population: 31,902,268
Capital: Ottawa
Languages: English, French
Currency: Canadian dollar

▲ Forestry is one of Canada's most important industries. Trees are cut down to make paper as well as to build homes.

The Rocky Mountains run down the west of Canada, and four of the five Great Lakes lie on its border with the United States. These, together with other Canadian lakes, contain about one fourth of the world's freshwater.

CANADIAN FORESTS
Forests cover 40 percent of the country. British Columbia is the leading province in timber production, with 250 ft. (75m)-high trees, such as Douglas fir, growing in its moist, coniferous forests. Maple syrup is collected from maple trees in Ontario and Quebec, and in the southwest there are orchards and vineyards.

THE GREAT PLAINS
Canada has vast grassland areas, or prairies, stretching across its center. Only about seven percent of Canada's land is used for growing crops, but these fertile plains produce enough to make Canada the world's second largest exporter of wheat. Cattle ranches on the drier grasslands supply beef and dairy produce.

▲ Moose are just one of the animals living in Canada's forests, which are also home to bears, beavers, bobcats, caribou, foxes, wolves, mountain lions, and goats.

INDUSTRY AND MINING
Manufacturing industries lie mostly in Ontario and Quebec. Products include cars, trucks, aircraft, machinery, steel, paper, and chemicals, as well as processed food and minerals. Among Canada's resources are gold, iron ore, copper, petroleum, and natural gas. Fishing is important, but overfishing has greatly reduced stocks.

SPORTS AND LEISURE
Most Canadians share a love of the outdoors, enjoying baseball, football, soccer, skiing, and ice skating. Competitive ice hockey is usually played indoors. Rodeo enthusiasts flock to the annual Calgary Stampede. There are over 30 national parks.

◀ In wintertime, temperatures can fall as low as –22°F (–30°C). Lakes and rivers freeze over, and people play games on the ice.

FAST FACTS

• The Yukon Territory is rich in metal ore. During the 1890s, it was the site of the Klondike gold rush

• Alberta has some of the world's best dinosaur remains. *Albertosaurus* is just one example

• The Canadian–U.S. border is the longest undefended border in the world

▶ The 1,814 ft. (553m)-high Canadian National (CN) Tower dominates Toronto's skyline. The city is Canada's financial, manufacturing, and communication center.

miles
0   500
0   500
km

ARCTIC OCEAN

Ellesmere I.

Melville I.   Bathurst I.   Devon I.

Banks I.   Somerset I.

Prince of Wales I.

Baffin I.

Victoria I.   NUNAVUT

ALASKA (U.S.A.)

YUKON TERRITORY

ARCTIC CIRCLE

Mt. Logan
Whitehorse

Great Bear Lake
NORTHWEST TERRITORIES

Iqaluit

LABRADOR SEA

Southampton I.

Hudson Strait

Yellowknife

Great Slave Lake

Hudson Bay

C A N A D A

Mackenzie

Peace

Churchill

Goose Bay

NEWFOUNDLAND

BRITISH COLUMBIA

ALBERTA

Athabasca

Edmonton

MANITOBA

James Bay

QUEBEC

St. John's

Gulf of St. Lawrence

PACIFIC OCEAN

Vancouver I.

Vancouver

Calgary

SASKATCHEWAN

Regina

Winnipeg

ONTARIO

NEW BRUNSWICK

PRINCE EDWARD I.

Quebec

Montréal

NOVA SCOTIA

Halifax

UNITED STATES OF AMERICA

Lake Superior

Lake Huron

Lake Michigan

Ottawa

Toronto

Lake Erie

Lake Ontario

Niagara Falls

St. Lawrence

ATLANTIC OCEAN

N

Canada's Horseshoe Falls is one of the two waterfalls that make up Niagara Falls.

CANADIAN PEOPLE

The ancestors of Canada's Native Americans arrived from Asia at least 13,500 years ago—possibly much longer. Those of the Inuit arrived much later and are not related to the earlier settlers. Europeans arrived during the 1500s. From 1754 to 1763, in the French and Indian War, Britain fought France for control of its Canadian territory (New France) and won. Since 1867, the country has been self-governing. Newfoundland became part of Canada in 1947.

THE GOVERNMENT

Canada is divided into ten provinces and two territories. The provinces make their own laws, but the territories are mainly under government control. National laws are made by an elected parliament that is located in Ottawa. There is also an unelected body of senators; they act as consultants and advise parliament.

TRANSPORTATION

Canada has a good system of roads, including the Trans-Canada Highway, which is more than 4,350 mi. (7,000km) long. The St. Lawrence Seaway, a waterway linking stretches of rivers and canals, allows ships to carry cargoes inland from the Atlantic Ocean as far as the Great Lakes.

▲ The Royal Canadian Mounted Police, nicknamed the Mounties, are Canada's national police force.

SEE ALSO

Arctic, Grassland, Native American, North America

CAR

Cars are motorized vehicles with an engine, wheels, and steering mechanism. They are designed to carry passengers or to race in competitions.

There are over 400 million cars on the road today. They have had a huge impact on society and are one of the world's most important inventions.

Cugnot's steam gun carriage of 1769 was the first motorized vehicle.

THE FIRST CARS
The first successful gasoline (gas)-powered vehicles were developed by the German engineers Karl Benz and Gottfried Daimler in the 1880s. Benz designed a complete vehicle. Daimler simply added his engine to a horseless carriage.

Daimler's first car, built in 1886, was a coach fitted with an engine.

HOW A CAR MOVES
Most cars today are powered by gas or diesel engines, or by electric motors. The engine turns a driveshaft, which is linked to the wheels by gears.

The Rolls Royce Silver Ghost of 1906 used automatic engine controls.

STREAMLINING
A car's shape is now designed using computers. It must look good, be safe, and comfortable, and work well. The sleeker or more streamlined the car, the faster and more economical it will be to drive.

The 1914 Model T Ford was the first car made on a moving assembly line.

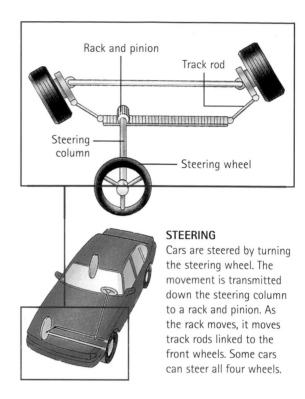

Rack and pinion — Track rod — Steering column — Steering wheel

STEERING
Cars are steered by turning the steering wheel. The movement is transmitted down the steering column to a rack and pinion. As the rack moves, it moves track rods linked to the front wheels. Some cars can steer all four wheels.

Objects that stick out, such as windshield wipers, can be hidden under panels to reduce wind resistance and wind noise. In some modern designs, front and rear panels on the car can be adjusted electronically to change the airflow around the car's body.

Over 20 million Volkswagen Beetles have been sold since 1938.

The 1984 Ferrari Testarossa can reach a speed of 180 mph (290kph).

The GM Sunraycer of 1987 uses solar energy from sunlight to power it.

▼ Racing cars are designed to have minimum air resistance. They have a sleek shape and pointed nose.

Battery — Air filter —

Rear spring

Water from the radiator cools the engine

Coiled spring and shock absorber for suspension

Brake pads apply pressure to discs to slow the car down

Gearshift for selecting the gears

Driveshaft

Gears connect driveshaft to wheels

Shock absorber

Exhaust pipe lets out used gases

Rubber tires filled with air cushion car from bumps

CONTROL SYSTEMS

Gearboxes have up to five forward gears to vary the speed and power of the car, and one gear for reversing. Gears are selected by a shift lever, although many gearboxes are automatic. An electrical system controls the engine, lights, and other instruments. The electric circuits are powered by a battery, which is charged from the engine. Computerized engine management systems in modern cars mean that problems can be diagnosed more easily.

ROAD SAFETY

Road safety is very important in the design of modern cars. Experiments using life-size dummies are carried out by safety experts to establish how a car collapses on impact and how this affects the passengers inside. These experiments have led manufacturers to introduce improvements in the design of the steering wheel, seats, and seat belts, and to the invention and use of new safety devices such as inflatable air bags.

KEY DATES

1891 René Panhard and Emile Levasor build first "horseless" carriage powered by a Daimler engine

1896 Karl Benz patents first automobile

1901 First mass-produced car, the Oldsmobile, is produced by Ransom Eli Olds in the United States

1906 First Grand Prix held at Le Mans, France

1908 Henry Ford introduces the Model T

1934 André Citroën introduces front-wheel drive

1979 Catalytic converter is introduced

IMPROVING COMFORT

Passenger comfort is improved by smooth braking and suspension. Brakes are linked to all four wheels to slow the car down. Modern cars use antilocking brakes to prevent skidding when roads are wet or slippery. The suspension system cushions the car from bumps in the road and usually consists of a coiled spring and shock absorber (to reduce the spring's vibrations) attached to each of the four wheels.

THE ENVIRONMENT

Cars have caused huge environmental and social changes, bringing mobility to millions of people. Thousands of miles of expressways have been built, and the ability to travel long distances to work has helped towns to spread. In some cities, however, poisonous gases from car exhausts and traffic congestion do cause serious problems. It is hoped that the use of new fuels, such as methanol or hydrogen, as well as electric motors, will reduce this pollution.

▼ Crash test dummies are used to test cars for road safety. Here an air bag is shown exploding after a crash. The dummy mimics how a person would be affected in the accident.

SEE ALSO

Invention, Transportation, Truck and bus

CARIBBEAN

The Caribbean islands lie between North and South America, forming a chain about 2,000 mi. (3,200km) long. They include Cuba, Jamaica, and Haiti.

ANTIGUA & BARBUDA
Area: 275 sq. mi.
Population: 67,448
Capital: St. John's
Language: English
Currency: East Caribbean dollar

BAHAMAS
Area: 3,900 sq. mi.
Population: 300,529
Capital: Nassau
Language: English
Currency: Bahamian dollar

BARBADOS
Area: 116 sq. mi.
Population: 276,607
Capital: Bridgetown
Language: English
Currency: East Caribbean dollar

CUBA
Area: 46,736 sq. mi.
Population: 11,224,321
Capital: Havana
Language: Spanish
Currency: Peso

DOMINICA
Area: 290 sq. mi.
Population: 70,158
Capital: Roseau
Language: English
Currency: East Caribbean dollar

The region known as the Caribbean includes three island groups: the Greater Antilles and the Lesser Antilles, which lie in the Caribbean Sea, and the Bahamas, in the Atlantic Ocean. These islands are also known as the West Indies because, when the explorer Christopher Columbus first saw them in 1492, he believed he was near India.

TROPICAL ISLANDS
The Caribbean's tropical climate and steady ocean winds mean that temperatures rarely drop below 77°F (25°C), although the hot days are often relieved by cooling sea breezes. Violent hurricanes sometimes strike the islands, causing great damage to property and crops.

FOREST ANIMALS
Vegetation on the islands includes palm trees and exotic flowers such as orchids. Some islands also have very dense rain forests—home to parrots and macaws, as well as bats, snakes, and insects. In many places, these forests have been cleared to make way for crop plantations.

▲ Bananas are one of the chief crops. They are picked while still green and exported in refrigerated cargo ships.

HOMEGROWN PRODUCE
Sugarcane is the main crop grown on the islands. Stalks are crushed for raw juice or refined to make crystallized sugar. Bananas and other fruits are important crops, as are coffee, cocoa, and cotton.

ISLAND INDUSTRY
As well as farming, there is some mining on the islands. Jamaica has bauxite (aluminum ore), and there is gold in the Dominican Republic. Cuba, Trinidad, and Barbados all have offshore oil and gas, and there is some manufacturing. Tourism is the largest industry, employing as many as one in five people on many of the islands.

THE ORIGINAL ISLANDERS
The first settlers in the Caribbean were the Caribs and Arawaks from South America. Most were killed by Europeans who arrived

▼ Large markets, where people sell homegrown goods, are a familiar aspect of island life.

DOMINICAN REPUBLIC
Area: 18,700 sq. mi.
Population: 8,721,594
Capital: Santo Domingo
Language: Spanish
Currency: Peso

GRENADA
Area: 133 sq. mi.
Population: 89,211
Capital: St. George's
Language: English
Currency: East Caribbean dollar

HAITI
Area: 16,714 sq. mi.
Population: 7,063,722
Capital: Port-au-Prince
Language: French, Creole
Currency: Gourde

JAMAICA
Area: 4,411 sq. mi.
Population: 2,680,029
Capital: Kingston
Language: English
Currency: Jamaican dollar

BAHAMAS

GREATER

ATLANTIC OCEAN

CUBA

CAYMAN IS. (U.K.)

JAMAICA

TURKS AND CAICOS IS. (U.K.)

ANTILLES

HAITI | DOMINICAN REPUBLIC

HISPANIOLA

CARIBBEAN SEA

◄ This square in Cuba has architecture typical of that built by the European colonials.

PUERTO RICO (U.S.)

ST. KITTS-NEVIS

ANTIGUA & BARBUDA

MONTSERRAT (U.K.)

GUADELOUPE (FRANCE)

DOMINICA

MARTINIQUE (FRANCE)

ST. LUCIA
BARBADOS

ST. VINCENT & THE GRENADINES

GRENADA

TRINIDAD & TOBAGO

LESSER

ANTILLES

KEY TO MAP
1 VIRGIN IS. (U.S.)
2 VIRGIN IS. (U.K.)
3 ANGUILLA (U.K.)

miles
0 — 100
0 — 100
km

Countries in parentheses are countries of which that island or group is a dependency. Aruba (Netherlands) is not shown.

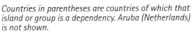

soon after Columbus sighted the islands. The Europeans brought slaves from Africa to work on sugar and cotton plantations. After the abolition of slavery in the 1800s, people from India and China came to work in the Caribbean.

A CULTURAL MIX
The people of the Caribbean reflect its mix of cultures. They speak Spanish, French, or English, often with a local dialect. Religion is an important part of life. As well as Christians, Hindus, and Muslims, there are Rastafarians, who worship Haile Selassie (emperor of Ethiopia until 1974) as a god. On Haiti, many people practice voodoo, a blend of African and Christian beliefs.

SELF-GOVERNING
Most larger islands are self-governing. Others are dependencies still linked to a colonial partner. They include Guadeloupe (France) and the two Virgin Island groups (U.K. and U.S.). The governments of the Caribbean are working to develop the islands, many of which are poor. In the last 50 years, many islanders have migrated to Britain, Canada, or the U.S. to find work.

ST. KITTS-NEVIS
Area: 152 sq. mi.
Population: 38,736
Capital: Basseterre
Language: English
Currency: East Caribbean dollar

ST. LUCIA
Area: 236 sq. mi.
Population: 160,145
Capital: Castries
Language: English
Currency: East Caribbean dollar

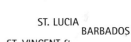

ST. VINCENT & THE GRENADINES
Area: 150 sq. mi.
Population: 116,394
Capital: Kingstown
Language: English
Currency: East Caribbean dollar

TRINIDAD & TOBAGO
Area: 1,864 sq. mi.
Population: 1,163,724
Capital: Port of Spain
Language: English
Currency: Trinidad dollar

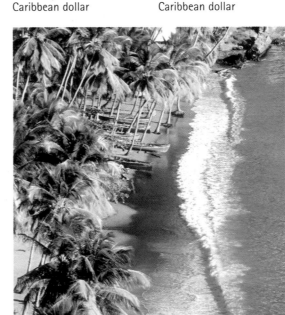

▲ The beautiful sandy beaches and warm waters of the Caribbean islands lure tourists from all over the world.

SEE ALSO
Empire, Explorer, North America, Slavery

CARTOON AND ANIMATION

A cartoon can be an animated film, a comic strip, or a single picture. The first printed cartoons, in the 1840s, ridiculed prominent people or political events.

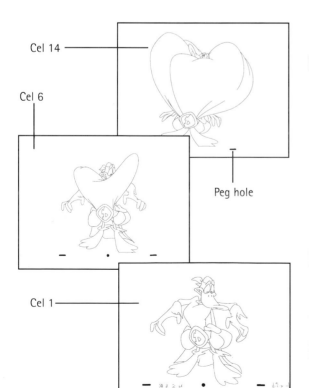

©Marvel Comics

▲ Spiderman, created in 1962, has crossed over from comic book to animated film.

The word "cartoon" was originally used by artists to describe the picture they produced as part of the preparation for a painting or tapestry. Today, cartoons are seen on screen and in print.

CEL ANIMATION

The traditional way of making cartoons for TV and film involves creating a moving sequence from a collection of individual images. This process is known as cel animation. Each action or change of expression of a character is made by using a number of slightly different hand-drawn pictures. When these are shown one after another on film, they give the viewer the illusion of movement by the character.

A CAST OF THOUSANDS

Between 15,000 and 20,000 images are used for a 20-minute animated film, so a whole studio of artists is often needed for longer films. Painters create a background picture for each scene, and illustrators draw the characters. Then other artists touch up the images. Disney's *Beauty and the Beast* had 90 artists whose only job was to touch up the lines. Once the image has been colored in, it is placed on a clear plastic sheet of celluloid, called an acetate, by a paint and trace artist. Then, finally, the animation is shot onto film.

COMPUTER ANIMATION

Many artists still draw by hand and use computers to add color. Computers also speed up the rendering (the planning of the movements and the creation of the frames). Disney's *Toy Story*, made in 1995, was the first full-length film to be made entirely by computer animation.

COMIC STRIPS

Comic strips use a smaller creative team than animated films. A strip tells a story in a series of pictures. Speech balloons are used to put words into the mouths of characters.

Cel 14

Cel 6

Peg hole

Cel 1

COMPUTER EFFECTS

In *The Duck* by Uli Meyer Animation, the figures were hand-drawn on transparent plastic, then scanned into a computer to be colored in and made three-dimensional. About 750 drawings were used in a five-second scene where Duck foils two robbers. The drawings (cels) are pegged one over the other to check the order of movement.

SEE ALSO

Computer, Design, Film, Newspaper and magazine

CASTLE

Castles are fortified homes that were owned by rich and powerful families during the Middle Ages. Some are still in use, but many are now in ruins.

Early castles, known as motte and baileys, were made of wood and soil.

Massive stone keeps began to be erected around 1070.

Concentric castles had two or more walls and strongly guarded gatehouses.

In the Middle Ages, castles were used to protect towns, river crossings, and frontiers. They were also used to guard against invasion and prevent rebellion.

MOTTE AND BAILEY
Castles were first built around A.D. 950 by knights or lords. The castles included a hill or mound surrounded by a ditch and topped by a wooden tower called a motte. A bailey, or courtyard, contained living quarters, stables, granaries, and barns. These early castles were protected by a high wooden fence, called a palisade.

STONE CASTLES
From about 1070, larger castles had a stone tower called a keep. The Tower of London, the first keep in England, was begun in 1078. Food and weapons were stored inside the tower, and the knight and his staff lived there. Prisoners were kept in dungeons.

TOWERS AND WALLS
From the 1100s onward, stone curtain walls were built to surround the keeps. Towers were added to the outside of the walls so that attackers could be shot at from different directions. After about 1270, a second outer wall was added to some castles to make them harder to attack. These castles, often built by Crusaders in the Middle East, were called concentric because of their double walls.

UNDER ATTACK
A castle was attacked with catapults, rams, and siege towers. Boulders and flaming missiles were hurled at it, and its walls undermined. If a castle was not captured quickly it was besieged. Most castles fell because of bribery, disease, or famine.

CANNON FIRE
By the 1450s, cannons and gunpowder became powerful enough to destroy walls. Castles were no longer safe from attack. Most fell into ruin, but some continued to be used as palaces or luxurious homes.

UNDER SIEGE
Armies attacked castles by smashing walls with catapults or rams and by digging out foundations so that the walls collapsed. The moat was drained and filled in so that siege machines could be wheeled right up to the walls. Attackers were shielded by frames covered with wet hides.

Keep

Curtain wall with towers

A giant catapult called a trebuchet hurled rocks

Rocks and soil, covered with wood, created a path across the moat

A battering ram was used to smash walls

Rocks and boiling water were poured on attackers

Soldiers used a siege tower to climb the walls

SEE ALSO
Crusades, Middle Ages, Warfare

67

CAT

Cats are agile, hunting mammals with keen senses and sharp teeth and claws. Domestic cats make some of the most popular pets.

The longhaired Persian needs regular grooming to keep its coat sleek.

The hairless sphinx was bred in the 1960s from a kitten born without fur.

The Manx cat from the Isle of Man, in the U.K., is famous for its lack of a tail.

The blue shorthair has copper eyes and a quiet, affectionate nature.

The Cornish rex has a curly coat of short, thin hair and large, open ears.

The Siamese has long been one of the most popular pedigreed (purebred) cats.

HUNTER IN THE HOME

Even a domestic cat, like this tabby, has the hunting instincts of its wild relations. Cats often toy with their prey, rather than killing it immediately. They hunt mostly at night, catching mice, small birds, and insects.

Whiskers are modified hairs with nerves at their base and are ultra-sensitive to touch

Extended

Retracted

THE CLAWS
Cats retract (pull back) their claws to keep them sharp when not in use. Each claw is attached to a toe bone. It is retracted by ligaments, which are worked by muscles.

Large, sensitive ears pick up sounds too faint for human ears to hear

Pupils open wide to let in a maximum amount of light. A mirrorlike layer at the back of the eye intensifies the light

The cat family is divided into two main groups, based largely on size. The first group is made up of big cats such as tigers, lions, and leopards. The second includes cougars, bobcats, and lynxes, as well as the many small wild cats and the domestic cat. In all there are about 37 species of cat.

PET CATS
It is thought that the domestic cat was originally a small wild cat living in Africa. By 2000 B.C. it had been tamed by the Ancient Egyptians, who used it to protect their stored food from mice and rats. Today, there are many breeds of domestic cat, including longhaired Persians and Angoras and the shorthaired Manx and Siamese.

CAT CHARACTERISTICS
Domestic cats resemble their wild relatives in many ways. They are excellent hunters, strong and agile, with a keen sense of hearing and very good eyesight. They have curved claws, strong jaws, sharp teeth, and whiskers that are sensitive to touch. Cats are naturally inquisitive and are expert climbers and jumpers. Their flexible backbones allow them to swivel their bodies into a wide range of positions.

CAT BEHAVIOR
Cats spend at least an hour a day grooming their fur by licking it with their rough tongues. This helps to keep their fur in good condition and keeps them cool in hot weather. Cats sleep, on the average, twice as long as other mammals, spending up to three fourths of the day asleep, usually in short intervals—hence "catnaps."

HUNTING TACTICS
Although most domestic cats do not have to catch their own food, their instinct (inborn behavior) is to hunt. A cat's sensitive nose quickly picks up the scent of its prey. With its soft, padded paws, a cat can stalk its prey without being noticed until it is close enough to pounce. Then it grabs the prey with its claws and kills it with a powerful bite—usually at the back of the head, breaking the victim's neck.

SEE ALSO
Animal, Mammal, Sight, Tiger

CAVE

Caves are hollows that are formed in rock and ice by erosion (wearing away), usually by water. The largest, most impressive caves are found in limestone rock.

Some caves consist of just one hole barely large enough for a person to enter; others are intricate mazes of passageways and chambers. The Mammoth Cave network in Kentucky is the world's longest. Its labyrinth of caves stretches for 350 mi. (560km).

ROCK, ICE, AND LAVA

Caves sometimes form in sea cliffs, where waves attack weak spots in the rock. The pressure of the water and the salty spray gradually erode the cliff structures. Long, tunnel-like caves can also develop in glaciers where streams of melted water run beneath the ice. Similar caves can be found in volcanoes, where a crust forms over a liquid stream of molten lava.

LIMESTONE CAVES

The largest and most impressive caves are found in limestone rock, where rainwater (which is slightly acidic) trickles through cracks in the rock. The rock slowly dissolves and the thin cracks get wider

and wider. The trickle of rainwater swells into a stream, which carves hollows in the stone to form caves and potholes.

THE INSIDE STORY

Where streams meet, they carve out very large caves, or caverns. The floor of the cavern may be filled by underground lakes, so that it can only be explored by diving. Water dripping from the ceilings of limestone caves is rich in minerals, such as calcium carbonate, from the dissolved rock. As the water drips, these mincrals are often deposited in dramatic columns—long, slender stalactites hang down from the ceiling; shorter, stumpier stalagmites grow up from the floor. Where they join together, a pillar is formed.

MAKING CAVES

It takes thousands of years for a limestone cave to form. The process begins when rainwater starts to wear away the stone and seep through cracks. Horizontal caverns are made where the water forms underground lakes. These are left dry when the level of groundwater falls.

1 Rain falls on the ground and seeps through cracks in the rock.

2 The cracks get wider and form a pothole.

3 Passages appear as the water continues to dissolve the rock.

4 The water becomes an underground stream, gradually eroding more rock to form a cave.

Stalactite

Stalagmite

Underground stream

5 Stalactites and stalagmites are formed from minerals deposited by the dripping water.

SEE ALSO

Glacier, Rock, Seashore, Volcano, Water

CELL

Cells are the smallest units capable of all the functions of life. Some living things are single cells; others (such as ourselves) are made up of billions of cells.

Bacteria have only one cell and can multiply fast.

Onions, like most plants, have box-shaped cells.

Sperm cells are used in reproduction.

Nerve cells take messages to and from the brain.

Muscle cells are long and thin and lie in bundles.

Every living thing is made up of tiny chambers, called cells—the basic building blocks of all organisms. Every cell has its job, but works with the others to keep the plant or animal alive. Some things, such as bacteria, are just one cell; this contains all they need to survive.

THROUGH THE WALLS
Each animal cell is surrounded by a thin membrane. This gives it shape and lets chemicals and waste pass in and out. Inside the membrane, tiny structures float in cytoplasm, a jellylike fluid.

INSIDE THE CHAMBER
Each tiny structure, or organelle, in a cell has a job. The nucleus, for example, contains genes (instructions that decide the cell's shape and function). Sausage-shaped structures called mitochondria release the energy in food. Other organelles store energy, make proteins, keep the cell clear of debris, or defend it against bacteria.

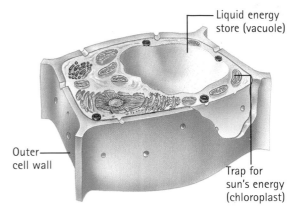

Liquid energy store (vacuole)

Outer cell wall

Trap for sun's energy (chloroplast)

▲ Plant cells have a thick wall of cellulose, which gives them a rigid shape. Up to 90 percent of their space is taken up by the vacuole—a sack full of sugary water.

PLANT CELLS
Unlike animal cells, plant cells have a thick cell wall and extra structures called chloroplasts. These structures are filled with a green pigment called chlorophyll. This traps the sun's energy and uses it to make food in a process called photosynthesis.

SPLITTING IN TWO
Cells multiply by splitting in two. Under a microscope, you can see some bacteria split as fast as once every 15 minutes. Most animal and plant cells multiply much more slowly than this for growth, to repair damage, and for reproduction.

Up to 800 mitochondria power the cell

Thin cell wall (membrane)

Cytoplasm (jellylike fluid)

Paired structures called centrioles help the cell to multiply

Substances leave or enter the cell in bubbles

ANIMAL CELLS
Every part of an animal—from its bones to its blood—is made of cells. Many of the cells are spherical, but unevenly shaped, because they do not have a thick outer wall like plant cells. They all have the same basic structures inside them, known as organelles.

Bean-shaped structures (lysosomes) clean up bacteria and debris in the cell

Little balls (ribosomes) make proteins (building blocks)

Structures called Golgi apparatuses pack proteins into bubbles

The nucleus is the cell's control center

SEE ALSO
Brain and nervous system, Disease, Genetics, Reproduction

CELT

The Celts are a group of people who lived in Europe from about 2,500 years ago. They were fierce warriors who fought frequently.

This Celtic silver and gold drinking cup was made in Ireland in the A.D. 700s.

A Celtic noble or priest would have worn this gold torque around his neck.

A brooch, from the 500s, used to fasten a woolen cloak around the shoulders.

The first Celts lived in central Europe from about 500 B.C. and came to live in countries such as Germany, France, Britain, and Spain. Most of what we know about Celtic life and culture has been passed down in accounts written by the Romans.

FARMING AND METALWORK
The Celts lived by farming the land, growing grain, root crops, and fruit, and breeding cattle, sheep, and pigs. They were skilled metalworkers, famous for gold jewelry. During the Iron Age, they made high-quality weapons and armor.

TRIBAL WARS
Celtic tribes fought fierce battles with their rivals. Warriors wore little armor, sometimes fighting naked to prove their bravery. Many tribes built fortifications on hills for protection. In Britain, Queen Boudicca (or Boadicea) led her tribe, the Iceni, in a failed attack on the Romans in A.D. 61.

▲ This map shows the major areas of Celtic settlement in about 200 B.C. Celtic people living in Turkey were called Galatians, while in France they were called Gauls.

GODS AND DRUIDS
The Celts had no written language, but passed on stories of their gods and history in songs and poems. They worshiped many different gods and goddesses, offering sacrifices in their honor. Ceremonies and rituals were performed by Druidic priests.

TODAY'S CELTS
Most Celtic tribes were conquered by about A.D. 150, during the spread of the Roman Empire. Today, Celtic people can be found in the British Isles and in Brittany, in France.

WARRIOR QUEEN
Queen Maeve ruled Celtic Connaught in Ireland in about A.D. 100. According to a later legendary story, "The Cattle Raid of Cooley," she attacked Ulster in order to capture a brown bull to complete her collection of prized items. She captured the animal, but was later defeated by another Celt, Cuchulainn.

SEE ALSO
France, Ireland (Republic of), Roman Empire

CENTRAL AMERICA

Central America is a strip of land between North and South America. It consists of Belize, Guatemala, Costa Rica, El Salvador, Honduras, Nicaragua, and Panama.

BELIZE
Area: 8,800 sq. mi.
Population: 262,999
Capital: Belmopan
Languages: English, Spanish
Currency: Belize dollar

COSTA RICA
Area: 19,238 sq. mi.
Population: 3,834,934
Capital: San José
Language: Spanish
Currency: Colón

EL SALVADOR
Area: 8,236 sq. mi.
Population: 6,353,681
Capital: San Salvador
Language: Spanish
Currency: Colón

GUATEMALA
Area: 42,042 sq. mi.
Population: 13,314,079
Capital: Guatemala City
Language: Spanish
Currency: Quetzal

Poverty, political instability, and civil war have troubled Central America for the last 100 years. All seven countries in this region are rich in natural resources, but wealth is spread unevenly. A growing number of people earn money from tourism, but 40 percent still work on the land, earning barely enough to survive.

LAND AND CLIMATE
Lowland forests, plains, and swamps lie along the Central American coasts, and rivers and mountains crisscross the region. Its many volcanoes include Guatemala's Tajumulco, the highest peak in Central America. The region's climate is hot and moist, with temperatures seldom dropping below 75°F (24°C). Land along the coast has the highest temperatures, with cooler areas inland on the mountains and plateaus (flat areas of land high above sea level). More than 12 in. (300mm) of rain per month falls in some areas from July to September.

FORESTS IN DANGER
Central America has some of the richest forests in the world, containing valuable hardwood trees, such as mahogany.

▲ The Mayan temple of Altun Ha lies deep in the rain forest of Belize. Hundreds of palaces and pyramids were built by the Maya in Central America between A.D. 300 and A.D. 900.

But in some places, including Costa Rica, the trees are being cut down so fast for timber, or to make space for farming, that national parks have been set up to protect the remaining trees. Jaguars, monkeys, snakes, caimans (like small alligators), iguanas, many species of bird, as well as colorful butterflies and other insects are all at risk from deforestation.

AGRICULTURAL LIFE
The majority of people in Central America are farmers. Cattle and sheep are raised in upland areas; export crops, such as bananas, sugarcane, cotton, and about one tenth of the world's coffee supply, are grown on plantations. Chicle (for chewing gum) is collected from sapodilla trees, and cacao beans are farmed for chocolate. Indian corn, beans, and rice are grown for food.

▼ Most Central Americans are Roman Catholic, but their religious festivals often have a local flavor. For example, All Saints' Day (November 1) is celebrated in Guatemala with riotous horse races.

◀ There are many Indian communities in Guatemala, each with its own distinct style of dress.

HONDURAS
Area: 59,160 sq. mi.
Population: 6,560,608
Capital: Tegucigalpa
Language: Spanish
Currency: Lempira

NICARAGUA
Area: 57,143 sq. mi.
Population: 5,023,818
Capital: Managua
Languages: Spanish
Currency: Gold córdoba

INDEPENDENT NATIONS

Honduras, Guatemala, El Salvador, Costa Rica, and Nicaragua gained independence from Spain in the 1800s. Panama separated from Colombia in 1903, and Belize was a British colony until 1981. In the 1960s, the Central American Common Market was set up to create unity between all the countries, but until recently, civil war and political instability have made this difficult. Today, renewed efforts are being made for greater cooperation between members.

PANAMA
Area: 29,300 sq. mi.
Population: 2,882,329
Capital: Panama City
Languages: Spanish, English
Currency: Balboa

INDUSTRIAL GROWTH

Migration to the cities in Central America is growing, but jobs are scarce since industry is still limited to small factories making clothing, household items, and shoes. Handmade pottery, woolen rugs, leatherwork, and hats are sold to tourists.

PEOPLE AND LANGUAGE

Most Central Americans are of mixed European and Indian descent. In the 1500s, Spanish soldiers and gold seekers conquered the region. Before then, it was home to various Indian tribes, including the Maya who ruled between A.D. 300 and A.D. 900. Many of the first European settlers brought African slaves, whose descendants still live in Belize, Nicaragua, and Panama. Spanish is spoken all over the region, although English is the official language in Belize. Many people also speak local Indian languages.

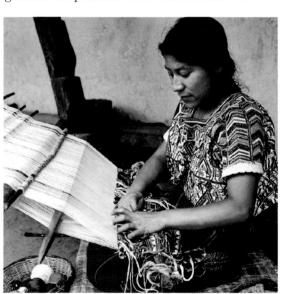

◀ Many Guatemalan village women weave traditional textiles to sell to tourists.

SEE ALSO

Aztec, Civil war, Conservation, Maya

CHEMISTRY

Chemistry is the study of chemicals. These are substances that are used in, or created by, a reaction involving changes to atoms or molecules.

ANTOINE LAVOISIER
(1743–94). Lavoisier was a French chemist. He explained how chemical reactions worked. He was the first to understand the role of oxygen in combustion (burning).

Oxygen is an element. The two atoms that make up its molecules are of the same kind. The chemical formula for oxygen is O_2.

Carbon dioxide gas is a compound of two oxygen atoms with one carbon atom. Its chemical formula is written CO_2.

A molecule of methane gas has a carbon atom in the middle bonded to four hydrogen atoms. Its formula is written CH_4.

Water has one oxygen atom and two hydrogen atoms, giving it probably the best-known chemical formula, H_2O.

CHEMICAL ANALYSIS

Chemists use flame tests as a way of identifying chemical elements—by seeing which color they give off when held in the flame of a Bunsen burner. A compound of an element is burned on the end of a piece of platinum wire or asbestos. The flame burns a distinctive color and so the element can be identified. This type of chemical analysis is called qualitative, and shows what elements a substance contains. To show how much of an element is present, chemists use quantitative analysis.

Barium

Potassium

Lithium

Sodium

Copper

Calcium

The compound is put into the flame on a platinum wire

Bunsen burner

Flame colors of elements

Chemistry explains the way substances behave and how they combine with each other. Chemists use chemical reactions to create many substances used in everyday life, including plastics, dyes, glues, detergents, and medicines.

ELEMENTS AND COMPOUNDS

An element is a substance in which all the atoms are of the same kind. A compound is a combination of two or more elements. The compound sodium chloride (common salt), for example, is a combination of the elements sodium and chlorine. Many compounds, including salt and water, occur naturally. Others, such as nylon and plastic, were first made artificially in laboratories.

CHEMICAL REACTIONS

When different substances combine to form new materials, a chemical reaction has taken place. A substance's atoms are bonded together into molecules. During a reaction, the bonds between atoms break, allowing new molecules to form. A rusting car is an example of a chemical reaction, as iron in the car and oxygen in the air form iron oxide, or rust. Chemists use symbols (such as Fe for iron and O for oxygen) to record what happens in a reaction.

ALCHEMISTS TO SCIENTISTS

Medieval alchemists studied reactions, but it was not until the 1770s that Antoine Lavoisier showed how reactions work. In 1869, Russian chemist Dmitri Mendeleyev worked out the periodic table, grouping elements by how they react with each other.

WEAPONS AND DRUGS

Today, chemical substances of all kinds are mined or manufactured. Chemists search for new reactions to create fertilizers or drugs, which may contain long chains of molecules. Industry mass-produces useful chemicals through large-scale reactions. Poison gas and other chemicals have been used as weapons, but they are now banned.

▲ Rust is the visible sign of a chemical reaction called oxidation. Oxygen in air or water combines with iron in metal to form iron oxide, or rust.

SEE ALSO
Atom and molecule, Metal, Paint and dye, Plastic, Warfare

CHINA

China is the third largest country in the world and the nation with the largest population. Almost a fourth of the Earth's people live in China.

Area: 3,691,502 sq. mi.
Population: 1,284,303,705
Capital: Beijing
Language: Mandarin
Currency: Yuan

China is one of the world's oldest civilizations. Its name comes from an ancient Chinese ruling family called Qin (pronounced Ch'in). The Chinese call their country Zhongguo, which means "middle land." China's 1.2 billion citizens are ruled by one of the world's few remaining communist governments.

NATURAL BARRIERS
China lies in eastern Asia; deserts and mountains form natural barriers with its neighbors. The Gobi Desert—502,000 sq. mi. (1,300,000sq km)—straddles the border with Mongolia. The Himalayas—the highest mountains on Earth, rising to almost 5 mi. (8,000m)—stretch along the border with India, Bhutan, and Nepal. The Chang (Yangtze) River is the longest in Asia and flows from the Tibetan uplands to the East China Sea, dividing the warm, moist southern regions from the drier and cooler north.

▲ The bicycle is China's main method of transportation. More than 17 million bicycles are made there each year.

▲ The giant panda lives in the bamboo forests of central and western China. So few now survive in the wild that it has become a worldwide symbol for conservation.

CHINA'S WILDLIFE
Plant life ranges from bamboos and other subtropical plants in the south to coniferous forests in the north. Garden plants now common around the world, such as wisteria, first came from China. With much of the country covered by mountains and desert, forests have been cleared to make way for villages and farms. This has reduced the habitats of animals such as the tiger (which is also prey to hunters) and the giant panda, making them rare in the wild. ▶

THE GREAT WALL OF CHINA
One of China's greatest early empires was ruled by the Qin dynasty. The first Qin emperor, Shi Huangdi, came to the throne in 221 B.C. He ordered the construction of the Great Wall to keep out invaders from the north. Stretching for 4,000 mi. (6,400km), the wall was built by joining together shorter walls that had been built earlier. The wall has been rebuilt many times. Most of the present wall was constructed during the Ming Dynasty (1368–1644).

RUSSIA

KAZAKHSTAN

RUSSIA

• Yining

Harbin •

KYRGYZSTAN

Tian Shan

MONGOLIA

MONGOLIAN UPLANDS

TAJIKISTAN

TAKLIMAKAN DESERT

Shenyang •

NORTH KOREA

PAKISTAN

• Hotan

GOBI DESERT

Beijing ■

Kunlun Mts.

Huang He

Tianjin •

INDIA

SOUTH KOREA

N

Xining •

• Lanzhou

C H I N A

YELLOW SEA

PLATEAU OF TIBET

• Xi'an

CENTRAL UPLANDS

Nanjing •

miles

0   500

NEPAL

0   500

km

Himalaya Mts.

Mt. Everest

BHUTAN

Wuhan •

• Shanghai

Chongqing •

Chang

EAST CHINA SEA

INDIA

Nanning •

Guangzhou •

TAIWAN

MYANMAR (BURMA)

LAOS

VIETNAM

MACAO   *HONG KONG*

SOUTH CHINA SEA

Hainan Island

A NATION OF FARMERS

About 70 percent of people farm the land. Many farms are run as collectives, with people working together and dividing crops between the government and themselves. Important crops include rice, which is the main food of the south, and wheat, which is used to make bread and noodles in the north.

Millet, tea, vegetables, soybeans, and cotton are also grown; and many farmers breed pigs, ducks, and chickens.

INDUSTRIAL GROWTH

Chinese industry has grown rapidly in the last 40 years. Factories produce machinery, transportation equipment, clothing, and electrical goods. Shanghai is the leading industrial city. In 1997, Hong Kong—then a British colony and wealthy financial and industrial center—was returned to China.

WRITING IN CHARACTERS

Over 90 percent of the people are Han Chinese, originally from the north of China. Mandarin is the main dialect, but many others are also spoken. Chinese writing does not use an alphabet. Instead, it uses symbols called characters that stand for words or ideas, not letters.

▼ Traditional ways of life are still strong in many parts of China. Here, fishermen use birds called cormorants to bring up fish from the water. They tie a thong around the bird's throat to stop it swallowing the catch.

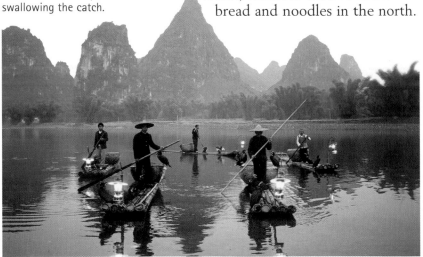

PHILOSOPHY AND FAMILY

For more than 2,000 years, Confucianism has been China's main religion. It teaches respect for parents and ancestors and has strongly influenced family life in China. At one time, several generations of the same family lived in the same house. Today, in an effort to curb China's population growth, the government rewards one-child families with priority housing and medical care. This has led to much smaller families.

RULED BY DYNASTIES

For thousands of years, China was an empire ruled by emperors from successive royal families called dynasties. Many great inventions were made by the Chinese, including paper, ink, silk, printing, and gunpowder. China remained isolated from most of the rest of the world until the 1800s, when foreign powers forced China to open its borders to trade. In 1911, dynastic rule was ended and the country became a republic.

COMMUNIST RULE

In 1949, China adopted a communist government and was renamed the People's Republic of China, under the leadership of Mao Tse-tung. His strict policies meant that there were many changes as all aspects of life came under state control, and people found their freedom restricted.

▲ Preparing food on a street stall. Rice, noodles, and vegetables are the main ingredients used in Chinese cooking.

◄ Shanghai is China's largest city, with a population of 13,400,000. It is also China's leading industrial center.

CHINA TODAY

Since Mao's death in 1976, China's government has encouraged economic reform and trade with foreign countries. More and more people are moving from the countryside to cities, attracted by factory jobs and higher standards of living. But political change is limited. In 1989, up to 1,000 protesting students were killed in Beijing's Tiananmen Square.

▶ This man is performing a traditional form of exercise that develops both mind and body. Called wushu, it is an ancient Chinese martial art.

◄ Farmers bring their produce to sell at a market in southern China. Here, farmers harvest three crops a year—two of rice and one of vegetables.

SEE ALSO

Asia, Communism, Mongol Empire, Paper, Zoology

CHRISTIANITY

Christianity is a religion based on the teachings of Jesus Christ, who lived in Palestine about 2,000 years ago. Today, it is practiced throughout the world.

▲ Upon entering the Christian faith, followers are baptized, or dipped in water. This symbolizes cleansing and reflects the way Jesus was baptized by John the Baptist.

More people follow the Christian religion than any other. About 1.5 billion people believe that there is only one God and that he sent his son to Earth to save people from sin.

The most well-known symbol of Christianity is the cross. It represents the cross on which Jesus was crucified.

THE LIFE OF CHRIST
The life and teachings of Jesus Christ are contained in the New Testament of the Bible, the Christians' holy book. (The Old Testament of the Bible contains the sacred writings of the Jews.) Jesus is said to have performed miracles and healed the sick. The Roman rulers of Jerusalem crucified him by nailing him to a cross. Christians believe that three days later Jesus was raised from the dead, and that some 40 days later he rose into Heaven.

Greek Christians used the fish as a code. The Greek word for fish spelled out the first letters of "Jesus Christ, God's Son, Savior."

CHRISTIANITY SPREADS
Jesus' teachings were spread by his disciples, or followers, who formed the early church. Despite persecution, Christianity became the religion of the Roman Empire in A.D. 324 and later spread across the world. Today, there are three main divisions in the Christian Church: Roman Catholic, Protestant, and

The Christian Bible consists of the Hebrew Bible (Old Testament) and Christ's life and teachings (New Testament).

Eastern Orthodox. About one billion people are Catholics.

THREE-IN-ONE GOD
Christians believe that God is a Trinity: the Father (God), the Son (Jesus), and the Holy Spirit (God's influence on Earth).

THE HOLY MEAL
Before his Crucifixion, Jesus ate the Last Supper with his disciples. Christians reenact this meal with bread and wine in a special church ceremony called Holy Communion, or Mass, when Christ "becomes present" again. They celebrate Christ's birth at Christmas and his Resurrection at Easter, and the coming of the Holy Spirit at Pentecost.

▲ On Palm Sunday (the Sunday before Easter), many Christians carry palms in church. This commemorates Jesus' entry into Jerusalem, when he was greeted with branches of palm.

▶ The leader of the Roman Catholic Church is the Pope. Catholics believe he is God's representative on Earth.

SEE ALSO

Crusades, Religion, Renaissance, Roman Empire

CITY

A city is a large community where thousands of people live and work. Nearly half of the world's population lives in cities.

Most cities are commercial or administrative centers. They are usually larger and more important than other towns in their region. Not all cities are huge. In Europe, a city is a town with a cathedral. In the United States, "city" is applied to an urban area with definite boundaries. The world's largest city is Tokyo in Japan, with over 25 million people, including those living in suburbs.

CITY LOCATIONS

The earliest cities grew in areas where the climate was suitable for growing crops. Access was also important so that trade could develop. Venice in Italy, London in England, and Kolkata (Calcutta) in India all grew because of their closeness to water, which provided transportation routes.

PLANNING AHEAD

Most of today's cities were not planned, but spread out as they grew. In 1692, William Penn, the founder of the state of Pennsylvania, drew a plan for Philadelphia that resembled a grid. This became the pattern for most U.S. cities. In the mid-1800s, a French administrator called Baron Georges-Eugene Haussmann redesigned Paris with wide boulevards and open squares rather than the chaotic maze of small streets that the city had been before.

CAPITAL CITIES

Every country has a capital city where the national government is located. During the 1900s, a few capital cities were designed and built from new, including Canberra in Australia, Brasília in Brazil, and Islamabad in Pakistan. But more often, capitals have grown over time and have a mixture of old and new buildings alongside each other. The oldest parts of a city often form the center. Many people live outside the city center in areas known as suburbs.

HOW CITIES WORK

With city centers becoming busier and more densely packed, high-rise buildings make the most of limited space. People working in the city often move farther out, where land is cheaper. This means that good road and train systems are necessary to bring them into the center.

▲ Large, elegant department stores attract tourists and shoppers to cities.

▲ The opera and other forms of entertainment bring people to the city center. They are often performed in grand and ornate buildings.

▲ Placing mass transit systems underground creates more space in cities.

▲ A good road network and public transportation are important to link the city with the suburbs.

SEE ALSO

Housing, Road, Skyscraper, Train, Transportation

CIVIL RIGHTS

Civil rights are the laws and customs that entitle everyone to fair and equal treatment. They give people the freedom to speak and act within the law.

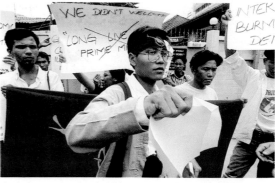
▲ A demonstration held in 1997 against the military government in Myanmar (Burma). The government had refused to recognize the results of recent elections.

▲ Amnesty International works for the freeing of political prisoners and prisoners of conscience. It campaigns against torture and the death penalty.

▲ The flag of the United Nations, which was set up in 1946, after the end of World War II. The aim of the UN is to maintain international peace and cooperation.

The idea of civil rights in the West dates back to the writings of Ancient Greek and Roman philosophers, and to the ideas of Judaism and Christianity. In some countries, civil rights are protected by a written constitution, as in the United States; in others, such as the United Kingdom, they consist of laws and customs built up over hundreds of years.

FAIR AND EQUAL
Civil rights mean people must be treated fairly and equally, no matter what their sex, religion, or ethnic origin. They are allowed freedom to express what they believe in speech or in the media. They also have the right to organize a political party, to have a fair trial if accused of a crime, and to vote in elections.

THE FIGHT FOR THE RIGHT
Many rights have been won only after a long and painful struggle. During the 1950s and 1960s, Dr. Martin Luther King led the civil rights campaign to win equality for black Americans. In South Africa, Nelson Mandela was imprisoned in 1962 for opposing apartheid (the separation of whites and nonwhites). He was finally released in 1991, when apartheid was abolished. In 1994, Mandela was elected South Africa's first black president.

CIVIL RIGHTS ABUSES
International bodies, such as the United Nations and the European Court of Human Rights, protect civil rights; other organizations, like Amnesty International, campaign on behalf of people who are persecuted. However, some governments continue to ban civil rights. Dictators and single-party states deny rights to their people because they do not want their power threatened. Communist countries, such as China, traditionally stress the importance of social rights—for example, the right to work—often at the expense of human rights like freedom of speech.

"I HAVE A DREAM"
In 1963, Martin Luther King led 200,000 people on a civil rights march in Washington, D.C. In his speech he declared, "I have a dream," demanding equal rights for black Americans. The Civil Rights Act of 1964 followed, and King was awarded the Nobel Peace Prize. In 1968 he was shot.

SEE ALSO
Communism, Democracy, Fascism, South Africa

CIVIL WAR

Civil war is an armed struggle between people who live in the same country or nation. Civil war is usually triggered by political, religious, or ethnic differences.

Families, communities, and whole countries have been divided by civil war. Because fighting takes place wholly within a country, no one escapes its effects. Prisoners are often murdered, homes destroyed, and civilians terrorized.

FIGHTING FOR RIGHTS

Civil wars erupt because of a difference in people's beliefs. They are often begun by minorities fighting for greater political or religious rights, for union with a similar group in a nearby state, or for the right to keep their way of life. These minorities are often led by strong figures.

OUTSIDE INFLUENCE

In some civil wars, outside countries give their support to one side, often for political gain or to protect human rights. During the 1980s, for example, a desperate civil war raged in Nicaragua between the socialist government and the right-wing Contras. The U.S.A. supported the Contras in order to combat the spread of left-wing socialist and communist regimes in Central America. Such foreign interference was typical of the Cold War, a period of rivalry and deep distrust between the Soviet Union, the U.S.A., and their supporters.

ETHNIC CLASHES

Civil wars started by ethnic (racial) hatred have produced some of the worst cruelties of recent times. In the early 1990s, fighting broke out in Yugoslavia, as three provinces—Bosnia, Croatia, and Slovenia—fought for independence from the Serbian-dominated state. During the long-running war, thousands of civilians became the innocent victims of ethnic cleansing—the murder or forced eviction of one racial group by another through the use of violence and terror.

AFRICAN UNREST

When colonial rule ended in many African nations in the 1960s and 1970s, civil war followed. Within countries like Nigeria and Angola, different peoples had been forced together by colonial boundaries and these differences caused conflict. Some of the bloodiest civil wars caused by political and ethnic differences have broken out in Somalia, Congo, and Chad.

▲ An Angolan UNITA rebel soldier pictured in 1986. Angola has suffered years of civil war, backed, until 1990, by countries such as Cuba, the Soviet Union, South Africa, and the United States.

▲ A United Nations soldier helps an old woman cross the main street in Sarajevo, in the former Yugoslavia. An armored vehicle shields them from sniper fire.

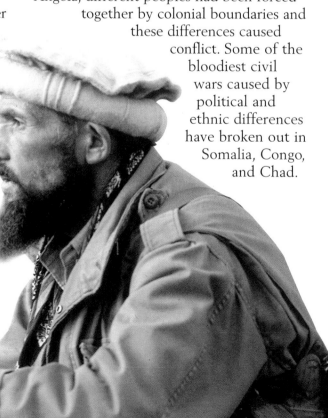

▶ A guerrilla fighter in Afghanistan. During the 1980s, Afghans fought to free their country from Soviet control. Guerrillas carried out surprise attacks on depots and patrols.

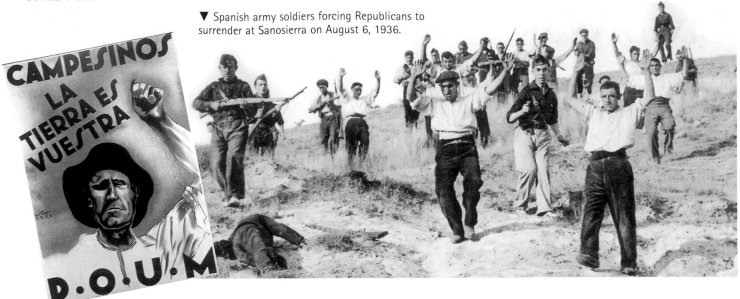

▼ Spanish army soldiers forcing Republicans to surrender at Sanosierra on August 6, 1936.

▲ Posters are often used to rally support. This poster declares, "Peasants, the land is yours." It was designed by Republicans in the Spanish Civil War.

CHARLES I
English ruler (1600–49), came to the throne in 1625. His execution ended the English Civil War.

OLIVER CROMWELL
(1599–1658) ruled England, Scotland, and Ireland as Lord Protector after the king's execution.

▶ The Roundheads' crushing defeat of Royalist forces at Naseby in 1645 was the decisive victory of the English Civil War.

ROMAN CIVIL WAR

Civil wars are not a new phenomenon. Many of the earliest civil wars were fought between influential individuals and their backers in the search for power. In 49 B.C., civil war was started in Rome when Julius Caesar ordered his armies to cross the Rubicon River and march on Rome. He drove out his opponents and succeeded in making himself dictator.

ENGLISH CIVIL WAR

The English Civil War, which lasted from 1642 to 1649, was a struggle between the English king, Charles I, and parliament over who should govern the country. Charles believed that kings were appointed by God and should rule alone. Parliament believed it should have greater power. Parliament refused to cooperate with the king and this caused civil war.

ROYALISTS AND ROUNDHEADS

England divided into two factions: the Royalists, or Cavaliers, supported the king; the Roundheads supported Parliament. Two great generals, Lord Fairfax and Oliver Cromwell, led the Roundheads, and eventually the king's forces were defeated. In 1649, Charles was executed and England was declared a republic.

THE SPANISH CIVIL WAR

In 1936, a left-wing Republican government was elected in Spain. Most of the right-wing army rebelled and tried to overthrow the government. France and the Soviet Union backed the Republicans. The right, led by General Franco, received support from Germany and Italy. Thousands of Spaniards died in the war. In 1939, the Republican army collapsed and Franco became dictator of Spain.

Royalist

Roundheads

SEE ALSO
Africa, Civil War (American) Greece and the Balkans, Refugee, Spain and Portugal, Warfare

CIVIL WAR, AMERICAN

More Americans died in the Civil War than in any other conflict. It was caused by the deep divisions between northern and southern states.

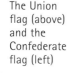

The Union flag (above) and the Confederate flag (left)

The American Civil War (1861–65) was caused by deep political differences. The southern states believed in the right of states, not Congress, to make their own laws, including the right to hold slaves. The South felt that this right was threatened by the election of Abraham Lincoln in 1860.

NORTH AND SOUTH
The North was a land of industry and manufacturing—and home to a strong movement against slavery. The South was a land of farms and plantations and depended on slaves for labor.

DECLARATION OF WAR
After Lincoln's election, 11 southern states seceded (separated) from the Union to create the Confederate States of America. Southern forces attacked Fort Sumter on April 12, 1861. Lincoln, determined to keep the nation intact, formed the Union army against the slaveholding states.

A Union soldier

A Confederate soldier

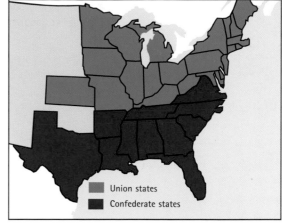

Union states
Confederate states

▲ The American Civil War was fought mainly in the East and Southeast between the southern, or Confederate states, and the northern, or Union states, including Oregon and California on the West Coast.

FOUR YEARS OF FIGHTING
The American Civil War was a fight the South could not win. More people lived in the North, it had a stronger industrial base, better communications, and a navy capable of stopping food and supplies reaching the South. In 1865, the South surrendered. More than 600,000 had died in the struggle, and most southern cities had been destroyed by the war. That same year, the 13th Amendment was added to the Constitution, abolishing slavery. Five days after the South's surrender, Lincoln was assassinated.

THE BATTLE OF GETTYSBURG

The Battle of Gettysburg in July 1863 was a major turning point in the American Civil War. About 85,000 Union troops, led by General George Meade, defeated some 75,000 Confederate soldiers led by General Robert E. Lee. The Confederates never truly recovered from the crushing defeat.

SEE ALSO
Slavery, United States of America, Warfare

CLIMATE

The climate of a region is its weather pattern over a long period of time. The weather may change from day to day, but the climate stays the same.

▼ The world can be divided into different climate zones. These vary from tropical regions, characterized by hot and humid weather, to freezing polar areas.

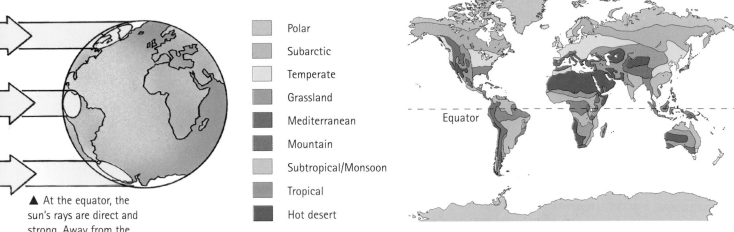

- Polar
- Subarctic
- Temperate
- Grassland
- Mediterranean
- Mountain
- Subtropical/Monsoon
- Tropical
- Hot desert

Equator

▲ At the equator, the sun's rays are direct and strong. Away from the equator, the sun's rays are weaker because they strike the Earth at an angle and must travel farther through the cool air of the atmosphere.

The climate of a region depends on how close the region is to the sea, how high up it is (its altitude), and, most importantly, how far it is from the equator (its latitude). Climate is usually measured as a combination of the average rainfall in an area and the temperature.

THE POWER OF THE SUN
The two extremes of climate on Earth are found at the equator and at the Poles. The climate is hottest in the zones on either side of the equator—the tropics—because the sun is almost directly overhead. The Poles are the coldest areas: temperatures drop below –58°F (–50°C).

THE TROPICS
The tropics are not only the hottest areas but also the wettest. The intense heat evaporates water from the rivers and oceans, forming rain clouds that drench the tropics. By the time the wet tropical air reaches deserts like the Sahara, in Africa, however, just the other side of the rain forests, it has lost most of its moisture.

COLDER HIGHER UP
Air is cooler the higher you go in the atmosphere. So mountainous regions have a colder climate than low areas. On a mountain, air cools by 42.8°F (6°C) for each 3,300 ft. (1,000m) climbed.

CHANGING CLIMATE
Climates can change over time. Volcanic eruptions may have a sudden, local effect, but deforestation and destruction of the ozone layer by pollutant gases may have long-term effects all over the world.

Polar front

Wind direction

Subtropical jet stream

Warm air from the equator

AFRICA

WIND CIRCULATION
At the Poles, cold air sinks and disperses and is replaced by warmer air flowing in from above. The cold air moving away from the Poles meets warm winds from the subtropics and pushes the warm air back to the equator.

SEE ALSO

Desert, Forest, Habitat, Mountain and valley, Pollution, Water, Weather

CLOCK

Clocks are instruments used to measure time in hours, minutes, and seconds down to the smallest fraction. They include mechanical, quartz, and atomic clocks.

Chinese candle clocks "chime" when the candle burns the string to release a weight onto the cymbal.

Sundials show the time by plotting the changing position of the sun's shadow during the day.

Chronometers, invented in the 1700s for use on ships, have a slowly unwinding spring, not a pendulum.

A quartz watch tells the time by recording the vibrations of a quartz crystal inside.

Atomic clocks count the vibrations of light given off by atoms, and are used in satellites and aircraft.

People first learned to tell the time using sundials, sandglasses, marked candles, and water clocks. But during the 1200s, the first mechanical clocks were made.

MECHANICAL CLOCKS
Mechanical clocks are set in motion in one of two ways—by winding up a spring or by raising a weight. Gearwheels with teeth move the hour, minute, and second hands—this is called the clock's movement. Some clocks need to be wound every day, but others can run for about a week.

THE PENDULUM
In 1582, the Italian scientist Galileo Galilei discovered that every swing of a pendulum, or hanging weight, takes the same length of time. The time the swing takes depends on the length of the pendulum arm. A Dutch astronomer called Christiaan Huygens used this knowledge to make the first pendulum clock 74 years later. In a pendulum clock, the swinging weight moves from side to side to regulate the movements of the clock's hands around the clock face.

QUARTZ CRYSTAL
Most of today's clocks and watches are battery-operated and have a tiny quartz crystal inside. The crystal vibrates when it receives a charge of electricity from the battery. It gives out regular, fast pulses of current, which are slowed down by a microchip to one per second.

ATOMIC CLOCKS
The most accurate clocks are cesium-beam atomic clocks, which were first made in 1955. These measure the frequency of an atom's vibrations. They lose only a fraction of a second every million years.

TURNING TIME
When a grandfather clock is wound up, a weight is pulled up to the top of its case. As the weight falls, tiny toothed gearwheels turn and move the hands around the clock face. The swing of the pendulum makes the weight fall evenly as the gears catch against the pallet at every swing, turning one notch of the escape wheel. This makes the "tick-tock" sound.

Pallet

Escape wheel

Gears

Weight

Pendulum

SEE ALSO

Atom and molecule, Electronics, Time

CLOTHING

Clothing is worn to protect the body and to make it look attractive. The kind of clothes people wear reflects where they live, their lifestyle, and their personality.

People started wearing clothes more than 100,000 years ago in colder parts of the world. Ice Age hunters 25,000 years ago stayed warm by sewing animal furs together. About 10,000 years ago, early farming communities learned how to spin plant and animal fibers to make thread that could be woven into cloth. Wool, cotton, silk, and flax for linen were used. Woolen cloth was used in cold northern areas; linen was preferred in hot countries such as Egypt.

THE FIRST PANTS

Among the first people to cut clothes into the kinds of shapes used today were the ancient tribes of Persia (Iran). Men wore coats with sleeves and an early form of pants designed for life on horseback.

READY TO WEAR

In 1785, the steam-powered loom marked the birth of the modern clothing industry; and in the 1850s, sewing machines

▲ Firefighters' protective suits were developed from space suit technology. The suits have many layers, which were originally intended to protect astronauts from the sun's lethal radiation while they worked in space.

arrived. Clothing factories soon started making large amounts of inexpensive, ready-to-wear clothes so that people could afford to buy garments instead of making their own or having expensive designs made up by dressmakers and tailors.

CHANGING SHAPES

Advances in technology have continued to shape fashion in the 1900s. Synthetic nylon was first used to make stockings in the 1940s, easy wash-and-wear polyester appeared in the 1960s, and Lycra became fashionable in the 1980s.

▲ In the 1960s, designers responded to a new teenage market, and the miniskirt arrived. Twiggy, shown here, was a British fashion model who became the symbol of the new look.

▲ Simple clothes, in natural fibers, worn in loose flowing styles, kept both women and men cool in Ancient Egypt.

▲ Richly embroidered fabrics were used to make clothes for wealthy people in the 1400s. Men's shoes had long, pointed toes.

▲ Knee breeches in pale colors were worn by gentlemen in the 1700s. Long pants became fashionable during the 1800s.

▲ In the mid-1800s, women wore tight corsets and hoops made of wicker or steel, called crinolines, to make their skirts stick out.

FASHION VICTIMS

Wearing the latest styles to be fashionable began as a way for rich people to show their wealth. But sometimes, staying in fashion was painful. During the 1800s, women in search of the "hourglass" figure wore laced corsets with whalebone inside. This compressed the waist, making it as tiny as possible. People still follow design trends, but since World War II, when many women started working in factories, clothes have become more practical.

WORKWEAR TO CLASSICS

Trends do not always come from designers. Tough denim jeans, originally made as workwear for Californian gold miners in the 1850s, have become fashion classics. Many people today choose clothes to express their personality.

NATIONAL DRESS

In many parts of the world, traditional dress is worn every day. The *sari*, worn by Hindu women, is a long wrap of light fabric worn over a tight-fitting top called a *choli*. In some countries, national dress is kept for festivals and family celebrations.

MIX AND MATCH

National dress has had a strong influence on Western fashion. American cowboys learned to make leather leggings (chaps) by watching Native Americans stretch and soak buffalo hides. Today, designers continue to borrow from different eras and cultures in a constant search for new ideas.

▲ This wet suit is made of neoprene (a synthetic rubber). It gives the diver protection and warmth under water. Clothes like these allow people to explore previously inaccessible places.

▲ Designers' creations are shown on the catwalk, then toned down and reproduced for the ready-to-wear market.

◀ Clothes for sports must be light, protective, and easy to move in. Uniforms often promote a sense of team spirit.

▶ Dressing outrageously is one way to express personality. This person's clothes and hairstyle show that he is a punk.

▲ In the 1800s, young boys and girls from wealthy families dressed alike. Both wore dresses over ankle-length pantaloons.

KEY DATES

1500s Whalebone is first used to stiffen corsets

1850s Tightly laced corsets and crinolines are used to create the "hourglass" figure

1870s The introduction of the bustle in women's dresses

1899 The "Gibson Girl" is created in the U.S.A.

1920s Coco Chanel revolutionizes women's fashion by creating short, simple shift dresses

1947 Christian Dior's "New Look" with very full skirts ends the austerity of the war years

1957 The sack dress dominates U.S. fashion

1960s André Courrèges (France) introduces the miniskirt, which is popularized in the U.K. by Mary Quant

SEE ALSO

Design, France, Material, Paint and dye, Textile

COAL

Coal is a rock formed under the ground from the remains of decayed prehistoric plants. It burns easily and is widely used as a fuel.

Anthracite is the highest quality coal. It gives the most heat but little smoke.

Most coal mined today is used in power plants to produce light and heat.

Some perfumes are made from coal tar—a black liquid produced from coal.

Coal, like petroleum and gas, is a fossil fuel. It was formed under the ground from the remains of plants over millions of years. It is used to make fires and to make electricity, chemicals, and steel.

CARBON CONTENT
Coal is made up of carbon, tar, oils, and minerals. There are three different types of coal, depending on the amount of carbon each contains. Lignite, or brown coal, contains less than 50 percent carbon; bituminous coal around 70 percent; and anthracite, the most valuable, has about 95 percent carbon. Over four billion tons of coal are mined each year and almost 4,000 billion tons remain underground.

INDUSTRIAL COAL
In about 1750, the Industrial Revolution led to a huge demand for coal as a fuel for steam engines. Today, many power plants burn coal to produce electricity. The iron industry uses coke—coal which has been heated to make the tar and oils evaporate—to produce iron and steel. The tar and oils are then used to produce dyes, fertilizers, and fibers such as nylon.

POLLUTION
When coal is burned, it releases smoke containing soot and poisonous gases, such as carbon monoxide. These can harm the environment, so most power plants have filters to clean the smoke.

▲ Different equipment is needed to mine coal. Cutting machines dig out coal within the mine while a conveyor belt transports it back up the shaft.

HOW COAL IS FORMED
About 300 million years ago, in an age known as the Carboniferous period, the climate was warm and wet, ideal for swampy forests. Dead plants rotted and formed peat, which was buried under layers of sand and mud as sea levels rose, flooding the swamps. These layers slowly turned to rock. Their weight squeezed the peat, turning it into coal.

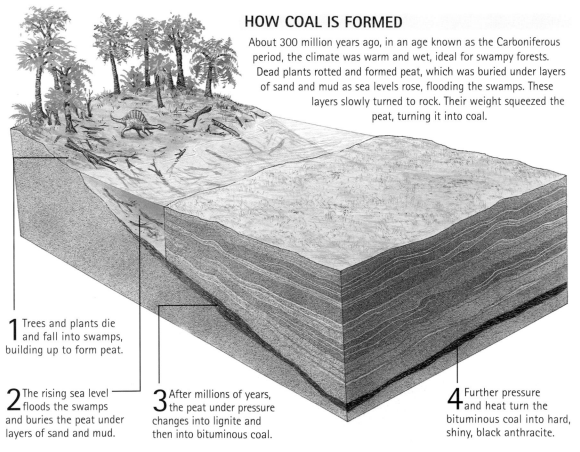

1 Trees and plants die and fall into swamps, building up to form peat.

2 The rising sea level floods the swamps and buries the peat under layers of sand and mud.

3 After millions of years, the peat under pressure changes into lignite and then into bituminous coal.

4 Further pressure and heat turn the bituminous coal into hard, shiny, black anthracite.

▲ A shaft is dug down to a seam many hundreds of feet below. A few mines are opencast—coal is mined at the surface.

SEE ALSO
Electricity, Fossil, Gas, Industrial Revolution, Iron and steel, Mining, Oil, Pollution

COLD WAR

The Cold War was a period of hostility between the capitalist and communist countries of the world. It began after the end of World War II.

▲ The U.S.S.R.'s Nikita Khrushchev (left) and U.S. President John F. Kennedy, fingers poised over their nuclear buttons, confront each other in this 1962 cartoon.

For more than 45 years, between 1945 and 1991, two superpowers, the United States and the Soviet Union (U.S.S.R.), fought each other using spies, alliances, trading bans, and local wars as their weapons.

IRON CURTAIN

After World War II, the U.S.S.R. and the U.S.A. distrusted each other. As communist governments took control of Eastern Europe, the Western nations reacted by forming a military alliance called the North Atlantic Treaty Organization (NATO). The frontier between West and East became known as the Iron Curtain.

CONFRONTATION

The Cold War was marked by a series of crises. The first was the Berlin Airlift in 1948, when the West flew in supplies to a Soviet-blockaded Berlin, the former capital of Germany. The superpowers began stockpiling nuclear weapons. Other countries took sides. In 1962, people feared that nuclear war would break out when the United States demanded that the U.S.S.R. withdraw nuclear weapons from Cuba. Eventually, the Soviets backed down and the crisis ended.

THE COLD WAR THAWS

After 1970, tension between the superpowers began to ease. The Cold War finally ended in the 1990s with the fall of communism in many European countries, and the breakup of the Soviet Union.

NO MAN'S LAND

After World War II, Germany was divided. The United States, France, and Britain controlled the West, and the U.S.S.R. controlled the East. The capital, Berlin, was also divided and, from 1949 to 1958, three million people escaped from East to West Berlin. In 1961, East Germany built the Berlin Wall to close off this escape route.

SEE ALSO

Communism, Democracy, Russia and the Baltic States, United States of America, World War II

COLOR

Color is what we see when light from an object reaches our eyes. White light seems colorless, but it is actually made up of a mixture of colors.

The primary colors of light are red, blue, and green. Mixed together they make up white light.

The primary colors of paint are yellow, blue, and red. Mixed together they produce black.

When you see a rainbow, you are seeing sunlight split apart by raindrops. The rainbow has seven colors: red, orange, yellow, green, blue, indigo, and violet. This range of colors is called the spectrum.

▲ Georges Seurat's *The Circus* (1891) is painted using a technique called pointillism. Pure color is applied as dots. These merge at a distance to create the subtler shades.

REFLECTING LIGHT

An object only appears to be a particular color because of the light it reflects. For example, a leaf looks green because it reflects green light and absorbs all the other colors in the spectrum.

PRIMARY COLORS

During the 1800s, scientists were amazed to discover that almost any color of light can be created by combining different amounts of a basic set of three colors—red, blue, and green. These are known as the primary colors of light.

MIXING IT UP

If equal amounts of red, blue, and green light are mixed together, they make white light. Mixing just red and green light together makes yellow; blue and green makes cyan (a green-blue); and blue and red makes magenta. In photography, printing, movies, and television, light is mixed to produce millions of different colors.

PAINTING A DIFFERENT PICTURE

Pigments (used in paints) have a different set of primary colors. The primary colors are yellow, blue, and red, and when they are mixed together they make black.

SEEING IN COLOR

We see color when light falls on the retina at the back of the eye. The retina is full of cells, called rods and cones, that are sensitive to light. Cones are sensitive to particular colors, and rods, which are not color sensitive, help us to see in dim light.

REFLECTION AND ABSORPTION

When light hits an object, the object absorbs (soaks up) some of the colors of the spectrum and reflects (throws off) others. A tomato, for example, looks red because it reflects red light back into our eyes, but absorbs the other colors of the rainbow: orange, yellow, green, blue, indigo, and violet light.

Light falls on the tomato

The tomato reflects red light

The tomato absorbs the orange, yellow, green, blue, indigo, and violet light

SEE ALSO

Art, Light, Paint and dye, Printing, Sight, Television, Wavelength

COMET, METEOR, AND ASTEROID

Comets, meteors, and asteroids are chunks of ice, rock, or metal that circle the Sun. As they travel closer to Earth, some can be seen lighting up the night sky.

Shooting stars are meteors burning up as they enter Earth's atmosphere.

The 12 mi.-long asteroid Gaspra was photographed by the *Galileo* space probe.

Arizona's Barringer Crater was made by a meteorite over 20,000 years ago.

The space between the planets is littered with debris left over from when the solar system formed. Balls of ice and rock with tails are called comets, small particles that blaze through Earth's atmosphere are meteors, and larger chunks of rock and metal are asteroids.

ICE-COLD COMETS

A comet has a fuzzy head and one or more tails. Its head is a lump of ice, dust, and rock, 6–18 mi. (10–30km) across. Surrounding it is a cloud of gas and dust called a coma. The Sun's heat and the solar wind (a stream of particles given off by the Sun) drive dust and gas out from the coma to form the comet's tails.

SHOOTING STARS AND SHOWERS
Many meteors have been around since our solar system formed, but others are chips off comets and asteroids, or even the Moon and Mars. These can be as small as grains of sand and most

burn up as they hurtle into Earth's atmosphere at speeds of up to 25 mi./sec. (40km/sec). These are called shooting stars. Some travel in swarms and create a meteor shower in the night sky. Such showers can appear at the same time each year, when Earth crosses the swarm's path. Every year, a few meteors hit Earth's surface and are called meteorites.

THE ASTEROID BELT
Asteroids (sometimes called minor planets) are chunks of rock and metal smaller than planets that circle the Sun. More than 4,000 have been found. The largest asteroid, Ceres, is 580 mi. (930km) across, but most are much smaller. They are usually found in the asteroid belt between Mars and Jupiter.

A COMET IN FLIGHT

Comets are surrounded by clouds of dust, called comas, which can be over 600,000 miles across. Comets travel in long loops around the Sun. Each time they approach the Sun, more gas and dust evaporate from their centers, making the comas grow larger and the comets form tails. Comets' tails always point away from the Sun.

Rocky crust

Dust tail

Gas tail

Coma

Ice core

▲ Halley's Comet is visible from Earth every 76 years. It was studied closely on its last return in 1986.

SEE ALSO
Astronomy, Moon, Planet, Solar system, Spacecraft, Space exploration, Sun, Universe

COMMUNICATION

Communication is the process of sending and receiving messages. This can be done by using spoken and written language or recognized signs and signals.

◄ Sign language for the deaf uses hand signals and is based on ideas, not words.

The Sumerians developed the first known writing system in about 3500 B.C.

From the 1400s, printing became a means of mass communication in Europe.

The telephone, invented in 1876, allowed long-distance communication.

A satellite dish receives images and sounds sent from around the world.

People usually communicate with each other individually or in small groups. However, they sometimes need to relay messages to a much larger audience. This is known as mass communication.

SIGNS AND SIGNALS
Humans have developed ingenious ways of conveying messages to each other, using signs and signals when language cannot be used. Some Native Americans sent smoke signals, and African tribes used drumbeats. Signals are still in use today—navies send messages using flags (known as semaphore), and road users rely on roadside signs and traffic lights.

POSTAL COMMUNICATIONS
One of the earliest, cheapest, and most reliable forms of communication was the mail. Stamps were first used in Britain in 1840. Letters today are sorted by machine, and then carried by truck, train, or airplane to their destination.

TELEGRAPH MESSAGES
For a long time, the fastest way to communicate over long distances was to deliver messages on foot, on horseback, or by boat. Then in 1840, the American inventor Samuel Morse introduced the first simple telegraph, which used electricity to send messages down wire cables. The messages were coded using a system of dots and dashes. This became known as Morse code.

FASTER THAN EVER
Since the 1800s, many inventions, such as the telephone, radio, and television, have made communication across the world faster and easier. Today, a message can be sent to the other side of the world in seconds by using satellite and computer links. The Internet lets all types of computers share services and communicate directly. Video conference centers allow people thousands of miles apart to see and talk to each other directly.

THE PONY EXPRESS

In 1860, the Pony Express was the fastest delivery system in the United States, delivering letters 2,000 mi. (3,200km) in less than ten days—it had previously taken over three weeks by boat or stagecoach. The riders rode in all weather, changing to fresh horses at every pony express station—spaced 10–12 miles apart. The service was closed in October 1861, once the telegraph and Morse code came into use.

SEE ALSO
Computer, Internet, Language, Media, Printing, Radio, Satellite, Telecommunication, Telephone, Television

COMMUNISM

Communism is a political theory based on the idea that everybody should share all wealth, property, and industry equally.

The German journalist Karl Marx developed the idea of communism in the 1800s.

Mao Tse-tung led the Communists to victory in China in the 1940s.

President Fidel Castro has led Cuba since 1959, after a three-year guerrilla war.

Ho Chi Min led North Vietnam for most of the Vietnam War.

► Vladimir Lenin, leader of the Bolshevik Party, led a revolution that overthrew czarist rule in Russia. He set up the world's first communist regime in 1917.

◄ Since North Korea became communist in 1948, many statues to heroic workers have been erected.

In 1848, Karl Marx and Friedrich Engels published the *Communist Manifesto*, which stated that private ownership should be replaced by common ownership. Marx wanted to see an end to the way of life in which most people worked for a low wage, while a few wealthy people owned the factories and land. He believed that the only way to achieve this was by revolution.

THE FIRST REVOLUTION
The first successful communist revolution took place in Russia in 1917, after which the Union of Soviet Socialist Republics (U.S.S.R.) was set up under the leadership of Vladimir Lenin. The state took control of farms, factories, mines, and railroads in the name of the people. Lenin and his successor, Joseph Stalin, ruled as dictators. Most people were better fed and housed, but personal freedoms were severely restricted.

SPREAD OF COMMUNISM
After World War II, communism spread to Eastern Europe, China, and countries in Africa, Asia, and Central America. During the Cold War, there was hostile rivalry between communist countries and the United States-led Western democracies.

THE COLLAPSE
From 1989 to 1992, communism in countries such as Poland, Hungary, and East Germany collapsed. With the break-up of the Soviet Union in the 1990s, China remains the only major nation with a communist government.

KEY DATES
1848 Journalist Karl Marx and philosopher Friedrich Engels publish the *Communist Manifesto*
1917 Lenin leads Russia's Bolshevik Revolution
1949 China becomes a communist state under Mao Tse-tung
1989 Communism collapses in Eastern Europe
1991 The breakup of the U.S.S.R. leaves only China, Cuba, Vietnam, and North Korea as communist states

SEE ALSO

China, Cold War, Democracy, Eastern Europe, Europe, Fascism, Revolution, Russia and the Baltic States

COMPUTER

Computers are machines that handle information according to sets of instructions. They then give the results in a form that people can understand.

In 1834, Charles Babbage (1792-1871) designed the first mechanical computer, but he never saw it built.

In the 1960s, computers used transistors and stored data on tape. They could fill a whole room.

The British Sinclair ZX81 was one of the first home computers to be launched on the world market.

Portable laptop computers, small enough to fit inside a briefcase, became available in the 1980s.

The process of miniaturization created electronic diaries called personal organizers.

The computer is an electronic device that can do calculations millions of times faster than the human brain. First, the computer receives data, or information, put in by the user; then it processes the data as simple electrical signals according to its program, and produces a result.

BINARY NUMBERS
All computers use a language called the binary system. Binary numbers are entirely made up of the digits 0 and 1. When a letter is typed on the keyboard or the mouse or joystick is moved, tiny electric currents are sent to the computer. These currents are stored by the computer as binary numbers.

MINIATURIZATION
The first computers took up a whole room, but by the 1960s, electronic components had become much smaller and computers began to shrink in size. The home computer became possible through the invention of the microchip, which contains tens of thousands of electronic components within a space no larger than a fingernail.

HIGHLY VERSATILE
A PC (personal computer) can tackle jobs from word processing to 3-D design and animation. Music can be recorded, edited, and played back on the PC. Desktop publishing means books and magazines can be designed on the PC.

HOW IT WORKS
Data (information) in a PC is usually stored in random-access memory (RAM). The central processing unit (CPU) calls it up when it is needed, according to a list of instructions (the program), which is also stored in memory. Data flows to and from the CPU along an electronic pathway called the bus. After processing, data is stored in RAM again.

SCIENCE FRONTIERS
Computers have revolutionized science and technology. Space probes, satellite TV, and weapons detection systems all rely on computers. Computers make it possible to test chemical and nuclear reactions without real-life experiments.

AUTOMATION
In the automotive industry, computers are used to design a car and then build it with the aid of robots. Inside the car itself, a computer can check the engine, the brakes, and the steering. Computers can even be used in the home to control temperature, lighting, and security.

GLOBAL LINKS
Computers are increasingly changing the way we live by connecting people and places. The Internet links up computers all over the world, allowing messages and information to be sent across the globe in a matter of seconds.

BILL GATES (born 1955) In 1975, American Bill Gates founded Microsoft, now the largest software company in the world.

HOW THE COMPUTER WORKS

A computer system has four basic parts. An input device such as the keyboard, mouse, or joystick enters information into the computer. Then the central processing unit (CPU), acting as the computer's brain, performs the tasks. The information is sent to an output device, such as the screen or printer, to display the results. And finally a memory unit stores programs and data.

A plasma screen is a light and quiet computer screen that provides sharp, vivid, high-quality images

The CPU is the brains of the computer

The CD-ROM drive uses compact discs to read and store data

Speakers are used to output sound from the computer

The keys on the keyboard act as switches, sending tiny electric currents to the computer when pressed

The hard disk is made up of magnetic layers that store information when the computer is turned off

A mouse is used to point to different areas of the screen.

COMPUTER ADD-ONS

Game Pad
A game pad is a powerful, dual-control input device used to play computer games.

Digital Camera
Photographs can be viewed on the screen of the camera and then imported to a computer for storage.

MP3 Player
This is a digital music player which can store and play songs downloaded from the computer.

SEE ALSO
Electronics, Internet, Robot, Satellite, Space exploration, Technology, Telecommunication

CONSERVATION

Conservation is the protection and careful use of natural resources, including animals, plants, and fossil fuels. It also includes care of historical treasures.

◀ The care and preservation of paintings is a painstaking process. An art conservator must understand a painting's history and content in the same way that an animal conservationist must know the habits of an endangered animal.

Conservationists try to find a balance between the needs of human beings and care of the environment. There are more than five billion people alive today and they all need land to live on, food to eat, and fuel for power. Without care, habitats can be destroyed, resources used up, and the Earth damaged.

▲ Recycling plastic, paper, tin, and glass conserves the Earth's resources. In many states, there are laws that specify that households can be fined for failing to separate trash for recycling.

GLOBAL AWARENESS

Some conservation issues are local, as when acres of forest are threatened with felling to make way for a new road. Others, such as recycling, saving energy, and stopping animals from becoming extinct, are shared worldwide. In 1992, world leaders got together at the Earth Summit in Brazil to draw up the very first global action plan to save the planet. One scheme that was introduced to encourage people to stop destroying their habitats— by logging trees or draining marshes—is the "debt-for-nature" idea. This means that a poor country has some of its international debt canceled in exchange for setting aside areas for conservation.

FACING EXTINCTION

As many as 100 rare plant and animal species become extinct each day—far more than when the dinosaurs died out, 65 million years ago. The tiger, rhinoceros, Asian snow leopard, and even some species of insects are all in danger of disappearing forever. The last few hundred mountain gorillas live on the borders of Rwanda, Uganda, and Zaire in Africa. Their rain forest home has been destroyed by farmers and timber firms, and they are killed by hungry villagers.

NATURE RESERVES

One of the best ways of protecting wildlife is to preserve an entire habitat in a national park. Zoos also help by breeding rare animals, such as the giant panda.

SAVING THE HELPLESS GIANT

Many species of large whale, such as the humpback whale (below), are threatened with extinction because they have been overhunted for their blubber, meat, oil, and bones. A global conservation body known as the International Whaling Commission (IWC) outlawed the killing of such rare whales in 1985, but not all countries have agreed to stop hunting.

SEE ALSO

Animal, Asia, Dinosaur, Ecology, Energy, Habitat, Pollution, Rain forest, Whale and dolphin, Zoology

CONSTELLATION

Constellations are groups of stars that form recognizable patterns in the night sky. Astronomers have named a total of 88 constellations.

▲ The Northern and Southern Hemispheres are domes of sky seen above and below the equator.

Thousands of years ago, people in Asia, Europe, and the Middle East realized that the stars formed patterns in the sky, and named them after characters and creatures in their lives and legends. By A.D. 300, the Greek astronomer Ptolemy had named 48 constellations. Many of the names he gave them are still in use, including Taurus (the Bull), Ursa Major (the Great Bear), and Andromeda (a mythical Greek heroine). Today, astronomers use the position of the constellations to map the stars.

THE ZODIAC

If we could see the stars during the day, the Sun would pass in front of 13 constellations over the course of the year. The ancient astronomers counted only 12 constellations and called them the signs of the zodiac—claiming that babies born under each sign would have certain traits.

NEAR AND FAR

Stars in a constellation seem close to each other, but are usually far apart. Orion contains the stars Betelgeuse (300 light years from Earth), Rigel (900 light years away), and Mintaka (2,300 light years away). One light year equals 5.88 trillion miles (9.46 trillion kilometers).

MAPS OF THE STARS

Two maps of the constellations are needed because people who live north of the equator (in the Northern Hemisphere) see different stars from those who live south of the equator (in the Southern Hemisphere). The constellations in the center of each map can usually be seen all year round, while those near the edge can be seen only during particular seasons or at certain times of the night.

SOUTHERN HEMISPHERE

NORTHERN HEMISPHERE

▲ Pegasus, the Flying Horse

▲ Phoenix, the Fire Bird

▲ Crux, the Southern Cross

▲ Libra, the Scales

▲ Scorpio, the Scorpion

▲ Hercules, the Giant

▲ Ursa Major, the Great Bear

▲ Leo, the Lion

SEE ALSO

Astronomy, Galaxy, Myth and legend, Solar system, Star

97

CONSTRUCTION

Construction is the process of putting something together. This can include houses, skyscrapers, bridges, dams, roads, and even ships.

▲ Hong Kong Harbor Bridge under construction in 1996. The last road section is being lifted from a barge below.

The construction industry is big business—it accounts for 15 percent of all jobs in the United States. The world's largest construction project, building a city in Saudi Arabia in the 1970s, employed nearly 52,000 people.

Bricks are still the most popular construction material in house building.

Carpentry is used to make the main frame, doors, and windows in many houses.

The frames of tall buildings and ships used to be fixed with hot nails, or rivets.

TRADITIONAL TECHNIQUES
In the past, most construction was domestic. Each family built a house, pens for animals, and dams to irrigate their crops. The materials were usually natural and found locally and included wood, clay, stone, bone, skin, or grass. Work was done by hand.

THE DAWN OF CIVILIZATION
As more complex civilizations developed, so did building skills. The first bricks were made in Palestine in 6000 B.C., and the construction of the pyramids in Egypt required thousands of workers, as well as skilled mathematicians. Ancient cranes were used on Roman building sites.

MODERN CONSTRUCTION
The size and height of constructions used to be limited by the skill of the stonemason or carpenter. But from the late 1800s, new techniques using steel frames and molded concrete allowed skyscrapers to be built.

A BUILDING GOES UP
There are two main stages in constructing a building. First, the foundations must be laid below ground to support the structure. Tough materials, concrete (poured in trenches) or steel columns (driven into the ground), are used. The second stage is the construction of the building above ground. Either the walls or a steel frame are constructed first to support floors and other features. Finally, the roof is added.

STEEL-FRAMED CONSTRUCTION

Modern high-rise buildings usually have a steel frame onto which floors and wall panels are bolted. The frame supports the weight of the building so walls can be thin with large windows.

▲ H-shaped, reinforced steel girders are bolted together to form the building's frame.

▲ Metal floor panels are bolted to the frame, then a wire mesh is laid and concrete is poured over it.

A crane, or derrick, is used for lifting building materials into place

Molded concrete wall panels are fixed to the outside of the frame

SEE ALSO
Architecture, Bridge, Dam, Housing, Road, Ship, Skyscraper, Tunnel

CONTINENT

Continents are large stretches of land unbroken by sea. There are seven continents on Earth.

The continents are attached to tectonic plates, the pieces that form the Earth's surface.

HOW CONTINENTS DRIFT

All the land on Earth is fixed to giant plates which float on a sea of magma (melted rock). As the magma moves slowly, so do the continents, but some toward each other and others apart. Where two giant plates rub together, a crack sometimes appears in the Earth's surface, allowing magma to escape. Two such cracks, known as mid-ocean ridges, run through the Atlantic and Indian oceans.

The Earth's crust is like a giant jigsaw puzzle made up of eight large pieces and several small pieces, called tectonic plates. On top of these plates sit seven land masses, or continents: Africa, Antarctica, Asia, Australia, Europe, North America, and South America. They make up 95 percent of Earth's land area; islands form the rest. The largest continent is Asia, with an area of just over 17 million sq. mi. (44 million sq km), and the smallest is Australia, covering about 3 million sq. mi. (7.7 million sq km).

CONTINENTAL CRUST

The continents are the thickest parts of the Earth's outer layer, or crust—in some places reaching down 38–45 mi. (60–70km). At the center, the continents contain the oldest rocks on the planet, with some dating back three billion years. As newer rocks were added around the fringes of these ancient cores, the continents grew.

FLOATING WORLD

The tectonic plates on which the continents sit are floating on a hot, molten layer called magma. Heat from deep inside the Earth keeps the magma moving slowly, and as it moves, so do the plates and continents. The slow movement of the continents is called continental drift.

VANISHED LANDS

More than 300 million years ago, all the land on Earth formed just one continent, called Pangaea. Then, about 180 million years ago, it split into two continents, called Gondwanaland and Laurasia. Slowly, North and South America broke away, India joined Asia, and Australia split from Antarctica and moved northward, until today's seven continents were created.

TOMORROW'S CONTINENTS

The movement is still continuing, and the continents we know today will look very different in 50 million years' time. Africa and the Americas, for example, will be even farther away from each other. North and South America will no longer be joined and Australia will have moved farther northward.

▼ At first there was just one large continent, then two, and finally the seven continents that we know were formed.

180 million years ago

65 million years ago

SEE ALSO

Africa, Antarctica, Asia, Australia, Earth, Europe, North America, Ocean and sea, South America

CRAB AND OTHER CRUSTACEANS

Crabs belong to a group of animals called crustaceans.
These creatures have no bones and are covered with
a hard shell called an exoskeleton.

The male fiddler crab has a very large claw, which it waves as part of a display to attract the female.

The hermit crab lives in an empty seashell, which it drags around with its two pairs of walking legs.

The lobster has one narrow claw for slicing dead fish, and a heavier claw for crushing clams.

The crayfish grows up to 16 in. (40cm) long. It lives in fresh water and has ten legs.

The water flea is one of the smallest crustaceans, growing to 0.008–0.7 in. (0.2–18mm) long.

The woodlouse is the only crustacean that lives entirely on land. It can roll itself up for defense.

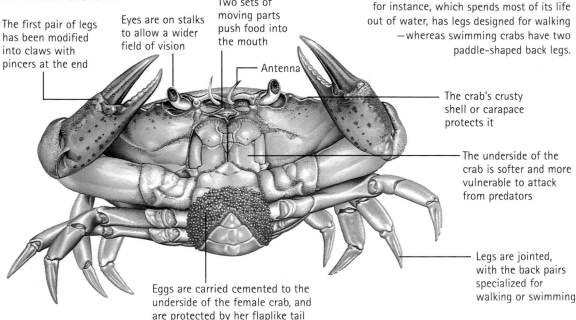

The first pair of legs has been modified into claws with pincers at the end

Eyes are on stalks to allow a wider field of vision

Two sets of moving parts push food into the mouth

Antenna

The crab's crusty shell or carapace protects it

The underside of the crab is softer and more vulnerable to attack from predators

Legs are jointed, with the back pairs specialized for walking or swimming

Eggs are carried cemented to the underside of the female crab, and are protected by her flaplike tail

LIVING ON THE SHORELINE

Most crabs live in or near the sea, but many have adapted to life on land. The shore crab for instance, which spends most of its life out of water, has legs designed for walking —whereas swimming crabs have two paddle-shaped back legs.

Crustaceans include shrimps, lobsters, woodlice, water fleas, and barnacles. Altogether, there are about 42,000 species of crustaceans. Beneath its hard body shell, a crustacean's body is divided into sections, with jointed legs attached. Crabs, lobsters, and barnacles have especially thick shells, which contain a lot of chalklike material. This makes their shells feel like crusts.

EYES ON STALKS
There are about 4,500 species of crab. The smallest are the tiny pea crabs, which are less than 0.4 in. (1cm) across. The biggest are spider crabs, which live on the seabed and measure up to 13 ft. (4m) across from the tip of one leg to another. Crabs have ten legs, two of which are claws, and their eyes can move up and down on the end of stalks.

CRAB HABITS
Crabs usually live in water or close to the shore. Large crabs feed mainly on dead animals, which they tear up with their claws; small crabs pick up tiny scraps of food from the seabed. Many crabs move sideways on land. The robber crab climbs palm trees to pick young coconuts, which it bores into with its powerful claws.

WITHOUT A SHELL
A crab's body is armored by a shell which molts as the crab grows. The hermit crab, however, does not have a shell and must inhabit empty mollusk shells to protect its soft abdomen. As it grows, it searches for a larger shell to make its home.

HATCHED FROM EGGS
Crabs and other crustaceans reproduce by laying eggs. On hatching, the tiny larvae drift about in water, passing through several body changes before they become adults. In a few species, including the woodlouse, the young hatch out looking like mini-adults.

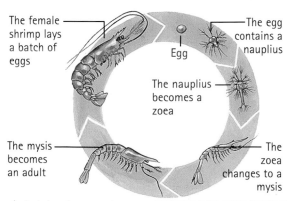

The female shrimp lays a batch of eggs

Egg

The egg contains a nauplius

The nauplius becomes a zoea

The mysis becomes an adult

The zoea changes to a mysis

▲ A shrimp larva must pass through several stages before becoming an adult.

SEE ALSO
Animal, Seashore

CROP

Crops are plants that are grown to provide food for people and animals. They are also grown for useful materials like cotton and linen.

◄ Cotton is a cash crop. It is grown for its fibers, which are spun to make thread or fabric. Its seeds are also crushed to produce oil and fodder.

Wheat grows worldwide, in areas with moist, mild winters and dry summers.

Rice grows best in warm, wet areas such as China, where it is a staple food.

Potatoes came from Peru, but have long been an important crop in Europe.

Sugar beet is grown for its sugar-rich root. Its leaves are used as animal fodder.

Coffee is the major cash crop in tropical regions. It is grown on plantations.

Grapes are grown in vineyards and harvested for wine, raisins, and fresh fruit.

The type of crop grown by farmers depends on the climate of the country, the quality of the soil, and its demand in the market. In developing countries, especially in tropical parts of the world, people grow just enough of a crop for their own needs. These are called subsistence crops. Other people, usually farmers, grow large amounts of crops so that they can be sold. These are called cash crops.

ESSENTIAL CEREALS

The most important food crops are cereals —large grasses grown for their seeds or grains. Cereals include wheat, rice, corn, oats, sorghum, and millet, which cover about three fourths of the world's farmland. Wheat is the most popular cereal, with about 590 million tons grown every year, mainly for people to eat, but also as animal feed. Rice is the main ingredient in the diet of over half the world's people, particularly in Asia.

ROOTS TO FRUITS

Another vital food source is root crops—plants with edible fleshy roots. The potato is an important root crop in Europe, and yams and cassavas are staples in many parts of Africa. Cotton and flax are grown for their fibrous flowers, which are used to make cotton and linen. Other major crops include tea and tobacco, which are grown for their leaves, and fruits such as bananas and apples.

WILD ANCESTORS

All crops have come from wild plants, but they have been bred over time to provide bigger and better yields in soils or climates that are not their natural homes. Some crops have changed so much that it is hard to say which wild plants were their ancestors. As field and crop sizes have grown, the use of fertilizers, insecticides, and fungicides has also risen.

HARVESTING THE CROP

Combine harvesters automatically cut, thresh, and clean cereals such as wheat ready for transportation to market. Special attachments can be added to harvest different crops such as soybeans and corn.

Grain husks (chaff) and straw are dumped

Grains shoot down a boom, into a truck

Threshing drum separates grains from stems

Controls are in the cab

Straw elevator moves cut wheat to the thresher

Grains are separated from chaff by a winnower, which blows air

Wheels straighten the wheat stalks before they reach the cutting wheel

SEE ALSO

Farming, Food, Fruit, Fungi, Genetics, Nutrition, Plant, Vegetable

CRUSADES

The Crusades were a series of religious wars that took place in the Holy Land in the Middle Ages. They were fought between Christians and Muslims.

▲ The Crusaders traveled to the Holy Land by land and sea from all the Christian kingdoms of Europe. They built more than 100 castles and fortresses in the area. One of the best preserved is Krak des Chevaliers in Syria, which withstood 12 sieges before falling to the Muslims in 1271.

——— First Crusade (1096–99)
——— Second Crusade (1147–49)
——— Third Crusade (1188–92)
——— Fourth Crusade (1202–4)

For nearly 200 years, starting in 1096, Christians from Europe marched to Palestine to fight the Muslims for control of the Holy Land, especially of Jerusalem. They carried the Pope's blessing, but many fought for power and wealth.

THE BEGINNING
From the 600s, Muslim Arabs ruled the Holy Land, but Christian pilgrims were allowed to visit Jerusalem. Then, in 1071, the Muslim Turks captured Jerusalem and threatened the Christian Byzantine Empire. Pope Urban II called for Christian soldiers to unite and march to the Holy Land to recapture Jerusalem and protect pilgrims.

PILGRIM PEASANTS
The response to the Pope's call was vast. With cries of *Deus Vult!* (meaning "God wills it" in Latin), thousands of people began the long march eastward. The first to set out for the Byzantine capital of Constantinople were bands of poorly armed pilgrim peasants under the leadership of Peter the Hermit and Walter

the Penniless. Many died on the way, and the rest were killed by the Muslims as soon as they reached Anatolia.

AN ARMY OF KNIGHTS
The First Crusade began in November 1096, when a large army, mostly of French and Norman knights under the leadership of noblemen such as Godfrey de Bouillon, gathered at Constantinople. It defeated the Muslims, capturing the cities of Antioch and Jerusalem, and set up a Christian kingdom along the Palestinian and Syrian coast.

Nuredin was the Muslim leader who united the Islamic forces that Saladin took into battle at Hattin.

Sultan Saladin led the united Muslim armies and took Christian strongholds after the Second Crusade.

THE BATTLE OF ARSUF
In 1191, King Richard I secured victory over the Muslim leader Saladin at Arsuf, with a charge of armored knights. The charge was led by the Knights Templars and Knights Hospitallers—two military orders of skilled knights who were fanatical enemies of Islam and, like monks, took religious vows.

JERUSALEM IS LOST

Muslim counterattacks started the Second Crusade (1147–49), in which King Louis VII of France and King Conrad II of Germany led separate attacks on Anatolia. These ended in failure for the Christians and weakened their hold on the Holy Land. In 1187, a new Muslim leader, Saladin, led Islamic opposition and wiped out the Crusaders at the Battle of the Horns of Hattin. He then captured Jerusalem and most of the Holy Land.

In 1212, thousands of children went on a children's crusade to the Holy Land. They did not reach their destination and many of them died or were sold as slaves.

RICHARD THE LIONHEARTED

The Third Crusade (1189–92) was led by Richard I (Richard the Lionhearted of England), Frederick I of Germany, and Philip II of France. Unfortunately, Frederick drowned on the way, but the Crusaders defeated Saladin and retook much of the Holy Land, except Jerusalem.

LATER CRUSADES

The Fourth Crusade (1202–4) ended in chaos. Its leaders wanted power and riches, and concentrated on Constantinople instead of fighting for the Holy Land. The Christians had little success in the Fifth Crusade (1217–21), but gained Jerusalem by treaty during the Sixth (1222–29). The Seventh Crusade (1248–54) ended with the capture of Louis IX of France, who was freed only after a ransom was paid.

FINAL BATTLE

During the Eighth Crusade (1270–72), the Muslims continued to advance. In 1291, they secured the last of the vital ports of Acre. No more Crusades took place and many of the knights retired to the island of Cyprus.

King Richard I of England led the Third Crusade and was given the nickname "Richard the Lionhearted."

▼ The Knights Hospitallers built many castles to defend land that they had captured. The largest was Krak des Chevaliers, which was built in the desert of modern-day Syria. It held a garrison of 2,000 men and only fell to the Saracens when, in 1271, its defenders surrendered after a year-long siege.

Louis IX ruled the coast around Acre, Syria, for four years between the Seventh and Eighth Crusades.

SEE ALSO

Castle, Christianity, Empire, Islam, Middle Ages, Middle East, Warfare

CUSTOM

Customs are the traditions, rituals, and ways of behaving in a society that are passed on from generation to generation and are sometimes turned into laws.

Some Portuguese fishermen paint eyes on their boats to watch over them at sea and bring them back safely.

The *haka*, performed by New Zealand rugby teams before a match, is based on a Maori war dance.

The custom of carving pumpkin faces comes from the Celtic Day of the Dead, celebrated on October 31.

The *chanoyu*, a Japanese tea ceremony which can last for four hours, came originally from China.

The painting of eggs is a symbol of new life which has been adopted by Christians at Easter.

DANCING DRAGON

During the Chinese New Year festival, dancers inside a dragon costume move through the streets while firecrackers are set off. The dragon is believed to bring rain for a successful crop, and so has become a symbol of good fortune for the coming year. The firecrackers are to frighten away evil spirits.

Every society has its own customs, waiting politely in line, for example, or wearing a particular costume during a celebration. Learning about different customs helps us to understand people from other countries or cultures.

RITES OF PASSAGE

Across the world, customs are different, but there are times of life, known as rites of passage, when a person's status changes. Such times include birth, coming of age, marriage, and death—occasions that are marked by elaborate customs in every society. The custom of keeping mother and baby secluded from society for a month after birth is a common custom in many countries, probably based on fear of infection. There are also many customs marking a young person's move from childhood to adulthood, ranging from throwing a party to a religious ritual.

LINKS WITH THE PAST

Customs may be adapted over time, often as a result of industrialization or contact with other cultures. A custom's original meaning may be forgotten, or it may continue as a way of keeping a link with the past. The special Thanksgiving meal, for example, is usually celebrated with the whole family and commemorates the survival of Pilgrim families long ago.

CUSTOMARY GREETINGS

Everyday customs help people to bond with other members of their society. For instance, every culture has a customary way of greeting—Europeans kiss or shake hands, the Inuit rub noses, and the Chinese bow. By taking part in customs, people demonstrate their membership of a group or society.

GOING AGAINST THE GRAIN

Refusing to follow a custom can offend; it may even lead to the exclusion of an individual from a group of society. Customs are not laws, but because they are designed to help us understand what is acceptable behavior in a society, customs are often included in laws or religious codes.

▲ In Hindu weddings, everything is brightly colored, and the bride usually wears a red sari with lots of gold jewelry.

SEE ALSO

Clothing, Dance, Food, Judaism

DAM

A dam is a barrier built across a river or stream to hold back water. The stored water may be used for irrigation, as drinking water, or to provide power.

Arch dams, used in tall, narrow canyons or gorges, are often surprisingly thin.

Concrete gravity dams are built to hold back water in broad, shallow valleys.

Embankment dams have a reinforced inner wall to hold back shallow lakes.

The earliest dams were built in the Middle East about 5,000 years ago. These dams were used to direct water to fields of crops, through canals called irrigation channels. A dam built on the Orontes River in Syria about 1300 B.C. still irrigates fields near the city of Homs.

CONTROLLING THE FLOW

Today, dams are still built for irrigation, as well as to stop flooding and to provide water power for electricity. In low-lying areas of China, Bangladesh, and the United States, dams have been built to stop flood disasters. Other dams are built so that water can be stored in artificial lakes, or reservoirs. The water is then supplied to homes and industry.

HYDROELECTRIC DAM

Hydroelectric dams use water power to produce electricity. They require large quantities of water and a very long drop from the top to the bottom of the dam. About 20 percent of the world's electricity is generated by hydroelectric dams.

EMBANKMENT DAMS

The simplest dams are embankment dams. They are made from earth and rock and have a waterproof core to stop water seeping through. The Aswan High Dam in Egypt controls the annual flooding of the Nile River and provides hydroelectric power for the whole country.

GRAVITY AND ARCH

Gravity dams are made of stone or concrete. They rely on their weight and strength to hold back the water. Arch dams are curved so that the weight of the water is pushed out from the dam to the canyon or gorge. They can be very thin—for example, the Vaiont Dam in the Italian Alps is 870 ft. (265m) high but only 75.5 ft. (23m) thick at its base.

ENVIRONMENTAL IMPACT

Dam building affects the surrounding environment, and wildlife can be destroyed. Some dams have fish ladders, which enable fish such as salmon to make their journey upstream to breed.

1 Water from the reservoir passes through a gate.

2 The flow of the water turns wheels (turbines).

3 The turbines turn dynamos to create electricity.

4 Cables carry the electricity away.

5 Excess water flows over a sluice.

FAST FACTS

- The world's largest dam is the Syncrude Tailings Dam in Alberta, Canada

- At 551 ft. (168m), the Grand Coulee Dam, in the state of Washington, is 200 ft. (20m) taller than the Great Pyramid in Egypt

- Dams were so important in ancient Mesopotamia that King Hammurabi's laws said that anyone who broke a dam should be sold into slavery to pay the farmer

SEE ALSO

Construction, Egypt, Waterpower

DANCE

Dance is one of the oldest art forms. It is the rhythmic movement of all or part of the body, and includes ballet, the waltz, flamenco, tap, rumba, and disco.

Dancing can express emotion, tell a story, create a specific atmosphere, or show off physical strength. There are two main types of dance: social dancing for enjoyment, and dance created to entertain an audience.

DANCING THROUGH HISTORY

People have been dancing for thousands of years—dancing figures appear in cave paintings in Europe and Africa dating back to prehistoric times. Many of the earliest dances that are still popular today were connected with religious ceremonies or superstitious beliefs. English morris dancing is based on ancient war rituals, and voodoo dancers in Haiti go into a trance in which they attempt to summon the spirits. The expressive dance drama of the Ancient Greeks has had a long-lasting influence in the West.

► Ice-skating competitions feature ice dancing in their freestyle section. Couples are not allowed to lift one another, but often imitate traditional ballroom dance routines using daring athletic poses.

GETTING TOGETHER

Formal social dances, where set steps are followed, go back many centuries. Bugaku dancing in Japan originated in the A.D. 600s. In medieval Europe, grand social dances were popular at court. Most were adapted from the simple country dances of ordinary people. As early as the 1400s, there were dance teachers who taught the steps to the latest dances.

CLASSIC BEAUTY

Ballet originated in the royal courts of Italy during the 1400s, but was developed in France. King Louis XIV was an enthusiastic dancer, and opened the first European dance academy in Paris in 1661. Until then, most dancers had been amateur, but professional dancers soon began to appear. The academy's director, Charles-Louis Beauchamp, helped to standardize the classic movements. He is thought to have set out the five basic ballet positions of the feet and arms. By the mid-1800s, romantic ballets such as *La Sylphide* were popular in Europe.

▲ Contemporary dance is less structured than ballet and does not always tell a story. It often uses choreography (arrangement) of the dancers' bodies to form striking poses.

▼ Ballet tells a story, whether it is a classical tale such as *Swan Lake*, or a favorite children's story like *Alice in Wonderland*. Here, Alice (far right) meets the fearsome Queen of Hearts during her journey through Wonderland.

◄ Music and dance are important in the cultures of many tribal countries, such as Zimbabwe, Africa. Here a Shangaan dancer, in an elaborate costume with wings, mask, and grass skirt, performs a tribal dance.

▲ Dancing to repetitive music with a powerful underlying beat, often in strobe lighting, swept clubs in the 1990s.

BREAKING AWAY

The second half of the 1800s was the era of classical Russian ballet, with great masterpieces such as Tchaikovsky's *Swan Lake*. But by the early 1900s, some dancers were beginning to create a freer style, breaking away from the rigid patterns and training of classical ballet. The American dancer Isadora Duncan was a big influence on contemporary dance. She performed barefoot, basing her moves on ideas inspired by Ancient Greece.

TAKE YOUR PARTNERS

As time went by, trends in social dances changed along with styles of music. In the 1800s, the waltz caused a scandal because the man and woman dancing held each other so close. Exciting new dances in the 1900s were based partly on African-American and Irish traditions, like jazz and tap. In the 1920s, while dramatic Russian ballets toured Europe, ordinary people in the United States were dancing the high-kicking Charleston.

DANCE FADS

Jitterbugging to the music of the big bands became popular in the 1930s and 1940s, developing into the sensational rock'n'roll jive of the 1940s and 1950s. The twist was popular in the 1960s, and the latter part of the last century was marked by disco, break dancing, and free expression.

► In the popular Japanese theater of Kabuki, an all-male cast performs comic dance, drama, and singing shows, often in female dress. To give a visual climax, each scene ends with a pose called the *mie*.

SEE ALSO

Africa, Custom, Music, Theater

DEMOCRACY

Democracy is a form of government in which the people take part in ruling the state. The people may rule directly or through elected officials.

◄ Two metal voting disks were given to each man in ancient Athens. They were used in criminal trials to vote guilty or not guilty.

People who live in a democracy either vote for officials who make laws for them, or they vote directly on laws in a meeting known as an assembly. Democracy allows people freedom of speech and the right to choose between competing political parties in regularly held elections.

◄ In some elections, a person votes by making a mark next to the candidate's name on a ballot paper. The papers (votes) are posted in a sealed ballot box, to be counted later.

POWER TO THE PEOPLE
The first democracy appeared in Ancient Greece in the 500s B.C., when men in cities could vote in assemblies. The word democracy is Greek for "rule by the people."

ELECTION VICTORY

India is the world's largest democracy, and election time plays an important part in the lives of the people. Candidates make speeches, distribute leaflets, advertise, and design posters to persuade people to vote for them. Most candidates belong to a political party whose members share the same ideas about how the country should be run.

ELECTED ASSEMBLIES
The reign of Alexander the Great and a succession of Roman emperors gradually put an end to democracy, and the Middle Ages saw the rise of feudalism and monarchy. Democracy reappeared in the 1600s, when elected assemblies began to take power in some countries. At first only wealthy men could vote, but today nearly every adult in a democracy is allowed to vote.

MAJORITY RULE
Voters choose people to represent them in legislatures (lawmaking bodies), such as the U.S. Senate or the House of Representatives. For a law to be passed, a majority in the legislature must vote for it. On important issues, there may be a vote of all the people: a referendum.

CHOOSING REPRESENTATIVES
Some elections are decided by a system in which the candidate with the most votes wins. Others are decided by proportional representation—each party gets candidates in parliament in relation to the number of votes it receives.

GOVERNMENTS AND THE LAW
There are many kinds of democracy. In Britain, there is a monarchy, but an elected parliament makes laws. France is a republic with a president and prime minister, as well as a legislature. Many former Soviet Union and Eastern European nations are becoming increasingly democratic since the fall of their communist governments.

SEE ALSO

Civil rights, Government, Greece (Ancient), Law, Politics

DESERT

Deserts are dry areas of land which have hardly any plants or animals. Most deserts are hot, get very little rain, and are sandy or rocky.

▲ Deserts are not always hot. Some places in Antarctica and Greenland are known as polar deserts because the ground there is so dry. For example, on the western side of Antarctica, there are areas that receive less than 5 in. (13cm) of snow each year.

More than a fifth of the world's land is so dry that it is known as desert. Most deserts receive less than 10 in. (250mm) of rain each year. Others receive more rain, but it quickly evaporates in the strong heat and winds, or sinks into the parched ground. The driest place in the world is Chile's Atacama Desert, parts of which have less than 0.004 in. (0.1mm) of rain each year.

WHERE DESERTS FORM

Most deserts, such as the Kalahari and Sahara in Africa, lie between the Tropic of Cancer and the Tropic of Capricorn (25° to the north and south of the equator). These are the tropics, where the air is often too hot and dry for rain clouds to form. The cold Gobi Desert in central Asia exists, however, because it is far from the sea's moist winds. Other deserts, like the Atacama, lie behind high mountains which block rain-bearing winds.

SURVIVAL TACTICS

Desert plants and animals have developed ways of coping with the lack of water. Plants usually have long, spreading roots to reach any available moisture. Most have spines or small leaves that are rolled or waxy to cut down on water loss through evaporation. Other plants spend most of their lives as seeds—only growing when rain falls. Desert animals often hide during the heat of the day and come out at night. Camels can go for many days without water.

POCKETS OF WATER

Oases are pockets of fertile land in a desert. These occur where an aquifer, or underground stream, comes to the surface. Plants such as palm trees thrive, and animals and people gather there.

CREEPING DESERTS

Deserts can spread. This may happen because the climate becomes drier or nearby land is overgrazed by farm animals.

IN THE SHADOW OF THE SIERRA NEVADA

The deserts of North America are shielded from rain by the towering mountain wall of the Sierra Nevada. In some areas, less than 4 in. (100mm) of rain falls, making the gravelly ground inhospitable except to a few plants and animals. Temperatures during the day can reach 212°F (100°C), but at night it is often near freezing because there is no cloud cover.

Scaly skin stops the rattlesnake from drying out

The kit fox sleeps in a cool burrow during the day

The roadrunner gets most of its water from the animals it catches

The prickly pear cactus stores water in its fleshy stem

With its shallow, wide-ranging roots, the saguaro cactus always finds water —

Some honeypot ants fill themselves with liquid, and act as reservoirs for the rest of the nest

SEE ALSO
Africa, Antarctica, Climate, Habitat, Plant, South America

DESIGN

Everything we use today, from a toothbrush to a car, has been designed according to its function, trends in fashion and art, and the latest available materials.

Spanish painter Salvador Dali designed this "Eye of Time" watch.

Even household appliances, such as the kettle, are always being redesigned.

Scottish designer and architect Charles Rennie Mackintosh designed all his chairs with unusually high backs.

Professional designers must create an object that does the job it is supposed to do as efficiently as possible. But they must also think carefully about the aesthetic value, or appearance, of the object, how and where it will be used, who will be using it, and changing trends in technology and materials.

AGE OF DESIGN
The word design comes from the Italian word *disegno*. From the 1300s to the mid-1500s, during the great Italian artistic era called the Renaissance, the word was used to describe the basic idea behind a work of art, as well as rough sketches of it. Today, the term covers a huge area, from detailed drawings and engineering plans for buildings to the graphic design of books, magazines, and product containers.

SKETCHING IT OUT
The first step for many designers, whether painters, architects, film set designers, or fashion designers, is to sketch out their

◀ Fashion designers draw their ideas on paper. They show the outfits from different angles and in a variety of colors, adding swatches of fabric.

ideas, or create storyboards on paper. If it is a building or product, they may then make up a small model to scale. Fashion designers often make up a sample garment, using inexpensive cloth.

DESIGNING ON COMPUTERS
Computers are now used extensively in design, especially for industry. They allow people to experiment with three-dimensional, often animated, models on the screen. Using CAD (computer-aided design), a designer can quickly change a detail and the computer will calculate and apply the changes to the rest of the design. Specialist programs help experts create cars, shoes, and electrical goods.

THE CREATIVE PROCESS
Computers can be used to highlight stress points, illustrate aerodynamics, and show other crucial design features of a prototype car. Newspapers and magazines are designed on computers, as was this book.

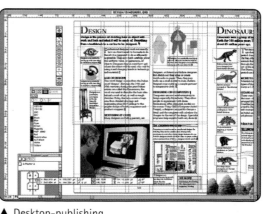

▲ Desktop-publishing software has revolutionized page design—changes can now be made in seconds.

SEE ALSO
Architecture, Art, Clothing, Computer

110

DINOSAUR

Dinosaurs were a type of reptile that lived on Earth for over 160 million years. They became extinct about 65 million years ago.

Tyrannosaurus rex was a theropod, or "beast-footed" dinosaur.

Diplodocus was a sauropod, or "lizard-footed" dinosaur.

Camptosaurus was an ornithopod, or "bird-footed" dinosaur.

Stegosaurus was a stegosaur, or "roofed" dinosaur.

Sauropelta was an ankylosaur, or "jointed" dinosaur.

Triceratops was a ceratopsian, or "horned-head" dinosaur.

The dinosaurs evolved 225 million years ago during a geological period known as the Triassic. Some were only the size of a chicken, others were the largest land animals that ever existed. They roamed the planet throughout the Jurassic period and died out at the end of the Cretaceous period. The Triassic, Jurassic, and Cretaceous periods are known as the "age of reptiles."

MORE TO COME

The same dinosaurs did not exist throughout the age of reptiles. For example, *Diplodocus* lived during the Jurassic and *Tyrannosaurus* reigned in the Cretaceous period. Scientists have found evidence of over 500 types of dinosaur, spanning all the periods, but it is believed that as many as 1,300 types may have existed—most of which are still undiscovered.

LIZARD OR BIRDLIKE

There were two main groups, or orders, of dinosaur—the Saurischia (with hipbones arranged like a lizard's) and the Ornithischia (with hipbones arranged like a bird's). The Saurischia can be divided into two smaller groups known as the theropods and the sauropods. The Ornithischia include four groups: the ornithopods, the stegosaurs, the ankylosaurs, and the ceratopsians.

MEAT-EATERS

The theropods were meat-eaters, all built to the same design. They had long mouths full of teeth for tearing flesh, they walked on their hind legs, and had small bodies which they balanced with long, heavy tails. Some, such as *Compsognathus*, were chicken-size, while the biggest were 39.4 ft. (12m)-long killers, such as *Tyrannosaurus*. ▶

KILLING MACHINE

The theropods were the meat-eating dinosaurs, which all had large jaws full of teeth for tearing flesh. *Deinonychus* was a terrifying killing machine equipped with deadly tools, including a slashing claw on the second toe of its back foot which gave it its name—"terrible claw."

Sharp teeth were used to tear flesh

Each toe and finger had a razor-sharp claw

The second toe of its back foot had a "terrible claw"

DINOSAUR GIANTS

Sauropods were plant-eaters. They had large, heavy bodies and moved around on all fours, using their long necks to reach leaves on trees. They were the largest land animals that ever lived and included *Diplodocus* and *Brachiosaurus*.

▲ A comparison between the size of mighty *Tyrannosaurus*'s feet and those of an average man.

PLANT-EATERS

The Ornithischia dinosaurs were also all plant-eaters. The only ones that could walk on their hind legs were the ornithopods. They had a more sophisticated chewing system than the long-necked sauropods, with cheeks for holding the food while they chewed it. *Iguanodon* is probably the most famous of the ornithopods.

▲ In 1978, a fossilized nest of 15 young *Maiasaura* was found in Montana. Evidence showed that the young were very small and would have had to be cared for by the mother to survive. *Maiasaura* means "good mother lizard."

BONY ARMOR

Three ornithischian groups evolved from the ornithopods (bird-footed dinosaurs). They all had armor of some kind that made them heavy, so they walked on four legs. The first was the stegosaurs—the "roofed" dinosaurs. They had large bodies and either a double row of bony plates down the back like *Stegosaurus*, or an arrangement of spines like *Kentrosaurus*.

▼ This fossil skeleton of *Tuojiangosaurus* was discovered in China in the 1970s. *Tuojiangosaurus* was a stegosaur that lived in the late Jurassic period, about 150 million years ago.

Archaeopteryx—one of the first birds

A SCENE FROM THE LATE JURASSIC

The late Jurassic is the period from 157 to 145 million years ago. It is known for its many plant-eating dinosaur species, such as spiny *Stegosaurus* and long-necked sauropods, including *Apatosaurus*. The main dinosaur predator was the meat-eating *Allosaurus*, but the reptile *Diplosaurus*, an ancestor of the crocodile, was also frightening.

A SCENE FROM THE LATE CRETACEOUS

The Late Cretaceous was a period from 95 to 65 million years ago. It was dominated by herds of duckbilled *Edmontosaura*, which had replaced the sauropods as the main plant-eaters. Meat-eating *Tyrannosaurus* probably hunted these animals, because other plant-eaters like *Triceratops* and *Ankylosaurus* had developed spectacular defensive armor. Large flying reptiles may have scavenged like vultures on the bodies of dead dinosaurs .

DINOSAUR FACTS

• The smaller meat-eating dinosaurs hunted in packs like wolves, preying on young or weak plant-eaters

• Large plant-eating dinosaurs like *Diplodocus* must have had to eat continuously to avoid starvation

• Dinosaurs may have been warm-blooded like mammals and birds

• Many different types of insect and mammal also lived during the time of the dinosaurs

• The dinosaurs' legs were not at the side like reptiles', but under their bodies like mammals'

JOINTED DINOSAURS

The second ornithischian group was the ankylosaurs, or "jointed" dinosaurs. They had bony armor that lay flat over their broad backs, and were also armed with spikes along the sides, as in *Edmontonia*, or a tail with a club, as in *Euoplocephalus*.

HORNED HEADS

The last ornithiscian group was the ceratopsians. They had armor on their faces and heads, where it formed big bony frills around the neck. These "horned-head" dinosaurs included *Triceratops*, which had a small horn on the nose and two long horns over the eyes, and *Styracosaurus*, which had an enormous horn on the nose and a series of smaller horns around the frill.

REPTILE NEIGHBORS

Dinosaurs were not the only reptiles that lived at the time. Many groups of swimming reptiles, such as the fish-shaped ichthyosaurs and the long-necked plesiosaurs, lived in the sea; pterosaurs flew in the air.

DEATH OF THE REPTILES

All of these unusual reptiles became extinct along with the dinosaurs at the end of the Cretaceous period. No one knows for sure how this happened, or why other reptiles, such as crocodiles and turtles, survived. It may have been a gradual process, due to a slow climatic change, or there may have been a sudden catastrophe, such as the Earth's being hit by a gigantic meteorite. The dinosaurs did leave some relatives, however. During the Jurassic period, birds evolved from the small meat-eating theropods, which means today's birds are the direct descendants of the dinosaurs.

Male

Female

▲ *Parasaurolophus* had a hollow crest extending upward from its nose, through which it may have hooted a warning or called its mate.

SEE ALSO

Evolution, Fossil, Mammal, Prehistoric animal, Reptile

DISEASE

A disease is an illness that disturbs the normal healthy functioning of a plant, animal, or person. Each disease produces symptoms (physical changes).

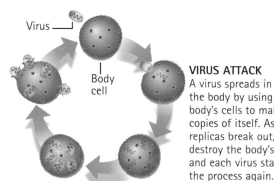

VIRUS ATTACK
A virus spreads in the body by using the body's cells to make copies of itself. As the replicas break out, they destroy the body's cell, and each virus starts the process again.

The human body may be attacked by thousands of diseases. These range from relatively harmless ones, such as the common cold and athlete's foot, to life-threatening diseases, such as typhoid and some cancers. Plants and animals also suffer from diseases—potatoes suffer from blight, and cats can get the flu (influenza).

▲ Many diseases have almost been wiped out by the widespread use of inoculation (also called immunization and vaccination). This is when a milder form of the disease is introduced into the body, by injection or via the mouth, so that the person develops long-term resistance to the disease.

BACTERIA AND VIRUSES
Flu, AIDS, and tetanus are all infectious diseases. They are caused by harmful microscopic organisms we call germs that invade the body and multiply. Tetanus is caused by bacteria (living creatures); flu and AIDS are caused by viruses (bundles of DNA wrapped in protein). Infectious diseases are spread from person to person by, for example, breathing in germs. A sudden outbreak of an infectious disease which affects many people is called an epidemic. Some infectious diseases can be prevented with vaccinations, and others can be treated with medicines such as antibiotics.

NONINFECTIOUS DISEASES
Many diseases are not caused by germs, but are the result of a poor diet. An example of this is scurvy, which is the result of not eating enough vitamin C. Others may be caused by an unhealthy lifestyle. For example, smoking and stress can lead to heart disease. Some diseases, such as hemophilia, run in families as a result of faulty genes.

LOOKING FOR CLUES
Symptoms such as pain or fever tell the person suffering from a disease that something is wrong, and give clues to doctors as to the cause. A doctor can also detect signs of disease by taking X rays or blood tests.

AFRICAN SLEEPING SICKNESS

In some areas of Africa, the tsetse fly spreads a disease called sleeping sickness. When it feeds on human blood, this tiny fly injects some of its saliva into the person's bloodstream. If its saliva contains microorganisms called *Trypanosoma brucei*, these enter the bloodstream also, and multiply inside the body, causing fever, headaches, and sleepiness. The person may die if not treated quickly.

Actual size of the tsetse fly

Tsetse fly

Trypanosoma brucei

Human red blood cell

Human skin

Proboscis used for sucking blood

SEE ALSO

Drug, Immune system, Medicine, Microorganism, Surgery

DOG

The domestic dog (*Canis familiaris*) belongs to the dog family, known as Canidae, and is believed to be descended from the gray wolf.

The chihuahua is the world's smallest dog: 10 in. (15cm) to the shoulder.

The poodle is an intelligent dog. There are three types: toy, miniature, and standard.

The greyhound, bred for speed, can reach 35 mph (57kph).

The bulldog was originally bred for the "sport" of bull-baiting in the Middle Ages.

The husky is a powerful sledge dog, able to pull twice its own weight.

The Airedale is the largest breed of terrier, probably bred for hunting otters.

Dogs do not sweat, but get rid of heat via their moist nose and tongue (panting)

Adult dogs have 42 teeth in a long muzzle, originally adapted for seizing prey on the run

Muscular, deep-chested bodies and long, slender legs, originally designed for chasing prey

The front paws have five toes, with strong, blunt, non-retractable claws

Dogs have a typical carnivore's digestive system, but they can also eat grain and cooked vegetables

Pointers have short, smooth coats, but many sporting dogs have long hair

When a pointer has located its quarry, its tail sticks straight out

All dogs' back paws have four toes, with a hidden fifth toe

SPORTING DOGS

Sporting dogs are bred for their acute sense of smell, which they use to track down game birds. The pointer (below) was popular during the 1800s, and gets its name from the way it stands with its tail straight and its nose pointing at the hiding bird. Other sporting dogs include setters, which crouch down, or "set," near hiding birds, and retrievers, which fetch dead game.

Dogs were the first animals to be tamed. Fossil remains of a domestic dog dating back 10,500 years have been found in Idaho. The relationship between human and dog probably began because dogs are natural scavengers, and hung around camps looking for food scraps.

BREEDS AND GROUPS

Since then, humans have selectively bred dogs—the American Kennel Club (AKC) recognizes 138 breeds of dog, and Great Britain's Kennel Club includes about 170. These breeds are divided into seven groups by appearance, use, and size: sporting dogs, herding dogs, hounds, nonsporting dogs, terriers, toy dogs, and working dogs. The dog's most acute senses—smell and hearing—were selectively bred early on for guarding and hunting. Other physical features were bred for specific uses. For example, the dachshund's short legs were selected for going down badger sets, and the bulldog's set-back nose was selected to help it breathe while biting. Nowadays, a gentle, nonaggressive nature is selected for pets.

A DOG'S LIFE

Most domestic dogs are fully grown by the age of 2, are old by the age of 12, and rarely live past 20. Female dogs can become pregnant from about seven months, and give birth to an average of three to six puppies, although some breeds may have up to ten puppies. The puppies open their eyes on the tenth day and are ready to leave their mother at six weeks. Dogs are pack animals and follow a leader. This loyalty can be transferred to a human, especially if the dog is trained while young.

▲ The border collie uses the hunting instincts of its wild ancestors to round up sheep.

SEE ALSO
Hearing, Wolf

DRUG

Drugs are substances that affect the way in which the body or mind works. Most drugs are used medicinally, to cure or prevent an illness.

Medicinal liquids called syrups make swallowing drugs easy for children.

Pills or capsules are the most common form of drug.

A drug is injected into the blood when a quick response is needed.

Eyedrops and inhalers act fast by sending the drug to the exact spot.

Creams and gels often contain drugs which disinfect a cut or graze.

Skin patches release drugs slowly through the skin into the blood.

Cigarettes are made from tobacco leaves, which contain the drug nicotine.

Over 4,000 years ago, Emperor Chi'en Nung of China put together a book of more than 300 medicinal plants, many of which are still used in medicine today. But it was not until the 1700s, when the English doctor William Withering studied the heart drug digitalis (extracted from foxgloves), that drugs were looked at scientifically. The modern drug industry began in 1899, when the German company Bayer manufactured the painkiller aspirin.

WHICH TYPE OF DRUG?
Doctors use many types of drugs to treat patients. For example, antibiotics such as penicillin kill the bacteria that cause infections. Analgesics (painkillers), such as aspirin and codeine, stop pain messages from reaching the brain. Sedatives have a calming effect and can help a person to sleep. Anesthetics deaden the body's nerves and are used in operations. Vaccines help the immune system to fight diseases, and insulin is given to people when their body fails to make enough of it naturally.

▶ The foxglove is listed in the oldest surviving book on drugs and their uses, written between A.D. 20 and A.D. 70 by the Ancient Greek doctor Dioscorides.

DANGERS AND ADDICTION
Some drugs, such as heroin or cocaine, are addictive, which means people cannot stop taking them. They are illegal because they are so dangerous. Even medicinal drugs or everyday drugs, such as alcohol, caffeine in tea and coffee, or nicotine in cigarettes, can be harmful if taken in large amounts.

TIMED-RELEASE CAPSULES
Drugs sometimes need to be released into the bloodstream slowly over a few hours, especially if they are painkillers. Timed-release capsules contain hundreds of tiny pellets with coatings of different thicknesses. Some of the pellets release the drug in the stomach, others release it later in the intestines.

Stomach

Intestines

1 The capsule (outer shell) breaks open in the stomach, releasing pellets which contain the drug. Each pellet looks like a tiny ball and is a different color according to the thickness of its coating.

2 The pellets with the thinnest coating dissolve first and release the drug in the stomach. The others move on to the intestines and release the drug later.

3 The drug is absorbed through the walls of the stomach and intestines into the bloodstream.

SEE ALSO

Medicine, Plant

EAGLE AND OTHER BIRDS OF PREY

Eagles and other birds of prey survive by hunting animals. They swoop down on their prey from the air, grabbing them with their sharp talons.

► Unlike hawks and eagles, owls, like this little owl, hunt their prey at night.

Birds of prey are born hunters. They have sharp eyesight to spot far-off prey, sharp, curved talons to catch their food, and strong, hooked beaks to tear at flesh. Most have large, broad wings with flight feathers that spread out when they soar in updrafts. As well as eagles, birds of prey include buzzards, falcons, hawks, kites, ospreys, and vultures. Owls are also often included, but belong to a different bird group.

The Andean condor is the largest bird of prey. It can weigh 26.5 lb (12kg).

A diving peregrine falcon can reach speeds of over 155 mph (250kph).

Northern goshawks can strike in midair, often attacking from below.

Vultures, such as this black vulture, feed on the bodies of dead animals.

Golden eagles carry prey equal to their own weight in their powerful talons.

HUNTING SKILLS
Most birds of prey soar high into the air and then swoop down on their prey on the ground at high speed. Some, such as the peregrine falcon, can also attack birds in midair. The kestrel is unusual because it hovers just a few yards above the ground before swooping. Vultures usually scavenge dead meat.

DIFFERENT TASTES
There are more than 50 species of eagle scattered throughout the world, although many are endangered. Most live in wild, remote places where humans cannot disturb them. Eagles eat a wide range of animals. The golden eagle attacks hares, small rodents, and other birds; the serpent eagle gorges on snakes. Some are experts at snaring fish, and the harpy eagle catches monkeys.

FISH FOR DINNER
The bald eagle, the national bird of the United States, is one of the most endangered birds of prey. It feeds on birds and small animals, but particularly likes fish. It scoops them from the surface of the water and flies off, gripping them in its powerful, sharp talons.

NEST RECYCLING
Many eagles use the same nest, or aerie, again and again, adding more material each time they breed. Their nests can become enormous—a bald eagle's can measure 10 ft. (3m) across and weigh over a ton. Most eagles lay just two eggs. Once the young have hatched, they do not leave the nest for up to two months.

SEE ALSO
Bird

117

EARTH

Our planet, Earth, is one of the nine planets that move around the Sun. It is made up of rock and metal, and is the only planet known to support life.

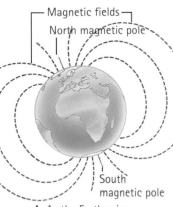

As the Earth spins, electrical currents beneath the surface turn the planet into a huge magnet, with a north and south pole just like any ordinary magnet.

Labels: Magnetic fields; North magnetic pole; South magnetic pole

Planet Earth is a not quite perfect ball of rock, with a metal core, which travels around the Sun. It is surrounded by a blanket of gases called the atmosphere, has one moon, and, as far as we know, is the only planet that supports life.

NIGHT AND DAY

Approximately every 24 hours, the Earth does a full circle on its axis—an imaginary line joining the North and South Poles. As it spins, one side turns to face the Sun and is in daylight, while the other side turns away, experiencing night. The Earth spins eastward, which is why the Sun seems to rise in the east and set in the west.

AROUND THE SUN

As well as spinning on its own axis, the Earth is constantly moving around the Sun. One complete path around the Sun is an orbit. The length of a year is determined by the time it takes a planet to make one orbit. This means that Earth travels 595 million miles (958 million km), at an average speed of 19 mi./sec. (30km/sec).

CHANGING SEASONS

The Earth is tilted toward the Sun at an angle of 23.5°. As the Earth orbits, those places that are tilted toward the Sun receive more warmth and light for the part of the year that is known as summer. As these places move farther around, they tilt away from the Sun, experiencing winter.

CORE TO CRUST

Beneath its thin shell, or crust, the interior of the Earth is very hot. Below about 45 mi. (70km), there is a mantle of rock that is semimolten (partly melted). The outer layer of the Earth's core is molten too, but enormous pressure keeps the inner core (the center) solid, even though temperatures here reach over 10,800°F (6,000°C). The upper layer of the mantle is made of plates, like pieces of a jigsaw, with the continents on top. Sometimes, the plates rub together, causing pressure which escapes through volcanoes or earthquakes.

FROM CORE TO CRUST

If we could cut a large section out of the Earth, we would see a planet made in four layers. At its center is a solid inner core of almost pure iron, surrounded by an outer core of liquid iron and nickel. Enveloping this is a mantle of silicon compounds, crystals, and lighter metals topped with a hard rock crust.

Labels: Enlarged section of mantle; Molten rock rising to surface; Continent; Continental plate; Mantle (1,864 mi. thick); Outer core (1,367 mi. thick); Inner core (1,553 mi. across)

The Earth is wrapped in a blanket of gases known as the atmosphere, which stretches up more than 310 mi. (500km) into space. It is held in place by the gravitational pull of the planet

THE EVOLVING EARTH

Astronomers believe that the Earth began to form about 4.6 billion years ago, when the solar nebula (a vast cloud of hot debris circling the newly formed Sun) began to cluster together into lumps that eventually became the planets of our solar system. The process took millions of years to complete, and Earth, like the other planets, developed a unique chemistry and atmosphere.

1 Hot clouds of dust and gases spin around the newly formed Sun. As the specks of dust collide, they stick together in lumps.

2 The forces of gravity pull more passing lumps into the spinning ball. Heavy elements such as iron sink to the center.

3 Lighter metals and rocks come to the surface and the red-hot Earth cools enough for a hard shell to form.

4 Gases escaping from the Earth form clouds and rain falls, creating oceans containing small oxygen-producing plants.

5 Originally one large mass, the Earth's land surface is now split into seven large bodies, known as continents.

LIFE ON EARTH

Why exactly there is life on Earth is still a mystery to scientists. The theories are numerous, but the answer is probably a combination of reasons. First, Earth's distance from the Sun is ideal—not too hot like Venus, nor too cold like Mars. Second, Earth is the only planet we know of that has water on its surface—over 70 percent of it is covered by water. Scientists believe that electrical storms on the newly formed planet caused chemical reactions between gases in the atmosphere. These created the first building blocks of life, which fell into the oceans, where they combined to become simple plant-like forms. All plants make oxygen, and so an ideal atmosphere was soon created for the evolution of oxygen-breathing life-forms.

Earth

▲ A day is the time it takes the Earth to turn once on its own axis: 23 hr., 56 min., and 4 sec.

Moon

▲ A lunar month is the time it takes the Moon to travel once around the Earth: 28 days.

Sun

Earth

▲ A year is the time it takes the Earth to travel once around the Sun: 365 days, 6 hr., and 9 min.

EARTH FACTS AND FIGURES

• Earth's diameter (the distance from Pole to Pole through the center) is 7,900 mi. (12,714km)

• Earth's circumference (the distance around its middle at the equator) is 24,901 mi. (40,075km)

• As Earth spins, places near the equator move much faster than places at the Poles, causing the planet to bulge slightly in the middle and be flattened at the top and bottom

• The temperature of Earth's inner core may be as hot as 11,200°F (6,200°C)

• Of the nine planets in our solar system, Earth is the third closest to the Sun

• The Sun and the Earth are about 93 million miles (150 million km) apart

• Earth's path around the Sun is not a circle but an ellipse (an oval), which means it is closer to the Sun on January 1 than on June 1

SEE ALSO

Atmosphere, Big Bang theory, Continent, Earthquake, Evolution, Gravity, Magnetism, Planet, Season, Solar system, Sun, Time, Volcano

EARTHQUAKE

An earthquake is a shaking of the Earth's surface. It is caused by the sudden release of pressure through weak parts of the Earth's crust.

The vast majority of earthquakes do not cause any serious damage. Small tremors can happen with an erupting volcano, an avalanche, or a landslide. However, the largest earthquakes occur as a result of pressure or tension deep under the ground being released through weak areas (fault lines) in the Earth's crust.

TECTONIC PLATES

The Earth's crust is broken into giant slabs called tectonic plates. Sometimes, pressure builds up underground as a result of the plates moving against each other. The pressure is suddenly released, sending out shock waves in all directions and causing the Earth's crust to shake and even crack.

EARTHQUAKE ZONES

There are two great earthquake zones. Both are where two tectonic plates meet. One stretches across southern Asia, through the Mediterranean, and into eastern Africa. The other is the "ring of fire" around the Pacific Ocean, which includes the United States. In 1906, a large part of San Francisco was destroyed by an earthquake in this zone.

▲ The shock waves begin underground in a region called the hypocenter, and reach the Earth's surface directly above, at the epicenter. From here, they radiate in all directions.

SHOCK WAVES

Earthquake shock waves are known as seismic waves. They are detected using a measuring instrument called a seismometer. A severe earthquake can be felt as much as 250 mi. (400km) away. The intensity of an earthquake is plotted on the Richter scale. An earthquake measuring over 7 on this scale can destroy buildings and take lives.

DISASTER IN JAPAN

In 1995, the Japanese city of Kobe was devastated by a violent earthquake that killed over 5,000 people. The earthquake measured 7.2 on the Richter scale. It caused houses and apartments to collapse, trains to be derailed, and roads to be ripped apart. The shaking lasted for about 20 seconds.

SEE ALSO
Continent, Earth, Mountain and valley, Ocean and sea

EASTERN EUROPE

Eastern Europe is a geographical region of eight countries that were once part of the communist bloc controlled by the Soviet Union.

BELARUS
Area: 88,044 sq. mi.
Population: 10,335,382
Capital: Minsk
Languages: Belarussian, Russian
Currency: Rouble

CZECH REPUBLIC
Area: 30,448 sq. mi.
Population: 10,256,760
Capital: Prague
Language: Czech
Currency: Koruna

HUNGARY
Area: 35,700 sq. mi.
Population: 10,075,034
Capital: Budapest
Language: Hungarian
Currency: Forint

MOLDOVA
Area: 13,000 sq. mi.
Population: 4,434,547
Capital: Chisinau
Language: Moldovan
Currency: Leu

POLAND
Area: 117,600 sq. mi.
Population: 38,625,478
Capital: Warsaw
Language: Polish
Currency: Zloty

Eastern Europe lies between the Baltic Sea, the Balkan Peninsula, the Black Sea, and Russia. It makes up more than one sixth of Europe's land area, and is a region of plains, low hills, and mountains.

PEAKS AND PLAINS
To the south lie the rugged Carpathian Mountains and Transylvanian Alps. The highest point is Gerlachovsky Stit, a peak of 8,713 ft. (2,656m) in the Carpathians. To the west is the Hungarian Plain, and to the east are the vast rolling steppes (treeless plains) of the Ukraine.

A REGION OF RIVERS
The area is watered by some of Europe's major rivers. The Danube, Europe's second longest river at 1,725 mi. (2,776km), forms much of Romania's southwestern border; the Dnieper and the Dniester both flow through the Ukraine. Europe's largest swamp, the Pripet Marshes, straddles the border between Belarus and the Ukraine.

▼ The medieval city of Prague, capital of the Czech Republic, has some of Europe's most beautiful and well-preserved architecture.

▲ Expanses of steppe once covered the Ukraine, but this land, covered with rich soil, is now heavily farmed.

CONTINENTAL CLIMATE
Away from the mountains, Eastern Europe has warm summers; temperatures average 68°F (20°C) or more in July. Winters get colder as you travel from west to east. Most of the region has moderate rainfall, with 20–40 in. (500–1,000mm) per year, but the southeast is drier, with less than 20 in. (500mm) of rain per year.

BREADBASKET OF EUROPE
In the lowlands, many of the region's forests have been cleared for farming. The fertile steppes, once an area of natural grassland, are also farmed. The Ukraine is sometimes called "the breadbasket of Europe" because of its high production of grain and other crops. ▶

N

BALTIC SEA

LATVIA

LITHUANIA

RUSSIA

GERMANY

miles
0   100
0   100
km

Vistula

Warsaw ■

POLAND

■ Minsk

BELARUS

RUSSIA

Pripet
Marshes

Kiev ■

■ Prague

CZECH REPUBLIC

Gerlachovsky
Stit ▲

SLOVAKIA

■ Bratislava

AUSTRIA

HUNGARY

■ Budapest

Danube

Hungarian Plain

SLOVENIA

CROATIA

Dniester

Carpathian

Mountains

UKRAINE

Dnieper

MOLDOVA

■ Chisinau

CASPIAN
SEA

ROMANIA

Transylvanian Alps

BLACK
SEA

Bucharest ■

SERBIA AND
MONTENEGRO

Danube

BULGARIA

BALKAN PENINSULA

ROMANIA
Area: 88,900 sq. mi.
Population: 22,317,730
Capital: Bucharest
Language: Romanian
Currency: Leu

SLOVAKIA
Area: 18,800 sq. mi.
Population: 5,422,366
Capital: Bratislava
Language: Slovak
Currency: Koruna

UKRAINE
Area: 222,600 sq. mi.
Population: 48,396,470
Capital: Kiev
Language: Ukrainian
Currency: Hryvna

▶ Old-fashioned factories,
such as this one in Romania,
cause air, water, and soil
pollution in many parts
of Eastern Europe.

DISAPPEARING WILDLIFE

As in the rest of Europe, the wildlife in
Eastern Europe has been reduced by the
destruction of forests and grasslands. A
number of large mammals that once grazed
on the steppes, such as the saiga antelope,
have now disappeared. The rare wisent
(European bison) is found in western
Belarus and central Poland; the Danube
Delta on the Black Sea is a major wetland
and home to many birds.

HEAVY AND LIGHT INDUSTRY

Coal, oil and natural gas, iron ore, and
other minerals are found in this region.
Heavy industry produces machinery,

▲ The practice of Eastern Orthodox Christianity is wide-spread in Belarus, Moldova, Romania, and the Ukraine. Here, priests celebrate the Eucharist in Kiev in the Ukraine.

transportation equipment, and steel and the manufacture of electronic goods, clothes, and processed food is increasing.

CITY DWELLERS
Many people live in rural areas, and a few people still follow nomadic lifestyles. But about two thirds of the people live and work in towns and cities. Kiev, in the Ukraine, is the largest city in Eastern Europe, with a population of 2,651,000.

RELIGIOUS WORSHIP
Religion is an important part of life for many people in Eastern Europe. The two dominant faiths in the region are Roman Catholic and Eastern Orthodox Christianity. There is a Muslim minority in Romania, which was once part of the Muslim Ottoman Empire.

FOREIGN POWERS
All of the countries of Eastern Europe have at times in their history been under the influence of a foreign power. In 1793, Poland disappeared after being divided up among Prussia, Austria, and Russia. Hungary and Czechoslovakia formed part of the Habsburg Empire until 1918. Romania gained its independence from Turkey in 1878. More recently, the Ukraine, Belarus, and Moldova were part of the Russian-dominated Soviet Union.

COMMUNIST RULE
After World War II, all the countries of Eastern Europe came under communist rule, either as part of the Soviet Union or as members of the Soviet bloc. Romania remained outside Soviet control, but under the communist dictator Nicolae Ceauşescu.

THE NEW MAP
In the late 1980s, the countries of Eastern Europe began to abandon communist rule in favor of their own democratically elected governments. Belarus, Moldova, and the Ukraine gained their independence in 1991, following the breakup of the Soviet Union. In 1993, Czechoslovakia split peacefully into two countries: the Czech Republic and Slovakia.

▲ Vacationers in Budapest play chess in one of Hungary's many natural hot springs.

DEMOCRACY IN HUNGARY
From the end of World War II, Hungary, like the rest of Eastern Europe, came under Soviet communist rule. However, demonstrations in favor of democracy, such as this one in Budapest in 1988, indicated people's unhappiness with the government. In 1989, Hungary was the first Eastern European country to shake off communism. In March 1990, it elected its first democratic government in 42 years.

EUROPA!

CAVE
CANEM

SEE ALSO

Cold War, Communism, Democracy, Europe, Russia and the Baltic States

ECOLOGY

Ecology is the study of how plants, animals, and humans live together in their natural surroundings, and the ways in which they affect one another.

THE FOOD CHAIN

Each organism in a food chain feeds on and gets energy from the previous level. Ecologists divide plants and animals in a chain into groups, depending on how they get their energy. Plants are energy producers, using the sun's energy to produce new growth. Animals are consumers, obtaining energy by eating plants or other animals.

2 PRIMARY CONSUMERS
Small herbivores (plant-eaters), such as freshwater shrimp and snails, form the second energy level.

1 PRODUCERS
Water plants form the beginning of the food chain, producing energy and growth from the sun, soil, and water.

3 SECONDARY CONSUMERS
The third level of energy usage is by larger carnivores (meat-eaters) such as trout, which feed on the shrimp and snails.

4 TOP PREDATOR
In the fourth level of energy transfer, a bigger carnivore such as an otter preys on the trout.

6 RECYCLERS
The otter's body is returned to the soil by detrivores (rotting material-eaters), such as fungi, bacteria, and flies and their maggots.

5 DEATH
The otter dies from old age or disease.

Every plant and animal depends on a cycle of food, energy, and waste disposal that links it to other plants and animals. Ecologists study how plants and animals are linked to each other in food chains and webs.

CHAINED TOGETHER

All living things need energy. Plants use light energy from the sun to turn substances in the soil, air, and water into food. Insects eat the plants and fish, birds, and other animals eat the insects. In this way, energy is passed along a food chain. When living things die, their bodies break down and release nutrients back into the ground to start the process again.

ECOSYSTEMS

An ecosystem consists of the plants and animals in a certain area, together with the air, soil, climate, and other nonliving things. A forest is one type of ecosystem, but there are many others. An ecosystem can be as small as a pond or as large as an ocean.

HUMANS INTERVENE

Humans are part of the biggest ecosystem of all—the Earth itself. Some human actions can affect the entire planet. Logging a rain forest, for example, affects the forest by destroying its plants and animals. Since trees produce the oxygen needed by humans and other life-forms, the world's oxygen supply is also affected.

GRAY SQUIRREL INVASION

The introduction of plants or animals from foreign lands can have harmful effects on ecology. When gray squirrels from North America were introduced to Britain, the native red squirrels were pushed out of the food chain in most areas.

▲ Many timber companies manage their forests ecologically, using a process known as artificial reforestation. This means that a constant supply of seed is sown in a nursery and transplanted to the forest to replace felled trees.

SEE ALSO

Animal, Brazil, Conservation, Forest, Habitat, Plant, Pollution

EDUCATION

Education is the development of skills and knowledge. It can be formal, as provided by schools, or informal—through playing, watching, and learning in everyday life.

Learning to play a musical instrument is free as part of the curriculum in some countries. In other places, pupils must pay for lessons.

Many people feel that the main reason for educating children is to benefit society, by teaching skills needed to keep the community going. Others feel that it is more important to develop an individual's talents and interests. The Ancient Greek philosopher Socrates believed that education could make people happier.

SCHOOL FOR ALL
The Ancient Greeks were the first to set up a formal education system, but only for boys of rich families. Lessons included the art of public speaking for budding politicians. In many countries, the church or charities governed schooling. It wasn't until the 1800s that governments began to take control, and the 1900s before education became free for most girls and boys. However, millions of people worldwide still do not possess the basic skills of reading and writing.

School trips are a fun and exciting way of relating subjects learned in the classroom to real-life objects and situations.

BEST YEARS OF YOUR LIFE
In most countries, it is compulsory for children to go to primary school at the age of 5 or 6, then on to a secondary (high) school at about 13 years of age. Some start earlier. Friedrich Froebel opened the first kindergarten (nursery) in Germany in 1837. In many parts of the world, attendance drops after the age of 11, but education can continue into adulthood at colleges or universities. Courses offer vocational (career) training or specialist qualifications.

THE CURRICULUM
The curriculum (subjects taught) varies in each country. It may emphasize religion, local crafts, or history. Many schools in the 1800s concentrated on reading, writing, and arithmetic. Subjects and teaching methods have changed over the years, as have educational theories. The Czech educationalist Comenius (1592–1670) thought pictures were a vital teaching tool. Italian reformer Maria Montessori (1870–1952) created wooden devices to help children learn through exploration.

SCHOOLS OF THOUGHT
Styles of teaching, subjects taught, and classroom settings have changed over the years. Once children had to sit in rows in silence while the teacher lectured them. Now, there is more emphasis on interaction and small-group tuition. Educators argue about which is best—formal instruction (presenting facts to learn) or learning through activity and experience.

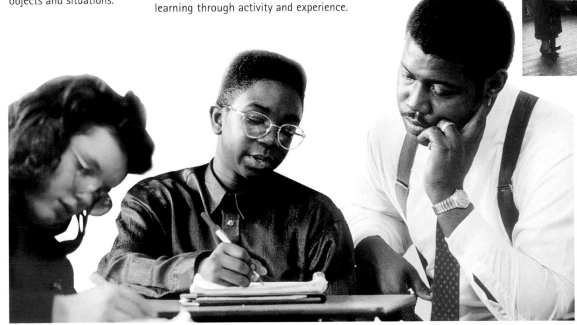

▲ A government health advisor known as the Food Fairy visits a classroom in the United States in 1925 to instruct children on healthy eating.

SEE ALSO

Greece (Ancient)

EGYPT

Egypt lies in the northeast of Africa. It has more people than any other African nation except Nigeria, yet most Egyptians live in just four percent of the country.

Area: 386,198 sq. mi.
Population: 70,712,345
Capital: Cairo
Language: Arabic
Currency: Egyptian pound

Traders, such as this man selling herbs and tea, set up their stalls in open street markets, or bazaars.

Most of Egypt's people live around the Nile Delta and Valley and along the Suez Canal, a vital shipping link for world trade. The Nile River, controlled by the Aswan High Dam, provides fertile land stretching from Egypt's border with Sudan right up to the Mediterranean Sea. Egypt's main cities are its capital, Cairo, and the port of Alexandria—two of the largest cities in Africa.

DESERT AREAS
On either side of the Nile lie two deserts that together cover more than 90 percent of the country—the vast, low-lying Western Desert and the hilly Eastern Desert, which borders the Red Sea.

AGRICULTURAL LIFE
Agriculture is the country's most important industry, employing over a third of all Egyptians. These farmers, known as *fellahin*, grow cotton and food crops such as corn and rice in the fertile Nile Delta. The manufacturing industry is growing, and tourists attracted by the ancient ruins also generate income for many Egyptians. Cotton, oil, and cloth are major exports.

A MUSLIM POPULATION
Most Egyptians are descended from the people of Ancient Egypt or from Arabs who invaded the country in the A.D. 600s. About 90 percent of the people are Muslim.

EGYPT TODAY
Egypt was part of the Ottoman Empire from 1517 until 1922. Britain controlled the Suez Canal and had administrative power in the country from the 1880s until the 1950s. Since the 1980s, Egypt has strengthened its ties with other Arab nations, including Saudi Arabia.

Egypt's main port of Alexandria was the world's greatest trading city 2,000 years ago.

▶ Triangular-sailed wooden boats called *feluccas* carry goods and passengers along the Nile.

SEE ALSO
Africa, Egypt (Ancient), Islam, Middle East

EGYPT, ANCIENT

Ancient Egypt developed along the Nile River around 5,000 years ago. Over the next 2,500 years, it grew into one of the greatest civilizations of all time.

▲ Pyramids were burial monuments for kings. The Sphinx (half man, half lion) stands beside the pyramids at Giza.

The funeral mask of Tutankhamen, boy-king of Egypt (1361-52 B.C.), was discovered in 1922.

The Ancient Egyptians chose to settle by the Nile in Africa because each year the river flooded, spreading mud over the banks. This provided them with fertile land to farm.

PYRAMID BUILDERS
The Ancient Egyptians were the first real engineers and built impressive temples, cities, and pyramids. The largest of the pyramids needed over 2 million blocks, each weighing as much as 2.5 tons. Some of the stones were from distant quarries and carried down the Nile on rafts.

The tombs of some important officials contained models of items that they might need in the next world.

A CREATIVE PEOPLE
The Ancient Egyptians used papyrus reeds to make shoes, boats, ropes, and writing paper. Papyrus scrolls preserve Ancient Egyptian hieroglyphic writing. The Egyptians also invented a 365-day calendar.

LIFE AFTER DEATH
Many gods were worshiped, including the sun god Ra and Osiris, god of the dead. The Egyptian kings, or pharaohs, were also believed to be gods. When they died, the kings and queens were buried in tombs full of things needed in the next world—food, jewelry, even small statues of servants (*shabtis*). Most royal tombs were robbed, but in 1922, the tomb of the boy pharaoh Tutankhamen was found, with most of its treasures untouched.

END OF A CIVILIZATION
Ancient Egypt included three great ages: the Old Kingdom, the Middle Kingdom, and the New Kingdom. In 31 B.C. Cleopatra died, and Egypt fell to the Roman Empire.

MUMMIFIED BODIES

The Ancient Egyptians believed in life after death. Their bodies were mummified (preserved) before burial to prevent decay. It took 70 days to mummify a body.

Charms (amulets) were wrapped into the bandages to ward off evil

This falcon-headed canopic jar held the intestines

The body was placed in salt for 40 days to dry. Before being bandaged, the dried body was rubbed with oils and spices

Most of the internal organs were put into canopic jars. This human-headed one held the liver

Linen bandages were soaked in resin (glue)

The jackal-headed canopic jar held the stomach

SEE ALSO
Archaeology, Egypt, Paper, Roman Empire

ELECTRICITY

Electricity is a form of energy. It can be stored in batteries or sent along wires to make electric trains, computers, lightbulbs, and other devices work.

Electricity is an invisible form of energy created by the movement of charged particles. It flows into our homes along wires and can be easily converted into other energy forms, such as heat and light.

▲ Each lightbulb in a circuit creates resistance to the flow of electric current, and so lightbulbs wired in series do not glow brightly.

▲ Lightbulbs wired in parallel all glow brightly, because each lightbulb is connected directly to the battery.

PASSING ON ELECTRONS
Everything in the world, including humans and the air they breathe, is made of atoms. Each of these tiny particles has a positively charged center (nucleus), with smaller, negatively charged electrons whizzing around it. Electricity is created when one of the electrons jumps to another atom. This can be caused by the magnetic field in a generator, by chemicals in a battery, or by friction (rubbing materials together).

THALES THE PHILOSOPHER
The discovery that an electric charge could be created by rubbing two materials together was first made by the Greek philosopher Thales over 2,600 years ago. He found that if he rubbed the fossilized tree sap, amber, with silk, it attracted feathers and dust. We now know that this happened because electrons had been passed between the silk and the amber,

Negative terminal, via which the electrons flow out of the battery

Positive terminal, via which the electrons return to the battery

Plates

▲ Wet batteries, like those in cars, store electricity and can be recharged. Six cells contain lead and lead dioxide plates in a solution of dilute sulfuric acid. The battery is first charged by an outside electrical source, but after that a generator, run by the car's engine, keeps it charged.

making them electrically charged. In recognition of his discovery, our word electron comes from the Greek word *elecktron*, meaning amber.

CONDUCTORS AND INSULATORS
The electricity of substances like amber is called static electricity, because the charge stays in place once the electrons have moved between the atoms. In other substances, the electrons carry on flowing. These substances are called conductors. Most electrical wires are made of copper because it is a good electrical conductor, as are all metals. Water also conducts electricity, which is why it is dangerous to

HOW A GENERATOR WORKS

An electric generator works by using the principle of electro-magnetic induction, discovered in 1831 by the British chemist and physicist Michael Faraday (1791–1867). He discovered that if a coil of wire is spun between two magnets, electrons begin to flow inside the wire coil. An alternating current (AC) and a direct current (DC) can be created in this way.

Wire coil — Carbon brush

N

S

Motion   Slip ring

▲ The two magnets naturally produce an alternating current (AC). As the coil spins, the magnetic field inside the coil points first one way and then the other. This makes the electric current change direction, or alternate.

Wire coil — Carbon brush

N

S

Commutator

Motion

▲ To create a direct current (DC), which flows in only one direction, the coil must be attached to a device called a commutator which is able to reverse the current.

▶ Practical DC generators are used to power large industrial motors. Unlike Faraday's simple model, a generator has many coils of wire wound on a rotor.

Coils

Magnet

Commutator

Rotor

Carbon brushes

ELECTRICAL TERMS

Conductor Any substance through which an electric current can flow

Coulomb (C) The measurement of electric charge

Current How fast electrons flow along a conductor—it is measured in amperes (A)

Insulator Any substance through which an electric current cannot flow

Resistance How hard it is for current to flow through a conductor—it is measured in ohms (Ω)

Static electricity Electric charge created by two objects rubbing together and exchanging electrons

Voltage (V) A unit of measurement describing how powerfully a battery sends electric current

Watt A unit of measurement that describes how much electrical energy can be converted into heat and light energy per second

PRODUCING ELECTRICITY

All power plants have a generator which produces electricity. In nuclear power plants, the nuclear reactor creates the heat needed to turn water into steam. The steam turns giant wheels, called turbines, which power the generator. The electricity it produces then flows along wires to homes, offices, schools, and stores.

THE POWER PLANT
The nuclear reactor splits atoms to create the heat needed to produce steam to spin the turbines.

Water heats and turns to steam

Nuclear reactor

Condenser

Cooling tower

Generator

Transformer

Steam spins the turbine which powers the generator

THE ELECTRICITY GRID
Electricity from the power plant travels via step-up and step-down transformers, which convert it to the voltage needed for distribution.

Nuclear power plant

Step-up transformer

Substation

Step-down transformer

Large factory

Underground transformer

Substation

Transformer

Homes

operate electrical appliances with wet hands. Other materials are made of atoms between which it is almost impossible for electrons to flow. These materials are known as insulators, and include plastic, wood, and amber. A flow of electrons is known as a current, and the term "resistance" is a measure of how difficult it is for current to flow through a conductor.

COMPLETING THE CIRCUIT

For an electrical appliance such as a flashlight to work, its electricity source (the battery) must be connected to the bulb by wires in an unbroken loop: a circuit. The job of the flashlight's on/off switch is to open or close a gap in the circuit. When the switch is on, electricity flows around the circuit, lighting the bulb. When the switch is off, the circuit is broken and the current cannot flow.

MAIN POWER SUPPLY

Batteries can provide only a limited amount of electricity. So most electrical devices receive their power from a main power supply, or electricity distribution mains. Wires connect millions of wall sockets to a power plant. An electric current flows from the plant, along the wires, out of the sockets, and into the equipment being used. To complete the circuit, the current returns to the power plant through other wires.

ALTERNATING CURRENT

The electricity that comes out of a power plant is in the form of alternating current (AC). Unlike a battery, which produces a steady one-way current called a direct current (DC), the main power supply flows first in one direction and then the other. The current changes direction very rapidly (about 60 times a second).

SEE ALSO
Atom and molecule, Electronics, Energy, Heat, Magnetism, Nuclear power

ELECTRONICS

Electronics is a branch of engineering which studies the components and circuits that make up modern electrical devices, like radios and toasters.

Until the 1950s, radios used glass tubes. They were bulky and fragile.

In the 1950s, the small, durable transistor began to replace the valve.

In the 1970s, microchips made hand-size radio-cassette players possible.

Modern electrical devices contain tiny electronic parts called components, which are joined together by lines of metallic paint on circuit boards. Electronic engineers know how to put the right components together to make circuits that can perform specific jobs.

WORKING PARTS
Components affect the way electrons (tiny charged particles) flow through a circuit. The simplest component, the switch, breaks the flow of electrons, or current. Resistors make it harder for the current to flow, while capacitors store current as electrical charge. Diodes let current flow in only one direction.

TRANSISTOR TECHNOLOGY
The first circuits used bulky glass vacuum tubes, which could magnify a current or switch it on or off. This ability to turn a current on or off electronically is the principle behind all computers. In the 1950s, the valve was replaced by a device called the transistor, which was much smaller, cheaper, and more durable, paving the way for the huge electronic advances that were to follow.

BIRTH OF THE MICROCHIP
In the 1970s, the invention of the microchip, which contained thousands of tiny transistors on a piece of material smaller than a stamp, allowed complex circuits to be squeezed into a tiny space. This made the home computer possible. More recently, very large-scale integration (VLSI) has enabled hundreds of millions of transistors to be put on a single chip, meaning that even smaller computers can be made.

ELECTRONICS TODAY
Electronics is now part of virtually all electrical devices. The microprocessor, a complex circuit on a single chip, is used in devices from robots and space rockets to videocassette recorders (VCRs), telephones, and digital watches.

HOW A DIGITAL WATCH WORKS
A digital watch is powered by a battery. Its timing is controlled by a quartz crystal, which vibrates thousands of times a second. The microchip uses these vibrations to keep time, which it displays in numbers.

Circuit board

Quartz crystal

Microchip

Battery cover

Battery

Liquid crystal display (LCD)

Outer casing

Plastic window

SEE ALSO
Atom and molecule, Clock, Computer, Electricity, Robot, Rocket, Telephone

ELEPHANT

Elephants are the largest animals on land. They have very thick skin, a trunk, and ivory tusks. There are two species of elephant: the African and the Asian.

Asian elephants are the smaller type, growing to 10 ft. (3m) at the shoulder and weighing up to 5 tons.

African elephants are the largest land animals. They can reach 13 ft. (4m) and weigh up to 6 tons.

The African elephant lives in forests and open grassland and is the largest living land animal. The Asian or Indian elephant is mainly a forest animal. It is also smaller, with smaller ears, a more rounded back, and a trunk that ends in one fingerlike tip, instead of two.

EATING MACHINES

Elephants live on leaves and bark, eating up to 440 lb. (200kg) of food a day. They use their trunks, which are giant, flexible nostrils, to pull up plants and to bring food and water to their mouths. They have 12 back teeth (molars), but only 4 are fully developed and in use at any one time. All elephants have tusks, or extra long, curved teeth, which they use to strip bark off trees and to dig for water.

PROTECTIVE INSTINCTS

Female elephants start to breed when they are about ten years of age. They are pregnant for 20 months, before giving birth to a single calf. When a calf is about to be born, other females gather around the mother and the herd stays in one place until the young calf, which stands nearly 3 ft. (1m) tall, is on its feet and ready to move on.

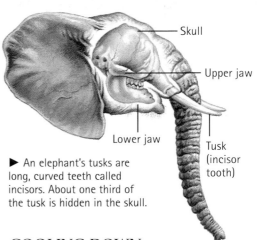

Skull

Upper jaw

Lower jaw

Tusk (incisor tooth)

▶ An elephant's tusks are long, curved teeth called incisors. About one third of the tusk is hidden in the skull.

COOLING DOWN

Because elephants have no sweat glands, they lose very little body heat. They cool down by hiding in the shade and flapping their ears, or by bathing in water and using their trunks to shower themselves.

OLD AGE

All elephants, except the old bull males, are sociable animals and live in herds led by the oldest females. They can live for over 60 years, but many are killed for their ivory tusks. In many places the bull elephants, which have the biggest tusks, have become rare. The spread of human settlements has also led to both Asian and African elephants becoming endangered.

SEE ALSO

Africa, Animal, Indian subcontinent, Mammal

EMPIRE

An empire is a group of nations or states under the control of a single power. Most empires are built up when one country conquers others.

Octavian, later called Augustus, became the first emperor of Rome in 27 B.C.

From A.D. 527 to 565, Justinian ruled the Byzantine Empire with his wife.

In 1525, Babar founded the Mughal Empire by conquering northern India.

Süleyman enlarged the Ottoman Empire in the 1500s.

Maria Theresa and Francis I unified the Hapsburg Empire in the 1740s.

Haile Selassie, emperor of Ethiopia, was overthrown by the army in 1974.

BRITISH INDIA

Over 600 small states, ruled by leaders including rajahs and maharajahs, came under the British Empire. They had their own laws, armies, and finances, but there were British troops in some states to guarantee loyalty.

Some of the greatest empires in history were the Roman, British, Byzantine, Japanese, Ottoman, and Russian empires. Each was ruled by an emperor or empress, but there have been other types of rule.

POWER GROWTH

Empires are usually built up when a country becomes richer or has larger armed forces than its neighbors, allowing it to spread its power and influence. The Greek king Alexander the Great trained his army with new weapons and tactics before conquering a vast empire from 334 to 323 B.C. The European Hapsburg dynasty used royal marriages and treaties to expand its Holy Roman Empire for more than 300 years from the 1400s. In the 1800s, the British Empire was won by economic strength, backed up by military superiority when needed.

IMPERIAL RULE

Many empires are ruled by a single state or nation, often with great brutality. The Assyrians in the ancient Middle East used their army to enforce the king's rule and to collect taxes. Those who disobeyed were cruelly punished. The Mongol Empire was run as a dictatorship in which the khan's wishes were enforced by the army. Other empires allowed some freedoms to their subjects. The states in the Athenian Empire of the 400s B.C. met each year to discuss events. Many of the cities and states in the Holy Roman Empire were free to run their own affairs, make their own laws, and even go to war.

KEY DATES

1500–1100 B.C. Egyptian New Kingdom rules an empire in southwest Asia

850–609 B.C. Assyria rules the Middle East

559–326 B.C. Persian Empire flourishes

264 B.C.–A.D. 410 Rome expands to rule vast areas before falling to barbarian invasion

228 B.C. China united under the Qin Dynasty

A.D. 800 Holy Roman Empire begins with the coronation of Charlemagne

1206 Genghis Khan founds the Mongol Empire

1492–1828 Spain conquers an empire in the Americas before colonies win independence

1880–1950s European powers build empires in Africa and Asia, then grant colonies independence

COLONIAL ADVENTURES

The Industrial Revolution made European states richer and better armed than other peoples. By 1850, several European nations owned colonies in Africa and Asia, which produced wealth and trade. In 1882, the British took over Egypt, prompting other European nations to conquer vast areas of Africa, Asia, and the Pacific and turn them into colonies. Within 40 years, it became clear that these colonies produced little wealth and were costly to maintain.

COLLAPSE OF EMPIRES

Empires may collapse as the result of foreign attack, member states breaking away, or internal dispute. The ancient Persian Empire was defeated in war by the Greeks under Alexander the Great. The Roman Empire was weakened by internal power struggles, and then fell to barbarian attacks during the 400s. In 1917, the German and Hapsburg empires were divided up into smaller states by the victorious Allies at the end of World War I, and the new states were racked by revolution, bringing an end to their empires.

A POSTIMPERIAL WORLD

Since 1945, very few empires have continued to exist. The colonial empires of the British, French, and other European

▲ The great palace of Persepolis was the center of the Persian Empire, founded by Darius the Great in 559 B.C. Nations subject to the Persian "King of Kings" brought tributes to Persepolis each spring as part of a great festival.

nations broke up when, weakened by World War II, they could not afford to keep the colonies in the face of nationalist independence movements. In 1990, the Soviet Union broke up, as the states of the old Russian Empire declared themselves independent. There are few multinational empires in the world today, because most nations are able to survive economically, and do not need to be part of an empire to be protected from invaders.

▲ The Forbidden City, inside the city of Beijing, includes palaces of the Chinese emperors from 1421 to 1911. They are now preserved as museums and galleries.

◀ The Assyrian Empire, with its capital at Nineveh, was a military state based on cruel and constant warfare. It collapsed in 609 B.C. when its enemies united to capture Nineveh.

SEE ALSO

Aztec, Babylon, Inca, Mongol Empire, Napoleonic Wars, Roman Empire

ENERGY

Energy is the ability to do work. An object or substance has energy if it can move or if it can generate such things as heat, sound, or electricity.

The Sun provides most of the heat and light energy that we use on Earth.

Energy is everywhere—in sunlight as heat and light energy, in a CD player as sound energy, even in a lump of coal as stored chemical energy. Energy can be converted from one form into another, but it can never be destroyed.

MOVING OBJECTS

One of the most basic forms of energy is the energy of movement, or kinetic energy. Heavy, fast-moving objects have more kinetic energy than light, slow-moving ones. The kinetic energy of a car is less than that of a truck traveling at the same speed. A parked car has no kinetic energy at all.

When things move, they are using kinetic energy—like this car.

HEAT ENERGY

Kinetic energy is also closely related to heat energy. An object is hot because its atoms (the tiny particles that it is made of) are constantly in motion. So an object's heat energy can be thought of as the kinetic energy of its atoms. The faster its atoms move, the hotter the object becomes.

Dynamite's explosive power comes from stored chemical energy.

SAVING IT FOR LATER

Energy can be stored to be used later. This energy in storage is called potential energy.

A radio produces sound energy by making the atoms in the air vibrate.

A hammer coming down to strike a nail uses the potential energy of gravity.

Nuclear energy takes its most dramatic form in a nuclear explosion.

▲ A runner waiting on the blocks to start a race is like a coiled spring ready to expand. When the starter's gun goes off, the potential (stored) energy in her muscles is converted into the kinetic (motion) energy of running.

Sun

Ancient forests turn the Sun's light energy into chemical energy

The chemical energy is stored as coal

The coal is mined and burned at a power plant

The heat energy released is changed to electrical energy

Four fifths of the energy is wasted as heat

Electrical energy becomes light energy

ENERGY CYCLE
The Sun is our main source of energy on Earth. Every time it is used, the energy changes form. Other natural sources include oil, gas, and coal, but we use them wastefully.

A spring stores energy as it is squeezed. When it is released and expands back to its original shape, the potential energy becomes motion (kinetic energy).

CHANGING FORM

The law of conservation of energy says that energy can never be destroyed or lost, but will change its form. For example, if a boy gliding on a pair of roller skates slowly comes to a halt, his kinetic energy will gradually decrease to zero. But the energy does not vanish, it is transformed into two other energy forms: heat and sound. The heat, created by the friction of the roller-skate wheels rubbing on the ground, warms up both the wheels and the ground. The sound energy can be heard as a swish or squeak of the wheels.

ENERGY AND POWER

Scientists measure energy using units called joules (J). Power—the rate at which energy is used—is measured in watts (W). The idea of power involves time. If two hotpots heat a pint of water from 50°F (10°C) to 212°F (100°C), they both give the water the same amount of heat energy. But if one hotpot does the job in half the time, it has twice the amount of power as the other. Nuclear power works by releasing the energy locked inside the nucleus of an atom and using it to do work.

MAKING IT WORK

Energy is never lost, but it can be wasted if not put to work. Heat is the main cause of energy wastage. For example, an ordinary lightbulb converts only one fifth of its electrical energy into light; the rest is wasted as heat. Inefficiency of car engines also means that the Earth's natural energy resources, such as oil, are constantly being wasted.

AN ENERGETIC GAME OF PINBALL

Energy is constantly changing its state. In a game of pinball, potential energy is converted into kinetic energy. The moving ball will tend to slow down through friction as it comes into contact with parts of the machine. Energy is used up in overcoming friction, but it is not lost—it is changed into heat. When the player adds energy to the ball, by pushing it with a flipper, the ball speeds up.

1 Pulling back the plunger coils a spring just behind the ball. In energy terms, the potential energy in the player's hand is transferred to the spring.

2 Letting go of the plunger shoots the ball into play. The spring's potential energy is changed into the kinetic energy of the moving ball.

3 As the ball moves inside the machine, it starts to slow down—its kinetic energy is being changed, mainly into heat. Flippers and obstacles have springs to speed up the ball.

SEE ALSO

Ecology, Electricity, Force and motion, Heat, Light, Magnetism, Nuclear power, Solar power, Sound

ENGINE

Engines are machines that convert energy into mechanical work to power vehicles, to drive other machines, or to generate electricity.

FRANK WHITTLE
(1907–87) An officer in the British Royal Air Force, designed a successful turbojet engine in 1941.

WERNHER VON BRAUN
(1912–77) Head of the team of German scientists during World War II that created the V2: the first rocket-powered guided missile, and the inspiration for later moon rockets.

The main types of engine are steam, gasoline (gas), diesel, jet, and rocket. Each one is supplied with energy by burning, or combusting, fuels such as coal, gas, and diesel oil. Nearly all engines are internal combustion engines, which means the fuel is burned inside the engine. The exception to this is the steam engine, which uses external combustion.

EARLY STEAM ENGINES

In the 1700s, much of the power for the Industrial Revolution was provided by the steam engine. In 1712, Englishman Thomas Newcomen developed the first practical steam engine for pumping water from mines. In 1765, a Scottish engineer, James Watt, began to improve the Newcomen steam engine and developed a much more efficient machine. Soon steam engines were powering factory machinery, as well as railroad cars, such as the *Rocket* locomotive, built by English engineer George Stephenson in 1829.

▲ An ultralight is a hang glider with an engine. It uses a two-stroke engine, which is lighter, cheaper, and more powerful for its size than a four-stroke engine.

THE POWER OF STEAM

In a steam engine, a fire is used to boil water to produce high-pressure steam. As the steam expands, it pushes a piston back and forth in a cylinder, or turns the blades of a fanlike wheel called a turbine. These then drive the machine. Most steam engines have been replaced by internal combustion engines. However, many power plant generators today are still worked by steam turbines.

GASOLINE ENGINES

Nowadays, cars, trucks, buses, and many trains and aircraft use internal combustion

STEAM LOCOMOTIVE

Steam locomotives powered the world's railroads for over 130 years. Hot gases from the burning coal surround the water tubes, turning the water to steam. The steam passes to the cylinder, driving the piston backward and forward. The piston in turn pushes the connecting rod backward and forward, which rotates a crank and drives the wheels. Water and coal are carried in the tender.

Steam chest · Regulator valve · Water tank · Steam tube · Safety valve · Coal

Waste steam

Cylinder · Piston · Connecting rod · Crank · Fire tube · Firebox

A FOUR-STROKE ENGINE

Cars have internal combustion engines with pistons that work in a four-stroke cycle (the piston makes two movements up and two down). Air and fuel are let into the piston cylinder by valves at the top. The explosion of ignited fuel moves the piston, which turns a crankshaft. This spins the driveshaft.

1 Induction. As the piston goes down, it draws a mixture of air and fuel into the cylinder.

2 Compression. The piston rises, compressing the air and fuel mixture ready for ignition.

3 Power. A spark lights the fuel, forcing the piston down and turning the crankshaft.

4 Exhaust. On the final stroke of the engine, the piston rises to expel exhaust (waste) gases.

engines fueled by diesel oil or gas. In a gas engine, the fuel mixes with air inside a cylinder, and a spark sets the mixture on fire, pushing the piston up and down in a four-stroke cycle (see above).

DIESEL ENGINES

Like gas engines, diesel engines have cylinders, pistons, valves, and a fuel supply, but there are no spark plugs or ignition system. The fuel explodes because of the heat created when the piston compresses the fuel and air inside a cylinder. The explosion pushes the piston up and down, which powers the vehicle.

THE GAS TURBINE

A jet, or gas turbine, engine does not have pistons. Instead, air is sucked in at the front of the engine and compressed, or squashed, by the rotating blades of the compressor. The air is blown into the combustion chamber and ignited with aviation fuel. The hot gases are expelled from the back of the engine, pushing the plane forward.

TO THE STARS

Like jet engines, rocket engines also use their exhaust gases to push the vehicle forward. Unlike jets, however, rockets cannot burn fuel by taking in oxygen from the air, since there is no air in space. Instead, they carry their oxygen supply with them, usually as liquid oxygen. The fuel either ignites spontaneously when mixed with the oxygen, or is lit by a spark.

A JET ENGINE

In a jet engine, air is sucked in at the front of the engine by giant rotating blades. The air is then compressed and passed into a combustion (burning) chamber, where it is ignited. The plane is thrust forward by the exhaust gases. These gases also turn a turbine, which drives the compressor.

KEY DATES

1862 Alphonse Beau de Rochas invents the four-stroke cycle

1876 Nikolaus Otto develops the prototype automobile engine

1878 Sir Dougald Clerk invents the two-stroke cycle

1892 Rudolph Diesel patents the diesel engine

1897 C.P. Steinmetz's *Future of Electricity* predicts air pollution from use of coal as fuel

1939 The first jet-engined aircraft, the Heinkel, flies in Germany

1944 The first V2 missile is fired on enemy targets

SEE ALSO

Aircraft, Car, Electricity, Energy, Rocket, Train, Transportation

EUROPE

Europe is the second smallest of the world's seven continents. It has 45 countries, including parts of Russia, Turkey, and Kazakhstan.

KEY FACTS

- **Area:** 8,964,540 sq. mi.
- **Population:** 728,950,000
- **Number of countries:** 45
- **Largest country:** Russia, 25 percent of which (1,648,200 sq. mi.) is in Europe
- **Smallest country:** Vatican City (108.7 acres)
- **Highest point:** Mount Elbrus (18,481 ft.)
- **Largest lake:** Lake Ladoga (7,000 sq. mi.)
- **Longest river:** Volga (2,287 sq. mi.)

Only the continent of Australia is smaller than Europe, but Europe's moderate climate, rich resources, and fertile land support a large population. Between them, the people speak about 50 languages and many more dialects. With its 45 countries, Europe is a continent of diverse cultures.

NEVER FAR FROM WATER
The northwest and west of Europe are bordered by the Arctic and Atlantic oceans, and the Mediterranean Sea surrounds the south. The coastline is broken up by thousands of fjords and other inlets, and only nine European countries have no access to the sea.

NORTH EUROPEAN PLAIN
Many of Europe's most populated areas lie on the North European Plain, which stretches from the southern part of the United Kingdom through northern France, Germany, and Poland to the Ural Mountains in Russia. To the north are

▲ Iceland in the North Atlantic Ocean is known as the "Land of Ice and Fire" because of its volcanoes and hot springs set against a landscape of ice fields and glaciers.

forests of coniferous trees such as fir, larch, and pine. Deciduous forests of ash, elm, and oak grow in central and southern Europe. In the southeast are large areas of dry grassland called steppes.

SCANDINAVIA
In the far north of Europe lies the cold and mountainous region of Scandinavia, which includes the countries of Norway, Sweden, Denmark, and Finland. The climate around the Arctic Ocean is cold and snowy, with temperatures in January averaging below 3°F (−16°C). Few trees grow in the extreme north, but the forests farther south contain large animals such as brown bears, reindeer, and wolves.

▼ Wine is produced throughout Europe, particularly in France (shown here), Germany, Spain, Italy, and Bulgaria.

miles
0   500
0   500
km

N

ARCTIC OCEAN

ICELAND

NORWEGIAN
SEA

NORTH
SEA

ATLANTIC
OCEAN

NORWAY

SWEDEN

FINLAND

Lake
Ladoga

BALTIC
SEA

ESTONIA

LATVIA

LITHUANIA

RUSSIA
(European part)

Ural Mountains

UNITED
KINGDOM

IRELAND

DENMARK

RUSSIA

BELARUS

PLAIN

NORTH
GERMANY

1

2

EUROPEAN

POLAND

KAZAKHSTAN
(European part)

Volga

CZECH
REPUBLIC

SLOVAKIA

UKRAINE

Caspian
Sea

FRANCE

5

4

AUSTRIA

HUNGARY

Carpathian Mts.

16

Mt. Elbrus

Alps

10   11

ROMANIA

Pyrenees

7

6

9

12

13

BLACK SEA

PORTUGAL

8

BULGARIA

Bosporus

SPAIN

ITALY

14

TURKEY
(European part)

MEDITERRANEAN SEA

15

GREECE

MALTA →

KEY TO MAP
1 THE NETHERLANDS
2 BELGIUM
3 LUXEMBOURG
4 SWITZERLAND
5 LIECHTENSTEIN
6 MONACO
7 ANDORRA
8 VATICAN CITY
9 SAN MARINO
10 SLOVENIA
11 CROATIA
12 BOSNIA–HERZEGOVINA
13 UNION OF SERBIA AND
    MONTENEGRO
14 MACEDONIA
15 ALBANIA
16 MOLDOVA

THE MEDITERRANEAN
The southern part of Europe is divided from the north by three mountain ranges: the Pyrenees, the Alps, and the Carpathian Mountains. The Mediterranean countries of southern Europe, including Italy, Spain, and Greece, have mild, rainy winters and hot, dry summers.

A FERTILE CONTINENT
Europe is a fertile continent; farms cover more than half the land. Crops include barley, oats, potatoes, and wheat, and citrus fruits and olives in the south. Vast areas of steppe in the Ukraine and southern Russia are heavily farmed for grain.

OIL, GAS, AND COAL
Oil and natural gas are produced in the North Sea, and coal is found in large quantities in Europe. These fuels help power the continent's many factories— Europe produces more manufactured goods than any other continent, including cars, electronic goods, ships, and steel.

A MIXED POPULATION
Most Europeans are the descendants of people who lived on the continent in prehistoric times, but there is a long history of immigration from Africa, Asia, and the Caribbean. About 70 percent of the population lives in cities and towns, working in factories or service industries, such as finance and tourism. ▶

▲ The number of red squirrels has decreased in Europe in the 1900s, following the introduction of the gray squirrel from North America and loss of large areas of woodland.

139

BRANCHES OF CHRISTIANITY

Christianity is Europe's leading religion. Many follow the Roman Catholic Church, which has its headquarters in Vatican City, in Rome, Italy. Protestantism is a branch of Christianity with its highest European representation in the north of the continent. The Orthodox Church flourishes in the east and southeast.

HISTORICAL CITIES

Many of Europe's large cities are steeped in history, but are also characterized by modern architecture and a modern way of life. Paris in France contains magnificent buildings dating from the Middle Ages, and is at the same time a leading fashion center. Moscow in Russia and London in England are important international cities, as well as historic sites. Athens and Rome, the capitals of Greece and Italy, have impressive ruins surviving from the days of Ancient Greece and the Roman Empire.

DEMOCRACY AND LAW

Throughout history, Europe has had an important influence on world politics. The system of democracy—where the government is chosen by the people— was first tried in Ancient Greece about 2,500 years ago. Similarly, many of the

▲ Istanbul in Turkey lies on the shores of the Bosporus, the strait that divides Europe from Asia. Its buildings reflect a mixture of Eastern and Western styles.

▲ The ruins of Delphi, a sacred site from as early as 1100 B.C., stand on Mount Parnassus in the southern part of mainland Greece.

laws developed during the Roman civilization (from 590 B.C. to A.D. 476) still influence legal systems today.

THE RENAISSANCE

From the 1300s, Europe became an increasingly important center of art and learning, with people interested in new ideas about art, science, and literature. This period is known as the Renaissance. At the same time, a desire for trade led European seafarers to set out to explore unknown lands and later to start colonies abroad. In the late 1700s, the continent was the birthplace of the Industrial Revolution, which brought great power and prosperity to the West.

END OF EMPIRES

The map of Europe has often changed throughout history, largely because of wars between rival countries. In the 1900s, two great world wars were fought between European powers. In the years following World War II (1939–45), the empires created in Africa and Asia by European countries such as Belgium, Britain, France,

◀ Many European countries, including Germany, the Netherlands, Romania, and Italy, have strong national soccer teams and attract enthusiastic fans, like these from Switzerland.

the Netherlands, and Portugal came to an end. Former colonies became independent countries, but many people living there continued to follow European customs and speak European languages. A large number of them have since made their homes in Europe.

EAST AND WEST

By the 1950s, Europe was divided between the noncommunist countries of the West and the Soviet-backed communist countries of the East. Until the 1980s, the two sides remained armed and

◀ German car-making factories are among the most highly automated in the world, and the cars they produce are exported worldwide.

hostile throughout the period known as the Cold War. But from the late 1980s, the Eastern European countries threw off their communist governments following the breakup of the Soviet Union in 1991. Yugoslavia also split up into five separate countries at this time, and a new map of Europe took shape, with new countries and partnerships. Today's Europe enjoys greater cooperation than at any other time during the 1900s.

▲ After World War II, about a seventh of Berlin was in ruins. The city was divided between East and West until 1990, when Germany was reunited.

THE EUROPEAN UNION

In the 1950s, a group of countries in Western Europe set up the European Community, or Common Market, to encourage greater economic unity in Europe. Over the years, the Community grew into the European Union, which aims for both economic and political unity. As of 2004, there are 25 member states.

SEE ALSO

Eastern Europe, France, Germany, Greece and the Balkans, Italy, Netherlands, Belgium, and Luxembourg, Scandinavia, Spain and Portugal, Switzerland and Austria, United Kingdom

EVOLUTION

Evolution is the way in which an organism changes over many generations, resulting in a species that is very different from its early ancestors.

JEAN BAPTISTE LAMARCK (1744–1829) was a French biologist who believed, mistakenly, that animals evolved during their own lifetimes. For example, each giraffe, by stretching, elongated its neck.

CHARLES DARWIN (1809–1882) shook the world, and especially the Church, with his theory of natural selection, which he published in *On the Origin of Species* in 1859.

Most scientists believe that the first simple organisms appeared on Earth over three billion years ago, and that all today's plants and animals have arisen from these by a process of gradual change. This process, which is constantly happening from one generation to the next, is known as evolution.

DARWIN'S THEORY

The idea of evolution has been around since the time of the Ancient Greeks. However, the first convincing theory of how evolution works was provided in the mid-1800s by the English naturalist Charles Darwin. He recognized that plants and animals produce lots of offspring, but that only a small number of these offspring survive. Darwin concluded that only the individual with the most useful characteristics is able to survive in a process that he called the struggle for existence.

SURVIVAL OF THE FITTEST

Darwin noticed that individuals that are not well suited to their surroundings die out. This leaves only the fittest individuals to breed and pass the useful characteristics

that have allowed them to survive on to their offspring. In popular terms, this process is known as "the survival of the fittest." It explains the enormous variety of plant and animal life that is found throughout the world—because the conditions vary from place to place, animals and plants adapt to fit their environment.

LITTLE BY LITTLE

With each new generation of plant and animal life, the struggle for existence continues. The result is that, over a long period of time, plants and animals gradually change and become better adapted to the place where they live

EVOLUTION FACTS AND FIGURES

- Scientists estimate that 99.9 percent of all the species that have ever lived are now extinct
- The idea of evolution was first suggested by the Ancient Greeks more than 2,500 years ago
- Another naturalist named Alfred Wallace came up with the same theory of evolution as Darwin (and at the same time), but Darwin published his ideas first
- By looking at fossilized animals in different layers of rock, scientists can see how the animals evolved
- When Darwin visited the Galapagos Islands he saw that all the finches had different beaks to suit their food, such as a long, hooked beak for catching insects or a nutcracker-shaped beak for eating seeds

THE EVOLUTION OF MAN

The earliest human beings probably evolved from ape-like creatures such as *Ramapithecus* (15 mya). *Australopithecus* (3.75 mya) walked upright on his back legs. *Homo habilis* (2 mya) made basic tools from stone and bone, while *Homo erectus* (1.75 mya) was probably the first human being to use fire. The Neanderthal people (*Homo sapiens*, 40,000 ya) lived alongside *Homo sapiens sapiens* who developed into modern man.

RAMAPITHECUS   **AUSTRALOPITHECUS**   **HOMO HABILIS**   **HOMO ERECTUS**   **HOMO SAPIENS**   **HOMO SAPIENS SAPIENS**

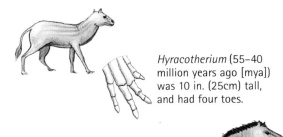

Hyracotherium (55–40 million years ago [mya]) was 10 in. (25cm) tall, and had four toes.

THE EVOLUTION OF THE HORSE

All life-forms probably developed from single-celled sea organisms. From there, evolution branched out in different directions. One group of fish, for example, evolved into amphibians, and one group of amphibians then gave rise to the reptiles. Birds and mammals evolved from different groups of reptiles. Today's hoofed horse evolved over millions of years from an animal the size of a dog.

Mesohippus (40–25 mya) was much larger and had three toes.

Merychippus (25–5 mya) was better suited to firm, grassy plains.

and the dangers that surround them. To an observer, each change may be almost invisible, but over millions of years they all make a big difference.

▲ Hungry Dutch explorers on the island of Mauritius in the 1500s were new predators for the trusting, flightless dodo, extinct by 1680.

NATURAL SELECTION

Conditions of habitat and climate are not the same everywhere, so a variation in the evolution of a plant or animal that is useful in one area of the world might be less useful in another. A species that spreads out may therefore evolve, or change, over a long period of time into several different species. Because this process of weeding out the inefficient individuals and favoring the fittest ones is an entirely natural one, Darwin gave it the name natural selection.

Pliohippus (5–2 mya) had stronger legs and single hooves.

EVIDENCE FROM THE ROCKS

Some of the strongest support for the idea of evolution comes from the fossilized remains of plants and animals that are found in rocks formed from layers of sand and mud on ancient seabeds. In each layer of rock, the organisms look slightly different from the ones below. This provides the evidence for a process of change over hundreds, thousands, or even millions of years.

Equus caballus (1.5 mya) was similar to today's horses.

A COMMON ANCESTOR

The bone structure of living animals also gives clues to evolution. A human's arm, a bird's wings, and a whale's flipper all look

very different and have different uses in everyday life. However, their bones are actually very similar. This suggests that these animals have all evolved from a common ancestor, which spread out over a wide geographical area. The arms then adapted for different jobs according to the demands of the different environments.

SEE ALSO

Dinosaur, Fossil, Genetics, Horse, Prehistoric animal, Prehistoric people

EXPLORER

People explore to discover the unknown. Through exploration we have learned much about the Earth. We are still exploring the oceans and outer space.

Christopher Columbus opened up America to European trade in 1492.

Captain Robert Scott died on the way back from the South Pole in 1912.

Jacques Cousteau helped invent the aqualung so he could explore under water.

The Phoenicians were among the first explorers, sailing the Mediterranean around 3,000 years ago. Pytheas, a Greek sailor, ventured into the Atlantic Ocean in 300 B.C. and, in A.D. 1000, Norway's Leif Ericsson reached North America.

THE SILK ROAD
Chinese and Arab travelers made long overland journeys. In 138 B.C., Zhang Qian became the first Chinese man to explore central Asia. Later, European merchants took the Silk Road to China, visited by the Italian Marco Polo in 1275 and described in his book *Description of the World*.

AGE OF DISCOVERY
In the 1400s, stronger ships and the invention of navigational aids such as the backstaff (used to plot the ship's position by the Sun and stars) prompted European explorers to head to sea. They went in search of lands to conquer and for trade,

riches, and slaves. Seeking a sea route to India, Portuguese sailors headed south along the African coast. In 1488, Bartholomeu Días reached the southern tip of Africa, and in 1498, Vasco da Gama crossed the Indian Ocean. Columbus arrived in America from Spain in 1492.

MAPMAKERS
In 1522, Ferdinand Magellan's ship from Spain completed the first voyage around the world. He died on the way, but the trip proved that the Earth was round. In the 1770s, James Cook of the British navy sailed the Pacific, mapping the coast of New Zealand and landing in Australia.

LAST FRONTIERS
Later explorers moved inland. The Scottish missionary David Livingstone traveled into Africa. Robert Peary of the United States conquered the North Pole in 1909, and Norway's Roald Amundsen reached the South Pole in 1911. In 1960, the *Trieste* dived 35,800 ft. (10,910m) under the sea, and in 1969 a human being walked on the Moon.

INTO THE UNKNOWN
Early sea voyages advanced navigational knowledge and helped mapmakers to produce more accurate maps. In the 1400s, Prince Henry the Navigator, of Portugal, skilled in mathematics and astronomy, helped organize 50 expeditions to West Africa. These trips pushed back the frontiers of navigation and paved the way for future trade and navigation.

SEE ALSO

Antarctica, Asia, Australia, Map, Ocean and sea, Space exploration, Submarine, Viking

EXPLOSIVE

An explosive is a substance such as gunpowder or dynamite that creates a huge burst of energy and a shock wave when it is triggered.

Demolition gangs use explosives to bring down old buildings. Mining companies use them to blast apart rocks, tunnelers to blow holes in mountains, and scientists to send rockets into space. Fireworks are pyrotechnic explosions that create a display of sound, light, and smoke.

GUY FAWKES
(1570–1606) A member of the Gunpowder Plot to blow up King James I of England and Parliament on November 5, 1605. He was caught returning to light the fuse and was hanged.

1 Sticks of dynamite are removed from their waxed wrappers and a detonating cap is inserted.

2 Holes are bored in the bricks and the dynamite is inserted. Fuse wire links each detonator cap.

CREATING SHOCK WAVES

When explosives release energy, they heat up the surrounding air. Fuels such as gas and coal release heat slowly, but an explosive heats the air rapidly. As the air around an explosive heats, it expands, creating a fast-moving shock wave that breaks apart any objects in its path. We hear the shock wave as a bang.

GUNPOWDER AND DYNAMITE

Gunpowder is the oldest explosive—it was discovered by the Chinese over 1,400 years ago. Its main ingredients are charcoal (charred wood), sulfur, and saltpeter, which are ground up and set on fire in air. Gunpowder is still used in fireworks today.

DETONATING SAFELY

The destructive power of an explosive is great, and it must therefore be controllable. When nitroglycerin (a combination of carbon, hydrogen, nitrogen, and oxygen) was invented in 1846, it was too dangerous to use, as it could detonate (ignite) by being shaken. The Swedish scientist Alfred Nobel solved the problem in 1867 by adding porous matter called kieselguhr, which created a new, safe explosive—dynamite. Dynamite does not need air to work and today is widely used for demolition.

UP THE CHIMNEY AND DOWN AGAIN

Demolishing a structure like a gas chimney, or smokestack, with explosives is an act of patience and precision. Preparation can take days, using tons of dynamite and yards of fuse wire. The skill lies in making sure that the construction falls safely, in the right direction, away from obstacles such as old gas pipes.

3 The structure is weakened by carefully knocking out rows of bricks near the ground, leaving a zigzag of concrete struts.

4 The demolition team has now finished its job, so everyone stands back and the electronic switch is flicked.

5 The dynamite has been placed so that the structure falls without damaging the nearby gas pipes.

SEE ALSO

Chemistry, Energy, Mining

FARMING

Farming is the business of growing crops and raising livestock on the land to produce food, drink, textiles, and other products.

Items such as food, leather, cotton, and rubber come from farms. Farming is the world's biggest employer, taking up more than half of the working population.

▲ Rows of green crops growing in the middle of a barren, sandy desert are evidence of the enormous achievements in farming and irrigation techniques.

ORIGINS OF FARMING
Archaeological evidence shows that farming began around 11,000 B.C., when Stone Age people began to herd wild animals. Later, in 7000 B.C., people learned that scattered seeds would grow and multiply, providing food for themselves and their animals. The first crops were probably wheat and barley, cultivated with simple hoes and sticks.

AGRICULTURAL REVOLUTIONS
Dramatic developments in farming have occurred since then. Irrigation of crops in Mesopotamia in 4000 B.C. and the ox-drawn plow, invented in about 3000 B.C., made it possible to work difficult soils.

▲ In the early 1700s, English politician Charles Townshend created a four-field crop rotation system, which meant that a field did not have to be left fallow (empty) each year.

From the A.D. 1400s, the potato, tomato, turkey, chili, and corn were brought from America to Europe and Asia. New machinery, such as Jethro Tull's seed drill (1700), Eli Whitney's cotton gin (1793), and steam-powered tractors (mid-1800s) made farming less labor-intensive.

NEW METHODS AND OUTLOOKS
Since the 1970s, a "green revolution" based on artificially improved crops and fertilizers has increased food production in poorer nations. In developed countries, new machines and the rearing of livestock on mechanized farms have increased production.

DAIRY FARMING

Milk is produced on dairy farms from cattle, although goats, buffalo (bison), and sheep may also be kept for milk. On modern dairy farms, cattle are milked by machine. The milk is cooled and stored in a large tank before being sent to a plant to be put into containers or processed into butter, cheese, and other products.

1 Cattle enter cowshed from fields.

2 Milking cups are attached, and milk is extracted automatically by vacuum.

3 Milk is piped to a chilled storage tank.

4 Tankers collect milk and take it to processing plants.

5 Cattle leave the shed and return to fields.

Computerized controls regulate operation of the milking

SEE ALSO
Crop, Food, Fruit, Mesopotamia, Vegetable

FASCISM

Fascism is a political belief which states that the government of a country is all-powerful and that the citizens must obey it for the good of the nation.

Juan Perón, with his wife Evita, ruled Argentina in the 1940s and 1950s.

Fascist ideas gained support after World War I (1914–18), with the first fascist government appearing in Italy in the 1920s. The term fascism comes from *fasces*, bundles of rods with an ax that were symbols of power in Ancient Rome.

SUCCESS THROUGH STRENGTH

Fascism is based on the idea that a nation will only succeed through disciplined, ruthless action and a determined will. Fascists believe that achieving a worthwhile aim makes all actions acceptable. Schools, religion, newspapers, the arts, and sciences are expected to serve the nation. Military power and a secret police back up a fascist government. Fascists often believe that their race or nation is superior to all others.

General Francisco Franco won a civil war before ruling Spain (1939–75).

SEIZING POWER

In 1922, the Italian fascist leader Benito Mussolini took advantage of chaos caused by a general strike to seize power. He called himself *Il Duce* (The Leader) and, with backing from big business, brought prosperity to Italy. But he led Italy to defeat in World War II and in 1945 was murdered by his own people. Fascist-style governments held power in Japan and Hungary in the 1930s and 1940s.

Antonio Salazar was dictator of Portugal from 1932 until 1968.

Oswald Mosley was the leader of the British Union of Fascists in the 1930s.

PACT OF STEEL

In May 1939, the two fascist dictators, Adolf Hitler in Germany and Benito Mussolini in Italy, agreed to a military treaty called The Pact of Steel. In 1940, Mussolini entered World War II on Hitler's side. They were later joined by other fascist states in Eastern Europe when Hitler invaded the Soviet Union in 1941. All shared in Hitler's downfall four years later at the end of World War II.

NAZI GERMANY

In Germany, the Nazi leader Adolf Hitler was voted into power in 1933, promising to end unemployment and poverty. As *Führer* (Leader), he crushed opposition, and ordered the murder of millions of Jews, gypsies, and others. In 1939, he started World War II, but killed himself in 1945 when Germany faced defeat.

MODERN EXTREMISTS

Some governments still follow fascist ideas, but none admits to fascism because of its association with the regimes of Hitler and Mussolini. Small, extremist political parties in many countries openly support racism and fascism, but win few votes in elections.

SEE ALSO
Government, Politics, World War I, World War II

FILM

A film is made up of a number of photos, or frames, projected in rapid sequence onto a screen to create moving images. It is a popular form of entertainment.

The kinetoscope, invented by Thomas Edison, was the first machine to produce moving pictures. Over 160 feet of film revolved on spools and the viewer looked through an eyehole to see the pictures move.

In 1877, British-American photographer Eadweard Muybridge took a series of photographs of a horse running, using 24 cameras. By putting the photos together in sequence, Muybridge created the concept of moving pictures on film. This became the movies—the most popular art and entertainment form of the 1900s.

THROUGH THE PEEPHOLE

Thomas Edison picked up Muybridge's idea and made a machine called a kinetoscope, which showed up to 90 seconds of moving pictures, viewed through a peephole. The French brothers Louis and Auguste Lumière took things one step further by inventing a machine that took these images, stored them on rolls of celluloid, and projected them onto a wall for an audience to see.

ADVENT OF AN INDUSTRY

Film screenings became popular all around the world, but especially in the United States. The film that broke new ground in movie history was Edwin Porter's dramatic 11-minute epic *The Great Train Robbery* (1903), in which a group of gunmen robs a train, and is then tracked down and brought to justice.

KEY DATES

1877 Photographer Eadweard Muybridge makes the first moving pictures on film

1893 Thomas Edison unveils his kinetoscope

1895 The movies are born in a Paris café as the Lumière brothers hold their first film screening

1903 Edwin Porter releases *The Great Train Robbery*

1905 Thousands of nickelodeon movie theaters (it cost a nickel to get in) opened across America

1927 First talking film, *The Jazz Singer*, appears

MAKING MOVIES

Making films can involve literally hundreds of technicians, actors, and cameramen, but it is the director of the film who controls what is seen on screen. He or she decides how a film should be shot, where the cameras should be set, and what kind of lighting to use. Today, many directors use computer-generated special effects in their films, and some of the footage shot in the conventional way with the camera is changed completely by computer enhancement.

Second camera takes shot from different angle

Cameraman

Director

Microphone

Console controls sound

SCREENPLAY

The principles of Porter's film still define filmmaking today. A written script details the scenes to be shot; these scenes are filmed, in any order, and then edited together in the order of the original script. This is known as postproduction. It is at this stage that computer effects and the soundtrack are added.

SUN AND STARS

The sunny weather and open landscape of a small suburb of Los Angeles, California, called Hollywood, made it the center of filmmaking in America, and later the world, from 1907. Once sound was added to films in 1927, other countries formed film industries, too.

SMALL SCREEN COMPETITION

The popularity of television in the 1950s left cinema in a slump. Filmmakers tried gimmicks such as 3-D (viewers wore green and red tinted glasses) or "smell-o-vision" to attract audiences. This slump continued until the 1970s when the modern blockbuster was born. These movies were just too big and too exciting to work successfully on the small screen. *Jaws*, Steven Spielberg's tale of a deadly killer shark, started the trend in 1975, but was eclipsed two years later by George Lucas's *Star Wars*.

SLAPSTICK MOVIES
Early movies were in black and white. Props and scenery provided the special effects, as in *Modern Times* (1936), one of Charlie Chaplin's first films with sound.

MUSICALS
Color was introduced in the 1930s, making films such as *The Wizard of Oz* (1939), shot in Technicolor, possible. However, until the 1950s, many films were still made in black and white.

WESTERNS
Films like Clint Eastwood's gritty *The Outlaw Josey Wales* (1976) continue to attract large audiences.

ANIMATED CARTOONS
Since their introduction to the screen in 1906, animated cartoons, such as *One Hundred and One Dalmatians*, have been popular, often appearing later on video.

SEE ALSO
Cartoon and animation

FISH

Fish are vertebrates (backboned animals) which breathe oxygen dissolved in water through their gills. They are found in salty and fresh water around the world.

▲ Mudskippers survive low tides in the swamps of Africa and Southeast Asia by breathing air. They use their strong pectoral fins as "arms" to climb trees in search of food.

FOUR TYPES OF FISH
Fish can be divided into groups by body structure. Examples are jawless fish, sharks and rays, and bony fish—primitive and modern.

Lampreys (above) and hagfish are ancient fish. They have no jaws, and, like sharks, their skeletons are made of soft cartilage.

Sharks usually have a torpedo-shaped body with a skeleton of cartilage. All have strong jaws, many with several rows of teeth.

Primitive bony fish, such as the coelacanth (above) and lungfish, are related to fish that lived over 400 million years ago.

Perch (above) are modern bony fish. Unlike primitive bony fish, they do not have a fleshy lobe at the base of each fin.

Most fish are streamlined for easy movement through water. The tail pushes the fish forward, and the fins are used for steering and balance. Most fish have two pairs of fins on their sides. There is one dorsal fin, running down the middle of the back, and another fin at the base of the tail. The tail is usually forked.

COLD-BLOODED CREATURES
As cold-blooded creatures, fish stay at the same temperature as the water they live in. If the water is very cold, fish slow down and may stop moving altogether. Apart from using sight and smell, fish also have a row of sensors on their sides, known as the lateral line, that picks up vibrations in the water even if the fish cannot see clearly.

BONE OR GRISTLE
There are over 22,000 known species of fish—more than all other vertebrates put together. Fish can be divided into cartilaginous fish and bony fish. Cartilaginous fish, whose skeletons are made of soft cartilage, or gristle, include sharks, skates, and rays. There are only about 800 species, all of which live in the

sea. Bony fish include some of the most colorful animals on earth, and the fastest—sailfish—can reach speeds of 60 mph (100kph).

BROWN AND GRISTLY
Most cartilaginous fish are brown or gray and have five or more gill slits on each side. Their fins are solid and their bodies are covered with rough, toothlike scales. Sailors once used shark skins to scrub the decks of wooden ships. The whale shark is the largest fish, measuring 40 ft. (12m) long and weighing up to 20 tons.

FISH BONES
Bony fish have smooth, overlapping scales. Their fins are delicate membranes stretched over slender spines. The gills are covered by a flap called an operculum, so there is only one gill opening on each side of the body. Most bony fish have an

TEMPERATE SEAS
Fish are adapted to suit their environment. Sea fish constantly lose water and must drink a lot, whereas freshwater fish take in water through their skin. Temperate waters, which get colder in winter, are home to dull-colored fish, commonly caught for food. These fish often swim deeper or migrate in cold weather.

KEY TO TEMPERATE SEA
1 FLOUNDER
2 SAND EEL
3 BASS
4 COD
5 CONGER EEL
6 HERRINGS
7 MACKEREL

Gill arch — Gills

Water flow

▲ Oxygen from the water passes through the thin walls of the gills (tiny blood-filled threads arranged in pockets on each side of the throat) and into the blood. The water then passes out through the gill slits.

INSIDE A TYPICAL FISH

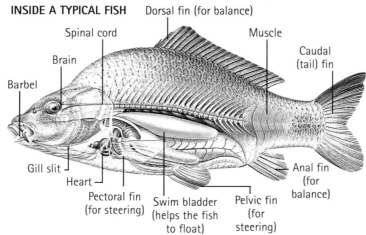

Spinal cord — Brain — Dorsal fin (for balance) — Muscle — Caudal (tail) fin — Barbel — Gill slit — Heart — Pectoral fin (for steering) — Swim bladder (helps the fish to float) — Pelvic fin (for steering) — Anal fin (for balance)

air-filled swim bladder, allowing them to float motionless in the water. Sharks have no swim bladder and would sink if they stopped swimming.

JAWLESS FISH

Another group of fish includes about 70 species of lampreys and hagfish. These are eel-shaped creatures without jaws. Lampreys have a round, suckerlike mouth and toothed tongue, used to rasp flesh from other fish. Hagfish have a slit-shaped mouth and sharp teeth. They eat dead fish.

MILLIONS OF EGGS

Some fish give birth to live young, but most species lay eggs. These are usually released into the water by the female, where they are fertilized by the male. Fish lay many eggs, as most get eaten. The ocean sunfish may lay 300 million eggs in its lifetime. Fish that protect their eggs do not lay many, and it is often the male that looks after them. The female sea horse lays eggs in a pouch on the male's abdomen, where they can be protected.

TROPICAL SEAS

The most brightly colored fish live in the tropics, blending in with the vivid coral reefs—their camouflaged colors hide them from predators.

FRESHWATER FISH

About two thirds of all fish live in freshwater streams, lakes, rivers, ponds, marshes, and swamps.

Guppies, native to the Caribbean islands, are attractive and popular aquarium fish.

Piranha live in South American rivers, feeding on fish or other animals with their razorlike teeth.

This African catfish is typical of its group, which has long barbels (whiskers) and fins that lock upright.

Rainbow trout are native to North America, but because of trout farming, now live in European rivers.

The climbing perch can be seen taking short "walks" across land—it has a gill chamber for breathing air.

KEY TO TROPICAL SEA
8 GROUPER
9 CLEANER WRASSE
10 LION FISH
11 FAIRY BASSLET
12 MANTA RAY (devilfish)
13 PARROT FISH
14 BUTTERFLY FISH
15 SEA HORSE
16 TOMATO CLOWNFISH

SEE ALSO

Animal, Fishing industry, Fossil, Jellyfish, Ocean and sea, Prehistoric animal, Shark

FISHING INDUSTRY

The fishing industry is the organized business of catching or breeding fish and shellfish for food, from seas, rivers, or lakes.

Gill nets hang like curtains beneath the surface with weights to hold them down.

Trawl nets are dragged along the bottom to catch demersal (seabed) fish.

Purse seines are nets pulled in a circle around pelagic (surface) fish.

Fishing is one of the world's most important industries. About 100 million tons of fish are caught each year. Japan, the U.S., China, Norway, India, Chile, and countries in the former U.S.S.R. catch the most. People have caught fish since prehistoric times, but commercial fishing did not begin until the 1600s.

FISHING GROUNDS

The oceans are vast, but most fish are caught in well-known fishing grounds within 60 mi. (100km) of land, in the shallower waters of the continental shelf. There are rich fishing grounds off Canada's east coast, near Iceland, and around Japan. Fish are attracted to these places by plentiful supplies of plankton to eat.

FISH TYPES

Two types of fish are caught at sea: pelagic and demersal. Pelagic fish, including herring, salmon, tuna, and anchovies, live near the sea's surface. Demersal fish, including cod, sole, and haddock, live near the seabed. Fishermen use different fishing methods and nets to catch the two types of fish. Nowadays, the size of fishing catches is limited by international agreements. This is because some species of fish have been overfished and are in danger of extinction.

FISH-FARMING

Keeping fish for food in tanks, ponds, or underwater cages is called fish-farming. Fish and shellfish, including salmon, trout, oysters, mussels, and scallops, are farmed. Fish-farming is one way of increasing fish catches without taking too many fish from the wild. About one tenth of fish sold now come from fish farms.

HARVESTING THE SEA

Many large fishing boats are equipped as floating fish factories. The net is winched in, and the haul is sorted into types of fish. Often they are cleaned and gutted before being placed in boxes of ice and stored in freezer compartments below deck to keep them fresh on the way to market. Long-range fishing boats may be at sea for several months at a time.

▲ Onboard trawlers, sonar equipment detects large groups of fish.

SEE ALSO

Fish, Ocean and sea

FLAG

There are 192 independent countries in the world. Each has a national flag that is flown at home and outside the country's embassies abroad.

Originally flags led the troops in warfare and identified friend or foe. The color and design of national flags reflect the nation's history or religion. In the U.S. flag the stars represent the states; the color red stands for courage, white for purity; and blue for justice and perseverance. In European heraldry white and yellow (representing metal) were never placed next to each other. Only the Vatican City flag breaks this rule.

Afghanistan

Albania

Algeria

Andorra

Angola

Antigua and Barbuda

Argentina

Armenia

Australia

Austria

Azerbaijan

The Bahamas

Bahrain

Bangladesh

Barbados

Belarus

Belgium

Belize

Benin

Bhutan

Bolivia

Bosnia-Herzegovina

Botswana

Brazil

Brunei

Bulgaria

Burkina Faso

Burundi

Cambodia

Cameroon

Canada

Cape Verde

Central African Republic

Chad

Chile

China

Colombia

Comoros

Congo Republic

Costa Rica

Côte d'Ivoire

Croatia

Cuba

Cyprus

Czech Republic

Democratic Rep. of the Congo

Denmark

Djibouti

Dominica

Dominican Republic

Ecuador

Egypt

El Salvador

Equatorial Guinea

Eritrea

Estonia

Ethiopia

Fiji

Finland

153

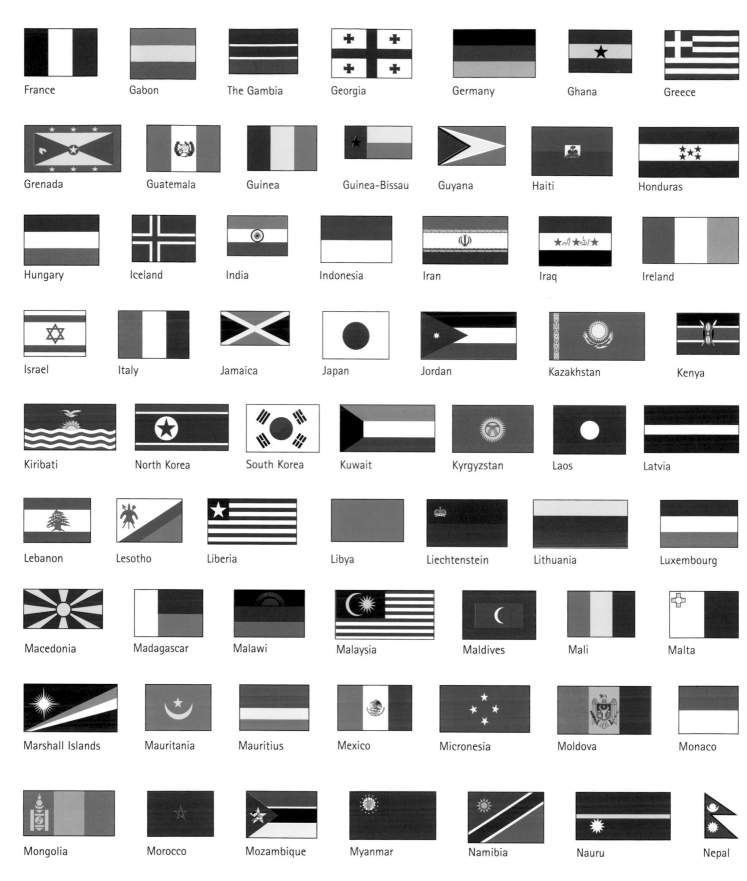

France	Gabon	The Gambia	Georgia	Germany	Ghana	Greece
Grenada	Guatemala	Guinea	Guinea-Bissau	Guyana	Haiti	Honduras
Hungary	Iceland	India	Indonesia	Iran	Iraq	Ireland
Israel	Italy	Jamaica	Japan	Jordan	Kazakhstan	Kenya
Kiribati	North Korea	South Korea	Kuwait	Kyrgyzstan	Laos	Latvia
Lebanon	Lesotho	Liberia	Libya	Liechtenstein	Lithuania	Luxembourg
Macedonia	Madagascar	Malawi	Malaysia	Maldives	Mali	Malta
Marshall Islands	Mauritania	Mauritius	Mexico	Micronesia	Moldova	Monaco
Mongolia	Morocco	Mozambique	Myanmar	Namibia	Nauru	Nepal
Netherlands	New Zealand	Nicaragua	Niger	Nigeria	Norway	Oman

Pakistan

 Palau

 Panama

 Papua New Guinea

 Paraguay

 Peru

 Philippines

 Poland

 Portugal

 Qatar

 Romania

 Russia

 Rwanda

 St. Kitts-Nevis

 St. Lucia

 St. Vincent and the Grenadines

 Samoa

 San Marino

 São Tomé and Príncipe

 Saudi Arabia

 Senegal

 Seychelles

 Sierra Leone

 Singapore

 Slovakia

 Slovenia

 Solomon Islands

 Somalia

 South Africa

 Spain

 Sri Lanka

 Sudan

 Suriname

 Swaziland

 Sweden

 Switzerland

 Syria

 Taiwan

 Tajikistan

 Tanzania

 Thailand

 Togo

 Tonga

 Trinidad and Tobago

 Tunisia

 Turkey

 Turkmenistan

 Tuvalu

 Uganda

 Ukraine

 United Arab Emirates

 United Kingdom

 United States of America

 Uruguay

 Uzbekistan

 Vanuatu

 Vatican City

 Venezuela

 Vietnam

 Yemen

 Yugoslavia

 Zambia

Zimbabwe

FLOWER

Flowers are the reproductive parts of some kinds of plants. They make seeds that will form a new generation of the same type of plant.

Flowers are really specialized leaves that have evolved over millions of years to help plants reproduce efficiently. There are more than 250,000 species of flowering plant, called angiosperms, which range from huge, long-lived trees to tiny annuals. Flowers may vary greatly in appearance, but they are all made up of the same basic parts.

Carpel:
Stigma
Style
Ovary

Stamen:
Anther
Filament

Petal

Sepal

Receptacle — Stem

Ovule (egg cell)

▲ Flowers have four main parts: sepals and petals (the outer parts), and carpels and stamens (the reproductive parts). The stamens are male and the carpels are female.

MALE AND FEMALE PARTS
The main reproductive parts of a flower are the female carpel and the male stamens. Each stamen is made up of the anther, which produces tiny powdery grains of pollen, and the filament, or stalk. The carpel has a stigma, which is often sticky and colored. The stigma is found at the end of a style—a kind of stalk that leads down to the ovary. Inside the ovary are egg cells that develop into the seeds that will later become new plants.

POLLINATION
For seeds to form, pollen grains from the anther must come into contact with the stigma. This process is called pollination. Most flowering plants are pollinated by insects. For example, as a bee pushes inside the flower looking for nectar, its body gets dusted with pollen from the anthers of the flower. The bee will then transfer this pollen dust to the stigma of the next flower it visits.

FLOWER APPEAL
The varying colors, scents, and shapes of individual flowers have developed to appeal to pollinators—usually insects, but also birds and small mammals, such as bats. Many flowers have glands called nectaries, which produce nectar—a sugary liquid on which the pollinators feed. The pollinators must push past the male and female parts of the flower to reach the nectar.

Bats are attracted to the nighttime scent and infrared colors of some tropical flowers.

Many alpine flowers are tough and lie low on the ground, to help them withstand the cold.

Desert plants, such as cacti, have bright flowers to attract insects for the few weeks they are in bloom.

Water flowers, such as white water lilies, float above the surface to attract insect pollinators.

▲ One of the petals of the bee orchid looks like a real bee. This signals to other pollinators that the flower is a good source of nectar, and they land on it. Other flowers attract bees with ultraviolet markings on their petals that only bees can see.

FLOWER FACTS
- The first flowering plant—thought to have been a magnolia—appeared about 160 million years ago
- The world's largest flower, *Rafflesia arnoldii*, grows in Indonesia and can measure up to 3 ft. (1m) in diameter. Its smell of rotting meat is irresistible to the flies that pollinate it
- Opium, which comes from the opium poppy, is used to make pain killing drugs like codeine
- The Madagascan periwinkle, once thought of as a weed, is now farmed to produce anticancer drugs

1 The poppy flower buds remain tightly closed until the pollen grains are ripe.

2 The buds begin to open, revealing the brightly colored petals and other flower parts.

Bee pollinator

3 The red flowers attract bees and flies, which climb into the flowers looking for nectar. Pollen from the carpels sticks to them and is carried to the stigma of the next flower that they visit. This is called pollination.

THE REPRODUCTIVE CYCLE

All flowering plants grow from seeds, which germinate into tiny plants, each with a root, shoot, and leaves. New buds on the shoot expand into leaves, branches, and more buds. When the plant is mature, some buds open to reveal flowers. The flower's male parts (anther and filament) release pollen grains. When these land on the stigma, a tiny tube grows down the style toward the egg cells in the ovary. When the tube meets an egg cell, the contents of both fuse together. This is fertilization, which results in a new seed.

BLOWN BY THE WIND

Some flowers are pollinated by the wind, which blows the pollen grains through the air. These flowers are rarely showy or scented. They often have feathery stigmas to catch the clouds of pollen as they fly through the air.

A GARDEN IN BLOOM

Particular flowering plants are selected for a garden because of when, and how often, they produce their flowers. This can depend on how long the flowering plants live. Annuals are plants that sprout, mature, flower, produce seeds, and die all in the same year. Biennials live for two years, and perennials live for three years or longer. Most garden plants are perennials, because once they have flowered, they flower every year for as long as they live.

4 After pollination, the showy petals and reproductive parts are discarded, leaving just the seed capsule.

Petals fall off to leave seed head

5 As it sways in the wind, the seed capsule shakes out the ripened seeds through holes.

6 Most poppies are annuals (plants that live for one year). This means that the plant puts all its energy into flowering and producing seeds, and then dies.

SEE ALSO

Desert, Fruit, Grassland, Leaf, Plant, Rain forest, Seed and pollination

FOOD

Food is any substance that is a source of nutrition to a living organism. Without it, nothing can live. The food we eat is supplied by plants and animals.

Modern diets contain a wide range of foods. Some, such as fruits and vegetables, are still in the original state in which they were grown. Others, such as bread and hamburgers, are processed foods, which means they arrive at our tables looking very different from the ingredients that were used to make them.

THE FIRST FARMERS

Until about 10,000 years ago, humans were hunter-gatherers, spending much of their time hunting animals and gathering fruits and vegetables for food. Then, by about 8000 B.C., people in fertile parts of the world began to manage the land for agriculture. They started to grow food crops and to domesticate animals such as cattle, sheep, and poultry for milk, meat, and eggs.

DIFFERENT DIETS

Meat and dairy products are a major part of the diet in developed countries, yet some people in the Far East have lost the ability to digest dairy produce because it has never been part of their diet. In tropical countries, people eat mainly rice, cassava, and potatoes, with very few vegetables, while in Mediterranean countries, it is usual to have a high intake of all kinds of different fruits and vegetables.

FOOD INTAKE WORLDWIDE

Although there is more than enough food to support the world's population, it does not always reach those in need. One in ten people does not get enough to eat, and every year, around 40 million people die of hunger—most of them in the poorer developing countries. In developed countries, people eat 30 to 40 percent more food than they need, which can cause its own set of health problems.

STAPLE FOODS

Our food comes from many different sources, either plant or animal. The main foods obtained from plants are grains, fruits, and vegetables. Products made from grains, or cereals, such as rice or bread, have been the basis of the human diet for thousands of years. Food from animals includes meat, eggs, and dairy products. They cost more to produce than plant foods.

▶ Cereals such as wheat (right), rice, and corn together make up about half of the world's food intake.

Bread

Flat bread

Noodles

Pasta

Cookies

Breakfast cereal

FOOD PROCESSING

Humans have been processing food—by cooking it—ever since the discovery of fire. Today, there are many other ways of processing food, such as milling, freezing, canning, and ultraheat treatment. Processing makes some foods, such as potatoes and wheat, easier to digest. It also stops food from rotting, which encourages germs to grow. Heat treatment kills germs, and chilling and freezing slow down their growth to a safe level.

ADDITIVES

Substances known as additives are usually added to foods during processing. Some, such as the vitamins and minerals added to bread and cereals, improve the nutritional value of food. Other additives include preservatives, which are added to foods to stop them going rotten, and colorings, such as the natural pigment of beets.

FOOD SAFETY

About six percent of the population suffers from food poisoning each year, usually caused by food contaminated with harmful bacteria such as *E. coli* or *Salmonella*. Preparing food hygienically lowers the risk of food poisoning. Foods such as meat, fish, milk, and eggs should be heated and cooked thoroughly before eating to kill any dangerous bacteria.

RELIGION AND CULTURE

The food people eat often depends on their culture or religion. For example, some Jews eat a kosher diet governed by religious laws, such as cooking and eating meat and dairy produce separately. In the Hindu religion, every living creature is believed to have a soul, so eating animals is often avoided. Many vegetarians believe animals should not be killed for humans to eat.

▲ Paella is a Spanish dish made with rice, shellfish, vegetables, and chicken, named after the shallow frying pan in which it is cooked. Each country has unique local ways of preparing food that have often been passed down through the generations, and are usually made from local produce.

FRUIT AND VEGETABLES

We eat fruits, such as oranges, and vegetables, such as cauliflowers, in their natural state. However, oranges can also be processed to make juice or preserved by canning. Vegetables such as peas can be frozen or dried to last longer.

DAIRY PRODUCTS

Dairy cattle produce milk, from which other products such as butter, cheese, and yogurt are made. Beef comes from cattle that have been specially reared for their meat. Beef is cut up into joints or steaks, or ground for foods such as burgers.

Picking in an orange grove

Cauliflower

Fresh oranges

Orange juice

Milk

Cheese

Butter

Hamburger

Yogurt

SEE ALSO

Crop, Custom, Farming, Nutrition, Prehistoric people

FORCE AND MOTION

A force changes the way an object moves. If the object is stationary, a force will set it in motion. If it is moving, a force will change its speed or direction.

Force is a word we use in everyday speech. For example, we may talk about forcing a door open or forcing a suitcase shut. In both, a force—either a push or pull—is being applied by a person to move the door or suitcase lid.

▲ An object's weight affects how fast it moves and how long it takes to stop. This is called its momentum, and it can be transferred from one object to another, as between two pool balls.

▲ This amusement park ride is kept spinning in a circle by two competing forces: centrifugal force, which pulls outward, and centripetal force, which pulls inward.

CHANGING VELOCITY
A force is anything that changes an object's velocity (speed in a given direction). A ball rolling along the ground has a certain velocity, but if it is kicked, the ball increases velocity. An increase in velocity is known as acceleration, and a decrease in speed is called deceleration.

STATE OF INERTIA
An object that stays at the same velocity— neither speeding up, nor slowing down or changing direction—is said to be in a state of inertia. This rarely happens, however, because moving objects usually slow down because they bump into something, come into contact with the ground, or are blown by the wind. The force created by wind, or when two items rub together, is known as friction. It works against motion, slowing things down.

MIGHTY FORCES
Pulling a door open or pushing it shut requires direct force and human strength. But sometimes we are not strong enough (do not have enough force) to move an object. People have invented machines such as levers and pulleys to increase the effect of human force. Powerful natural forces such as electricity and magnetism have also been harnessed to work for us. Another natural force, gravity, literally keeps our feet on the ground.

NEWTON'S LAWS
Most of the principles of force and motion were first discovered in the 1660s by the English scientist Isaac Newton. Today, in honor of his work, we measure force in newtons (N). One newton is roughly the force that you feel when you hold a large orange in the palm of your hand.

ACTION AND REACTION
Whenever force is applied to an object, it always creates another force, called a reactionary force, that works in the opposite direction. A kayaker paddling through water moves forward by such action and reaction. The kayaker's paddle pushing the water backward is the action, while the reaction is the force exerted by the water on the paddle, which pushes the kayak forward through the water.

Action: the paddle pushes against the water

Reaction: the kayak moves forward in the water

SEE ALSO
Bridge, Electricity, Gravity, Heat, Invention, Machine, Magnetism

FORENSIC SCIENCE

Forensic science is the scientific investigation of a crime, such as theft or murder, by scientifically trained specialists—doctors, dentists, chemists, and biologists.

▲ Surfaces are dusted for fingerprints. Victims have their fingerprints taken, so that only unknown prints are included in a search.

▲ Dried blood is scraped off the murder weapon, diluted, and analyzed for blood type and DNA code.

No matter how careful a criminal may be, he or she will leave clues behind. It is the job of the forensic team to examine the scene of the crime for fingerprints and footprints, bloodstains, and other evidence.

AT THE SCENE OF THE CRIME

Equipment such as cameras, lasers, and materials for casts make a record of the position of everything at the scene. Samples of hair, paint, glass, and other substances are also taken away for analysis. These samples have to be handled very carefully. The investigating team wears paper bodysuits, overshoes, and gloves so that they do not contaminate the samples. They will also wrap and seal the samples in plastic before sending them for analysis.

ANALYZING CLUES

Fingerprints can reveal the identity of a criminal, if they can be matched to samples kept on a computer network. Analysis of DNA (genetic code) from blood and other samples taken from the scene of the crime has been used since 1986 for more serious crimes. Each person has a unique DNA fingerprint or profile, which can be checked against samples taken at the scene. Laboratory analysis of a single fleck of paint is enough to identify a car used in a crime, for example. Similarly, bite marks in food found at the scene can lead to an arrest, if they can be matched with dental records.

CAUSE OF DEATH

Suspicious deaths involving murder, suicide, or an accident are usually investigated by a coroner (an official who specializes in forensics). The coroner will order an autopsy (an examination of the body to determine the cause of death). The forensic pathologist (a doctor who specializes in autopsies) examines the appearance of the body and then dissects it, looking at each organ in turn. He or she also analyzes blood and flesh samples.

WHO DUNNIT?

Every item at the scene of the crime tells a story. Criminals often wear gloves, so fingerprints are rare, but clothing fibers caught on the corner of a photocopier in a scuffle may lead police to the murderer.

FIBERS
Fibers from clothing worn by the criminal and the victim are taken away and studied under a microscope.

FINGERPRINTS
Finding just one print can solve the crime—even identical twins have different fingerprints.

BLOOD
Originally, only the blood group could be established, but now a unique DNA code can be found.

FOOTPRINTS
Footprints can reveal the criminal's shoe size and the store where the shoes were bought.

SEE ALSO
Chemistry, Genetics

FOREST

Forests are large areas of land covered mainly by trees and other plants. Today, they occupy almost 30 percent of the world's land area.

There are three basic types of forest: coniferous (boreal), broad-leaved deciduous, and dense, tropical rain forests. Many forests include a combination of coniferous and deciduous trees.

CONIFEROUS FORESTS

Coniferous forests are found in the cold northern areas of Canada, Europe, and Asia and include spruce, fir, or pine. These trees are evergreens (do not shed their leaves in winter) and carry their seeds in cones.

DECIDUOUS FORESTS

The temperate regions of the United States and Europe have warm summers, mild winters, and rain all year round. Here, the native forest trees, such as oak, ash, and beech, are all deciduous, which means they drop their leaves in the fall.

THE TROPICS

In the hot, permanently wet regions of the tropics, there are dense rain forests full of teak, ebony, rosewood, mahogany, and other evergreen trees. Often the trees grow so closely together that sunlight cannot reach the ground. Other regions in the tropics with both wet and dry seasons have deciduous woodlands and savanna—grasslands with scattered clumps of trees.

WHY WE NEED FORESTS

Forests provide food and shelter for animals and refresh the atmosphere by turning carbon dioxide into oxygen. More than two billion people use firewood for cooking and heating. There is also a large trade in forest products: softwoods (conifers) for building and making paper, and hardwoods (deciduous) for furniture. Other products include fruits, nuts, and spices, gums and resins, rubber, and many vital medicines.

▲ In deciduous forests, the fallen leaves form a carpet on the floor which nourishes new growth.

FAST FACTS

• Before forests were cleared to make way for farms and cities, forests covered about 60% of the world's land area

• 25% of the forests are boreal, 21% temperate, and 54% tropical

• Some rain forests have over 150 different trees in 1,076 sq. ft. (100 sq m)

• In the United States, only 5% of the original forests remain

THE LIFE OF THE FOREST

A forest's highest layer is formed by the treetops and is called the canopy. Below this are shorter trees, then a layer of bushes and shrubs. Lower still, there are ferns, grasses, and wildflowers, and then the mosses and fungi that grow on the forest floor. In addition to the larger animals, such as deer and squirrels, there are thousands of smaller creatures living under the leaves, and in the bark and forest soil.

1 At first, there is a grassy meadow, into which pine seeds fall and grow to become seedlings.

2 Pine trees need full sun to grow, so they form the top layer of forest, with deciduous trees beneath.

3 The type of forest changes as old pines die and deciduous trees fill in gaps in the canopy.

4 In the final stage, a totally deciduous forest develops. It is the climax of this ecological succession.

SEE ALSO

Brazil, Habitat, Plant, Rain forest, Tree

FOSSIL

Fossils are the remains of once-living things found in rocks. They are preserved in different ways and show us what conditions were like in the past.

◀ An ancient leaf's shape is often preserved on stone as a black outline, or trace of carbon.

Dead insects can be preserved whole in tree resin (sap) that has turned into amber over time.

Ammonites (fossilized shells of extinct mollusks) are often found as molds or casts in rock.

A dinosaur footprint, made over 65 million years ago, may be preserved in rock as a trace fossil.

Fossils can include shells, bones, teeth, leaves, skeletons, or even whole animals. Most fossils are found in areas that were once in, or near, water, such as the sea or a river. Layers of mud in the water settle over the animal, creating the perfect conditions for its remains to be preserved.

TYPES OF FOSSIL

A living substance can be preserved whole, but more often it is changed in some way over time. It can be replaced by another material, such as stone, or may rot away leaving an empty mold of the organism.

PRESERVED WHOLE

An insect stuck in resin (sap) oozing from a tree will be preserved whole when that resin turns to the semiprecious stone amber. When larger animals die, usually only the hard parts like bones and teeth are preserved. Sometimes, pools of natural tar can preserve mammoth bones unaltered since the Ice Age (over 10,000 years ago).

PETRIFIED WOOD

Fossilized wood is petrified. This means that the wood has been replaced, molecule by molecule, by a stony material. The carbon in a leaf can survive as a black outline on a stone surface. Millions of leaves preserved in this way produce coal.

A STONE REPLICA

Stone copies of plants or animals are created when water seeps through the rock in which they lie, removing all of the remains. This leaves an empty mold in the shape of the living creature, which is filled by minerals seeping into the rock—creating an exact copy of the creature, known as a cast. Seashells are often fossilized as casts in limestone. Trace fossils are marks in the rock that show where an animal once existed, as in the case of wormholes.

USEFUL FOSSILS

We can tell how old a rock is from its fossils. Many animals existed for only a short time in history and, when we find their fossils in rock, we can tell the age of that rock. Other fossils tell us about the climate or habitat of an area in the past. For example, finding a fossil palm leaf in a cool region indicates it once had a tropical climate, and fossil seashells found far inland reveal that the area was once under the sea.

HOW FOSSILS ARE FORMED

When a dinosaur dies, its flesh rots away, leaving only the bones behind. Scavengers may also remove parts of the body, so complete fossilized remains are rare. Over time, the bones are covered by layers of soil, which harden into rock. Millions of years later, the fossil is exposed by wind and rain or movements in the Earth's crust.

1 The dinosaur's body falls into a sea, river, lake, or swamp. Under water the remains are more likely to be buried fast by soil and sand deposited by the water.

2 The dinosaur's flesh rots away or is eaten by water animals. Its bones and teeth are covered by many layers of sand and soil, which change to rock over time.

3 Thousands of years later, the strata of rock shift, bringing the bones to the surface.

SEE ALSO

Coal, Dinosaur, Evolution, Oil, Prehistoric animal, Rock

FRANCE

France is Europe's third largest country. Only Russia and the Ukraine are larger. France has a rich cultural tradition and a turbulent history.

Area: 210,700 sq. mi.
Population: 59,765,983
Capital: Paris
Language: French
Currency: Euro

Most French landscape is plains or low hills. Three of its borders are high mountain ranges: the Vosges in the northeast; the Pyrenees in the southwest; and the Alps, including France's highest point, Mont Blanc (15,771 ft./4,807m), in the southeast. The Massif Central rises in central France. Paris, the capital, lies in flat country on the Seine River. Other major rivers include the Loire, Rhône, and Gironde.

A NATION OF FARMERS
France is Europe's leading farming nation. Its soil and climate are generally good for crops. The north country is cool and moist, averaging about 1.5 in. (35mm) of rainfall per month. The south is drier and hotter, with summer temperatures above 77°F (25°C). Farmers grow wheat, barley, oats, flax, sugar beet, fruit, and vegetables, and raise cattle and sheep. France is famous for its wines and cheeses, and French cooking is admired and copied all over the world.

PARIS THE CAPITAL
Paris is the center of government, arts, and fashion. It is France's largest city—home to about a sixth of the nation's people. Its 2,000-year-long history means the buildings are a mixture of old and new. Visitors come to see the Louvre Museum, the tomb of Napoleon, Notre Dame Cathedral, the Eiffel Tower, and other famous sights.

▲ Peaceful rural communities are farm-based. Typical crops include wheat, apples, and grapes.

FRENCH LIFE
Although France is a land of forests and green countryside, three fourths of the people live in towns and cities. They meet in sidewalk cafés and restaurants, or enjoy a game of *boules* (a kind of outdoor bowling). Favorite sports include bicycle racing, soccer, rugby, and tennis. There are parades and speeches on Bastille Day (July 14), France's national holiday commemorating the beginning of the French Revolution in 1789.

AN INDUSTRIAL GIANT
After Paris, the largest French cities are Marseilles (the main seaport), Lyons, Toulouse, and Nice. France has a highly developed industrial economy. French factories produce many goods, including cars, aircraft, chemicals, machinery, and textiles. Fishing and mining are important. France also has an international reputation for luxury goods, such as perfume and elegant clothes. Europe's fastest trains speed between French cities, and there is also a fine road system.

▲ Many French people, and other Europeans, ski in the Alps on the border between France and Italy.

► This spectacular glass pyramid, finished in 1989, is the entrance to the Louvre Museum in Paris. The Louvre, originally built as a residence for the kings of France, now houses one of the world's largest art collections.

France is famous for its chic style of fashion, with French designs being copied the world over.

ANCIENT TIMES

In ancient times, France was part of a Celtic territory called Gaul or Gallia. It was conquered by Julius Caesar and was part of the Roman Empire for 500 years, until the fall of the Western Roman Empire in the 400s. A Germanic people called the Franks then conquered the area, bringing it within their empire. France gets its name from the Latin *Francia*, meaning "country of the Franks."

▲ Each summer, the world's top riders take part in the Tour de France, a bicycle race across France. The final stage is in Paris, from Disneyland to the Champs-Élysées.

A TURBULENT HISTORY

France became an independent country in the 800s, but there was no common language until the founding of the French Academy in the 1630s. France has had a turbulent history, including wars with England and Spain and rule by greedy or inept kings. The Revolution of 1789 removed the king and many of the old ways, and during the rule of Napoleon Bonaparte (1799–1815), France dominated Europe. France suffered great damage and loss of life in two world wars, but recovered to become a founding member of the European Union (EU) and a strong voice in world affairs.

ACROSS THE WORLD

France also ruled colonies overseas, which is why today the French language and culture are found in places as far apart as Quebec and North Africa. There are still many French dependencies all over the world. The island of Corsica, which lies off the southeast coast, is also an official region of France.

▲ The 984 ft. (300m)-high Eiffel Tower in Paris won a design competition for the World's Fair in 1889.

SEE ALSO

Celt, Europe, Napoleonic Wars, Revolution, World War I, World War II

FROG AND TOAD

Frogs and toads belong to the group of animals known as amphibians. Most spend their early life as tadpoles in water, but the adults live mainly on land.

◄ The male edible frog has large vocal sacs to call females in the mating season.

Frogs are related to toads, but frogs generally have a slimmer body with smooth skin, and toads have drier, warty skin. All amphibians have thin skin; their lungs are inefficient and they breathe mainly through their skin. Oxygen from the air passes through the skin and into tiny blood vessels just under the surface. This can happen only if the skin is moist, so they are usually found in damp places.

Gliding frogs have rounded sucker pads to help them climb.

Bullfrogs can grow up to 8 in. (20cm), and may even eat newly hatched alligators.

South American arrow-poison frogs are extremely dangerous.

STICKY TONGUE
Most frogs feed on slugs, insects, and worms, which they catch with a long, sticky tongue. Larger frogs, such as the American bullfrog, also feed on prey such as mice, and even small ducklings.

MUSCULAR LEGS
Frogs are great jumpers. Their long, muscle-packed hind legs can send them shooting over 12 times their own length through the air. Webbed feet help frogs swim; tree frogs make huge leaps from branch to branch, aided by sticky pads on their toes. Toads have less powerful back legs than most frogs and waddle.

BRIGHT COLORS
Green or brown is the typical color of most frogs, but some tropical frogs are brilliantly colored. Some species change their skin color with changes in light or temperature, and all frogs shed the outer layer of their skin several times a year, pulling it over their head with their legs.

NOISY COURTSHIP
Frogs and toads can be very noisy at breeding time, when males croak to attract females. The European marsh frog is one of the noisiest—a colony sounds like a crowd of people laughing.

INSIDE A FROG

A frog's internal organs are similar to those of higher animals such as dogs. Externally, their bulging eyes help them look around in many directions, while the disk above the eyes is the eardrum (called a tympanum). Some frogs have a sticky-tipped tongue fixed to the front of their mouth that they flick out to capture prey.

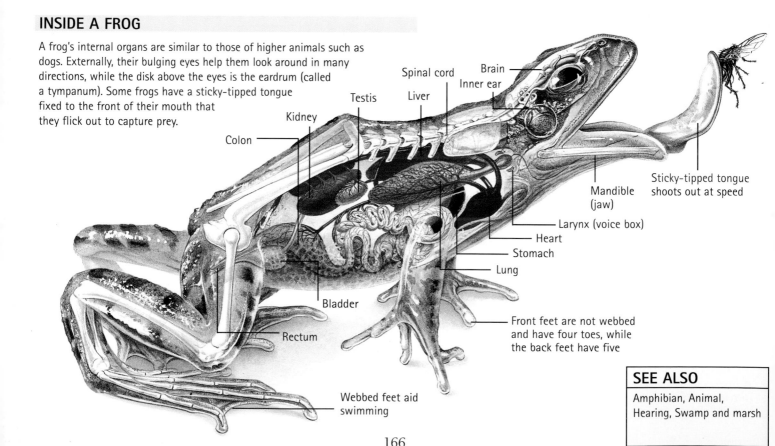

Testis
Spinal cord
Brain
Inner ear
Liver
Kidney
Colon
Mandible (jaw)
Sticky-tipped tongue shoots out at speed
Larynx (voice box)
Heart
Stomach
Lung
Bladder
Front feet are not webbed and have four toes, while the back feet have five
Rectum
Webbed feet aid swimming

SEE ALSO

Amphibian, Animal, Hearing, Swamp and marsh

FRUIT

Fruits contain the seeds of flowering plants. They protect the developing seeds and help them to reach a suitable place to grow into new plants.

Pomes are fleshy fruits like pears which have their seeds in a core formed from the flower stem.

Berries, such as tomatoes, cucumbers, and oranges, hold many seeds inside a single fruit with soft pulp.

Drupes have a single stone which contains the seed. Blackberries are a cluster of many small drupes.

Dry fruits range from chestnuts to corncobs, but all are seed-bearing.

For a new generation of plants to grow successfully, the seed must be spread away from the parent plant so that the new plants are not all grouped together. Fruits are the means by which flowering plants ensure that their ripe seeds get to new, fertile locations.

FLESHY FRUITS

Fruits can be divided into two basic groups: fleshy and dry. Fleshy fruits are juicy and taste good to mammals and birds, which eat the seeds along with the fruit. The seeds pass through the animals' bodies undigested and drop to the ground, where they grow into new plants. Strawberries are false fruits. They develop from a swollen stem. The seeds on the surface are the real fruits.

DRY FRUITS

Fruits such as poppy seedheads or walnuts become dry as the seed ripens. Some, such as pea pods, split open so that the seed is scattered in all directions. Others, such as the maple key, are light and can be blown by the wind. Nuts are also fruits. They have a hard outer casing that rots when the seed inside is ripe and ready to germinate (start growing).

SEED CONTAINERS

Fruits develop from the ovary of the flower after it has been pollinated. The seeds inside the fruit develop from the fertilized egg cells within the ovary. Some fruits, including peaches, cherries, and plums, contain a single seed. However, most fruits, such as apples, raspberries, tomatoes, and squashes, contain more than one seed. Occasionally, the sepals (leaves outside the flower petals) remain after the petals of the flower have fallen, and enclose the fruits, as in acorns.

FRUIT TO EAT

Some fruits are poisonous to humans, but there are many that are delicious and nutritious. Fleshy fruits often contain fruit sugars, which are a useful source of energy, and the fiber provided by the skin, flesh, and sometimes the seeds, aids healthy digestion. Fruits contain vitamins, minerals, and other nutrients that help the body fight off illness. Nuts are also an excellent source of protein.

EATING THE FRUIT

The bright color and pleasant smell of fruits such as blackberries attract birds and animals to eat them. After digesting the soft outer part, they pass the seeds out of their body with the rest of their waste. By this time, they will often be at some distance from the original plant.

1 The dispersed seed falls on fertile soil and the first shoots appear.

2 Flowers on the mature plant are pollinated and produce seeds.

3 The petals drop off and the fruit forms. It is hard and unappealing to birds.

4 The fruit becomes succulent and sweet when it is ready to be eaten.

SEE ALSO
Flower, Food, Leaf, Nutrition, Plant, Seed and pollination

FUNGI

Fungi are neither plants nor animals, but have their own kingdom, which has over 100,000 species and includes mushrooms, toadstools, molds, and yeasts.

◄ The mold on these nectarines comes from airborne spores that have started to breed.

The earth star lifts its fruit body clear off the ground on starlike rays.

The giant puffball is as big as a man's head and makes billions of spores.

Truffles, which grow close to tree roots, are considered the tastiest of fungi.

Unlike plants, fungi need a supply of organic food in order to grow and reproduce. Plants have a green pigment, called chlorophyll, which allows them to make their own food using the Sun's energy. Fungi have no chlorophyll, so they take food from plants and animals.

WHERE THEY LIVE
There are more than 100,000 different types of fungus. Some, like yeast, are only a single cell. Most form masses of threads, called mycelium, which spread inside whatever they feed on. Many live inside plants or in the soil, where they help to break down dead plant and animal matter.

HOW THEY BREED
To reproduce, fungi must release minute spores into the air. Some fungi, such as mushrooms and toadstools, grow large fruit bodies to help the spores travel farther. Others grow tall, threadlike stalks with spore capsules at the end. If they land in a suitable place, the spores will grow to form new fungi of the same type. There are fungus spores around us all the time.

USEFUL FUNGI
Some fungi are useful because they help to break down the remains of dead plants and animals or make medicines. An example is the antibiotic penicillin. Certain yeast fungi are used to make bread and alcohol. Some mushrooms are good to eat, but others contain deadly poison, and it is difficult to tell them apart.

NO-FUN FUNGI
Fungi can grow on and spoil food, paper, wood in buildings, and damp clothes. Fungal diseases can damage and even kill plants, including crops such as potatoes and strawberries. Some affect animals and people: athlete's foot is a common fungal disease that causes itchy, flaky skin between the toes.

HOW FUNGI BREED

Like most fungi, the poisonous fly agaric has a web of threadlike mycelium through which it feeds on decaying matter. To reproduce, it releases spores from the surface of its gills into the air. When the spores land, they develop their own mycelium. But they can only grow fruit bodies by joining up with mycelium from the same species of fungus.

Cap

Developing gills

Developing cap

Mycelium

Upturned cap allows spores to disperse farther

Gills, where spores are produced

Spores

Stipe (stem)

SEE ALSO
Medicine, Microorganism, Plant

GALAXY

A galaxy is a huge collection of stars held together by gravity. The Sun is just one of about 200 billion stars contained within our home galaxy, the Milky Way.

There are probably over a billion galaxies in the universe. They come in three basic shapes: spiral, elliptical, and irregular.

Barred-spiral galaxies have a well-defined bar with arms attached to it.

Elliptical galaxies can be round or oval, and have very little gas or dust.

Irregular galaxies are small and shapeless, and contain a great quantity of gas.

THE NUCLEUS

The central part of a galaxy is called the nucleus. Here, stars are crowded much closer together than on the galactic outskirts. Astronomers now believe that massive black holes may lie deep within the nucleus of many large galaxies. There is probably a black hole at the center of our own galaxy.

LIGHT-YEARS AWAY

Enormous distances separate galaxies. The closest large galaxy to the Milky Way is the Andromeda Galaxy, located about two million light-years away. It is the farthest object visible to the naked eye.

CLUSTERS AND SUPERCLUSTERS

Galaxies are arranged in clusters, which are themselves part of superclusters. The Milky Way and the Andromeda Galaxy are the two largest members of a small cluster of about 30 galaxies known as the Local Group. This, in turn, forms a tiny part of the Local Supercluster.

ACTIVE GALAXIES

Galaxies vary greatly in the amount of energy they give off. Some galaxies, known as active galaxies, are so-called because they give out more energy than is available from all the stars they contain. The extra energy is believed to be supplied by matter falling into a black hole at their center.

ELLIPTICAL

Elliptical galaxies are round or oval in appearance and usually have very little gas or dust. They vary greatly in size, from giants to dwarfs. Giant ellipticals may contain up to ten trillion stars and are the largest type of galaxy.

THE MILKY WAY

The Milky Way is a large spiral galaxy measuring about 100,000 light-years across (a light-year equals 5.88 trillion mi./ 9.46 trillion km). It is about 14 billion years old and takes 225 million years to rotate once. Like all spirals, it contains plenty of gas and dust, from which new stars are formed. The dense nucleus is the oldest part and has no gas left for new stars.

Nucleus

Planet Earth

Gas from which new stars form

Spiral arm

SEE ALSO

Astronomy, Big Bang theory, Black hole, Constellation, Solar system, Star, Universe

GAS

Gas that is burned for cooking and heating is a fossil fuel consisting mainly of methane. It is usually brought into homes and industries via pipelines.

Gas is useful because it releases heat when it burns. It is used for heating and cooking in homes, and many industries burn gas for welding or smelting.

FOSSIL FUEL

Most domestic gas is natural gas, found underground, often with oil or coal but sometimes on its own. Like oil, gas was formed over millions of years from the remains of plants and animals. These organisms are made up largely of hydrogen and carbon, which change to a hydrocarbon called methane when they decay. The natural gas is then mined. Bottled gas, used by campers, is not natural gas. It is propane or butane, two by-products of oil refining.

PROCESSING GAS

Most natural gas is found under the sea. It flows under pressure through a pipe connected to a gas terminal on land, although some is made into a liquid and shipped across the sea. There are a few unwanted substances in natural gas, which are removed at the terminal. The resulting gas does not smell, and a leak could go unnoticed. So a chemical with a distinct smell called a thiol is added.

92 percent Methane
3.5 percent Ethane
2.5 percent Nitrogen
1 percent Propane
1 percent Other

◄ The composition of natural gas varies, although its main ingredient is always methane. These are the percentages for gas from the North Sea.

GAS—THE BURNING ISSUE

The Chinese used natural gas thousands of years ago to evaporate seawater to obtain salt. In the early 1800s, oil prospectors set alight wells which produced only gas because it was worthless to them. Then, in the 1870s, experiments were carried out in which natural gas was piped into U.S. homes.

1 Exploration teams search for gas by drilling from rigs in areas with the right rock formation. Gas is often found with oil.

2 The gas reaches terminals in seamless steel pipes.

3 Smaller pipes then supply homes and industries.

4 The gas is used in stoves and heating systems.

DRILLING FOR GAS

Gas is usually found many thousands of feet below the Earth's surface in a rock such as sandstone. A layer of hard, impermeable rock above it prevents the gas from reaching the surface unless it is drilled by a gas or oil company.

SEE ALSO

Mining, Oil, Rock

GENETICS

Genetics is the science that studies how animals and plants pass their features to their offspring, generation after generation.

Gregor Mendel (1822–84) bred pea plants and studied how they passed features on to offspring.

Nobel Prize-winning scientists James Watson of the U.S.A. and Francis Crick of the U.K. discovered the structure of DNA in 1953.

Babies look like their parents. This tendency for offspring to resemble their parents was known in ancient times. People bred particular plants or animals with features they wanted, such as cows that gave the most milk. Over many generations, this selective breeding led to cows that gave even more milk.

PATTERNS OF INHERITANCE
In the 1850s, an Austrian monk called Gregor Mendel discovered the basics of inheritance by breeding pea plants. He found that some features of pea plants, such as height and color, were not passed on to the next generation as a blend of both parents' features. Instead, a feature from one parent was dominant.

IT IS IN THE GENES
We now know that the features inherited by the peas were decided by their genes.

▶ Dolly, an artificially cloned sheep, was created from a cell taken from another adult sheep. This means that both sheep have exactly the same genes.

Genes are the instructions which decide the appearance and function of each living cell or organism. They are arranged on corkscrew-shaped chemicals called DNA (deoxyribonucleic acid), visible only under an electron microscope.

PASSING ON GENES
When a human or other living thing reproduces, it passes on a copy of half of its genes to its offspring. Each reproductive cell (sperm or egg) contains a different combination of genes, guaranteeing that each offspring will be unique.

GENETIC ENGINEERING
Scientists can now change animals and plants by genetic engineering. The required gene is extracted from the DNA using chemicals called enzymes and inserted into a host organism to obtain the desired characteristic.

PASSING ON THE MESSAGE

DNA is made of thousands of chemical subunits (known as bases), strung in a line like beads on a necklace. There are four different bases, called A, T, G, and C, which are arranged along the DNA. Their sequence determines the cell's genetic code, in the same way that letters of the alphabet arranged in a certain order become a sentence.

The DNA strands are separated while the code is copied during reproduction

C = Cytosine, which always links to Guanine

T = Thymine

G = Guanine

A = Adenine, which always links to Thymine

A gene is made up of three pairs of subunits

Genes are contained inside the nucleus of each microscopic living cell

Nucleus

The DNA strand looks like a twisted ladder—a shape known as a double helix

The DNA strands are coiled up into chromosomes —human cells contain 23 pairs

The DNA is wrapped around a core of proteins

SEE ALSO
Atom and molecule, Cell, Crop, Farming, Forensic science

GERMANY

Germany is a large country which lies in the middle of Europe and borders nine other countries. East and West Germany were reunified in 1990.

Area: 137,830 sq. mi.
Population: 83,251,851
Capital: Berlin
Language: German
Currency: Euro

Germany has a varied landscape, with a broad, flat plain in the north and uplands in the central region. The south is mountainous and includes the South German Hills, Black Forest, and Bavarian Alps. The country is crossed by several major rivers, including the Danube, Rhine, Oder, Weser, Ems, and Elbe. The climate is rarely severe, with warm summers and mild winters, and most places receive from 20–40 in. (500–1,000mm) of rain a year.

FARMING AND INDUSTRY

Only about six percent of Germans are farmers, growing crops such as wheat, barley, rye, and potatoes, as well as grapes to make wine. Many more people work in manufacturing or service industries. There are factories almost everywhere, especially in the Ruhr region—the heart of the iron, steel, and chemical industries. German goods include cars, cameras, computers, and textiles. Factories in the east are being modernized to match those in the west, the most prosperous part of the country.

GETTING AROUND

Germany has a high standard of living and many people own cars. Expressways, called

▲ Many locals wear Bavarian national costume during the famous Munich Beer Festival, held every October. It attracts thousands of people from all over the world.

▶ Germany is the world's third largest producer of cars after Japan and the United States. Car manufacturers from all over the world exhibit their latest models at the Frankfurt Motor Show each year.

▲ The Rhine is one of Europe's most important rivers. Its banks are lined with vineyards and picturesque towns.

autobahns, were built from the 1930s, and the country also has an efficient modern railroad system. Barges carry heavy goods along the Rhine and other waterways.

FOOD AND RECREATION

Germans enjoy good, hearty cooking. A famous annual celebration is the Munich Beer Festival, held in October. Popular foods include wurst (sausage), sauerkraut (pickled cabbage), rich pastries with whipped cream, and smoked cheeses. For recreation, many people enjoy soccer, tennis, athletics, hiking, climbing, and boating.

ARTS AND ARCHITECTURE

Germany has produced philosophers such as Kant and Hegel, and writers such as Goethe and Schiller. Bach, Beethoven, Brahms, and Wagner were all German. The automobile was invented by the German engineers Daimler and Benz, and German scientists pioneered the jet engine and space rocket. The country is also famous for Meissen china, and for its architecture, which includes many magnificent churches and palaces.

WARS AND RECOVERY

For hundreds of years, Germany was a patchwork of independent states, each with its own rulers. By the 1700s, Prussia emerged as the strongest, uniting most of the other states to form a German Empire, in 1871. Germany suffered defeat in World War I (1914–18) and was then ruled by the Nazi dictator Adolf Hitler, who led the country into World War II (1939–45). Defeat in this war left Germany divided. East Germany was under communist rule, and West Germany became the richest capitalist democracy in Europe. In 1990, the two parts—an economically prosperous west and an impoverished east —were reunited, bringing many economic and social problems. However, Germany is still a powerful economic and political force within the European Union (EU).

▲ An East Berlin guard hands a flower to West Berliners sitting on top of the Berlin Wall in 1990—the year the Wall came down, after dividing the city for over 25 years.

▼ Sigmaringen Castle, built on top of a mountain in the Black Forest region, is typical of many castles that dot the German landscape.

SEE ALSO

Europe, Fascism, Industrial Revolution, Industry, World War I, World War II

GLACIER

A glacier is a mass of ice that flows slowly, under the influence of gravity, either from high in the mountains or in polar regions where it is very cold.

Take a handful of snow and squeeze it hard. It turns to ice in your hand. This is what happens when snow falls, year after year, in the valleys of high mountains. The snow at the bottom of the valley is compressed by the weight of the snow above, until it turns to ice.

ICE RIVERS

As the ice comes under greater pressure from the snow above, it begins to soften and flow like putty. At this point, a glacier has formed. The glacier moves slowly—perhaps 10 ft. (3m) per year.

DESTRUCTIVE POWER

A heavy glacier is a powerful force of erosion. As it moves downward, it grinds the valley into a distinct U-shape. A valley that once held a glacier is obvious from its flat bottom and vertical sides.

POLAR ICE CAPS

Glaciers that form near the North and South poles can cover whole countries or continents, and are usually known as ice caps or ice sheets. Snow falls at the center of the continent and spreads out toward the sea. Antarctica and Greenland are both covered by ice sheets.

THE ICE AGE

Between 1,600,000 and 10,000 years ago, the Earth went through periods of intense cold, known as ice ages. For thousands of years in each ice age, vast glaciers covered much of North America, Asia, and Europe as far south as London, England. Many of the lakes, valleys, and hills that we see today were carved by these ice sheets. The first people to settle the Americas crossed from Asia to what is now Alaska on 3,300 ft. (1,000m)-high ice bridges.

GATHERING RUBBLE

The debris that is worn away by the glacier is carried along, either embedded in the ice or lying on the top. This rubble is called moraine. When it is dropped at the glacier's snout (front edge) as the ice melts, moraine forms a landscape of irregular heaps of sand, clay, and rocks.

1 The top of the valley is eroded by the glacier into a sheer-sided basin called a cirque.

2 As the glacier travels, its surface cracks to form crevasses.

3 The glacier picks up soil and rocks (moraine), which pile into ridges.

4 Melting ice forms a lake at the bottom of the glacier.

Snout

This is also moraine

SEE ALSO

Antarctica, Arctic, Lake, Mountain and valley, Prehistoric animal, Prehistoric people

GLAND

Glands are organs that make and release chemicals that the body needs. One group of glands makes hormones, which control growth, life, and development.

▲ The skin has two exocrine glands beneath its surface: sebaceous glands, which make oil to keep skin and hair soft, and sweat glands, which keep the body cool.

Sebaceous gland

Sweat gland

FAST FACTS

• Tear glands are exocrine glands that release tears to clean the front of the eye

• Human endocrine glands produce over 50 hormones

• Women's breasts are mammary glands, which produce milk

Some glands in the body have little tubes known as ducts, through which they release chemicals directly to an area where they are needed. These are the exocrine glands. They include sweat glands in the skin and salivary glands in the mouth. Other glands have no ducts and release chemicals called hormones into the blood. These are the endocrine glands.

THE MASTER GLAND
The pituitary gland is the smallest but most important gland in the body. It is attached to part of the lower brain called the hypothalamus. Together, these two areas of the brain control all of the body's nerves and endocrine glands.

SUGAR IN THE BLOOD
The body stores and uses energy as glucose (blood sugar). A gland in the neck, called the thyroid gland, makes a hormone called thyroxine which controls metabolic rate (how fast the cells use up glucose). The amount of glucose in the blood is regulated by two more hormones, called insulin and glucagon, which are made in the pancreas.

HEALTHY TEETH AND BONES
On the thyroid gland are four tiny, pea-size glands called parathyroids. Together, the thyroid and parathyroids make hormones which affect levels of calcium for healthy teeth and bones.

PUMPING UP THE ADRENALINE
There is an adrenal gland on top of each kidney. The outside of each gland makes steroid hormones that control the body's water balance and bodily reactions to stress and illness. The inside makes adrenaline (epinephrine), the hormone that gets the body ready for emergency action. A fast heartbeat, more sweat, and the need to urinate frequently are all effects of adrenaline. Today, we may feel these effects in a stressful situation, such as an exam, but their original purpose was to prepare the body to run from danger, such as a wild animal.

ENDOCRINE GLANDS

Hormones circulate around the body in the bloodstream. Their levels are often regulated by a system known as feedback. This means that sensor cells check how much of each hormone is present in the blood, and tell the glands to release more or less, as is needed.

The pituitary gland makes over 12 hormones

The thyroid gland makes thyroxine, which controls the body's use of energy

Four parathyroids are embedded in the thyroid gland

The thymus gland helps the immune system to develop in childhood, then gradually shrinks

As well as being an endocrine gland, the pancreas is also an exocrine gland which makes digestive juices

An adrenal gland sits on the top of each kidney

Ovaries

▲ Ovaries make female hormones which control the menstrual cycle and breast development.

Testes

▲ Testes make male hormones which control sperm production and growth of facial hair.

SEE ALSO

Brain and nervous system, Hearing, Human body, Mammal, Reproduction, Sight, Skin and hair

GLASS

Glass is a transparent material made by melting together sand, salt, and other substances at high temperatures, then leaving them to cool gradually.

People first made glass over 6,000 years ago, to use as a colored glaze on stone or clay beads. The earliest surviving glass containers, dating from about 1500 B.C., came from Egypt and Mesopotamia. They were molded around stones as they cooled, or carved once they had set. There are many more ways to make glass today. It can be molded, blown into shape, or rolled into flat sheets like pastry.

USES FOR GLASS

Glass is used to make countless objects around us—from windowpanes and lenses in eyeglasses to cookware and ornaments. It can also be pulled into long strands, like spaghetti, to make fiberglass. Fiberglass can be spun into thicker strands, called fiber-optic cables, that carry information as pulses of light over vast distances. It can also be matted to make glass wool, a material that traps heat like a blanket. Glass wool is often used to insulate attics.

SODA-LIME GLASS

Modern, manufactured glass is about 72 percent silica (the main ingredient of sand), but also contains other substances to make it easier to produce. Ninety percent of all glass is a type called soda-lime glass. This contains soda (sodium carbonate) to reduce its melting temperature from 2,372 to 1,292°F (1,300 to 700°C), and lime to stop it dissolving in water.

TOUGHENING IT UP

Tiny amounts of other chemicals can change glass properties. Boron, for example, can make it ovenproof, copper can make it a red color, and lead can make it more transparent. Because glass shatters, it can be laminated (toughened by sandwiching acrylic plastic or wire meshwork between layers of glass). Such glass can be made to withstand bullets.

FLOAT GLASS FOR WINDOWS

Traditionally, window glass was made by hand, either by spinning or blowing a lump of melted glass flat and cutting it. Then, at the beginning of the 1900s, sheet glass began to be made by drawing melted glass straight from the furnace through rollers. The surface was rough, though, and needed costly polishing, so in the 1950s, English glass manufacturer Alistair Pilkington invented the float process shown here.

1 A powder containing about 72 percent silica (the quartzlike part of sand), 15 percent soda, 6 percent lime, 4 percent magnesia, 2 percent alumina, and 1 percent boric oxide is poured into the furnace.

2 The glass is heated until soft and workable. The soda gives a melting point of about 1,292°F (700°C).

3 The glass passes between rollers and onto a bath of hot metal, usually tin, where it floats until its surface is smooth and hard.

4 The glass passes over cooling rollers until its surface is hard enough not to be scratched by handling.

5 The glass is cut for use in windows and mirrors.

▲ Stained-glass windows are made from small pieces of colored glass, joined together with lead strips. The colors come from metal oxides which are added to the glass during smelting. For example, red is from copper, and yellow is from manganese and ferrous oxide. Features are painted on later.

SEE ALSO

Materials,
Telecommunication

GOLD

Gold is a shiny, yellow precious metal. It is a stable chemical element that is not affected by air or water, which means that it never rusts or tarnishes.

Unlike most metals, gold occurs in its pure state. Some of it is found as grains in sand or gravel, but most of it occurs as veins in rock. It has been valued by people for thousands of years because of its qualities as an attractive metal that never tarnishes and is easy to shape.

▲ Most gold is found in lodes, or veins, in rock. This must be crushed before the gold can be collected.

GOLD MINING

Most gold—about 2,000 tons a year—is extracted by mining. After crushing the rock in which it is found, gold is collected using one of several chemical methods, the most common of which is the cyanide process. Sodium cyanide is added to a pulp of powdered rock and water. This dissolves the gold, which is filtered before zinc is added. The gold settles as a fine mud, and the zinc is dissolved.

ORNAMENTAL AND PRACTICAL

Gold has been used for making jewelry and ornaments for thousands of years. Today, it is used for many other things, including wiring electronic circuits, making dental fillings, and forming part of satellite reflector shields.

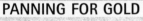

► Ornate gold knife belonging to the Ashanti king Kofi Karikari in the 1800s. Kings of this West African empire were also enthroned on the Golden Stool, a gold throne used as a symbol of power.

STRENGTHENING GOLD

Pure gold is very soft and needs to be hardened by mixing it with other elements, such as copper, nickel, or silver. The amount of gold in an object is measured in carats. Eighteen-carat gold contains 18 parts of gold and 6 parts of silver and copper. The purest gold is 24-carat gold.

THE GOLD RUSHES

Nearly half of the world's gold is held by governments as ingots (gold bars). Gold has always been prized. From 1840 to 1900, thousands sought their fortune in California, Colorado, the Yukon in Canada, South Africa, and Australia in what came to be called gold rushes.

PANNING FOR GOLD

Rocks containing tiny nuggets, veins, or flakes of gold may become eroded (worn away) by rain or ice. When this happens, the gold can be carried into streams. During a gold rush, prospectors would be seen standing in streams panning for gold. After dipping the pan into the stream they would swirl and tip it gently to throw off water, leaving gravel—and, with luck, gold.

► If the prospector was lucky, he would find small grains of gold mixed in with the gravel at the bottom of the pan.

SEE ALSO
Australia, Chemistry, Metal, Mineral and gem

GOVERNMENT

The government of a country is the system by which laws are made, social services provided, and the country organized.

The structure of governments varies, but most governments are responsible for the same tasks and have a constitution (a set of rules which they must obey).

BRANCHES OF GOVERNMENT

Most governments today have three branches: the executive (a president or prime minister), the legislative (a congress, assembly, or parliament), and the judiciary (the highest courts of law). The legislature is composed of elected representatives and it makes the laws by which the country is governed. New laws are debated by the legislature, then a vote is taken. Once a law is passed it is enforced by the judiciary.

THE JOB OF GOVERNMENT

National matters, such as defense or foreign policy, come under the national government. Services such as education, police, fire, parks, trash collection, road-building, transportation, and urban planning come under local (municipal) administration. Governments may also provide social services to help the aged, the unemployed, or those on low incomes. Costs for such services may be shared between national and local governments.

DICTATORS AND OLIGARCHS

In Ancient Rome, an oligarchy (men from a small number of noble families) met in the Senate to run the government. In 82 B.C., Lucius Sulla was made dictator with supreme power to solve disputes. Against strong opposition, he reformed the constitution and the legal system and cut government power. In 79 B.C., Sulla retired to his country estate.

RAISING TAXES

Running a country is expensive. Governments raise money by placing taxes on how much people earn or inherit and on how much they spend. In Korea, 18 percent of earnings are taken in taxes; in France it is 44 percent. To pay for local services, local governments may collect additional taxes. These often take the form of a property tax or local sales tax.

▲ The House of Commons, inside the Houses of Parliament at Westminster, London, is where elected members of the British parliament sit and vote on new laws.

TYPES OF GOVERNMENT

Communism A system based on the political theories of Karl Marx and Friedrich Engels in the 1800s. They advocated class war and a society in which all property is owned by the people. Communist states are usually dictatorial.

Dictatorship Rule by one person, a group, or a committee whose word is law. Often accompanied by censorship and restricted rights. The idea of dictatorship comes from Ancient Rome, when the Roman Senate could appoint individuals as dictators in times of national emergency.

Federalism A union of two or more states which can pass individual state laws, but which accept the national government's rule in matters such as the country's defense. The United States, Australia, Canada, and Switzerland all have federal governments.

Monarchy Rule by a king, queen, emperor, or empress. Traditionally, a monarch would have supreme power, but nowadays most monarchs have only constitutional power. This means that their power is limited by the country's constitution or government to ceremonial duties. The U.K. has this system.

Oligarchy Government by a small ruling group. A republic would be an oligarchy if only a few people were entitled to vote for the leader. Most Ancient Greek city-states were oligarchies because only the free men (not slaves or women) could vote. Ancient Rome was an oligarchy ruled by a few nobles.

Republic A state or country where power is held by elected representatives acting on behalf of the people who elected them. An elected president is head of state and sometimes of the government. This is the most common form of government in the world today.

SEE ALSO

Civil rights, Democracy, Empire, Revolution, Women's rights

GRASSLAND

Grasslands are large areas of flat or gently rolling land covered by grasses, often with trees and bushes scattered across them or clustered along streams.

▲ Damp, long-grass prairies are rich in bluestem, switch grass, and needlegrass.

Between dry, rainless deserts and dense, wet forests there are usually areas known as grasslands. These regions have definite wet and dry seasons. The grasses grow quickly, flower, and produce seeds in the wet season, then die back or do not grow in the dry season. Most of a grass plant is below ground. This means that it can survive droughts and fires better than other plants.

GRASSLAND TYPES

Different types of grass grow all over the world, and grasslands are given different names wherever they exist. In North America, they are called prairies or plains; in Africa, savanna. The cooler grasslands of Argentina are called pampas, and in Russia they are steppes.

AFRICAN SAVANNA

Temperatures on the savanna are hot all year, and rain falls only during the summer. The long red oat, bluestems, and dropseed grasses plus scattered trees produce up to 18.2 tons of vegetation per acre (45 tons per hectare) each year, providing food for animals that include zebras, antelope, and ostriches. Frequent fires encourage fresh growth of grasses and trees.

ANIMALS AND PLANTS

Antelope in Africa, kangaroos in Australia, and bison in the United States graze the grasslands. Marmots, rabbits, and ground squirrels burrow for roots and shelter. These plant-eaters are hunted by lions, wolves, hyenas, and birds of prey such as hawks and eagles. Invertebrates (animals without backbones), such as insects, are the largest group of grassland animal. These provide food for rodents and small birds.

HARVESTING THE LAND

Wild grasslands once covered almost a third of the world's land, but most have been changed by humans. Sheep farmers in Australia, cattle ranchers in the U.S., dairy farmers in Europe, and nomadic goat herders in North Africa all depend on natural or cultivated grasslands to feed their animals. Grasslands have also been plowed to produce cereal crops such as wheat, corn, and oats.

FAST FACTS

- There are more than 7,500 kinds of grass
- Grasses are very adaptable. They grow in the sea, in swamps, in deserts, on mountaintops, and in the frozen Arctic wilderness
- The biggest grasses are bamboos. They can grow up to 130 ft. (40m) tall and 12 in. (30cm) thick at the bottom

Scattered trees grow where roots can reach deep, permanent water

Waterholes fill during the wet season, storing water for the dry season

Grazing animals wander across the grasslands in herds, usually settling near a source of water

SEE ALSO
Africa, Animal, Argentina, Canada, Crop, Farming, Food, Habitat

GRAVITY

Gravity is a force that exists between any two objects, pulling them together. On Earth, the force of gravity pulls you toward the ground and gives you weight.

When you jump up in the air, you come back down again. This is because Earth's gravity pulls you down toward the planet. If there were no gravity, we would drift off the Earth and into space. Gravity explains why the stars and planets move in the way that they do, and how the Moon affects the tides each day. It is also the force that gives us our weight.

▲ Astronauts and fighter pilots feel the effects of g-forces (gravity) during takeoff. Not only does gravity distort their faces, but it can also send all the blood to their legs, sometimes making them feel faint.

MASS AND WEIGHT

The less gravity there is, the less you weigh. If you were in outer space, far away from any other objects, you would not feel any gravity. This means you would be completely weightless, even though your mass (quantity of matter) would not have changed. On Earth, the weight of something depends on its mass. A walrus has more mass than a mouse, for example, so it feels a greater force of gravity. That is why a walrus weighs more than a mouse.

FREE FALL

Sky divers experience a feeling of weightlessness in a free fall from a high airplane. In fact, they are still being pulled by the Earth's gravity, but the air resistance is pushing against them. Only outside the Earth's atmosphere, in space, are we truly weightless.

FAST FACTS

• Isaac Newton (1643–1727) discovered the law of gravity, supposedly when he saw an apple fall from a tree

• Gravity keeps the rings of Saturn in orbit around the planet

• To escape the Earth's gravity, a spacecraft must reach 7 mi./sec. (11.2km/sec). This is called escape velocity

◀ The speed at which a rocket is launched determines whether it escapes Earth's gravity and flies into space or plummets back to Earth.

▶ Early space rockets used the Earth's gravitational pull to go into orbit around the planet. Today, all satellites use this same principle.

PULLING TOGETHER

We normally think about gravity only as it applies to the Earth, but gravity exists between any two objects. The greater their mass and the closer they are together, the larger the force of gravity between them. Two ships at sea, for example, will attract each other, but their gravitational pull is so small compared to other forces on Earth that it is not noticeable. However, two nearby spaceships, far away from other objects in space, will create a noticeable gravitational attraction, called microgravity.

DROPPED FROM ON HIGH

Like all forces, gravity alters the velocity (speed) of objects. Near the Earth's surface, gravity makes all objects accelerate at the same rate—105 ft./sec.^{2} (9.81m/sec^2)—no matter how heavy. If a full and an empty box fall from the top of a tall building, they reach the ground together.

SEE ALSO

Earth, Force and motion, Moon, Solar system, Spacecraft

GREAT DEPRESSION

The Great Depression was a worldwide slump in trade and economies. It began with the Wall Street stock market crash in 1929 and lasted well into the 1930s.

In the 1930s, trade between nations collapsed, businesses closed, and millions of people lost their savings and their jobs. This worldwide slump was known as the Great Depression.

THE CAUSES
Trouble began after World War I (1914–18). The loser, Germany, was ruined by having to make huge payments to the victorious Allies. Many Germans lost all of their savings as the value of their money collapsed. There were fears of a revolution like the one in communist Russia (1917).

HOME FROM WAR
In Britain, France, and the United States, factories struggled to adjust to peacetime trade. Millions of soldiers came home and looked for jobs. Trade unions called workers to strike against employers who demanded wage cuts. In 1926, a general strike (all

workers) happened in Britain. Food prices fell so low that many farmers were ruined and were forced to give up their land.

THE CRASH
In 1929, the United States's financial market crashed after a period of frantic buying. Share prices fell sharply, ruining many investors. Banks and businesses shut down. The Wall Street Crash (named after New York's financial district) affected money markets around the world. World trade plunged. The Great Depression had begun.

EFFECTS OF THE SLUMP
The Great Depression cast a shadow across the 1930s. Jobless people lined up for food and clothing handouts. Some lost their homes and wandered the streets, begging or looking for work. Droughts and dust storms brought more misery to farming communities in the United States.

► President Franklin D. Roosevelt launched the New Deal: a national program to aid the poor through community projects. Preparations for World War II aided recovery in Europe.

▲ Few were immune to the effects of the Great Depression. Many well-qualified people were out of work.

FLEEING THE DUST BOWL
In 1930, a drought hit large areas around Oklahoma, where grassland had been plowed to produce wheat. By 1933, the soil had turned to dust, leaving farms useless. Thousands of poverty-stricken families fled the Dust Bowl looking for work in California and elsewhere. By the 1940s, the grassland had regrown.

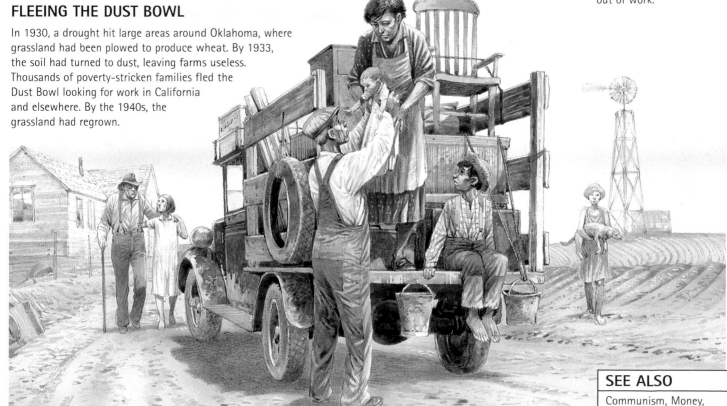

SEE ALSO

Communism, Money, Revolution, World War I, World War II

GREECE AND THE BALKANS

Nine countries make up the Balkans, a mountainous region in southwest Europe named after the Balkan mountain range that runs through it.

ALBANIA
Area: 10,630 sq. mi.
Population: 3,544,841
Capital: Tirané
Languages: Albanian, Greek
Currency: Drachma

BOSNIA-HERZEGOVINA
Area: 19,700 sq. mi.
Population: 3,964,388
Capital: Sarajevo
Language: Serbo-Croatian
Currency: Convertible Mark

BULGARIA
Area: 42,858 sq. mi.
Population: 7,621,337
Capital: Sofia
Language: Bulgarian
Currency: Lev

CROATIA
Area: 21,800 sq. mi.
Population: 4,390,751
Capital: Zagreb
Language: Croatian
Currency: Kuna

GREECE
Area: 50,500 sq. mi.
Population: 10,645,343
Capital: Athens
Language: Greek
Currency: Euro

▶ Remains of the Parthenon, a temple built in the 400s B.C. for the goddess Athena, stand on the Acropolis in the center of Athens.

The Balkan peninsula has seas on three sides: the Adriatic and Ionian to the west, the Mediterranean to the south, and the Aegean and Black seas to the east.

MOUNTAIN COUNTRY
Apart from the Balkan Mountains, there are several other mountain ranges. One famous peak is Mount Olympus in Greece, which is 9,950 ft. (2,911m) high. The Danube River is the most important waterway, forming the border between Romania and Bulgaria. The Balkan region has a mild climate. Summer temperatures reach 86°F (30°C); winters can be cold and snowy in the mountains.

LAND OF THE SLAVS
There is a rich cultural and religious diversity as a result of many invaders to the region. Ancient Greece ruled an empire until the Roman invasion in 146 B.C. Then, in the A.D. 300s, the Roman Empire became split into east and west, and the Balkans fell into the eastern part, known as the Byzantine Empire. During the 500s, Slavs came down from the north, scattering into distinct tribes, which are reflected in the languages present today: Bulgarian, Serbian, Croatian, Slovenian, and Macedonian. The Ottoman Turks ruled the region from the 1400s, but most Balkan people stayed Christian under Islamic rule.

▲ Fish is important in the diet of many Greek people, especially on the islands. Here, a fisherman rows out from the harbor of Symi, a Greek island near the Turkish coast.

THE BALKANS TODAY
In 1929, King Alexander I became dictator of Yugoslavia, a nation made up of Bosnia-Herzegovina, Croatia, Montenegro, Serbia, and Slovenia, and introduced a common language, Serbo-Croatian. After World War II (1939–45), Yugoslavia, Bulgaria, and Albania became communist countries. Marshal Tito was leader of the communist Federal People's Republic of Yugoslavia until he died in 1980. Savage civil wars began in 1991, and the former Republic of Yugoslavia broke up. It is now divided into five independent countries. All the Balkan

◀ 150,000 Serb refugees flee from a Croatian attack in the Krajina region of Bosnia during the civil war, in 1995.

MACEDONIA
Area: 9,900 sq. mi.
Population: 2,054,800
Capital: Skopje
Languages: Macedonian, Albanian, Turkish, Serbian, Croatian
Currency: Denar

SLOVENIA
Area: 7,800 sq. mi.
Population: 1,932,917
Capital: Ljubljana
Languages: Slovenian, Serbian, Croatian
Currency: Tolar

TURKEY
Area: 297,600 sq. mi.
Population: 67,308,928
Capital: Ankara
Language: Turkish
Currency: Turkish Lira

▲ The Festival of Roses is held each year in Kazanluk, Bulgaria, one day before rose picking begins. The petals are crushed for their oil (attar), used in perfume.

countries are striving to modernize their economies. Several hope to join Greece as members of the European Union (EU).

HOW PEOPLE LIVE
Many of the Balkan people are farmers, living in small towns and villages as their ancestors did 100 years ago. They grow corn, barley, fruits, and vegetables, and raise sheep, goats, cattle, and pigs. Donkeys and horse-drawn wagons can still be seen carrying produce to market. There are few big cities, apart from national capitals such as Athens (Greece) and Belgrade (former Yugoslavia), where skyscrapers tower over older buildings. Factories make vehicles, textiles, chemicals, and electronic goods, and mines produce coal, iron, and lead.

WHERE EAST MEETS WEST
Along the sunny Balkan coasts, with their beaches and medieval towns, tourism is an important industry. New hotels and roads are being built to cater for the growing tide of visitors. Eastern and Western building styles can be seen side by side: here a Christian church in Byzantine style, there an Islamic mosque. Bulgaria is famous for growing roses to make perfume. Visitors from all over the world visit Greece to see the wonders of its ancient civilization.

SERBIA AND MONTENEGRO
Area: 34,100 sq. mi.
Population: 9,979,752
Capital: Belgrade
Languages: Serbo-Croatian, Albanian
Currency: New Dinar

▼ Albanian children standing in front of an air raid shelter built during the rule of communist dictator Enver Hoxha from 1946 to 1985.

SEE ALSO
Civil war, Empire, Europe, Greece (Ancient), Refugee

GREECE, ANCIENT

The Ancient Greeks created one of the world's greatest civilizations. They gave us enduring styles of architecture, art, literature, and government.

Not many paintings are left from Ancient Greece, but there are many decorated pots—usually showing myths or festivals.

This silver, four-drachma coin, made in Athens, was used all over Ancient Greece. The owl symbolized Athena, goddess of wisdom.

Corrupt politicians were ostracized (sent into exile) if enough voters scratched their name onto *ostraca* (pieces of broken pottery).

The Greeks moved south into what is now Greece some 4,000 years ago. The Minoans developed a great civilization around 2000 B.C., on the island of Crete, but most achievements in the arts, sciences, and government were made during the Golden Age. This was a period between 477 and 431 B.C., when Athens was the ruling city-state.

A RUGGED COUNTRY

The nature of the Greek countryside helped to shape the country's history. Its mountain ranges made travel by land difficult. Fiercely independent and patriotic communities grew up in the fertile pockets between the mountains, and Ancient Greece became a country divided into many city-states.

THE OLYMPIANS

The people were deeply religious. They believed in many gods—all of whom had human form, but possessed superhuman powers and were, of course, immortal. The chief gods were known as the Olympians because they were believed to live at the top of Mount Olympus in northern Greece. Zeus ruled the gods with his wife Hera. Other gods and goddesses included Aphrodite, goddess of love; Apollo, god of the sun, music, and poetry; Ares, god of war; and Athena, goddess of wisdom. The Ancient Greeks built temples to their gods, in which they made offerings of food, wine, and sometimes live animals. Rich families had shrines in their homes to less important household gods.

▲ Women were usually married at the age of 13, often to men over twice their age. They were in charge of the house and wove all the material for the loose-fitting garments, known as *chitons*, worn by men and women.

DECORATIVE ARTS AND FESTIVALS

The Greeks decorated their temples and palaces in a new, natural style of marble statues and reliefs. Music, drama, dance, and sports were celebrated at festivals, such as the Olympic Games, held every four years from 776 B.C. in honor of the gods.

LITERATURE AND LEARNING

The poet Homer, who created the epic poems the *Odyssey* and *Iliad*, was just one of many great writers. Dramatists such as Aeschylus, Euripedes, and Sophocles wrote plays for open-air theaters. Socrates, Plato, and Aristotle discussed philosophy in *agoras* (marketplaces) and academies, while scientific discoveries were made by Pythagoras, Archimedes, and others.

◀ The ruggedness of the Greek terrain meant that most trade and warfare were carried out at sea. Greek warships, known as *triremes* (above), had up to 170 oarsmen arranged on three decks, which gave them great speed.

ATHENS VERSUS SPARTA
The two most powerful city-states were
Athens and Sparta, which were constantly
at war with each other. They had different
approaches to education, the arts, and
warfare. Athens and other city-states had
democratic governments where all male
citizens could vote, and their children were
educated in the arts and sciences. Sparta
was a military state with a tough, warlike
people. Boys were sent away to military
camps at the age of seven, and girls were
also trained in gymnastics and warfare—
a fact which shocked the Athenians.

EMPIRE AND LEGACY
Early in the 400s B.C., Athens and Sparta
united against a new common enemy,
Persia. The Ancient Greeks won, but
fighting resumed and the city-states began
to crumble. Then, in 335 B.C., Alexander the
Great united Ancient Greece once more,
and went on to conquer almost the entire
Middle East, from Egypt to northern India.
In 146 B.C., the Romans conquered Greece,
but adopted much of its culture.

▲ The actors in the amphitheaters wore clay masks so that even people in the top rows could tell the characters apart.

▲ Lyres were stringed instruments made from turtle shells. Athenian boys learned to sing and play the lyre and *aulos* (flute) at music schools.

▲ Amphitheaters, like this one at Delphi, were carved into the sides of hills. Their clever design meant that a whisper on stage could be heard by the whole audience.

KEY DATES
2000 B.C. Minoan civilization in Crete flourishes

1600-1200 B.C. Mycenaean civilization on the mainland rules Greece

900-800 B.C. Homer writes *Iliad* and *Odyssey*

490 B.C. Persian army invades Greece—the Greeks win at the battle of Marathon

480 B.C. Battles of Thermopylae and Salamis

431-404 B.C. Peloponnesian War between Athens and Sparta. Plague kills a third of Athenians. Sparta wins

356-323 B.C. Reign of Alexander the Great

146 B.C. Roman Empire conquers Greece

BATTLE OF THERMOPYLAE
The Greek cities fought frequent wars with each other, but in 480 B.C.
they united against an invasion by the Persian emperor Xerxes. A force
of 300 *hoplites* (armored infantry) from Sparta held thousands of
Persians at the mountain pass of Thermopylae for three days
before being wiped out. This gave the Greek fleet of
ships time to gather at the Straits of Salamis
and defeat the invasion.

SEE ALSO
Architecture, Astronomy, Democracy, Europe, Greece and the Balkans, Medicine, Mesopotamia, Myth and legend, Olympic Games, Sculpture, Seven Wonders of the World, Theater

HABITAT

A habitat is the home of particular species of animal or plant. It provides them with the food, shelter, and conditions that allow them to survive.

◄ Oystercatchers living on the coast of the Netherlands depend on clean seas for the survival of the shellfish they feed on.

◄ Sure-footed mountain goats live among the crags of the Rockies, Canada.

▲ An orangutan sits in a rain-forest canopy in Borneo—a threatened habitat.

▲ Only a few swamp habitats support alligators. Here, two bask in the sun in the Everglades.

▲ Antarctica's inhospitable habitat is home to animals with a thick layer of fat, such as this Weddell seal and pup.

▲ A beetle scuttles across the cold desert of Turkmenistan. Its small size helps it keep warm.

Key

Cold desert: cold region with little rain. Animals and plants must be able to survive the lack of water and cold.

Tundra: treeless plains near Arctic. Snow-covered in winter. Migratory animals, moss, and lichens in summer.

Temperate woodland: tree-covered areas in climate that changes between winter and summer. Trees usually shed their leaves.

Coniferous forest: areas (usually northern) with trees bearing pine cones. Wildlife includes deer, bears, wolves.

Savanna grassland: grassland areas with scattered trees, lying between desert and rain forest. Large predators and herbivores.

Tropical rain forest: dense forest around equator in Asia, Africa, and South America. Habitat with the most wildlife.

Steppe and dry grassland: hot summers and cold winters. Short grasses, with many snakes and rodents.

Hot desert: hot with little rain. Can be sandy or rocky. Many animals hide during the day.

Climate, soil, plants, and animals—from the tiniest insect to the tallest tree—all create a habitat. Scientists classify them into types, such as grassland, forest, desert, mountaintop, river, swamp, or sea. These groups show great variation.

HABITATS AND BIOMES
When scientists talk about a habitat in general, they use the word biome. For example, a grassland is a biome, but a specific grassland such as the Argentinian Pampas is known as a habitat. Within each habitat there are also thousands of small, specialized living spaces, such as the dark, damp world under a rock on a riverbank, or a pool of water in the fork of a forest tree. These are known as microhabitats.

OCEAN WORLDS
The biggest biome of all is the oceans, which cover 71 percent of the Earth's surface. This biome is divided into layers according to how warm or salty the water is and how far down the sunlight reaches. It also varies from place to place—from the warm, blue seas of the Caribbean to the cold, windswept Antarctic Ocean. Around the edges of the seas are other special habitats, such as coral reefs, rocky and sandy shores, and river mouths.

UPSETTING THE BALANCE
Each habitat is a complex system, with all the plants and animals perfectly suited to, and yet dependent on, their environment, as well as on one another. When something upsets the balance, a habitat can be badly damaged. Parts of Africa's savannas have been turned into desert because too many people, goats, and cattle have stripped off the vegetation. Lakes and rivers in many countries have been poisoned by industrial chemicals. Forests may be damaged by acid rain, and some seashores are being scarred by oil spillages.

SEE ALSO
Desert, Forest, Grassland, Ocean and sea, Pollution, Rain forest, Seashore

186

HEARING

Hearing is one of the five senses. It depends on the detection of sound waves in the air which are changed into nerve signals and sent to the brain for processing.

Bats use their high-pitched (100,000Hz) squeaks to locate flying insects to eat.

Frogs can hear only low frequency sounds of 5,000Hz and below.

Dogs hear both high and low-pitched sounds. Dog whistles are 35,000Hz.

Human ears hear frequencies from about 30 to 18,000Hz.

For most people, hearing is the second most important sense, after sight. It allows communication, warns us of danger, and gives pleasure, from music to birdsong.

THE OUTER EAR
We hear with our ears. The outer ear is just a skin-covered flap of gristle, or cartilage, that catches sound waves in the air. Most of the delicate working parts are behind it, protected inside the skull.

INSIDE THE EAR
Sound waves funnel into the ear canal. At its end, they hit a small patch of flexible skin, the eardrum. The sound waves bounce off it and make the eardrum vibrate (shake back and forth). Vibrations pass from the eardrum, along a chain of three tiny bones, called the hammer (malleus), anvil (incus), and stirrup (stapes). These bones pass the vibration to the oval window.

THE COCHLEA
The oval window is a membrane in the wall of a fluid-filled chamber, the cochlea, which is coiled like a snail, small enough to sit on your fingernail. Vibrations of the oval window push ripples into the fluid inside the cochlea. As the ripples go around the coil, they shake almost two million tiny hairs protruding from 25,000 hair cells.

SOUND TO ELECTRICITY
The hair cells send signals to the brain. Here they are analyzed for volume and frequency, and compared with soundprints in the memory. Sound waves travel at about 1,115 ft./sec. (340m/sec). If sound comes from the side, waves reach the closer ear a fraction of a second before the farther ear. From this tiny difference, the brain works out the direction of the sound source. This is only possible with two (or more) ears and is called stereophonic hearing. Frequency of sound is measured in vibrations per second, hertz (Hz), and our ears can hear only certain frequencies.

CAPTURING SOUNDS ON THE AIRWAVES

The outer ear collects sound waves in the air and sends them toward the eardrum. They travel through the middle ear, via the hammer, anvil, and stirrup to the cochlea, where they become electrical messages that are sent to the brain along the cochlear nerve.

Pinna (earflap)
Cartilage
Bone
Outer ear
Ear canal
Wax-producing gland
Eardrum
Hammer
Anvil
Middle ear
Stirrup
Oval window
Eustachian tube (leading to throat)
Inner ear
Semicircular canals
Cochlear nerve (to brain)
Cochlea
Tiny branches of the cochlear nerve
Inner hair cell
Outer hair cell

▲ Movement of the hairs inside the cochlea sends electrical signals to the brain. Inner and outer hair cells register different frequencies of sound.

SEE ALSO
Bat, Human body, Sound

187

HEART AND CIRCULATORY SYSTEM

The heart is a hollow, muscle-walled pump in the chest. It squeezes at least once every second to pump blood around the body. If it stops, so will life.

The heart is a muscular pump with four chambers (pockets) which drives the blood around the body by means of a network of arteries, veins, and capillaries known as the circulatory system.

WILLIAM HARVEY
(1578–1657) The English doctor who showed that blood circulates (moves around the body) in only one direction, along arteries and veins.

IN AND OUT
As the muscles in the heart contract, blood is squeezed from the heart into arteries, which carry the blood around the body. As the heart muscles relax, blood flows into the heart from the body, via veins. Each squeeze–relax cycle is a heartbeat.

A TIRELESS MUSCLE
The cardiac (heart) muscle never tires. In an average lifetime, the heart beats more than 2.5 billion times. On average,

the heart beats 70 times per minute, although heartbeat rate varies with age or health. Each beat pumps about 2.5 fl. oz. (70ml) of blood. As the body has only about 5.3 qt. (5 l) of blood, all the blood passes through the heart in one minute. An active body uses more energy and oxygen, so the heart beats faster and pumps more blood with each beat.

CHECKING THE HEART
Each heartbeat starts in a small area of the wall in the right atrium. This is the heart's natural pacemaker. It sends tiny electrical signals through the heart's walls, telling them to contract. The action is controlled by nerve signals from the brain and chemicals in the blood called hormones. Electronic sensors placed on the skin can detect the electrical signals of the heart. The signals are displayed as a graph on an ECG (electrocardiograph) machine.

TWO PUMPS IN ONE
The heart is not one pump but two, separated by a muscular dividing wall. The right pump receives low-oxygen blood from the body, along the main veins. It sends this blood out through the pulmonary arteries to the lungs, where it receives oxygen, and returns to the heart's left pump. This sends it out around the body again.

Brachial artery

Cephalic vein

Jugular vein

Carotid artery to head

Aorta

Pulmonary arteries to the lungs

Superior vena cava

Pulmonary veins from the lungs

Renal artery to kidney

Renal vein from kidney

Iliac artery

Iliac vein

Femoral artery

Femoral vein

Tibial artery

Tibial vein

■ Blood with oxygen

■ Blood without oxygen

The superior vena cava carries blood from the upper body

Blood to head and neck

Aorta carries blood to the body's cells

Pulmonary arteries to the lungs

Pulmonary arteries

Pulmonary veins from the lungs

Left atrium

Pulmonary veins

Valve

Right atrium

Right ventricle

Left ventricle

The inferior vena cava carries blood from the lower body

Blood to the lower body

SEE ALSO
Blood, Gland, Human body, Muscle

HEAT

Heat is a form of energy that is created by the vibration of atoms within a substance. Heat always moves from warm places to cooler ones.

Only a fraction of the Sun's rays reaches us, yet it is our most important heat source.

Everything is made up of atoms and molecules that are always moving, even when an object is perfectly still. Their motion gives the object internal energy, or heat. The faster the atoms and molecules move, the hotter an object is. We usually measure heat with a thermometer.

By striking a match, we start a chemical reaction which produces heat.

CONDUCTION

If two objects of different temperatures touch each other, the hotter object will always transfer some of its heat to the cooler object. For example, when you stir hot coffee with a cold teaspoon, the heat from the coffee flows into the teaspoon. This happens because atoms in the coffee touch atoms in the spoon, making them vibrate more. This is called conduction. Metal is a good conductor of heat but some materials, such as polystyrene, transfer heat poorly. They are called insulators.

Pressure deep inside the Earth produces heat that escapes via volcanoes.

The flow of electricity through wires creates heat that we use to toast bread.

Friction (two objects rubbing together) creates heat used to start a fire.

▲ The Earth's inner heat escapes through cracks in the crust, creating hot springs in Iceland. People bathe in them, and geothermal plants use the heat to make electricity.

RADIATION AND CONVECTION

Heat also travels by radiation and convection. The Earth is warmed by heat which radiates (spreads out) through space from the Sun to the Earth. Heat radiates very fast—it takes just over eight minutes for heat to radiate from the Sun to the Earth. Convection occurs only in liquids or gases that are unevenly heated. Warm parts of a liquid or gas flow into cooler ones, spreading heat with them.

HEAT IN OUR LIVES

When we eat food, our bodies break it down, releasing energy that heats us inside. We burn fuels, such as wood and coal, to help us stay warm, or to make heat to drive machines. Power plants make electricity, which we convert into heat in our homes.

FEELING THE HEAT

Boiling water in a kettle over an open fire requires heat to travel in each of its three ways: radiation, conduction, and convection. Air molecules are set in motion by heat, radiating from the fire. The hot air molecules hit the kettle bottom, making its molecules vibrate. The heat travels through the metal via conduction and through the water by convection.

Heat travels up the cold handle of the kettle via conduction. If the handle was wood it would not become hot, because wood is a poor heat conductor

Heat circulates through the water via convection until all of the water is the same temperature

Heat from the fire radiates through the air until it hits the bottom of the kettle

SEE ALSO

Atom and molecule, Electricity, Energy, Solid, liquid, and gas

HELICOPTER

Helicopters are aircraft with spinning rotor blades instead of wings. These make them able to fly in ways that are impossible for most other aircraft.

Rotor blade
Rotor shaft
Lower swash plate
Control rod
Upper swash plate
Hydraulic controls
Blade pitch adjuster
Blade attachment
Engine exhaust
Gearing
Control panel
Cockpit
Engine
Tail rotor shaft
Tailplane
Tail rotor

BELL 407

The Bell 407 helicopter is a popular commercial helicopter, capable of carrying six passengers as well as the pilot. It has one main rotor and a small vertical tail rotor. It is used as an air taxi and for many light tasks such as police searches and traffic surveillance.

The Ka-26 Kamov Hoodlum has two sets of main rotors, rotating in opposite directions.

The Russian Mil-24 gunship has one main rotor on top and a small vertical rotor at the back.

The Boeing Vertol Chinook military helicopter has two rotors—one at each end.

Helicopters are very maneuverable aircraft—they can take off and land vertically in a small space, hover in one place, and fly in any direction: forward, sideways, even backward!

ONE ROTOR OR TWO
Most helicopters have one set of long, thin rotor blades (the main rotor) on top and a smaller tail rotor. The main rotor provides lift to keep the helicopter in the air. The tail rotor is used for changing direction. It also stops the helicopter from being spun around by the main rotor. Some helicopters have two main rotors which rotate in opposite directions to prevent the vehicle from spinning around.

TAKING OFF
The angle of the rotor blades is called the pitch. By changing the pitch of the blades, with a control lever in the cockpit, the pilot can make the helicopter take off, land, climb, or hover. Raising and twisting the end of the lever makes the rotor blades spin faster and also tilts each one so that together they create more lift. When the lift is greater than the helicopter's weight, it takes off or climbs; when the lift and weight are equal, it hovers; and when the lift is less than the weight, it descends.

MOVING AND STEERING
A helicopter moves forward when the whole of the main rotor is tipped forward. To slow down, the rotor is tipped back. Tipping the blades to the side makes the helicopter fly sideways. To turn, the tail-rotor angle is altered with foot controls.

SPINNING INTO ACTION
The first helicopters flew in the early 1900s, but they were clumsy and could barely take off. The first successful modern helicopter was the Vought-Sikorsky VS-300, built by Igor Sikorsky in 1940.

HELICOPTERS AT WORK
The helicopter's versatility in flight means it can be used for search and rescue at sea, police observation, or as an air ambulance. Military helicopters can fly lower than planes, and take off from small clearings or the decks of ships.

SEE ALSO
Aircraft

HIBERNATION

In the cooler parts of the world, many mammals pass the winter months in a very deep sleep. This is called hibernation.

Many types of bat are active during the night and go into a type of hibernation each daytime.

Some butterflies, such as the monarch, hibernate in groups in hollow trees or attics over the winter.

The deep winter sleep of some bears is hibernation, but their body temperature only drops slightly.

Snakes, such as adders, hibernate under rocks or in holes under the ground when the weather is cold.

Some animals, such as the lungfish, estivate (become inactive in summer to survive drought).

Many animals hibernate during the winter when it is cold and there is little food. While hibernating, their body temperature falls greatly until it is little more than that of the surroundings.

GETTING READY

During the autumn, an animal will eat a lot to increase its body fat; this will give it energy while hibernating. It then looks for a safe spot in which to settle down. Most rodents take food supplies into their sleeping quarters to hibernate.

ONLY JUST ALIVE

While hibernating, an animal's heart and breathing rates drop until it is only just alive. It may stir and stretch itself from time to time, but does not really wake up until the outside temperature rises in the spring. By this time, most animals have used up all their food reserves and are very thin. They have to look for food right away and will die if they do not find any.

WHO HIBERNATES?

Insect-eating bats in cool climates have to hibernate because there are not enough insects for them to eat in the winter. Ground squirrels, such as the prairie dog, also hibernate. Among birds, only the whippoorwill and some other nightjars are known to hibernate. Small hummingbirds also huddle together at night in a type of nightly hibernation.

COLD-BLOODED ANIMALS

Reptiles, amphibians, and many fish living in cold climates become inactive in the winter. As the air or water temperature falls, the animals get slower and slower and then come to a complete stop. But there is not such a dramatic change as in the hibernating mammals, because they are cold-blooded animals, and their temperature is always similar to that of the surroundings.

WARM WINTER SLEEP

Before hibernating, the chipmunk tunnels underground and builds a nesting place. It also collects seeds and nuts, which it stores in the tunnel. After it has pushed the earth out, it often loosely plugs up the entrance with earth. The chipmunk sleeps through most of the winter but may wake up on warm winter days, when it will eat some of its food.

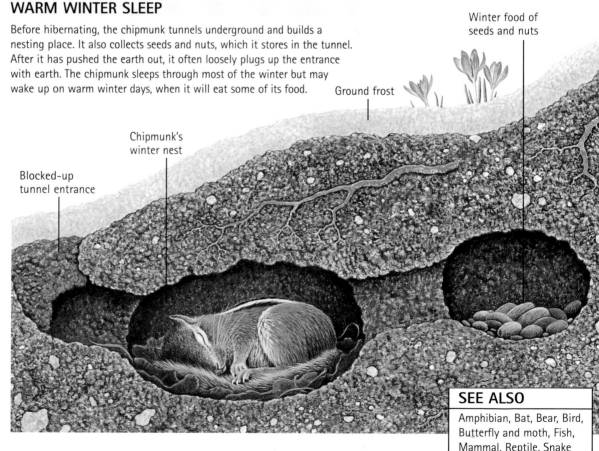

Winter food of seeds and nuts

Ground frost

Chipmunk's winter nest

Blocked-up tunnel entrance

SEE ALSO
Amphibian, Bat, Bear, Bird, Butterfly and moth, Fish, Mammal, Reptile, Snake

191

HINDUISM

Hinduism is one of the oldest existing religions. It began in northern India about 4,000 years ago and is now the most popular religion in southern Asia.

▲ Many small shrines exist by the sides of roads as well as in most Hindu homes. Here, food and flowers are offered and incense and candles burned.

Today, about 80 percent of Indians are Hindu and there are over 800 million Hindus worldwide. Much of Hinduism was developed by people called Aryans, who settled in India from about 1500 B.C.

▲ Shiva is one of the most important of Hindu gods and represents destruction and rebirth.

EARLIEST WRITINGS
The Aryans produced the earliest Hindu writings, called the *Vedas*, in about 1000 B.C. Later there were the famous epic stories, the *Ramayana* and *Mahabharata*. Other important writings led to the creation of the Indian caste system. This is a social and religious system where people are divided into different groups by birth.

MANY GODS
Hindus have three main gods: Brahma (the creator of the universe), Shiva (the destroyer), and Vishnu (the preserver). But they also worship many other gods

and goddesses and believe that all kinds of people and objects can become divine. The cow and the crow, for example, are sacred to Hindus and cannot be killed.

CYCLE OF LIFE
Like Buddhists, all Hindus believe in reincarnation, or being born again after death. They also believe in the importance of living a good life, and in karma, which means that one is punished or rewarded for one's past actions in the next life.

HINDU TEMPLES
Like most Hindu temples, this one in India's capital city, Delhi, is highly ornate. The goddess of good fortune, Lakshmi, is worshiped here in religious rituals, which are usually led by Hindu priests and teachers, who are members of the Brahman caste.

FAST FACTS

• Unlike Buddhism, Hinduism does not have a founder or a rigid system of beliefs

• There are all kinds of religious festivals and pilgrimages. Thousands travel to bathe in the sacred waters of the Ganges River every year

• Hindu wedding celebrations are very colorful and elaborate. When Hindus die, they are cremated

SEE ALSO
Buddhism, Religion

HIPPOPOTAMUS

Hippopotamuses are large, thick-skinned animals with short legs and a massive head and muzzle. They live in the lakes and rivers of tropical Africa.

▲ Hippos normally stay under water for up to six minutes without breathing, and they can actually run under water.

The large, or river, hippo has thick, gray skin and spends much of its time wallowing in shallow water.

The small pygmy hippo has oily, blackish skin and spends less time in the water than the river hippo.

Hippopotamus means "riverine horse" and comes from the Greek words *hippos* (horse) and *potamus* (river). In reality, however, the animal is more like a giant pig.

BARREL ON SHORT LEGS

After the elephant and rhinoceros, the hippopotamus is the world's largest land animal. It is like a barrel with short legs—about 11.5 ft. (3.5m) long, weighing up to 4 tons, and only about 5 ft. (1.5m) high. Hippos generally live in groups of around 5 to 30 strong. They spend most of the daytime wallowing in pools of mud or shallow water, usually with their heads appearing just above the surface. Their eyes, ears, and nostrils are all at the top of the head, so they can see, hear, and breathe without being seen. They have a good sense of smell, although their eyesight is relatively poor.

FEEDING HABITS

In the evening, hippos leave the water to feed. Grass is their favorite food, but they also eat crops and often damage them by trampling through fields. Adult hippos have no enemies apart from people. Calves (young hippos) are sometimes eaten by lions on land and by crocodiles in the water, but they are usually well protected by the adults. An adult hippo can easily bite a crocodile in half with its huge jaws.

A SMALL COUSIN

The pygmy hippopotamus is no more than about 5.75 ft. (1.75m) long, has oily, blackish skin and a rounded head. It lives in the swamps and damp forests of West Africa, but spends less time in the water than its larger, gray-skinned cousin.

FEROCIOUS FIGHTERS

The hippopotamus has a huge head and can open its mouth very wide to reveal curved, daggerlike teeth up to 20 in. (50cm) long. With its mouth wide open, the hippo looks as if it is yawning, but this is really a challenge made by one male to another. The males often fight and can cause terrible wounds with their teeth.

▲ Huge tusklike teeth are used for fighting.

▲ The ears remain closed when under water.

▲ Each hoofed foot has four webbed toes.

▲ The hippo's nostrils close up under water.

SEE ALSO

Africa, Animal, Mammal

HORSE

Horses are four-legged, plant-eating mammals with a single hoof on each foot. Long ago they were wild but today almost all horses are domesticated.

THE HORSE FAMILY
All animals that have a single-toed hoof on the end of each leg belong to the horse family—the group called *Equidae*.

The common zebra has black-and-white stripes and lives wild in Africa.

The ass is smaller than the horse, has long ears, and is usually colored gray.

The Shetland pony is a hardy breed of horse with thick coat and long mane.

Przewalski's horse, found in Mongolia in 1870, is the only truly wild horse left.

Most grazing mammals are cloven-hoofed, which means that their feet end in a pair of hoofed toes. Horses' feet, however, end in a large single hoof. This feature, combined with long and powerful legs, makes horses fast and tireless runners. They are therefore perfectly suited to life in open places, where there is nowhere to hide from danger.

WILD HORSES

Horses are sociable animals, and in the wild live in herds of about 10 to 20. Mares (female horses) usually breed at the age of about two or three years, and normally have one foal a year. At one time, herds of wild horses roamed across the grassy plains of eastern Europe and central Asia. They were preyed upon by wolves and other predators, and hunted by people for food. But about 6,000 years ago, humans began to tame horses. From that moment, the history of the horse abruptly changed.

PRZEWALSKI'S HORSE

Domesticated horses soon outnumbered wild ones, which became increasingly rare. There were originally three different kinds of wild horse. But by the late 1800s, only one was left, called Przewalski's horse, which lived in a remote part of Mongolia. Today, there are over 700 Przewalski's horses in zoos around the world.

PULLING POWER

Horses have been bred for a wide variety of uses. Some of them were originally bred for their pulling power, and were used by farmers to pull plows and farm carts in the days before tractors were invented. Today, there are nearly 200 different breeds of horse. They include huge draft horses, which can measure nearly 6.5 ft. (2m) high at the shoulder, Shetland ponies, and the Falabella horse from Argentina, which is smaller than many dogs.

▲ Many North American rodeo events such as steer wrestling have evolved from working with cattle.

HORSES TODAY

Today, horses are used in every continent except Antarctica. In many countries, they still carry on traditional roles of providing transportation and a livelihood for their owners. In North America, they have played a vital role in cattle herding for over 350 years; Australians still use hardy horses called walers that were bred by early settlers. Other uses today include policing, ceremonial and sports events, hunting, and riding for fun. But one of the most popular events is horse racing. For this, thoroughbreds descended from Arabian stallions of the 1700s are mostly used.

▲ Horses used for showjumping need to have a combination of power, stamina, boldness, and agility in order to handle the tough demands of the sport.

PARTS OF THE HORSE

The overall shape and appearance of a horse is called its conformation, while the parts of the horse's body are called the points. A horse's skeleton gives clues about its breed. For example, a draft horse has large, thick bones to support its weight whereas a racehorse has long, fine bones that help it to run swiftly.

Quarters
Dock
Croup
Flank
Back
Withers
Mane
Crest
Poll
Forelock
Muzzle
Thigh
Chest
Molar teeth
Incisor teeth
Stifle
Forearm
Shoulder
Knee
Fetlock
Hoof

▲ The incisor (front) teeth can be used to tell a horse's age. As the horse grows older, they change in shape, becoming longer and projecting farther forward. The gap between the incisor and molar teeth is where the bit (mouthpiece) is placed when the horse is bridled.

Hock joint
Cannon bone
Splint bone
Long pastern bone
Short pastern bone
Coffin bone

Heel
Frog
Hoof wall
Sole
Shoe

FAST FACTS

• The Roman Emperor Caligula is said to have made his horse, Incitatus, consul—a very high rank in Roman government

• The earliest ancestor of the horse had four toes and was the size of a fox

• Horses are measured in hands from the ground to the top of the withers. A hand is 4 in. (10cm)

• A horse goes through four gaits, from slow to fast: walk, trot, canter, and gallop

▲ The modern horse stands on only one toe (its hoof), but the two splint bones on either side of the cannon bone are remnants of the early horse's other toes.

▲ Horses have metal shoes nailed to their hooves to protect the hoof wall from wearing down on rough or hard ground. Shoes must be replaced every few weeks. Before they can be fitted, the new growth of hoof has to be trimmed and the hoof reshaped.

SEE ALSO

Animal, Evolution, Mammal, Mongol Empire, Sports, Transportation, World War I

HOUSEHOLD APPLIANCE

Household appliances are devices that make day-to-day jobs around the house easier. They have changed our lifestyles and improved public hygiene and diet.

Most toasters pop up when sensors inside detect that a set temperature has been reached.

Stoves can be designed to burn any fuel. Modern ceramic stove tops like this use electricity.

The first washing machine (invented by Hamilton Smith, U.S.A., 1858) relied on muscle power.

Early refrigerators (invented by Ferdinand Carre, France, 1858) were cooled by blocks of ice.

Irons have been used for centuries, first heated on a stove, then by gas, then, in 1891, by electricity.

Houses in developed countries contain a wide range of appliances. Many, including stoves, refrigerators, freezers, food processors, and microwave ovens, are used in the kitchen to preserve and prepare food. Others, such as washing machines, tumble dryers, dishwashers, and vacuum cleaners, help with cleaning. Since the invention of electricity—a form of energy that can be converted into movement or heat—more sophisticated appliances have beeen produced.

WASH DAY
Before labor-saving appliances, routine housekeeping was a full-time job. A day was set aside to wash clothes using a washboard and a mangle. Perishable food could not be stored easily, so people shopped almost every day, and preparing meals

VACUUM CLEANERS

While the suction pulls dirty air in, a spinning brush helps dislodge dirt. Bags are finely perforated and act as a filter, while bagless designs (right) use a whirling vortex of air to spin dirt out—air is pushed out, but dirt is trapped inside.

Air spins at up to 923 mph (1486kph)

Air minus dirt and dust

Brush

Dirty air

▶ Percy Spenser (U.S.A.) invented the microwave oven in 1945 using technology developed for military defense during World War II.

took longer. Rugs had to be hung up outside and beaten to get the dust out.

MAKING A MEAL OF IT
Most stoves use gas or electricity, and these are easy to control. Methane, butane, or propane gas goes through a valve and burns in the air, releasing heat. Electric stoves have elements containing wire which resists the flow of electricity. As the current is forced along this wire, electrical energy is turned into heat energy. Coffeemakers and toasters work in the same way.

MICROWAVE OVENS
Microwave ovens contain a magnetron, which turns electricity into microwaves, or high-frequency radio waves. Microwaves make molecules of water and fat in the surface of the food vibrate very fast, producing heat. This heat spreads from the outside to the middle of the food.

WASHING MACHINES
These have microprocessor control systems. A powerful electric motor turns the drum full of wet clothing back and forth through a series of cycles, which duplicate the stages of washing by hand. The clothes are agitated in hot detergent, then rinsed and spun at high speed, which forces out most of the water.

Dust particles

The electric motor turns a fan which creates a partial vacuum and causes air to rush in, pulling dust with it

SEE ALSO
Design, Electricity, Invention, Machine, Technology, Wavelength

HOUSING

Housing includes any form of building or structure in which people live. It can provide shelter for a single person, a family, or several family groups.

Since at least 50,000 years ago, people have built tents or shelters from sticks, animals hides, or turf. When people settled down to farming, they began to build more permanent houses.

Gypsies of Europe live in horse-drawn wagons.

Indonesians build houses on stilts in damp areas.

The Mongolian *yurt* can be folded and moved.

Native American *pueblos* are made of mud bricks.

Sudanese huts have small windows to keep out heat.

Suburban houses have garages and yards.

BUILDING MATERIALS
For thousands of years, people used natural materials, such as wood or stone, that they found nearby. Clay and chopped straw were mixed, then shaped into bricks, and dried in the sun. Later, people learned to bake the bricks in ovens to make them tougher and more waterproof. Modern houses may still be made of bricks, or of modern materials such as concrete, steel, and glass.

INTO THE CITY
In the 1700s and 1800s, during the Industrial Revolution, people crowded into cities to find work. Whole streets of new houses were built, often by mill or factory owners, to meet demand. Today, cities continue to expand, but homes in outlying surburbs take advantage of space by having front or back yards.

CLIMATE AND DESIGN
In forested areas of North America and Scandinavia, wood is an important building material. Elsewhere, houses are more likely to be built of bricks or stone.

▲ The shanty homes of beggars contrast sharply with apartments for the wealthy in Mumbai (Bombay), India.

In hot countries, houses have thick walls to keep the inside cool. Houses in areas with a lot of snow or rain usually have sloping roofs so the water can run off.

COMPUTER CONTROL
Modern houses are equipped with gas, electricity, water, and drainage systems. Soon houses may be computer-controlled, with lighting, heating, security, TV, and other features run automatically.

◄ Millions of people around the world live in tall apartment buildings, many of which were built during the 1950s and 1960s, especially in heavily populated areas.

▼ Energy-saving ideas, such as these solar panels, make modern houses more efficient.

SEE ALSO
Architecture, Castle, City, Construction, Materials

HOVERCRAFT

Hovercraft travel on a cushion of air, which greatly reduces water resistance. They can travel over both water and land, something no other craft can do.

The British *SRN6* hovercraft, built in 1965, is still in service over 30 years later.

The *ABS* hovercraft circumnavigated the Baltic Sea in 1994.

The Russian giant assault hovercraft delivers troops and equipment onto land.

The American *Hovermarine* is designed to seat up to 150 passengers.

When a boat moves, the surrounding water pushes against it and slows it down. It could go much faster if it could travel above the water instead of through it. The hovercraft and its cousin, the hydrofoil, both provide a solution to this problem.

CUSHIONS AND SKIRTS

The air cushion that holds a hovercraft up is created by one or more powerful lift fans. Air pumped by these fans is prevented from escaping too quickly by a flexible rubber skirt all around the edge. Hydrofoils, on the other hand, use winglike foils to lift them from the water.

THE FIRST HOVERCRAFT

People experimented with vehicles supported by air cushions as long ago as 1877, but the technology to build a

▲ Hydrofoils have aerofoil-shaped underwater wings, or foils, which lift the craft's hull out of the water as it speeds up. They are powered by propellers or water jets.

hovercraft was not available until the 1900s. The first successful hovercraft was built by the British engineer Christopher Cockerell in 1959.

SKIMMING WAVES

Hovercraft have a number of uses. The largest hovercraft carry passengers and their cars across short stretches of water such as the English Channel. Small, one-person hovercraft often race against each other in sports events. Military hovercraft transport troops and equipment onto beaches.

HOW THE HOVERCRAFT WORKS

Because a hovercraft is raised up on a cushion of air, it can travel over water or land and reach speeds of up to 80 mph (130kph), much faster than an ordinary ship. Two large fans on each side of the hovercraft suck in air and push it underneath the craft to lift it up. Another two large fans at the rear, with rudders for steering, propel the craft forward.

Radar aerial · Control cabin · Door · Rotating bow thruster · Passenger seat · Propeller · Rudder · Driveshaft · Luggage holders · Flexible rubber skirt · Passenger door · Drive belt · Lift fans · Diesel engine

SEE ALSO

Boat, Ship

HUMAN BODY

The human body is made up of a skeleton, organs, outer skin, and specialized systems, all of which work together to make it one of the most complex of all life–forms.

▼ Different ethnic groups vary in appearance, often as a result of adapting over thousands of years to climates and conditions.

Arabian

African

European

Chinese

Indian

The human body is similar to the bodies of other large mammals, especially apes. But it is also unique in many ways. It can walk upright on its two back legs. Its fingers are capable of precise, delicate movements, and its large brain is far more complex than that of any other creature. These features make humans a separate species in the animal kingdom, called *Homo sapiens*.

BUILDING BLOCKS
The human body is made up of more than 50 trillion tiny building blocks, called cells. These are all microscopic in size, and vary in shape and structure according to their functions. Every second, the body makes more than five million cells of various kinds, to replace those that wear out and die.

BODY TISSUES
Cells of the same kind are grouped together to form tissues. For example, bone tissue is strong and stiff, to provide the body with an inner supporting framework—the skeleton.

▶ Through regular stretching exercises, the human body can become very supple and capable of bending and twisting in extreme ways.

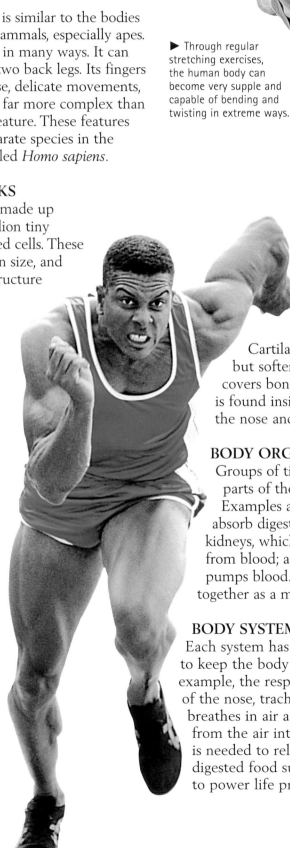

▶ Athletes train hard in order to build up their muscles and reach peak body fitness.

Cartilage tissue is also strong, but softer and smoother. It covers bones where they join, and is found inside flexible parts like the nose and ears.

BODY ORGANS
Groups of tissue make up the main parts of the body, called organs. Examples are the intestines, which absorb digested food into blood; the kidneys, which filter waste products from blood; and the heart, which pumps blood. Several organs work together as a major body system.

BODY SYSTEMS
Each system has a very important job to keep the body alive and healthy. For example, the respiratory system consists of the nose, trachea, and lungs. It breathes in air and absorbs oxygen from the air into the blood. Oxygen is needed to release the energy from digested food substances, in order to power life processes. ▶

DIGESTIVE SYSTEM

The body needs to maintain its cells and tissues, and repair worn-out parts. The raw materials for growth and repair come from food, which is processed by the digestive system: the mouth, teeth, esophagus, stomach, and intestines. Food is broken down into nutrients and energy-rich chemicals, which pass into the blood. Waste matter passes out of the body as feces.

URINARY SYSTEM

The life processes inside cells produce waste products, some of which are removed by the urinary system. This consists of the kidneys, which filter the wastes from the blood to form urine, and the bladder, which stores the urine before it is removed from the body.

COORDINATION AND CONTROL

The body parts and organs do not work on their own. Two main control systems keep them functioning together in a coordinated fashion. The hormonal system consists of body parts called endocrine glands that make substances called hormones. These pass into the blood and around the body. Each hormone affects the chemical activity of certain cells and tissues, making them speed up or slow down.

NERVOUS SYSTEM

The second control system, the nervous system, is a network of wirelike nerves throughout the body, with the brain as the control center. The brain receives information as tiny nerve signals from the sensory system—mainly the eyes, ears,

SKIN AND MUSCLES

The skin protects the inside of the body from dirt, too much dryness or wetness, injury, harmful rays, and germs. It also helps to keep the body warm in cold weather and cool in hot conditions. The muscular system consists of more than 640 muscles. In most cases, each end of a muscle is joined to a bone. When the muscle shortens or contracts, it pulls on the bones and moves that part of the body.

Face muscles

Neck muscle

Deltoid (shoulder muscle)

Biceps (upper arm muscle)

Pectorals (chest muscles)

Rectus abdominis (abdominal muscles)

Quadriceps (front thigh muscle)

Gastrocnemius (calf muscles)

BODY ORGANS

An organ is made up of two or more types of tissue that work together to perform a specific function. The heart, for example, is an organ whose function is to pump blood around the body. It is made up of muscle tissue, connective tissue, and epithelial tissue.

Liver

Lung

Small intestine

Large intestine

Stomach

Pancreas

Heart

nose, tongue, and skin. These sense organs detect what is happening around the body. The brain also sends signals to muscles, telling them when and how to contract and produce movements. It is also the site of mental processes such as thoughts, feelings, emotions, and memories.

REPRODUCTION

The human body reproduces like any other mammal's. The reproductive system consists of either female or male sex organs. The male ones make sperm cells; the female ones contain egg cells. When a sperm cell fertilizes an egg cell, the egg begins to multiply rapidly. Over a period of nine months, it grows and develops within the mother's body into an embryo, then a fetus, and is born as a baby.

◀ The average body reaches its peak physical power and maximum size around the age of 18 to 25 years. After this it begins to age. Signs of aging include wrinkled skin, gray hair, balding in men, shrinking, weaker muscles, slower reactions, and less sharp senses.

GROWING UP

Some animals are active and independent within minutes of birth. But a human baby needs food, warmth and care for many months. As it grows into a child, it learns to sit, stand, walk, talk, read, write and acquire many other skills. This takes years because human society is very complex, with many customs, traditions, rules and laws.

CIRCULATORY AND LYMPHATIC SYSTEMS

The circulatory system consists of the heart, blood vessels, and blood. It transports oxygen from the lungs, and nutrients and energy-rich substances to all parts of the body. The lymphatic and immune systems produce antibodies which are released into the bloodstream to fight off disease.

- Oxygenated blood
- Deoxygenated blood
- Lymphatic system

Peripheral blood vessels in limbs

Lymph vessels

Lymph nodes

Heart

Aorta (main artery from heart)

Phalanges (finger bones)

Metacarpals (palm bones)

Cranium (skull)

Humerus (upper arm bone)

Ulna (near little finger)

Radius (near thumb)

Clavicle (collarbone)

Sternum (breastbone)

Rib

Spine (backbone)

Ilium (hipbone)

Coccyx (tailbone)

Femur (thighbone)

Patella (kneecap)

Fibula (calf bone)

Tibia (shinbone)

Tarsals (anklebones)

Phalanges (toe bones)

Calcaneus (heel)

THE SKELETON

The human skeleton consists of 206 bones. These are rigid and tough, and provide a strong supporting framework inside the body. They are linked at joints, which allow the bones to move in certain ways without coming apart.

SEE ALSO

Blood, Brain and nervous system, Heart and circulatory system, Immune system, Reproduction

IMMUNE SYSTEM

The body protects itself from illness and disease using its immune system, which constantly cleans the blood and body tissues and attacks invading germs.

EDWARD JENNER
Jenner was a British doctor (1749-1823) who developed the technique of vaccination—a way to provide artificial immunity against disease. In 1796 he vaccinated patients with harmless cowpox to protect them against deadly smallpox.

The immune system is one of the body's most complicated systems. It includes a series of glands—known as lymph glands, or lymph nodes—that are found throughout the body, but especially in the neck, armpits, and groin. These glands are connected by a network of tubes called lymph vessels, and both glands and vessels contain a pale, milky fluid called lymph.

MILLIONS OF CELLS

Lymph and lymph glands are home to the main kind of cell in the immune system, called the lymphocyte. These cells are also found in large quantities in the blood, where they form one kind of white blood cell, and in the fluids that bathe all the body parts. There are about two trillion lymphocytes in the human body.

RECOGNIZING INVADERS

Germs such as bacteria and viruses are continually entering the body by being breathed in, or swallowed, or through a cut. As soon as germs enter, lymphocytes called T- and B-cells identify them as "nonself," or foreign particles. They do this by detecting unfamiliar substances, or antigens, on the germs' outer surface.

ON THE ATTACK

Some of the B-cells then start to multiply and form plasma cells. These cells produce Y-shaped substances known as antibodies that attach themselves to the antigens and cause the germs to burst, or clump together so they cannot multiply. T-cells produce chemicals that kill infected cells. They also help another type of white blood cell, called a macrophage, to destroy germs by engulfing, or eating, them.

LONG MEMORIES

Different germs carry different antigens. When a germ infects the body, causing an illness, B-cells known as memory cells remember its antigens so that, if the germ enters again, the memory cells can quickly activate the immune system to fight off the illness. This protection against disease is called immunity.

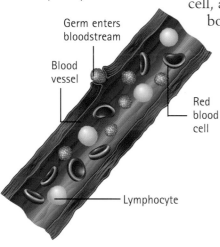

Germ enters bloodstream

Blood vessel

Red blood cell

Lymphocyte

1 When a germ enters the bloodstream—for example, through a cut—white blood cells, known as lymphocytes, are drawn to the site.

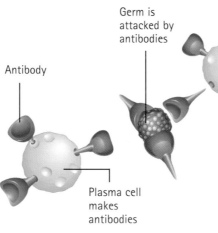

Germ is attacked by antibodies

Antibody

Plasma cell makes antibodies

2 Some lymphocytes multiply and form plasma cells which make antibodies that attack the germ.

Germ is engulfed by a macrophage

3 Other lymphocytes— certain types of T-cell— help to attract macrophages to the site. These swallow the germ and dissolve it.

IMMUNITY AGAINST DISEASE

Lymphocytes and macrophages work together to destroy germs that cause disease. Often, they do not succeed in killing a new germ before it has multiplied and caused an illness. However, once the memory cells have been primed, the immune system is ready for action. Next time it meets the germ it can quickly make the right antibodies to fight off the infection. Immunity can also be artificially induced. A specially weakened form of the germ is swallowed or injected into the body. It is not strong enough to cause illness, but it activates the immune system to remember the real germ in the future.

SEE ALSO
Disease, Gland, Human body, Medicine

INCA

The Inca were people who lived in the Andes Mountains of South America. From about 1200 to the mid-1500s, they ruled a rich and sophisticated empire.

KEY DATES

c.1300 The Inca make Cuzco their capital city

1438 The Inca Pachacuti Yupanqui becomes ruler and begins the conquest of an empire

1525 Huayna Capac expands the empire to its largest extent

1532 The Spanish invasion begins

1572 The death of the last Inca, Tupac Amaru

The Inca had no writing system. They used knotted, colored strings, called *quipus*, to keep records.

Gold, silver, and precious stones were used to craft beautiful objects used by noble families and in religious rituals.

The Inca Empire was centered around Cuzco—an upland valley in the Andes Mountains of Peru. The empire stretched into present-day Ecuador, Colombia, Bolivia, Argentina, and Chile. Although made up of many tribes, its ruling emperor and nobles were members of the Inca tribe. The empire collapsed after the Spanish invaded in 1532.

GOD ON EARTH

The first great Inca emperor was Pachacuti Yupanqui, a warrior who came to power in 1438. His son, Tupac, and grandson, Huayna Capac, extended the empire. The emperor was known as "Inca." He was considered a god, a descendant of the sun.

RUNNING AN EMPIRE

The empire was strictly governed. The ordinary people worked many days each year for the emperor, planting crops, fighting battles, or building bridges and roads. The roads ran throughout the empire, crossing mountain ravines by rope bridges. In places, roads were carved from rock, elsewhere they were paved. The roads were mostly used by *chasquis*, the royal messengers, and merchants, who used llamas to carry goods. There were no wheeled vehicles.

EVERYDAY LIFE

Most of the 12 million people were farmers. They kept llamas and alpacas for wool and meat, and grew Indian corn, potatoes, and other vegetables in terraced fields. Wool and cotton cloth was woven by hand, and pots made from clay. Stone fortresses guarded cities and roads, but most families lived in houses made from mud bricks.

GREAT FESTIVAL OF THE SUN

The Capac Raymi, the Great Festival of the Sun, was held in Cuzco on the longest and shortest days of the year. At dawn, the emperor offered a golden cup of sacred beer and sacrificed a white llama to Inti, the sun god, to gain his help and protection. Other important gods included the supreme deity Viracocha and the goddesses of the earth and the sea.

SEE ALSO

Empire, South America

INDIAN SUBCONTINENT

The Indian subcontinent is a huge land mass which includes the countries of India, Pakistan, Bangladesh, Nepal, and Bhutan. It makes up one tenth of Asia.

BANGLADESH
Area: 51,700 sq. mi.
Population: 133,376,684
Capital: Dhaka
Language: Bengali
Currency: Taka

BHUTAN
Area: 18,000 sq. mi.
Population: 2,094,176
Capital: Thimphu
Language: Dzongkha
Currency: Ngultrum,
Indian rupee

INDIA
Area: 1,148,000 sq. mi.
Population: 1,045,845,226
Capital: New Delhi
Languages: Hindi, English
Currency: Rupee

MALDIVES
Area: 115 sq. mi.
Population: 320,165
Capital: Male (Male Island)
Language: Divehi
Currency: Rufiyaa

NEPAL
Area: 52,800 sq. mi.
Population: 25,873,917
Capital: Kathmandu
Language: Nepali
Currency: Nepalese rupee

Three quarters of the Indian subcontinent is covered by India itself. As well as Pakistan, Bangladesh, Nepal, and Bhutan on the mainland, there are two island nations in the south—Sri Lanka and the Maldives.

FROM HIGH TO LOW
High mountain ranges lie in the north of the region, including the Himalayas, which contain the world's highest peak, Mount Everest (29,028 ft./8,848m), on the border between Nepal and China. Southern India consists largely of a plateau called the Deccan. Bordering the Deccan are two low mountain ranges, the Eastern and Western Ghats, edged by narrow coastal plains.

WATER AND WINDS
The longest river in the region, the Indus (1,800 mi./2,897km), flows from the Himalayas through Pakistan. The Brahmaputra (1,680 mi./2,704km) and Ganges rivers (1,550 mi./2,494km) join in Bangladesh and flow across the world's largest delta, into the Bay of Bengal. Cherrapunji, near Shillong, just north

▲ Religion and festivals play an important part in Indian life. Many people go on pilgrimages to holy places like the city of Varanasi on the banks of the Ganges river. The waters of the river are considered sacred.

of Bangladesh, is the rainiest place on Earth, receiving an average of 426 in. (10,820mm) a year. Most rain falls from June to October, when monsoon winds blow from the sea. These have little effect on the dry northwest—the Thar Desert along the Pakistan–India border has less than 10 in. (250mm) of rain a year.

TROPICAL TREES
Few plants grow in the northwest, except on the wetter mountain slopes, but most of the Indian subcontinent has plenty of farming and grazing land. Valuable trees in tropical forests include ironwood, rosewood, and teak. Bamboo also grows in many areas.

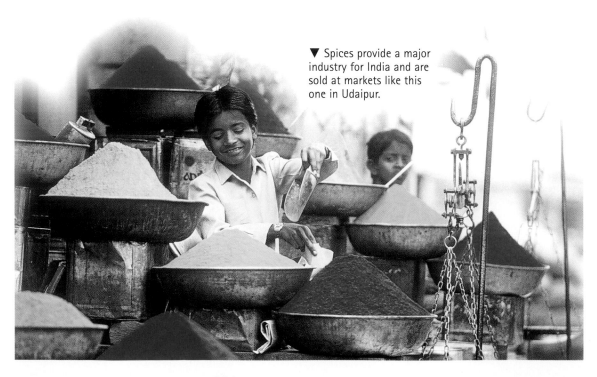

▼ Spices provide a major industry for India and are sold at markets like this one in Udaipur.

ENDANGERED SPECIES

Some wild elephants still live in the forests, but many have been tamed and work as beasts of burden. Overhunting and the destruction of forests and other habitats have meant that some animals—including Asian lions, cheetahs, and tigers—have become endangered species. Others, such as the one-horned Indian rhinoceros, came close to extinction, but are now protected.

MORE WILDLIFE

Wild boar and buffalo are common, and mongooses are found throughout the region. The cobra is the best-known reptile, and the region's many birds include the myna bird, which can imitate human speech. Mountain animals include brown and black bears, deer, the rare snow leopard, the markhor (a kind of wild goat), various kinds of wild sheep, and wild yaks.

▼ Bangladesh has few industries apart from jute processing. It grows the best-quality jute in the world, which is made into rope and string.

▲ Ihuhu Island is one of 1,200 coral islands that make up the Maldives. Most are just 6.5 ft. (2m) above sea level.

GROWING POPULATIONS

With a population of over one billion, India has more people than any other country apart from China. Pakistan, with a population of 147 million, ranks sixth in the world and Bangladesh, with 133 million people, is the world's eighth largest country.

INDIA'S LANGUAGES

India has 19 major languages and more than 1,650 dialects and minor languages. The two main language groups are the Indo-European, which includes Hindi—the most widely spoken language—and the Dravidian languages, including Tamil, which are spoken mainly in the south. English is also spoken by many Indians.

PAKISTAN
Area: 300,700 sq. mi.
Population: 147,663,429
Capital: Islamabad
Language: Urdu
Currency: Pakistani rupee

SRI LANKA
Area: 25,332 sq. mi.
Population: 19,576,783
Capital: Colombo
Languages: Sinhala,Tamil
Currency: Sri Lankan rupee

▲ The Taj Mahal at Agra was built between 1632 and 1653 at the request of the Mogul emperor Shah Jahan, who wanted it as a tomb for his wife.

URDU AND BENGALI

Pakistan's official language is Urdu, but less than a tenth of the people speak it as their first language. Instead, they speak the language of their community. The largest communities are the Punjabi, Sindhi, Pushtun, and Baluchi. In Bangladesh, more than 95 percent of the people speak the official language, Bengali.

RELIGIONS OF INDIA

Beautiful temples, mosques, and other religious buildings are everywhere. In places such as Udaipur, India, there are spectacular palaces built hundreds of years ago for princes. Today, Hindus make up 82 percent of India's population, with Muslims forming another 12 percent. India also has large numbers of Christians, Sikhs, Buddhists, and Jains. Islam, the Muslim religion, is the chief religion in Pakistan, Bangladesh, and the Maldives.

INFLUENCE OF BUDDHA

Hinduism is the official religion of Nepal, but the country was the birthplace of Buddha, so many Nepalese have combined the beliefs and practices of the two religions. Buddhism is the chief religion in Bhutan and of the Sinhalese in Sri Lanka, although a minority group in Sri Lanka, the Tamils, mainly follows Hinduism. Differences between these groups have led to fighting between government troops and Tamil guerrillas.

FARM LIFE

More than three fifths of the people of the Indian subcontinent are farmers who live in villages and farm the land around them. Farming is the leading activity, and rice is the main crop in India, Bangladesh, and Sri Lanka. In Pakistan, wheat is the leading food crop. Tea is grown in northeast India, around Darjeeling and in Assam, as well as in Sri Lanka.

▲ Agriculture is Sri Lanka's main economic activity. Important crops, including tea, are grown on large plantations.

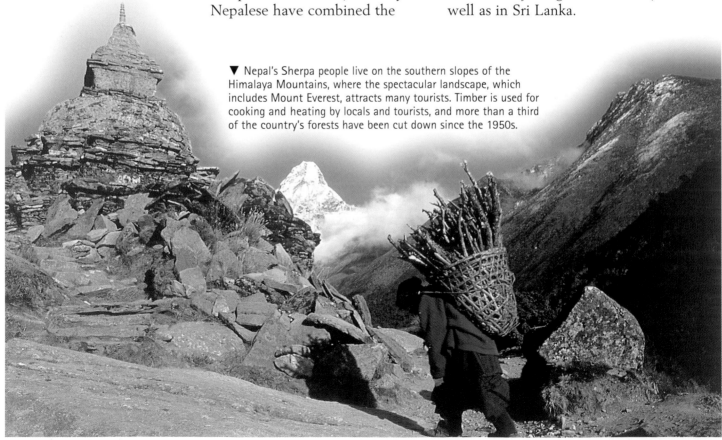

▼ Nepal's Sherpa people live on the southern slopes of the Himalaya Mountains, where the spectacular landscape, which includes Mount Everest, attracts many tourists. Timber is used for cooking and heating by locals and tourists, and more than a third of the country's forests have been cut down since the 1950s.

▲ In Bhutan, local women make cheese from yaks' milk.

Most farmers have a low standard of living and live in houses made of mud and straw. India has more cattle and buffalo than any other country, but Hindus consider them sacred and they cannot be killed for food. Fishing is also a major activity.

DEVELOPING INDUSTRY
The Indian subcontinent has plenty of coal, iron ore, and other minerals. There is some oil, and petroleum refining is an important industry. Textiles are leading products, and Mumbai and Delhi are developing large electronics industries.

CITY LIFE AND EDUCATION
The region has six cities with more than five million people. These are the four Indian cities of Mumbai (formerly Bombay), Kolkata (Calcutta), Delhi (made up of the walled city of Old Delhi and the capital New Delhi), and Chennai (formerly Madras), as well as the Bangladeshi capital Dhaka and Karachi in Pakistan. Sri Lanka has a good education system, but in the rest of the Indian subcontinent there are millions of people who cannot read or write. The education system in India is, however, gradually improving.

EARLY TIMES
From the late 1700s, India, Pakistan, and Bangladesh formed part of a huge colony called British India. In 1947, British India became independent, splitting into two parts—modern India and Pakistan, which was created for Muslims. In 1971, East Pakistan broke away and became the separate country of Bangladesh. Sri Lanka became independent from Britain in 1948, as did the Maldives in 1968.

DIFFICULT DIVISION
At the time of the partition of British India, the status of Kashmir in the north was not satisfactorily settled. Part of this territory now falls within northeast Pakistan, but the bulk lies within the Indian states of Jammu and Kashmir. Guerrillas and governments are in dispute over whether Kashmir should remain part of India, become part of Pakistan, or become independent.

◀ Pakistan's national cricket team is world famous. Children play the game from an early age.

GANDHI
Mohandas K. Gandhi was born in India in 1869. From the 1920s, he used peaceful protests to lead India to independence. He became known as Mahatma, meaning "great soul." He was assassinated in 1948.

FAST FACTS
• Indians call their country Bharat after a legendary monarch
• The name India comes from an ancient word *Sindhu* meaning "river"
• India is the world's seventh largest country
• India's railroad system is the largest in Asia

SEE ALSO
Asia, Buddhism, Hinduism, Islam, Mountain and valley

INDONESIA

Indonesia, in Southeast Asia, is the world's largest island group. There are more than 17,000 islands, about half of which are inhabited.

Area: 705,200 sq. mi.
Population: 232,073,071
Capital: Jakarta
Language: Bahasa Indonesia
Currency: Rupiah

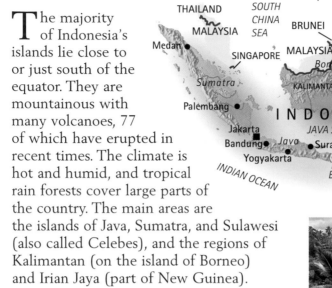

The majority of Indonesia's islands lie close to or just south of the equator. They are mountainous with many volcanoes, 77 of which have erupted in recent times. The climate is hot and humid, and tropical rain forests cover large parts of the country. The main areas are the islands of Java, Sumatra, and Sulawesi (also called Celebes), and the regions of Kalimantan (on the island of Borneo) and Irian Jaya (part of New Guinea).

WILDLIFE

The western islands of Indonesia were once linked by land to Asia, and many Asian animals such as elephants and orangutans can be found there. The eastern islands, once linked to Australia, contain animals such as cockatoos and birds of paradise.

▲ A group of Hindu temples at Prambanan near Yogyakarta are some of Java's important ruins.

▲ Rice, Indonesia's main food, is grown on terraced fields. Volcanic ash makes the soil rich and fertile.

WEALTH OF LANGUAGES

Most of Indonesia's people are Malays. Apart from the national language, about 300 other languages and dialects are spoken. More than 80 percent of the people are Muslims, making Indonesia the world's largest Islamic country.

LIFE AND WORK

Many Indonesians live in rural villages, some in houses raised on stilts. Industry is growing rapidly, however, leading to the development of large modern cities such as Jakarta and Surabaya on Java. The forests are rich in timber and the seas provide good fishing. Minerals include tin, nickel, copper, and oil. Factories make clothing and electrical goods for export.

PREHISTORIC PEOPLES

People have lived in Indonesia since prehistoric times. There were Hindu and Buddhist kingdoms from the 700s, before the arrival of Islam. Portuguese traders came in the 1500s, then the Dutch colonized the area in the late 1800s, calling it the East Indies. Eventually, in 1949, Indonesia became a republic.

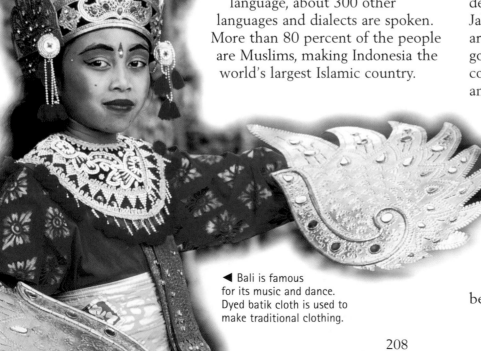

◄ Bali is famous for its music and dance. Dyed batik cloth is used to make traditional clothing.

SEE ALSO

Asia, Islam, Malaysia, Rain forest, Southeast Asia, Volcano

INDUSTRIAL REVOLUTION

The Industrial Revolution is the name given to the great changes that took place when people began to use steam power to make goods in factories.

Thomas Newcomen built the first steam engine in 1712 to pump water.

In the 1700s, society in Britain began to change from being based on agriculture, with people working at home, to being dominated by factories and industrial cities. The changes were caused by the invention of machines that made goods faster and more cheaply than before. The owners of the new machines employed other people to work on them. In this way, the factory came into existence, surrounded by houses for the workers. Often several factories were built together, from which a new town developed.

The spinning jenny of 1764 could spin several threads at one time.

In 1777, the world's first iron bridge was erected in Shropshire, England.

Eli Whitney's cotton gin of 1794 separated cotton seeds from fiber at speed.

Locomotives, such as the German *Der Adler* of 1835, powered the rail boom.

WOMEN'S WORK

Factory jobs often required skill rather than strength. Women were as good as men for such work, and many single women gained independence by earning a wage for themselves. Most women gave up work when they married, to run the household and family.

KING COTTON

The Industrial Revolution began around 1760 when new machines that could quickly spin cotton thread were invented in Britain. These made thread so fast that hand weavers could not keep up. So weaving machines were invented.

THE POWER OF STEAM

At first, waterwheels powered the weaving machines, but by 1780 these could not cope. Simple steam engines were being used to pump water out of mines. Between 1764 and 1790, Scottish engineer James Watt improved the steam engine so it could drive machines. By 1800, there were about 500 steam engines at work in Britain. For the first time, people had an artificial source of power.

RAW MATERIALS

The Industrial Revolution required three things: iron to make machines, coal to burn in steam engines, and money to pay for ▶

BRUNEL
The British engineer Isambard Kingdom Brunel (1806–59) built railroads, bridges, and the world's largest ship.

RAW MATERIALS

The Industrial Revolution required iron for machines, coal to burn in steam engines, and money to pay for them both. By 1750, Britain had all three and became the first country to industrialize. The iron industry grew quickly after 1709, when Abraham Darby first used coke to smelt iron (melt the iron ore). This was cheaper and more efficient than the old way using charcoal. New coal mines were dug to supply coal for steam engines and coke for ironworks.

CANALS AND RAILROADS

The new industrial products required a transportation system to move them to people. Between 1750 and 1830, canals were dug, linking major cities and rivers. Most roads remained poor, but in 1804, Richard Trevithick built the world's first steam locomotive. By the 1830s, Britain had embarked on a railroad craze, and railroads were soon being built across western Europe and North America. By 1870, many of their cities had been linked by rail. Belgium, France, Germany, and the United States began industrializing after 1815. By 1900, the U.S. and Germany had overtaken Britain in steel production.

BUSINESS BOOM

The new machines made goods faster and more cheaply. Factory and mine owners made huge profits, some of which they spent on more machines, so creating new jobs. Investors saved small amounts of money in banks, which then lent large amounts to industrialists. This developing "capitalist" system raised money to build factories, offices, and houses.

A HARD LIFE

For many workers, life in the factories and mines was hard and dangerous. Men, women, and children worked 13 or more hours a day, often for low wages. Many workers

DEVELOPING INDUSTRIAL AREAS

The new factories were built near canals and railroads so that raw materials could be brought in and finished goods taken to markets easily. Houses were built to accommodate the workers, but many industrial areas became slums, and lacked running water, drains, and other basic services.

KEY DATES

1769 James Watt perfects the steam engine

1794 Eli Whitney invents the cotton gin

1807 Robert Fulton's first steamboat

1831 First U.S. steam-powered railroad (South Carolina)

1834 Cyrus McCormick demonstrates his reaper

1844 Samuel Morse sends first telegraph message

1849 Elias Howe patents the sewing machine

were killed or injured by unsafe machinery before new safety laws were enforced. Towns grew rapidly and without proper planning, leaving some areas without drains or clean water. Diseases that were caught from unclean water (like cholera) or in crowded conditions (tuberculosis) became common and killed thousands of people. These conditions caused social unrest and even riots.

CAMPAIGNERS AND REFORMERS

Gradually, laws to shorten working hours and stop child labor were introduced. Trade unions, at first banned, campaigned for better pay and conditions for workers.

In time, reformers won improved working conditions and schooling for all children. Slums were cleared and new laws controlled factory and housing development.

LONG-TERM EFFECTS

During the Industrial Revolution, cities grew rapidly as people began to leave the countryside to find work. Industrialization spread worldwide during the 1900s, and the world economy today is geared to the production of goods, though some countries in Africa and Southeast Asia remain dependent on agriculture or services. People now enjoy higher standards of living than ever before, but at a high cost to the environment. Industrialization has caused pollution and used up resources such as coal, oil, and minerals. However, new technology is being developed to solve some of the problems created by industrialization.

URBAN DEVELOPMENT

Streets of attached houses were built around factories to house the workers. Gradually, some factory owners or town councils improved conditions for the workers by building schools and churches.

CHILD LABOR
In the 1700s and 1800s, factory owners employed children, many of them under ten years of age, to work in factories and mines. They had to work long hours in dangerous and unhealthy conditions. However, by 1900, most industrialized countries had banned child labor.

SEE ALSO

Coal, Engine, Iron and steel, Machine, Pollution, Train, Transportation, Water power

INDUSTRY

Industry covers all the different kinds of work people do, from producing raw materials and manufacturing goods to providing services.

► Researchers in the chemical industry develop new materials such as drugs and plastics.

Borer

Grinder

Puncher

Turning machine

▲ Machine tools such as these are widely used to manufacture machinery and motor components.

Manufacturing industries, such as the aircraft and automotive industries, make goods for people to buy. The electronics industry, for example, produces tiny wafers of silicon that are the brains of our desktop computers, and the chemical industry manufactures a wide range of chemicals, from fertilizers to lifesaving antibiotics. The steel industry is one of the most important of all industries because it produces the metal that many other industries rely on. The construction industry uses steel to build towering skyscrapers and massive dams and bridges.

PRIMARY INDUSTRIES
Mining produces the raw materials, such as ores and petroleum, on which manufacturing industries depend. It marks the beginning of the industrial production process and is therefore called a primary industry. Agriculture, forestry, and fishing are also primary industries. Manufacturing is next in the production chain, and is called a secondary industry.

GETTING SERVICE
When the manufacturing industries have produced the goods, they have to be sold to the consumer. This is the job of stores. They do not produce goods, but they provide a service by buying goods from the manufacturers and selling them on to customers. Stores are an example of a service industry, often called a tertiary (third) industry. Other examples of service industries include transportation and tourism, insurance and banks, restaurants and hotels, hospitals, and local government.

MASS PRODUCTION
A key feature of modern industry is mass production—the manufacture of goods in large quantities at a relatively low cost. In a typical mass-production operation, goods are built up piece by piece on an assembly line, with people often working side by side with industrial robots.

▲ Some industries, such as this shoe factory in India, involve hundreds of people working together. Others have people working in smaller groups, or alone at home.

AUTOMATION TAKES OVER
Today, many assembly lines are fully automated, with machines now controlled by computers instead of humans. Robots are increasingly being used, particularly in the automotive industry. They are ideal for performing highly repetitive, hazardous, or awkward tasks, such as spot welding or paint spraying. Fitted with a gripper, they can also be used to move objects.

SEE ALSO
Construction, Farming, Fishing industry, Industrial Revolution, Mining, Robot

INSECT

Insects belong to the large group of animals called arthropods, which means "jointed feet." An insect's legs are made up of small segments and flexible joints.

Male stag beetles have large jaws that look like the antlers of a stag.

Crickets have long hind legs for hopping, and rub their wings together to "sing."

Earwigs are flat with pincers at their tail and wings that fold away.

Aphids have soft brown or green bodies up to 1 in. (3mm) long.

A human louse, like all sucking lice, feeds on the blood of mammals.

IDENTIFYING AN INSECT

All adult insects have a body that is divided into three parts: the head, the thorax (where legs and wings are joined), and the abdomen (where the insect digests its food and makes its eggs). They also have three pairs of legs and a tough body case, or exoskeleton.

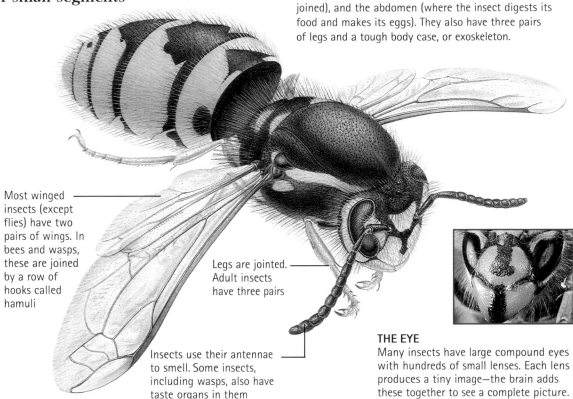

Most winged insects (except flies) have two pairs of wings. In bees and wasps, these are joined by a row of hooks called hamuli

Legs are jointed. Adult insects have three pairs

Insects use their antennae to smell. Some insects, including wasps, also have taste organs in them

THE EYE
Many insects have large compound eyes with hundreds of small lenses. Each lens produces a tiny image—the brain adds these together to see a complete picture.

More than a million kinds of insect have been found on Earth. That's more than all the other types of animal put together. They are split into around 29 groups and include grasshoppers, beetles, butterflies, flies, and bees. Insects have no backbone or skeleton inside the body, but the whole insect is covered with a tough, horny material called chitin. This forms an external skeleton rather like a suit of armor. It is made up of segments, some of which are loosely connected by soft membranes so that the insect can move.

WITH OR WITHOUT WINGS

Most insects have two pairs of wings, but some, including fleas and worker ants, never have wings. Flying ants only have wings for a short time, then lose them. Beetles and many bugs look as if they have no wings because their front wings form hard cases and completely cover the delicate hind wings.

BREATHING WITH TUBES

Insects do not have lungs. They breathe by way of a system of fine tubes, called tracheae. These branch through the body and carry air and oxygen. In most insects, air enters the tubes through small holes on the sides of the body—mainly on the abdomen. The openings are called spiracles and they are best seen in large caterpillars, which are the young stages of butterflies and moths.

WATER BUGS

Insects that live in water usually have to come to the surface to renew the air in their breathing tubes, but many young insects can absorb dissolved oxygen straight from the water into their tracheae. ▶

▶ Beetles form the largest insect order, with more than 250,000 species.

◀ The praying mantis has powerful jaws so it can munch through the hard outer case of insects.

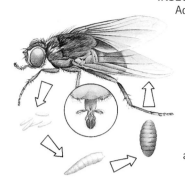

INSECT LIFE CYCLE
Advanced insects, such as flies, have a four-part life cycle. The eggs hatch into larvae which change their skins twice as they grow. Then comes the pupa stage where they change into the adult form.

MOUTHPARTS
Insects have a variety of mouthparts adapted to suit their diets. Some have chewing jaws, others suck up their food, and some have piercing needles.

Tiger beetles are fierce carnivores (meat-eaters), with prominent biting mandibles (or jaws).

Weevils' mouthparts are extended into a snout. They can be serious pests, infesting flour and grain.

A fly's proboscis is like a straw with a sponge tip. It dribbles on food to dissolve it, then sucks it back up.

INSECTS ARE EVERYWHERE
Very few insects live in the sea, but they live everywhere else, and they feed on just about everything. Many are pests and cause a lot of damage by eating our food and crops. Termites and other insects, such as the woodworm and deathwatch beetle, can even destroy our houses. Fleas and mosquitoes suck our blood and carry dangerous diseases. But there are also some very useful insects. Honeybees pollinate many of our crops and give us honey, silkmoths give us silk, ladybug beetles eat huge numbers of greenflies (aphids) and other plant pests, and dung beetles and their grubs help to keep the countryside clean by eating the dung of cows and other animals.

AN INSECT GROWS UP
Most insects start life as eggs, but the insect that hatches from an egg does not usually look much like its parents. A caterpillar, for example, looks nothing like an adult butterfly or moth: it has no wings, and instead of sipping nectar from flowers it munches its way through leaves with its biting jaws. Before it becomes an adult, the caterpillar has to pass through a chrysalis, or pupa stage, during which its body is broken down and rebuilt in the adult form. Bees, flies, and beetles pass through similar stages as they grow up.

THE EMERGING INSECT
Insects molt several times as they grow up, because their tough outer coats, or exoskeletons, cannot grow. At each molt, the old skin splits open and the insect crawls out.

Young insects of this kind are called larvae, and this way of growing up is called a complete metamorphosis, meaning "a complete change."

SMALL ADULTS
Grasshoppers and dragonflies have a slightly different kind of life cycle. The young insects do not have wings, but they do look fairly like the adults apart from being smaller. They are called nymphs, and they gradually turn into adults without passing through a chrysalis stage. This way of growing up is called an incomplete metamorphosis—"an incomplete change."

INSECT HOMES

Ants are the most successful social insects. In the leaf-cutter ant's communal home, the queen lays the eggs, nursery workers look after them, and larger workers cut leaves and bring them back, leaving scent trails by touching the ground with the tips of their abdomen. Soldier ants have a big head with strong jaws and bite to protect the nest, while smaller workers build new tunnels and tend the fungus gardens to feed the others.

Soldier ants use their sting and powerful jaws to defend the colony

Nursery worker

1 The nest has its own air conditioning system—air tunnels keep it at a constant temperature and humidity.

Smaller worker protects leaf

2 A large leaf-cutter can grow up to 3/4 in. (2cm) and carry a gigantic weight in its mouth.

3 A worker takes the eggs to the nursery chambers and tends the growing larvae.

4 Ants chew the leaves to pulp, and mix it with their droppings. A fungus grows on the mixture and the ants eat the fungus.

5 Waste chamber.

6 A queen ant can lay one egg every ten seconds.

GETTING FATTER

As insects grow they shed their old body cases—but not before growing a soft new one. The insect pumps itself up with air or water for a few hours until the new skin has hardened, and then gets rid of the air or water to leave enough space for the next stage of growth. Most insects molt between 4 and 10 times as they grow up, but some may molt as many as 50 times before they are fully grown adults.

LARGE AND LITTLE

The heaviest species is the African Goliath beetle, which is about as big as a man's fist and weighs about 3.5 oz. (100g). Some stick insects are longer, but their bodies are extremely thin. The tiniest insects are smaller than a period on this page.

HOME ALONE

Most insects are solitary—living alone and finding a safe place to lay their eggs. This could be inside the body of another insect, in the case of the tarantula hawk wasp which lays an egg on a paralyzed but living spider. Social insects always live together in large family groups. Each insect has its own job, and only the queen lays eggs.

◄ Bumblebees are social insects that have pollen baskets (hairs) on their hind legs to collect pollen.

FAST FACTS

• Ants and bees recognize members of their own colony through smell

• The number of lenses in an insect's eye varies from about 6 in a worker ant to 30,000 in some dragonflies

• There are around 3,500 species of cockroach. Most live in tropical countries

SEE ALSO

Black Death, Butterfly and moth, Disease, Fossil, Prehistoric animal

INTERNET

The Internet is a globe-spanning computer network, giving people rapid access to information, knowledge, entertainment, and opinions from around the world.

▲ Cybercafés allow people to make use of the Internet in comfortable surroundings.

FAST FACTS

• The Internet began to grow explosively when the World Wide Web was made available to the public in 1993

• Newsgroups allow people with common interests to keep in contact by E-mail

• The Internet is often called "cyberspace," a word first used in 1984 in William Gibson's science-fiction novel *Neuromancer*

The Internet, or "Net," is often referred to as the Information Superhighway. It allows vast amounts of information to stream around the world from computer to computer, letting the general public have easy and quick access to it.

WHAT THE INTERNET CAN DO
School students can call up pictures and information from galleries in, for example, France, Japan, and Britain. They can check unfamiliar words and historical dates in computerized reference libraries based in almost any country. Alternatively, they can listen to a clip from an album while printing out the guitar chords to go with it. A major use of the Internet is to carry electronic mail, or E-mail. An E-mail message can include pictures and audio clips, as well as words, and can be sent to hundreds of computers as easily and as cheaply as to one.

BIRTH OF THE INTERNET
The Internet began as a military network for communications. In the early 1970s, American engineers designed a system that could keep working even if a nuclear attack knocked out some of the computers. Signals could automatically be rerouted through the surviving computers. This design was later used to set up computer networks linking universities, and now it is used in the Internet.

THE WORLD WIDE WEB

The World Wide Web was invented in 1990 so that users could "surf the Net" quickly. By clicking on hot spots on the screen, the user jumps to pages of information consisting of words and pictures located on various computers around the world. Each of these has its own hot spots which lead to further pages.

▼ Search engines greatly speed up the process of finding Web pages and specific pieces of information on the Web.

▼ People can view live video clips of a current space mission from NASA.

▲ Many goods and services can be ordered and paid for over the Internet.

▶ Using E-mail, people can send letters and pictures to one another across the world within minutes.

◀ Information on plays, movies, zoos, circuses, and many other forms of entertainment can be found on the Internet.

SEE ALSO
Communication, Computer, Technology, Telecommunication

INVENTION

An invention is the creation of something new. In the past 200 years, the number of inventions has boomed, changing the world dramatically.

▲ Wheels were used in Mesopotamia about 3200 B.C. The cart wheel was developed from the earlier potter's wheel.

Civilization has been driven forward by inventions. Each invention has been based on those that came before it, and has made further progress possible.

GETTING THE BASICS RIGHT
Prehistoric people were the first inventors. They learned how to farm and to make fire, pottery, the wheel, and metal tools. One invention often leads to others. Without the wheel, for example, there could be no wagons, watermills, or machines driven by gears. Key inventions of the 1800s included photography, electric light, plastics, and automobiles. In 1946, the first electronic computer was built, changing the way we live.

THE INVENTORS
Some people stand out as lone inventors. In the late 1400s, the Italian Leonardo da Vinci designed a flying machine, but could not build it because there was no suitable engine. The American Thomas Alva Edison is credited with more than 1,000 inventions, including the lightbulb and the phonograph. Other pioneers who worked alone were Alexander Graham Bell (the telephone), Guglielmo Marconi (the radio), and Karl Benz and Gottfried Daimler (the automobile). More recent inventions, such as the television and computers, were developed by large research teams with many specialists.

GOOD OR BAD?
Most people would agree that painkilling drugs are "good" inventions and that poison gas is "bad," but poison gas can be put to good use to kill pests that eat our food. It is how inventions are used that makes them useful or harmful.

The flushing toilet was developed in the 1840s.

Safety matches were invented in 1844.

An early experimental photocopier of 1940.

John Logie Baird invented the television in 1926.

Alexander Graham Bell invented the telephone in 1876.

PHONOGRAPH
Thomas Edison's phonograph of 1877 used a cylinder of tinfoil to record sound.

RECORDED SOUND
Sound recording has traditionally been by analogue means. The sound waves in the air are reproduced as peaks and troughs in a groove on a solid object. These were read by passing a needle along the groove. Modern CDs treat sound as digital computer data which is recorded as a series of pits on the disc.

78RPM GRAMOPHONE
In 1921, a flat plastic disc, or record, with sound fed through electric speakers gave better quality sound.

COMPACT DISC
The compact disc, or CD, of the early 1980s contained digital music, read by a laser beam for accurate reproduction.

HI-FI VINYL
In 1958, stereo sound from long-playing records produced high-fidelity sound, or hi-fi, for the first time.

SEE ALSO
Aircraft, Car, Clock, Electronics, Industrial Revolution, Nuclear power, Printing, Warfare

IRELAND, REPUBLIC OF

The Republic of Ireland occupies 80 percent of the island of Ireland, which lies off the west coast of Britain. It is also called by its Gaelic name, Eire.

Area: 26,600 sq. mi.
Population: 3,883,159
Capital: Dublin
Languages: English, Irish Gaelic
Currency: Euro

Ireland is a land of green fields, rolling hills, lakes, known as loughs, and winding rivers. The center of the country is flat, and low mountain ranges line the coasts. The Shannon, at 240 mi. (386km) the longest river in the British Isles, is used for hydroelectric power. Ireland has a mild, moist climate, and rich green grass grows on the limestone that forms much of the country, giving it the name Emerald Isle.

FARMING AND EUROPE
Ireland is a farming country famous for dairy foods such as butter. Wide bogs in the midlands are full of peat (decayed plants), which is cut and dried for fuel. After joining the European Union (EU), the republic prospered as EU money helped it to modernize farm machinery and farming methods.

INDUSTRY AND CITIES
Irish factories make electronic equipment, textiles, plastics, and other goods. The country also brews alcoholic beverages. Industry is centered mainly around Dublin, Cork, and Limerick—three fifths of the people now live in towns or cities, where they are more likely to find work.

IRELAND AND BRITAIN
England gained control of Ireland in the 1500s, after which Protestants from England and Scotland settled there. When Ireland became self-governing in 1921, the six Protestant-dominated counties of Northern Ireland stayed part of the United Kingdom. In the republic, most people are Roman Catholics. The division of the island causes continuing tensions.

▲ Live music, traditional and modern, is a large part of Irish culture. The country has also produced many great writers.

▼ The city of Dublin is popular with tourists. Landmarks include the Ha'penny Bridge over the Liffey River.

▲ The Irish are famous for breeding horses. Their thoroughbred yearlings are often used as racehorses.

SEE ALSO

Christianity, Civil war, Europe, U.K.

IRON AND STEEL

Iron is one of the most common metals in the Earth's crust. It is often used mixed with other ingredients in the form of steel—a cheap, strong building material.

Steel can be shaped in various ways. It can be rolled into tubes . . .

. . . or drawn through a hole to make wire.

A series of rollers shapes solid steel into girders.

Steel is used for a wide range of everyday objects.

In its natural state, iron is found combined with other elements, such as oxygen, as a rocky material called iron ore. Before it can be used, the iron has to be extracted (removed) from its ore by a process called smelting.

EXTRACTING THE IRON

The iron ore is mixed with coke (a form of carbon) and limestone (a chalky rock). Then it is blasted with hot air until it reaches a temperature of over 2732°F (1500°C). The iron melts and most of the impurities (unwanted materials) float to its surface. The impurities, known as "slag," are then removed. The iron remaining is called pig iron. This still contains some impurities, especially carbon, but after further heat treatment, it can be poured into molds to make cast-iron parts such as engine blocks.

▲ Glowing red-hot, molten iron is poured from a giant ladle into molds and left to cool as ingots.

MAKING STEEL

Most pig iron goes for refining, or purifying, to make steel. This involves mixing it with scrap steel and blasting it with oxygen so that most of the carbon burns off. Steel is a tough, strong material that is used to make bridges, buildings, and many other objects that carry heavy loads. Manufacturers often add other elements to steel to give it special properties. Adding chromium and nickel makes stainless steel—a material that never rusts. This is used to make such things as engine parts and surgical tools.

PROCESSING THE IRON

Iron is extracted from its ore in a blast furnace. The resulting pig iron contains about four percent carbon, which comes from the coke in the furnace. This carbon makes the iron very brittle, so the iron is processed again before it is used. Steel is made by blasting the pig iron with oxygen inside a furnace called a converter. The oxygen combines with the carbon in the iron to form gases that are easily removed.

The raw materials are put into the furnace

Limestone

Coke

Iron ore

Blast furnace

Waste gases are removed

Mixed raw materials

Hot air is blasted into the furnace

Molten slag is removed

Iron

Oxygen is blown onto the molten metal

Pig iron and scrap steel are poured into the converter

Molten pig iron pours into ladle

Converter

1 As the coke burns inside the furnace, it removes the oxygen from the iron ore to leave pig iron.

2 Inside the converter, oxygen is used to burn off most of the carbon, leaving steel.

3 The molten steel can be poured into molds to make ingots, or it can be cast into shapes while still fluid.

SEE ALSO
Bridge, Construction, Earth, Metal, Skyscraper

ISLAM

Islam is the second most common religion in the world after Christianity. People who follow Islam are called Muslims.

▲ The crescent and star are the symbols of Islam.

There are more than one billion Muslims across the world, many in the Middle East and Africa. They believe in one all-powerful god, who created everything. Their name for this god is Allah. Islam means "submission" in Arabic, and devout Muslims try to live their lives according to Allah's word.

THE STORY OF MUHAMMAD

Islam began with the prophet Muhammad, an Arab born in about A.D. 570 in the city of Mecca (in what is now Saudi Arabia). When he was 40, Muhammad was called by Allah to preach his words, and he spread Islam throughout much of the Arab world. He died in 632.

▲ Islam has no organized church and no priests. Instead, there are holy men and teachers.

PILGRIMAGE TO MECCA

The pilgrimage to Mecca, called the hajj, takes place during the 12th month of the Muslim year. About two million Muslims from across the world converge on Mecca to perform rituals, such as walking around the holy shrine, or Kaaba (the black structure seen below), which contains a black stone dating from ancient times.

THE FIVE PILLARS OF ISLAM

- There is no god but Allah, and Muhammad is God's messenger
- A formal prayer must be said five times every day, while facing the holy city of Mecca
- Those who can afford it should give to the poor each year
- Followers must fast during the month of Ramadan
- Followers must make a pilgrimage to Mecca, if possible, at least once during their lifetime

LAWS OF ISLAM

Islamic Law, or the Shariah, is very important to Muslims. It was laid down by early Islamic teachers and tells Muslims how they should live their lives. The holy book of Islam is the Koran (or Qur'an), said to be Allah's exact words, as told to Muhammad. A Muslim's main religious duties are the "Five Pillars of Islam"—faith, prayer, almsgiving, fasting, and pilgrimage.

MUSLIMS AT PRAYER

The Muslim place of worship is called a mosque. Five times a day, criers known as *muezzins* call the people to prayer from minarets, or towers, on the mosques. Muslims do not have to go to the mosque to pray, except on Fridays, but can pray in any clean place.

SEE ALSO
Crusades, Middle East, Pilgrim, Religion

ISRAEL

Israel occupies a narrow strip of land in southwest Asia, on the eastern shore of the Mediterranean Sea. It makes up most of the area once called the Holy Land.

Area: 7,800 sq. mi.
Population: 6,029,529
Capital: Jerusalem
Languages: Hebrew, Arabic
Currency: Shekel

The hills of Galilee lie in northern Israel, and lowlands and fertile plains lie to the west. Most of the south is made up of the Negev Desert.

SALTY SEA

The Jordan River flows along the country's eastern border from the north, into the Sea of Galilee and then into the Dead Sea. The Dead Sea is in fact a lake and contains useful minerals, such as potash, used to make soap. The water is so dense that swimmers can float easily. Summers are dry and hot; winters are cool.

WATERING THE LAND

Irrigation schemes have brought water to dry land, making it lush with crops. On collective farms called *kibbutzim*, families live and work together growing fruits such as oranges—Israel is a major producer of citrus fruits. Other crops include vegetables, cotton, and olives. Israel is a highly developed country, however, and about 90 percent of Israelis live in towns and cities. Many of them work in factories or service industries.

▲ The Dome of the Rock shrine, sacred to Muslims, stands in East Jerusalem. It is on the site where Muhammad is said to have risen into heaven.

▲ The Dead Sea is the saltiest body of water in the world. The salt crystallizes and forms lumps in the water.

THE HOLY LAND

Jews, Christians, and Muslims all regard Jerusalem as a holy place. Its religious sites include the Western Wall, at the site of the ancient Jewish Temple. When the Romans conquered the land and called it Palestine, most Jewish people were forced to leave. Modern Israel was founded in 1948 as a homeland for the Jews. Several wars between Jews and Palestinian Arabs followed, involving neighboring Arab states. Today, some 900,000 Arabs live in Israel and an uneasy peace is maintained.

◄ Since 1993, Palestinians have had limited control over the West Bank and Gaza Strip. Jewish children attend separate schools.

SEE ALSO
Asia, Christianity, Islam, Judaism, Middle East, Pilgrim

ITALY

As the seat of the Roman Empire and cradle of the Renaissance, Italy has been at the center of European civilization for centuries.

Area: 113,500 sq. mi.
Population: 57,715,625
Capital: Rome
Language: Italian
Currency: Euro

▲ ▼ Venice's annual carnival is a major event, and carnival-goers dress flamboyantly for the occasion. Boats known as gondolas are used for transport in Venice, where the main "streets" are canals—the Grand Canal at the Rialto Bridge has been the scene of many regattas, or races.

Some of the highest mountains in Europe, the Alps, tower across northern Italy. Another mountain chain, the Apennines, stretches from north to south. The independent state of San Marino lies at the bottom of Mount Titano in the Apennines—it is the oldest republic in Europe, founded in the A.D. 300s, and has an area of just 24 sq. mi. (61sq km).

POWER FROM WATER
Rushing mountain streams are used in hydroelectric schemes to provide much-needed power for a country with little coal or oil of its own. Italy's largest rivers, the Po, Arno, and Tiber, are all in northern Italy, as are lakes Garda, Como, and Maggiore. Southern Italy, which includes the islands of Sardinia and Sicily, is hotter and drier than the north.

FOOD AND DRINK
Italy is the world's largest wine producer. Italian dishes vary from north to south, and range from veal in subtle, light sauces to seafood in rich, spicy tomato sauces. Italian recipes have inspired cooking around the world, and pizza and pasta have become international dishes.

▲ Italy has many old and beautiful churches. Even a tiny country church, like this one near Siena, may have a priceless medieval *fresco* (painting on plaster) or a carving.

AGRICULTURE
Many Italians are farmers. The major crop is wheat, used to make pasta and bread. Others are olives, grapes, corn, and sugar beets. Cattle are reared mainly in the north, and many sheep and goats are kept on rough pastures in Sardinia and Sicily.

INDUSTRIOUS NORTH
In northern Italy, industry is based around the cities of Turin, Milan, and Genoa. Factories make a wide range of goods including automobiles, clothing, machinery, and chemicals. Milan is particularly famous for its fashion houses, where clothes are designed. Many raw materials have to be imported, and Italy has a large fleet of merchant ships.

SPEAKING ITALIAN
Almost everyone in Italy speaks Italian, although a few communities speak another language—German is the first language of people

▲ Italy is rich in artistic treasures, spectacular buildings, and historic remains such as those of the Colosseum, an ancient amphitheater in Rome.

living near the Austrian border. Most Italians are Roman Catholics, and the head of the Catholic Church, the pope, lives in Vatican City, in Rome.

VATICAN CITY
Vatican City, the smallest independent state in the world, is under one fifth of a square mile (0.44sq km). St. Peter's Basilica, at its center, is almost 690 ft. (210m) long, and is shaped like a cross.

VARIETY FOR VISITORS
Tourism is one of Italy's main industries. Every year, millions of people visit the country to enjoy its peaceful countryside, sunny beaches, snowcapped mountains, and historic cities such as Venice, Florence, Naples, and Rome.

ROME TO RENAISSANCE
Italy was where the Roman Empire was founded. Roman rule ended in A.D. 476, but Rome remained the headquarters of the Roman Catholic Church. Italy broke up into smaller city-states, and from the 1300s to the early 1500s, it was the center of the Renaissance. The country has produced explorers such as Marco Polo, artists such as Leonardo da Vinci, and scientists such as Galileo.

UNITING THE STATES
From the 1500s, France and Austria tried to control Italy. During the 1800s, Giuseppe Garibaldi and other patriots led the fight to unite the Italian states. They drove out the Austrians and, in 1861, Italy became an independent and united kingdom.

MODERN ITALY
During the 1920s and 1930s, the Fascists, led by Benito Mussolini, held power. After World War II (1939–45), Italy held its first free election for 20 years and a republic replaced the monarchy. The country has prospered as a member of the European Union, despite having had many changes of government. Today, the south of Italy is poorer than the north, but modern Italy is a major industrial nation.

◀ Motorcycles are a popular form of transportation with young Italians, meeting here at the Piazza del Popolo in Rome.

▲ Modern opera began in Italy in the early 1600s, with the composer Claudio Monteverdi. Today, Italian singers such as Luciano Pavarotti are popular all over the world.

SEE ALSO
Art, Christianity, Europe, Fascism, Renaissance, Roman Empire, Volcano

JAPAN

Japan is an island country in northeast Asia, off the east coast of China. The Japanese call their country Nippon or Nihon, which means "source of the sun."

Area: 152,400 sq. mi.
Population: 126,974,628
Capital: Tokyo
Language: Japanese
Currency: Yen

By area, Japan is Asia's 18th largest country. Its largest island is Honshu, followed by Hokkaido, Kyushu, and Shikoku. There are also thousands of small islands, such as the chain of Ryukyu Islands.

▲ Today, Japan's leading industries include the manufacture of electrical goods such as televisions.

ERUPTIONS AND EARTHQUAKES

Most of Japan is hilly or mountainous and the rivers are fast flowing, providing water power for electricity. Japan's highest peak, Mount Fuji at 12,388 ft. (3,776m), is a volcano which last erupted in 1707–8. Over 60 of Japan's volcanoes are active, earthquakes are also common.

VARIED CLIMATE

The northernmost island of Hokkaido, just south of the Russian territory, is cool and snow is common in winter; Kyushu in the south is much warmer. Most of Japan has plenty of rainfall.

PINK-FACED MONKEYS

Forests cover about two thirds of the land and many animals, including bears, wild boar, deer, and foxes, live in them. Pink-faced monkeys called Japanese macaques live as far north as the northern tip of Honshu. They have long, thick fur and swim in hot springs in the snow to keep warm.

FIRST ARRIVALS

The first people in Japan were probably descendants of a group of people called the Ainu, a few thousand of whom live in Hokkaido today. The ancestors of most modern Japanese people probably reached the islands from mainland Asia around 2,200 years ago. The country ranks seventh in the world by population.

SHARED RELIGIONS

Over three quarters of the people live in crowded cities and towns. The largest city is Tokyo, and other large cities include Yokohama and Osaka, all situated on Honshu, where 80 percent of the people live. Japan follows two main religions: Shinto and Buddhism. Many people follow both.

▲ Japan is a leading fishing nation. It supplies not only its own people with fish, but also many other countries.

▼ Many beautiful temples, like the Kinkaka Ji with its spectacular gardens, can be found in Japan's former capital, Kyoto.

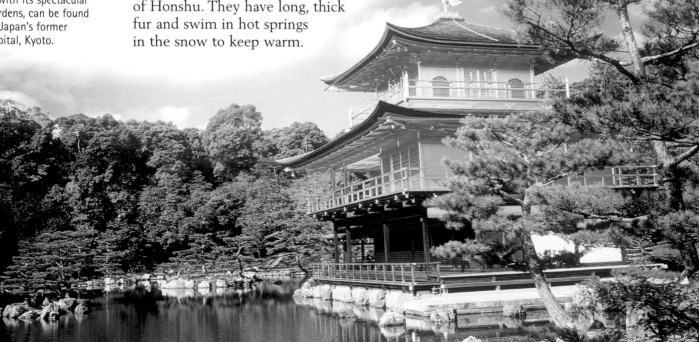

MEETING ITS NEEDS

Although it lacks natural resources, Japan is a wealthy country. Because it is so hilly, only about 15 percent of the land is farmed. But Japan produces about 70 percent of the food it needs. Rice is the leading crop and food. Fruit, sugar beet, tea, and vegetables are also important.

MADE IN JAPAN

Manufacturing is the most valuable activity, and Japan ranks second only to the United States among the world's top industrial countries. Its products are sold around the world and include chemicals, electrical and electronic equipment, iron and steel, machinery, ships, textiles, vehicles and transportation equipment.

POWERFUL NATION

Japan became a powerful nation during the late 1800s. It won some important battles against China in 1894 and defeated Russia in 1905. In 1937, it attacked China and, in 1941, it attacked the American naval base in Pearl Harbor, Hawaii. This act drew it and the United States into World War II.

MOVING TO DEMOCRACY

In 1945, after the United States had dropped atomic bombs on Hiroshima and Nagasaki, Japan surrendered. The United States occupied Japan until 1952. During this time, Japan became a democratic country, and the once all-powerful emperor became the head of state with only ceremonial duties. The country is now ruled by an elected prime minister and government, and is one of the world's great economic powers.

SEA OF OKHOTSK

Hokkaido

● Sapporo

● Hakodate

N

JAPAN

Sendai ●

miles
0　　　　125

0　　　125
km

SEA OF JAPAN

Honshu

Shinano

Mt. Fuji ▲　■ Tokyo
● Yokohama

Kyoto ●　　● Nagoya
Kobe ●
　　　● Osaka

Hiroshima ●

Shikoku

PACIFIC OCEAN

Nagasaki ●

Kyushu

EAST
CHINA
SEA

Osumi Is.

Ryukyu Is.

Okinawa

Sakishima Is.

► Sumo, a Japanese style of wrestling in which opponents try to push each other out of a ring, is a popular national sport.

◄ Japan's bullet train, here seen against a backdrop of Mt. Fuji, is one of the fastest in the world. It runs on the island of Honshu.

SEE ALSO

Asia, Buddhism, China, Industry, Southeast Asia, Volcano, World War II

JELLYFISH AND OTHER COELENTERATES

Jellyfish, sea anemones, and corals belong to a group of animals called coelenterates. They all have soft bodies armed with stinging tentacles.

▶ Jellyfish move by pumping water backward with their bodies.

A Portuguese man-of-war is not a true jellyfish. Like corals, it is a colony of animals living together.

The hydra is a freshwater coelenterate. It forms new buds that break off and grow into new animals.

Sea anemones are tube-shaped animals that attach themselves, with a suckerlike base, to rocks in the sea.

Coelenterates are invertebrates—which means "no backbone." In fact they have no trace of a skeleton at all—except for corals, whose soft bodies are surrounded by a hard case made of limestone. Coelenterates have no brain, but have simple nerves and muscles. The largest individuals are found among the jellyfish, which are nearly all umbrella- or bell-shaped animals with a mouth on the underside. There are about 250 different kinds. Most of them are no bigger than a saucer, but there are a few real giants, with bodies up to 6.5 ft. (2m) across and tentacles as long as 230 ft. (70m).

STINGING STRINGS

Most coelenterates use tentacles to catch prey. Even corals are carnivores, or meat-eaters, using stinging cells on their tentacles to paralyze microscopic animals in the water. The stings of some jellyfish are very dangerous to swimmers. Those of the Australian sea wasp jellyfish can kill a person in minutes.

A STICKY END

Some jellyfish have bodies covered with sticky slime that traps any small animals they touch. Aurelia, the common jellyfish found washed up on beaches, uses stinging cells and then envelops its paralyzed prey in mucus.

BREAKING UP

Jellyfish scatter eggs or tiny babies into the water, but these do not grow directly into jellyfish. Instead, they settle on a rock or seaweed and grow into cone shapes. They gradually divide until they look like piles of miniature saucers. Each saucer floats away and grows into a new jellyfish.

ENTANGLING PREY

The jellyfish's tentacles are covered with powerful stinging cells and are used to catch and kill fish, shrimp, and other small animals. The lion's mane jellyfish, here, can have a 6.5-ft. (2-m) body and tentacles reaching 130 ft. (40m). The tentacles pull the victim into the mouth, which is hidden under its bell-like body.

Tentacles are covered with stinging cells containing tightly coiled stinging threads

The stinging cell is fired into the prey like a tiny harpoon. Once fired, it cannot be used again. It is cast off and new cells grow

226

SEE ALSO
Animal, Evolution, Ocean and sea

JUDAISM

Judaism is the religion of the Jewish people. It teaches that there is one true God, who revealed himself to the Jews and has given the human race rules to live by.

The six-pointed star became a symbol of Judaism during the Middle Ages. It signifies the protection of God given to David, king of Israel in about 970 B.C.

Jews believe that there is one eternal, invisible God who created the universe. There are about 18 million Jews living in Israel and all over the world.

MOSES AND THE HEBREWS

The first followers of Judaism were the Hebrew people of the Middle East. According to the Bible (Old Testament), the Jewish holy book, God made an agreement with Abraham and his descendants in about the year 1900 B.C. In about 1200 B.C., God sent Moses to lead the Hebrews out of slavery in Egypt. God revealed his teachings about how to live and serve God to Moses. These teachings are the basis of Judaism and are contained in the Torah, laws based on the first five books of the Bible. Later works, the Talmud, tell people how to lead good lives and how to observe rituals.

THE HOLY SABBATH

The Hebrews worshiped at the Temple in Jerusalem, but this was destroyed in a war with the Roman Empire in A.D. 70. Modern Jews study their faith in buildings called synagogues. Here, they are guided by teachers known as rabbis. The most religious day of the week is the Sabbath, which lasts from sunset Friday to sunset Saturday. Jews cannot work on this day, because they believe this was the day when God rested after creating the world.

Jewish women pray at Jerusalem's Western Wall, at the site of the ancient Temple.

Jews light a candle a day during the eight days of Hanukkah, to celebrate the rededication of the Temple in 165 B.C.

▲ A rabbi preparing to sound the *shofar* (ram's horn) at Yom Kippur wears a *tallith* (prayer shawl) and phylactery boxes.

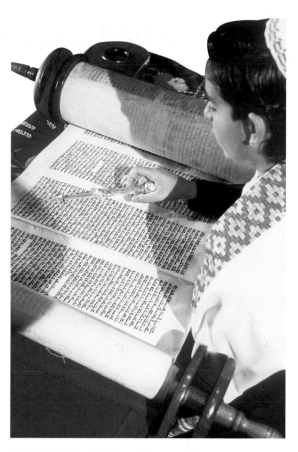

BAR MITZVAH

When a Jewish boy officially becomes a man, at the age of 13, the bar mitzvah ceremony is held. The boy reads from the books of the prophets during the Sabbath service. The service is often followed by prayers and a family celebration. A girl of 13 has a similar ceremony, the bat mitzvah. She is not yet officially a woman, but now has religious responsibilities.

KOSHER RITUALS

Jews observe various festivals, including Yom Kippur in September or October, when sins are confessed and forgiveness asked. At Passover, in March or April, the departure from Egypt is celebrated. Orthodox Jews have strict rules about what they eat, how their food is prepared, and the way ritual objects should be treated. These rules are called kosher.

PERSECUTION

For centuries, Jews have lived among other nations, which have sometimes persecuted them. During World War II, the Nazis murdered millions of Jews in what is called the Holocaust. After this, many Jews created a new homeland, Israel, in the area where the Hebrews lived.

SEE ALSO
Israel, Religion, World War II

KANGAROO AND OTHER MARSUPIALS

Marsupials are mammals that normally carry their young in pouches. There are about 250 different kinds, most of which live in Australia and New Guinea.

Koalas live in and feed off of eucalyptus trees.

Common opossums are found in North America.

Wombats are nocturnal burrowing animals.

The Tasmanian devil is stocky with sharp teeth.

Kangaroos are the biggest of the marsupials, some of them reaching nearly 6.5 ft. (2m) tall. They are Australia's equivalent of the herds of antelope that live on the African plains. Kangaroos are not hoofed animals and they move by leaping instead of running, but they graze and browse like antelope and they have a similar head and jaws. Farmers do not like kangaroos because they eat the grass intended for sheep.

ALL KINDS OF KANGAROO

There are about 60 kinds of kangaroo. The smallest are about the size of a rabbit and are called rat kangaroos. The middle-size ones are often called wallabies. The red kangaroo and the gray kangaroo are the biggest species. They usually live in small groups called mobs. Although they are about as tall as a man when they stand upright, their young, called joeys, are only about 1 in. (2.5cm) long when they are born.

A WIDE VARIETY

Not all marsupials are grazers. Just like the mammals in other parts of the world, Australia's marsupials have adopted all sorts of habits. Possums and gliders live in the trees like monkeys and squirrels; the koala is like a small bear. There is even a marsupial mole. There are also many carnivorous, or meat-eating, marsupials, including the doglike Tasmanian devil.

EXTINCT SPECIES

The Tasmanian wolf, or thylacine, is another doglike carnivore, but it has not been seen alive since 1936 and is probably extinct. Farmers hunted it because they thought it killed their sheep. Many other Australian marsupials have died out because they were killed by cats and dogs and other mammals introduced by man.

▲ Red kangaroos can bound along on their huge back legs at speeds of about 24 mph (40kph) and can cover 26 ft. (8m) in a single leap.

THE LONG JOURNEY

A kangaroo is born blind and helpless, and looks more like a grub than a kangaroo. As soon as it is born it has to climb up to its mother's pouch, where it starts to feed and grow. It develops long back legs and a long tail, and by six months it is ready to leave the pouch for the first time.

1 The newly born kangaroo crawls up its mother's body until it reaches the security of the pouch.

2 Inside the pouch, the baby suckles on its mother's milk and starts to grow rapidly.

3 By six months, the joey is old enough to leave its mother's pouch, but it soon jumps back inside if danger threatens.

SEE ALSO

Animal, Australia, Mammal

228

KENYA

Kenya is a country on the east coast of Africa with beautiful scenery and spectacular wild animals. The equator runs through its center.

Area: 219,800 sq. mi.
Population: 31,138,735
Capital: Nairobi
Languages: English, Swahili
Currency: Kenyan shilling

Most of northern Kenya is made up of dry plains. There are also forested uplands in the west and savannas (grasslands) to the south. Part of Africa's largest lake, Victoria, is in the west.

MOUNT KENYA

Volcanic mountains lie in the middle of the country, close to the equator. They include Mount Kenya, now extinct. At 17,058 ft. (5,199m), it is the country's highest peak, second only to Tanzania's Mount Kilimanjaro in the whole of Africa.

FARMS AND CITIES

The mountainous areas have fertile soil which is good for farming. On large plantations, Kenyan farmers grow coffee, tea, vegetables, and fruit for export. On small plots of land, people raise crops of corn, beans, cassava, and potatoes for food. Only one fifth of the land is suitable for farming, and many Kenyans have left their villages to seek jobs in towns and cities such as Mombasa—the main port— and the capital city, Nairobi.

▲ The Kenyan capital of Nairobi has many modern buildings.

▲ Kenya's many national parks and their wildlife are major tourist attractions.

NATIONAL PARKS

Kenya's wildlife is threatened by poaching. There are several national parks where animals are protected, and these attract visitors from all over the world. Tourism plays an important part in Kenya's developing economy.

KENYA'S PEOPLE

Most Kenyans are black Africans, although a small number are of European, Asian, and Arab descent. There are about 50 different ethnic groups, including the Kikuyu, Masai, and Samburu. Kenyans are enthusiastic about soccer and athletics. Kenyan runners have won many medals at the Olympic Games.

MODERN KENYA

Some of the earliest-known fossil remains of human beings have been found in parts of Kenya. Kenya became a British colony in 1920. It gained its independence in 1963, and became a republic in 1964. The country's most famous leader of modern times was Jomo Kenyatta, president from 1964 until his death in 1978.

▶ People such as the Samburu live in Kenya's semidesert areas.

SEE ALSO
Africa, Animal, Fossil, Mountain and valley

229

KIDNEY

The kidneys are vital organs that clean the blood by filtering out unwanted substances and excess water. These are then removed from the body as urine.

▲ A young girl whose kidneys are not working properly is given regular "dialysis" treatment. This involves linking her up to a special machine called a hemodialyzer which filters out the waste materials in her blood. Once a suitable donor has been found, she can be given a kidney transplant.

Body processes, such as digesting food or burning energy, produce various waste substances. These are collected from all parts of the body by the blood system, and are carried to the kidneys, where they are filtered out. The kidneys are the most important part of the body's excretory system, which is responsible for getting rid of, or excreting, liquid wastes.

A MILLION MICROFILTERS

Inside each kidney are two layers. The outer layer—the renal cortex—contains about a million tiny filtering units, called nephrons. Each nephron has a tiny knot of microscopic blood vessels, or capillaries, called a glomerulus, which is surrounded by a double-layered cup—Bowman's capsule. As blood flows through the glomerulus, water, minerals, salts, and wastes seep out into Bowman's capsule. These substances ooze from the capsule through a long, thin U-shaped tube, called the nephron loop, or loop of

Henle, which lies in the kidney's inner layer—the renal medulla.

KEEPING USEFUL SUBSTANCES

Each nephron loop is surrounded by more capillaries, so that useful substances such as minerals and salts can pass from the loop back into the blood. A certain amount of water is also taken back, or reabsorbed. The amount depends on the body's water supplies and is controlled by chemical messengers called hormones.

COLLECTING THE WASTES

The unwanted substances that are left form the urine. This trickles into larger tubes, or collecting ducts, and gathers in the renal pelvis—a space in the middle of the kidney. From here it dribbles into a tube called the ureter and is carried down to the bladder, a small muscular sac in the lower abdomen. The bladder empties by squeezing its muscular walls to force the urine along another tube, the urethra, to the outside.

THE KIDNEYS AT WORK

The kidneys, which are bean-shaped, are positioned centrally in the rear of the body, one on either side of the spine. They receive blood via the renal arteries and, after the blood has been filtered, it is carried away by the renal veins. All of the body's blood flows through the kidneys about 350 times a day—that's more than 1,870 qts. (1,700l)! This is constantly cleaned and filtered to produce about 3 pts. (1.5l) of urine each day.

Glomerulus
Blood vessel
Capillaries
Nephron loop (loop of Henle)
Bowman's capsule

Renal vein
Renal artery
Renal pelvis
Renal cortex
Renal medulla
Kidney
Ureter
Bladder
Urethra

SEE ALSO

Blood, Heart and circulatory system, Human body

230

LAKE

A lake is a body of still water that fills a hollow in the Earth's surface. These hollows form in a number of ways, and the water in them can be fresh or salty.

An oxbow lake is a curved section cut off from a meandering river.

Crater lakes form in the tops of old volcanoes or in meteorite craters.

The water that fills a lake comes from rain, inflowing streams, or, sometimes, from underground springs. As well as providing an important habitat for many kinds of plant and wildlife, lakes are used by people as a source of water, for fishing, for transportation, or for fun.

GREAT DEPTHS
The deepest lakes lie in rift valleys, where parts of the Earth's crust have cracked and sunk. Lake Baikal in Siberia is over 5,200 ft. (1,600m) deep and was formed more than 30 million years ago. It is the world's oldest and deepest lake. Other such lakes include Lake Nyasa in Malawi and Lake Turkana (Rudolf) in Kenya.

THE DEATH OF A LAKE

Lakes begin to die as soon as they form. Rivers entering the lake bring sand and gravel that form a delta, and silt that fills up the bottom of the lake. At the same time, rivers leaving the lake cut a gorge, lowering the water level. Eventually, the falling water level and rising deposits combine to turn the lake into dry land.

GLACIAL WATERS
Most lakes were formed in hollows left behind by the retreating glaciers of the last Ice Age, about 10,000 years ago. Others were formed in depressions between heaps of rocky debris dumped by the glaciers. The Great Lakes of North America and most of the Scottish lochs were formed in this way.

SALT LAKES
Sometimes a lake forms in a hollow with no outlet. Water can then escape only by evaporating, which leaves behind large deposits of salt. The lake between Israel and Jordan known as the Dead Sea is eight times saltier than seawater.

UNIQUE WILDLIFE
Larger lakes support their own wildlife. Lake Baikal is home to about 1,500 plant and animal species found nowhere else. But pollution has become a major problem in many lakes, wiping out numerous species.

The deepest lakes are fault valley lakes that form where rocks subside.

Gorge

Hollow carved by glaciers fills to form lake

Silt

Marshy delta

River enters lake

SEE ALSO
Dam, Glacier, Mountain and valley, River, Swamp and marsh

LANGUAGE

Language is how humans communicate with one another, either through speech, writing, or even sign language. It comes from the Latin word *lingua*, meaning tongue.

▲ "Happy New Year" written in a number of different languages.

Language starts as a collection of sounds, arranged so that they mean something. Over time, people developed different languages and then organized the sounds into alphabets. An alphabet is a collection of signs that represent the sounds we use.

▲ The Rosetta Stone, found in Egypt in 1799, helped scholars to read Ancient Egyptian hieroglyphs (left), as the same inscription was written in three languages, including Ancient Greek.

ABCDE
Roman

ابتث ج ح
Arabic (read right to left)

АБВГД
Cyrillic (Russian)

ABΓΔE
Greek

בגדהו
Hebrew (read right to left)

▲ The first five written symbols of five different alphabets.

香氣治療
Chinese characters

▲ Chinese has no alphabet, but consists of 50,000 characters, each of which represents an object or idea.

WORLD LANGUAGES

Today, there are between 4,000 and 5,000 languages in the world. Mandarin Chinese is the language spoken by the largest number of people. Next comes English, which is spoken in more countries than any other language. About 845 languages are spoken in India. People have tried to make up artificial "universal" languages. The best-known is Esperanto, invented in 1887.

HOW LANGUAGES CHANGE

Languages constantly change. New words, such as "Internet," come into use. Old words disappear, for example, "bombard," meaning a cannon. Latin, the language of the Ancient Romans, is not spoken, but people can read it. Words can also move from one language to another. English contains many of these words, such as "video" (I see) from Latin and "planet" (wanderer) from Greek.

LANGUAGE FAMILIES

Languages belong to families—groups of related languages which developed from an original parent language. English belongs to the Germanic branch of the large Indo-European language family; French belongs to the Romance branch.

SIGNS AND CODES

Language is not just confined to spoken or written words. Deaf people use sign language and blind people read Braille, a special alphabet using raised dots. Even codes, such as those used by computers, are called languages.

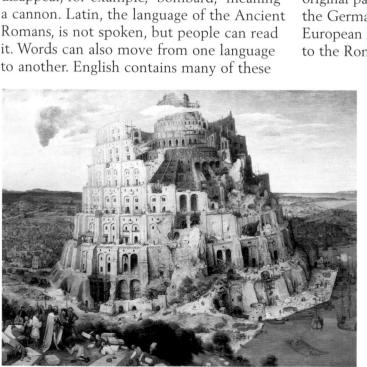

◄ "The Tower of Babel" story tells how people tried to build a huge tower to reach Heaven. God stopped it from being built by making everyone speak different languages, so that they could not understand each other.

SEE ALSO

Communication, Internet, Literature, Media, Newspaper and magazine

LASER

A laser is a machine that produces a powerful beam of concentrated light. The word "laser" is short for Light Amplification by Stimulated Emission of Radiation.

Lasers give out light in a narrow, concentrated beam which is all one wavelength—unlike light from a bulb which goes out in all directions. And while ordinary light spreads out and fades away over long distances, a beam of laser light does not. It can travel for thousands of miles as a strong, straight beam.

Light shows use beams and holograms (3-D images) created by lasers.

Sensors in the nose of a bomb can home in on laser light aimed at a target.

In industry, the high temperature of the laser cuts holes in solid steel.

▲ A laser seals as it cuts, so there is less bleeding, making lasers useful for making precision cuts in surgery.

RUBY OR GAS LASERS
The most common type of laser produces a beam of red light. It is the "ruby laser," which has a rod-shaped red crystal inside of it. Ruby lasers produce flashes or pulses of powerful light. Gas lasers produce a continuous beam. These use colored liquids or gases instead of crystals. Lasers that use colored liquids are called "dye lasers."

DIRECTING THE BEAM
As laser beams are narrow and intense, they have hundreds of uses. Low-powered laser beams can be reflected (bounced) off objects to find out if they are dark or light, smooth or pitted, still or vibrating. They are used in this way in stores to read bar codes on products, to register the pits on CDs, or to monitor the vibrations of machines. Since laser beams are completely straight, they can also be used as guides on construction sites to help build walls and floors.

THE CUTTING EDGE
High-powered laser beams create enough energy to burn exact holes through solid metal. They are used to cut precise parts for machines

and clothes. Laser beams may also replace the surgeon's knife in delicate operations, such as those on the eye.

3–D IMAGES
One of the most amazing uses of the laser is the hologram. This is a set of ridges that creates a three-dimensional picture (image with depth) when it is seen in the right light. A hologram is produced by scanning a laser beam across the surface of an object. The ridges of the hologram record the way the object reflects light, so they can create a 3–D image when light shines on them.

Totally reflecting mirror

Artificial ruby rod

A coiled fluorescent light provides the energy

Laser beam

Semisilvered mirror

INSIDE A RUBY LASER
A rod of artificial ruby is used as a "lasing medium." A powerful lamp directed at the ruby crystal energizes the atoms inside it, so it flashes light. This light is reflected back and forth between two mirrors so that the light waves become coherent (all the same wavelength). It escapes through a tiny hole in one of the mirrors as a narrow "laser beam" ready to be focused.

SEE ALSO
Astronomy, Light, Surgery, Technology, Telescope

LAW

Laws are the rules people live by. Governments make laws, and law officers and courts see that laws are obeyed and disputes settled.

COURT AND LEGAL SYSTEMS

Civil law Deals with disputes between individuals, as in medical malpractice suits

Criminal law Protects all of society and punishes those who break the law

State courts Deal only with issues that involve state law

Federal courts There are 94 federal district courts; the U.S. Supreme Court is the highest court in the country, and is the court of final appeal for federal and state cases

▲ A traffic policeman in Samoa controls the flow of pedestrians across the road. Police act on behalf of the government to enforce the laws of a country and maintain order. They investigate crimes and arrest suspects, patrol the streets, direct traffic, find missing persons, and help in times of disaster.

About 4,000 years ago in Babylon, King Hammurabi issued a list of laws dealing with such things as stealing and bad workmanship. The Ancient Jews based their laws on the Ten Commandments given to Moses by God, as told in the Bible. The early Greeks invented democracy—lawmaking by all the people—and the Romans gave us most of the kinds of law we still use today, such as family law, property law, and criminal law. Emperor Justinian I of the Byzantine Empire drew up his famous Code of Civil Law in A.D. 534.

TOWARD MODERN LAW

A big step toward modern law came in 1215, when King John of England signed the Magna Carta—an agreement to govern according to laws. Later, parliaments rather than kings began to make laws. In 1804, Emperor Napoleon I of France introduced the Napoleonic Code, still the basis for much French law today.

UPHOLDING THE LAW

In a democracy, laws are proposed by governments, passed by legislatures (a congress or parliament), and enforced by the police and courts. People accused of breaking a law may have to go to court, where lawyers argue the case, presenting evidence and questioning witnesses. A group of ordinary people, called the jury, decides whether the accused is guilty or not guilty. The judge decides the punishment—perhaps a number of years in prison, a fine, or community service.

COURT PROCEDURE

A person accused of breaking the criminal law is innocent until proven guilty by a court of law. The lawyers put the case to the jury. The prosecution tries to prove that the defendant is guilty, and the defense tries to show that he or she is innocent. Then it is up to the jury to decide.

Jury A body of people (usually 12) who swear under oath to listen to the evidence and make an unbiased decision based on it alone

Prosecution lawyer He or she provides evidence of the defendant's guilt, questioning witnesses and scientific experts, and presenting physical evidence

Judge The person who oversees court proceedings, rules on law, and, where guilt is proven, decides on the form of punishment

Defendant The person accused of breaking the law. In the witness box he or she can be questioned by lawyers

Stenotypist The person who keeps a record of everything that is said during the course of a trial

Defense lawyer The lawyer who acts on behalf of the defendant to show his or her innocence

Physical evidence Items which are put before the jury, presented to prove the defendant's guilt or innocence

SEE ALSO

Civil rights, Democracy, Mesopotamia, Roman Empire

LEAF

Leaves use energy from sunlight to make food for plants, and are themselves a source of food for animals. They also produce the oxygen we need to breathe.

The horse chestnut has a compound leaf made up of separate leaflets.

Maple leaves are hand-shaped, or palmate, with no separate leaflets.

The ash leaf is made up of several leaflets.

The cherry has a pinnate (feather-shaped) leaf.

Pine needles are long, thin evergreen leaves that grow in clusters.

Leaves are the food factories of green plants. They come in a variety of shapes and sizes, and help us to identify the different plant species. The branching pattern of veins on the surface of a leaf is part of a network of tubes that carry water and food to all parts of the plant. The large vein that runs across the center of the leaf is called the midrib.

MAKING FOOD

The main function of leaves is to make food for the plant. This process, known as photosynthesis, takes place in tiny bodies, called chloroplasts, in the leaf cells. These contain a green-colored substance called chlorophyll that absorbs light energy. The energy is used to turn water and the gas

LEAF DESIGN

Leaves are designed to catch as much sunlight and lose as little water as possible. Stiff veins hold the leaf out to the light, and cells are transparent so that light can reach the chloroplasts. The outer layer, or cuticle, is waterproof, and most of the stomata are on the underside of the leaf, shielded from drying breezes.

carbon dioxide from the air into food molecules, such as starch and sugar. The by-product of this process is oxygen gas, some of which is used by the plant for respiration. The rest passes into the air. Nearly all living things need oxygen to survive.

TRANSPIRATION

Leaves also help the plant to draw water up from the soil, by a process called transpiration. As the water evaporates (dries) from tiny pores, or stomata, in the leaf's surface, more water is sucked up from the roots to replace it. Each pore is bound by two special "guard" cells that can open or close the opening to control water loss. The water moves up the stem through fine tubes called xylem vessels. Another set of tubes, the phloem vessels, carries food around the plant.

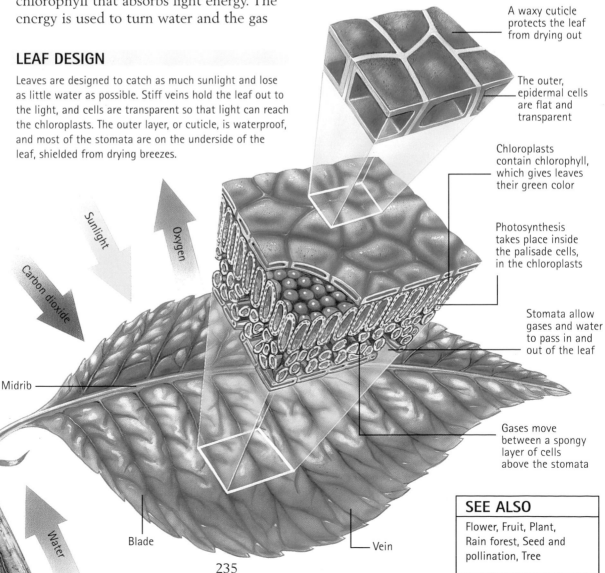

A waxy cuticle protects the leaf from drying out

The outer, epidermal cells are flat and transparent

Chloroplasts contain chlorophyll, which gives leaves their green color

Photosynthesis takes place inside the palisade cells, in the chloroplasts

Stomata allow gases and water to pass in and out of the leaf

Gases move between a spongy layer of cells above the stomata

Sunlight

Oxygen

Carbon dioxide

Water

Midrib

Blade

Vein

SEE ALSO

Flower, Fruit, Plant, Rain forest, Seed and pollination, Tree

LENS

A lens is a transparent object with at least one curved surface that helps us focus on an image by bending rays of light. It is normally made of glass or plastic.

Glasses help us see if our eye lenses don't work properly.

The lens in a camera focuses light onto the film inside.

Microscopes use lenses to magnify objects from 100 to 1,600 times.

Lenses in a pair of binoculars help you see things that are far away.

Some periscopes use lenses to enlarge the image reflected from the mirrors at either end.

When light travels through a lens, it slows down. This is because light travels faster through air than through other transparent substances like water, glass, and plastic. As it slows down it bends off course. This effect, called "refraction," is why a straw put in a glass of water at an angle looks bent. The bending distorts the image seen by the eye and can be used to make an object seem bigger or smaller.

DISTORTED IMAGES

If you put a magnifying glass close to the page of a book, you'll see a larger-than-life version of the page below it. This happens

BENDING LIGHT

There are two kinds of simple lens: convex (or converging) lenses which enlarge the image and concave (or diverging) lenses which are thicker at the edges than the middle and reduce the image.

Focal length—distance from lens center to the focus

Virtual image

Actual image

Virtual image

Actual image

CONVEX LENS
Rays of light passing through the lens are bent inward. A magnified image is produced behind the object.

CONCAVE LENS
Light rays are bent outward, so they spread out (diverge), producing a reduced image between the object and the lens.

▶ A magnifying glass has a convex lens—a lens much thicker at the middle than the edges. The image seen depends on how close you hold the glass.

because light rays from the page have been bent away from each other by the lens. Light rays from distant objects are bent toward each other by a magnifying glass. If it's dark enough, you can catch these rays on a sheet of paper. If you put the paper the right distance from the lens, they will form a focused (sharp) image.

GETTING FOCUSED

The distance from the lens to the piece of paper is called the "focal length" of the lens. In general, a thick lens bends light more than a thin one, so it has a shorter focal length. A camera uses a convex lens to produce sharp images on photographic film. Specialist cameras also use concave lenses (that are thicker at the edges than the middle). These are used to compress large images, like landscapes, onto a photograph.

EYE LENSES

Our eyeballs act like giant convex lenses that focus (bend) light onto the backs of our eyes. The muscles of our eyes pull the lenses flatter when we want to focus on objects in the distance, or make the lenses thicker to focus on nearby objects.

SEE ALSO
Astronomy, Laser, Light, Microscope, Photography, Sight, Telescope

LIGHT

Light is a visible form of energy. It moves faster than anything else in the universe, traveling 186,000 miles in a single second. Without light we cannot see.

▲ The Moon has no light of its own—it shines only because it reflects the Sun's light. Stars, however, are luminous because they produce their own light.

SIR ISAAC NEWTON
The English scientist and mathematician (1642-1726) demonstrated that light was broken into different colors by shining light through a prism.

The Sun, our nearest star, is our main source of light. Although it is nearly 93 million miles (150 million km) away, the light it makes reaches the Earth in eight minutes and is so strong that it damages our eyes if we look straight at it. At night, when our part of Earth faces away from the Sun, we have to use lightbulbs or candles for light. Compared to the Sun, the light energy made by these is tiny. They can only light up objects a few yards away.

CASTING SHADOWS

Light can travel through air, water, and other transparent (see-through) materials. Unlike sound, it can also travel through a vacuum, or empty space. Materials that only allow some light through, and are not transparent, are said to be translucent.

Many materials, like wood and metal, are opaque—they block light. If you shine a light at an opaque object, you will see a dark area behind it—the shadow. This has exactly the same outline as the object, because light travels in straight lines.

INVISIBLE ENERGY

There are many other types of energy, including radio waves, microwaves, and X rays, that travel just like light. In fact, light is only one tiny part of a huge range of energy forms, called the electromagnetic spectrum. Over the last 100 years, people have built a variety of machines, such as scanning equipment, microwave ovens, and radios, that can detect or make use of the invisible parts of this spectrum.

▲ When light shines through a prism (a 3-D glass triangle), it splits into the colors of the spectrum.
▶ This also happens when light shines through water (like rain) causing a rainbow.

▲ There are two basic ways to produce artificial light: through heat (known as incandescence), as in an electric lightbulb, or by making a gas glow, as in a fluorescent light.

▲ Glowworms, the glowing larvae of fireflies, have light organs under their abdomen which produce a heatless light known as bioluminescence.
▶ Many deep-sea fish have similar light organs on their sides to help them find food and mates in the dark.

SEE ALSO

Color, Electricity, Energy, Laser, Lens, Microscope, Moon, Sun, Wavelength

LITERATURE

Literature is the art of writing fine prose or poetry. This often involves storytelling, but may also include history, biography, and information books.

People told each other stories and poems long before they learned to write. This is "oral" (spoken) literature. Most modern literature is written in the form of books or is performed as drama.

► Rapunzel used her hair as a climbing rope in a German tale recorded by the Grimm Brothers.

▲ Good literature is written to be enjoyed, and it provides hours of entertainment for the cost of a single book.

GREAT STORYTELLERS
The Ancient Greeks told stories in poetry and in drama about heroes and gods. The poem by Homer called the *Iliad* tells of the heroes who fought at the siege of Troy. In China and India, poets told tales of how the world began and of the mysteries of life and death.

► Long John Silver, the charming but deadly pirate, appeared in *Treasure Island*, a novel written by the Scottish author Robert Louis Stevenson in 1881.

WRITING IT DOWN
A few oral works were written down, such as the epic English poem *Beowulf* in about A.D. 750. Books were copied by hand throughout the Middle Ages, when Geoffrey Chaucer (c.1342–1400) wrote a collection of stories called the *Canterbury Tales*. After 1455, the printing press made it possible to copy books cheaply and easily. A "golden age" of literature began in many countries.

THE NOVEL
The novel is a long story in prose. During the 1800s, ordinary people learned to read, and the novel became popular. Some novels were published as serials in magazines. Leading novelists of the time included Britain's Charles Dickens, France's Victor Hugo, and Leo Tolstoy in Russia.

POETRY
Poets aim to raise emotions in the reader by putting words together in striking ways. Often poetry has a rhythmical "beat," and line endings may rhyme. A poem may be short, like a Japanese three-line *haiku*, or long, like

► The mischievous country boy Tom Sawyer, who appeared in 1876, is one of the most popular characters created by American humorist Mark Twain.

◄ Hamlet, the moody Danish prince, was created by the English playwright William Shakespeare, based on an old Danish tale.

John Milton's 12-book *Paradise Lost*. A poem can tell a story, make the reader laugh, or reveal the poet's innermost feelings.

DRAMA

Plays were performed in Ancient Greece, but modern drama dates from the 1500s. Although there may be stage directions, dramatic literature is largely dialogue and relies on acting for its power. Movie scripts use special effects, lighting, and camera angles to make the dialogue more effective.

HOW WRITERS WORK

Writers watch and listen, invent plots and characters, and note down interesting things that happen. Many writers stick to one kind of book, such as humor, horror, crime, romance, religion, art, or philosophy. Some writers tell their own life story in an autobiography, others write about famous people in a biography, or about the past as history. Writers work in every

▶ D'Artagnan, hero of the French novel *The Three Musketeers*, was created by Alexandre Dumas in 1844 and has featured in several movies.

field, from aviation to zoology. Writers' works may appear in articles in newspapers and magazines, as scripts on film and television, and on new media such as the Internet.

CHILDREN'S WRITERS

There were few books written for children before the 1700s. Today, some of the best writers create stories for children. A few books, such as A. A. Milne's *Winnie the Pooh*, become classics, with their characters known around the world.

PUBLISHING A WORK

There are two main kinds of literature: fiction (stories) and nonfiction (factual books, from cookbooks to encyclopedias). Every book starts with a writer who either thinks up an idea or is asked to write a book by a publishing company. The publisher pays the writer for the book, and sees to the editing, design, illustration, and printing. By selling large quantities of books to readers, the publisher hopes to make a profit.

Charles Dickens (1812–70) was a great English novelist.

Dante (1265–1321) began modern Italian literature with his *Divine Comedy*.

American writer Edgar Allan Poe (1809–49) mastered the horror story.

Murasaki Shikibu (c.978– c.1014) wrote the *Tale of Genji* in Japan, about 1005.

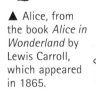

▲ Alice, from the book *Alice in Wonderland* by Lewis Carroll, which appeared in 1865.

▶ The story of Don Quixote and his servant Sancho Panza, by the Spanish author Miguel de Cervantes, has been translated into over 60 languages.

SEE ALSO

Film, Greece (Ancient), Language, Myth and legend, Printing, Theater

LUNGS AND RESPIRATORY SYSTEM

The lungs are two pinkish-gray, spongy, cone-shaped organs inside the chest. The respiratory system consists of the nose, throat, trachea, lower airways, and lungs.

▲ When breathing in, the rib cage expands and the diaphragm is lowered. These actions happen in reverse when breathing out.

FAST FACTS

• The lungs cover an area as large as a tennis court

• At rest, an average person takes about 12-15 breaths every minute. Each breath consists of just over a pint of air

• After great activity, the breathing rate can rise to 60 breaths per minute, with over six pints of air per breath

Oxygen is essential for almost every living thing, including the human body. When we breathe in, our lungs take in fresh air, absorb oxygen from it, and pass it to the blood, which carries it to all the parts of the body. Fresh air is taken into the lungs by breathing, or respiration. This process is powered by two sets of muscles—the diaphragm below the lungs and the intercostal muscles between the ribs, in front of the lungs.

IN AND OUT

To breathe in, the diaphragm tenses, shortens, and flattens. The intercostals also shorten and pull the ribs upward and forward. These movements stretch the lungs, making them larger, and suck fresh air in through the nose and mouth, down the throat and trachea, into the lungs. To breathe out, the diaphragm relaxes, and the stretched lungs spring back to their normal size, pushing stale air out.

OXYGEN IN

Dark, bluish-red, low-oxygen blood flows to each lung along the pulmonary artery. This divides many times to form a network of microscopic blood vessels, or capillaries, which enclose tiny balloons called alveoli. Oxygen from the air inside each alveolus seeps easily through its thin lining and the thin capillary wall, into the blood. This makes the blood bright red. The capillaries join to form the pulmonary vein, which carries the high-oxygen blood away.

CARBON DIOXIDE OUT

In addition to taking in oxygen, the respiratory system also removes one of the body's waste products, carbon dioxide. This seeps the opposite way to oxygen—from the blood into the alveolus—and is breathed out as stale air.

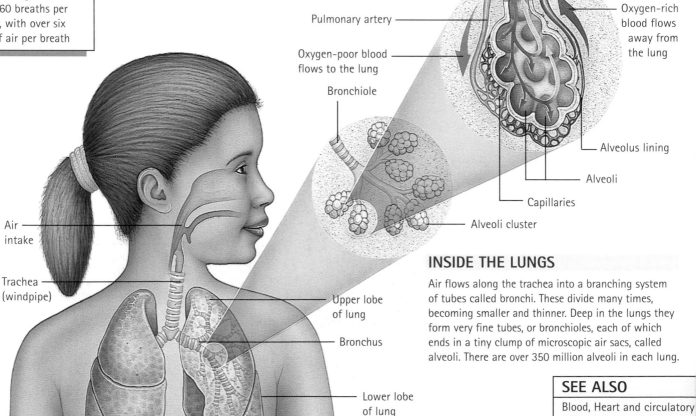

INSIDE THE LUNGS

Air flows along the trachea into a branching system of tubes called bronchi. These divide many times, becoming smaller and thinner. Deep in the lungs they form very fine tubes, or bronchioles, each of which ends in a tiny clump of microscopic air sacs, called alveoli. There are over 350 million alveoli in each lung.

SEE ALSO

Blood, Heart and circulatory system, Human body, Muscle

MACHINE

A machine is a device that makes work easier by allowing us to use force to complete a task. It can be simple, like a screwdriver, or complicated, like a car.

Simple machines make work easier and can be used as parts of more complex devices. There are six main types of machine: the lever, pulley, and wheel and axle (which are all forms of levers); and the screw, inclined or sloping plane, and wedge (all forms of inclined planes).

BASIC MACHINES

By using a lever, you can increase the effect of the force, or effort, you apply. The machine needs a fulcrum (a fixed point) to support it. By positioning the fulcrum carefully, you can apply a small effort at one end of the lever to raise a big load at the other end. Heavy weights can be moved using an inclined plane (pushing goods up a ramp is easier than lifting them); on rollers, like the logs used by pyramid builders to move slabs; or by a wheel turning on an axle.

MAGNIFIED FORCE

A screw can either pull things together or push them apart (like a jack). A pulley system uses wheels to change the direction of a force produced by pulling on a rope. The wedge (an ax, for example) can be used to split materials.

Corkscrews make use of screw and lever actions. The screw's spiral thread gives a tight grip.

A pair of scissors is a double lever. The screw is the fixed point or fulcrum; the blades pivot around it.

A can opener acts as a wedge, forcing its way into the lid while cogged wheels turn the cutter.

THE FIRST MACHINES

The potter's wheel, invented around 3500 B.C., was one of the earliest machines. Others include the spindle, for spinning fibers into yarn; the loom, for weaving yarn into cloth; the plow, for turning heavy soil; and bellows, for blowing air into fires.

WAR AND WORK

Early war inventions include the battering ram (a wedge) and the catapult (a lever). An important development of the wheel was the gear. A gearwheel combines the principles of wheel and lever. As it turns, its teeth, or cogs, mesh with other toothed wheels. In this way it can change the speed and direction of the force applied, depending on the number and spacing of the teeth.

Pulley wheels

INVENTIVE PAST

The Ancient Greeks used screws, lathes (used for turning wood), construction cranes, and watermills—the first machines to use nonanimal power. They discovered that steam could be used to drive machines. But neither the Greeks nor the equally inventive Chinese were interested in labor-saving machines, because slaves were cheap and plentiful. ▶

Having four wheels allows four times the load to be lifted with the same effort

Effort

RAISING THE LOAD

The simplest type of pulley is a wheel with a grooved rim. A rope or chain is passed around the groove. The pulley changes the direction of a force, so by pulling down on the rope, a person can raise a heavy weight. The more pulleys there are with one rope running through them, the greater the load that can be lifted with the same effort.

Load

TAKING THE STRAIN

Elevators can be hydraulic or operated by electric traction, like the one here. Hoisting ropes, made of steel cables, are raised or lowered by a pulley wheel, turned by an electric motor. In the 1850s, engineer Elisha G. Otis invented the first elevator featuring an automatic safety device—a safety clamp—which would prevent the elevator from falling if the rope broke.

MEDIEVAL MACHINES

Important mechanical inventions of the Middle Ages included the crossbow, windmill, clockwork, and the printing press. During the 1200s, the English monk Roger Bacon predicted the use of cars, airplanes, and submarines long before the technology and materials required for such inventions were even available.

MACHINES REPLACE WORKERS

As labor became more expensive, it made economic sense to make machines do more work. From the 1700s, a new kind of mechanized industry developed. The Federal Armory in Springfield, Massachusetts, pioneered the mechanized manufacture of muskets for the army. In Britain, the engineer Marc Brunel designed 43 machines that could make 10,000 pulley blocks a year, enabling the Royal Navy dockyard to reduce the workforce required for the task from 110 to just 10 men.

▲ From the invention of the potter's wheel, someone got the idea for the cart wheel. Fitted with pots, a wheel could also raise water from one level to another, for irrigation.

Elevator drive and speed controls

Hoisting ropes

Car guide rails

Car: this observation elevator has glass sides

Safety clamp

Traveling cable

Counterweight

RAW POWER

The invention of the coal-burning steam engine provided a new source of power. Unlike humans and animals, a steam engine never tired, and, unlike wind and water power, was not reliant on the weather. Steam engines could generate power in factories, mines, ships, and railroad locomotives.

THE FACTORY AGE

To make machines, machine tools were needed to stamp out metal plates, cut screws and gears, and shape metals by cutting, drilling, grinding, or polishing. Standardization of parts made it easier to keep machines working and repair them quickly. Important new inventions included the dynamo, the electric motor, and the hydraulic press and ram. The clothing and shoemaking industries were transformed by the sewing machine, invented in 1846.

THREAT TO JOBS

The use of machines in industry greatly increased output and made factory goods cheaper. But there was a human cost. Workers, including women and children, toiled for low pay in bad conditions. In the 1880s, social critics like the Englishman William Morris complained that machines were destroying craftsmanship, reducing people to a form of slavery. Some people smashed machines they thought were going to take away their work.

WORK REVOLUTION

The machine revolution affected farming, where machines took over harvesting, baling, and threshing. Transportation and trade were revolutionized in the mid–1800s by the locomotive, steamship, and conveyor belt. Machines invaded offices and stores, at first in the form of typewriters and cash registers.

THE MODERN WORLD

New machines, such as the car and the airplane, began to transform the world at the beginning of the 1900s. The invention of the jet engine and the rocket allowed people to travel at speeds that had been unimaginable before. In the home, old-fashioned devices were being discarded in favor of new time- and energy-saving appliances such as the washing machine, vacuum cleaner, and the food processor. In industry, robots and increasingly efficient computers took over many basic production processes. New materials, such as plastic, ceramics, and carbon fibers, are today replacing metals to make machines that are smaller, yet more efficient.

▲ Car jacks can be manual (like the screw car jack above) or hydraulic. They are machines that are designed to raise and support a heavy load, like a car, little by little. By turning a handle many times, the operator applies a small force pushing a long way; this force is converted to pushing a large force (the car) a short way.

▶ A forklift truck is a machine that raises weights using liquid pressure (hydraulics). Simple hydraulic machines have a cylinder with a large and a small piston inside. The cylinder is filled with fluid. A force applied to the small piston is transferred to the larger one, increasing the force.

◀ A snowblower has two engines: one drives the truck, the other turns the drum. As it turns, blades on the drum churn the snow, forcing it upward through the chutes. As the truck moves forward, it takes in more snow.

SEE ALSO

Car, Engine, Household appliance, Industrial Revolution, Industry, Invention, Robot

MAGNETISM

Magnetism is a force that pulls objects made of iron, nickel, or cobalt toward magnets. Scientists do not fully understand how this force is created.

The horseshoe magnet has a pole at each end.

So does the simple bar magnet.

A ring magnet has one pole on its outer surface and another pole on its inner one.

If you have ever moved a magnet toward a pin, you have experienced magnetism. Pins are made of steel—a material that consists mainly of iron—and they feel a strong force pulling them toward the magnet, which may even be strong enough to make them stick to it. Any material, like steel, that is attracted toward a magnet in this way is called a magnetic material.

MAGNETIC POLES

When an object is attracted to a magnet, it sticks to its ends—this is where the magnet exerts, or gives out, the greatest force. The two ends of the magnet are called its poles. One of them is north-seeking and the other is south-seeking. They should be marked in some way so you can tell them apart. If you bring the same poles of two magnets face to face, they will repel each other; and if you bring different poles of two magnets face to face, they will attract each other.

► Industrial-strength electromagnets can lift heavy pieces of scrap iron.

ELECTRO-MAGNETISM

In 1820, a Danish physicist, Hans Christian Ørsted, discovered that magnetism was produced by an electric current. This led to the development of the electromagnet—a temporary magnet formed when an electric current passes through a conductor such as wire, which is wrapped around an iron core. Electromagnets are useful because they can be turned on or off and altered in strength. They can produce magnetic fields strong enough to drive generators and electric motors. Smaller ones are used to make doorbells and buzzers work.

MAGNETIC EARTH

The Earth itself acts like a huge magnet with magnetic poles at its north and south ends—known as the magnetic north pole and the magnetic south pole. These poles act like the ends of a magnet and make compass needles point north. They are close to the geographic North and South Poles, which are at the top and bottom of the imaginary line, or axis, around which the Earth spins.

Iron filings scattered around two magnets show that a south-facing and a north-facing pole are pulled toward each other

When the north-facing poles of two magnets are put together, they repel each other and the force pushes out the iron filings

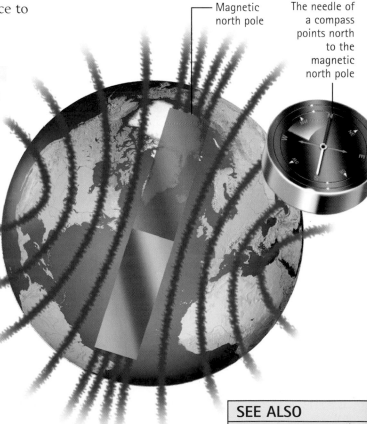
Magnetic north pole

The needle of a compass points north to the magnetic north pole

SEE ALSO

Antarctica, Arctic, Earth, Electricity, Iron and steel, Metal

MALAYSIA

Malaysia is a fast-growing nation in Southeast Asia, consisting of Peninsular Malaysia and the areas of Sabah and Sarawak on the island of Borneo.

Area: 126,900 sq. mi.
Population: 22,662,365
Capital: Kuala Lumpur
Language: Malay
Currency: Ringgit (Malaysian dollar)

The two regions that make up Malaysia lie 400 mi. (650km) apart, across the South China Sea. The climate is hot, humid, and rainy and there are swamps, rain forests, and golden beaches. The many mountains include Mount Kinabalu (13,445 ft./4,100m), the highest peak in Southeast Asia.

▲ Sarawak has a swampy coastal plain and many rivers. In some villages, people live in houses raised on stilts.

▲ Workers tap rubber trees for their latex. Rubber is a major export, as well as tin, gas, oil, palm oil, hardwood, tea, cocoa, and pineapples.

RURAL AND CITY LIFE
Wildlife includes giant turtles and over a thousand types of orchid. Traditionally, Malays lived in rural areas, in villages called *kampongs*, but half the population now lives in towns and cities. The capital, Kuala Lumpur, has many modern buildings, including one of the world's tallest skyscrapers, and is Malaysia's largest city.

GROWING INDUSTRIES
Malaysia has fertile soil, and the most important food crop is rice. There are also large deposits of minerals. The country is growing rapidly as an industrial power, and is a major producer of components for the electronics industry, textiles, cement, cars, and tires. Tourism is also growing.

MALAYSIA'S PEOPLE
Just over half the people are Malay, and a third are Chinese. Other groups include Tamils from India and Sri Lanka and the native peoples of Sarawak and Sabah: Dayaks, Ibans, and Kadazans. Malay is the national language, but Chinese, Tamil, and English are also widely spoken. Islam is the official religion, but about half the people practice other religions, including Buddhism and Hinduism.

CHINESE ANCESTORS
The ancestors of today's Malays came from China around 2000 B.C. The Arabs, Portuguese, and Dutch all occupied the area before the British seized control in the early 1800s, eventually granting independence in 1957. Today's Malaysia was eventually formed in 1963.

▲ Traditional crafts include working with textiles. In the north of Peninsular Malaysia, batik work is popular.

SEE ALSO
Indonesia, Rain forest, Southeast Asia

MAMMAL

Mammals are vertebrates (they have backbones). They have adapted to a wider range of habitats and show a greater variety of forms than any other animal group.

◄ The armadillo is covered in bony plates that protect it from predators. When attacked, it curls up into a tight ball.

Orangutans are one of about 180 primates. This group includes humans.

The bat is the only mammal that can fly. Its forelimbs act as wings.

There are about 250 types of marsupial, mostly found in the Australian region.

Mammals like the hyena have strong teeth called canines for stabbing flesh.

Marine mammals like the seal have short fur and streamlined bodies.

The duck-billed platypus is one of only three species of egg-laying mammal.

All mammals are warm-blooded, which means they can keep their bodies warm and stay active even in the coldest weather. The only other animals that can do this are birds. Most mammals are covered with hair or fur, which helps keep them warm. Unlike other animal babies, young mammals feed on their mother's milk. Mammals also have larger brains than other animals.

A SUCCESSFUL GROUP

The first mammals appeared on Earth about 200 million years ago as small, insect-eating creatures. When dinosaurs died out about 65 million years ago, mammals began to explore different habitats and try different foods. They became larger and took on many different shapes. Thousands of "experimental" mammals have come and gone during the last 50 million years, but only about 4,200 different species live in the world today.

VARIETY OF HABITATS

Mammals are not as numerous as birds or fish, but they can be found in almost every habitat: some live in seas and rivers; some spend their lives high up in the trees of the forest; antelopes and other grazing mammals form huge herds on grasslands. Some mammals manage to survive in the driest deserts and on the coldest mountaintops. Bats have taken to the air; seals, whales, and dolphins to the seas.

THE RIGHT TEETH

Mammals eat a wide range of foods and most have teeth designed to suit their diets. Most plant-eating mammals (herbivores), such as horses and elephants, have large grinding teeth at the back of the mouth. Rodents have sharp, chisel-like front teeth for gnawing nuts and other hard foodstuffs. Flesh-eating mammals (carnivores), such as lions and wolves, have large, sharp canines for stabbing and seizing prey, and sharp-edged cheek teeth for slicing through flesh.

CARE OF THE YOUNG

Young mammals learn many of their survival skills during the period that they are with their mother, feeding on her milk. At birth, lion cubs are blind and helpless, weighing only about 3.3 lb. (1.5kg). The mother carries them in her mouth from one hiding place to another, and the male protects his family from intruders. Only when the cubs are between 18 and 24 months old will the lioness have another litter.

MAMMAL OF THE DESERT

The two-humped Bactrian camel of central Asia is well adapted to life in the desert. It can travel for days or even weeks with no food or water because it carries a large store of fat in its humps, which it converts into food. At the end of a long period without food, the humps lose much of their firmness, and may even flop to one side. With its bushy eyebrows and long lashes, the camel can shield its eyes from the sand. It can even close its nostrils during a sandstorm. A close relative of the Bactrian camel is the Arabian camel, or dromedary, which has only one hump.

COVERED IN FUR
One of a mammal's main characteristics is its fur. A Bactrian camel's fur can grow to 10 in. (25cm) on its head, neck, and humps. Camels grow a new coat once a year.

NECK BONES
All mammals, apart from the manatee and sloth, but including the giraffe, have seven cervical vertebrae (bones that make up the neck).

A MOTHER'S MILK
Mammals are the only animals to feed their young with milk, produced in special glands called mammae.

Omnivorous mammals, which include humans, eat plants and animals. Insect-eaters, such as shrews and hedgehogs, have lots of small, sharply pointed teeth, but anteaters have no teeth at all: they lap up ants with their sticky tongue. Some whales have no teeth: they feed on small animals which they sift from the water with plates of horny material in the roof of their mouth called baleen or whalebone.

EGGS AND POUCHES

A tiny number of mammals, such as the duck-billed platypus, are unusual because they lay eggs. Others, called marsupials, are also known as pouched mammals, because the female nurses her babies in a pouch or pocket on her body. About 50 million years ago, marsupials lived all over the world, but they are now found mainly in the Australian region, with a few in North and South America. All other mammals, known as placental mammals, give birth to live young.

THE LARGEST GROUP

Placental mammals are by far the biggest group of mammal. While the baby is inside its mother, it gets food and oxygen from her blood through a structure called the placenta. A placental mammal baby can stay inside its mother's body for much longer than a marsupial baby. A baby elephant, for example, grows inside its mother for about 22 months and is well developed when it is born. Some baby mammals can run around soon after they are born, but many others, including human babies, are quite helpless at birth.

FAST FACTS

• With their relatively large brains, mammals have a greater ability to learn than other animals

• Special mammal senses include the bat's sonar and the mole's ultrasensitive whiskers

• The largest mammal, the blue whale, can be 100 ft. (30m) long

SEE ALSO

Animal, Bat, Bear, Cat, Dog, Hippopotamus, Horse, Kangaroo, Monkey, Platypus, Prehistoric animal, Rat, Rhinoceros, Tiger, Whale and dolphin, Wolf

MAP

Maps show the Earth, or a part of it, on paper. They may show travelers a route or they may display weather patterns, land use, and other information.

A pedometer is used to measure distance.

A theodolite gives the direction of distant objects.

Stereo viewers give a 3-D image from aerial photos.

From the earliest times, people have drawn sketch maps to describe a route or place. Only in the past 400 years has science made it possible to draw accurate maps of the entire world.

CHARTS IN CLAY

The first maps were drawn on clay tablets about 2300 B.C. in Mesopotamia. They showed nearby towns and how to reach them, but were not at all accurate. In about A.D. 140 the scientist Claudius Ptolemy produced a book on geography which contained many maps. Soon afterward, the Roman army produced a map of cities and forts based on accurate measurements of the roads in between.

SEA CHARTS

The European sailors who traveled to other continents from the 1450s onward needed charts that included information such as depth of the sea, strength of currents, and how best to enter a harbor.

READING THE MEANING

Maps may contain many different types of information. The most familiar maps are those showing road routes for travelers. Scientists may create maps showing how many people live in different areas, what land is used for, or the types of soil to be found. Maps showing temperatures and air conditions are used for weather forecasting. All maps rely on accurate surveying, the collection of information by people on the ground and the transfer of this to the maps.

▲ Maps using Mercator projection, invented in 1569, allow sailors and pilots to plot their course accurately, but distort areas close to the North and South Poles.

► Maps using Peters projection, developed in 1973, give accurate areas but distort shapes.

Modern charts contain similar information, together with locations of lighthouses and radio beacons.

MAPS TO SCALE

Most maps are made to a scale, meaning that distances on the map are related to distances on the ground. For example, a map of scale 1:100,000 means that 1 inch on the map is equal to 100,000 inches on the ground, or 1.6 mi. Some maps are deliberately inaccurate. For example, a map of an expressway may not show corners or distances, but only which towns can be reached from each exit.

▲ Relief maps show physical features, such as rivers, plains, hills, and mountains.

▲ Here, population density is shown by colors. Dark colors are areas with the most people.

▲ Route maps may show roads, railroads, and built-up areas to help travelers find their way.

SEE ALSO

Mesopotamia, Navigation, Weather

MATERIALS

People use a huge range of different materials with which to make things. These include metal, plastic, rubber, ceramics, glass, and wood.

Leather is strong but soft, and easily cut to shape.

Rubber can be stretched, but bounces back to shape.

Plastic may be soft or hard and can take any shape.

Glass is hard but shatters easily when hit.

Wood is relatively light and strong.

Bricks of clay can bear heavy weights.

All the materials people use originally come from the Earth. Materials that are used in their natural state are called raw materials. These may be processed or mixed together to make manufactured or "synthetic" materials.

RAW AND SYNTHETIC
Wood, which comes from trees, is a raw material. It can be used in its original state or processed to make manufactured materials such as cardboard and paper. Glass is a synthetic material made by mixing together sand, salt, and other raw materials at a high temperature.

PROPERTIES
Materials must be chosen carefully. A ladder, for example, must be made of something strong and rigid, like steel. If it is made of something soft and stretchy, like rubber, it will bend when people walk up it, making it dangerous to use. Every material has properties, such as strength and hardness. Other properties

▲ A lathe spins an object quickly, so that it can easily be smoothed to a perfect round shape.

▲ Metal is heated until it becomes liquid, then poured into a mold. When it cools and hardens, the metal takes the shape of the mold.

characterize a material as ductile, elastic, or plastic. A ductile material is one that can be stretched easily. Metal is ductile when it is hot; it can be pulled into thin wires. Materials like rubber that go back to their original shape after stretching are elastic. Wet clay and other materials that can be pushed into any shape, and then stay like that, are plastic. Most plastics have this property when they are hot, which is how they got their name.

COMPOSITES
Sometimes people need to combine materials to benefit from two properties which a single material does not have. For example, car windshields need to be transparent like glass, but as strong as steel. Manufacturers often mix materials or sandwich them together to make new ones called composites. Laminated glass is a composite material. The strongest type has a thin steel mesh sandwiched between panes of glass. It is almost completely transparent, but is strong enough to stand or walk on.

◄ Clay is an example of a material that changes easily. As clay it is soft and weak. But when heated, or fired, it changes to pottery, which is very hard and strong. Adding different substances, such as bone ash or white clay, gives pottery different properties.

SEE ALSO
Bridge, Construction, Design, Housing, Solid, liquid, and gas; Textile

MAYA

The Maya Indians dominated Central America from about A.D. 250 to A.D. 850, building cities deep in the rain forest. Their descendants still live in the region.

The Maya were great astronomers and carved dates of religious ceremonies on stones.

The Maya wrote using glyphs (picture symbols) to show sounds of words or to convey ideas.

The Maya were among the most highly developed civilizations in Central America. Their achievements in art, architecture, astronomy, and mathematics were outstanding.

▲ Modern Maya at a market on the steps of a church in Guatemala.

MIGHTY MAYA

The first Maya lived in city-states, probably led by priest-kings. Evidence of these states dates back to around A.D. 250, with stone pillars erected by the rulers to record their achievements. Within a few generations, the Maya were building vast cities, such as Tikal (now in Guatemala), with populations of up to 50,000 people. These spread across the Yucatan Peninsula to the Pacific Ocean. This was known as the Classic Period.

WEALTH FROM THE EARTH

The wealth of the Maya was based on trade and farming. As early as 1500 B.C., people in the area were growing Indian corn, the basic food of the Maya. The seeds were either boiled or ground into a powder to make a porridge. Mayan farmers grew tomatoes, string beans, avocados, and sweet potatoes. They had no farm animals, but hunted wild game and fish. Most people lived in forest huts, coming into the city only to attend markets or religious ceremonies.

SCIENCE OF THE STARS

Mayan priests learned how to calculate the solar year, lunar months, and even the movements of the planet Venus. For these calculations, the Maya developed complex mathematics and used writing more skillfully than any other American people.

DEATH OF A CULTURE

In about A.D. 800, some of the southern cities were abandoned. By 950, most of the great cities had collapsed. The reasons for this are unknown. People continued to live in their homeland, but in villages. There was a revival around 1200, and then, in the 1500s, the Maya were conquered by Spanish invaders.

MAYAN MONUMENTS

With only stone hand tools, the Maya managed to build great pyramids and palaces. The Castillo Pyramid in Chichén Itzá reached 100 ft. (30m) above the ground. Chichén Itzá survived longer than most Mayan cities—it was inhabited until about 1440.

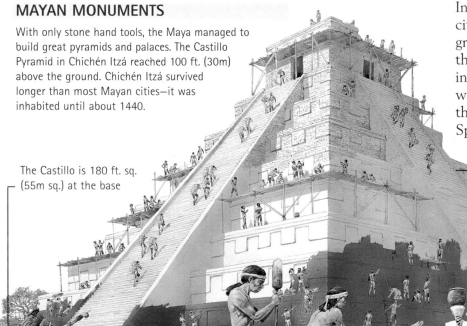

The Castillo is 180 ft. sq. (55m sq.) at the base

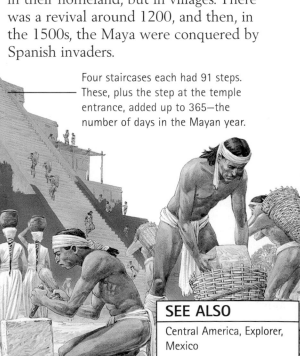

Four staircases each had 91 steps. These, plus the step at the temple entrance, added up to 365—the number of days in the Mayan year.

SEE ALSO

Central America, Explorer, Mexico

MEDIA

The media are the channels through which news and views are publicized. They include radio, television, newspapers, magazines, teletext and the Internet.

▲ Paparazzi photographers spy on celebrities and take photographs for international papers and magazines.

The media offer a window on the world, bringing events from other countries close to home. Media can be printed (newspapers, magazines or books), broadcast (on radio, television or cinema) or electronic, such as the Internet. It can be aimed at informing and entertaining, or advertising something or someone.

CENSORSHIP
News put out through media can affect public opinion. Some governments try to censor the media, others use them for propaganda. The freedom of the press to print or broadcast what it likes, so long as it is true, is an important civil right. In democratic countries such as the USA, there are laws to protect the press from pressure to print a particular thing. A free press can question the actions of a government and make it difficult for dictators. Most dictators or one-party states allow only news favourable to themselves to be broadcast.

CONTROLLING THE MEDIA
Usually the media are owned by private businesses. Reporters or programme-makers may do as they please, as long as their work fits in with the style and tone of the programme or publication, which may support a particular political party.

MEDIA INFLUENCE
Companies and personalities may try to influence what appears in the media by offering gifts, trips or parties. Journalists may also be threatened with being sued for libel or having access to events withdrawn if unpleasant stories are broadcast.

Game, set and match to Rusedski

British tennis ace Greg Rusedski wowed spectators with his powerful style on court yesterday to win through to the finals.

By JANE SMITH

CANADIAN-BORN Rusedski beat his opponent 6-0, 6-4 in straight sets, then faced a gruelling fifth set when he eventually took match point on 14-12.

GIRLFRIEND IN CROWD
Rusedski's girlfriend Lucy Connors was among the crowd cheering ecstatically on centre court. He now heads Britain's

NEWSPAPER
A reporter and photographer will go along to a match to record results and comments from players.

COVERING AN EVENT
A news event will be covered in different ways by the various media: newspapers send a reporter and photographer; radio shows may have just one broadcaster with an outside broadcast unit; television needs visual images and sound.

TELEVISION
Television coverage of a news event demands camera operators, sound technicians and a commentator on site.

RADIO
Results are given during a radio news bulletin, while sports programmes are recorded live from events.

THE EVENT
Major sports attractions, such as the Wimbledon or the US Open tennis tournaments, give press passes to TV and radio stations and accredited journalists.

SEE ALSO
Internet, Newspaper and magazine, Photography, Radio, Television

MEDICINE

Medicine is the scientific study of human disease. It covers the causes, prevention, diagnosis, and treatment of all types of different sicknesses.

The name of the Ancient Greek Hippocrates (c.460–377 B.C.) lives on in the Hippocratic oath, a code of principles for doctors.

French chemist Louis Pasteur (1822–95) invented pasteurization—a process of killing germs in liquids such as milk.

English surgeon Joseph Lister (1827–1912) introduced antiseptics into surgery, reducing the risk of bacterial infection.

Alexander Fleming (1881–1955) was a British bacteriologist who discovered the antibiotic drug penicillin.

The Greek physician Hippocrates is often called the "founding father of medicine." He examined patients and recorded their symptoms. He also prescribed many remedies, including willow bark tea—later shown to be the source of aspirin. But medicine could not progress in a scientific way until doctors understood how the body works.

UNDERSTANDING THE BODY
In the 1500s, the Belgian anatomist Andreas Vesalius was the first to show where bones, muscles, blood vessels, and organs were situated in the body. Then William Harvey (1578–1657), a British doctor, discovered that the blood was pumped around the body by the heart. During the 1800s, scientists showed that microbes (microscopic organisms such as bacteria) could cause disease, and medicine began to progress as a modern science.

MAKING A DIAGNOSIS
The identification, or diagnosis, of a disease begins with the doctor taking a history of the illness. This includes asking about symptoms, previous illnesses, and details of the patient's lifestyle. Then the doctor carries out a physical examination.

MILESTONES IN MODERN MEDICINE

1905 First blood transfusion

1922 Frederick Banting and Charles Best first treat a diabetic patient with insulin

1928 Discovery of penicillin by Alexander Fleming

1938 First artificial hip replacement

1943 First renal dialysis or artificial kidney machine

1955 Polio vaccine introduced by Jonas Salk

1967 First heart transplant operation done by Dr. Christiaan Barnard in Cape Town, South Africa

1979 World declared free of smallpox following worldwide vaccination program

1981 First cases of AIDS diagnosed

This may include listening to the sounds of the patient's chest and abdomen with a stethoscope, feeling organs such as the liver, and looking into the eyes, ears, and throat with special instruments. Most illnesses can be diagnosed from the history and physical examination alone. The doctor may also send blood, urine, and other samples to a hospital laboratory for testing. Sometimes the patient will need to have an X ray or a scan. These create pictures of the inside of the body which can give a better idea of what is wrong.

MEDICAL TREATMENT
Most illnesses are treated by drugs or surgery. There are around 6,000 drugs available today, including painkillers,

◀ Computer technology is widely used in the development of new drugs. Here, a "virtual reality" system is being used to create a 3-D image of a drug, which can then be manipulated by the researcher.

antibiotics, anticancer drugs, and drugs for mental illness. Surgery is often used in the treatment of heart disease and cancer to remove or repair diseased tissue. It is now also possible to replace major organs such as the heart, lungs, kidneys, and liver by transplant surgery.

PREVENTATIVE MEDICINE
Prevention is always better than a cure. Doctors and nurses use what they know about the causes of disease to help stop patients getting sick in the first place. Smoking is known to cause both heart disease and lung cancer, so the medical profession tries to discourage patients from smoking. Smokers can attend antismoking clinics, for example, and there are health warnings on cigarette packs. People can also look after themselves by eating a healthy diet, exercising, getting enough rest, and having regular checkups.

Vaccination protects people from diseases such as polio.

ALTERNATIVE TREATMENT
There are also complementary or alternative medicines, which take a different approach to healing. Acupuncture comes from the Chinese medical tradition. It depends upon balancing the body's lifeforce, or *chi*, which flows along invisible channels in the body called meridians. During treatment, an acupuncturist uses needles to help the chi flow more freely. This and other forms of alternative medicine, such as reflexology, homeopathy, and aromatherapy, are popular with patients, although their effects may not be scientifically proven.

▲ Acupuncture involves thin metal needles being inserted into selected points in a patient's body. In China, where the technique originated, it is used as an anaesthetic during surgical operations.

VIEWING THE BODY IN CROSS SECTIONS
One of today's fastest and most accurate forms of imaging (to help diagnosis) is the computerized tomography (CT) scanner, which creates a "virtual reality" image of the patient's body. The patient is moved slowly through the scanner, inside of which an X-ray source rotates around the body. A ring of detectors relay the information to a powerful computer for processing. The information is then displayed on screens on the main console as a series of cross sections, or slices, through the patient's body.

Revolving X-ray source

Continuous spiral (ring) of detectors

X-ray beam

Computer screen

Movable patient couch

Main console

▲ This image, produced by a CT scanner, provides details of a slice through the patient's brain.

SEE ALSO
Disease, Drug, Human body, Immune system, Nutrition, Surgery, X ray

253

MESOPOTAMIA

Mesopotamia lies along the valleys of the Tigris and Euphrates rivers in the Middle East. The world's earliest cities and organized civilizations grew up here.

Cast copper work, a bust of King Sargon of Akkad.

A wooden lyre shows the importance of music at Ur.

Elaborate gold jewellery was worn by the nobles.

Cylinder seals were used by merchants and priests.

After 2000 B.C., chariots dominated warfare.

Watered by the mighty Tigris and Euphrates rivers, Mesopotamia (a Greek word meaning "between the rivers") was a fertile and wealthy land. It was here that early farmers developed writing, founded cities, and built a series of empires which dominated surrounding lands.

FIRST FARMERS
Farming spread into Mesopotamia from the hills to the north and west. By about 6000 B.C., people living along the rivers had learned how to irrigate fields to grow barley, wheat, dates, and beans. Sheep and goats were kept for their meat and wool. In the fertile valley more food could be grown, and the population boomed. By about 3500 B.C., villages along the twin rivers had grown into cities of over 10,000 people.

CITY-STATES
The buildings in the cities were made of mud bricks, with only a few being built of kiln-baked bricks. The people learned how to weave wool and flax into clothing, make copper tools, and produce high-quality pottery for the first time. Each city was independent, but traded with other towns and people, even importing ivory and

▲ A number of powerful cities ruled the area that surrounded them until the growth of empires.

▶ A ceremonial helmet made of an alloy of gold and silver, which belonged to King Meskalamdug of Kish in about 2200 B.C.

gemstones from India.

THE WORLD OF GILGAMESH
The need to organize irrigation schemes led to the growth of strong central governments by kings or priests. Gradually, a few powerful cities, such as Eridu, Kish, and Uruk, came to dominate the surrounding area, known as Sumer. Writing was invented to keep track of government and temple records, but was soon used to record events and the deeds of kings. In about 2700 B.C., Gilgamesh became king of Uruk and fought several wars. He was so famous that many stories were told and written about him.

SACRED CITIES
At the center of each city was a *ziggurat*, a massive artificial hill topped by a temple. Built of layers of mud brick and straw, the ziggurats were up to 330 ft. (100m) across

THE LAW CODES

Rulers set out law codes, often carved on a stone pillar and set up for public display. The oldest known was made by Ur-Nammu, who ruled Ur in about 2100 B.C. The code dealt with slaves, personal injury, and witchcraft. Ur was also famous for its ziggurat, an enormous stepped temple to the Moon god Nanna, also built by Ur-Nammu.

and 300 ft. tall. Mud bricks were not strong enough to support these structures for long, and most ziggurats were repaired about every 100 years. The ziggurat was dedicated to the god or goddess of the city, whose prestige depended on the power of his or her city. Gods could win or lose worshipers if their city won or lost a battle. Many rulers were both kings and priests, or the posts were held by the same family.

WARRIOR EMPIRES

In about 2370 B.C., King Sargon of Akkad, the area around Nippur, conquered Mesopotamia. He and his successors conquered lands as far as Syria. Soon after 2000 B.C., invaders from the

north and west destroyed the empire and overran several cities. The invaders settled in Mesopotamia and adopted local customs. By about 1792 B.C., King Hammurabi of Babylon claimed to rule all of Mesopotamia. Gradually the northern cities grew more wealthy and powerful. In 1250 B.C. the Assyrians, based at Nineveh, conquered a new empire covering Mesopotamia, Syria, Palestine, and Egypt.

END OF AN ERA

Mesopotamia enjoyed a final period of power from 626 B.C. to 539 B.C., under the Chaldean rulers. It was then conquered by Persia and became a part of larger empires. Mesopotamia is now divided among Iraq, Syria, and Turkey.

◄ Cuneiform writing and a carving of a king. Cuneiform symbols represent an object and the sound of its name. They were used to write a variety of languages from 3200 B.C. to A.D. 100.

▲ One of two statues of goats made of gold, silver, and lapis lazuli found in one of the royal tombs at Ur.

SEE ALSO

Babylon, Egypt (Ancient), Empire, Middle East, Seven Wonders of the World

METAL

A metal is a shiny material such as iron, gold, or copper. Most are solid at room temperature, easy to shape when hot, and good at conducting heat and electricity.

▲ Metals can be joined by welding—the application of heat, pressure, or both. Here, an electrical current is being used to heat steel in a process called arc welding.

▼ Aluminum alloys are used in aircraft construction because they are light but strong.

The Earth has a huge supply of some metals, such as tin and iron —used to make tools, machines, and large structures. Other metals, such as gold and platinum, are rare. They are usually used in small quantities.

WORKING WITH METAL
People have known how to extract and use metals since about 8000 B.C. If a metal is heated until it becomes molten (liquid), it can be poured into a mold. As soon as it cools, it hardens and keeps its shape until melted again. Metals can also be hammered into any shape or pulled into long strands. Most solid metals are very strong and hard, which is why they are used to make things like building frames and engine parts that have to keep their shape when put under pressure.

METALS THAT RUST
If something made of iron is left outside, it will go rusty. This is because the surface of the iron reacts with oxygen in the air to form a new compound —iron oxide. Many other metals react with oxygen or other elements, and so are not found in their pure state in the ground. Instead, they are found as ores— compounds of metal and oxygen. A common way of extracting metal from oxide ores is to heat them with charcoal to remove the oxygen, leaving the pure metal.

ALLOYS
People have discovered many ways to mix metals both with each other, and with nonmetals, to make useful materials. These mixtures are called alloys. Steel is an alloy made from iron and small amounts of carbon and other metals. It is harder and stronger than pure iron. Bronze is a hard alloy made from copper and tin.

METAL FATIGUE
You need a large force to break a lump of metal apart all at once. But some metals break when bent many times by a small force. This way of breaking a metal, called metal fatigue, is a serious hazard. Machines like airplanes that must not fail are checked for signs of metal fatigue.

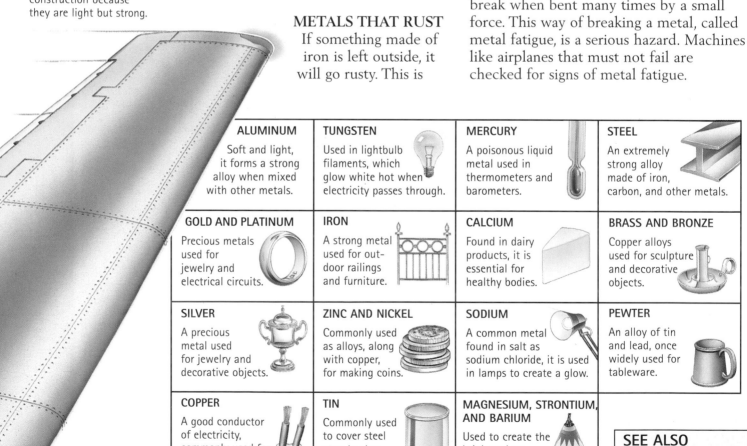

ALUMINUM Soft and light, it forms a strong alloy when mixed with other metals.	**TUNGSTEN** Used in lightbulb filaments, which glow white hot when electricity passes through.	**MERCURY** A poisonous liquid metal used in thermometers and barometers.	**STEEL** An extremely strong alloy made of iron, carbon, and other metals.
GOLD AND PLATINUM Precious metals used for jewelry and electrical circuits.	**IRON** A strong metal used for outdoor railings and furniture.	**CALCIUM** Found in dairy products, it is essential for healthy bodies.	**BRASS AND BRONZE** Copper alloys used for sculpture and decorative objects.
SILVER A precious metal used for jewelry and decorative objects.	**ZINC AND NICKEL** Commonly used as alloys, along with copper, for making coins.	**SODIUM** A common metal found in salt as sodium chloride, it is used in lamps to create a glow.	**PEWTER** An alloy of tin and lead, once widely used for tableware.
COPPER A good conductor of electricity, commonly used for electrical wiring.	**TIN** Commonly used to cover steel cans to stop them rusting.	**MAGNESIUM, STRONTIUM, AND BARIUM** Used to create the bright colors in fireworks.	

SEE ALSO
Construction, Gold, Iron and steel, Mineral and gem, Mining, Silver

MEXICO

Mexico, North America's third largest country, lies between the United States to the north and Central America to the south.

Area: 742,500 sq. mi.
Population: 103,400,165
Capital: Mexico City
Language: Spanish
Currency: Mexican peso

In north and central Mexico, mountain ranges called *sierras* enclose a high plateau. This plateau, Mexico's most thickly populated region, contains active volcanoes. Mexico's highest peak, Mount Citlaltepetl (18,700 ft./ 5,700m), also called Orizaba, is a dormant volcano.

▲ At Christmas, children try to burst a papier-mâché *piñata*, which is full of candy.

▲ Tourists visit Mexico to see ancient ruins such as the Great Pyramid and *chacmool* figure in the Yucatan Peninsula.

DESERTS AND FORESTS
Seven tenths of Mexico has little rainfall. The north is largely desert, but rain forests grow in the south. Temperatures vary according to the height of the land. Acapulco on the coast is much warmer than Mexico City, which is 7,550 ft. (2,300m) above sea level. Mexico City was built on the site of the ancient Aztec capital Tenochtitlán, founded around 1325.

MESTIZOS
Many Mexicans are *mestizos*, of mixed European and Native American origin. Most white people are descendants of Spaniards who arrived in Mexico in 1519. Spanish is the official language, but some Mexicans speak Native American languages. Most Mexicans are Roman Catholics, and about three fourths of the people live in cities and towns.

TRADE AND FOOD
Mexico is rich in minerals, including silver. Oil, gas, and oil products are the main exports. Factories also produce chemicals, clothing, iron and steel, processed foods, and vehicles. Food crops include corn (used to make flour for pancakes called *tortillas*), beans, rice, and wheat. Coffee, cotton, vegetables, and fruits are also important.

MODERN TIMES
Mexico became independent from Spain in 1821. It lost land to the United States in the Mexican War (1846-48), and this war ruined Mexico's economy. There were revolutions between 1910 and 1921, but since then Mexico has been mainly at peace. Poverty has led many people to illegally enter Mexico's rich neighbor, the United States, in search of jobs.

◄ Cattle are reared in the northern part of Mexico's plateau, where there is little rainfall.

SEE ALSO
Aztec, Central America, Maya, North America

MICROORGANISM

Microorganisms are tiny living creatures that cannot be seen without a microscope. They can be bacteria, viruses, protists (protozoans), or tiny algae or fungi.

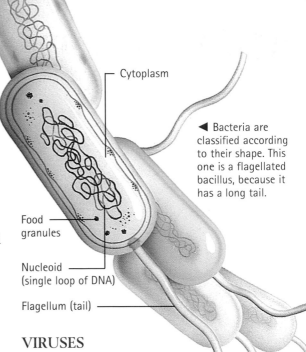

Cytoplasm

◄ Bacteria are classified according to their shape. This one is a flagellated bacillus, because it has a long tail.

Food granules

Nucleoid (single loop of DNA)

Flagellum (tail)

The Ebola virus is long and wormlike in shape. It is often deadly.

A colony of rodlike, food-poisoning bacteria growing on cooked roast beef.

Yeast cells are fungi and can be used to ferment alcohol and make bread.

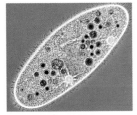

Paramecium protists are abundant in water and soil and feed on bacteria.

Many varieties of single-celled algae form colonies in or on top of water.

Bacteria are single-celled specks of living matter, mostly well under one hundredth of a millimeter long. There are three main shapes: rods, spheres, and spirals. Bacterial cells differ from other cells because their DNA, which controls all living things, floats free through the cells instead of being contained in a nucleus. They get food and energy by breaking down all kinds of living or dead substances and, unlike most other living things, many of them can survive without oxygen.

GOOD AND BAD

Bacteria reproduce by simply splitting into two. This can happen every 15 minutes in good conditions, so bacteria exist in huge numbers. Many bacteria cause illnesses, including tuberculosis, cholera, and food poisoning. These are often called germs or microbes. But not all bacteria are harmful. Some help to keep the soil in good condition, and others can be used to manufacture yogurt and other foods.

PROTISTS

Protists are single-celled organisms in which the DNA is wrapped up in a nucleus near the cell's center. They live everywhere, especially in watery surroundings. The best-known members of the group are amoeba, which continually change shape as they move. Some live harmlessly in water and swallow bacteria by simply flowing over them. Others live inside animals and cause illness. Many protists cause diseases such as malaria and sleeping sickness.

VIRUSES

Viruses are even smaller than bacteria. On the border between living and nonliving things, most consist of a piece of DNA inside an envelope of protein. Viruses can form crystals like salt and other chemicals, and can survive in this state for a long time. But they can reproduce only when they get inside other living things. In such cases, the DNA of a virus invades the cells, forcing them to make more viruses. All viruses therefore cause disease in other living things. Human illnesses caused by viruses include measles, AIDS, and the common cold. Prions are even smaller than viruses and have only recently been discovered. BSE, or mad-cow disease, is thought to be caused by prions.

Vacuole of digestive chemicals

Arms

Food particle

Nutrients are absorbed and used

Chemicals attack and break down food

Waste products are expelled

SEE ALSO

Cell, Disease, Fungi, Genetics, Microscope

MICROSCOPE

Microscopes are instruments that magnify tiny objects or reveal fine details on larger objects. They have opened up a whole world that was invisible to our eyes.

An electron scan (x20) of Velcro, used as a clothes fastener, showing the nylon hooks and loops.

A false-color electron scan (x200) of a sweat pore from a blister on the palm of a man's hand.

An electron scan (x500) of individual cotton fibers, which make up a single thread of cotton.

An electron scan (x1,300) of human hairs protruding from the surface of the scalp (colored pink).

The first microscope was made by the Dutch eyeglass maker Zacharias Janssen in 1609. The first scientist to see bacteria was the Dutchman Anton van Leeuwenhoek, who made his own microscopes in the 1670s. The first microscopes were optical, which means that the object, or specimen, being studied was viewed through an eyepiece. For this to work, the specimen needed to be thin enough to let light through.

ELECTRON MICROSCOPES
Electron microscopes first appeared in the 1930s. Instead of light, they use a beam of electrons controlled by magnetic fields. Electron microscopes are very powerful and can show details 1,000 times larger than optical microscopes can show. However, the specimen must be dried out

OPTICAL MICROSCOPES
In an optical microscope, light shining through an object is bent as it passes through a lens. This makes the object appear much bigger. Adding a second lens makes the magnification even greater. Optical microscopes with several lenses are called compound microscopes and can magnify things by up to about 2,000 times their real size.

▲ In an electron microscope, the electrons are invisible, so a fluorescent screen is used instead of an eyepiece.

and sliced very thinly—about a thousandth of the thickness of this page. In addition, the air must be removed from inside an electron microscope and from around the specimen, as electrons are easily scattered.

OTHER MICROSCOPES
Scanning electron microscopes move a beam of electrons over the surface of the specimen. The electrons that bounce off are collected to make an image. Scanning probe microscopes and atomic force microscopes were invented in the late 1980s. They can magnify a million times, showing up individual atoms. An extremely sharp probe moves over the surface of the specimen, "feeling" its shape in tiny detail. A computer turns signals from the probe into a 3-D image, which is displayed on a monitor screen.

Binocular lenses

Specimen mounted on a rectangular slide

Magnification and focusing are electronically adjustable

Dyes are used to make the specimen visible

Eyepiece lenses

Path of light

Body

Objective lens

Specimen tray

Focusing knob

Electric bulb lights up specimen

SEE ALSO
Atom and molecule, Lens, Microorganism, Telescope

MIDDLE AGES

The Middle Ages was the period in European history which began in about A.D. 750 and ended in the 1400s, with the dawn of the period known as the Renaissance.

▶ During the 1400s in France, Christine de Pisan wrote for a living. This was unusual in an age when few people, particularly women, knew how to read and write.

Society was divided into three estates: the clergy and the nobility...

... and the third estate, made up of farm workers, traders, and craftspeople.

Following the collapse of the Roman Empire during the A.D. 400s, western Europe was overrun by pagans (non-Christians). By 1400, Europe shared a common Christian culture and was about to begin centuries of expansion through exploration, trade, and conquest.

EMPEROR AND POPE
In 800, Charlemagne, king of the Franks, was crowned emperor by the pope. This was an attempt to reunite Europe under a Christian ruler. The power of pope and emperor dominated the Middle Ages.

FEUDAL SOCIETY
In this period, Europe was divided into many kingdoms, dukedoms, bishoprics, and other states. The source of most wealth was farmland. The feudal system of controlling land and people was developed in France during the 900s. Kings gave land to lords and knights in return for military services. Each lord had to swear fealty (loyalty) to his overlord. The lord's land was farmed by peasants, who paid him in labor and surplus crops. The Church also held a lot of land, and many monasteries used their wealth to encourage learning and the arts.

A VIOLENT PERIOD
After defeating invading Vikings, Muslims, and Avars, the rulers of Europe fought each other for power and wealth. The Hundred Years' War (1337-1453) was fought between the kings of England and France over who should rule France. The Hapsburg family of Austria and the Hohenzollerns of Germany fought long wars to conquer new lands.

TRADE AND INDUSTRY
After about 1100, Europe became increasingly wealthy. Merchants and craftspeople formed guilds—organizations that imposed regulations and controlled prices. They helped to spread skills and encourage trade between regions. By 1400, a growing number of people were working in manufacturing and trade.

MEDIEVAL BANQUETS

The wealthy lords and ladies of the Middle Ages held banquets for special occasions. These formal meals began early in the day—around 10 or 11 A.M.—and continued for several hours. Guests ate with their fingers or with knives and spoons (forks had yet to be invented). The food included a great many meat dishes and was often heavily spiced.

SEE ALSO

Castle, Crusades, Renaissance, Roman Empire

MIDDLE EAST

The Middle East is a group of countries in southwest Asia lying between Africa and Europe. It has great economic importance and is an area of unrest.

AFGHANISTAN
Area: 250,000 sq. mi.
Population: 27,755,775
Capital: Kabul
Languages: Pashto, Dari
Currency: Afghani

BAHRAIN
Area: 239 sq. mi.
Population: 656,397
Capital: Manamah
Language: Arabic
Currency: Bahraini dinar

CYPRUS
Area: 3,572 sq. mi.
Population: 767,314
Capital: Nicosia
Languages: Greek, Turkish
Currency: Cyprus pound and Turkish lira

IRAN
Area: 631,700 sq. mi.
Population: 66,622,704
Capital: Tehran
Language: Farsi
Currency: Rial

IRAQ
Area: 167,600 sq. mi.
Population: 24,001,816
Capital: Baghdad
Languages: Arabic, Kurdish
Currency: Iraqi dinar

Much of the Middle East is desert, with rugged mountain ranges in eastern Turkey, Iran, and northern Afghanistan. Afghanistan contains the region's highest peak, Nowshak (24,560 ft./7,485m), in a range called the Hindu Kush. Most people live along the coasts, in inland valleys, or around oases.

ANCIENT RIVERS
The main rivers, the Tigris and Euphrates, rise in Turkey and flow through Syria and Iraq. They join to form a river called the Shatt al Arab, which empties into the Persian Gulf. The world's first city-states were founded along these rivers in Mesopotamia, by a people called the Sumerians, in around 3500 B.C. The Middle East's most famous inland body of water is the Dead Sea, which lies in a deep valley between Israel and Jordan. Its shoreline is the world's lowest point on land, 1,300 ft. (400m) below sea level.

▲ The Elburz Mountains in Iran, close to the Caspian Sea, make up one of the Middle East's many mountain ranges.

RAIN, SNOW, AND DESERT
The areas with the highest rainfall are in the northeast: the Turkish city of Istanbul has an average rainfall of more than 30 in. (800mm) a year; Saudi Arabia's capital Riyadh has only 3 in. (80mm). Snow falls on the mountains, and temperatures drop below freezing in the winter. The desert plains are hot. Few plants grow in the deserts, but date palms flourish around oases. ▶

▼ The Middle East has been transformed by the discovery of oil. In Kuwait, the oil industry provides jobs for women as well as men.

ISRAEL
Area: 7,800 sq. mi.
Population: 6,029,529
Capital: Jerusalem
Languages: Hebrew, Arabic
Currency: Shekel

JORDAN
Area: 35,300 sq. mi.
Population: 5,307,470
Capital: Amman
Language: Arabic
Currency: Jordanian dinar

KUWAIT
Area: 6,900 sq. mi.
Population: 2,111,561
Capital: Kuwait City
Language: Arabic
Currency: Kuwaiti dinar

LEBANON
Area: 4,105 sq. mi.
Population: 3,667,780
Capital: Beirut
Language: Arabic
Currency: Lebanese pound

OMAN
Area: 82,000 sq. mi.
Population: 2,713,462
Capital: Muscat
Language: Arabic
Currency: Omani rial

QATAR
Area: 4,200 sq. mi.
Population: 793,341
Capital: Doha
Language: Arabic
Currency: Qatari riyal

SAUDI ARABIA
Area: 830,000 sq. mi.
Population: 23,513,330
Capital: Riyadh
Language: Arabic
Currency: Riyal

SYRIA
Area: 72,234 sq. mi.
Population: 17,155,814
Capital: Damascus
Language: Arabic
Currency: Syrian pound

▲ In Saudi Arabia, men often relax and drink tea together. Tradition means that women do not attend such gatherings.

DESERT ANIMALS

In some areas, nomadic tribes herding camels, goats, and sheep move around in search of pastures. The best-known animal of the Middle East is the camel, which can go for long periods without water. Another desert animal, the Arabian oryx, once lived throughout the Arabian Peninsula and in Lebanon, Iran, and Iraq. By 1972, it was extinct in the wild because people had overhunted it in their cars. Arabian oryxes bred in captivity have now been released in Oman and are increasing in number.

PEOPLE AND RELIGION

Many of the people of the Middle East are Arabs, and Arabic is their chief language. There are also Afghanis, Armenians, Greeks, Iranians, Jews, Kurds, and Turks. The Middle East was the birthplace of Judaism, Christianity, and Islam, and all three religions regard Jerusalem in Israel as a holy city. Muslims also make pilgrimages to Mecca and Medina in Saudi Arabia. Islam is now the main religion, although Christians live in Cyprus and Lebanon, and Judaism is the chief religion in Israel.

In cities such as Damascus in Syria, handicrafts are sold at markets called *souks*.

HOW PEOPLE LIVE
Until about 50 years ago, most people lived on farms or in farming villages. Today, three fifths of the people live in towns and cities. The largest cities are Istanbul in Turkey and Tehran, the capital of Iran. Many cities have tall modern buildings as well as older areas.

OIL POWER
The region's chief resource is oil, and Saudi Arabia has about a fourth of the world's known oil reserves. Other leading oil producers are Iraq, Iran, Kuwait, Oman, Qatar, and the United Arab Emirates. Bahrain also depends on oil exports. Money from oil sales has been used to build new cities and roads, and to develop new industries to make oil products such as chemicals and plastics.

INDUSTRY AND FARMING
Iran and Turkey have many other industries and Israel, the most developed country in the Middle East, is known for its aircraft, electrical goods, electronics, precision instruments, and textiles. About two fifths of the people are employed in agriculture. Barley, citrus fruits, cotton, sugarcane, and wheat are leading products.

Kuwait's water towers are part of a desalination plant, where fresh water is produced by removing salt from seawater.

MIDDLE-EASTERN WARS
The boundaries of many Middle Eastern countries were set after World War I (1914-1918). Israel was created in 1948, leading to several Arab-Israeli wars. Civil war occured in Lebanon between 1975 and 1991, while Cyprus has been divided since 1974 into a Turkish-speaking Muslim area and a Greek-speaking Christian area. In 1991 and 2003, U.S.-led coalitions battled Saddam Hussein's military regime in Iraq. Another conflict involves a people called the Kurds, who live in parts of Armenia, Iran, Iraq, Syria, and Turkey. They are fighting to have their own country, Kurdistan.

SADDAM HUSSEIN
Saddam Hussein (born in 1937) became Iraq's president in 1979. He led Iraq into war with Iran, which lasted from 1980 to 1988. In 1990, Iraq invaded Kuwait, but an international force drove the Iraqis out during the Gulf War in 1991. In 2003, a U.S.-led coalition invaded Iraq and overthrew Hussein and his government.

TURKEY
Area: 297,600 sq. mi.
Population: 67,308,928
Capital: Ankara
Language: Turkish
Currency: Turkish lira

UNITED ARAB EMIRATES
Area: 32,300 sq. mi.
Population: 2,445,989
Capital: Abu Dhabi
Language: Arabic
Currency: Dirham

YEMEN
Area: 203,800 sq. mi.
Population: 18,701,257
Capital: Sana
Language: Arabic
Currencies: Rial

SEE ALSO
Asia, Christianity, Europe, Islam, Israel, Judaism, Mesopotamia, Oil

MIGRATION

Migration is the regular, instinctive movement of animals between one place and another. Their journeys are usually made to tie in with the seasons.

► Caribou (also known as reindeer) migrate from the Arctic tundra in vast herds to winter in the great coniferous forests farther south.

▲ Humpback whales migrate thousands of miles to reach warm waters, but they do not cross the equator.

► Monarch butterflies fly more than 1,860 mi. (3,000km) to reach their winter home.

▼ When the insects on which swallows feed die out in the autumn, the birds fly south to find a fres supply.

FINDING THE WAY

The map shows the routes taken by various migratory animals. Migrants are believed to use a range of methods to find their way. Some follow geographical features such as mountains and coastlines, others use their sense of smell. Birds, in particular, may be guided by the sun or the stars, or by sensing the Earth's magnetic field.

◄ The Arctic tern is a long-distance flyer, making an annual round trip of up to 25,000 mi. (40,000km).

◄——►	Swallow
◄——►	Caribou/reindeer
◄——►	Monarch butterfly
◄——►	Arctic tern
◄——►	Humpback whale

▲ Salmon battle their way upstream to reach their breeding grounds.

Every year, many animals journey hundreds, sometimes thousands, of miles to avoid cold winters—when food is hard to find—or to reach their summer breeding grounds. The animals usually travel in one direction before the onset of winter, then make the return journey the following spring.

BIRD MIGRANTS

Birds are among the most common migrants. Cuckoos, swallows, and many other insect-eating birds live in Europe and North America during the summer, when insects are plentiful, then fly south to spend the winter in warmer lands. Certain geese and ducks breed during the summer in the far north, but when the lakes begin to freeze, they fly south in search of food. The Arctic tern makes the longest journey of all. Each year, it flies from the Arctic to the Antarctic and back again, so that it can enjoy the summer months in both places.

BREEDING TIME

Whales commonly feed in cold waters in the far north and south, but they migrate to warmer subtropical waters to breed. Seals travel long distances across the sea to rocky islands where they bear their young, and turtles head for warm sandy beaches in which to lay their eggs. Some fish also migrate, though not annually. Salmon live in the sea, but return to the same river in which they hatched in order to spawn (breed). European eels, on the other hand, live in fresh water but travel to the Sargasso Sea, east of Florida, to breed.

INSECT MIGRANTS

Some insects migrate. Millions of monarch butterflies, for example, fly south from Canada and the northern United States to winter in warmer areas. They breed in the spring and die soon afterward, but their young complete the journey north.

SEE ALSO
Bird, Butterfly and moth, Reptile, Whale and dolphin

MILLIPEDE AND CENTIPEDE

Millipedes and centipedes are long-bodied animals with many pairs of legs. Millipedes feed mainly on rotting vegetation, but centipedes are active hunters.

▶ When threatened, millipedes usually coil up tightly to protect their legs.

The word millipede means "thousand legs," whereas centipede means "hundred legs." Neither animal tends to have as many legs as its name suggests, but both have an impressive number, which makes them easy to identify.

Two of the 6,500 species of millipede. Most have 120 to 160 legs, but the record is 750.

SEGMENTED BODIES

Millipedes and centipedes belong to a group of animals called arthropods. Like other arthropods, they have a tough outer case, or exoskeleton, and their bodies are divided into segments. In most millipedes, the segments are circular in cross section, and each one carries two pairs of tiny legs. In centipedes, the segments are flatter and, instead of carrying four legs, each segment carries just two.

DANGERS OF DRYING OUT

Millipedes and centipedes do not have fully waterproof bodies, which means they have to be careful not to dry out. To avoid this they tend to live in damp places, such as scattered or piled leaves and soil, and are active mainly at night.

DIFFERENT LIFESTYLES

In other ways, these animals live quite differently. Millipedes have small jaws and they feed on the remains of decaying plants. They move quite slowly and, if they are threatened, rarely run away. Instead, they often protect themselves by coiling up into a spiral. Some millipedes have special glands that produce a poisonous fluid. If another animal tries to eat them, the fluid soon puts the attacker off its meal. Centipedes, on the other hand, are aggressive hunters with large claws surrounding their head. Many can move quite fast, either to scurry after their prey or to escape danger.

FEROCIOUS HUNTERS

A centipede's flattened body allows it to slip easily in and out of crevices while it is hunting. Centipedes are armed with special claws on either side of the head that inject poison into their prey. Most centipedes feed on small creatures such as worms, snails, and beetles, but large tropical species—which can reach over 10 in. (25cm) long—sometimes attack frogs, mice, and even birds. Their claws are strong enough to pierce human skin, with very painful results.

Two of nearly 3,000 types of centipede. Most have 30 to 50 legs, though one species has 177 pairs.

Leg muscles anchored to the rigid body wall allow the limbs to move freely

The poisonous claws around a centipede's head are actually modified front legs

Overlapping membranes between the segments allow greater flexibility of movement

A centipede has long antennae which it uses to search for food

SEE ALSO

Animal, Insect

MINERAL AND GEM

Minerals are the natural elements or compounds that make up rocks in the Earth's crust. Gems, metal ores, sand, salt, and even talc are all types of mineral.

Jade is a hard, usually green, semiprecious gemstone that can be carved to form fine ornaments.

Turquoise ranges in color from blue to gray-green. Sky blue specimens are popular as gems.

The gem opal shows a characteristic play of colors, known as opalescence.

There are over 3,000 different minerals, but only 30 of them make up the majority of rocks, soil, and sand on Earth. Some minerals form glassy crystals, others are like brightly colored rocks. They vary in color, density, and hardness, and also in their ability to reflect light and conduct heat or electricity.

MINERAL COMPOUNDS

Some minerals, such as gold, consist of one pure element. Many others are made up of two or more elements, combined to form a compound. The most common mineral—quartz—is a combination of silicon and oxygen. Most grains of sand are quartz, which is used for making glass.

MINERAL ORES

Many mineral compounds contain metals. The mineral hematite, for example, is iron oxide and galena is lead sulphide. Minerals such as these, from which the metals can easily be removed, or extracted, are called ores and are widely mined.

FORMING CRYSTALS

Many minerals form distinct three-dimensional shapes called crystals. The shapes are the result of the arrangement of atoms and molecules inside the mineral. Minerals that produce fine, hardwearing crystals that can be cut and polished to a beautiful finish are called gemstones.

PRECIOUS GEMS

Gems are most commonly worn as jewelry. They include diamonds, rubies, sapphires, and emeralds. Diamonds, because they are incredibly hard, are also used in industry and mining for drilling, cutting, and grinding. Industrial-grade diamonds can now be made artificially.

SCALE OF HARDNESS

An Austrian scientist, Friedrich Mohs (1773–1839), devised a scale to grade the hardness of minerals. His scale ranges from grade 1 for talc, the softest, to grade 10 for diamond, the hardest.

On Mohs's scale, a fingernail rates as 2.5, a copper coin as 3.5, and a steel penknife as 5.5.

A SELECTION OF MINERALS

The iron ore hematite often forms kidney-shaped lumps, which earn it the name kidney ore.

Quartz forms fine crystals and comes in many colors. The colorless variety is called rock crystal.

Galena has a metallic gray color and forms cubic crystals. It is the main ore of lead, and is commonly found with quartz.

Talc (magnesium silicate) is the softest mineral on Mohs's scale. It is widely used as talcum powder.

Gold is a soft, malleable (easily worked) metal which has been used since ancient times to make jewelry.

Malachite is a copper ore, well known for its bright green color. It is often granular, and rarely forms crystals.

SEE ALSO
Earth, Gold, Metal, Mining, Oil, Rock, Silver, Soil

MINING

Mining is the process of taking from the Earth useful or valuable substances such as coal, gas, salt, mineral ores, gemstones, or building stone.

The earliest mines were built to find useful metals like lead, copper, iron, and tin and precious metals such as silver or gold. But, because there were no effective methods for removing excess water or supplying workers with air, the mines always had to be near the surface.

MINING AND MACHINES

Over the last two centuries, problems with drainage and ventilation have been solved by using machines, and mines can now be sunk deep into the ground. As well as pumping out water and circulating air, machines are used for drilling and cutting and carry materials, men, and equipment to and from the surface. Deep mining has always involved dangers from cave-ins, flooding, and poisonous gases. In the future, work in dangerous conditions is likely to be done by robots controlled from the surface.

REACHING THE DEPOSITS

There are many different methods of mining—the type and depth of deposit usually determine the method used. Materials such as stone, gravel, and sand are mined in quarries. Mineral deposits near the surface can be removed by opencast mining, using mechanical diggers or high-pressure water jets. Deep deposits are reached by sinking vertical shafts into the ground, or by driving a tunnel into the side of a hill or mountain—called drift mining. Explosives are often used to blast rocks apart so the minerals can be broken up.

▲ Gold is found as small grains, or nuggets, of pure metal. Here, gold nuggets are being washed out of the soil using water.

▶ A vast bucket-wheel excavator is used to dig up rocks and minerals in an opencast mine.

MINING METHODS

A shaft mine is used to reach deep deposits. Where deposits are closer to the surface, minerals can be hauled up a slope in wagons. Drift mines are used where the seam reaches the surface, as on a hillside. Deposits close to the surface are removed in an opencast mine, and oil beneath the sea is tapped by an oil rig.

Shaft mine
Air ventilation house
Winding gear
Slope mine
Drift mine
Excavator
Opencast mine
Oil rig
age (elevator)   Main shaft   Tunnel   Ore vein (or coal seam)   Oil reservoir

SEE ALSO

Coal, Gas, Gold, Industry, Iron and steel, Metal, Mineral and gem, Oil, Rock, Silver

MONEY

Money is used to buy things or to save wealth for future needs. Money may take the form of bills, coins, or anything accepted as payment.

Native Americans used beads and shells made into decorative patterns.

The Ancient Chinese used bronze cast into spade, knife, and other shapes.

Coins are popular because they are easy to produce and last a long time.

Paper money began as promises by banks to pay a certain amount of coins.

Credit cards and checks are useful because they can be used instead of cash.

Before there was money, trade took place through barter, the exchange of one item or service for another. Barter only works if the person with one item wants what the other has to offer. Money allows people to sell things for money, then swap the money for what they want. It also makes borrowing possible, so that exchanges can be spread over time.

BEADS TO COINS

Many things have served as money. Useful products, such as salt or knives, have been used, as have decorative beads or even natural items such as shells or cattle. Coins made of precious metals and stamped with a design to show how much metal they contain were probably invented in Lydia (part of modern Turkey) around 700 B.C.

PROMISES TO PAY

Paper money is not valuable itself, but is a promise to pay real money. It was invented in China in around A.D. 1000. Until the 1900s, bills could be exchanged for gold. Most modern bills represent promises made by a bank or government, as do checks or credit cards.

▶ In 1923, German money lost value rapidly. Money became so worthless that bundles of bills were used as toys.

MAKING COINS

Coins are made from metals such as bronze or copper, which are stamped with a design showing how much they are worth and which country produced them. First, an artist draws the design on paper.

The design is engraved, in reverse, onto metal dies.

The metal for the coins is melted into thin sheets.

Round "blanks" are cut from the metal sheets.

The dies stamp the coin design onto the blanks.

THE MEASURE OF WEALTH

Money can be used to store and measure wealth, but the value of money is not stable. Wars may cause governments to collapse, so that their money becomes worthless. If a government prints too many bills, or allows excessive borrowing, the money loses value and inflation occurs.

HIGH FINANCE

Large sums are lent and borrowed by governments and large companies in the money markets. Brokers and banks arrange loans or sell shares, allowing businesses to trade and grow.

SEE ALSO

Gold, Great Depression, Silver, Trade

MONGOL EMPIRE

The Mongol Empire was created by the Mongols of eastern Asia. During the 1200s, they conquered vast areas of Asia and Europe to form a powerful empire.

Genghis Khan (c.1162-1227) united the Mongols and founded the empire.

Kublai Khan (c.1217-94) organized the conquests in China into a stable state.

Tamerlane (1336-1405) conquered an empire in central and western Asia.

The speed and brutality of the Mongol conquests stunned and terrified their enemies. But the Mongols failed to organize their new empire, and it collapsed as quickly as it had been created.

THE TIDE OF CONQUEST
In 1206, Temujin, leader of the Mongols, united the nomadic Asian tribes, taking the title Genghis Khan, or supreme ruler. By 1215, he had conquered northern China, killing about 35 million Chinese. Genghis Khan then turned west, taking western Asia, the Caucasus region, and southern Russia before his death in 1227. Genghis's son Ogedai then became khan, smashing Russia, Hungary, and Poland by 1241. That year Ogedai died, and the new khan, Mongke, turned on China and Persia.

MONGOL WARFARE

Mongols were mounted on hardy ponies, able to travel long distances in a short time. The light cavalry was armed with bows and trained to shoot while galloping. Heavier cavalry had lances and armor. This combination of speed and shock smashed every army they met.

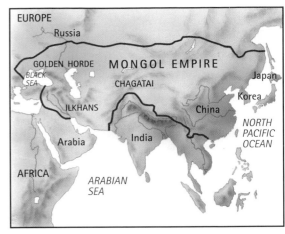

▲ The Mongol Empire at its largest in 1280 under Kublai Khan. The Golden Horde, Chagatai, and Ilkhans later became smaller independent empires.

THE NEW EMPIRE
By 1279, all of China had been conquered, and the Mongol Empire stretched from Korea in the east to the Black Sea in the west. Kublai Khan moved his capital to China, from where he was able to enjoy the wealth and luxuries of the conquests.

COLLAPSE OF THE KHANS
After 1300, the khan in China lost control of Mongol rulers elsewhere. The Mongols abandoned the tough life of warriors, and in 1368 were driven out by the Chinese. In the west, Mongol power was broken by the early 1400s. Today, Mongolia is a vast but poor country north of China.

SEE ALSO
Asia, China, Empire

MONKEY AND OTHER PRIMATES

Monkeys and apes belong to a group of mammals known as the primates, which also includes lorises, lemurs, and galagos, as well as human beings.

Monkeys differ from apes in having a tail, although this is sometimes very short. Both have their eyes at the front of the head, giving them human-looking faces. They are intelligent creatures with good brains, and they learn quickly. They live in family groups or larger colonies and spend a lot of time grooming each other and looking after their babies. Apes are the nearest living relatives of human beings.

The woolly monkey is a New World monkey.

The South American spider monkey uses its tail as an extra hand.

The Old World colobus monkey rarely comes down from the trees.

The mandrill is one of the largest Old World monkeys.

LIFE IN THE TREES
Monkeys and apes are very active and nimble animals, with excellent eyesight. Except for the South American night monkey, or douroucouli, they feed in the daytime and sleep at night. Most of them live in the trees, where they can run along branches and swing from branch to branch with amazing ease. They grasp branches with hands and feet, and some South American monkeys can even hold on to the branches with their tail. Baboons, the largest of the monkeys, live mainly on the ground, although they usually sleep in the trees at night. With their pointed muzzle and large teeth, they look more like domestic dogs than monkeys.

TWO MONKEY GROUPS
There are about 130 kinds, or species, of monkey, nearly all of which live in the tropical and subtropical parts of the world. They fall into two main groups—the New World monkeys of South and Central America and the Old World monkeys of Africa and Asia. New World monkeys, which include the little tamarins and marmosets, have a

◄ Baboons live in close family groups called troops. As with other monkeys and apes, the female carries her babies until they are old enough to look after themselves.

▲ Ring-tailed lemurs walk on the ground holding their long tail up in the air. The word lemur means "ghost," a name derived from the weird cry of some species.

broad nose with the nostrils facing to the sides. Old World monkeys have a narrower nose with the nostrils pointing downward.

THE BIGGEST APE
Thirteen different kinds of ape live in the forests of the Old World; no apes are found in the Americas. The gorilla, the chimpanzee, and the pygmy chimpanzee, or bonobo live in Africa. Weighing up to 440 lb. (200kg), the gorilla is the largest and strongest of all the primates. It usually walks on all fours, with its knuckles on the ground. Gorillas are not the fierce creatures that people once thought them to be. In fact, they live peacefully in the forest in small family groups.

▲ An adult chimpanzee, closely observed by its young, uses a stick as a tool to probe for termites. Chimpanzees are among the most intelligent apes, able to imitate humans and solve simple problems.

INTELLIGENT CREATURES

Chimpanzees look like small gorillas, but usually have a paler face. They live in large communities, often with over 100 individuals. They are probably the most intelligent of the apes, often using simple tools to help them find food.

ORIENTAL APES

The orangutan and the nine species of gibbon live in Southeast Asia. Orangutans reach up to 4.3 ft. (1.3m) when upright, and their bodies are covered in sparse, reddish-brown hair. Gibbons are small apes, rarely weighing over 13–15 lb. (6–7kg), and they are wonderful acrobats. They use their long arms to swing and leap through the branches at high speed. Unlike chimps, gibbons and orangutans rarely come down to the ground.

FAMILY LIVING

Gorillas live in family groups, or troops. Each group is made up of one or more males and several females with their young. The group is ruled by a large mature male, known as a silverback because of the silver-gray hairs on his back. Gorillas are vegetarian, eating a diet consisting mainly of leaves and shoots, but also of bark, stems, roots, and fruit. They may live for up to 37 years.

VEGETARIAN DIETS

Monkeys and apes are basically vegetarian, although they often eat insects and other small animals. Chimpanzees even catch monkeys and small antelopes. Fruit is plentiful at all times of the year in the tropical areas, and is the main food of most monkeys and apes. The gorilla and a few monkeys feed mainly on leaves and shoots.

OTHER PRIMATES

Galagos, or bush babies, lorises, and lemurs have smaller brains than monkeys and apes, and are often called lower primates. Their snouts are more pointed than those of most other primates. They live mainly in the trees and feed mostly on fruit, leaves, or insects. Galagos live in tropical Africa and lorises in southern Asia. Both are active at night and have very large eyes. Lemurs are found only on the island of Madagascar, off the east coast of Africa.

▲ The loris is a slow-moving primate that lives in Southeast Asia. It has huge, forward-pointing eyes and broad, grasping hands and feet.

▲ The orangutan is an endangered species. Special rehabilitation centers in Sumatra and Borneo care for young animals and introduce them back into the wild.

SEE ALSO

Animal, Conservation, Mammal

MOON

The Moon is Earth's only natural satellite. Its diameter is 2,160 mi. and it lies at an average distance of 238,855 mi. from Earth.

Crescent Moon (waxing)

Half Moon (first quarter)

Full Moon (appears round)

Half Moon (last quarter)

Crescent Moon (waning)

The Moon shines because it reflects light from the Sun. The phase of the Moon (how much of its surface we can see) depends on the position of the Moon in its orbit.

SOLAR ECLIPSE

Sometimes the Moon passes exactly between the Earth and the Sun. When this happens, there is a total solar eclipse and, for a few minutes, the Sun's bright disk is blotted out. Since the Moon takes exactly the same time (27.3 days) to complete one orbit of the Earth as it does to spin around once on its axis, it always keeps the same side facing toward us.

BLEAK AND LIFELESS

The Moon is a bleak place with no atmosphere, which means there is no weather either. There is no life, though ice has now been found on the dark side. The Moon consists mostly of solid rock with a small central core of molten rock or iron. A thin layer of dust covers its surface. During the day, the surface temperature may climb to 260°F (127°C), but at night it can plunge to as low as –279°F (–173°C).

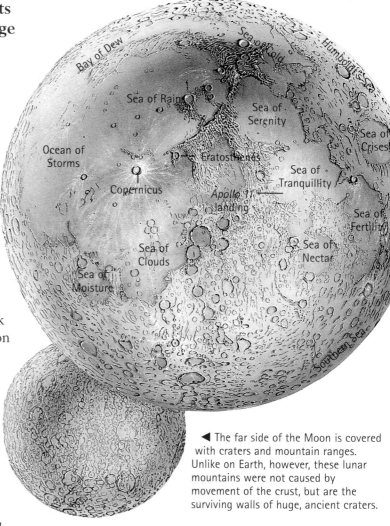

◄ The far side of the Moon is covered with craters and mountain ranges. Unlike on Earth, however, these lunar mountains were not caused by movement of the crust, but are the surviving walls of huge, ancient craters.

ORIGIN OF THE MOON

The Moon was formed just over four and a half billion years ago. It may have been gouged out of our own world when a large object struck Earth. Another possibility is that the Moon has always been a separate body and was captured by the Earth when it strayed too close.

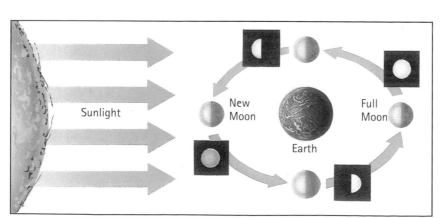

◄ At New Moon, the unlit side of the Moon, which is invisible to us, faces Earth. It grows (Crescent Moon) until half, then all, of the unlit side becomes visible (Full Moon). The phases then continue in reverse until the Moon is new again.

PLAINS AND CRATERS

The dark regions of the Moon's surface, known as maria (seas), are low-lying plains of solidified lava surrounded by brighter, mountainous areas. Craters, formed by the impact of meteorites and asteroids, occur everywhere on the Moon,

▼ The Collision Theory suggests that the Moon was formed when a large body struck Earth.

but are especially common in the uplands. They range in size from a few yards to 685 mi. (1,100km) across—Imbrium Basin in the Sea of Rains.

PULL OF THE MOON

Just as the Moon is held in orbit around the Earth by gravity, so Earth itself is affected by the Moon's gravity. The oceans and seas are pulled up when the Moon is directly above them. As Earth rotates, these tidal bulges shift from east to west twice daily, causing high tides.

MYTHS AND LEGENDS

For centuries, the Moon has given rise to various myths and legends. Early people saw it as a god or goddess, and some philosophers thought it was linked with birth and death, because it waxed and waned. It was also feared that eclipses signaled war or famine. In astrology, the Moon is believed to have an important influence over our lives and destinies.

▼ Moon rocks brought back from the Apollo missions range in age from about 4.5 billion years, just after the Moon was formed, to 3.1 billion years, when the lava plains were created.

Anorthosite

Vasicular basalt

Typical basalt

◄ This body added its own material to the debris thrown off into space (1). The debris formed an orbiting cloud (2), which finally solidified into a solid mass—the Moon (3).

▶ The Capture Theory suggests that the Moon was a passing body caught by the Earth's gravity. This explains its different composition, although calculations show that a collision with another body was more likely.

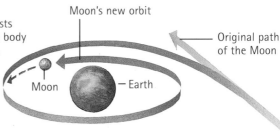

Moon's new orbit

Original path of the Moon

Moon — Earth

▲ Earth and the Moon may have formed together as a double planet from the cloud of debris left over after the formation of the Sun. However, this argument does not explain why their surface rocks are so different, and why the Moon has such a small iron core compared with Earth's.

SEE ALSO

Astronaut, Earth, Gravity, Planet, Solar system, Space exploration

MOUNTAIN AND VALLEY

A mountain is a mass of land that is much higher than its surroundings, pushed upward by movement of the Earth's crust. Valleys are formed on mountain slopes.

As glaciers melt, they leave deep U-shaped valleys gouged out by the ice.

Erupting volcanoes build up mountains made of lava and ash.

Block mountains form along breaks, or faults, in the Earth's crust.

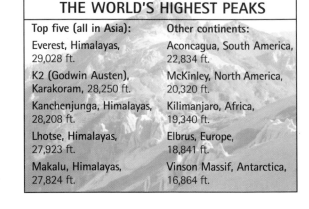

A mountain is higher than a hill, but there is no strict distinction between the two. Mountains are natural barriers to communication, and valleys offer trade routes, places for settlement, and pastures for farming. Some mountains are found under the sea. One of them, Mauna Kea in the Pacific Ocean, is higher than Everest.

HIGHEST PEAKS

Mountains are formed over millions of years through plate tectonics—movement of the Earth's crust. The crust is made up of rigid plates which are continuously moving. The highest mountains are the youngest. The longest mountain range on Earth, the Andes (4,475 mi./7,200km long), is being formed as the Pacific plate plunges beneath the South American plate. The highest range, the Himalayas, is being formed as the Indian plate crushes up against the Asian plate.

FOREVER WEARING AWAY

All the time a mountain is being pushed up, forces of erosion (such as wind and water) are wearing it down. Water flowing down the slopes gathers in streams and rivers, which carve out deep V-shaped valleys. Flat-bottomed, U-shaped valleys are formed by glaciers. Some straight valleys like the Great Rift Valley, East Africa, are formed along a crack or fault in the Earth.

MOVING THE EARTH

The highest mountains are fold mountains. These are found in chains, or ranges, and are formed like folds in a blanket when the ends are pushed together. They are pushed up when rocky plates of the Earth's crust collide. When one plate plunges beneath another, the rocks of the uppermost plate crumple up, making the mountain range.

Rocks that best resist weathering survive as high peaks

Mountain river valleys are deep and V-shaped, with a zigzag course, many waterfalls, and rapids

Collisions cause layers in the crust to crumple in wavelike patterns

SEE ALSO

Africa, Continent, Earth, Earthquake, Glacier, Lake, Ocean and sea, Volcano

MUSCLE

The body has 640 muscles, each specialized to contract (become shorter) to make the body move. All body actions, from blinking to sprinting, are muscle-powered.

▼ Inside a muscle are bundles of long muscle fibers (myofibers), thinner than human hair, joined by connective tissue.

Skeletal muscle

Smooth muscle

Cardiac muscle

Biceps relaxes

Skeletal muscles pull on the bones—they move fingers, arms, and other parts of the skeleton

Biceps contracts

Triceps contracts

Triceps relaxes

are made of bundles of threadlike structures, called actins and myosins.

MUSCLE POWER

For a muscle to pull, each myosin "grabs" its neighboring actin and makes it slide past— like pulling in a rope with a hand-over-hand movement. Millions of myosins and actins doing this make the whole muscle shorten. The amount and strength of contraction are controlled by nerve signals to each muscle from the brain.

THREE MUSCLE TYPES

Skeletal muscles have a striped appearance under the microscope, so they are known as striped, or striated, muscles. As we can make them contract when we want to (by thinking), they are called voluntary muscles. Cardiac muscle (called the myocardium) forms the thick walls of the heart. It contracts regularly to pump blood. Visceral muscle forms layers and sheets in the walls of the body's inner parts—viscera—such as the stomach, intestines, and bladder. Both of these work automatically, so they are known as involuntary muscles.

The human body's muscles vary in size and shape. They can be thinner than cotton thread, long and bulging in the middle, or wide and slablike—the largest, the gluteus maximus, is in the buttocks. Most are firmly attached to the skeleton by their tapering ends, called tendons.

WORKING IN PAIRS

Muscles can only pull, not push. So they are arranged in opposing pairs. One of the pair pulls the body part one way. To move the part back again, its opposing partner pulls it the other way. Animal muscles have the same structure, and work in the same way as human muscles.

INSIDE A MUSCLE

Muscles are made up of bundles of long fibers called muscle fibers, or myofibers. Each contains bundles of even thinner microscopic parts—muscle filaments, or myofilaments. In turn, muscle filaments

The eye has six muscles which help rotate the eyeball in its socket

Ligaments

Tendons and ligaments are tough elastic tissues. Ligaments connect one bone to another; tendons connect a muscle to a bone

Achilles tendon

Tendons

▲ When you bend your arm, the biceps muscle in the upper arm pulls the forearm, and so bends the elbow. Its opposing partner, the triceps, pulls the forearm the other way and straightens the elbow.

SEE ALSO

Heart and circulatory system, Human body, Lens, Sight, Touch

MUSIC

The word "music" comes from the Greek muses (goddesses), who were said to inspire song and dance. In more scientific terms, music is the art of organized sounds.

As painters or sculptors use lines, colors, and shapes, so musicians use the properties of sound. They use notes of different pitch (highness or lowness) and combine them with the beat of a rhythm to make a melody, or tune. They can add harmony—the sounding together of two or more notes of different pitch. Tone, or timbre, the special quality of sound produced by different instruments or voices, is another aspect of music.

African tribal music is one of the oldest surviving musical forms and is always accompanied by the rhythm of drums.

MUSIC WITH A PURPOSE
The earliest music was probably functional. People danced and sang or chanted because the strange power of music gave them courage to hunt wild animals. They also sang and danced to honor their gods, or to accompany themselves as they worked. All of these ancient types of music are still with us.

John Lee Hooker was a leading player of the blues, which have greatly influenced U.S. pop music.

MUSIC AS ART
With the growth of civilizations, people turned music into an art. The ancient *ragas* of India—rhythmic or melodic patterns—are a fine example of this. In the Western world, music as an art grew and changed rapidly. In medieval Europe, music still had a functional purpose, since it was sung in church and so served religion. But there was also the singing and the playing of minstrels, whose music was intended for pleasure and entertainment.

Elvis Presley revolutionized pop music in the 1950s, becoming one of the first stars of rock'n'roll music.

► British musician Evelyn Glennie (born 1965) is one of the top percussionists in the world. She is deaf, but feels the vibrations of the music through her sense of touch.

▲ Jazz music originated in New Orleans during the early 1900s, and has remained a major form of music ever since. Unlike written music, it requires musicians to improvise, or make up music on the spur of the moment.

THE RENAISSANCE
From about 1400 to the present day, Western music has been divided into periods. The Renaissance, about 1400-1600, was a period when the rich had more time to enjoy themselves. There was a big increase in secular (nonreligious) music, and much more music for instruments, including the harpsichord and lute, by such composers as William Byrd and John Dowland.

◄ Notation for an E major chord on guitar.

Treble clef

C D E F G A B C D E F G A B C

C D E F G A B C D E F G A B C

Bass clef

♯ — a "sharp" symbol before a note raises its pitch by one (semitone) note
♭ — a "flat" symbol before a note lowers its pitch by one (semitone) note
♮ — a "natural" symbol before a note cancels the previous sharp or flat symbol

Whole note Half note Quarter note Eighth note Sixteenth note

Whole note (or bar) rest Half note rest Quarter note rest Eighth note rest Sixteenth note rest

N.B. A dot after any note increases the time value of that note by half its length again

Two quarter notes per bar Three quarter notes per bar Four quarter notes per bar Six eighth notes per bar

MAJOR KEY SIGNATURES

G D A E B

F B♭ E♭ A♭ D♭

MUSICAL MARKS

ff	very loud	*sfz*	emphasis
f	loud	*tr*	trill
mf	moderately loud	⌢	pause
mp	moderately quiet	**cresc.**	get louder
p	quiet	**dim.**	get quieter
pp	very quiet	**rit.**	slow down

Staccato: a dot above or below a note shortens the sounding length of that note
Legato: a curved line, or slur, between two notes of different pitch means that they should be played smoothly

THE BAROQUE PERIOD

During the baroque period, about 1600-1750, much music was composed on a grand and opulent scale. There were operas by Monteverdi and Handel, great choral works by Handel and J. S. Bach, and clear-sounding music for string orchestras by Vivaldi and others.

CLASSICAL ERA

The classical period, about 1750-1820, focused on new music forms for orchestras and instrumental groups: string quartets, sonatas, concertos, and symphonies. Haydn, Mozart, and Beethoven were masters of these new forms, with their emphasis on systematic development and "classical" order and proportion.

THE ROMANTICS

Beethoven's dramatic and expressive music also opened the way for the romantic period, about 1820-1900. Composers now wanted to express their own thoughts and feelings through poetic songs, descriptive pieces, or operas full of passion and drama. Schubert, Mendelssohn, Schumann, Chopin, Berlioz, Wagner, Verdi, Brahms, and Tchaikovsky all lived during this period.

GROWTH OF WORLD MUSIC

The last century has seen an explosion of musical styles. It has also seen the growth of blues and jazz, which gave rise to rock and pop. Composers have been influenced by jazz and music from the Far East and elsewhere. Every type of music has been touched by electronics and computers. TV, radio, satellites, cassettes, CDs, and the Internet make it instantly available to people all around the world.

► Traditional instruments, as well as synthesizers, can be connected to a computer using MIDI (Musical Instrument Digital Interface). Once stored in the computer's memory, the notes can be made to trigger any sound or effect.

J. S. Bach (1685-1750) influenced almost every composer who followed.

Mozart (1756-91) was a child prodigy who began to compose at the age of five.

Beethoven (1770-1827) composed very powerful music, despite being deaf.

Liszt (1811-86) was a brilliant pianist who wrote very difficult piano music.

Wagner (1813-83) wrote dramatic operas of a highly romantic nature.

Gershwin (1898-1937) was famous for his popular songs and musicals.

SEE ALSO

Dance, Film, Musical instrument, Radio, Sound

MUSICAL INSTRUMENT

Musical instruments create vibrations that are turned into sound. Most have their own range of pitched (high or low) notes. All have their own tone, timbre, or "voice."

Musical instruments may be classified scientifically as: aerophones, in which the air itself vibrates; chordophones, in which one or more strings vibrate; membranophones, in which a stretched skin, or membrane, vibrates; and idiophones, in which the whole body of the instrument vibrates as one. The better-known way of classifying them is: strings, woodwind, brass, percussion, as well as keyboard instruments, electronic instruments, and the voice.

Irish harps were carried from town to town by wandering minstrels.

The 6 ft. (1.8m)-long serpent was very popular during the 1600s and 1700s.

From the 1100s, the hurdy-gurdy accompanied singers at feasts and dances.

The Jew's harp is placed inside the mouth, while a finger plucks its tongue.

STRINGED INSTRUMENTS

Stringed instruments produce their sounds from vibrating strings. With violins, violas, cellos, and double basses, the strings are usually scraped with a bow to make them vibrate. In other stringed instruments, notably the guitar, the strings are plucked. The player presses down on the strings with his or her fingers to change their "playing length," which is the section that vibrates. This is called "stopping." The wooden body vibrates in sympathy with the strings, giving them volume and tone.

▶ VIOLIN

Fingerboard

Scroll

Tuning peg

Bow

Horsehair

The four violin strings are made of metal, gut wound with thin wire, or plastic

Bridge

Chin rest

Sound post

Tailpiece holds strings to belly

Back

End pin

◀ CELLO

SYMPHONY ORCHESTRA

A typical orchestra includes a string section of violins, violas, cellos, and double basses; a brass section of French horns, trumpets, trombones, and tuba; a wind section of clarinets, oboes, bassoons, flutes, and piccolos; and a percussion section of timpani, gong, glockenspiel, bass drum, and various other percussive instruments.

▲ TROMBONE

Flared bell

Cupped mouthpiece

◄ TUBA

Outer tube

▼ TRUMPET

Inner tube

Key for water outlet

The trombone uses a sliding tube instead of piston valves

BRASS INSTRUMENTS

Brass instruments are nearly all made from brass or other metal. The player's lips vibrate in a cup-shaped mouthpiece and the tube magnifies these vibrations and changes their tone. Modern horns, trumpets, and tubas have valves that shorten the length of the tube to produce notes. The length of tube, size of bore, and the shape of the bell (flared end) determine the range of notes and their special tone.

The electric guitar has a flat, solid body and electric pickups under each string.

WOODWIND INSTRUMENTS

Woodwind instruments make air vibrate in a tube. Many are made from wood, but this is not what classifies them as woodwind—it is the way they are played. Some, like the flute and recorder, have a mouthpiece that turns the player's breath directly into vibrations. The oboe, clarinet, and bassoon have small vibrating reeds. The player sounds different notes by opening or closing holes in the tube's side, and so changing the length of the tube in which the air vibrates.

▼ FLUTE

Finger key

Foot joint

Finger hole covered by key

Cork pads make airtight seal

Head joint

Body joint

Lip plate

Mouth hole

▼ CLARINET

▼ OBOE

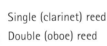

Single (clarinet) reed

Double (oboe) reed

The saxophone has a flared bell, single-reed mouthpiece, and is very popular in jazz.

The rock drum kit includes a bass drum, floor toms, cymbals, and a snare drum.

PERCUSSION INSTRUMENTS

Percussion instruments are struck. Drums have a tight membrane across a frame, which the player strikes with hands, fingers, or sticks. The air inside the frame, or the frame itself, makes the vibrating membrane sound louder. Bells, cymbals, and gongs are all made from a single piece of material and vibrate as a whole when struck. Some percussion instruments, such as drums and bells, sound notes of definite pitch. But with gongs and cymbals it is difficult to place the pitch.

▼ TIMPANI (KETTLEDRUM)

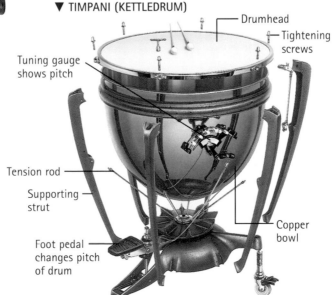

Drumhead

Tightening screws

Tuning gauge shows pitch

Tension rod

Supporting strut

Foot pedal changes pitch of drum

Copper bowl

The powerful church organ has one or more keyboards and several banks of pipes.

SEE ALSO

Dance, Music, Sound

MYTH AND LEGEND

Myths and legends are the names given to the stories which early people told about their heroes and religious beliefs, and to explain the world about them.

In earlier times, when people knew little about science or nature, they explained things like how the sun rose and set or how the world began through stories called myths. Before writing was developed, myths were passed down from generation to generation by word of mouth. By studying myths, we can learn much about a people's way of life, customs, and values.

▲ Baba Yaga is a witch in Slavic mythology who guards the gate to the Other World. She has power over animals and birds, and day and night.

HEROIC EXPLOITS

Unlike myths, which early people regarded as sacred and true, legends are folktales about the imaginary exploits of a hero. The hero often existed, but over many tellings the story became exaggerated. The earliest recorded literature in the world is the Sumerian legend *The Epic of Gilgamesh*. It was based on a real person, King Gilgamesh, who lived around 2700 B.C. However, in the legend, the hero Gilgamesh is described as being half-god.

▲ In Greek legend, the magical winged stallion Pegasus was ridden by the hero Bellerophon. Pegasus later became a carrier of thunderbolts for Zeus.

THE UNKNOWN EXPLAINED

All early people had their own myths to explain how natural events happened. The Ancient Greeks believed that the sun was their god Apollo driving a flaming chariot across the sky each day. The Ancient Egyptians believed that the sun god Ra sailed across the sky in a boat.

▲ The Japanese often placed clay figures of ferocious, warriorlike gods in holy places to frighten off the demons.

▲ The Zuni Indians of the Southwest believe that the first people came from underground and were trained by the medicine man Yanauluha to farm the land and maintain order.

CREATION MYTHS

Most early people had their own myths to explain how the world began. Many myths start with nothingness, darkness, or water. Out of this comes a god, who then starts the process of creation. According to an Indian myth, the world began when a creature shaped like a man divided into man and woman. From their marriage came the human race and, later, animals.

FAVORITE GODS

At the center of most myths was a group of people's gods. The functions of particular gods depended on what was important to the people. For instance, farming was very important to the Aztecs of Mexico and so they worshiped, among others, a group of corn gods. The gods of the seafaring Vikings were mostly concerned with war.

HOMES OF THE GODS

People's gods usually belonged to one "family." Often they looked and behaved like people. They had mythical homes, usually in the sky or on a mountaintop, as gods needed to be all-seeing. Some gods inhabited sacred groves or the sea. However, the chief god in African mythologies lived on the Earth.

EPIC TALES

The Greeks and Romans also told long stories to entertain. Among them are the Greek poet Homer's epic poems about Troy—the *Iliad* and *Odyssey*. He wrote these during the 700s B.C. and they are great works of literature. Such myths have inspired artists and writers ever since.

▶ The Norse (Scandinavians) believed that giants were a constant threat to both gods and human beings. Here, Surt leads the fire giants of Muspell against the gods at Ragnarok in what would be the last battle—and the end of the world.

▲ According to Greek legend, Perseus, son of Zeus, killed the Gorgon Medusa by cutting off her head. The sight of her head, which had snakes for hair, turned people to stone. Here, Perseus holds it up to King Polydectes and his courtiers in anger.

◀ In Hindu mythology, the half-man, half-eagle creature Garuda was said to be the sun in the form of a bird. Here, he carries the god Vishnu and his wife Lakshmi.

SEE ALSO

Greece (Ancient), Language, Literature, Mesopotamia

291

NAPOLEONIC WARS

The Napoleonic Wars were fought between Napoleon, ruler of France from 1799 to 1814, and his allies, and other European states, such as Britain and Russia.

Napoleon was helped on campaigns by marshals like Michel Ney (1769-1815).

Cavalry Marshal Joachim Murat (1767-1815) became king of Naples.

Marshal Louis-Alexander Berthier (1753-1815) was chief of staff from 1805.

In 1799, General Napoleon Bonaparte (1769-1821) seized power in France. He introduced liberal freedoms and went to war with countries who opposed his rule. In 1804, he crowned himself emperor of France and crowned his wife empress.

THE CONQUEST OF EUROPE

In 1805, Napoleon defeated Austria at Ulm and Austerlitz. Prussia was defeated at Jena in 1806, and in 1807 the Russian army lost at Friedland. From 1808 to 1814, a British army fought in Portugal and Spain against a French invasion. In 1812, Napoleon invaded Russia, but was cut off by winter weather. Of his 500,000 men, only 75,000 returned. In 1814, Napoleon was forced to go into exile.

STRATEGY AND TACTICS

Napoleon tried to cut the enemy off from supplies and force them to fight where and when he chose. On the battlefield, he relied on artillery to pound the enemy before columns of infantry broke through the enemy lines, followed by cavalry to hunt fugitives. Bright uniforms helped soldiers to recognize each other through the dense battlefield smoke.

DEFEAT AT WATERLOO

In 1815, Napoleon returned to France. His new army marched quickly, but was defeated by the British and Prussians at Waterloo. He was banished to the Atlantic island of St. Helena, where he died in 1821.

BATTLE OF MARENGO

Napoleon made his reputation at the Battle of Marengo in Italy on June 14, 1800. Attacked by 31,000 Austrians, Napoleon led a fierce defense by his 18,000 men until 10,000 reinforcements arrived under General Louis Desaix. Napoleon's brilliant counterattack crushed the Austrians.

SEE ALSO
France, Revolution, Warfare

NATIVE AMERICAN

Native Americans were the first people to settle the Americas, before the discovery and settlement of those lands by Europeans.

The Tlingit lived along the northwest coast.

Navajo farmed the southwest of North America.

The Creek lived in the eastern woodland area.

Native Americans developed many different cultures and civilizations, but were overwhelmed by European invaders after the 1400s. Today they make up a minority of the American population.

EARLY ARRIVALS
Before 20,000 B.C., humans crossed into the Americas along a land bridge that stretched from eastern Asia across the Bering Strait. By about 10,000 B.C., they had spread south to the tip of South America. The Inuit of Canada and Alaska came from Asia only 3,000 to 5,000 years ago.

NATIVE CULTURES
The earliest Native Americans hunted wild animals and gathered wild plants. About 1500 B.C., some groups began farming. The main crop was Indian corn, or maize, but beans and squash were also grown. In addition, they continued to gather nuts, berries, and wild grains. They rarely domesticated animals. Although some groups, or tribes, lived in a fixed place, many tribes moved as they followed the animals they hunted—the bison, or buffalo, of the great plains, for example. Along the northwest coast, cultures based on fishing developed.

DISEASE AND MASSACRE
In 1492, Christopher Columbus sailed to America from Europe. Over the next 400 years, the European settlers spread over most of the Americas. European diseases killed many Native Americans, who had no immunity. About 80 percent of the Mandan tribe in the northern plains was killed by smallpox.

▲ This thriving smoked-fish business in Wisconsin shows how traditional skills have been adapted to modern times.

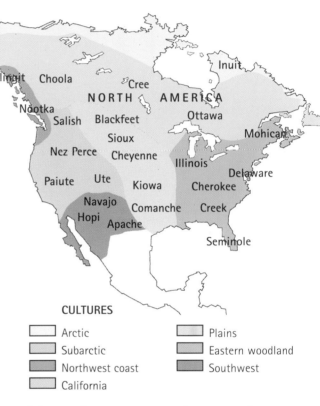

CULTURES

Arctic	Plains
Subarctic	Eastern woodland
Northwest coast	Southwest
California	

Many other surviving tribes were driven from their lands or killed in warfare. The last battle of the Indian Wars was fought at Wounded Knee, South Dakota in 1890.

TRIBAL LANDS
In the late 1970s, some tribes started legal battles against the U.S. federal government to try to reclaim land that had been taken from them. Today, North America is home to about 2 million Native Americans. Many still live on reservations, keeping alive their traditional cultures. Some of these remain poor, others run thriving businesses.

◀ The Cheyenne were one of the plains tribes. During war, the warriors were organized into seven societies, with the "dog soldiers" acting as scouts and forward troops.

SEE ALSO
Canada, North America

NAVIGATION

Navigation is the science of finding the way. It is used mainly to guide ships, aircraft, and spacecraft, but can also be used for vehicles on land.

The magnetic compass was invented in China around A.D. 1000.

The backstaff helped to find latitude by measuring the height of the sun and stars.

The astrolabe was used by navigators before the invention of the sextant.

The sextant, which also determines latitude, is still in use today.

For thousands of years, ever since people began to travel by sea, navigation has been necessary. Early navigators relied on skill and guesswork, but today they are helped by satellite technology and computers.

ANCIENT ARTS
Many early people traveled for trade or war, but the first to navigate seriously were the Phoenicians and Greeks, who sailed throughout the Mediterranean from about 750 B.C. By 300 B.C., some Greeks could find latitude by studying the stars, but after the fall of the Roman Empire, most navigational skills were lost.

HENRY THE NAVIGATOR
In 1418, Prince Henry of Portugal set up a school of navigation, which made many

MODERN NAVIGATIONAL SYSTEMS
The idea of bearings from beacons is used with satellite technology. The U.S. military Geostat system has satellites in orbit around the Earth positioned so that at least two are within radio range from any place on Earth. It is claimed a soldier with a computerized, handheld receiver can find his or her position to within 6.5 ft. (2m).

◄ The lines of latitude and longitude marked on globes and atlases can be used to pinpoint specific places. Lines of latitude show how far north or south of the equator a place is. Lines of longitude run from the North to the South Pole.

Lines of longitude

Lines of latitude

advances in exploration and navigation. The tools developed depended on compass readings and sightings of the stars and sun. Although this early equipment underwent many changes, it remained the basis of navigation until well into the 1900s.

PINPOINTING A TARGET
World War II brought a major boost to navigation. Bomber aircraft needed to find their way to a target accurately. One way was to direct two radio beams into enemy territory so they crossed over the target. Aircraft followed one beam until they found the second. Another system was based on radio beacons. By taking a bearing on two beacons, the navigator could find his position to within a few hundred yards. The system was adapted to cover shipping lanes as well as air routes, and remains in use today as a major navigational aid for boats and ships.

Signals from satellites help aircraft pinpoint their position to within 300 ft. (100m)

Navigation satellites beam radio signals to Earth

A receiver on board uses signals from land-based radio beacons to calculate the boat's position

Radar reflectors on floating buoys warn of hidden dangers

A computer on board uses satellite radio signals to guide the boat with great accuracy

An echo sounder measures the water depth by beaming high-pitched sound waves toward the seabed

SEE ALSO
Explorer, Magnetism

NETHERLANDS, BELGIUM, AND LUXEMBOURG

The Netherlands, Belgium, and Luxembourg make up a group of countries in northwest Europe called the Low Countries. The Netherlands is also known as Holland.

BELGIUM
Area: 11,700 sq. mi.
Population: 10,274,595
Capital: Brussels
Languages: Dutch, French
Currency: Euro

LUXEMBOURG
Area: 999 sq. mi.
Population: 448,569
Capital: Luxembourg
Languages: French, German, Letzebuergesch
Currency: Euro

NETHERLANDS
Area: 15,785 sq. mi.
Population: 16,067,754
Capital: Amsterdam
Language: Dutch
Currency: Euro

The name Netherlands means "lowlands"—two fifths of the country lies below sea level and the countryside is crisscrossed with canals. Half the country's freight is carried on the inland waterways. The landscape is dotted with windmills, originally built for controlling the water level. Belgium is also low-lying and mostly flat, rising to hills called the Ardennes in the south, which extend across the border into the small country of Luxembourg.

TRADE AND NEW LAND
From the 1500s, the Dutch became seafarers, growing rich from fishing and trade, and built up an empire in Southeast Asia. Rotterdam is now the world's largest port. The Dutch became experts at flood control, draining the land, and reclaiming it from the sea by building dikes and using pumps. This has created rich farmland—cheese and butter are major exports.

INDUSTRIES AND CITIES
Belgium's textile industry dates back to the Middle Ages. Today, the country is a heavily industrialized nation. Belgium and Luxembourg are both leading steel producers. The city of Luxembourg is a major center of banking, and Luxembourg is one of the wealthiest nations in Europe. The Netherlands is Europe's most densely populated country. Amsterdam, its largest city, is the national capital, although the government sits at The Hague.

HISTORY AND HERITAGE
The Netherlands fought for freedom from Spanish rule during the 1500s. Belgium and Luxembourg were part of the Netherlands until the 1800s. These three countries remain closely linked as members of the European Union, which has its headquarters in Brussels.

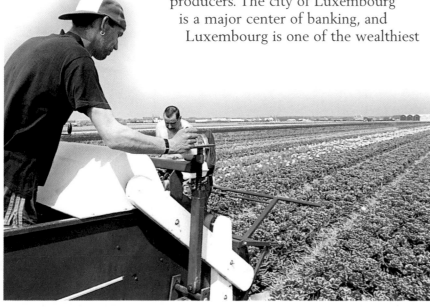

◄ Cut flowers and bulbs are important crops in the Netherlands, as well as fruit and vegetables.

SEE ALSO

Europe

NEWSPAPER AND MAGAZINE

Newspapers and magazines are publications that print international or local news, alongside comments on important events and interviews with celebrities.

People all over the world find out about events by reading newspapers and magazines. National daily and weekly newspapers carry news from around the world. Some magazines specialize in one subject, such as football or medicine.

TABLOIDS AND BROADSHEETS
The first newspapers were printed in Europe in about 1650, after the introduction of the printing press. They may be printed every day or once a week, and may concentrate on local events or cover worldwide news. Most newspapers are either tabloid, with a page size of about 11.5x14 in. (30x40cm), or broadsheet, about twice as large. Tabloids tend to print short stories, often about film stars and popular events. Broadsheets usually print

longer stories, looking at serious events in more detail. Although newspapers are all different, most have similar features. Sports news is usually printed toward the end of a paper and national, political, and international news stories are at the front.

GATHERING NEWS
News is gathered by reporters who may visit events, such as political conventions and baseball games, and interview people taking part. Personalities and commercial companies often write a press release and send it to reporters to let them know about events or new products.

MAGAZINES
Magazines may be published weekly or monthly. They often feature full-color, glossy pages with in-depth interviews and features. Some magazines cover a wide range of subjects, but some can be highly specialized. They may deal with fashion, sports, or celebrities. Those which concentrate on a particular business are called "trade press." Magazines often have a long lead time (written several weeks or months in advance).

Children's comics appeared in the late 1800s. This one started in 1937.

Superheroes, popularized by DC Comics, include Wonder Woman from 1941.

Magazines may concentrate on particular subjects or age groups.

Tabloids are small-size newspapers with a more sensationalist style.

Broadsheets are larger and the news reports have a more serious tone.

▲ Using computers, newspaper designers decide on the look of a page, choosing the style of type and the size and number of pictures.

▶ An editor and designer discuss the content of the lead, or front, page.

Game, set, and match to Rusedski

◀ A photographer brings in shots of an event he has covered to show the picture editor, who will select the best shots to be used.

◀ Reporters write their stories straight onto the computer network. They are cut to length by a copy editor, who also checks facts and spellings.

CREATING A NEWSPAPER
Most newspapers, magazines, and books are put together on computers (desktop publishing) before they are sent to be printed. A newspaper staff includes writers, photographers, designers, and copy editors working under a chief editor.

SEE ALSO
Cartoon and animation, Design, Language, Media, Printing

NEW ZEALAND

New Zealand lies in the South Pacific, 1,180 mi. (1,900km) southeast of its nearest neighbor, Australia. It has two main islands, both of which are long and narrow.

Area: 103,700 sq. mi.
Population: 3,908,037
Capital: Wellington
Language: English
Currency: New Zealand dollar

◀ Most of New Zealand's landscape is hilly, but there are fertile valleys and plains, such as South Island's Canterbury Plains.

▲ In the greeting *hongi*, Maoris rub noses. Other traditions include carving, weaving, and tattooing.

Over four fifths of New Zealanders live in towns or cities. Three quarters of the population lives on North Island, where it is warmest, but South Island is the largest of the two main islands.

LANDSCAPE AND WILDLIFE
The coasts are ideal for sailing, surfing, and fishing, and the mountains attract many skiers. There are active volcanoes, geysers, and pools of bubbling mud. Because New Zealand has been isolated from other land masses for millions of years, it has developed distinct native wildlife such as the kiwi, a flightless bird, and many different kinds of fern.

EARNING A LIVING
Most of New Zealand's wealth comes from farming, but this employs fewer than one in six people. Major exports include cheese, fruit, meat, wool, and wine, as well as seafood, timber products, and aluminum. There are large reserves of coal and gas, and industry is concentrated around Auckland, the largest city. Tourism is a fast-growing business.

TWO TRADITIONS
New Zealand was first settled by Maoris from Polynesia around A.D. 900, and they still account for about an eighth of the population. Permanent British settlement began in 1840. Settlers transformed the country by founding cities and introducing cereal crops, sheep, and cattle. Independence came in 1907, but ties between New Zealand and Britain remain close through trade and sport.

◀ The All Blacks is New Zealand's national rugby football team. It is one of the best in the world.

SEE ALSO
Custom, Pacific Islands

287

NIGERIA

Nigeria is a republic on the west coast of Africa. It has a greater population than any other African country and a rich blend of cultures.

Area: 356,670 sq. mi.
Population: 129,934,911
Capital: Abuja
Language: English
Currency: Naira

Nigeria's coastline consists of mangrove swamps. To the north of these lies a belt of dense tropical rain forest. Farther north, open woodland and savanna grassland merge into areas of semidesert.

RICH IN RESOURCES
Nigeria's most valuable natural resources are oil and gas. Other important products are palm oil (used for making soap), tin, cacao (used for making cocoa), peanuts, rubber, cotton, and timber. In the dry north, livestock and cereals such as millet and sorghum are important. In the wetter south, fish, rice, yams, and cassava are the main foods. The biggest city is the former capital Lagos, a major port.

ARTS AND CRAFTS
Nigeria has a rich tradition in arts, music, and literature. The craftspeople of the kingdom of Benin were famous for casting fine sculptures in bronze 500 years ago. Wood carving and weaving are other traditional crafts. Nigerian authors writing in English, such as Chinua Achebe, have won fame, and in 1986, Wole Soyinka was the first African to be awarded the Nobel Prize for Literature.

NEW NATION OF OLD PEOPLES
Nigeria's boundaries were established by its British colonizers in the early 1900s. The new nation brought together over 200 ancient tribes and kingdoms, as well as many different languages and religions. Most Nigerians live in small villages. Over half the people are Muslims who make up most of the population in the north. The other main religion is Christianity. The three main ethnic groups are the Hausa, living in the north, and the Ibo and Yoruba in the south. Nigeria became independent from British rule in 1960.

▲ Each of Nigeria's 30 states is headed by a governor. Although elections have been held— in 1979 and in 1993—the army has ruled the country for most of the time since the 1960s. Political parties are now banned.

◄ Zuma Rock dominates the landscape at Abuja. The city, which was built in 1979 to replace Lagos as the capital, is centrally located.

SEE ALSO

Africa

NORTH AMERICA

North America is the third largest of the world's seven continents and the fourth largest in population. It stretches from the Arctic Ocean to Central America.

▲ In the Canadian province of Quebec, average January temperatures range from 10°F (–12°C) to –20°F (–29°C).

KEY FACTS

- **Area:** 8,391,630 sq. mi.
- **Population:** 491,519,000
- **Number of countries:** 23
- **Largest country:** Canada (3,560,200 sq. mi.)
- **Smallest country:.** St. Kitts-Nevis (139 sq. mi.)
- **Highest point:** Mount McKinley (20,320 ft.)
- **Largest lake:** Superior (31,700 sq. mi.)
- **Longest river:** Missouri (2,700 mi.)

▼ The world's first skyscraper was built in Chicago in 1884. It no longer stands, but two other early skyscrapers, the Wrigley Building (left) and the Tribune Tower (right), are still Chicago landmarks.

The largest part of North America is made up of Canada and the United States. The rest consists of Mexico, the seven countries in Central America, and the islands in the Caribbean Sea, which include 13 independent countries and 11 overseas territories still linked to a colonial partner. The U.K. territory of Bermuda lies in the North Atlantic Ocean and is also part of North America.

LARGEST ISLAND

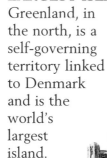

Greenland, in the north, is a self-governing territory linked to Denmark and is the world's largest island.

MOUNTAINS AND PLAINS

In the western half of the continent are the Rocky Mountains, the world's second longest mountain chain. The continent's highest peak, Mount McKinley at 20,320 feet (6,194m), is in Alaska. There are smaller mountain ranges in the east, including the Appalachians. The Canadian Shield is a huge area of ancient rock with poor soil, but it is rich in minerals. Across the center of the continent is the vast grassland region known as the prairies.

GREAT LAKES AND RIVERS

The five Great Lakes—Superior, Huron, Erie, Ontario, and Michigan—form the world's largest grouping of this kind. The thundering waters of Niagara Falls, on a strait between lakes Erie and Ontario, are an impressive spectacle. The Mississippi, Missouri, and Ohio rivers together form the continent's longest river system, over 4,600 mi. (7,500km) long.

COLD AND HOT

North America has every kind of climate. The north has bitterly cold winters—in the Arctic regions of Canada and Alaska it is too cold for trees to grow. In the south, huge forests of evergreen and deciduous trees cover the land. Still farther south, there are hot deserts and tropical forests.

GIANT TREES

Some of the world's tallest trees, the giant redwood and the sequoia, grow on the west coast of North America. In the eastern forests, the leaves of maple, hickory, and other deciduous trees provide a brilliant color show in the autumn. Mesquite, prickly pear, and saguaro cactus grow in desert regions. ▶

KEY TO MAP
1 ST. KITTS-NEVIS
2 ANTIGUA & BARBUDA
3 DOMINICA
4 BARBADOS
5 ST. LUCIA
6 ST. VINCENT & THE GRENADINES
7 GRENADA
8 TRINIDAD & TOBAGO

ANIMAL LIFE

Wildlife has been reduced by hunting and settlement, so bison (buffalo), wolves, and bears are no longer widespread. There are caribou, moose, mountain lions, wild goats, porcupines, beavers, rattlesnakes, and alligators. Birds include the turkey, macaw, roadrunner, and bald eagle—the national symbol of the United States.

FARMING

North America is rich in farmland, and the continent provides about half the world's grain exports. The vast prairies have been plowed for cereals or are used as grazing land for cattle and sheep. Important crops are corn, soya, cotton, wheat, and flax. There are also plantations growing bananas, coffee, cotton, and sugarcane, and huge orchards of apples, oranges, cherries, and other fruits.

▼ North American bison, also known as buffalo, graze in Yellowstone National Park. These animals live mostly in reserves. Their numbers have been greatly reduced by overhunting, and strict laws now exist to protect them.

GOODS AND RESOURCES

Only Europe makes more factory goods than North America, which is a major producer of vehicles, aircraft, electronics, and chemicals. It is rich in minerals, including silver, natural gas, oil, copper, and coal. Some of the world's leading companies are based here.

CITIES AND TRANSPORT

Most North Americans live in towns and cities. The continent has some of the world's largest cities, including Mexico City, New York, and Los Angeles, where skyscrapers form dramatic skylines and

▲ At carnival time in Mexico, people dress in traditional costumes. Many Mexicans are of Spanish ancestry, but there are also descendants of the Ancient Mayan people living in Mexico and Central America.

where cars and trucks move along multi-lane expressways. In this huge continent, trains and airplanes carry passengers and freight long distances. Many North Americans enjoy a high standard of living, but in the inner cities of the United States, and in Mexico and parts of the Caribbean, people are relatively poor.

VARIED ROOTS
North America has been a "melting pot" for people from many parts of the world. English is the main language, but French is used in parts of Canada, and Spanish is spoken in Mexico and by many people in Central America and the United States. Many North Americans have European or Asian roots. African Americans are the descendants of black people brought from Africa as slaves.

THE FIRST AMERICANS
People came to North America from Asia, possibly as early as 30,000 B.C., and settled across the continent. They were hunters, some of whom, over the ages, became farmers and town-builders. Another group was the ancestors of the Inuit people, who settled in the far north. The Maya and Aztecs of Mexico created civilizations of which impressive ruins still remain.

EUROPEANS ARRIVE
Vikings came to North America about 1,000 years ago but did not settle for long. In 1492, the explorer Christopher Columbus "discovered" the American continent, which soon became known as the New World. He was followed by explorers from Spain, who came seeking gold. From the 1600s, the British and French settled in Canada and along the east coast. Spain ruled Mexico, Florida, and Central America. Canada and Mexico became independent in the 1800s.

THE UNITED STATES
The United States was created in 1776 when the 13 colonies broke away from Britain. It rapidly grew into an industrial giant. Native Americans were driven from their lands as settlers moved west across the Great Plains and reached the Pacific coast. Immigrants from Africa, Europe, Asia, and Central America have helped to shape the modern United States.

▲ Sequoias, growing on North America's west coast, are some of the world's tallest trees.

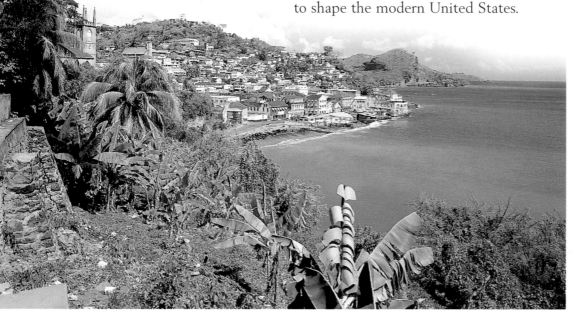

◀ Grenada is one of 13 independent island nations in the Caribbean. Its capital, St. George's, lies on the southwest coast among forested hills.

SEE ALSO
Aztec, Caribbean, Central America, Explorer, Maya, Mexico, Native American, Slavery, United States of America, Viking

NUCLEAR POWER

Nuclear power is the generation of electricity using heat released by changes in the nuclei of atoms. The process is known as a controlled nuclear reaction.

Lise Meitner (1878–1968) proved that heavy atoms can be split into lighter ones—a process she called "nuclear fission."

Otto Hahn (1879–1968) worked with Meitner to split the atom, for which he was awarded the 1944 Nobel Prize for Chemistry.

Enrico Fermi (1901–54) built the first nuclear reactor in a squash court in 1942 and later worked on the atomic bomb project.

The center of an atom is called the nucleus. Radioactive elements, such as uranium, have nuclei which sometimes split, releasing energy including heat. When these nuclei split, they throw out two or three tiny particles called neutrons. These can hit other nuclei, making them split, shooting out more neutrons.

AN IDEAL FUEL
Compared to coal, oil, or gas, very small amounts of uranium can make a lot of electricity, and no oxygen is needed. Nuclear power is ideal for spacecraft and submarines: a nuclear-powered spacecraft can keep its instruments working for years,

▲ The mushroom cloud from a nuclear explosion is made up of particles of rock, soil, water, and other materials that eventually fall back to Earth as radioactive "fall-out."

and a nuclear-powered submarine can travel around the world without refueling or polluting the air with waste gases.

HOPEFUL SOLUTION
In the 1950s, nuclear power was seen as the solution to the world's energy needs. The world's first commercial nuclear power plant, Calder Hall in England, started generating electricity in 1956. Some countries, including France, rely heavily on nuclear power. But few nuclear power plants are now being built because of the dangers.

NUCLEAR HAZARDS
Nuclear waste is hard to dispose of, remaining dangerously radioactive for thousands of years. Making old nuclear reactors safe is expensive. There is also the chance of an accident, such as the one in 1986 at Chernobyl in the Soviet Union, when an explosion contaminated thousands of square miles. Nuclear fusion, which releases energy by joining nuclei together rather than splitting them apart, may provide safe and clean energy in the future.

Reactor vessel

Water and steam separator

Control rod

Steam outlet

Core (nuclear fuel assembly)

Pump

Water inlet

Control rod drive

Concrete shield

THE NUCLEAR REACTOR

In a reactor, a moderator such as graphite or water is used to slow down the neutrons released from fuel rods containing uranium. Slowed neutrons are much better at splitting other uranium atoms, causing a sustained chain reaction that releases huge amounts of heat. Control rods stop the reaction going too fast by absorbing neutrons. The heat boils water into steam, which turns turbines to make electricity.

▲ In nuclear fission, neutrons are used to split heavy atoms, such as those in uranium, which in turn release more free neutrons and energy.

▲ In nuclear fusion, two nuclei of a lightweight substance such as hydrogen combine to form heavier ones, releasing a further neutron and energy.

SEE ALSO
Atom and molecule, Electricity, Energy, Submarine, World War II

NUTRITION

Nutrition is the process by which we take in and use food. Chemical substances found in food, called nutrients, provide energy and help the body function.

▲ Children in the Sudan collecting ants to eat during famine. Not eating enough food can result in malnutrition, draining energy and lowering resistance to disease.

There are five important nutrients—carbohydrates, proteins, fats (in small quantities), vitamins, and minerals. In addition, we cannot live without water.

ENERGY AND GROWTH
Carbohydrates and fats provide the body with energy. Proteins are necessary for growth and repair of cells. Vitamins and minerals like calcium, potassium, and iron are essential for the health of nerves, skin, bones, muscles, and brain. Research has shown that eating food rich in vitamins A, C, E, and beta-carotene can help protect against the cell damage that causes cancer.

FIBER AND WATER
Fiber, the indigestible part of fruits and vegetables, is essential in the diet. It adds bulk to food and helps it move through the large intestine during digestion. Water

is vital. The human body is made up of about 65 percent water. Its cells need water to keep chemical reactions going. We need about 3.5 pt. (2 l) of water a day.

A BALANCED DIET
The energy value of food is measured in calories. The more work your body does, the more calories you need. A man needs, on average, 2,700 calories a day and a woman 1,900; a 16-year-old boy needs 3,200 calories a day and a girl 2,100.

FOOD SHORTAGES
Many people do not get enough to eat. Malnutrition (not getting sufficient nutrients) causes weakness and disease, accounting for around 54 percent of deaths in under-fives in developing countries, which is about 6.6 million deaths a year.

Fruits and vegetables are rich in vitamins. We should eat five portions each day.

Carbohydrate foods contain natural sugars and starches for energy.

Fats can be animal (butter, milk, cheese) or vegetable—from plants and nuts.

Meat, fish, cheese, and pulses and nuts are sources of protein.

A BALANCED DIET

A healthy meal can take many forms. Most national diets are based on locally grown produce, animals or fish, and a traditional staple food that is usually starchy and relatively cheap, such as rice, bread, or pasta.

▼ Pasta is a good energy source; adding cheese increases protein. Tomato sauce provides vitamin C.

▼ The traditional Thanksgiving dinner in America is a typical well-balanced meal.

◄ Research shows the Japanese diet is especially beneficial to long-term health. Tofu (bean curd) contains protein, calcium, and other minerals. Raw fish is used to make sushi.

► Many of our most popular foods originally come from South America.

▲ Fresh, raw vegetables are simply prepared in hot countries like Australia. Broiling meat reduces fat.

◄ A healthy meal in one bowl. In parts of West Africa, meat, beans, and nuts are mixed in a stew (gumbo) along with yam, a root vegetable.

SEE ALSO
Farming, Food, Fruit, Vegetable

293

OCEAN AND SEA

Seventy-one percent of the Earth's surface is covered by water. Nearly all of this vast area is made up of saltwater oceans and seas.

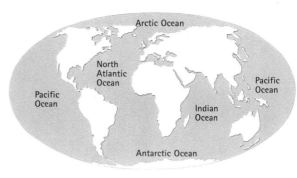

▲ The main oceans of the world cover more than two thirds of the Earth's surface.

High spring tides are caused by the combined gravitational pull of the Sun and Moon when they are in line with the Earth. This occurs at the full Moon and new Moon.

Weak neap tides occur during the Moon's first and third quarters, when the gravitational forces of the Sun and Moon are at right angles and their combined force is less.

The Earth's crust is of two types: dense oceanic crust and lighter continental crust. The continental crust forms the great land masses of the Earth, and these, being relatively light, stand high above the general level of the Earth's surface. The water-filled hollows that lie between the continents are called oceans.

OCEAN FOUNDATIONS

The ocean floor is made of denser crustal material, which is constantly being created and destroyed through the process of plate tectonics. Along each ocean lies a volcanic ridge, forming a vast underwater network that encircles the Earth. This is where new crustal material is generated. The old material is destroyed along the edges of some of the oceans as one crustal plate is drawn down and swallowed up beneath the edge of another.

OCEAN FEATURES

This movement creates the basic features of an ocean: the oceanic ridge, which can rise to about 3,000 ft. (1,000m) beneath the surface; the abyssal plains, the greatest area of ocean floor, on average 16,500–20,000 ft. (5,000–6,000m) deep; and the oceanic trenches, many over 30,000 ft. (9,000m) deep, with the deepest—the Marianas Trench—plunging to over 36,000 ft. (11,000m).

THE SOFT COVERING

The sediments of the ocean floor consist of tiny skeletons and shells, volcanic dust, and mud that has washed off the land. Sediments close to oceanic ridges are thin, but thicker farther away. This is because the new ocean crust close to the ridges has not had enough time to collect much debris.

SHALLOW SEAS

Seas differ from oceans in that they are much shallower. They are the areas of the continents that happen to be below sea level—the continents' flooded edges. Sea floors tend to be thickly covered in sediment, such as sand and mud, brought

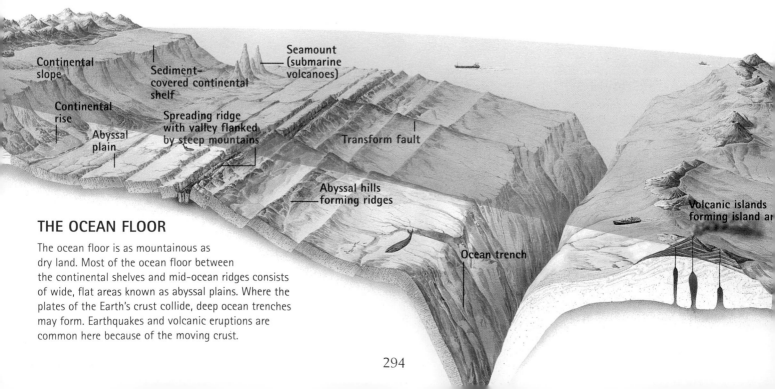

Continental slope

Continental rise

Abyssal plain

Sediment-covered continental shelf

Spreading ridge with valley flanked by steep mountains

Seamount (submarine volcanoes)

Abyssal hills forming ridges

Transform fault

Ocean trench

Volcanic islands forming island ar

THE OCEAN FLOOR

The ocean floor is as mountainous as dry land. Most of the ocean floor between the continental shelves and mid-ocean ridges consists of wide, flat areas known as abyssal plains. Where the plates of the Earth's crust collide, deep ocean trenches may form. Earthquakes and volcanic eruptions are common here because of the moving crust.

294

down by the rivers. Some seas do not lie on the continental shelf but are inland. The Caspian Sea is completely landlocked, and the Black Sea is only narrowly connected to the Mediterranean Sea. The Red Sea is an oddity—although it is small and almost landlocked, its floor is true oceanic crust and it has a central ridge.

LIVING THINGS

Most ocean life is found within a layer of water about 300 ft. (100m) deep, where sunlight penetrates. Plankton is the mass of tiny plants and animals that drifts in the sea and is the basis of the entire ocean food chain. All sea creatures depend directly on plankton for food, or on animals that feed on plankton. Planktonic

MARINE LIFE

Life-forms in the ocean are more varied than those on land. New creatures are often discovered in the deep sea.
1 Herring **2** Sperm whale **3** Shrimp **4** Rat-tail **5** Anglerfish **6** Grenadier **7** Cod **8** Gulper eel **9** Sea spider, tube worms, clam, white ghost crab **10** Tripod fish **11** Viperfish **12** Swallower **13** Lanternfish **14** Swordfish **15** Yellowfin tuna **16** Giant squid **17** Hammerhead **18** Barracuda **19** Portuguese man-of-war **20** Plankton **21** Green turtle **22** Sea lion **23** Common dolphin

plants (*phytoplankton*) grow here and also planktonic animals (*zooplankton*), which include one-celled animals, baby crabs, and fish. Larger creatures feed upon these animals, and even larger predators feed upon them in turn. The final link in the food chain is humans—the sea provides a source of food for much of the world's population.

MYSTERIOUS DEPTHS

Although the oceans have been traveled by many generations, the sea retains its mystery. It has been the source of many legends, including the mermaid and the sea serpent, and has inspired artists throughout the centuries. Scuba divers and scientists in submersibles are still learning about the sea, studying its creatures and geological features, and discovering submerged cities and shipwrecks.

ATOLLS

An atoll begins as a coral reef surrounding a volcanic island. As the island sinks, the reef grows upward. Eventually, the island disappears completely, and all that remains is a ring-shaped reef, or atoll, surrounding a lagoon.

SEE ALSO

Crab, Explorer, Jellyfish, River, Seashore, Shark, Snail, Starfish, Swamp and marsh, Water

295

OIL

Oil, or petroleum, is a thick, black liquid, sometimes called crude oil. It is a valuable raw material for fuels such as gasoline, and in the chemical industry.

Animal fats, such as pig lard, are used for cooking.

Vitamin-rich cod liver oil is used in medicine.

Most of the world's olive crop is grown for its oil.

Oil from sunflower seeds is used to make margarine.

Oil is a complex mixture of chemical compounds consisting of the elements hydrogen and carbon. These hydrocarbons release heat when they burn. This is what makes them useful as fuels.

THE ORIGINS OF OIL
The story of oil began millions of years ago, with plants and animals that lived in the ancient seas. After they died, the bodies of these plants and animals decayed and gradually turned into oil. The oil has remained trapped in rocks ever since. Like coal and gas, oil is a fossil fuel.

FINDING OIL
The search for oil is called oil exploration. Crude oil is always found in certain patterns of rock, so geologists look for

► In a refinery, parts, or fractions, of the crude oil are separated out in a process called fractional distillation. Fuels such as kerosene and gasoline are made by mixing these fractions. Other fractions are sent to chemical plants to be made into drugs, paints, plastics, and other products.

these patterns in areas where oil is likely to be found. They use magnetic and seismic surveys (which send sounds from explosions at ground level to bounce off rocks underground) to find rock formations that may contain oil.

DRILLING FOR OIL
To get the oil out, a hole is drilled down through the rocks. This is an oil well. The most expensive method is using oil rigs at sea (offshore), although onshore drilling is also common. The oil is sent by pipeline or by ship to an oil refinery for processing.

THE FUTURE OF OIL
Like other fossil fuels, oil pollutes the environment when it is burned. It also contributes to acid rain and to global warming. The modern world uses increasing amounts of oil for automobiles, power generation, heating, and industry. New oil finds are being made, but known reserves may only last about 50 years. In the future, alternative fuels will be needed so that the world's oil reserves do not completely run out.

OFFSHORE DRILLING
It is more dangerous to work on an offshore oil rig than a land rig because storms can damage the structure. It also costs about ten times more to build. The rig itself has to be floated out to sea in sections and then assembled; the equipment and crew are carried out to the site by helicopter. Because of the huge expense involved, several test drillings are done to make sure that there are enough oil reserves to justify the cost of setting up a permanent rig.

— Crown block

A crane is used for raising and lowering drilling equipment to the seabed

— Derrick

◄ A large-toothed bit is used to drill through soft rock.

► The drill shaft rotates within an outer casing. Mud is pumped down to clean the bit and bring up the rocks.

SEE ALSO
Coal, Gas, Medicine, Mining, Plastic, Pollution

OLYMPIC GAMES

The Olympic Games are a world athletic and sports competition that takes place every four years. About 200 nations enter competitors in about 270 events.

▲ The ancient Olympians, such as this discus thrower, competed naked.

The first modern Olympic Games were opened by King George I of Greece in Athens on April 5, 1896. They were a huge success, but it took several attempts to get them established as a successful global event. The modern Olympics were inspired by the ancient Olympic Games, which were first held in Olympia, Greece in 776 B.C.

OLYMPIC SPIRIT

The aim of the Olympic Games is to promote peace, equality, and friendship, and to inspire athletes around the world. Competition between individuals rather than countries is encouraged, and on the scoreboard at every Olympic Games is the message: "The most important thing in the Olympic Games is not to win but to take part…."

▲ The Olympic symbol of five linked rings represents the five continents of Africa, Asia, Australia, Europe, and North America. It was designed so that at least one of the six colors in the symbol (including the white background) would appear in all the flags of the competing nations.

OPENING CEREMONY

At every Olympic opening ceremony, a parade of nations is led by Greece, the founder nation, with the host country coming last and the nations in between appearing in alphabetical order. During the celebrations, the athletes and officials take the Olympic oath, the Olympic torch is lit, and the Olympic flag raised. As a sign of peace, doves are released into the stadium. ▶

THE 1996 ATLANTA GAMES

The 1996 Games, which marked the 100th anniversary of the start of the modern Olympics, were held at Atlanta, Georgia. The opening ceremony was the most spectacular to date, and new events for the Games included mountain biking, beach volleyball, women's soccer, and women's fencing.

FAST FACTS

• Since 1896, only five countries have been at all the Games: Australia, France, Greece, Great Britain, and Switzerland

• The marathon used to be 25 miles, but in the 1908 London Games it was extended to over 26 miles so that Princess Mary could see it start from the nursery window at Windsor Castle

• The newest Olympic sports include beach volleyball, women's soccer, tae kwondo, and the triathlon (introduced for Sydney 2000)

• The Roman Emperor Nero was so desperate for Olympic victory that he introduced music and poetry competitions and announced himself the winner in six events

▲ U.S. athlete Jesse Owens became the star of the 1936 Games at Berlin, Germany, when he won four gold medals. In the face of Nazi propaganda for white superiority, Owens's victory was a huge embarrassment for Nazi officials.

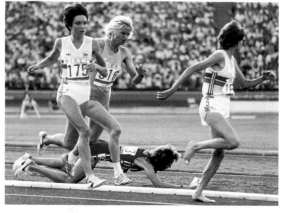

▲ Not all Olympic events go smoothly, as was the case when Britain's Zola Budd (right) collided with America's Mary Decker in the women's 3,000m event in 1984 in Los Angeles. Mary Decker fell and lost her chance of victory. This caused a great uproar.

THE OLYMPIC TORCH

Four weeks before the start of the Games, the Olympic flame is lit in Greece by magnifying the sun's rays with mirrors. It is then carried across the world in a torch by a series of runners. On the opening day of the Games, the last runner enters the stadium and the arena flame is lit. It stays burning until the close of the Games.

THE ANCIENT GAMES

The ancient Olympic Games were first organized as a religious, sporting, and cultural festival held in honor of Zeus, the ruler of the Greek gods. Every four years, Greek athletes traveled from all over the country to Olympia, a village near Mount Olympus (home of the gods) in Greece. Only Greek citizens could compete, although no women were allowed to take part in or even watch the Games on pain of death. The Games were taken so seriously that a truce between any warring states within Greece was called so that competitors could travel safely to Olympia.

BANNING OF THE GAMES

At the first ancient Olympic Games, in 776 B.C., there was only one event, a 200m stadium race. Gradually, more events were added, including chariot racing in 680 B.C. The Games were finally banned in A.D. 394 by the Roman emperor Theodosius. The Romans had conquered Greece, and Theodosius banned all pagan festivals, including the Olympic Games.

THE WINTER OLYMPICS

The modern Olympics fall into two parts: the Winter and the Summer Olympics. The first Winter Olympics were held in Chamonix, France, in 1924. Until 1994, they were always held in the same year

Thomas Burke (U.S.A.) wins the 100m event in the 1896 Olympics in Athens, Greece.

The Canadian ice hockey team triumphs in the first-ever Winter Olympics in Chamonix, France in 1924.

Attilio Pavesi (Italy) wins the cycling road race in the 1932 Games in Los Angeles.

Dawn Fraser (Australia) wins the 100m freestyle swimming event in Melbourne, Australia, in 1956.

Joe Frazier (U.S.A.) is heavyweight boxing champion at the 1964 Games in Tokyo, Japan.

as the Summer Olympics but are now held two years earlier. Winter Olympic sports include ice hockey, luge (small sled), skating, skiing, and bobsled.

THE SUMMER OLYMPICS

The Summer Olympics include nearly 30 sports: combat sports include judo and boxing; ball games include volleyball and handball; court games include tennis and badminton; and water sports include rowing and swimming. Athletics is classified as one sport in the Olympics, but includes 24 men's events and 20 women's events. As well as running events, athletics includes the high jump and long jump, the discus and javelin, and the decathlon (ten athletic events spread over two days).

POLITICAL PROBLEMS

Because the Olympic Games are the world's greatest sporting event, they have sometimes been used as a political tool. In 1972, Israeli competitors were attacked and killed by Arab terrorists at the Olympics in Munich, Germany. Eight years

later, the Games in Moscow were boycotted by the United States and its allies because of the Soviet invasion of Afghanistan. In 1984, the Soviet Union and its allies refused to compete in the Olympics in Los Angeles because of fears over security arrangements.

TODAY'S GAMES

At recent Games, there have been problems over athletes taking drugs. In 2000 a gymnast, four weightlifters, and a wrestler were stripped of their medals because they had taken drugs. Despite such controversies, the Olympic Games are still considered to be the ultimate sporting event and attract athletes from all over the world.

▲ The Paralympics is a competition for disabled competitors. It is separate from, and held after, the main Olympics, although it takes place in the Olympic stadium and is no less competitive. Here, the 4 x 400m wheelchair relay event at Atlanta was won by the German team.

▲ Yaping Deng, from China, was the winner of the women's table tennis singles competition at Barcelona, Spain, in 1992 and at Atlanta in 1996.

Fourteen-year-old Nadia Comaneci (Romania) is gold medalist in the combined athletics event in the 1976 Games in Montreal, Canada.

Steffi Graf (Germany) wins the women's tennis singles event in the 1988 Games held in Seoul, South Korea.

Jan Zelezny (Czech Republic) wins the javelin event in the 1996 Games in Atlanta.

SEE ALSO

Greece (Ancient), Sports

PACIFIC ISLANDS

Before the 1960s, most of the islands in the Pacific Ocean were ruled by Britain, the United States, or France. There are now 13 independent countries.

 FIJI
Area: 7,100 sq. mi.
Population: 856,346
Capital: Suva
Languages: English, Fijian
Currency: Fiji dollar

 KIRIBATI
Area: 277 sq. mi.
Population: 96,335
Capital: Tarawa
Languages: English, Gilbertese
Currency: Australian dollar

 MARSHALL ISLANDS
Area: 70 sq. mi.
Population: 73,630
Capital: Majuro
Languages: Marshallese, English
Currency: U.S. dollar

The Pacific Islands are part of a vast region called Oceania (which also includes Australia). Some of the islands are the mountainous tips of volcanoes, and others are coral islands that rest on the tops of sunken volcanoes.

ISLAND GROUPS
The Pacific Islands are divided into three areas. Melanesia, meaning "black islands" after the dark skin of the people, includes Fiji, Papua New Guinea, and the Solomon Islands. Micronesia, meaning "tiny islands," includes part of Kiribati, the Federated States of Micronesia, and several island groups associated with the United States. Polynesia, meaning "many islands," includes the islands in a triangle formed by New Zealand, Hawaii, and Easter Island.

 FEDERATED STATES OF MICRONESIA
Area: 271 sq. mi.
Population: 135,869
Capital: Palikir
Language: English
Currency: U.S. dollar

 NAURU
Area: 8 sq. mi.
Population: 12,329
Capital: None, but Yaren is the seat of government
Language: Nauruan
Currency: Australian dollar

 NEW ZEALAND
Area: 103,700 sq. mi.
Population: 3,908,037
Capital: Wellington
Language: English
Currency: N.Z. dollar

 PALAU
Area: 177 sq. mi.
Population: 19,409
Capital: Koror
Languages: Palauan, English
Currency: U.S. dollar

 PAPUA NEW GUINEA
Area: 182,700 sq. mi.
Population: 5,172,033
Capital: Port Moresby
Language: English
Currency: Kina

 SOLOMON ISLANDS
Area: 10,600 sq. mi.
Population: 494,786
Capital: Honiara
Language: English
Currency: Solomon Islands dollar

TONGA
Area: 270 sq. mi.
Population: 106,137
Capital: Nukualofa
Languages: English, Tongan
Currency: Pa'anga

 TUVALU
Area: 9 sq. mi.
Population: 11,146
Capital: Funafuti
Languages: Tuvaluan, English
Currency: Australian dollar

VANUATU
Area: 5,700 sq. mi.
Population: 196,178
Capital: Port-Vila
Languages: Bislama, English, French
Currency: Vatu

SAMOA
Area: 1,100 sq. mi.
Population: 178,631
Capital: Apia
Languages: Samoan, English
Currency: Tala

miles
0   1000

0   1000
km

N

KEY TO MAP
1 WALLIS AND FUTUNA ISLANDS (FRANCE)
2 SAMOA
3 AMERICAN SAMOA (U.S.)
4 NIUE (N.Z.)

SEE ALSO
Australia, New Zealand, United States of America

PAINT AND DYE

Paint is a coloring which is used to cover a surface, usually to protect or decorate it. A dye is a substance that sinks into the material, coloring it inside and out.

Paints and dyes were traditionally produced in small batches from natural substances such as ocher, fruits, or flowers. Today, most are mass-produced in factories.

INSIDE PAINT

Paint is usually applied as a liquid. It dries by evaporation and forms a thin layer. It consists of a liquid—called a binder or medium—which may be water, an oil, or a resin and a solid—the pigment which gives paint its color. Chemicals are often added to improve the paint. They may prevent the paint from becoming solid in the can, or make the paint resistant to damage from exposure to the sun or frost once applied. Buildings or furniture may be treated with paints that, in the event of fire, break down chemically to slow up the spread of the flames.

MAKING PAINT

In the first stage of making paint, oils, resins, and solvents (thinners) are blended together. Colored pigment is then added, and the mixture is ground in a ball mill until the paint is thoroughly mixed.

▲ In textile dyeing, the cloth is immersed in the dyeing solution and the temperature is raised until enough dye has moved out of the solution and into the cloth fibers.

▶ Pigment gives paint its color. Today's pigments are usually made from chemicals, but artists often grind their own paints by hand.

◀ In 1856, English chemist William Perkin accidentally invented the world's first artificial chemical dye, a mauve derived from coal-tar waste.

ORIGINAL MAUVENE PREPARED BY SIR WILLIAM PERKIN IN 1856

USING DYES

Dyes are used to color plastics and paper as well as textiles. They usually need a fixative, or mordant, to help them penetrate fibers and stay in them. Most mordants are chemical solutions of metal salts. Until the 1850s, dyes were derived from natural substances such as leaves and berries. Indigo, a plant, was used to dye cloth blue, the cheapest color, usually worn by servants in Europe in the 1700s. By 1880, chemists had learned how to make an artificial indigo. Nowadays, almost all dyes are industrially produced. To make sure the color is even, the material being dyed must not resist the dye, and it must be moved continually during dyeing.

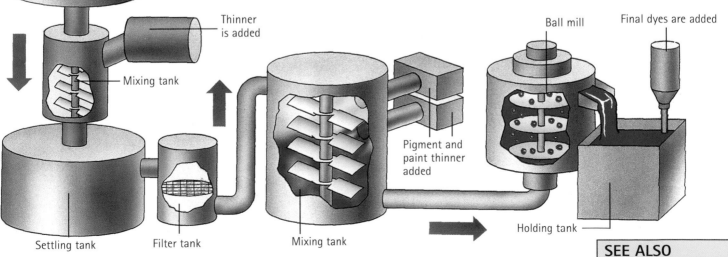

Oil and resin are blended together

Thinner is added

Mixing tank

Settling tank

Filter tank

Mixing tank

Pigment and paint thinner added

Ball mill

Final dyes are added

Holding tank

SEE ALSO

Color, Textile

PAPER

Paper is a material made from plant fibers that are webbed together to form sheets. It is used for many different purposes, including writing and packaging.

Waxed paper can be used to make cartons for holding liquids.

Filter paper is used inside cars to stop grit from entering the engine.

Furnishings such as lampshades and wallpaper can be made from paper.

Paper is used for communication—it can be printed or written on.

Paper is used to mop up liquids, both in industry and in the home.

People have known how to make paper for over 2,000 years. The earliest papermakers lived in Ancient China. They made thick, coarse sheets of paper by flattening and drying out a pulp (mush) of water, chopped bark, plants, and fishing nets. Some 500 years before them, the Egyptians had discovered they could make something like paper by pressing papyrus strips together. Our term "paper" comes from the word papyrus.

STRONG FIBERS

Like Ancient Chinese paper, modern paper is made from a pulp, but most of it contains shredded, softened wood from coniferous trees such as pine, spruce, or fir. The fibers in wood, or any other plant, are made of a strong material called cellulose. This makes the paper very strong, so that it does not fall apart easily when pressed, folded, or stretched.

MAKING PAPER TODAY

In a papermaking machine, wood chips are boiled with sodium hydroxide or another chemical to soften them and strip them of everything but their long, stringy fibers. This pulp is spread over a conveyor belt, blasted with air, then squeezed between rollers to turn it into dry paper.

DIFFERENT SOURCES

Over the years, people have experimented with cellulose from sources other than wood. Paper currency and expensive writing paper often contain fibers from cotton rags, which are made from cotton plants. The fibers make the paper very smooth and tough.

WASTE PAPER

On average, every person in the United States uses about 660 lb. (300kg) of paper a year. About half the paper we use is recycled to make newspapers, toilet paper, and other low-quality papers. The rest is dumped in landfill sites.

Pulp from recycled paper added

Bark removed

Wood chipped

Water and chemicals added and wood chips cooked into pulp

Pulp beaten to break down fibers so they will mat together easily

Pulp cleaned and bleached to make it white

Pulp drained on fine mesh belt

Heated rollers dry paper and press fibers firmly together to form a sheet

Finished paper is wound onto reel

SEE ALSO

Conservation, Egypt (Ancient)

PHILIPPINES

The Republic of the Philippines is a country in the southwest Pacific Ocean, off the coast of mainland Asia. It consists of more than 7,000 islands.

Area: 114,830 sq. mi.
Population: 84,525,639
Capital: Manila
Languages: Filipino, English
Currency: Peso

The Philippines lie in one of the most violent geological zones, the "ring of fire," where there are many volcanoes. The dormant volcano Mount Apo (969 ft./ 2,954m) is the country's highest peak. The two largest islands are Luzon and Mindanao. Off the northeast coast of Mindanao is one of the deepest points in the Pacific, the Philippine Trench, reaching 34,248 ft. (10,439m) below the surface. The climate is tropical, with monsoon rains in July and August.

FORESTS AND FARMING
Forests cover half the land. The fiber from kapok trees is used for insulation, and bamboo provides a useful building material. With many trees being felled for timber, deforestation is a problem. In the fertile soil, farmers grow rice, corn, cassava, sweet potatoes, sugarcane, and abaca (Manila hemp). The seas provide fish, clams, and shrimp.

▲ Three fifths of the people live in rural areas and many are farmers. The carabao, a type of water buffalo, is used to pull plows and haul loads.

▲ Gold is one of the Philippines' valuable resources. The country also has large reserves of copper, chromium, nickel, oil, and natural gas.

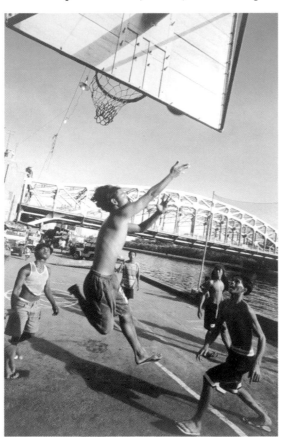

BOOMING CITY
Manila, founded in 1571, grew from a collection of shore villages into a teeming metropolis. It symbolizes the country's growth as an industrial nation. More than 7.8 million people now live in and around it, and it is the busiest port. Factories make clothing and electronic goods for export.

THE FILIPINOS
The people of the Philippines, Filipinos, are related to Malays. Chinese, Indians, Japanese, and mountain people called Negritos also live there. Catholicism has been the main religion since the Spanish took over the islands in 1565. The islands take their name from King Philip II of Spain. They were ruled by the U.S. after 1898 and invaded by Japan during World War II, becoming independent in 1946.

◄ More than half of the population is under 20 years old. Basketball is the country's national sport.

SEE ALSO
Asia, Volcano, World War II

PHOTOGRAPHY

Photography is the process of capturing images by focusing light onto a light-sensitive surface using a camera. It is used in the arts, media, and sciences.

Louis Daguerre produced the first successful photographs with his prototype camera.

The first popular camera by Kodak had an internal box to hold the film. The lens was part of the case.

A Polaroid camera takes a picture, develops the negative, and makes a print inside the camera.

The IXUS camera stores picture data on film, making it easy to improve the quality of prints.

► Julia Margaret Cameron's *The Parting of Sir Lancelot and Queen Guinevere* (1860s) is an example of early art photography. Cameron often posed her subjects as characters from stories.

As early as 1515, Leonardo da Vinci described how an image could be made on the wall of a darkened room by letting light through a tiny hole in the opposite wall. This was called a *camera obscura*, meaning dark chamber. Apart from sketching it by hand, there was no way of recording the image until the 1700s, when the British scientists Sir Humphry Davy (1778–1829) and Thomas Wedgwood (1771–1805) caught outlines of leaves and faces on paper or leather coated with light-sensitive silver chloride.

THE FIRST PHOTOGRAPHS
The first photographs, called heliograms, were made in the 1820s by the French doctor Joseph Niépce (1765–1833) on bitumen-coated pewter plates using a camera obscura. In the 1830s, the French painter Louis Daguerre (1787–1851) made photographs on plates coated with light-sensitive silver iodide. The British inventor William Fox Talbot (1800–77) found a way to "fix" the silver iodide permanently so that it would not react to light and darken after a picture was taken. He also invented a process that made it possible to make many copies of one photograph.

PHOTOGRAPHY FOR EVERYONE
Photography was a complex procedure until 1889, when the American George Eastman (1854–1932) invented roll film and the small box camera. It soon became a hobby that any amateur could take up. More technical advances, such as the invention of flashbulbs and color film in the 1930s, led to the growing popularity of photography as it is enjoyed today.

PHOTOJOURNALISM

Journalists quickly learned that a good photograph could often tell a story with more impact than written words. The first British war correspondent, Roger Fenton (1819–69), began taking battlefield photographs of the Crimean War in the 1850s. In the 1860s, the American Matthew Brady (1823–96) captured the grim reality of the U.S. Civil War.

SOCIAL REALISM

American sociologist Lewis Hine (1874–1940) was one of the first to use photography to show the terrible living conditions of poor people. His striking portraits of children at work in factories and mills helped to change child labor laws. Modern photojournalists often risk their lives to take pictures of war-torn countries or to reveal injustices in society.

ART PHOTOGRAPHY

Some early photographers used the principles of painting in their photographs. In the 1860s, the British photographer Julia Margaret Cameron (1815–79) created stunning portraits using blur and soft focus. The French photographer Nadar (1820–1910) captured many Paris intellectuals and artists, encouraging them to pose naturally. In the 1920s, the American photographer Man Ray (1890–1976) experimented with artistic effects. His original style combined fantasy with reality, inspiring succeeding generations of budding photographers.

FUTURE PHOTOGRAPHY

Today, cameras are becoming smaller and easier to use. Images from digital cameras can be viewed on a television or loaded onto a computer for editing, printing, or sending across the Internet. An image can be processed in many ways to change its color, shape, size, and composition. Holography is a method of photography that uses lasers to show all sides of a subject in 3-D.

▲ Lewis Hine captured the poverty-stricken conditions that many immigrant families in the United States endured during the early 1900s.

▲ Fast shutter speeds freeze a moving image, but blur still occurs with a racing amusement park ride.

HOW A CAMERA WORKS

When you take a picture, the camera's shutter flicks open and shut to let light hit the film for the correct length of time. The lens does the focusing, either automatically or by hand. The aperture controls how much light gets through to the piece of film, or frame, so that it is exposed to a focused image at the correct level of brightness.

Film advance

Viewfinder

Light

Lens

Diaphragm

Shutter

Film

▲ When light hits the film, it changes the chemicals coating the film. Other chemicals make the negative image appear (with colors and areas of dark and light reversed). The photo is printed onto paper by shining light through the negative. The final picture is positive (colors appearing correctly).

▲ Digital cameras do not use film—the image is converted into digital form and stored on disk.

SEE ALSO

Art, Computer, Film, Internet, Lens, Newspaper and magazine, Printing

PILGRIM

Pilgrims are people who travel to take part in religious or spiritual events. Often they travel along a specific route or path known as a pilgrim way.

▲ Muslims who have completed the hajj pilgrimage decorate their homes with paintings of the journey.

Many religions have places which are considered sacred or where holy rituals are held. The most popular ritual of ancient times was the Greek festival of Demeter, the farming goddess. Each year people traveled to the town of Eleusis, where secret ceremonies, called the Mysteries, took place.

Holy relics of Christian saints are often stored in jeweled boxes.

CULT OF THE SAINTS

Many Christians believe that visiting the grave of a saint brings them closer to God. During the Middle Ages, Canterbury drew pilgrims from Britain and northern Europe to the tomb of St. Thomas à Becket, and Compostela in Spain held the tomb of St. James. But the greatest pilgrimage was to Jerusalem, where Christ was crucified. Today, Christians visit holy places such as Fatima in Portugal or Lourdes in France.

Buddhists climb Mount Fuji to view the dawn in the summer months.

THE HAJJ

Muslims have a duty to visit Mecca at least once. This pilgrimage, the *hajj*, centers on a sacred black stone—which Muslims believe was given by God to Adam to absorb the sins of mankind—and on sacred pillars and hills.

Followers of Shinto in Japan return to their family shrine once a year.

PILGRIMS IN THE NEW WORLD

Sometimes people have to travel to a new place in search of religious freedom. In the early 1600s, a group of Puritans sailed from England on the *Mayflower* to set up a simplified, or "purified," church in America. They established Plymouth Colony in 1620, and became known as the Pilgrims.

Ancient Egyptians held festivals at Bubastis for the cat goddess Bastet.

PILGRIM WAYS

During the Middle Ages, a network of roads, called pilgrim ways, ran across Europe, linking major sites of pilgrimage. Pilgrims made donations and bought badges and relics, creating wealth for the churches and cities they visited. Monasteries were built along most routes to provide shelter for travelers.

SEE ALSO
Buddhism, Christianity, Crusades, Hinduism, Islam, Middle Ages, Religion

PLANET

Planets are the largest objects that circle around stars. They may be rocky, like Earth, or made mostly of gas and liquid, like Jupiter.

Sir William Herschel (1738–1822) discovered Uranus in 1781.

In 1846, Urbain Le Verrier (1811–77) found the position of Neptune.

John Couch Adams (1819–92) predicted in 1845 that an eighth planet existed.

Percival Lowell (1855–1916) began the search for Pluto in 1905.

Clyde Tombaugh (b.1906) discovered Pluto in 1930 near its predicted position.

The Sun is orbited by nine planets, most of which have moons. They range in size from Pluto, less than one fifth as wide as Earth, to Jupiter, which is 11 times wider than Earth.

THE WANDERERS

The word planet is Greek for "wanderer." The name comes from the way planets appear to move against the stars over time. It is thought that the planets formed at about the same time as the Sun. As the original cloud of gas and dust collapsed to form the Sun, some matter was spun out into a flattened disk. Over several million years, the dust and gas gathered together to form the planets and moons. Denser rocks gathered near the Sun and lighter gases farther out.

MERCURY

Mercury is the planet closest to the Sun, at an average distance of 36 million miles

PLANETARY NAMES

Mercury The Roman god of merchants and travelers

Venus The Roman goddess of love

Mars The Roman god of war

Jupiter The king of the Roman gods

Saturn The Roman god of seeds and sowing

Uranus The Greek god of the sky

Neptune The Roman god of the sea

Pluto The Roman god of the dead

PLANET SYSTEMS

Planets in the solar system and around other stars share several features. The solid center is often surrounded by layers of gas forming an atmosphere. Circling the planet may be smaller planetlike objects called moons. Around the equator may be bright rings consisting of tiny particles of rock and ice.

(58 million km). Its diameter is just 3,031 miles (4,878km). During the day, its temperature soars to 806°F (430°C), hot enough to melt lead. At night it cools down to –274°F (–170°C). Mercury's day, the time it takes to spin around once on its axis, is equal to 59 Earth days. Its year, the time it takes to go once around the Sun, is equal to 88 Earth days.

VENUS

With a diameter of 7,545 miles (12,142km), Venus is nearly the same size as Earth. But in other ways the two are completely different. Most of Venus's atmosphere consists of carbon dioxide, a gas that traps the Sun's heat. This "greenhouse effect" makes Venus even hotter than Mercury, although it is about twice as far from the Sun. Most of the surface is covered in lava that flowed out of giant volcanoes millions of years ago. Venus is the only planet to spin in the opposite way to the direction of its orbit. It spins so slowly that one of its days lasts for 243 Earth days. ▶

▲ The space probe *Voyager 2* was launched in 1977 and by 1989 had passed close to Jupiter, Saturn, Uranus, and Neptune, sending data back to Earth.

MARS

The fourth planet from the Sun, Mars is only about half the size of the Earth and is much cooler. Its strong red colour is due to rust in the rocks on its surface. Its atmosphere consists mostly of carbon dioxide and is about 100 times thinner than Earth's. The largest volcano and the largest canyon ever discovered are to be found on the Martian surface. There are also features on Mars that look like dried-up river beds. This suggests that Mars was once warmer and wetter than it is now. Under these conditions, life may have developed and there is even a chance that primitive life may exist there today. Mars has two tiny moons: Phobos and Deimos. The larger of these, Phobos, is only about 15 miles (24km) across.

JUPITER

The biggest of the planets, Jupiter, could swallow up over 1,000 Earths. It has a

MERCURY
The surface of Mercury is rocky, often covered in sand, and marked by large meteorite craters. There is no atmosphere and the planet is roasted by the nearness of the Sun.

VENUS
Venus has broken slabs of rock and some dust on its surface. Most sunlight is blocked by the clouds of sulfuric acid in the atmosphere of carbon dioxide and nitrogen.

EARTH
Only Earth is known to support life. The rocky surface is covered by water and soil. The atmosphere of nitrogen and oxygen contains clouds of water vapor.

MARS
The reddish surface of Mars is made up of rock and sand. The atmosphere is thin and consists mostly of carbon dioxide. Both poles are covered with caps of ice.

JUPITER
As a gas giant, Jupiter has no surface. Instead, dense layers of gas surround a core. Io, one of 16 moons, has a rocky surface dyed red by sulfur from its many volcanoes.

SATURN
Like Jupiter, Saturn is a gas giant. The 91 per cent hydrogen atmosphere has dense clouds of ammonia, water, and methane colored by phosphorus and other elements.

URANUS
Hydrogen and helium make up most of the gas giant Uranus. The planet is surrounded by rings of blackish particles "shepherded" by two small moons.

NEPTUNE
Gas giant Neptune's blue color is from methane gas. The surface of the moon Triton is frozen methane and nitrogen. Geysers of nitrogen gas erupt to 5 mi. (8km).

PLUTO
Pluto is made of frozen nitrogen and methane. Its moon Charon is almost large enough to be a twin planet. The Sun is so far away that it appears as a bright star.

diameter of 88,235 miles (142,800km), but most of this is made of gases and liquids rather than solid rock. Like the Sun, Jupiter contains a great deal of hydrogen. Jupiter spins so fast that its day lasts less than ten hours. But one year on Jupiter is nearly 12 times longer than one of ours. Jupiter has a single ring and 16 satellites. One of these, Ganymede, is the largest moon in the solar system—bigger than Mercury.

SATURN

Measuring 74,565 (120,000km) across, Saturn is second only to Jupiter in size. Like Jupiter, Uranus, and Neptune, it is a gas giant. It is famous for its bright rings, made up of billions of particles of rock and ice. The rings are more than 169,000 miles (272,000km) across, but they are very thin. Saturn has at least 18 moons. The largest of these, Titan, is the only moon known to have an atmosphere.

URANUS

Orbiting the Sun 19 times farther out than the Earth, Uranus receives very little heat. The temperature at the top of its clouds is –364°F (–220°C). With a diameter of 32,300 miles (52,000km), Uranus is less than half the size of Saturn but still four times bigger than the Earth. Uranus has a set of thin, dark rings and 15 moons.

NEPTUNE

Similar in size and appearance to Uranus, the blue-green planet Neptune orbits the Sun at an average distance of 1.7 billion miles (2.8 billion km). It is bitterly cold and 85 percent of its atmosphere is hydrogen. Neptune has several thin rings and eight moons.

PLUTO

With a diameter of about 1,430 miles (2,300km), Pluto is the smallest planet in the solar system. It is also the coldest and the farthest from the Sun, on average 40 times farther out than Earth. One year on Pluto lasts about 248 Earth years. Pluto's moon, Charon, discovered in 1978, has a diameter of about 810 miles (1,300km).

PLANETS OF OTHER STARS

Although planets around other stars have never been seen, scientists know they exist because they cause the stars they orbit to wobble slightly. As more and more are found, the chances grow that billions of planets may exist, and that there may be life on some of them. In 1961, astronomers at the Green Bank Observatory in West Virginia estimated that the nearest intelligent life should exist within about 300 light years of Earth. Radio telescopes are used to monitor stars with planets for radio broadcasts.

▲ Life from other planets has featured in the movies. The alien in the movie *E.T.* was friendly, but other movie aliens are warlike.

▲ Saturn's rings are made up of dust, ice crystals, and rocks up to 33 ft. (10m) across. The rings are 41,000 mi. (66,000km) wide, but only 0.6 mi. (1km) deep. As Saturn orbits the Sun, the rings are seen from Earth from different angles.

GREAT RED SPOT

The Great Red Spot on Jupiter has existed since at least 1665. It is a circular storm with winds blowing at about 260 ft. per second (80m per second). The red color may be due to sulfur in the clouds.

SEE ALSO

Astronomy, Moon, Solar system, Spacecraft, Space exploration, Sun

PLANT

Plants are living organisms that harness the energy of the Sun to feed themselves. Without plants for animals to feed on, there would be no animal life on Earth.

Ferns are among the oldest plants, appearing about 350 million years ago.

The dodder is a parasitic plant. It inserts suckers into other plants to get food.

The carnivorous Venus flytrap feeds on insects that it traps in its leaves.

We make textiles from the ripe fruit of the cotton plant.

Some plants are dangerous to eat—hemlock can be used to make poison.

Plants provide timber. Wood from the oak tree is heavy, hard, and strong.

Most plants are able to absorb sunlight by means of a green substance inside them called chlorophyll. They use the energy from the Sun's light to make food by a chemical process called photosynthesis. This results in the production of oxygen, which all plants and animals, including humans, need to live.

PLANTS OF ALL KINDS

There are about 400,000 different kinds of plant, ranging in size from tiny mosses only a few millimeters long to giant redwood trees, which grow to over 300 feet (100m) tall. Each has adapted to absorb light, find water and minerals, and withstand the temperature range in its own habitat. Desert plants such as cacti have long, widely spreading roots to collect water, which they store in their expandable stems. Succulent plants store water in swollen, fleshy leaves. Plants in cold places grow in thick, low clumps which protect them from the cold and wind.

DESIGNED TO CATCH LIGHT

Plants need to catch as much light as possible. Each one has leaves which are shaped and arranged on the stem so they overshadow the leaves below as little as possible. Tall trees have strong, woody trunks to hold their leaves high above the ground and other plants. Plants like vines climb up through the trees with clinging tendrils. Plants called epiphytes grow entirely suspended in tree branches, never touching the ground.

OTHER SOURCES OF FOOD

Some parasitic plants, such as mistletoe, obtain extra nourishment by growing into the tissues of larger plants. Some plants, such as the dodder, cannot make any of their own food. The dodder attaches itself to another plant for nourishment. There are also carnivorous plants, such as the pitcher plant and the Venus flytrap, which can catch and digest insects.

PLANTS AND PEOPLE

People learned to grow plants as crops about 10,000 years ago. Today, over four fifths of the world's food comes from

GERMINATION

Inside the seed are all the parts needed to form a new plant. The stage when a seed starts to sprout is called germination. In order to begin the germination process, a seed must have warmth, moisture, and oxygen.

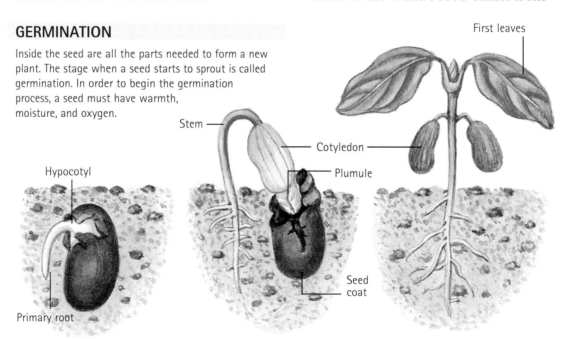

Stage 1	Stage 2	Stage 3
When a seed starts to germinate, it splits and the primary root is formed from the hypocotyl.	The stem pushes up through the soil and the cotyledon starts to break out of the seed coat.	The plumule breaks free of the cotyledon, the stem grows upwards and the first leaves are formed.

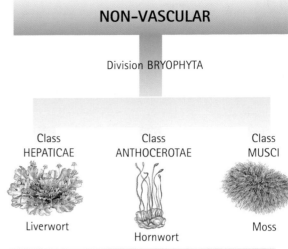

NON-VASCULAR

Division BRYOPHYTA

Class HEPATICAE — Liverwort

Class ANTHOCEROTAE — Hornwort

Class MUSCI — Moss

CLASSIFYING PLANTS

Plants are classified according to certain similarities they share. One way is to divide them into ten groups, or divisions. The division Bryophyta is made up of nonvascular plants. These plants do not have the tissues that carry food and water from one part of the plant to another. The other nine divisions are all vascular. The division Anthophyta contains all flowering plants (also called angiosperms), which contain their reproductive cells in flowers. Angiosperms are divided into two classes, monocots and dicots. The basic difference is in the number of cotyledons, or seed leaves. Monocots have one and dicots have two. Monocots, such as grasses, normally have long narrow leaves, whereas dicot leaves are usually broad.

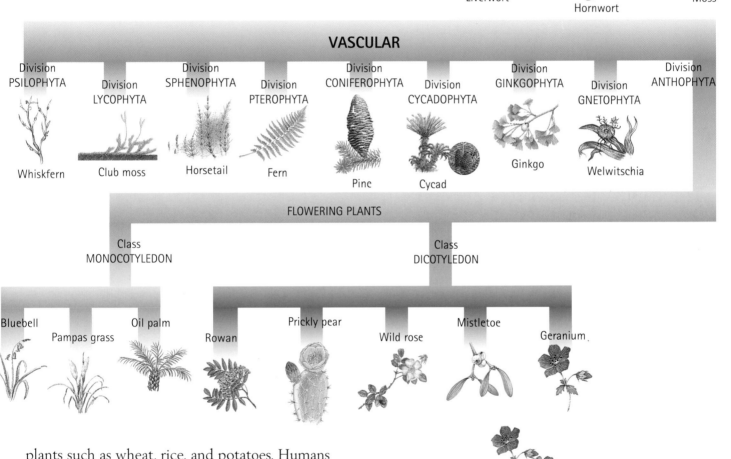

VASCULAR

Division PSILOPHYTA — Whiskfern

Division LYCOPHYTA — Club moss

Division SPHENOPHYTA — Horsetail

Division PTEROPHYTA — Fern

Division CONIFEROPHYTA — Pine

Division CYCADOPHYTA — Cycad

Division GINKGOPHYTA — Ginkgo

Division GNETOPHYTA — Welwitschia

Division ANTHOPHYTA

FLOWERING PLANTS

Class MONOCOTYLEDON — Bluebell, Pampas grass, Oil palm

Class DICOTYLEDON — Rowan, Prickly pear, Wild rose, Mistletoe, Geranium

plants such as wheat, rice, and potatoes. Humans eat a variety of fruits, nuts, and vegetables and make drinks from tea, coffee, and grains. Plants also provide products such as vegetable oils, cotton, rubber, and—perhaps the most useful of all—wood. Many of the drugs we use to treat disease come from plants. Even fuels such as coal are the fossilized remains of prehistoric plants.

PLANT BREEDING

Most plants we use today are quite different from their ancestors. Using methods such as genetic engineering, plant breeders have made improvements to cereals such as wheat to make them more productive or more resistant to pests.

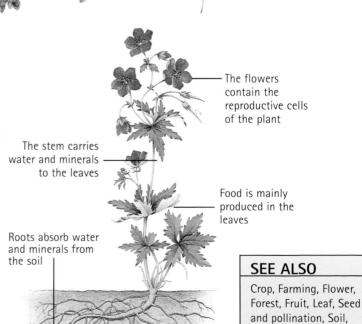

The flowers contain the reproductive cells of the plant

The stem carries water and minerals to the leaves

Food is mainly produced in the leaves

Roots absorb water and minerals from the soil

311

SEE ALSO

Crop, Farming, Flower, Forest, Fruit, Leaf, Seed and pollination, Soil, Tree, Vegetable

PLASTIC

Plastics are materials that can easily be stretched or molded into shape. Most are made from the chemicals obtained from petroleum oil.

Plastic replaces many metal items because it is light and durable.

Many items are wrapped and sealed in plastic rather than paper bags.

Strong and lightweight plastics can replace the metal bodywork in cars.

Polyester is a plastic widely used in clothing manufacturing.

Instead of wood, boats today are often made of strong, lightweight plastic.

Plastic is used for replacement body parts, such as false teeth.

Plastics are man-made and consist of long chains of molecules called polymers. The way these chains are arranged gives plastics their different qualities. Hard plastics can be used to replace metals, such as car parts. Soft plastics can be used to create fabrics, leather, suedes, and even fur.

NATURAL INGREDIENTS
John W. Hyatt, a New York chemist, developed the first plastic in the late 1860s. The plastic, which was called celluloid, did not last well. It changed color and became brittle if left in strong light. Even so, it was used to make numerous objects, from billiard balls and shirt collars to false teeth and photographic film.

CHEMICALLY BASED PLASTIC
The first plastic to be chemically based was a material called Bakelite, which was invented in 1909. More modern plastics, however, such as polyvinyl chloride (PVC) and polyester, have become lighter and easier to color. They can also be flexible and are able to withstand moisture and strong sunlight.

HARD OR SOFT
Plastics do not all behave the same way when reheated. Some, called "thermoplastics," melt and can be reshaped

PLASTIC MOLDING

Two common methods for molding plastic are that of injection molding, in which plastic pellets are heated and then injected into a mold, and hot extrusion, in which hot plastic is forced through openings to make rods or sheets.

INJECTION MOLDING
Plastic pellets
Mold for bowl
Finished bowl
Heating element
Plunger

HOT EXTRUSION MOLDING
Plastic pellets
Extruded plastic sheet
Heating element
Completed plastic sheets
Mechanical screw

after reheating. Polyethylene, a material used to make plastic bowls, is like this, which is why it often loses its shape if something hot is placed on it. Other plastics are "thermosetting." Once they have cooled and set during manufacture, they cannot be reshaped. In fact, if a thermosetting plastic is heated up, it gets harder. Electric plugs are made of thermosetting plastics, which is why they do not melt if the wires inside them overheat.

◄ Plexiglas is an ideal plastic for a squash court, as it is transparent like glass but much stronger.

SEE ALSO
Atom and molecule, Clothing, Materials, Oil

PLATYPUS

The platypus is an unusual mammal with a beak like a duck and a tail like a beaver. It lays eggs, but has fur, and it feeds its young with milk like other mammals.

▲ Echidnas are found in Australia and New Guinea. The female lays one egg a year, which hatches in a pouch on her belly. The young echidna stays in the pouch for several weeks, feeding on its mother's milk.

The platypus is often called the duck-billed platypus because of the shape of its jaws, which resemble a duck's bill. It is one of only three mammals that lays eggs. The others are two species of echidna, or spiny anteater. The platypus is found in Australia and Tasmania. It lives near rivers and lakes. Each occupies its own stretch of water, where it digs a burrow in the bank with its strong claws. It sleeps in its burrow for most of the day and comes out to feed mainly at night, when it uses its flat bill to catch large numbers of insects and worms.

A FAKE?

The platypus is up to 30 in. (75cm) long, including its tail, and it weighs up to 5.5 lb. (2.5kg). When European scientists first saw the skin of a platypus, they thought it was a fake—as if someone had sewn a duck's beak and a beaver's tail onto the

▲ Platypuses are very good swimmers, pushing themselves through the water with their broad, paddlelike front feet and steering with their hind feet and tail.

body of another animal. The platypus's bill is not hard like that of a duck. It is soft and leathery and very sensitive, and it has no teeth. The platypus stores energy-giving fat in its broad tail.

DEFENSE TACTICS

The male platypus has a poisonous spine on each back leg. The animals use their spines when they fight each other during the breeding season. Wounded platypuses are not seriously hurt by the poison, but there is enough in each spine to kill a dog.

HATCHING FROM EGGS

When the female is ready to lay her eggs, she makes a tunnel in the riverbank up to 100 ft. (30m) long. At the end of it she makes a nest of leaves for her eggs. Three or four months after hatching, the young leave the burrow, but they stay a few more weeks while they learn to swim and find food.

▶ The female platypus has no teats (nipples)—instead, the babies lap up the milk as it oozes from pores on her body.

▲ Babies, about 0.8 in. (2cm) long, break out of the eggs after ten days and start to feed on their mother's milk.

SEE ALSO
Animal, Mammal

POLITICS

Politics is the art and science of seeking public office through elections or appointment, controlling government policies, and influencing those in power.

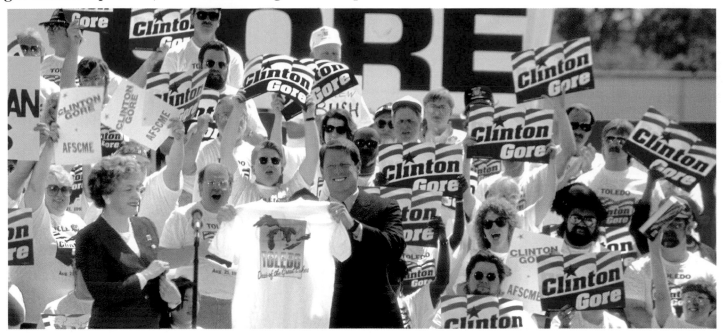

Politics is about power in government. People who seek to form governments or affect policy are politicians.

▲ Vice presidential candidate Al Gore at a rally during the 1996 presidential election in the United States. Campaign rallies gain television coverage, encourage party workers, and allow politicians to get their message across.

▼ A meeting of Chartists in London in 1848. The Chartists staged mass meetings and organized petitions demanding political reform, in particular universal suffrage and vote by secret ballot.

ELECTION POLITICS
During elections, parties put forward candidates and publish their ideas and programs. Politicians make speeches, appear on radio and television, and go out to meet the people. There are two main election systems: the "winner-takes-all" system (the candidate with the most votes wins) and proportional representation (where voters may vote for more than one candidate, and for more than one party).

Politics today has much to do with media management—the skillful use of TV and advertising.

LEFT AND RIGHT
Politics is often divided into left and right. These terms come from the French Revolution: those supporting the king sat on the right side of the assembly; those supporting a republic sat on the left. Today, right-wing politicians tend to support tough law and order, economic freedom, and existing institutions. Left-wingers often want a more liberal justice system, more government control of the economy, and changes to existing institutions.

PILING ON THE PRESSURE
Pressure groups and lobbyists usually represent an organization, such as a union or manufacturer, or a single issue, such as stricter laws against drunk drivers. They mobilize opinion through the press or by organizing public demonstrations.

SEE ALSO
Communism, Democracy, Government, Revolution

POLLUTION

Pollution happens when a harmful substance is released into the environment in such large quantities that it causes damage to people, wildlife, or habitats.

The control of pollution is a major problem facing the world. Large areas may soon become uninhabitable and many plants and animals may become extinct. Public opinion is now forcing governments and industry to combat pollution.

SMOKES AND SMELLS
Car exhausts and factories pump fumes into the air. Some of these gases mix with clouds to form acid rain, which kills plants. Carbon dioxide traps the sun's heat, and may lead to global warming. Other gases, called CFCs, are thought to destroy ozone—the gas barrier that blocks harmful radiation from the sun. Noise can also be a form of pollution, with traffic or aircraft noise ruining the quality of life.

OIL SPILL
Oil tankers carry up to 550,000 tons of oil, so accidents may be devastating. The oil floats on the sea, forming a slick that blocks the sunlight required by seaweed and algae. Birds and fish may be trapped or poisoned by the oil. Thousands of creatures die, but most areas recover within a few years.

▲ Liquid waste dumped into rivers may poison wildlife and threaten supplies of drinking water for humans.

WASTE NOT . . .
Trash is created in large quantities, and the world is running out of places to put it all. Recycling glass, paper, and other waste reduces the need for dumping. Radioactive waste created by nuclear power plants remains dangerous for thousands of years.

DEAD RIVERS
Industrial waste dumped into rivers can kill all life. Fertilizers can produce growths of algae, which absorb the oxygen in the water, killing fish and plants. International agreements have been drawn up to stop countries dumping waste at sea and to reduce the pollution of lakes and rivers.

▲ Smoke and other pollutants can travel thousands of miles before falling as deposits or as acid rain.

SEE ALSO
Conservation, Ecology, Habitat

315

PREHISTORIC ANIMAL

Prehistoric animals are animals that lived before people began to record things in writing. Animal life began around 3.5 billion years ago in the oceans.

▼ *Diplocaulus*—an amphibian from the Permian period, was a pond dweller. His head shape would have made him hard to swallow.

We know that prehistoric animals existed because some of their remains have been preserved in rocks as fossils. The fossils tell us a lot about the shape and size of the animals. From this, scientists can work out how they lived and what they ate.

ARMORED CREATURES

The first living things appeared about 3.5 billion years ago. We don't know much about them because their soft bodies did not leave many traces in the rocks. About 600 million years ago, animals began to develop shells or other hard coverings, and these hard parts were often preserved as fossils. Trilobites were among the earliest of the armored creatures. They looked like woodlice and lived mainly on the seabed. Corals and many kinds of shellfish lived with trilobites. Huge sea scorpions, or eurypterids, up to 6.5 ft. (2m) long, fed on smaller animals.

OUT OF THE WATER

The first animals with backbones were fish that appeared about 500 million years ago. Many of them had bony armor to protect them from sea scorpions. The earliest prehistoric animals all lived in the sea, but they gradually spread into fresh water and then onto the land. The amphibians were the first backboned animals to move onto the land. These early amphibians were like fish with stumpy legs that could only just about lift their bodies off the ground—some of them looked like big newts or salamanders. The early amphibians all lived in damp places and, just like today's frogs and toads, they had to go back to the water to breed. One group of amphibians started to change: their skins got thicker and they laid eggs with tough shells. These animals became the first reptiles. They could live in drier places and they spread all over the land.

TAKING TO THE SKIES

Some reptiles, called pterosaurs, learned to fly. Others went back to the sea, where they lived like today's dolphins. The best-known prehistoric reptiles were the dinosaurs, which ruled the Earth for over 100 million years during the Triassic, Jurassic, and Cretaceous periods. Many small, ratlike mammals wandered over the land at the same time as the dinosaurs. Some probably fed on dinosaur eggs, but only when the dinosaurs died out, about 65 million years ago, could mammals really have a chance of survival.

▶ *Meganeura* was like a giant dragonfly, with a wingspan reaching to about 30 in. (75cm). It probably grew large because of the warm Carboniferous forests.

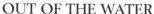

Pleistocene
(ice ages)
2 million years ago (mya)

Pliocene
Cattle, sheep
5 mya

Mammoths lived around 5 million years ago (mya)

Miocene
Mice, rats, apes
24 mya

Oligocene
Deer, pigs, monkeys, rhinos
37 mya

Eocene
Horses, dogs, cats, elephants, rabbits
58 mya

Hyracotherium—first horse (size of a terrier)

Paleocene
Owls, shrews
65 mya

Paramys—early rodent of 55 mya

Cretaceous
Snakes, first modern mammals
144 mya

Jurassic
First birds
208 mya

Archaeopteryx—first bird with feathers

Triassic
Dinosaurs, mammals, frogs
245 mya

Permian
286 mya

Sailback reptile—from Permian period

Carboniferous
First reptiles
360 mya

Devonian
Insects, spiders
408 mya

Oldest land vertebrate from Devonian period

Silurian
First land plants
438 mya

Ordovician
505 mya

Cambrian
Shellfish, corals
570 mya

Trilobites from 570 mya

Precambrian
Life begins in the sea. First jellyfish, worms
3.5 billion years ago

CENOZOIC 65–0 MILLION YEARS AGO

MESOZOIC 245–65

PALEOZOIC 570–245

PRECAMBRIAN

Dzungaripterus's pincerlike beak crushed shellfish

Dimorphodon had strong jaws and sharp teeth

Tropeognathus fed on fish caught by the mouthful

▲ Scientists get clues to these pterosaurs' diets by studying their jaws. Strong jaws and sharp teeth were used for meat, and *Tropeognathus*'s odd beak steadied it in the water.

FLYING GIANTS

Quetzalcoatlus was the largest pterosaur. It lived in Europe about 150 million years ago. Its wingspan was at least 40 ft. (12m)—almost five times bigger than our largest bird's —and its loose throat pouch could have held fish.

▲ Evidence of prehistoric animals comes from fossils and ancient cave paintings like those at Lascaux, France, showing deer, horses, elephants, and bison, which lived in Europe up to 50,000 years ago.

EXPERIMENTAL MAMMALS

As nature experimented with different shapes and sizes, many very strange prehistoric mammals appeared. *Baluchitherium* was a giant, giraffe-shaped rhinoceros that lived in Asia between 20 million and 30 million years ago. With its huge head carried about 25 ft. (8m) above the ground, it was probably the largest mammal ever to live on land. Most of these "experimental" mammals died out completely, but some of them survived and gradually evolved into the mammals that we see around us. Like the reptiles

before them, some invaded the sea and became whales and seals, and some, such as bats, developed wings and learned how to fly.

MAMMALS IN THE ICE AGES

During the last two million years, there have been several very cold periods called ice ages. Many northern parts of the world were covered with ice. Most animals moved south to avoid the cold, but some managed to survive close to the ice because they were able to grow thick coats, like the woolly rhinoceros and the woolly mammoth. These cold-climate mammals died out when the climate began to warm up about 10,000 years ago, and new species evolved to replace them.

▼ *Smilodon* was one of the saber-toothed cats of the Pleistocene period. They had massive fangs, about 6 in. (15cm) long, and huge neck muscles to power their jaws.

SEE ALSO
Animal, Dinosaur, Evolution, Fossil, Mammal, Prehistoric people

317

PREHISTORIC PEOPLE

Prehistoric people lived in "pre-history," that is, before about 3500 B.C. when people first began to write and so record their lives. They include our earliest ancestors.

Neanderthals first shaped sophisticated hand tools.

Cro-Magnons made arrowheads from flint.

A bone needle used in the Palaeolithic era.

The first human beings lived in Africa more than two million years ago. But small, humanlike creatures who walked upright on their hind legs were living more than four million years ago. Today, scientists have named them australopithecines, and we know about them because their bones and footprints have been discovered. One of the most famous finds was the skeleton of a female, nicknamed "Lucy," who lived about 3.75 million years ago in Ethiopia.

APE MEN AND WOMEN
Australopithecus probably looked and lived very like the apes. This species was overtaken by a more advanced species, known as *Homo habilis* (skillful man), who

MODERN MAN APPEARS

The Cro-Magnons (named after the site in France where their bones were first discovered) were the first modern humans, appearing around 40,000 years ago. They were taller (67 in./1.7m tall) and more slender than the Neanderthals, and had bony chins and domed heads.

▼ The various species of australopithecines, around 3.5 million years ago, were probably proficient hunters, using sticks and stones to kill prey and dig up edible roots.

was certainly a toolmaker, able to shape stones to make cutting and scraping tools. Animal bones have been found with scratches on them, suggesting that *Homo habilis* cut off the skins and meat from dead animals with stone tools.

STONE AGE PEOPLE
The early Stone Age, or Paleolithic period, began with *Homo habilis*. Some 1.75 million years ago, a new human species appeared. This was *Homo erectus* (upright man), who spread from Africa as far as Europe and Asia. *Homo erectus* had a bigger brain, made better tools, and

▲ An encampment of hunters in Eastern Europe, about 25,000 years ago. Hunting together they could kill large animals.

was probably the first human being to use fire. Some time after 400,000 years ago, yet another human species came on the scene. This was *Homo sapiens* (wise man). One group, the Neanderthal people (named after a valley in Germany), lived in Europe and the Middle East until about 35,000 years ago, surviving the cold of the Pleistocene Ice Age by living in caves.

PREHISTORIC CULTURES
At least two types of *Homo sapiens* lived side by side—early *Homo sapiens* (the Neanderthals) and a subspecies, *Homo sapiens sapiens*, who looked more like modern human beings. The Neanderthals were much larger and lacked a chin. They used simple tools and had probably developed a language to speak to one

another. For some reason, the Neanderthals died out, leaving our species as the only humans on Earth. The surviving peoples, such as the Cro-Magnons, lived all over Europe during the Stone Age. They built simple wooden huts, fished, and hunted deer and wild cattle, moving on in search of food. They began to express themselves through art, drawing pictures on cave walls and carving stones into human shapes. There are famous examples of cave paintings in Lascaux in France and Altamira in Spain.

SETTLING DOWN
In the Neolithic, or late Stone Age, people moved from a nomadic life based on food gathering and hunting to a more settled existence, growing crops and domesticating animals. This happened by about 11,000 years ago. People began to make metal tools about 5,500 years ago. The timing of events differs from area to area. The Ancient Greeks were living in the Bronze Age at the height of their success 3,000 years ago, historical times for them, but in Britain, prehistory lasted until the Romans invaded 2,000 years ago in the Romans' Iron Age.

◄ This mummy, found in 1991 in the Similaun glacier in Austria, is estimated to be 5,300 years old. Such finds tell us about our ancestors' lifestyles.

Mesolithic people learnt to attach blades to handles.

Mesolithic antler spear thrower, still used by the Inuit.

FAST FACTS
- The Paleolithic period (early Stone Age) goes back two million years to the time of *Homo habilis*
- Mesolithic times were known as the middle Stone Age, when Europe was recovering from the Ice Age, c.18,000 B.C.
- The Neolithic period (late Stone Age) was marked by the beginning of agriculture

SEE ALSO
Evolution, Fossil, Prehistoric animal

PRINTING

Printing is the mass production of identical images of writing or pictures on books, posters, packaging, and fabrics. It is used in education, business, art, and fashion.

The first attempts at printing were made in China during the A.D. 700s. Wooden blocks were carved with characters and pictures, which were then inked and pressed onto paper.

▲ With the Gutenberg press, books could be printed and circulated on a large scale. As printing became quicker and less expensive, books became cheaper, spreading information to a greater number of people. Printing inventions during the 1800s aided revolutions in science and mechanics.

EARLY PRESSES

The German Johann Gutenberg (c.1390–1468) invented the first printing press around 1455. Gutenberg used movable type, with raised pieces of metal for each letter so that words could be rearranged easily. The type was laid on a form and then covered with ink. A sheet of paper was placed over it, held down by screws to give a clear, even image. Later inventors added mechanisms for automating the printing press. By 1830, a steam press could produce 1,000 sheets per hour.

MODERN PRINTING

In 1904, the American printer Ira Rubel invented offset lithography printing. He discovered that the inked image from a printing plate could be offset, or stamped, onto a rubber roller, which could then be printed onto paper. In 1930, this system was combined with a method of making pictures up from small dots. When used with four basic ink colors, this made mass-production color printing possible. Today, many publications are printed from computer-generated pages. Laser printers work by spraying ink onto the page; dot matrix printers form images from tiny dots.

PICTURE PRINTS

Artists use intaglio to make engravings: they cut a design into the printing plate. Gravure printing uses a copperplate, which is engraved with a picture using a photographic process. Different tones and strengths of color are produced by engraving more deeply or shallowly.

OFFSET LITHOGRAPHY PRINTING

Rubber rollers are offset with a printing image, one for each of four basic colors: yellow, magenta, cyan (blue), and black. Paper is then printed with the colored inks alternating in turn until the complete picture is built up.

Paper • Water rollers • Printing plate • Yellow plate • Magenta plate • Cyan plate • Black plate • Ink rollers • Offset cylinder

◄ In silk-screen printing, a mesh made of silk, nylon, or copper is marked so that dyes can be pressed through onto fabric in a clear design. Silkscreen is used for fashion, art, and advertising.

SEE ALSO

Communication, Newspaper and magazine, Paint and dye, Paper, Textile

RADAR AND SONAR

Radar and sonar are systems that locate objects. They work by sending out waves, detecting echoes from objects, and measuring the distance in between.

Bad weather detected from radar in nose of aircraft warns pilot

Pulses sent and received from secondary scanner

Pulses sent and received from primary radar scanner

Radar altimeter measures height of aircraft above ground

Receiver

Oscillator

Transmitter

Antenna

Antenna

Radar and sonar are used to find the location of objects that are difficult to see. They also help people to judge how fast objects are moving. Radar is used at airports to track aircraft in the surrounding airspace. Boats use sonar to measure the depth of the seabed or riverbed and to spot any obstacles under water.

HOW RADAR WORKS

Radar, which is short for Radio Detection And Ranging, works by sending out a narrow pulse of radio waves. Any car, aircraft, or other large metal object in the way of this pulse will reflect it, just like a mirror reflects light. A receiver on the radar system picks up the reflected

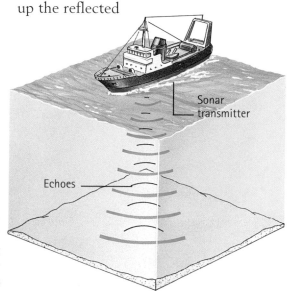

Sonar transmitter

Echoes

AIRCRAFT RADAR

Air traffic controllers need to know the height and position of aircraft around busy airports to prevent collisions between planes. They have small display screens that relay information they have found. The displays show a realistic map of the area, marked with objects. Large aircraft have onboard radar to detect other planes and bad weather.

waves and measures how long the radio wave took to bounce back. This information can be used to calculate the object's distance. Radar is used by scientists to calculate the distance to other planets and by police to catch speeding drivers. It is also used to track storm fronts and forecast the weather.

HOW SONAR WORKS

Sonar, meaning Sound Navigation And Ranging, works in a similar way to radar. Instead of radio waves, it sends out a pulse of high-pitched sound. Known as ultrasound, the sound from a sonar system is so high that humans cannot hear it. The ultrasound bounces off any dense objects in its path, such as rocks, shipwrecks, and schools of fish, back toward the ship. Hydrophones (underwater microphones) pick up the reflected sound and use it to calculate the distance of the objects.

◄ Survey ships use sonar to chart the contours of the seabed. The time it takes sound waves to reflect back to the ship indicates the depth of the seabed.

▲ Radar was first used to detect enemy aircraft during World War II. Information was sent to a central control room, where it was used to track enemy action and plot battle strategies on a map.

SEE ALSO
Aircraft, Medicine, Navigation, Radio, Ship, Sound, Submarine, Weather, World War II

RADIO

Radio is an invention we can use to send and receive information through air, and even deep into space, without connecting wires.

A radio wave is a form of energy that travels through the air. There are radio waves around all the time. But you are unaware of them until you turn on your radio (technically, your radio receiver) and tune in to one of them.

GUGLIELMO MARCONI
In 1895, this Italian inventor (1874–1937) was the first to send telegraph signals through the air without the use of wires.

DIFFERENT FREQUENCIES

All waves vibrate back and forth. The rate at which they do this is their "frequency." Radio waves vibrate at amazingly high frequencies—anything from a few thousand to a few billion times a second. Radio stations broadcast on different frequencies from each other so that their transmissions do not get mixed up. Most stations advertise the frequency they use. When you tune your radio in to a station, you alter its circuits so that it is able to pick up the right frequency.

AM AND FM

There are two ways in which radio waves can be transmitted: one method is called AM (amplitude modulation), the other is called FM (frequency modulation). An AM broadcast sends out a radio program by varying the amplitude (extent of vibration) of a radio wave. An FM broadcast sends it out by varying the radio wave's frequency. Your radio can pick up these changes and turn them back into sounds.

A VARIETY OF USES

Radio is regularly used by the police and by the crews onboard ships and airplanes to keep in touch with people back at base or ground control. Entertainers often use radio microphones on stage to relay their voices to amplifiers. Radio waves are also used to send signals to remote-controlled model cars, boats, and planes.

1 A microphone turns sound waves from the DJ's voice into a vibrating electric current.

2 This current combines with another current that vibrates very rapidly.

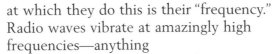

3 The combined currents are turned into radio waves, which are beamed through the air. A tuned-in radio picks up these waves.

4 The radio waves are amplified.

5 Circuits inside the radio pick out the current originally made by the DJ's microphone.

6 A loudspeaker turns this current into sound waves again.

MAKING A RADIO BROADCAST

When a disc jockey, or DJ, makes a radio broadcast, a microphone picks up his or her voice and turns it into an electric current. This current, which vibrates exactly as his or her voice does, is sent to a transmitter for broadcasting. In the transmitter, the vibrating current is mixed with another one that vibrates millions of times a second. This very rapid current is called a "carrier wave." Once they are mixed together, the two currents are turned into a radio wave which can be beamed out through the air.

SEE ALSO

Communication, Electronics, Sound, Telecommunication, Wavelength

RAIN FOREST

These dense, damp forests are mainly found near the equator. They contain more types of plants and animals than all other habitats put together.

The world's largest rain forests are the tropical rain forests of South America, Africa, and Southeast Asia, where the climate is always warm and wet. There is no winter at the equator, so there is nothing to stop the plants growing. The result is a huge variety of trees, ferns, vines, and epiphytes (plants that grow on other plants).

TROPICAL RAIN FORESTS

Although they cover only six percent of the Earth's surface, tropical rain forests contain about three fourths of all known plant and animal species. Wherever you look, there are always some plants in flower or producing fruit, so there is a constant supply of food for birds, bats, insects, snakes, tree frogs, monkeys, and a host of other animals. Most of the animals live in the trees.

◀ Tropical forest animals have adapted to life in the trees. The sloth uses its hooked claws to move from branch to branch.

RAIN-FOREST LIFE CYCLE

Tropical rain forests are made up of several layers. The main canopy (treetop layer) is usually 100–165 ft. (30-50m) above ground, where the slender trunks break out into a cluster of branches, but the tallest trees reach 200 ft. (60m). The understory, dark beneath the canopy, consists of tree trunks covered with lianas (woody vines) and laced together by creepers. The forest floor is surprisingly clear. Leaves, fruit, animal droppings, and bodies decompose quickly when they fall to the ground, and their chemical building blocks are immediately absorbed by plant roots and used to make new growth. It is nature's most efficient recycling system.

TEMPERATE RAIN FORESTS

Farther from the equator are temperate rain forests, formed in coastal regions where onshore winds bring constant rain. These lie chiefly in northwestern North America, southern Chile, Tasmania, southeastern Australia, and New Zealand. The dominant trees are redwoods and Sitka spruce in the Northern Hemisphere and eucalyptus and Antarctic beech in the Southern Hemisphere. Some temperate rain forest trees are even taller than those in the tropical forests, but the plant and animal life is not as rich.

THREATS TO THE FOREST

Large areas of the Amazon, Congo, and Malaysian rain forests have been destroyed by logging for timber. Vast areas have also been cut down to make way for plantations of rubber, coffee, bananas, and sugarcane, or to provide pastures for cattle. Rain forests play an important part in keeping the Earth's climate healthy, and they contain many medicinal plants. International organizations are trying to protect the remaining forests before it is too late.

Emergent tree

Canopy

Understory

Lianas wind around the tree trunks, and rafflesias grow on the forest floor

SEE ALSO
Brazil, Conservation, Forest, Habitat, Plant

RAT AND OTHER RODENTS

Rodents are mammals that have sharp, chisel-like front teeth. They use these for gnawing through food, as well as through anything that gets in their way.

▲ In order to supply wood for its lodge (nest) and its winter food store, the beaver uses its sharp incisors to trim branches and even to fell small trees.

Black (and brown) rats carry the germs of several diseases, including typhus.

The European red squirrel is one of several species of tree squirrel.

House mice live among people—"mouse" comes from a word meaning thief.

Most hamsters have large cheek pouches. They use these to carry food in.

Porcupines use their sharp, spiny quills to defend themselves.

Found in cold, northern regions, lemmings migrate to prevent overpopulation.

Rats belong to a large group of mammals called rodents. There are about 1,500 different rodents; they include rats, mice, voles, hamsters, squirrels, beavers, and porcupines. The smallest rodent is the harvest mouse from Europe and Asia, which could easily sit in an egg cup. The biggest is the capybara from South America, which can weigh over 65 lb. (75kg). Rodents make up about 40 percent of the world's mammal species.

SHARP TEETH
All rodents share one important feature—a set of four sharp front teeth, called incisors, which work like chisels. They use these to gnaw their way through their food, to chop up nesting material, and to get through anything that blocks their path. Beavers use their incisors to gnaw through solid tree trunks, and rats and mice use them to gnaw through household

▲ Like all rodents, rats have four sharp front teeth. These are self-sharpening, and grow throughout the rodent's life.

WIRE CUTTERS
Both the black rat and the much more common brown rat (shown right) eat almost any kind of plant or animal. With their strong teeth, they are able to cut through materials as strong as wire to get to food. When eating, they often use their front feet to hold their food while their teeth gnaw at it.

lumber, food packaging, and even electric wiring, which can set off fires.

FAST BREEDERS
Compared with many other mammals, rodents often breed very rapidly if they have enough food. A female brown rat can start to breed when only two months old, and can produce as many as five litters a year, with up to 12 in each litter. Poisons or traps are often used to keep rats under control, but their fast breeding rate makes this difficult.

SEE ALSO
Animal, Black Death, Mammal

REFORMATION

The Reformation was a period in Europe's history when the Christian Church in the West was split by disagreements and Protestantism became established.

LUTHER'S 95 THESES

In 1517, the German priest Martin Luther (1483–1546) was so upset at the scandal of the sale of indulgences (pardons for sins) by corrupt Church officials that he listed 95 theses, or arguments, against the practice and nailed them to the door of the church in Wittenberg.

John Calvin (1509–64) was influenced by Luther and set up a Protestant church in Geneva, Switzerland.

King Henry VIII of England (1491–1547) broke away from the Catholic Church in order to get a divorce.

John Knox (1514–72) established the Protestant faith in Scotland with help from Elizabeth I.

▶ During the 1200s, the Catholic Church set up the Inquisition (meaning "inquiry") to deal with heresy. In 1542, the pope created a Roman Inquisition to cope with Protestantism. Like the civil courts, the Inquisition used torture as a form of questioning—sometimes to excess.

The Reformation grew out of the ideas of the Renaissance. People no longer shared the same beliefs about religion and wanted greater freedom of worship. Religious arguments became mixed with political struggles, leading to bitter wars. The Reformation led to great changes within the Roman Catholic Church.

BEGINNINGS

The pope in Rome was the head of the Catholic Church. However, by 1500, many people saw the Church as corrupt. Early protesters, such as Jan Huss (c.1370–1415) in Bohemia and John Wycliffe (c.1330–84) in England, spoke out against the Church. But the Reformation really began in 1517 when Martin Luther attacked Church corruption with his 95 theses. The pope expelled Luther from the Church. But Luther continued to lead the Protestant revolt until his death in 1546.

PROTESTANTISM SPREADS

Religious leaders, including Huldreich Zwingli and John Calvin in Switzerland, took up Luther's cause. In England, King Henry VIII broke with the pope over his divorce (which the Church refused), and made himself head of the Church of England. In the Netherlands, many Dutch people took up Protestantism in order to break free from Spanish (Catholic) rule.

MARTYRS AND WARS

Europe was split into two religious camps, often at war, with cruelties on both sides. Under Queen Mary I in England, Catholics persecuted Protestants. Under Mary's sister, Queen Elizabeth I, Protestants did the same to Catholics. France was torn by civil wars between Catholics and Protestants, and religious conflict reached its height during the Thirty Years' War (1618–48), which killed about half the people of Germany.

SEE ALSO

Christianity, Crusades, Religion, Renaissance

REFUGEE

Refugees are people who are driven from their homes by war, revolution, natural disasters like floods, or because of political, racial, or religious persecution.

▲ Frequent famines in Ethiopia, like this one in the mid-1980s, force many villagers to congregate in camps, reliant on food aid.

When refugees flee from war or famine they can carry little with them. They travel in large, sudden movements, often bringing problems with them. Some refugees are welcomed in their new homelands, others are treated badly.

▲ Some refugees are forced to flee for religious reasons. The Huguenots in France suffered for 250 years. Many were murdered in the Massacre of St. Bartholemew's Day, 1572.

MASS MOVEMENTS

In the past, refugees were often met with hostility and forced to act brutally themselves. In A.D. 370, when the Huns invaded Europe from Asia, the Goths and Germans were defeated and fled west into the Roman Empire. A lack of land and food led to fighting and the Roman Empire was destroyed. Other refugees have been made more welcome. In the 1700s, the Protestants in Catholic France were persecuted and moved to nearby countries, like the Netherlands and Britain, bringing with them weaving and banking skills.

INTERNATIONAL HELP

In the 1920s, recognizing that refugees could disrupt stable nations and lead to further wars, the League of Nations set up an international agency for refugees. The United Nations formed a new commission after World War II to help resettle millions of displaced people—15 million in Europe, and 4.5 million Polish people who were moved from Russia. The aim was to provide food and shelter until the refugees could return home or find somewhere to settle. A similar crisis struck in 1947 when Britain withdrew from India and it was divided into two new states, India and Pakistan. Religious riots led to thousands of deaths and millions of refugees.

HUMAN DISASTERS

The breakup of Yugoslavia into a number of independent states in the 1990s created bitter fighting and refugees. Civil war based on ethnic differences meant thousands of people had to leave their homes. The nations of Western Europe sent economic aid—and troops to try to make sure that it got to the refugees.

FAST FACTS

• About 5 million Hindus and Sikhs moved from West Pakistan into India in 1947, and Muslims left India for Pakistan

• After the Vietnam War ended in 1975, hundreds of thousands of Vietnamese fled by boat

• Almost 4 million Afghans left their homeland following Soviet invasion in 1979

UNWANTED VICTIMS

Some of these Rwandan refugees had been walking for a month before reaching the border at Zaire. Most had taken refuge in Zaire in 1995, to escape conflict between Rwanda and Burundi, only to be forced back on the road in November 1996, when civil war broke out in Zaire.

SEE ALSO

Greece and the Balkans, Israel, Judaism, United Nations, Warfare

RELIGION

A religion usually involves a belief in a god or gods. It may have rituals, regard certain places as holy, and prescribe rules for living.

There have been, and still are, many religions around the world. Most religions teach that people should lead good lives and behave in certain ways.

Zoroaster (c.600 B.C.) believed the Earth was fought over by good and evil gods.

GODS

Gods are thought to be greatly superior to humans, endowed with wonderful powers. The Ancient Greeks had hundreds of gods, each for a different thing—such as the sea, wind, or love. This group of gods is known as a pantheon. Many people, including the Vikings and Ancient Egyptians, had such a pantheon. Other religions, including Judaism, Christianity, and Islam, have only one god.

Siddhartha Gautama (c.500 B.C.), the Enlightened One, founded Buddhism.

REVELATIONS

Some religions are based on a revelation—the passing on of sacred knowledge—from a god or gods to a human. Islam is based on the teachings of God as given to the prophet Muhammad in Arabia nearly 1,400 years ago. The Mormon Church of Latter-Day Saints is based on visions and a holy book revealed to Joseph Smith in Palmyra, New York in the 1820s.

Confucius (551–479 B.C.) established the way of life now called Confucianism.

TALKING TO THE GODS

The Ancient Greeks believed that the Oracle at Delphi, dedicated to the sun god Apollo, could foretell the future. The chief priestess gave answers to questions in a trance. These answers were often ambiguous, but even the government of the day sometimes consulted the Oracle.

PRIESTS AND TEMPLES

Many religions have priests, who study holy teachings and make sure that rituals are carried out properly and that holy places are respected. Other religions, such as Islam, have no priests. The Ancient Egyptians built vast temples that were considered to be the home of a god. In many societies, great wealth is lavished on the temple or church. However, Australian Aborigines believe that certain places are sacred to the spirits and should not be built on.

HOLY COMMUNITIES

The followers of some religions may form a special community and treat non-believers as outsiders. In some religions, people form communities where they follow the teachings of the religion very strictly. Such dedicated communities include the monasteries and convents of Christianity and Buddhism.

Jesus Christ (c.4 B.C.– c.A.D. 30) preached and taught in Palestine.

▼ In New Guinea, dancers in colorful costumes take the roles of spirits during ceremonies.

Abu Bakr (c.573–634) led Islam after the death of the prophet Muhammad.

SEE ALSO

Buddhism, Christianity, Hinduism, Islam, Myth and legend, Pilgrim

327

RENAISSANCE

The Renaissance was a revival in arts and sciences which began in Italy around 1350 and spread across Europe. It marked the end of the Middle Ages.

In the late 1300s, Italy was the richest and most populated area in Europe. However, Italy was not a unified country at this time—the region was divided up into about 250 states, and each state was based around a city and governed by the wealthiest families in that particular area.

Astronomers developed more accurate telescopes to observe the stars.

The invention of printing (1440) made the spread of learning possible.

THE REBIRTH

The word "renaissance" means rebirth. Italy had preserved much of the Ancient Roman civilization, but this had been largely ignored until the 1300s. Then, around 1350, Italian scholars began to copy old manuscripts and circulate them. These manuscripts contained the history of the ancient (classical) world and passed on its knowledge of architecture, science, and art. There was also an influx of Ancient Greek learning from the city of Constantinople after it fell to the Turks in 1453. Renaissance thinkers were increasingly influenced by the way ancient scholars studied subjects such as philosophy, literature, and science, and wanted to recreate the spirit of the classical age. During the Middle Ages which had immediately preceded the Renaissance, people had been much more concerned with theology (religion).

POWERFUL BACKERS

The rich noblemen who ruled the Italian cities paid for the classical manuscripts to be copied. In Florence, the powerful Medici family of bankers spent lavishly as patrons of the arts. Lorenzo Medici, who ruled Florence from 1469 to 1492, was called "the Magnificent" because he attracted the finest scientists and artists to the area. Francesco Sforza, a mercenary who became Duke of Milan in 1450, was another great Italian patron.

GREAT ARTISTS

Renaissance artists began painting and sculpting in a completely new style. Instead of stiff, formal poses, they drew people more naturally and put them in real landscapes and rooms. By 1424, Tomasso Masaccio was decorating churches in Florence with beautiful frescos. At the same time, Filippo Brunelleschi was building startling new structures. His masterpiece is the dome on the cathedral in Florence, which he began in 1420. It blends excellent engineering with graceful design and was the largest dome in the world at the time.

◀ Hans Holbein's *The Ambassadors* (1533) typifies the spirit of the Renaissance: the richly robed ambassadors are surrounded by objects from science and the arts.

328

FUTURISTIC IDEAS OF FLYING MACHINES

The great minds of the Renaissance, like Leonardo Da Vinci, didn't take all their inspiration from the past. His sketch books show a fascination with flight and the possibility of flying machines long before the invention of the first successful aircraft.

LEONARDO DA VINCI
As well as being a painter (masterpieces include the *Mona Lisa*) and inventor, da Vinci (1452–1519) studied biology, anatomy, and mechanics.

▲ A modern artist's impression of Leonardo's flying machine—turning paddles moved the wings.

▲ Leonardo's original sketches

Scientists began to make their own detailed observations instead of simply accepting the teachings of the Church. The Polish astronomer Nicolaus Copernicus (1473–1543) realized that the Earth moved around the Sun. However, he was afraid to publish his findings until he was very close to death, because they opposed the Church view that the Earth was the center of the universe.

DESIDERIUS ERASMUS
(1466–1536) was a Dutch priest and leading Christian humanist whose writings attacked the morals of church leaders.

THE SPREAD OF LEARNING

As the new art and learning developed in Italy, other countries took note. The universities of Oxford, Cambridge, and Paris became centers of the Renaissance in England and France. Scholars such as Erasmus of Rotterdam in Holland and Thomas More of England developed and spread the ideas. In both Holland and Germany, artists such as the van Eycks, Dürer, and Holbein took Renaissance ideals and developed a distinct northern European style. In England, Shakespeare and Spenser began a revolution in poetry and drama. Then, in 1600, Marie de Medici married King Henri IV of France, taking Italian craftsmen, artists, and cooks with her, which further spread the ideas through Europe.

▲ Michelangelo's statue of Moses shows veins and muscles typical of the realistic style of Renaissance sculpture.

COMBINING SKILLS

The ability to mix very different skills was typical of the artists and scientists of the Renaissance. Michelangelo Buonarroti is best known for his marble sculptures, such as the famous *Pietá*, but he was also a painter and poet. He even worked as an architect on St. Peter's Basilica in Rome in 1547. Most versatile of all was Leonardo da Vinci, who created several great paintings, studied science, and designed irrigation systems for farms. Other famous figures of the era include the artists Giotto, Botticelli, and Raphael; sculptors Donatello and Ghiberti and the architect Bramante.

◄ Bramante's Tempietto in Rome reflects classical building styles.

SEE ALSO
Architecture, Art, Astronomy, Dance, Design, Explorer, Invention, Italy, Printing, Sculpture

REPRODUCTION

Reproduction is the process of producing new organisms so that life continues from one generation to the next. All living things make more of their own kind.

Reproduction is one of the most important functions of all living organisms—from the tiniest microbes to the largest trees, elephants, and whales. It means making more of your own kind, or species. There are two main types of reproduction: asexual and sexual.

ONE BECOMES TWO

The simplest form of asexual reproduction is that of organisms consisting of a single cell, such as amoebas or bacteria. These reproduce by simply dividing into two. Each offspring cell grows larger and then also divides, and so on. In suitable conditions, some bacteria can double their numbers like this every 15 to 20 minutes.

ONE-PARENT REPRODUCTION

Many plants reproduce asexually by vegetative propagation. A part of the plant grows roots into the soil and sprouts a stem, which then becomes a separate individual. Gardeners make use of this process by slicing off a part of a plant and growing it into a new individual. Some simple animals reproduce in a similar way, by budding. The parent sprouts a "bud" that grows into a new individual. Hydras, tiny anemonelike water creatures, multiply by budding.

▲ Single-celled organisms, such as the amoeba, reproduce asexually by dividing in two—a process called "binary fission."

AVERAGE PREGNANCY TIME FOR MAMMALS	
Species	Days
Common shrew	15
House mouse	17
Horseshoe bat	45
Cat	63
Dog	63
Tiger	103
Goat	150
Moose	245
Gorilla	260
Human	266
Horse	333
Blue whale	350
Asian elephant	660

FERTILIZATION

Reproduction is very similar in all mammals, including humans. The female or mother has reproductive organs called ovaries that make hundreds of tiny eggs. The male or father has reproductive organs called testes (testicles) that make millions of even tinier sperm. During mating, the male passes his sperm cells into the reproductive tubes, or tract, of the female. Here, one of the sperm joins with, or fertilizes, an egg. The genes in the egg and sperm come together to create a new individual.

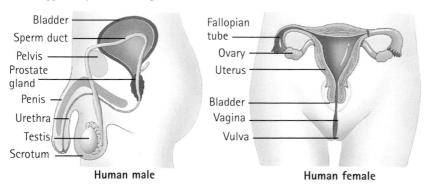

Human male

Bladder
Sperm duct
Pelvis
Prostate gland
Penis
Urethra
Testis
Scrotum

Human female

Fallopian tube
Ovary
Uterus
Bladder
Vagina
Vulva

Sperm — Egg — Nucleus — Membrane — Sperm nucleus

1 Day 1: a sperm cell penetrates and fertilizes an egg inside the Fallopian tube, forming a zygote.

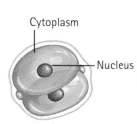

Cytoplasm — Nucleus

2 The zygote divides into two and continues to travel along the Fallopian tube toward the uterus.

▲ Ultrasound scans, as of this 20-week-old fetus, are used to check on a baby's development in the uterus.

DIFFERENT GENES—VARIATION

Most plants and animals breed by sexual reproduction. This requires two parents—female and male. Each parent contributes a unique selection of genes, so the offspring vary in the genes they inherit and grow up to be slightly different from each other. This variation means that at least some offspring will be suited to the world's ever-changing conditions, and so will survive in the struggle for life.

HAVING BABIES

Some young mammals, such as mice, are born without fur, with eyes closed, and depend totally on their parents. A human baby is also helpless, although it does have certain reflexes, such as crying when it is hungry or cold. Other mammal babies, such as whales, giraffes, and antelope, are alert and able to move about within minutes of birth. The number of young born at one time varies. Mother seals, dolphins, bats, and humans usually have one baby. Mother dogs, cats, and rats have several babies. A mother opossum may give birth to more than 30 babies.

Yolk sac
Amniotic cavity
Body stalk

Embryo Yolk sac

Placenta

3 The cells continue to divide until, after 4 to 5 days, a tiny ball of 16 cells has formed.

4 Day 13: the ball settles into the lining of the uterus, which forms supportive structures.

5 Day 21: the embryo feeds off the yolk sac and its spine and brain begin to form.

6 Day 28: the stomach and arm and leg buds have all begun to form and the heart starts pumping blood.

7 Day 35: bones and muscles start to form, and the arms and legs continue to grow.

HOW THE HUMAN BABY DEVELOPS

During development, the cells multiply rapidly, move around, and change into specialized shapes, gradually forming the basic body organs. This rapid growth is called the embryo stage. As the tiny, tadpolelike body develops, it takes on a recognizable shape. It develops muscles, bones, skin, and other features. Eight weeks after fertilization, it is called a fetus. It is nourished by the mother through a specialized organ, the placenta. Finally, it leaves the uterus through the birth canal to begin life in the outside world.

Amniotic cavity

Umbilical cord

8 Day 56: the 0.8-in. (2-cm) fetus has developed its main body parts, including fingers and toes; some muscles and nerves function.

9 After four months, the baby has doubled in size and has well-developed features such as fingers and toes.

10 After five months, the lungs and most of the other body organs are working properly. The fetus usually repositions itself, so that at the end of nine months (above) it is ready to be born head first.

LAYING EGGS

Mammals, some snakes and fish, and a few insects give birth to their young. But the vast majority of animal mothers reproduce by laying eggs, out of which the offspring hatch. On land, the eggs are usually encased in a tough shell for protection and to prevent drying out. Examples are bird and reptile eggs. These contain a yolk, which is the food store for nourishing the baby as it develops. Insects, spiders, and similar smaller creatures also lay tough-cased eggs, but without large food stores inside. The offspring must hatch out and feed immediately.

REPRODUCING IN WATER

Eggs laid in water do not need a waterproof casing. Amphibians' eggs are jellylike, and the eggs of most fish, crabs, and similar creatures have thin walls. On land, the male usually transfers his sperm into the female's body during mating, otherwise the sperm would dry out and die. In water, females can release their eggs, and males their sperm, without the risk of their drying out. Male and female cast their sperm and eggs into the water and fertilization is left to chance. In many fish and crabs, males and females come together and release their eggs and sperm into one place.

SEE ALSO

Amphibian, Animal, Butterfly and moth, Evolution, Fish, Flower, Human body, Insect, Mammal, Microorganism, Seed and pollination

REPTILE

Reptiles are air-breathing animals with backbones and a covering of tough scales. Most of them live on land, but some live in the sea or in fresh water.

▲ The Australian frilled lizard raises its collar in a display of aggression that frightens its attacker away.

Reptiles are usually described as cold-blooded creatures, and this means that their body temperature goes up and down as the air or water temperature changes. Most reptiles live in warm places, but they are found everywhere except in the far north or south. Those living in cooler places make themselves warm in the morning by sitting in the sun. Reptiles are vertebrates (they have backbones), and there are 6,500 different species divided into four main groups: turtles and tortoises; alligators and crocodiles; lizards and snakes; and the tuatara, a species in its own group. The tuatara is described as a living fossil—it has hardly changed in 200 million years.

When frightened, the poisonous cobra rises and spreads its hood.

The crocodile is a large meat-eater that seizes its prey with powerful jaws.

TORTOISES—AN ANCIENT GROUP

Reptiles first appeared on the Earth over 300 million years ago, and many different kinds have come and gone since then. The oldest group of reptiles still living is the turtles and tortoises, which have not changed much in 200 million years. They are easily recognized by their shells, which are made of bone and usually have a horny covering. There are about 240 different species. Those living in the sea are usually called turtles and those living on land tortoises. Freshwater species are called terrapins. In the United States, however, the name turtle is often used for all the shelled reptiles. Land-living tortoises feed mainly on plants, but the other species are mainly meat-eaters.

OCEANGOING CREATURES

Most reptiles lay eggs. **1** The oceangoing marine turtle comes ashore to find a safe place in the sand for her young. **2** She lays her eggs in a sheltered spot. **3** Weeks later, the hatchlings break out of their shells. **4** They scramble out and race for the safety of the water. **5** Aquatic turtles all have limbs that act as paddles or flippers, making them excellent swimmers.

Tortoises have no teeth, and they bite their food with sharp, horny beaks.

DINOSAUR RELATIVES

The huge dinosaurs that roamed the Earth millions of year ago were reptiles. Their nearest living reptile relatives are the alligators and crocodiles. These dangerous meat-eaters live in and around tropical rivers. There are 22 to 23 species, which are about 9 to 18 ft. (3-6m) long.

LIZARDS AND SNAKES

These animals form the largest group of reptiles alive today. There are about 3,750 species of lizard and 2,400 species of snake. Scientists believe that snakes descended from a group of burrowing lizards that gradually lost their legs about 100 million years ago. Some snakes are poisonous and bite with grooved fangs that inject venom from saclike glands. Lizards nearly all live on land and are mostly very active animals. They include both vegetarians and meat-eaters. The world's biggest lizard is the Komodo dragon, which lives in Indonesia. Up to 10 ft. (3m) long, it eats animals as large as pigs. It is one of the monitor lizards, which have long necks and powerful teeth. Some monitors steal crocodile eggs and even eat young crocodiles. Small lizards feed mainly on insects, slugs, and other species of invertebrate animals.

Orbit (eye socket)
Radius
Ulna
Humerus
Thoracic vertebrae
Ribs
Femur
Caudal (tail) vertebrae
Tibia
Phalanges

ANATOMY OF A TYPICAL LIZARD

Unlike snakes, lizards have an outer ear opening and moveable eyelids. They cannot unhinge their jaws like snakes to swallow large prey. Lizards usually have four well-developed limbs, but some have limbs modified to help them run, climb, or burrow. A typical lizard has a very long tail.

The slowworm looks like a snake but is really a lizard without legs.

The tortoise can pull its head, legs, and tail into its hard, protective shell.

The gecko can climb walls using suckerlike pads on its feet.

CHAMELEONS

These are slow-moving lizards, some of which are famous for their ability to change color. A chameleon surrounded by green leaves is usually some shade of green, but if it is then put among brown leaves or bare twigs it will gradually turn brown. Chameleons feed on insects, which they catch by firing out their long, sticky tongue at great speed. Their bulging eyes are also very unusual because each one can be moved separately: one eye can look forward while the other one looks behind. This is very useful for finding insects and also for spotting enemies.

A STRANGE SURVIVAL TRICK

Many birds and mammals like to eat lizards, but most lizards run away quickly when they are frightened. Their enemies often manage to grab no more than the tail—and then a surprising thing happens. The lizard snaps off its tail and races away, leaving the predator with just a wriggling tail. The lizard grows a new one.

▲ A chameleon lashes out its tongue to catch a hapless insect. Its tongue is almost the same length as its body.

FAST FACTS

• Some tortoises have been known to live for well over 120 years

• The Gila monster and the beaded lizard can kill people with their poisonous saliva

• The only oceangoing lizard is the marine iguana, which lives in the Galapagos Islands

SEE ALSO

Alligator and crocodile, Desert, Ocean and sea, Snake

REVOLUTION

A revolution is an overwhelming uprising by the people that aims to destroy the social or political system of a country and replace it with a new system.

Wat Tyler (d.1381) led the Peasants' Revolt of southern England in 1381.

George Washington (1732–99) led colonial troops in the American Revolution.

Simon Bolivar (1783–1830) led many revolts in South America.

Georges Danton (1759–94) led the republican faction in the French Revolution.

Giuseppe Garibaldi (1807–82) led revolutions in Italy to create a united nation.

Revolutions are unpredictable. They may achieve all their aims or lose sight of the ideals that were fought for. Their leaders may go down in history as heroes or traitors.

MASS MOVEMENTS
Revolutions occur when most of the people in a country are suffering hardship, or when they want changes to be made. If they cannot gain what they want, anger and the demand for more radical change builds up. However, revolutions need an incident to start them. The uprising of Sicilians against French rulers in 1282 began when a Sicilian stabbed a Frenchman who had insulted his wife.

REASONS FOR FAILURE
Most revolutions fail. The government has many advantages over ordinary people, including wealth, control of the army, and better organization. Revolutions are often disorganized, starting as separate protests

▲ Medieval peasant revolts were generally aimed at abolishing harsh taxes. Rebels often burned the books in which taxes were recorded.

that can be put down by force. Even if rebel forces unite, they often argue later. The revolutions that succeed are those with a clear aim and strong leadership. But even these may fail. In 133 B.C., the Roman army officer Tiberius Gracchus led the poorer citizens in demands for reform of land and property laws. The revolution failed when noblemen killed Gracchus, his brother, and over 300 supporters.

MEDIEVAL PEASANTS
During the Middle Ages, the peasants of Europe had to pay taxes and work long hours for their masters. Some nobles treated their peasants harshly. In 1381, the

FARMERS AGAINST SOLDIERS
During the American Revolution the British hired 30,000 German soldiers, mostly Hessians. The colonial militias, largely made up of farmers, won many skirmishes, but, compared with the soldiers, they were poorly trained. It was only after George Washington took charge of the Continental Army and began serious training that the rebelling forces won major battles and, eventually, the war.

peasants of England demanded an end to such conditions. The uprising collapsed, but reforms were slowly introduced. In 1524, German peasants launched a violent uprising. They murdered nobles and organized an army. The nobles hired foreign troops and defeated the peasants at Frankenhausen in 1525. Most of the rebels were killed.

THE AMERICAN REVOLUTION

The American Revolution began in 1775 when British colonists protested against being taxed by Britain with no representation in Parliament. At first, the uprising aimed at changing the status of the colonies, but in 1776 the colonies declared independence. After full-scale war with Britain, the new United States established a democratic republic.

THE FRENCH REVOLUTION

In the France of 1789, the king was seen as someone who spent vast sums of money on luxuries. Involvement in wars, including the American Revolution, had drained the treasury. At the same time, food prices had doubled after the harvest failed, and many were close to starvation. The middle

classes demanded an end to the injustices. In May 1789, Louis XVI called a meeting of the States General (parliament) for the first time in about 175 years. This body demanded tax reforms. Food riots broke out, and mob violence spread. The new government introduced radical measures to please the mob. The king tried to flee the country, was arrested, and beheaded. In the Reign of Terror that followed, almost 20,000 people were executed as enemies of the Revolution. Ten months later, moderates established a new government based on the ideals of the Revolution. ▶

● Centers of revolution in 1848

◀ In 1848, people supporting democracy and social reforms rose against the monarchies of Europe. King Louis Philippe was overthrown in France, and major reforms were introduced in Belgium, Denmark, and the Netherlands. Elsewhere, the armies and peasants remained loyal to their monarchs. Revolts were crushed in Prussia and Italy, though some reforms were made. Only in Austria, Poland, and the smaller German states did the revolutions fail totally.

TO THE BARRICADES

The *sans-culottes*, the working class of Paris, formed the shock troops of the French Revolution. On July 14, 1789 they attacked the royal prison of the Bastille, marking the start of violence. July 14 is now the most important public holiday in France. During fighting, the *sans-culottes* built barricades across the narrow streets of Paris, from which to defy troops and police.

▲ Demonstrations of over one million people in Tehran led to the rise to power of religious leader Ayatollah Khomeini in Iran.

▲ Government symbols may be destroyed by revolutionaries, as was this portrait of Stalin by Hungarians in 1956.

▶ Civilians may take over military weapons in a revolution. The Hungarian uprising of 1956 failed when trained Soviet troops invaded.

REVOLUTION IN RUSSIA

In 1917, Russia was ruled by a czar, or emperor. The peasants were tied to their land, and the urban poor had no civil rights. In the spring, the czar was overthrown and replaced by democrats from the middle classes, but many social problems remained. Vladimir Lenin, leader of the Communist Party, took advantage of this to begin uprisings in major cities. These spread and rapidly became a civil war, which ended in 1921 with complete Communist victory.

REVOLUTION FROM ABOVE

In 1959, a force of Communist guerrillas united with popular discontent to overthrow the Cuban government. The guerrilla leader, Fidel Castro, then began a revolution from above by overthrowing the economic and social systems of the country in favor of communism.

VELVET REVOLUTIONS

In 1956, the Hungarians launched a peaceful uprising to overthrow their communist government. But this uprising was crushed by Soviet troops. By 1989, however, Russia was too weak to interfere in Eastern Europe. Massive peaceful protests began in Poland, East Germany, Czechoslovakia, Bulgaria, and Hungary. Known as "velvet revolutions," these movements replaced communism with democracy within a few months.

STORMING THE PALACE

Taking key buildings and communication centers is vital to any successful revolution. On October 25, 1917, Russian Communists and supporting troops seized government buildings, including the famous Winter Palace in St. Petersburg. Within days, the government of Russia was communist.

SEE ALSO
Civil war, Communism, Fascism, France, Russia and the Baltic States, United States of America

RHINOCEROS

Rhinoceroses are large, thick-skinned mammals that are distantly related to the horse. They have one or two horns on the nose and three hoofed toes on each foot.

▲ Rhinos may fight each other with their horns, which can sometimes be torn from the nose in the struggle.

There are five species of rhinoceros (or rhino). Two live in Africa and three in southern Asia. They are all plant-eaters. The African white rhino, which is actually gray like all the others, lives mainly on scrubland, where it feeds on grass. Nearly 6.5 ft. (2m) high, up to 13 ft. (4m) long, and over 2 tons, it is the largest of the five. The Sumatran rhino is the smallest, weighing only 1 ton; unlike the others it is very hairy.

HORN OR HAIR?

A rhino's horn is not made of bone or horn. It is actually made of very coarse hairs which are firmly stuck together. African black rhinos and white rhinos have two horns, and the one farthest foward can be nearly 5 ft. (1.5m) long. The Sumatran rhino also has two horns, but Indian and Javan rhinos have only one. A young rhino begins to grow horns when it is four or five weeks old.

ENDANGERED SPECIES

All rhinos are rare animals. There are probably only about 50 Javan rhinos left in the world, and about 150 Sumatran rhinos. The animals have been hunted for their horns, which are often ground up and used to make traditional medicines in Asia. The white rhino lives in various national parks in Africa and is the most numerous, but the other rhinos are in serious danger of becoming extinct.

The two-horned black rhino has a hooked upper lip and lives on the African plains.

The one-horned African white rhino has square lips and lives on the scrubland.

The one-horned Indian rhino has large folds of skin and lives in marshy jungles.

The two-horned Sumatran rhino has hairy skin and lives in rain forests.

The one-horned Javan rhino lives in the rain forests, but is now nearly extinct.

A rhino's horns are used for self-defense and for digging up bushes and shrubs.

A black rhino uses its hooked upper lip for grasping leaves.

A rhino's foot has three toes, each of which ends in a hoof. The middle toe takes most of the rhino's weight.

THE BLACK RHINOCEROS

Like all rhinos, the African black has excellent hearing and a good sense of smell. Its eyesight is not good, however, and the animal often charges almost blindly when it is disturbed by an unfamiliar smell or sound. A charging black rhino is terrifying, since it can run more than 28 mph (45kph), faster than a human.

SEE ALSO
Africa, Animal, Indian subcontinent, Mammal

RIVER

When water falls as rain and snow over the land, it eventually flows back to the seas and oceans. Usually, it flows back in the form of a river.

A river that flows quickly down a steep slope, over hard rocks, cuts a deep gorge in the land.

When a river flows more slowly over softer rocks, the valley is worn back into an open V-shape.

▲ Waterfalls occur when a river tumbles over the edge of a steep cliff or ledge, as in the powerful Dettifoss Falls in Iceland.

A river goes through many stages in its development. First, water falls as rain on hills and mountainsides and seeps into the ground until the soil and rock are completely saturated with it—so full that they cannot hold any more. The top level of this saturated zone is called the water table. When the water table reaches the surface of the soil—on a steep slope, for example—water pours out, forming into a spring. Water from the spring runs downhill as a stream, and in time, many streams unite to form a river.

YOUNG RIVER

When a river is young, it runs swiftly down the hill or mountainside. High up, close to the springs, the falling water is full of energy and can carry rocks and boulders with it. This rocky debris scrapes and crashes along the bed of the river, carving out a deep V-shaped valley or gorge. This constant erosion is typical of

WORLD'S LONGEST RIVERS		
Name	Outflow	Length
Nile	Mediterranean Sea (Egypt)	4,160 mi.
Amazon	Atlantic Ocean (Brazil)	4,000 mi.
Chang	East China Sea (China)	3,964 mi.
Ob	Gulf of Ob (Russia)	3,362 mi.
Amur	Tartar Strait (Russia)	2,744 mi.
Yenisey	Kara Sea (Russia)	2,543 mi.
Missouri	Mississippi River (U.S.A.)	2,540 mi.

a river in its early stage, and waterfalls and rapids (fast currents) are common.

MATURE RIVER

In the next stage of the river's development, some of the rocky debris begins to settle out in a process called deposition. However, erosion still takes place. The river valley becomes broad and flat, and the river winds, or meanders, around in it. When the course of the river swings toward the valley's edge, the sides are worn back, and the valley becomes wider. At the same time, rocks and sand are deposited on the valley floor, forming what is known as a floodplain. This whole area can be under water during flooding. As it flows, the river constantly changes direction, and eats into the sediment (solid matter) which has already been dropped, lifting it, and depositing it elsewhere.

▼ Rivers are used all over the world to move goods and people. This river market in Zaire is part of a river trade route, where people travel by boat to buy and sell goods.

LOOPING CURRENTS

When a river flows in a loop, its current is faster on the outside. The faster current can erode more quickly than the slower current on the inside, so the outside bank of the loop is worn back. At the same time, sand and pebbles are deposited by the slower current, and build up the inside bank. The loop gradually becomes more pronounced, and the course of the river changes.

OLD MAN RIVER

In its final stage of development, the river becomes so slow that there is no erosion anywhere, only deposition. The river is now a long way from its source high up in the mountains, and is meandering slowly across a flat plain. The river overflows its banks during times of flood,

depositing fertile sediment on the plains as the water slows down away from the main current. The banks can get built up so that the river may actually flow at a higher level than the plain around it. Such a river alters its course continually during flooding, spreading valuable fertile soil on the plain, but making the water difficult to manage.

MEETING THE SEA

Eventually, the river reaches the sea at its mouth. If there are no currents at this point, the river's sediment is deposited as sandbanks. These sandbanks may form islands, and the river water splits up into individual streams between them, forming a delta. More often, the sediment is carried away, and the river has a broad tidal mouth called an estuary.

When the channel of a river flows in a snakelike pattern across its valley, it is said to meander.

1 Some meanders swell to broader loops than others.

2 The neck of the loop then becomes very narrow.

3 The old channel is cut off to form an oxbow lake.

Glacier · Meltwater · Waterfall · Rapids · Stream · Tributary stream · River · Oxbow lake · Estuary · Meander · Floodplain · River mouth

THE IMPORTANCE OF RIVERS

Although rivers make up only a tiny percentage of the Earth's surface water, they are very important. Rivers form the landscape and provide natural barriers. They also provide vital links from seas to inland areas, and are used for transporting goods. Most inland villages, towns, and cities began as settlements around rivers; when bridges were built, the settlements grew. Rivers supply food, and water for drinking, washing, and crop irrigation.

SEE ALSO
Lake, Mountain and valley, Transportation, Water

ROAD

People build and use roads for travel and for moving freight. Cars and trucks on the roads now carry most of the world's passengers and goods.

Interchanges are systems of roads that allow traffic to switch between expressways smoothly and safely.

Unpaved roads have stony or earthen surfaces and can be muddy after rain.

Track surfaces are often gravel. They are in remote areas with little traffic.

Main roads have all-weather surfaces and can support heavy trucks.

The earliest roads were rough tracks, made by people's feet as they traveled between villages. Sometimes, trackways of timber were laid over swampy ground. Few early roads were suitable for wheeled carts, especially in wet weather.

ROMAN ROADS
The Romans were among the first people to build good roads. Surveyors planned the route, following old tracks or setting out a new, straight line. The roads were suitable for wagons or an army on the march. Towns grew at points where roads crossed.

DECLINE AND REVIVAL
After the Romans, road building stopped in the Western world. Both the Inca of South America and the Chinese had advanced road systems, but in Europe, most roads were no better than rough tracks. Improvements were not made until

Natural soil

Compacted soil

Subbase

Base course

Pavement

Shoulder

ROAD CONSTRUCTION
The lowest layer in modern highways is the subbase of stone which levels the ground. The base course is stones of about 1.5 in. (4cm). The top pavement may be made of concrete or of tar and small stones. Lane markings, lights, and signs make roads safer for driving.

the 1700s, when armies built better roads to move supplies. In 1816, British engineer John MacAdam (1756–1836) published new designs for roads. He used well-drained layers of stones and gravel bound together by sand. The design was used around the world for major routes.

AUTOMOBILES
In the 1890s, early drivers demanded better roads, because cars could not cope with cart tracks. By the 1930s, the first highway systems had been built in Italy and Germany. Today, many towns are dominated by roads and traffic, causing pollution and safety problems. Road building has opened up regions such as the Amazon, causing environmental damage. Roads are needed for business and pleasure, but urban planners need to solve the problems that roads create.

◀ Roman roads were built with flat stones laid over concrete. They were built and used by the army.

SEE ALSO
Car, Transportation, Truck and bus

ROBOT

A robot is a machine designed to imitate human actions. It can perform a range of tasks that are often too dangerous or monotonous for a human to do.

Robots are widely used in factories. Here, robotic hands solder parts onto electronic circuit boards.

Radio-controlled bomb disposal robots check out suspect packages and make controlled explosions.

Robots have taken on cult status in films. Robby the Robot starred in *Forbidden Planet* (1956).

▶ Tiny robots are used in microsurgery. Here a "bugbot" is sweeping away fatty cholesterol deposits clogging up human arteries.

The name "robot" comes from *robota*, the Czech word for the work peasants had to do for their landlords. Robots free humans from heavy and boring work; they perform routine tasks in industry, such as painting or welding. They can be used in dangerous conditions, for example where there are poisonous fumes or around volcanoes. Robots equipped with electronic "eyes" can also inspect or sort goods.

ROBOTS IN INDUSTRY

The first robot was introduced in 1961 by General Motors in New Jersey. Although they were invented in America, Japan is now the world's leading maker and user of industrial robots. The first robot in Japan was brought from the U.S. in 1967. By 1978, Japan was making 10,000 robots a year, by 1980 twice as many. By the 1990s, half the world's working robots were in Japan— mostly in the car and electronics industries.

ROBOTS VERSUS HUMANS

Uses are being developed for robots outside industry. In 1990, the U.S. Army

▲ Early robots and movie robots (left) looked like humans. Later, useful robots were tiny and buglike or resembled industrial machines. By the 1990s, robotic research seemed to have gone full circle. Honda's (right) can walk, climb, and make simple decisions.

introduced the Robo-spy, a remote-controlled, all-terrain vehicle equipped with a video camera. This was designed to roam enemy territory and send back information about forces and equipment. In 1991, a robotic sheepshearer was introduced in Australia; it could work almost twice as fast as a human shearer. In 1993, a dairy farm in the Netherlands became the first to install a computer-controlled robot milking machine.

SEE ALSO

Computer, Industry, Spacecraft, Space exploration

ROCK

Rocks are the solid substances that make up the surface of the Earth. There are three types of rock, each of which forms in a different way.

Granite is a coarse-grained igneous rock that has formed slowly underground.

Pumice is a light igneous rock that often forms in a volcanic eruption.

Marble is a medium-grained rock that forms in metamorphic terrains.

Slate is a dense, fine-grained metamorphic rock that splits into thin slabs.

Limestone is a sedimentary rock that often contains tiny fossilized remains.

Sandstone is a sedimentary rock made of fine or coarse grains cemented into beds.

Igneous rocks are those that have formed from heat. Sedimentary rocks are formed under water from layers of materials and organic remains. Metamorphic rocks are the result of changes made to existing rocks.

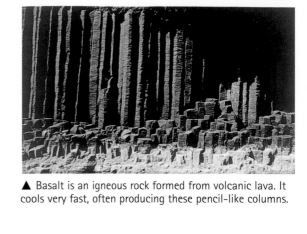

▲ Basalt is an igneous rock formed from volcanic lava. It cools very fast, often producing these pencil-like columns.

ROCKS FROM HEAT

Hot molten magma from inside the Earth can break out at the surface through a volcano as lava. It then cools and solidifies quickly, forming very fine rock such as basalt. Or, it may cool slowly underground, forming big, coarse mineral crystals. Granite is formed this way. In both cases, the rock is igneous—formed from fire.

ROCKS FROM WATER

Loose materials, such as sand or mud, can build up in layers at the bottom of the sea. These layers, or beds, may eventually be buried, compressed, and cemented into a solid mass. The resulting rock is called a sedimentary rock—built from layers. The layers may consist of small fragments such as sand, creating sandstone. Or they may be built from minerals dissolved in the seawater, like limestone, or built up from things that were once alive, like coal. We find fossils in sedimentary rocks.

NEW ROCKS FROM OLD

The third kind of rock forms when a rock that already exists is heated or squeezed. This may occur in the heart of a mountain chain when it is being pushed up, as the heat and pressure change the minerals that it contains. This produces a metamorphic rock—a rock of change. Great heat gives a rock with an even, crystalline structure, such as marble. Great pressure produces a rock in which the crystals are all twisted and deformed—schist, for example.

ROCK CYCLE

New rock is constantly being pushed up toward the Earth's surface, where it is broken down by the elements and deposited at the bottom of lakes, rivers, and seas. These sedimentary layers are compressed into new rock, which may later be uplifted or sink to depths where it melts to form igneous rocks. It can also become so roasted and compressed that it forms metamorphic rock.

Uplift

Erosion by ice

Uplift

Extrusive (surface) igneous rock

River carries rock fragments to sea

Material deposited on seabed

Sedimentary rock layer

Metamorphism creates new rock

Intrusive (non-surface) igneous rock

Buried rock layer

SEE ALSO
Earth, Fossil, Mineral and gem, Mining, Oil, Soil

ROCKET

Rockets provide the thrust needed to lift spacecraft above Earth's atmosphere. They do this by burning fuel and shooting out the exhaust gases behind them.

Rockets make use of a law of physics: a force in one direction gives rise to an equal force in the opposite direction. The backward force of the escaping gases leads to an equal and opposite thrust that pushes the rocket forward. Because rockets have a supply of liquid oxygen, they can work in the emptiness of space.

MULTISTAGE ROCKETS

Most space rockets consist of three separate sections, or stages. After the powerful first stage has run out of fuel, it falls away and the second-stage engines ignite. After this fuel has been used up, the spacecraft completes its journey away from Earth, with the help of the third-stage engines.

Height in feet

Launch escape system	360
Command module	330
Propulsion engine	
Service module	
Lunar module	300
Instrument unit	
THIRD STAGE	260
Liquid oxygen	
	230
1 rocket engine	
Liquid hydrogen	200
SECOND STAGE	
Liquid oxygen	160
5 rocket engines	
	130
Liquid oxygen	100
FIRST STAGE	
	60
Kerosene fuel	
Solid-fuel motor	30
5 rocket engines	0

SPACE SHUTTLE

The rockets that power the U.S. space shuttle are reusable. The shuttle consists of an orbiter; an external fuel tank, which supplies the orbiter's main engines; and two solid rocket boosters. When these boosters have run out of fuel, they fall into the ocean on parachutes, to be recovered. The empty fuel tank is jettisoned next, and burns up on reentry into Earth's atmosphere. The orbiter continues into space to carry out its mission, returning to Earth to land on a runway like an airplane.

FUTURE ROCKETS

Almost all rocket engines today use chemical fuels, but their use in long-distance space travel is limited. In the future, nuclear rockets may be the answer, if scientists can eliminate the risk of accidents during takeoff. Another idea for deep-space missions is the use of a matter-annihilation device, which emits a beam of photons.

▲ The U.S. space shuttle program came to an abrupt halt in 1986, when the orbiter *Challenger* blew up 73 seconds after liftoff, killing all seven of its crew members.

MILESTONES IN ROCKETRY

c.1000 Chinese fireworks propelled by gunpowder

1805 Englishman William Congreve develops a rocket for use in battle

1903 Russian Konstantin Tsiolkovsky designs a spacecraft powered by liquid fuel

1926 American Robert Goddard launches first liquid-fueled rocket

1944 Germany launches its destructive V2 rockets

1957 First rocket to lift a spacecraft into Earth's orbit

1981 Shuttle becomes first reusable rocket system

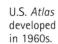

German V2 first tested in 1942.

U.S. *Atlas* developed in 1960s.

Soviet *Soyuz II* launched in 1968.

European *Ariane IV* makes first flight in 1986.

U.S. *Titan* launched *Viking* spacecraft to Mars in 1974.

Reusable U.S. space shuttle makes first flight in 1981.

Saturn V takes U.S. *Apollo II* crew to Moon in 1969.

SEE ALSO
Engine, Spacecraft, Space exploration, Warfare

ROMAN EMPIRE

The Romans ruled the Mediterranean and much of Europe for hundreds of years. Many modern legal and government systems are based on those of Rome.

Julius Caesar (c.100–44 B.C.) was a dictator, taking power from the Senate.

Caligula (A.D. 12–41) ordered many executions and may have been insane.

Hadrian (76–138) ordered the building of defenses along the empire's borders.

Septimus Severus (146–211) reformed the empire into a military state.

The cruelty of Commodus (161–192) plunged the empire into civil war.

Constantine the Great (c.280–337) was the first Christian emperor.

The Roman Empire was built up by the people of Rome from about 250 B.C. and lasted until A.D. 476. The Romans were good at organization and were feared for their powerful army and navy. The empire had one language, one economy, and one government.

THE REPUBLIC
According to legend, Rome was founded in 753 B.C., and in 509 B.C. became a republic. Rome's main rival was Carthage, a city in North Africa, and in 218 B.C. the two went to war. The Carthaginian leader, Hannibal, wiped out the main Roman army at Cannae in 216 B.C., but he could not capture Rome, and Carthage was defeated. By 44 B.C., Rome had conquered Greece and large areas of the Near East, North Africa, Spain, and France.

AGE OF AUGUSTUS
As the Roman Empire grew, patricians, or noblemen, gained vast wealth and the ordinary citizens, or plebeians, lost political power. The army was more loyal to successful commanders than to the government. These tensions led to a series

▲ The territory of the Roman Empire expanded rapidly during wars with Egypt, Carthage, and Greece. After A.D. 117, remote areas, such as Mesopotamia, were abandoned.

of civil wars from 49 B.C. to 30 B.C. The wars were won by Octavian, nephew of the dictator Julius Caesar. He took the title Augustus, meaning "the sacred one," and established a new type of government, giving power to the emperor.

CITIZENS OF ROME
Being a citizen of Rome had many advantages. Citizens could vote, stand in elections, or work in the government. At first only people from Rome were citizens, but gradually men from other cities or who had served in the army for 30 years became citizens. Finally, in A.D. 212, every free man in the empire became a citizen of Rome.

THE ROMAN ARMY

The Roman army was organized into legions of about 6,000 armored infantry, with a few archers and cavalry. In battle, the legion was trained to fight in tight formations, such as the *testudo*, or tortoise (below). The army was skilled at building forts to guard the frontiers. Each legionary had to carry all his equipment, including weapons, cooking pot, blanket, and tools (right).

ROMAN HOUSING

Most Romans lived in the countryside or in apartment blocks (*insulae*), but wealthy families would have a town house, or *domus*. The front rooms were rented out to shopkeepers. The family lived in rooms around the atrium courtyard or the peristyle garden. The *triclinium* (dining room) was close to the kitchen.

Peristyle
Private fountain
Private shrine
Triclinium
Public fountain
Room for entertaining
Atrium
Impluvium
Front door
Shop
Kitchen

BREAD AND CIRCUSES

Most people in the Roman Empire lived in country areas and worked on farms. The cities were centers for business and government. To keep the people entertained, games were held in which gladiators fought each other or wild beasts in the arena. Criminals might be thrown to the lions as a form of execution. Also popular were chariot races held in an oval-shaped arena called a *circus*. Free bread was distributed in Rome to the poorer citizens.

BARBARIAN ONSLAUGHT

After about A.D. 300, plagues and famines reduced the population, and heavy taxation and bad government reduced trade and wealth. In 395, the empire was divided in two, with capitals at Rome and Constantinople. The Eastern Empire became the Byzantine Empire, which had strong Greek influences. After 370, waves of Germanic Goths, Saxons, and Franks invaded and raided the empire. The Roman army kept the invaders under control for a while, but in 410 the Goths captured Rome. In 447, the Huns, under Attila, invaded the empire. Although the Huns were defeated in 453, the power of Rome had been broken. The last Roman emperor, Romulus Augustulus, abdicated in 476 and the empire split into small Germanic kingdoms. The Byzantine Empire survived until conquered by the Turks in 1453.

THE LEGACY OF ROME

The laws of Rome influenced legal codes in many countries, and Latin, the Roman language, developed into French, Italian, and Spanish. It was the discovery of Roman art and architecture that laid the foundations for the Renaissance, and for the modern world.

▲ A gold coin of the later empire. Coins of known value were essential for trade and prosperity.

▲ The ruins of a temple in Ephesus, in modern Turkey, one of the richest cities in the Roman Empire.

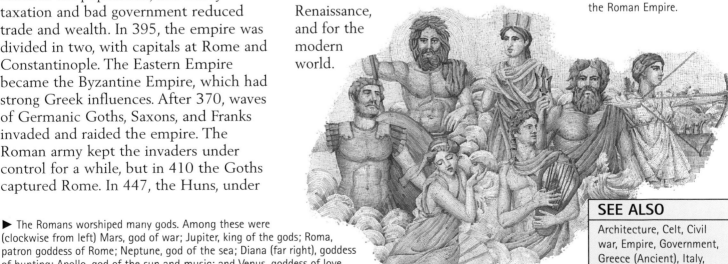

▶ The Romans worshiped many gods. Among these were (clockwise from left) Mars, god of war; Jupiter, king of the gods; Roma, patron goddess of Rome; Neptune, god of the sea; Diana (far right), goddess of hunting; Apollo, god of the sun and music; and Venus, goddess of love.

SEE ALSO

Architecture, Celt, Civil war, Empire, Government, Greece (Ancient), Italy, Revolution, Slavery, Warfare

RUSSIA AND THE BALTIC STATES

The Russian Federation is the largest country in the world. Its western neighbors—Estonia, Latvia, and Lithuania—are known as the Baltic States.

ESTONIA
Area: 17,400 sq. mi.
Population: 1,415,681
Capital: Tallinn
Language: Estonian
Currency: Kroon

LATVIA
Area: 24,900 sq. mi.
Population: 2,366,515
Capital: Riga
Language: Latvian
Currency: Lats

LITHUANIA
Area: 31,200 sq. mi.
Population: 3,601,138
Capital: Vilnius
Language: Lithuanian
Currency: Litas

RUSSIA
Area: 6,592,800 sq. mi.
Population: 144,978,573
Capital: Moscow
Language: Russian
Currency: Rouble

Western Russia is mostly flat and low-lying, and is separated from the east by the Ural Mountains. In the east, Siberia consists of plateaus and ridges, and to the south, the landscape is mountainous. Much of the north is tundra—treeless land where the soil is frozen below the surface. The north is bounded by the world's longest Arctic coastline. Estonia is flat, and almost half of it is farmland; Latvia has low, wooded hills. Lithuania's coast of white sand dunes is popular with tourists.

WINTER AND SUMMER
Most of Russia has long, cold winters, with half the country covered with snow for six months. Summers are mild or warm, but short. In the winter, most northern ports, such as St. Petersburg, are closed by ice. Rivers such as the Volga, Don, and Dnieper are an important part of the transportation system and are joined by major canals.

▲ Russian ballet became internationally famous in the 1800s. The Moscow Academic School of Choreography is one of the training centers for children.

RICH IN RESOURCES
Russia's resources include coal, oil, gas, iron, copper, gold, and platinum. But many of these reserves are in remote areas and their use is hampered by the climate and transportation problems. The railroads radiate out from Moscow and St. Petersburg, around which industry is concentrated. Three fourths of the population lives in towns and cities. Agricultural output ranges from cattle

▶ Riga, on the Western Dvina River, is Latvia's capital city and its main industrial center.

miles
0 500

0 500
km

N

ARCTIC OCEAN

Franz Josef Land

Severnaya
Zemlya

New Siberian
Islands

BERING SEA

Novaya Zemlya

NORWAY

ESTONIA
LATVIA
LITHUANIA
RUSSIA
POLAND
BELARUS

FINLAND

Murmansk

Tallinn

Riga

Vilnius

St. Petersburg

Arkhangel'sk

Kolyma

Indigirka

Lena

SEA OF
OKHOTSK

W. Dvina

Dnieper

Moscow

Nizhniy Novgorod

Kazan

Perm

Ural Mts.

CENTRAL SIBERIAN PLATEAU

Sakhalin

Kuril Islands

UKRAINE

Don

Volga

Samara

Yekaterinburg

Chelyabinsk

Ob

Yenisey

R U S S I A

Rostov-na-Donu

KAZAKHSTAN

Omsk

Novosibirsk

Lake Baikal

Amur

CHINA

Vladivostok

JAPAN

GEORGIA

CASPIAN
SEA

CHINA

MONGOLIA

AZERBAIJAN

and cotton to barley, corn, sunflower seeds, tobacco, wine, and reindeer. The main exports of the Baltic States are foods, chemicals, and manufactured goods.

PEOPLE AND RELIGION

Russians account for 87.5 percent of the population of Russia. Important minorities include Tatars, Ukrainians, and Germans. There are 130 different nationalities in all. Despite over half a century of campaigns by communist governments against religion, many people are strongly loyal to the Russian Orthodox Church. In the Baltic States, most people belong to either the Lutheran, Roman Catholic, or Russian Orthodox Church. Average levels of education are high, although researchers, especially in technology and medicine, have been held back by shortages of funds.

RUSSIA'S EXPANSION

The Russian state emerged from the Rus civilization in the A.D. 800s. Its rulers took the title of czar. Peter the Great, czar from 1682 to 1725, introduced Western European culture and technology and founded a new capital, St. Petersburg. By conquering Estonia and Latvia, he began a program of expansion that his successors extended to Lithuania, Belarus, the Ukraine, and the Crimea. Russian settlement of Siberia began in the 1700s, and in the 1800s Finland, the Caucasus, and Central Asia were added to the Russian Empire. ▶

▼ Lake Baikal in Siberia is the world's deepest lake—5,712 ft. (1,731m).

▲ Like Latvia and Lithuania, Estonia became independent in 1991. It had been taken into the Soviet Union in 1940.

▲ Boris Yeltsin (above) became president after Mikhail Gorbachev resigned in 1991. Yeltsin retired in 1991, and Vladimir Putin took over the presidency.

▲ Long, harsh winters are an accepted part of life in Siberia. Local people use sleds to carry shopping.

EARLY 20TH-CENTURY RUSSIA

Russia was held back by its very size and a lack of resources. Poverty increased as the population grew within overcrowded settlements. Russian achievements, nevertheless, included the development of modern ballet, the music of Tchaikovsky, and the writings of Tolstoy and Chekhov.

RUSSIAN REVOLUTION

Revolution finally came in 1917, in two stages. Alexander Kerensky—a moderate —was brought to power, then overthrown by the Bolsheviks, led by Vladimir Ilyich Ulyanov (Lenin). Lenin ruthlessly led the Bolsheviks to victory and, in 1922, established the communist-run Union of Soviet Socialist Republics (U.S.S.R.), or Soviet Union. This covered almost all of the former Russian Empire, except Finland and the Baltic States.

SOVIET CONTROL

After Lenin's death in 1924, Joseph Stalin ruled as a brutal dictator. He took the peasants' land to create government-run farms, and built up heavy industry, dams, railroads, and an electric power system. After World War II, the U.S.S.R. gained control over much

▶ The Kremlin, in Moscow's Red Square, was originally a fortress. Under communist rule, it became the government headquarters.

of Eastern Europe, either by forcing countries to become Soviet republics or by controlling their governments. After Stalin's death in 1953, Soviet life was dominated by the Cold War between the Soviet-led communist countries and the U.S.-led Western democracies.

TOWARD DEMOCRACY

Mikhail Gorbachev became Soviet leader in 1985 and introduced political reforms. He encouraged other Eastern European countries to do the same, and many of these abandoned communism. The Soviet Union broke up at the end of 1991, and countries including the Baltic States became independent. Gorbachev gave way to Boris Yeltsin. He was the first Russian leader to be democratically elected.

SEE ALSO

Asia, Astronaut, Cold War, Communism, Eastern Europe, Europe, Revolution

348

SATELLITE

Satellites are objects that move in orbit around other objects of greater mass. A satellite may be natural, like the Moon, or artificial, like an orbiting spacecraft.

Spacecraft orbiting high above the Earth can be used to relay messages over very long distances. Some satellites are used to send television signals around the world or to track the movement of hurricanes and large weather fronts. Communication satellites are used to pass on telephone conversations and computer data. These satellites receive signals from a transmitting station on Earth, amplify them, and beam the signals down to another Earth station, which may be thousands of miles away.

▲ *Sputnik 1*, the world's first artificial satellite, was launched by Russia on October 4, 1957. It was used to broadcast scientific data and orbited the Earth for six months.

▼ Satellites can sometimes give us a clearer picture of activity on the Earth's surface than we can get from the ground. The Earth is surrounded by craft designed specifically for different purposes.

GEOSYNCHRONOUS ORBIT
Most communication satellites move in a special orbit known as a geosynchronous orbit, which is about 24,550 mi. (35,900km) above the equator. This orbit allows the satellite to remain over the same point on the Earth's surface at all times.

ASTRONOMICAL SATELLITES
By carrying telescopes and other instruments above the Earth's atmosphere, astronomical satellites can see distant objects, such as stars, nebulae, and galaxies, much more clearly than we can from the ground. They can also pick up types of waves, such as infrared, ultraviolet, X rays, and gamma rays, which are partly or totally blocked by the atmosphere. For example, X-ray satellites have helped scientists to study black holes and dense, remote binary (double) stars.

SURVEYING THE EARTH
Remote-sensing satellites, equipped with powerful cameras and other equipment, provide valuable information about our planet's natural resources. They can reveal changes to the polar ice caps or the rate at which human beings are destroying the rain forests. Weather satellites can track the movement of hurricanes and supply data that allows accurate weather forecasts several days in advance.

Landsat 4 can spot areas where the Brazilian rain forest has been cleared

The European Remote Sensing satellite (ERS) helps to predict earthquakes by using radar to detect changes in fault lines

Spy satellites use powerful telescopes to detect potential trouble spots

The space shuttle carries sensing equipment that can detect volcanoes erupting

The Meteostat Second Generation (MSG) satellite stays in geostationary orbit above the Atlantic to track weather fronts such as hurricanes and cyclones

SEE ALSO
Communication, Telecommunication, Telephone, Television, Weather

SCANDINAVIA

Scandinavia consists of the neighboring northern European countries of Denmark, Norway, Sweden, Finland, Iceland, and the Faeroe Islands.

DENMARK
Area: 16,576 sq. mi.
Population: 5,368,854
Capital: Copenhagen
Language: Danish
Currency: Krone

FINLAND
Area: 117,900 sq. mi.
Population: 5,183,545
Capital: Helsinki
Languages: Finnish, Swedish
Currency: Euro

ICELAND
Area: 39,709 sq. mi.
Population: 279,834
Capital: Reykjavik
Language: Icelandic
Currency: Krona

NORWAY
Area: 118,900 sq. mi.
Population: 4,525,116
Capital: Oslo
Language: Norwegian
Currency: Kroner

SWEDEN
Area: 173,349 sq. mi.
Population: 8,876,744
Capital: Stockholm
Language: Swedish
Currency: Krona

► Stockholm, capital of Sweden, is built on 14 small islands connected by about 50 bridges.

The name Scandinavia refers to the large peninsula made up of Sweden and Norway. Often included in this term are the neighboring countries of Denmark and Finland, as well as Iceland and the Faeroe Islands, which have cultural and language links with the region. Danish, Swedish, Norwegian, and Icelandic all come from a common ancestor language, but Finnish is distinctly different.

THE FAEROE ISLANDS
These islands in the North Atlantic Ocean, of which 18 are inhabited, have a population of over 43,000. They were ruled by Norway until 1380, and many of the inhabitants are of Norse origin. For the last 600 years, they have been under Danish control. In 1948, they became self-governing. The representatives of their *Lagting* (assembly or parliament) sit in the Danish assembly in Copenhagen.

LONG SUMMER DAYS
Due to their northerly location, the countries of Scandinavia have long, cold, snowy winters. In Iceland and the northernmost parts of Finland, Norway, and Sweden around the Arctic Circle, it is light for 24 hours a day around midsummer and dark for most of the day toward the end of December.

RICH IN RESOURCES
Flat Denmark is famous for its agriculture, Finland for its lakes, Sweden for its forests, Norway for its spectacular coastal fjords (inlets), and Iceland for its dramatic geysers (hot springs) and volcanoes. The region is rich in natural resources, including oil, gas, iron, and timber. Since oil was discovered in the North Sea in the 1960s, Norway has become self-sufficient in natural gas and oil, and expert at oil rig construction. Sweden is the most industrial of the Scandinavian nations and is one of the

▲ Norway's coast is famous for its many fjords—long, narrow inlets of the sea that make fine natural harbors.

wealthiest countries in Europe. Fishing and shipbuilding have been important industries for the whole region. Modern Scandinavian styles of architecture and design, especially of furniture, metalwork, and glassware, are influential worldwide.

NORTHERN PEOPLE

Most Scandinavians are descendants of Germanic people who moved into the area around 2,000 years ago, while most Finns migrated around the same time from western Russia. North of the Arctic Circle are the Sami—descendants of the earliest inhabitants of Sweden and Finland. Today, a small number of Sami live a traditional way of life herding reindeer, which they keep for their meat, milk, and hides. But most earn a living from farming, fishing, or mining. Since 1993, the Sami have had their own council called the *Sameting*.

▼ In Denmark, surrounded as it is by sea, both fishing and shipbuilding are important. Danish fishing fleets bring in mackerel, herring, cod, shrimp, and flatfish.

SCANDINAVIAN POLICIES

Norway, Denmark, and Sweden are all constitutional monarchies, but Finland and Iceland are republics. The Scandinavian countries have traditionally been strong supporters of international organizations, human rights, health and welfare programs, and conservation. Many of these efforts are coordinated by the Nordic Council, founded in 1953.

NORSE MYTHOLOGY

In pre-Christian times, early Scandinavian and Germanic people shared a common mythology, known as Norse mythology. The myths, originally passed on by word of mouth, were first written down in the 1200s. Four of the early Norse gods—Tiw, Odin, Thor, and Freya—are remembered in the days of the week: Tuesday, Wednesday, Thursday, and Friday. Today, Lutheran Protestant Christianity is the main religion in all Scandinavian countries.

▲ Found in arctic regions, reindeer migrate several hundred miles a year in search of food.

SEE ALSO

Arctic, Europe, Myth and legend, Viking

SCULPTURE

Sculpture is a piece of three-dimensional art that gives you different views as you walk around it. It can be carved, molded, or shaped out of a range of materials.

▲ Rachel Whiteread's award-winning *House* (1995) used a house in East London as a mold.

The two traditional ways of making a sculpture are carving and molding. Carving means cutting into wood or stone; molding involves making a model in clay and using it to cast a replica in concrete or a metal. Sculpture can also be carved in relief, by cutting a raised picture into flat stone or wood. Modern sculptures have been made from plastic, glass, and everyday objects—one British artist, David Mach, uses papers and magazines.

GODS AND IDOLS
Since people began using tools, they have made figures of people and animals, or religious idols to please their gods and scare away evil spirits. Tiny figures made by shamans (magician-priests) about 30,000 years ago are among the earliest known sculptures. The Ancient Egyptians cut huge figures out of solid rock, and there are other massive ancient sculptures in the Americas and Asia. Tribal totem poles are a form of sculpture. The Ancient Greeks created impressive lifelike figures.

CHANGING IMAGES
In the Middle Ages, European sculpture was mostly religious—the architectural decoration in and on church buildings. During the Renaissance, artists returned to the realism of the classical Greeks. Their works were for religious and private patrons who paid for marble and bronze sculptures.

BREAK WITH TRADITION
In the 1900s, sculptors began to explore new styles, using solid shapes to represent abstract ideas and feelings. This included using ordinary objects in unusual ways, like assembling moving pieces or mobiles—known as installation art. American artist Christo wrapped buildings in plastic, which linked art and architecture in a new way.

▲ Michelangelo's bold and lifelike marble statue of *David* (1504) followed the classical Greek style.

▲ American sculptor Andy Goldsworthy's *Slits Cut Into Frozen Snow* (1988), a form of land art, shows that art isn't confined to museums.

▶ Hundreds of years ago, Easter Islanders carved more than 600 huge stone statues, known as *moai*, using handpicks.

SEE ALSO
Art, Renaissance

SEASHORE

There are many types of seashore, from rocky cliffs to sandy beaches. Each habitat has its own creatures and plant life, specially adapted to live there.

Tidal pools contain plants and small marine animals.

Rocky cliffs are a favorite nesting place for kittiwakes.

Many salt-resistant grasses thrive on sand dunes.

The seashore, the narrow zone where land and sea meet, is one of the most varied and fascinating habitats on Earth. It contains creatures that have evolved to live half their lives on land and half at sea.

BEACHES
The most common type of shore is the sandy beach, made of tiny particles of rock (sand) worn down by being constantly rolled together by waves. Plants can't grow in the loose sand between high- and low-water marks, but just below the surface, sandworms and burrowing shellfish feed on tiny food particles washed in with the tide. Sandy and muddy shores are favorite feeding places for shorebirds.

CLIFFS
Where waves hammer against hard rocks, a steep cliff may form. Here, the tiny ledges and cracks are home to specialized plants that can survive the salt spray and cold winter winds. Cliff ledges also provide nesting places for many seabirds such as gulls, guillemots, and gannets, and puffins live in burrows in the soil on the cliff top.

ROCKY SHORES
Rocky coasts are home to a huge variety of red, brown, and green seaweeds, some like long leather belts, some like mosses. The seaweed fronds provide a cool, damp hiding place for sand hoppers (beach fleas), crabs, barnacles, winkles, and limpets. Rock pools provide another place in which sea creatures can survive while the tide is out. Some mollusks, such as mussels and limpets, attach themselves to rocks.

SANDY SEASHORES
A vast array of birds, plants, mollusks, and crustaceans live around the world's seashores. Crashing waves constantly change the shape of sandy beaches, so all forms of life must be adaptable—most shore plants and animals are able to live in and out of water. Shorebirds feed on worms, fish, and other small creatures.

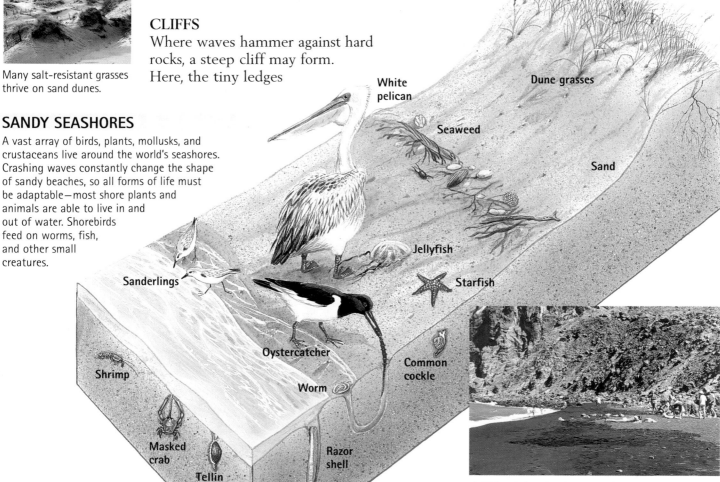

White pelican

Dune grasses

Seaweed

Sand

Jellyfish

Starfish

Sanderlings

Oystercatcher

Common cockle

Worm

Shrimp

Masked crab

Tellin

Razor shell

▲ Volcanic beaches have black sand. An example is the Playa Anglais, Canary Islands.

SEE ALSO

Bird, Crab, Fish, Jellyfish, Ocean and sea, Snail, Starfish, Volcano, Worm

SEASON

As the Earth orbits the Sun, the tilt of its axis causes changes in the length of day and the temperature. This creates what we call the seasons.

MARCH 21
Spring begins in the Northern Hemisphere, autumn in the Southern Hemisphere. Days and nights are of equal length.

DECEMBER 21
Winter begins in the Northern Hemisphere, summer begins in the Southern Hemisphere.

JUNE 21
Summer begins in the Northern Hemisphere, winter begins in the Southern Hemisphere.

SEPTEMBER 23
Autumn begins in the Northern Hemisphere, spring begins in the Southern Hemisphere. Days and nights are of equal length again.

▲ December in Alberta, Canada, brings the typically snowy and cold weather of a Northern Hemisphere winter.

The seasons affect everything we do. They determine when we plant our crops and harvest them, what kind of clothes we wear, what we eat, how much energy we use for heating and lighting, and even how we feel. The seasons are caused by the tilt of the Earth's axis during its yearly journey around the Sun.

THE EARTH'S TILT
The Earth is always spinning, tilted at an angle of 23.5°, so that the North Pole tilts toward the Sun for part of the year. In the Northern Hemisphere, the Sun is high in the sky and the days are long and warm, resulting in summer. At the same time, the South Pole is tilted away from the Sun, and the Southern Hemisphere has its winter.

THE SOLSTICES
As the Earth orbits the Sun, its axis points toward the same spot in space, so that six months later, the North Pole tilts away from the Sun. It is now winter in the Northern Hemisphere and summer in the Southern Hemisphere. In the Northern Hemisphere, the longest day (the summer solstice) is June 21 and the shortest day (the winter solstice) is December 21. For the Southern Hemisphere, the longest day of the year is December 21 and the shortest day is June 21.

THE EQUINOXES
Halfway between the solstices are the autumn and spring equinoxes. On March 21 and September 23, the tilted Earth is sideways-on to the Sun, and day and night are of equal length. Spring in the Northern Hemisphere begins on March 21, when the Southern Hemisphere has autumn. On September 23, the Northern Hemisphere's autumn begins, and it is spring south of the equator.

▲ Southern Hemisphere areas like Green Island Beach, Australia, enjoy the beginning of their summer season in December.

SEE ALSO
Climate, Earth, Hibernation, Sun, Weather, Wind

SEED AND POLLINATION

Seeds are the means by which flowering plants reproduce to make other plants of the same species. But pollination must take place before a seed is formed.

Stone fruits (drupes) such as the peach have a large stone that contains a seed.

The coconut is a very large seed, with edible flesh and milk inside its tough husk.

The acorn is the fruit of the oak tree. Its woody cup holds a hard, smooth nut.

Maple seeds have papery wings that help them scatter on the wind.

An apple has several seeds in its core, to increase its chances of reproduction.

A seed consists of a tiny new plant, called an embryo, and a store of food, all contained within a tough protective coat. Some seeds can remain dormant (in a resting state) for over 100 years before they grow into new plants. To make a seed, pollen (male cells) from one plant must fertilize, or pollinate, the eggs (female cells) of another plant.

POLLINATION

Some plants, like grasses and trees, rely on the wind to blow their pollen from one plant to the next. Other plants have large flowers, with bright colors, scents, and nectar, to attract insects, bats, birds, or small animals. These visitors feed on the nectar, and as they do so, the pollen sticks to them and is carried to the next flower they visit. When a pollen grain sticks to another flower's stigma, it sends out a pollen tube that grows down inside the stalk leading to the ovary, so male cells can reach the egg and fertilize it. Once the egg has been fertilized, it develops into a seed.

GERMINATION

A seed must have moisture, warmth, and oxygen to grow into a new plant. This process, called germination, begins with the seed absorbing water. The embryo begins to grow, and its root pushes its way through the seed coat. The seed leaves, or cotyledons, and the shoot soon follow.

SEEDS AS FOOD

When a seed falls to the ground, its starchy food store feeds the young plant, and it is this starch that people use as food. The seeds of wheat, barley, corn, rice, and other members of the grass family are cooked to make basic foods, or ground into flour to make bread and pasta.

SEED DISPERSAL

Plants scatter, or disperse, seeds using many methods. Mice and other small animals eat grass seeds (grain) and berries, and spiky burrs from plants such as thistles stick to their fur. Later, mouse droppings move seeds to a different area, and burrs drop off along the way. Dandelion seeds have soft, feathery tufts, and poppies have tiny, light seeds, which make it easy for them to become windborne.

▶ A wheat grain is a seed made up of starch (used to make flour), covered with a shell (bran).

Bran
Starch
Husk
Embryo

▲ When a windborne seed falls to the ground, its food store gives it the nutrients it needs to take root.

▲ The soil provides additional nutrients so that the plant can push above ground level and grow to full size.

SEE ALSO

Crop, Flower, Fruit, Plant, Tree, Vegetable

SEVEN WONDERS OF THE WORLD

The Seven Wonders of the World were the most impressive and famous buildings and monuments known to the Ancient Greeks.

In about 146 B.C., the Greek architect Philo of Byzantium produced a list of the finest engineering feats of the known world. Of these, only the Great Pyramid, the ruins of the Temple of Artemis, the Mausoleum, and the Pharos remain.

IN MEMORY

The greatest of the Egyptian pyramids were built at Giza as tombs for the pharaohs Cheops (Khufu), Chephren (Khafre), and Mycerinus (Menkure) between 2600 B.C. and 2500 B.C.

The Mausoleum was built as the tomb of King Mausolus of Caria in 353 B.C. by his widow, Artemisia, in the city of Halicarnassus in Egypt. The tomb was so stunningly beautiful that even today, elaborate tombs are called mausoleums. The Hanging Gardens of Babylon were built in about 580 B.C. by King Nebuchadrezzar II of Babylon to remind his wife, a princess from the mountain kingdom of Media, of home.

BUILT FOR THE GODS

The Temple at Ephesus, Turkey, was built in 350 B.C. by the Greek architects Scopas and Apelles. It had over 100 columns, each 65 ft. (20m) tall and decorated with sculptures. It was dedicated to Artemis, goddess of nature. The statue of Zeus at Olympia, home of the Olympic Games, was made in 433 B.C. by Phidias of Athens. The wooden statue, covered in ivory and gold, stood 43 ft. (13m) tall. The Colossus of Rhodes was a 108 ft. (33m)-tall bronze statue of the sun god Helios, erected by the city of Rhodes after invaders were defeated in 305 B.C. It fell in an earthquake in 224 B.C. and was sold for scrap in A.D. 653.

THE FIRST LIGHTHOUSE

The approach to the harbor of Alexandria in Egypt was extremely dangerous. To help ships arrive safely, the great Pharos was built in about 280 B.C. The tower stood over 384 ft. (117m) tall and was topped by a statue of a god, thought to be Zeus Soter. The tower could be seen from far out to sea and led ships into harbor. At night, it is said, a fire was lit to guide ships. The tower gradually crumbled into ruins after 1,500 years.

The pyramids of Egypt at Giza.

The Colossus on the island of Rhodes.

The Mausoleum of Halicarnassus.

The statue of Zeus at Olympia.

The Hanging Gardens of Babylon.

The Temple of Artemis at Ephesus.

SEE ALSO

Babylon, Egypt (Ancient), Greece (Ancient)

SHARK

Sharks are fish whose skeletons are made of gristly cartilage instead of bone. Almost all of them live in the sea and they feed mainly on other fish.

The aggressive tiger shark can grow to over 16 ft. (5m) long and has been known to attack human beings.

The hammerhead shark can grow up to 20 ft. (6m) long and has a flattened head like the head of a hammer.

The basking shark can grow to over 33 ft. (10m) long and swims close to the surface to feed on plankton.

The fast and powerful mako shark grows up to 11.5 ft. (3.5m) long and is a popular catch for sea fishermen.

The thresher shark grows to about 20 ft. (6m) long and uses its long tail to stun the fish it feeds on.

The harmless whale shark grows up to 40 ft. (12m) long but feeds only on plankton and small fish.

There are about 370 kinds of shark, from the little dogfish, less than 19 in. (0.5m) long, to the huge whale shark, which is 40 ft. (12m) long and weighs 14 tons. Most sharks are fast swimmers, with streamlined bodies. Their fins are thick and leathery, and cannot be folded like those of other fish.

GILL SLITS FOR BREATHING
A shark has five to seven gill slits just behind the head on each side. Water taken in through the mouth flows out through these slits after passing over the gills, where life-giving oxygen is taken from it. Most sharks must keep swimming to keep this oxygen flow going.

SKIN LIKE SANDPAPER
The skin of a shark is covered with denticles—toothlike scales that make it very rough. In fact, sailors once used shark skins as sandpaper to scrub the decks of their wooden ships. A shark's teeth have

serrated, razor-sharp edges and can easily slice through flesh. Its digestive juices are strong enough to corrode steel.

THE LARGEST FISH
Although most sharks are ferocious hunters, the largest ones are actually harmless. The whale shark is the largest fish in the world. It has a huge mouth, but it feeds by straining tiny animals and plants from the water, just as many whales do.

SKATES AND RAYS
Skates and rays are closely related to sharks, but their bodies are very flat. Their head and body and massive front fins are all fused together to form a circular or diamond-shaped disk. They live mainly on the seabed and feed on shellfish and other bottom-dwelling animals, which they crush with rows of flat teeth. Some of them are armed with poisonous spines.

Sense pores on the nose can detect the electrical signals given off by the twitching muscles of the shark's prey

THE GREAT WHITE
Up to 26 ft. (8m) long, the great white is the most dangerous of all sharks. It preys on large animals such as dolphins, sea lions, and other sharks. It will also attack human beings and even fishing boats.

The skin consists of tiny, toothlike scales and is used to make rough shark leather

Gill slits open and close to take in oxygen from the water

Razorlike teeth are continuously replaced by new ones. During its lifetime, a shark will get through thousands of teeth

SEE ALSO
Fish, Ocean and sea, Whale and dolphin

SHIP

Ships are craft that weigh more than 1,000 tons. They are used to carry passengers and freight or to catch fish. They may also be used in warfare.

▲ Tankers transport liquids, usually oil, in bulk. The liquid is stored in tanks, and empty chambers give added buoyancy. The engines and crew quarters are usually placed at the rear.

Viking longships of A.D. 900 had open decks and were powered by sails and oars.

Galleons during the 1500s had high sides on which to mount guns.

Clippers of the 1800s had streamlined hulls for extra speed.

The *Great Eastern* of 1855 combined steam and sail power and was the first liner.

Large wooden ships were first made in the countries around the Mediterranean Sea and in the Far East about 300 B.C. These ships were powered by sails or oars and were up to 165 ft. (50m) in length. Later wooden ships, with tall masts and several sails, reached 380 ft. (115m).

IRON AND STEAM

Modern ships were made possible by two important developments. The first was the use of iron or steel construction, which is strong enough for very large ships. The second was the steam engine, which made ships independent of the direction in which the wind was blowing. The only practical limit to the size of a steel ship is the depth of coastal waters and the size of docks. The largest ships now afloat are the supertankers. These sail between oil fields and refineries in Europe, America, and Japan. Supertankers are far bigger than any liner or warship, weighing up to one million tons when fully loaded and measuring over 1,300 ft. (400m) long.

CARGO CARRIERS

Modern cargo ships include bulk carriers and container ships. The bulk carrier transports large, solid cargoes such as coal or iron ore, using special equipment to load and unload. The container ship carries pre-loaded containers, each small enough to be loaded onto a truck. A very large ship may carry several thousand containers. These big merchant ships have an "island" at the back (the stern) containing the bridge, the crew quarters, and the engine room. They also have a long center deck above the cargo holds, and a further small island close to the front (the bow).

PASSENGER SHIPS

Luxurious passenger ships called liners were used to carry passengers between continents, but today, large passenger-carrying ships are used for cruising. They take people on vacation, allowing them to visit different ports while enjoying a luxurious life on board. Another passenger ship is the ferry, used for carrying people and vehicles on short sea crossings. Ferries are designed to load and unload their passengers quickly, usually through huge doors at the bow and stern. A modern cruise liner may weigh 80,000 tons, and some ferries weigh over 20,000 tons.

WARSHIPS

As trade by sea became more important and nations competed for dominance, they began to develop navies of fighting ships. Warships now include destroyers, cruisers, and submarines, armed with guns, missiles, and torpedoes. The largest warships are aircraft carriers, which can weigh 80,000 tons or more. They act as offshore air bases from which air strikes on enemy targets can be made.

ENGINES AND STEERING
Most modern ships are driven by one or two propellers, powered by large diesel engines or by gas turbines, although some warships use nuclear power. The diesel engine is cheaper and more reliable, and the gas turbine is small and light. A rudder is used for steering, but small propellers, or thrusters, are used to control the ship when it is maneuvering.

SKIMMING THE SURFACE
A ship uses most of its energy pushing the water aside, so some modern craft skim above the water. Hydrofoils are supported by "wings" under the water, and hovercraft float on a cushion of air. Both are fast, but cannot be built too large.

Air strikes against enemy fleets are launched from aircraft carriers.

Cruise ships are luxurious floating hotels that carry thousands of passengers.

Missiles and torpedoes are launched from submarines beneath the sea surface.

▲ A multipurpose cargo ship carrying containers, tanks, and crates. Lifting equipment along the center of the ship is used to load and unload the cargo.

FACTORY FISHING
Factory ships catch large numbers of fish and waste almost nothing. The net is hauled in, spilling the catch into the fish bin where it is sorted before passing to the cleaning room where heads and guts are removed. The waste is processed into fish meal, while the clean fillets are packed and frozen. The frozen fish is stored in the refrigerated hold until the ship reaches port. The entire operation is controlled from the bridge, where sonar and other electronic aids help the captain, or skipper, find giant shoals of fish.

Net

Fish bin

Cleaning room

Net winch arms

Radar and radio antennae

Bridge

Net roll

Anchor

Refrigerated hold

Packing and freezing unit

Fish meal storage

Fish meal processor

Engines

Propeller

Rudder

SEE ALSO
Boat, Explorer, Fishing industry, Hovercraft, Navigation, Warfare

SIGHT

Sight is the ability to detect light and form it into an accurate view of the shapes, colors, and distances of surrounding objects.

Insect compound eyes have a mosaic of cells which build up an image.

Flatworms have cupped organs able to detect the direction of a light source.

Sight is the most important sense for most animals, providing over half of all the information that enters the brain. Animals use their eyes to look for food and mates and to watch for danger. Most invertebrates (creatures without backbones) have simple eyes, able to give only a rough picture of their surroundings.

ADVANCED VISION

Animals with backbones (vertebrates) have eyes that are able to see clearly. At the front of the eye is a transparent area, known as the cornea, through which light enters. Behind the cornea is a colored ring of muscle, the iris, with a central hole, the pupil. The iris changes shape to make the pupil wider in dim light, so that more light enters the eye, for clearer vision. Behind the pupil is the lens, which focuses light rays. A ring of ciliary muscles changes the shape of the lens to adjust the focus.

▲ A cat's eyes stand out in poor light (left). They have an extra layer, the guanine, which reflects light back past the retina. The guanine allows cats to see clearly in poor light (right), although they cannot distinguish colors.

LIGHT TO NERVE SIGNALS

Light rays focused by the lens shine onto the retina. This contains millions of light-sensitive cells, known as rods and cones. They send nerve signals to the brain, which forms them into a picture. The rods are sensitive in dim light, and detect movement and the contrast between black and white. The cones, which are clustered in one small area, see color. Only humans and a few other types of animal can see in full color.

TWO EYES

Most animals have two eyes, which help to judge distance in two ways. Each eye sees an object from a slightly different point. The brain compares these two views, and the more different they are, the nearer the object. Also, when looking at closer objects, the eyes swivel inward, and the brain can measure the distance of the object from the amount of swivel.

THE HUMAN EYE

The human eyeball, about 1 in. (25mm) across, is set into a bowl-shaped socket in the skull. Six small muscles move the eye up, down, and sideways. The eye's whitish outer layer, the sclera, is strong and tough. Inside is the choroid layer, soft and blood-rich, which nourishes the inner parts of the eye. The main bulk of the eyeball is filled with clear jelly, or vitreous humor, which keeps it firm.

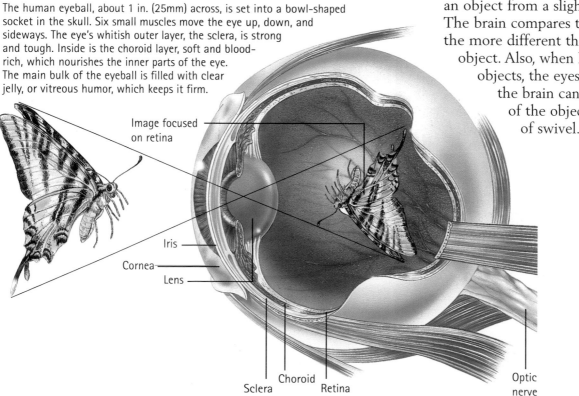

Image focused on retina

Iris

Cornea

Lens

Sclera

Choroid

Retina

Optic nerve

▲ Nerve cells on the retina react to light. They send signals along the optic nerve to the brain.

SEE ALSO
Brain, Cat, Eagle, Human body, Insect, Lens, Light, Wavelength

SILVER

Silver is a white-colored precious metal. It is best known for its use in jewelry, coins, and silverware, but it is also used in electronics and photography.

Silver on calcite.

Silver ore.

Silver wiry form.

In addition to its beauty, silver has important properties that make it unique. One of the most important is its conductivity: it allows heat and electric current to pass through it (conduct) more easily than any other metal.

MINING SILVER
The amount of silver in the Earth is tiny, but it occurs in many types of rock. Some rocks contain pure silver metal. Others combine silver with other chemical elements in silver ores. Silver is separated from these ores (smelted) using heat and electricity. Like gold, silver is a by-product of copper and lead mines. Mexico leads in the world's production, followed by the United States and then Peru.

SILVER JEWELRY AND COINS
Silver jewelry has been made for at least 6,000 years, even before the smelting of metals began. Most modern silver jewelry is made of an alloy (mixture) of 80 percent silver and 20 percent copper.

◄ Silver is often used with turquoise in Native American jewelry such as necklaces.

This ewer from the ▼ 1600s is an example of Spanish silver tableware.

▼ Pegasus features on this ancient silver coin from Corinth, c.350 B.C.

Like gold, silver is used as a form of money. Coins have been made out of silver for at least 2,800 years. For much of that time, large quantities of silver have been held in reserve by governments as a sign of their wealth. Today, however, silver has other more important uses.

OTHER USES OF SILVER
Around 40 percent of the world's silver production is used in photography. Compounds of silver, called silver halides, are used to make photographic film. Silver is also used in modern electronic circuit boards and in some surgical equipment. Most mirrors are made by coating glass with a thin layer of silver.

SILVER ELECTROPLATING
In electroplating, a metal object is coated with a plate (thin layer) of another metal, such as silver or gold, using an electric current. The pitcher is immersed in a water and silver solution. One wire is connected to a strip of silver, and another is connected to the pitcher. The wires are both connected to a power source. When the current is switched on, electrolysis occurs: silver moves from the solution to coat the pitcher with a smooth layer.

Pitcher made of base metal

Electric power pack with negative and positive currents

Pitcher is completely immersed

Bath containing solution of water and silver salts

Silver particles stick to pitcher via electric current

Silver strip

Finished silver-plated pitcher

SEE ALSO
Electronics, Metal, Mineral and gem, Mining, Money

SINGAPORE

Singapore is a small island nation in Southeast Asia. It lies at the southern tip of the Malay Peninsula, to which it is connected by a causeway.

SINGAPORE
Area: 241 sq. mi.
Population: 4,452,732
Capital: Singapore City
Languages: English, Malay, Chinese, Tamil
Currency: Singapore dollar

▲ Traditional life mixes with modern—Chinese rickshaws ferry passengers along Singapore's main highways.

The Republic of Singapore consists of over 50 islands, of which the largest is linked to Malaysia by road across the Johor Strait. It is a flat country with a warm, wet, tropical climate. Only about five percent of the island is still wooded—the natural rain forest has been cleared to make space for homes, offices, and parks.

PROSPERITY

Singaporeans enjoy one of the highest living standards in Asia. Lacking raw materials of its own, Singapore has prospered from the skills of its well-educated, hardworking people. Although 78 percent of the population is Chinese, 14 percent Malay, and most of the rest from India, English is the main language of government, business, and education. Singapore is one of Asia's leading international financial centers. Other main industries include electronics, building and repairing ships, refining oil, fishing, and tourism.

NEW COUNTRY, NEW NATION

Singapore supported small farmers and fishermen until Sir Stamford Raffles, a British trader, saw the advantages of its natural harbor and location on major trade routes, and made it a British possession in 1819. Under British rule, the population grew, gaining many Chinese and Indians, who came as traders and laborers. The port handled products like rubber, tin, and timber from Malaya. British rule ended in 1959, and Singapore became part of the Federation of Malaysia (1963–65). Since then, it has been an independent republic.

MALAYSIA

Johor Strait

SINGAPORE
Choa Chu Kang
Nee Soon
Bukit Panjang
Serangoon
Ubin I.
Pulau Tekong I.
Changi
Paya Lebar
Tuas
Jurong
Singapore City
Bedok
Strait of Singapore
N
Sentosa I.

miles
0   5
0   5
km

▼ The city of Singapore developed around its harbor. It is one of the largest and busiest ports in the world, used by over 500 shipping lines.

SEE ALSO

Asia, Southeast Asia

SKELETON

The strong framework of more than 200 bones called the skeleton gives the body shape, support, and protection, and allows it to move.

A bird's skeleton is very light in weight, making flight easier.

Large mammals such as cows need strong bones to carry their body weight.

Fish have spiny bones to support fins and flexible backbones for swimming.

The body's firmness, shape, and strength are due to its skeleton. The skeleton has two main parts. The skull, backbone, and ribs form the central, or axial, skeleton and the arms and legs make up the appendicular skeleton. This system of 206 tough, rigid parts, called bones, forms the body's internal framework and protects delicate organs such as the brain, heart, and lungs. Bones are linked to each other at joints and are anchored to muscles, which pull on them to move the body.

BONE STRENGTH

Each bone's size, shape, and strength depend on how it supports its part of the body and its muscle attachments. Bones are stiff because they contain crystals of minerals such as calcium and phosphate. But they are also slightly flexible, because they contain fibers of the body protein collagen, so that they bend slightly under stress, rather than crack.

INSIDE A BONE

Bones are pale yellow and have their own blood vessels and nerves. Bones are a combination of living cells and minerals. Bone cells, called osteocytes, produce tiny rodlike structures of bone minerals, called osteons (Haversian systems). Most bones have a strong outer layer of compact bone, with the osteons packed together. Inside this is a layer of spongy, or cancellous, bone.

BONE MARROW

In the middle of some bones is jellylike marrow. This makes new cells for the blood, producing millions every second. All of a baby's bones contain marrow, but by adulthood, marrow is found mainly in the sternum, backbone, ribs, and skull.

THE HUMAN SKELETON

The skull consists of 8 bones joined together; the face has 14 bones. Inside each ear are 3 of the body's tiniest bones called ossicles. The backbone has 26 bones called vertebrae; 12 pairs of ribs join the sternum at the front of the chest. Each shoulder and arm has 32 bones, including 8 carpals in the wrist. Each hip and leg has 31 bones, including 7 tarsal bones in the ankle.

Head

Spongy bone

Shaft

Compact bone

◀ About one third of bone is living tissue. The rest consists of minerals like calcium and phosphate, which produce a hard, yet slightly elastic, material.

Haversian canals (ringed by bone cells)

Marrow

▲ Human thighbone.

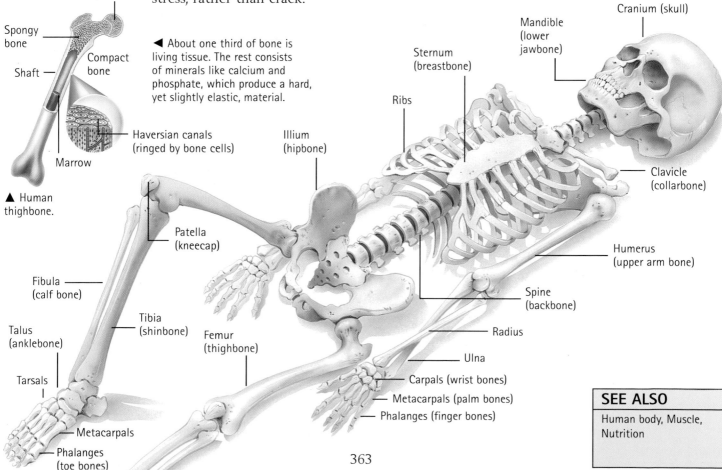

Mandible (lower jawbone)

Cranium (skull)

Sternum (breastbone)

Ribs

Illium (hipbone)

Clavicle (collarbone)

Patella (kneecap)

Humerus (upper arm bone)

Fibula (calf bone)

Spine (backbone)

Tibia (shinbone)

Talus (anklebone)

Femur (thighbone)

Radius

Tarsals

Ulna

Carpals (wrist bones)

Metacarpals (palm bones)

Phalanges (finger bones)

Metacarpals

Phalanges (toe bones)

SEE ALSO

Human body, Muscle, Nutrition

SKIN AND HAIR

Skin protects our delicate insides from wear, damage, dirt, germs, and rain. It also helps to cool or warm the body, and gives us our sense of touch.

Reptiles such as lizards have dry, scaly skin.

Pigskin: only mammals' skin is covered with hair.

Slug skin: glands secrete slime on the skin.

Skin is a hard-wearing, living tissue, covering about 6.5 sq. ft. (2m sq). It weighs almost 9 lb. (4kg). The eyelids are 0.02 in. (0.5mm) thick, the soles of the feet 0.2 in. (5mm); average thickness is 0.08–0.1 in. (1–2mm). Skin continuously grows and renews; with pressure and wear, it becomes thicker and tougher.

THE OUTER LAYER

The skin's surface, the epidermis, is dead, but just underneath it is one of the body's busiest parts, the dermis. Microscopic cells at the base of the epidermis continually multiply, which pushes old cells upward. Over about four weeks, these cells fill with the tough body protein, keratin (which also makes up hair and nails), flatten, and die. The dead cells then reach the surface, and rub and flake off with daily wear and tear.

GETTING UNDER YOUR SKIN

There is an outer and inner layer of skin. The outer layer is the epidermis, underneath is the thicker dermis. This contains fibers of stiff collagen and stretchy elastin, making it strong yet flexible. In the dermis are sweat glands, hair roots, tiny blood vessels, and microscopic nerve endings for our sense of touch. Each hair is anchored in a follicle. It has a sebaceous gland that makes a natural wax or oil called sebum.

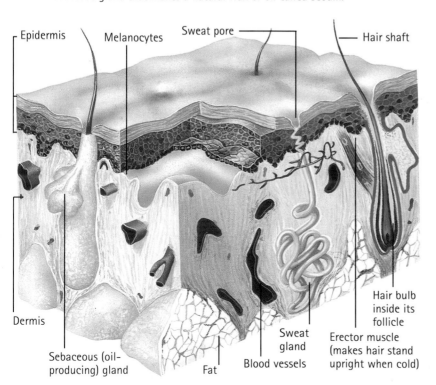

- Epidermis
- Melanocytes
- Sweat pore
- Hair shaft
- Dermis
- Sebaceous (oil-producing) gland
- Fat
- Sweat gland
- Blood vessels
- Hair bulb inside its follicle
- Erector muscle (makes hair stand upright when cold)

When skin is damaged, a scab forms to protect the body from germs while new skin develops under it.

1 Broken blood vessels become narrow to stop blood loss. White blood cells destroy bacteria.

2 Substances in the blood called platelets cause it to clot. This clot hardens into a scab.

3 In the dermis, cells called fibroblasts produce new tissue. When healed, the scab falls off.

SKIN COLOR

Our melanocyte cells produce tiny flecks of dark brown melanin (pigment). More active melanocytes make more melanin and thus produce darker skin. We inherit our normal level of melanocyte activity, and therefore our skin color, from our parents. However, strong sunlight makes melanocytes more active to protect the body from the sun's ultraviolet rays— and this produces a suntan.

COOLING SWEAT

Skin helps to control our temperature. If the body is too hot, tiny blood vessels in the dermis widen, allowing more blood to lose heat to the air. The microscopic sweat glands also ooze sweat through the pores (tiny holes) onto the skin. As this dries, it draws more warmth from the body.

HAIR AND GOOSE BUMPS

If the body is too cold, the blood vessels narrow, to reduce heat loss. The erector muscle, attached to a hair, pulls it upright. This traps air near the skin's surface which keeps warmth in, and causes goose bumps. Hairs are long rods of dead, keratin-filled cells. The only living part is the hair bulb.

SEE ALSO
Amphibian, Blood, Cell, Gland, Human body, Snail, Touch

SKYSCRAPER

Skyscrapers are very tall buildings found in cities where land is expensive. Usually built from concrete on a metal frame, they contain offices and apartments.

▲ High-rise building is a risky operation. A builder climbs a steeple during construction of the Bank of China in 1989.

When U.S. mechanic Elisha Graves Otis created an elevator with a safety device in 1852, he made skyscrapers possible—tall buildings could now be used comfortably. In 1884, William Le Baron Jenney built the world's first skyscraper in Chicago (now demolished). Its ten stories would not qualify as a skyscraper today, but its metal frame structure set a new trend.

HIGH-RISE LIVING

From 1895, the lead in skyscraper-building passed to New York. Famous examples include the Woolworth Building (1914), the Chrysler Building (1930), and the Empire State Building (1931), which was the world's tallest building until the 1960s.

SWAYING WEIGHT

Skyscrapers must support a heavy weight (the Empire State Building weighs around 400,000 tons) and resist strong winds, so a strong, stable frame is vital. It can be made of prestressed or reinforced concrete, although steel girders form the skeleton of most skyscrapers. Chicago's John Hancock Center (1970) used crisscross beams; the Sears Tower (1974) is made from nine huge steel tubes welded together to form one structure.

UNDERGROUND SUPPORT

The right foundation is crucial to stop a skyscraper falling over or collapsing. Piles (columns of concrete and metal) are driven deep into the ground. London's National Westminster Tower has 59 ft. (18m)-deep foundations with piles driven down a further 79 ft. (24m).

GOING UP

Some skyscrapers (like the John Hancock Center) have their steel skeleton on the outside; others show a wall of glass. During construction, manufactured sections of glass, concrete, and steel are brought onto the site and put into place by cranes. The wiring and service ducts go between the floors.

Canary Wharf, London, 800 ft., 50 stories

Bank of China, Hong Kong, 1,033 ft., 72 stories

Chrysler Building, New York, 1,046 ft., 77 stories

John Hancock Center, Chicago, 1,127 ft., 100 stories

Empire State Building, New York, 1,250 ft., 102 stories

Sears Tower, Chicago, 1,450 ft., 110 stories

Petronas Towers, Kuala Lumpur, 1,483 ft., 88 stories

Canadian National Tower—not really a skyscraper, but the world's tallest building at 1,821 ft.

SEE ALSO

Architecture, City, Construction, North America

SLAVERY

Slavery is when one person becomes the property, or slave, of another. The slave must do as the owner wishes and has few, if any, rights under the law.

William Wilberforce (1759–1833) led Britain to abolish slavery in 1833.

Ex-slave Harriet Tubman (c.1820–1913) helped 300 slaves escape in the U.S.A.

Nat Turner (1800–31) led a failed uprising of slaves in America in 1831.

Slavery is now illegal in all countries, but was once a normal part of society. Slaves were kept as servants or as workers on farms or in factories.

BONDAGE OF WAR
In early times, prisoners captured in battle belonged to the victors. In 146 B.C., the Greek city of Corinth rebelled against the Roman Empire. When the city was recaptured, its entire population of about 80,000 was sold into slavery. In some areas of the Roman Empire, over half the people were slaves. From 1250 until the 1800s, Egypt was ruled by slaves called Mamelukes. Children captured on raids were made slaves and trained to be the next generation of Mameluke rulers.

PLANTATIONS
In the United States, many African slaves were plantation workers in the South. Although some slaves were treated well, others experienced harsh conditions. A movement to abolish slavery grew in northern states after about 1800. In 1861, several southern states seceded (left the

▲ An Arabian slave market in the 1200s. The Arabs traded slaves from Africa, Europe, and Asia through the great markets of Zanzibar, Samarkand, and Mombasa.

Union), partly because they wanted to keep slavery, and this began the American Civil War (1861–65). Slavery was abolished after the victory of the northern states.

SLAVERY CONDEMNED
After about 1780, public opinion in many countries began to turn against slavery. Slavery was abolished in the British Empire in 1833, and by the 1890s most other countries had followed. Some tribal societies in Africa and South America continue to use slaves. People captured in local wars or who break certain laws are made slaves. Most Arab and Islamic countries have made slavery illegal, but sometimes slaves are used as servants by rich and powerful families.

THE TRIANGULAR TRADE
The largest slave trade was between West Africa and the Americas—the Triangular Trade. Ships left Bristol or Liverpool in England with weapons and tools to be traded in Africa for slaves. The slaves were so tightly packed onto ships (above) that many died during the voyage to the Americas, where they were sold for sugar or tobacco destined for England. Between 1680 and 1800, about seven million slaves were traded.

SEE ALSO
Civil rights, Civil War (American)

SLEEP

Sleep is a state of decreased consciousness, during which the body rests from its normal activities. It is essential for a healthy body and mind.

SLEEP CYCLES

Laboratory studies show the electrical patterns the brain produces during sleep. Electrodes from an EEG, or electroencephalograph, are attached to the sleeper's head —these record changes in brain activity, shown as a wavy line on the graph. In an 8-hour sleep period, sleepers go through REM and NREM cycles every 90 minutes, starting with NREM in Stage 1. Sleep gets deeper until Stage 4, the deepest sleep. After 60 to 90 minutes, dreaming (REM) occurs during Stage 2, when the brain becomes more active again. Longer REM periods occur as sleep continues.

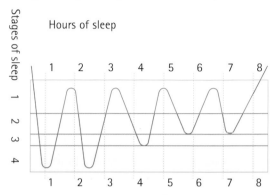

Hours of sleep

Stages of sleep

When we sleep, the electrical activity of the brain slows down in stages, along with heart rate, temperature, and breathing. However, when we dream, the brain's activity increases again, and the eyes move rapidly under the eyelids in REM (rapid eye movement) sleep. We go through several cycles of non-dreaming (NREM, or non-rapid eye movement) and dreaming sleep every night.

SLEEP AND GROWTH

Although we spend a third of our lives asleep, no one really knows why it is so important. Sleep rests the body, but we use almost as much energy asleep as when we are awake. Sleep is important for growth, which is why children need more than adults. It may also help with learning and memory. As people age, they need less sleep. A baby sleeps most of the time, and a four-year-old needs 10 to 14 hours of sleep a night. A young adult may sleep for 8 hours, but people over 60 sleep only about 5 to 6 hours, and wake often during the night.

SLEEP DISTURBANCES

Sleep is essential. When a person has insomnia (the inability to sleep) for even one night, he or she feels irritable and clumsy. If insomnia continues, lack of concentration and hallucinations (seeing things that are not real) can occur. Some people have nightmares; others get out of bed and walk around while they are asleep (sleepwalking). Jet lag is the disruption of sleep caused by air travel across time zones.

DREAMS

Many people believe that dreams are the working through of thoughts and feelings that happen during the day. Some people remember dreams and some do not. Dreams are often fantastic and colorful, and provide people with inspiration for art, music, stories, and movies.

SLEEP FACTS

- Human beings are mostly diurnal—they are awake during the day and they sleep at night

- Some animals, such as badgers, are nocturnal— they sleep by day and are active at night

- Reptiles, fish, and insects have periods of inactivity that resemble a sleeping state

- Donkeys need 3 hours of sleep per day

- Bats need 20 hours of sleep per day

◀ The Spanish painter Salvador Dali (1904–89) was inspired by his dreams and called his art "hand-painted dream photographs." In *The Persistence of Memory* (1931), he illustrates his idea of time.

SEE ALSO

Animal, Hibernation, Human body, Season, Time

367

SNAIL AND OTHER MOLLUSKS

Mollusks are soft-bodied, invertebrate animals that have no bones and no legs. They include snails, slugs, clams, cockles, limpets, oysters, octopuses, and cuttlefish.

The great black slug (which can be orange) has a tough skin flap on top.

The common mussel, a bivalve, has a shell in two parts, hinged at the front.

The spiny murex, a type of sea snail, is a univalve—it has a single, coiled shell.

Cuttlefish, octopuses, and squid are among the most active and mobile mollusks.

Most mollusks are protected by hard shells. Snails have a one-piece shell that is usually coiled; bivalves, such as cockles and mussels, have a two-piece shell hinged along one side. Cuttlefish and squid have a shell that grows inside their body, and some slugs have a small, flat shell under the skin. A few kinds of mollusk, like octopuses and some kinds of slug, have no shell at all, just a tough skin cover protecting the organs.

SLIMY TRAILS

A snail moves from place to place by gliding along on a muscular part of its body called the foot. It lubricates its path with slime poured out from glands near the front. The head is at the front and carries one or two pairs of feelers or tentacles. Land snails have eyes at the tips of their tentacles; sea snails' eyes are at the base.

▲ A baby leopard slug emerges from a pearl-like cluster of eggs. It takes about 30 days for the eggs to hatch.

THOUSANDS OF TEETH

Land snails are usually active at night or in damp weather. They feed mainly on plants. A snail's tongue, called a radula, carries thousands of tiny teeth and it works like a strip of sandpaper to shred up the stems and leaves of the plants. The tongues of some sea snails are so strong that they can drill through the shells of other animals.

MOLLUSKS WITH HINGED SHELLS

Bivalves all live in water, most of them in the sea. Some are fixed to rocks and never move, but others can burrow in sand and mud. They feed by drawing a current of water into the open shell and filtering small particles of food from it, taking oxygen from the water at the same time.

LIFE SUPPORT BACKPACK

Mollusks have a skinlike mantle that makes the shell. Most of the snail's internal organs are in its coiled hump, which stays inside the shell. When it is alarmed, the snail can also pull its head and foot right inside its shell.

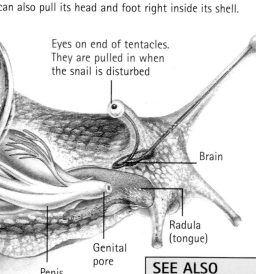

Heart

Intestine

Kidney

Stomach

Digestive gland

Mucous glands

Hermaphrodite gland. (Most land snails are hermaphrodite —they have both male and female sex organs)

Hermaphrodite duct

Salivary glands

Foot

Penis

Genital pore

Eyes on end of tentacles. They are pulled in when the snail is disturbed

Brain

Radula (tongue)

SEE ALSO

Animal, Evolution, Ocean and sea, Soil

SNAKE

Snakes are slender reptiles with no legs and, like all reptiles, they are covered with scales. There are about 2,800 species and all of them prey on other animals.

Although they have no legs, snakes can slither surprisingly quickly over the ground. Most of them move by throwing their bodies into curves and pushing backward against the ground. Some also push themselves along by digging their belly scales into the ground. Many snakes can even climb trees in this way. Snakes are generally inactive and are seldom seen except when they are hunting or disturbed.

Most snakes live alone, but rattlesnakes and corn snakes hibernate in groups.

HUG OF DEATH
A snake finds its food largely by smell. It picks up scent particles from the air by flicking out its forked tongue, and it homes in on the scent of its prey. Some snakes merely grab their prey in their jaws and swallow it live. Others poison or suffocate their prey first. Snakes that suffocate their prey are called constrictors. They include boas, pythons, and the anaconda—the largest snake, which can grow to 30 ft. (9m). They coil powerful bodies around their victims and squeeze.

The bright yellow eyelash viper is well camouflaged in the golden palm fruit.

▲ Snakes shed their skins (epidermis), including the scale covering their eyes (the brille), in order to grow.

DEADLY INJECTION
Poisonous snakes, which include vipers and cobras, inject venom into their prey through large teeth called fangs. The venom of around 270 snakes is harmful or fatal to humans. The saw-scaled viper of Africa, Indian cobra, and Australian taipan are among the world's most dangerous snakes.

SWALLOW IT WHOLE
All snakes swallow prey whole since they have no broad back teeth for crushing and cannot chew. A snake can swallow animals larger than itself because it can open its mouth extremely wide. And, since its ribs are not joined together, they open out to let the food pass along the body.

A huge meal, like a baby zebra, could last a python more than six months.

Snakes have one eye on each side to give them a wide view

Fangs

Venom canal

Venom gland

Hinged jaw

Elastic ligaments stretch between the bones

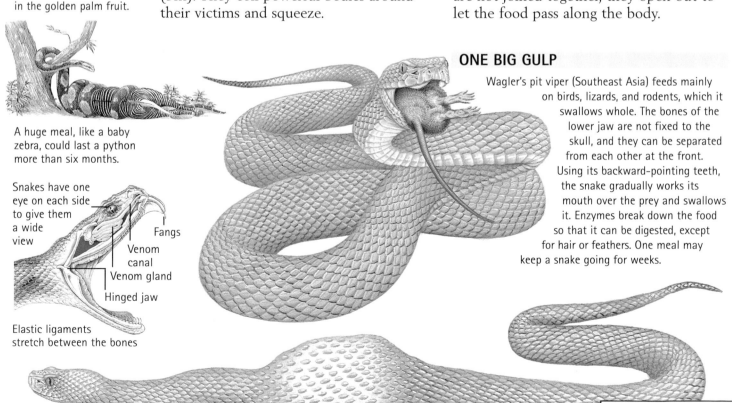

ONE BIG GULP
Wagler's pit viper (Southeast Asia) feeds mainly on birds, lizards, and rodents, which it swallows whole. The bones of the lower jaw are not fixed to the skull, and they can be separated from each other at the front. Using its backward-pointing teeth, the snake gradually works its mouth over the prey and swallows it. Enzymes break down the food so that it can be digested, except for hair or feathers. One meal may keep a snake going for weeks.

SEE ALSO

Animal, Desert, Hibernation, Reptile

SOIL

Soil is the loose material that lies on the Earth's surface and in which plants grow. It consists mainly of small particles of broken-down rock and plant material.

Water table   Topsoil   Subsoil

Deciduous forests form deep, humus-rich soils.

Dry, lime-rich soils form on grasslands.

Mountains have only a thin covering of poor soil.

Desert soils are rich in salts, but lack humus.

Tropical rain forests form fertile, but thin, soils.

Swamps have wet and often acidic soils.

► Farmers add manure and other organic matter to soil to boost the fertility of their land.

Soil covers the rocks of the Earth and is sometimes very deep. It consists of small pieces of rock, along with plant material, fungi, bacteria, and a host of tiny animals.

HOW SOILS FORM
Rocks are broken down by rain and wind to produce a layer of grit. Leaves and stems falling on the grit rot away to provide food for fungi, worms, and microscopic organisms. Some plant fibers remain in the soil as humus, which holds the grit together and helps it hold water. The rest of the plants, and the remains of animals, are broken down by fungi and bacteria into simple chemicals that provide nutrients for new plants.

A MATTER OF LAYERS
Soil is made up of layers. The dark topsoil is rich in humus and nutrients. Below that is the subsoil, a layer of fine material containing a lot of clay. The thickness of the layers and their chemical composition vary according to the climate, the type of rock the soil is made from, and the kind of vegetation growing in it.

Broken rock   Bedrock

A HIDDEN WORLD
Living within the soil are creatures that break down plant and animal matter into nutrients that can be absorbed by plant roots. Earthworms pull plant waste into the soil and are eaten by moles whose tunnels help to circulate air. Microscopic beetles, centipedes, and other creatures feed on rotting plant and animal matter, and on each other.

VALUABLE RESOURCE
The plants that take root in soil form the basis of the food chain for all land animals. People plant food crops in the soil as well as fodder crops to feed farm animals. Most farmers care for their soil, but in some areas, cutting down trees or intensive farming leads to soil erosion and crop failure.

SEE ALSO
Climate, Conservation, Crop, Farming, Habitat, Seed and pollination

SOLAR POWER

Solar power harnesses the energy in the sun's rays. It is a nonpolluting source of energy that will not run out until the sun dies, billions of years from now.

The sun is our chief source of energy. Coal, oil, and gas come from the fossilized remains of ancient plants that used sunlight to grow. The sun's energy is stored in oceans and rivers, and in the winds. All living things need the sun. Yet we use only a fraction of the energy reaching us from the sun.

SOLAR POWER PLANTS

By using mirrors, the sun's rays can be used to heat a water-filled boiler. Steam from the boiler turns a turbine which makes electricity. A power plant called Solar 1 in California uses 1,818 computer-controlled mirrors to concentrate the sunlight onto a boiler tower 300 ft. (91m) high. Solar power plants need to be in sunny places, and much of the electricity they make is lost during distribution.

▼ Solar cells mounted in winglike panels are used to power satellites because they require almost no maintenance.

SOLAR HEATING

Sunlight can provide heat for the home, saving other energy resources. Modern buildings with large windows and heat-absorbing collectors on the roof can take in enough energy from sunlight to provide room and water heating, even on cloudy days. Just a simple, insulated glass panel with a black-coated bottom will collect enough solar energy to warm the water inside, since black absorbs the most sunlight.

▲ A solar furnace uses a huge curved mirror to focus the sun's rays. It uses the sun's energy to provide a clean, nonpolluting source of heat.

▼ Energy from the sun can be used directly to heat water for a home's hot-water system through the use of solar panels.

SOLAR PANEL

Sunlight · Black metal plate · Glass sheets · Fiberglass insulation · Channels for liquid · Pump · Solar-heated liquid · Heat exchanger · Cooled liquid · Hot water out · Storage tank · Cold water in

ELECTRICITY FROM SUNLIGHT

Solar cells, first developed in the 1950s, make electricity when light shines on them. They are made of wafers of silicon, like computer chips. The cells change some of the energy in sunlight into electrical energy. They are ideal for places where there is plenty of sunlight but no electricity supply, such as orbiting space satellites like the Hubble Space Telescope (below) and space stations. In the future, there may be a huge, orbiting solar power plant which beams microwave energy down to an antenna on Earth.

SEE ALSO

Electricity, Electronics, Gas, Oil, Satellite, Sun

SOLAR SYSTEM

Our solar system is made up of the Sun and the objects that orbit it. These include the nine planets and their moons, as well as asteroids, comets, and meteors.

THE PLANETS	
Distance from Sun (million mi.)	Average time to orbit Sun
Mercury	
36	88 days
Venus	
67	225 days
Earth	
93	1 year
Mars	
141	1.9 years
Jupiter	
480	11.9 years
Saturn	
900	29.5 years
Uranus	
1,800	84 years
Neptune	
2,800	164.8 years
Pluto	
3,666	247.7 years

The Sun is at the center of the solar system and has a mass 740 times greater than all the planets combined. It is this mass that holds the planets and other objects in their orbits by gravity.

ROCKY WORLDS AND GAS GIANTS
Most of the matter from which the planets formed consisted of hydrogen and helium. The planets nearest the Sun—Mercury, Venus, Earth, and Mars—were too warm to hold on to these plentiful light gases, and instead became small worlds of rock and metal. Farther from the Sun, where temperatures were very low, the planets attracted huge amounts of hydrogen and helium. They became the gas giants— Jupiter, Saturn, Uranus, and Neptune.

ASTEROIDS AND COMETS
Between the orbits of Mars and Jupiter is a band of space where asteroids—rocks as big as mountains—are common. This is the asteroid belt. Occasionally asteroids collide. When this happens, bits break off that may eventually arrive on Earth as meteorites. A vast cloud of frozen comets is thought to lie much farther from the Sun than Pluto. This cloud, which may be 100 times farther from the Sun than the Earth is, marks the outer edge of the solar system.

HOW THE SOLAR SYSTEM FORMED
The Sun was born about five billion years ago out of a great cloud of gas and dust in space. Scientists believe that the planets, as well as the asteroids and comets, gradually formed out of this spinning cloud.

1 Material that was left over from the cloud of dust and gas formed a disk that circled the Sun.

2 As particles within the disk collided, they began to stick together, forming larger objects.

3 The objects grew into planets, moons, asteroids, and comets, which often collided.

4 Eventually, the remaining objects circled the Sun in orbits that rarely crossed.

◄ The planets of our solar system drawn to scale:
1 Mercury; 2 Venus; 3 Earth; 4 Mars; 5 Jupiter; 6 Saturn; 7 Uranus; 8 Neptune; and 9 Pluto.

SEE ALSO
Astronomy, Big Bang theory, Comet, meteor, and asteroid, Constellation, Galaxy, Planet, Star, Sun, Universe

SOLID, LIQUID, AND GAS

Solid, liquid, and gas are the three states in which substances, or matter, can exist. Each state depends on how strongly the molecules are bound together.

BOILING POINTS (at sea level)		
Substance	°C	°F
Iron	2,800	5,072
Mercury	357	675
Water	100	212
Ethanol	78	172
Oxygen	−183	−297
Nitrogen	−195	−319

MELTING POINTS (at sea level)		
Substance	°C	°F
Iron	1,535	2,795
Mercury	−39	−38.2
Water	0	32
Ethanol	−117	−179
Oxygen	−218	−360
Nitrogen	−210	−346

As you read this book, you may be sitting at a table or desk. It is probably made of wood, plastic, or steel. At room temperature, these materials are all solids. They are made of molecules that are strongly bound together. That is why the table keeps its shape. Scientists call a solid a state of matter.

LIQUIDS
If you have a filled glass, you can see another state of matter: liquid. Water, milk, and ethanol (ordinary alcohol) are all liquid at room temperature. Like all other liquids, they are made of molecules that are only loosely bound together. When you pour a liquid into a glass, its molecules are able to flow around the bottom of it. That is why the liquid fills the container evenly, forming a level surface.

GASES
All around you is air. Air is in another state, called a gas. Gases are made of molecules that are hardly bound to each other at all. When you release a gas into any space, its molecules are free to move around the space randomly, spreading around and filling the whole space evenly. That is why a beach ball forms a spherical shape even though you only blow air into one end of it.

CHANGING STATE
If we change a substance's temperature enough, its state will usually change. When iron is over 2,795°F (1,535°C), for instance, it melts into a liquid. Similarly, if water is below 32°F (0°C), it freezes to form ice, a solid. Oxygen, one of the gases that makes up air, will condense to form a liquid if we cool it to a chilly −297°F (−183°C).

HOW TEMPERATURE CHANGES MATTER

At room temperature, water is in a liquid state. However, water can be turned into a gas by heating it until it boils and turns into water vapor. Alternatively, if the water's temperature is lowered to below freezing point, it will turn into ice, which is its solid state. These changes take place because temperature affects the way in which the individual atoms and molecules of a substance are bound together.

Gas molecules move randomly and independently of one another

The molecules in liquids are free to move around

LIQUID
Liquids, such as water, have a fixed size, or volume, but no fixed shape.

The molecules and atoms in solids are tightly bound together

SOLID
Solids, such as ice, have a fixed shape and size.

GAS
Gases, such as water vapor from boiling water, have no fixed shape or size.

SEE ALSO

Atom and molecule,
Heat, Iron and steel

SOUND

Sound is a form of energy that can be heard. It is caused by vibrations and travels in waves through solids, liquids, and gases.

▼ When you tap a tuning fork against a hard surface, it starts to vibrate rapidly, giving out a constant pitch. When the prongs vibrate outward, they compress the air near them, creating high pressure. When they vibrate inward, the air expands, leaving an area of low pressure.

— Air compressed

— Air expanded

We usually think of sound traveling only through air, but it can also move through other substances. When you are swimming under water in a pool, you can still hear the sounds going on around the pool. That is because sound can travel through water—or any other liquid. Noisy neighbors are a problem because the sounds they make can travel through walls and floors—solid materials.

MAKING SOUND

You can make a sound in the air if you hit two objects together, a pair of pot lids, for example. The objects create sound because you give them some energy, making them vibrate (shake). As the objects vibrate, they compress, then release the air each side of them, over and over again. This makes the air pressure around them rise and fall repeatedly.

THE HUMAN VOICE

The human voice produces sound when air from the lungs is forced past the vocal cords. How high or low the voice is depends on how quickly or slowly these cords vibrate. The diaphragm controls the flow of air in and out of the lungs. The muscles around the mouth turn the noise produced by the vocal cords into recognizable sounds. The cavities in the nose, throat, and chest help the sounds to resonate.

Diaphragm — Speaker wire

Magnet

Metal core with coiled wiring

Cone amplifies diaphragm's vibrations

▲ Loudspeakers turn electrical signals back into sounds. The signals cause a diaphragm inside the speaker to vibrate, and this motion reproduces the original sound.

AIR VIBRATIONS

Sound is caused by only tiny changes of air pressure. When someone nearby talks to you, they make the air pressure rise and fall by about 1/10,000 of normal air pressure. That is roughly the pressure change you feel when you put a single sheet of paper in your palm. As air vibrates, it shakes a thin membrane in the ear—the eardrum. That is why we hear the vibrations as sound. Our ears cannot pick up all kinds of vibration. They have to be loud enough for us to hear. They also have to happen at a rate that our ears can detect—in other words, they have to be the right frequency.

SPREAD OF SOUND

When an object vibrates, sound waves spread out from it. The farther you are from the object, the more the energy from it has spread, so the quieter it is. Sound waves bounce off hard objects such as brick walls or windows. When you listen to someone speaking in a room, for example, you hear both the sound that has come directly from their voice and the sound that has bounced off the walls, ceiling, and floor. This effect is reverberation.

LOUDNESS

The harder you hit something, the louder the sound you make with it. That is because it vibrates more, creating a greater pressure change in the air around it. Our

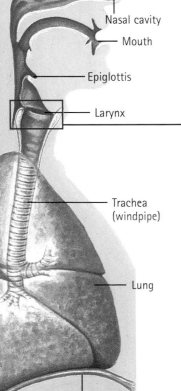

Nasal cavity

Mouth

Epiglottis

Larynx

Trachea (windpipe)

Lung

Diaphragm

▲ The vocal cords are tightened when someone speaks or sings. Breathing out makes the cords vibrate and produce sound.

▲ The vocal cords produce low notes when they are relaxed.

▲ The vocal cords produce high notes when they are taut.

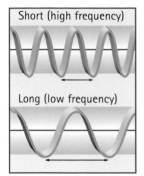

▲ The pitch of a sound—whether it is high or low—depends on its frequency or wavelength. Long waves have a lower frequency and pitch than short waves.

▲ A sound's loudness depends on the height of its waves, called its amplitude. Quiet sounds have a smaller amplitude than loud sounds.

▲ A visual display of three different sounds: a complete symphony orchestra (top); the spoken word "hello" (above left); and two hand claps (above right). Rich, complex sounds involve thousands of waveforms, of differing amplitudes and frequencies, all intermingling at the same time to make up the waveform shapes above.

ears can pick up a wide range of pressure changes. At best, they can detect sounds made by pressure changes that are a mere 5 billionths of normal air pressure. A pin dropping is this quiet. At the other extreme, our ears can detect pressure changes about one fifth of normal air pressure. A pneumatic drill is this loud.

FREQUENCY AND PITCH

Whistles and women's voices make sounds that are much higher in pitch than bass guitars and men's voices. That is because they make sounds that have a higher

frequency, or shorter wavelength. Frequency is measured in hertz (Hz). Our ears can only pick up sounds that are between 20 Hz and 20,000 Hz. A car horn makes a sound with a frequency of about 200 Hz, women can sing notes as high as 1,200 Hz, and men can sing notes as low as 60 Hz.

SPEED OF SOUND

On a warm day, sound travels through air at about 1,082 ft./sec. (330m/sec). On colder days, it travels more slowly. Sound travels at different speeds through other materials. It travels four times faster through water than air. Sound travels through solid concrete (such as the concrete partition between two offices) over ten times faster than it travels through air.

BREAKING THE SOUND BARRIER

When a vehicle, such as the British jet car Thrust SSC (below), travels at the speed of sound, pressure waves build up in front of the vehicle and form a shock wave. As the car accelerates through the sound barrier and travels faster than sound, the shock wave breaks away and can be heard, after the car has passed, as a sonic boom. You cannot hear a vehicle approaching at supersonic speeds.

LOUDNESS SCALE

Loudness is measured in decibels (dB). Since the sound energy increases ten times, the decibels go up by the number ten. The following table shows the loudness of some sounds.

• Rocket liftoff	150–190 dB
• Jet takeoff	120–140 dB
• Thunder	95–115 dB
• Motorcycle	70–90 dB
• Vacuum cleaner	60–80 dB
• Orchestra	50–70 dB
• Talking	30–60 dB
• Whispering	20–30 dB
• Falling leaves	20 dB

Shock wave

Sound waves

SEE ALSO

Hearing, Musical instrument, Radar and sonar, Radio, Wavelength

SOUTH AFRICA

Occupying the southernmost tip of the African continent, the country of South Africa consists mostly of a vast plateau, 3,940 ft. (1,200m) above sea level.

Area: 471,400 sq. mi.
Population: 43,647,658
Capital: Cape Town (legislative), Pretoria (administrative), Bloemfontein (judicial)
Languages: Afrikaans, English
Currency: Rand

South Africa's high, flat-topped hills are surrounded by fertile, low-lying coastlands from 34–150 mi. (55–240km) across. The spectacular Drakensberg Mountains rise to 11,425 ft. (3,482m), and the Limpopo River marks much of the country's northern boundary. The separate, mountainous kingdom of Lesotho is entirely surrounded by South African territory. The climate is mostly dry and sunny, averaging 63°F (17°C).

DESERT, GRASSLAND, AND SCRUB

In the north, the Kalahari Desert stretches into neighboring Botswana. Most of the vast central plateau is occupied by an area of coarse grassland called the Highveld. The Middleveld, in the northwest, is more suited to livestock than crops because of its poor soil, owing to erosion and little rain. The northeast of the plateau is the Transvaal Basin, where farmers grow citrus fruits, corn, and tobacco. Elephants, lions, leopards, and great herds of antelope and zebras live on Transvaal's thorny scrub and are protected in the Kruger National Park.

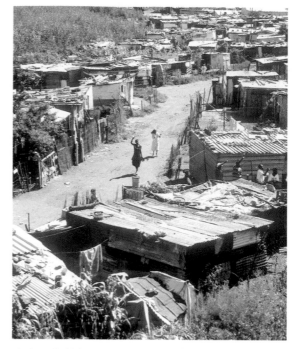

▲ Apartheid forced many blacks to live in sprawling slums, called townships. One is Soweto—South Africa's largest black residential area.

PRECIOUS RESOURCES

South Africa has a vast wealth of natural resources, in particular minerals. It exports more diamonds than any other country, and is the world's largest producer of gold, platinum, chrome, and manganese. It also has large reserves of gas, coal, copper, iron, asbestos, silver, nickel, and uranium. It is Africa's most industrial country and could be one of the world's richest nations. It can provide enough of its own grain and meat to feed its population, and a quarter of its wealth comes from industries such as chemicals, textiles, and machinery.

▲ The Drakensberg Mountains form a long line of sharp cliffs where South Africa's high central plateau drops down toward coastal lowlands.

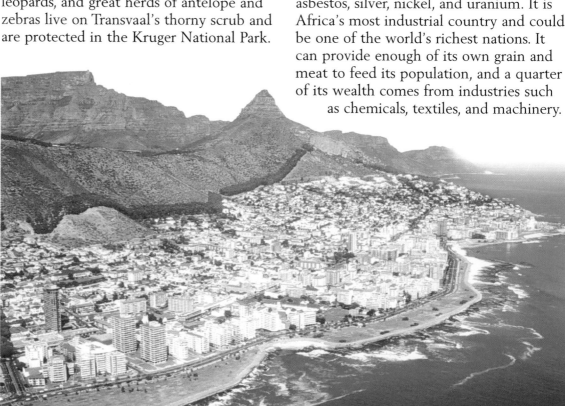

▶ For many visitors, the first sight of South Africa is Cape Town, set against the dramatic backdrop of Table Mountain, at the southern tip of the country.

POLICY OF APARTHEID
The wealth of South Africa's natural resources has benefited only a minority of the population. This is because a policy of apartheid (separateness) was introduced in 1950 by the white government; this separated blacks from whites and refused blacks equal rights. With black people making up almost three fourths of the population, millions of people were left in abject poverty. Many other countries protested against the cruelty of apartheid, and imposed sanctions which limited South Africa's overseas trade.

THE AFTERMATH OF APARTHEID
The process of apartheid began to collapse in 1990, under the presidency of F. W. de Klerk. In 1994, the first multiracial elections were held in South Africa, bringing to power a majority black government. Although this struck a blow for equality, the new democracy still faces enormous problems: 2 million children have no schooling at all; half the population still lives in homes without electricity; 12 million still need clean water supplies; and a third of the population is unemployed. The great gap between rich and poor creates a major problem of violent street crime.

▲ The elections of 1994 brought to power the African National Congress (ANC), headed by Nelson Mandela. Between 1964 and 1990, Mandela had been imprisoned for his opposition to the apartheid regime.

FIGHTING FOR TERRITORY
The first South Africans were the San and the Khoi peoples. From about A.D. 300, Bantu-speaking peoples such as the Zulus, Xhosa, and Sesotho moved into the region. From 1652, Dutch settlers came by sea, soon followed by other Europeans. In 1806, the British took over the coastal areas, where the Dutch farmers (called Boers or Afrikaners) had settled. In order to keep their independence and claim new land for themselves, the Afrikaners made the Great Trek inland in 1834–38; during this time they founded Transvaal and the Orange Free State. The discovery of gold and diamonds on Afrikaner territory led to two wars between the Boers and the British. Final Afrikaner defeat in 1902 led to a united South Africa in 1910.

PLANS FOR THE FUTURE
South Africa's population is 77.4 percent black, 12.2 percent white, 8 percent of mixed descent, and 2.4 percent Asian (subcontinent). The government wants a "rainbow society" where all people can live in harmony. Public holidays celebrate Human Rights, the Family, Freedom, Workers, Youth, Women, Heritage, Reconciliation, and Goodwill.

▲ One of the main peoples of South Africa is the Zulus. About 7 million of them live here, mainly in the province of Natal.

SEE ALSO
Africa, Civil rights

SOUTH AMERICA

Covering 12 percent of the planet's land area, South America is the fourth largest continent. Its people make up 6 percent of the world's population.

▲ Ecuador's Cotopaxi (19,347 ft./5,897m), seen from the volcano Illinizais, is the continent's highest active volcano.

KEY FACTS

- **Area:** 6,949,410 sq. mi.
- **Population:** 355,068,000
- **Number of countries:** 12
- **Largest country:** Brazil (3,265,100 sq. mi.)
- **Smallest country:** French Guiana (34,400 sq. mi.)
- **Highest point:** Aconcagua (22,834 ft.)
- **Largest lake:** Lake Maracaibo (6,300 sq. mi.)
- **Longest river:** Amazon (3,900 mi.)

South America's varied landscape includes the rocky islands of Tierra del Fuego (belonging to Argentina and Chile) and the immense grasslands of Argentina and Venezuela. There are also snowcapped mountains and active volcanoes. The Andes, running along the Pacific coast for 12,900 mi. (8,000km), form the longest mountain range in the world. Aconcagua in Argentina is the highest peak.

WET AND DRY

The Amazon River basin holds half of the world's fresh water. It occupies two fifths of the continent and is the world's largest tropical rain forest. The Amazon is second to the Nile in length. Quibdo in Colombia is South America's rainiest place, with more than 350 in. (8,900mm) of rain a year. The Atacama Desert in Chile is one of the world's driest places—the port of Arica in northern Chile averages less than 0.04 in. (1mm) of rain a year—but the hottest temperatures are recorded in the Gran Chaco region of northern Argentina.

CLIMATIC DIFFERENCES

The great range of climates is because there is a wide variation in the distance of the different countries from the equator, and in the height of different areas above sea level. Lake Titicaca, between Bolivia and Peru, is the highest lake in the world, 12,500 ft. (3,812m) above sea level.

COASTAL CITIES

High mountains, dense forests, and vast distances make overland transportation difficult and costly. Most major cities lie along the coast or on large rivers, where they can be served by shipping. Only a

▲ Venezuela's Angel Falls has a longer drop (3,212 ft./979m) than any other waterfall in the world.

▶ In Bolivia, llamas graze high up in the Andes and are kept for their wool and meat. They are also able to carry heavy loads.

GALAPAGOS IS.
(Ecuador)

▲ The giant tortoise is one of the many unusual forms of wildlife on the Galapagos Islands, which lie 600 mi. (960km) off the coast of Ecuador.

tenth of all roads are paved, and in rural areas, donkeys and carts drawn by oxen or horses are used to carry goods. Aviation has developed rapidly since about 1950, especially in Brazil, which has 1,500 airports and landing grounds.

UNIQUE WILDLIFE

South America's isolation from the rest of the world has led to the evolution of many unique forms of wildlife. These include the rhea (a large, flightless bird), the capybara (the world's largest rodent), and the llama. Other South American creatures include the tapir, armadillo, jaguar, condor, iguana, giant anteater, tree sloth, vicuña, piranha fish, manatee, and many varieties of parrot and monkey.

PLANTS AND PRODUCTS

The Amazon region contains more kinds of plants than anywhere else in the world, including 2,500 types of tree and hundreds of species of orchid. South American plants yield products such as rubber, quinine, sisal, and chocolate and woods such as mahogany and balsa.

▼ The Pan-American highway, which runs through the Atacama Desert, links most South American countries to each other and to North America.

CARIBBEAN SEA

PANAMA

Caracas

Lake Maracaibo

VENEZUELA

Georgetown

GUYANA

Paramaribo — Kourou

Quibdo

Bogotá

Angel Falls

Cayenne

San Agustin

COLOMBIA

SURINAM

FRENCH GUIANA
(France)

Quito

ECUADOR

Cotopaxi ▲

Amazon

B R A Z I L

PERU

Andes

BOLIVIA

Lima

Lake Titicaca

La Paz (seat of government)

Brasilia

Arica

Sucre (legal)

São Paulo

PACIFIC OCEAN

GRAN CHACO

PARAGUAY

Rio de Janeiro

ATACAMA DESERT

Asunción

Andes

ARGENTINA

URUGUAY

Aconcagua ▲

Buenos Aires

Montevideo

Santiago

CHILE

ATLANTIC OCEAN

N

miles
0   500

0   500
km

FALKLAND IS. (U.K.)

Stanley

SOUTH GEORGIA
(U.K.)

Tierra del Fuego

SOUTH SANDWICH
IS. (U.K.)

VARIED DESCENT

The native people of South America came from Asia by way of North America. From 1500 onward, Europeans came to settle, mostly from Spain and Portugal. Many intermarried with local people, producing children of mixed race known as *mestizos*. In Andean countries such as Bolivia and Peru, native people still make up a large proportion of the population. Argentina's population is largely white, with many people of Italian, German, or British descent, while Brazil's population includes many descendants of African slaves brought to work on sugar plantations. Since 1940, South America's population has tripled.

▲ Sugarcane is Guyana's most important crop. It is grown near the coast.

TODAY'S PEOPLE

One person in three in South America is under 15. About three fourths of the population now lives in cities, the three largest cities being Brazil's São Paolo and Rio de Janeiro, and Argentina's Buenos Aires. Four fifths of adults can read and write. Most of the people are Roman Catholics. In most South American countries, there is a small governing class of officials, businessmen, landowners, and military leaders; a growing professional middle class; and a poor majority, many of whom are unemployed and living in overcrowded conditions. Living standards are lower in rural areas, many of which still lack electricity, telephones, schools, and medical care. Official development programs are trying to improve rural conditions to reverse the movement of people to the cities.

▲ Indians make up much of the population in Bolivia. Many wear traditional clothes, especially for festivals. Panpipes are a popular local instrument.

SPORT AND LEISURE

Soccer has passionate fans throughout the continent—Brazil's Pelé has been called the world's greatest soccer player of all time. Bullfighting is still popular in Colombia, Venezuela, and Peru. South

▲ Brazil produces a third of the world's coffee. The beans must be washed in order to remove the outer skin.

America has produced many popular forms of music and dance, such as the tango and samba. Colorful *fiestas* (festivals) are held on national and religious holidays. South American writers who have won the Nobel Prize for Literature include Chilean poets Gabriela Mistral and Pablo Neruda, and Colombian novelist Gabriel Garcia Marquez.

MINERAL RESOURCES

Since European settlement began, South America has developed as a supplier of raw materials. At first this meant gold and silver, then timber, sugar, coffee, and

▼ Bolivia is rich in tin. Local people sift through the mountains of slag for tin ore.

rubber, and, after the coming of railroads and steamships, beef, wheat, and wool. Venezuela is rich in oil and iron, Brazil in manganese and bauxite. Colombia has emeralds and coal, and Chile has copper as well as guano (bird droppings) and nitrates, used as fertilizer and to make explosives. Mineral exports pay for imports of manufactured goods, but modern mining is highly mechanized and creates few jobs.

INDUSTRIALIZATION

Brazil is the most industrialized South American country, producing cars and trucks, light planes, televisions, and machinery for the rest of the continent. Shortages of money and skills hold back industry in other countries, but most now produce basic items such as clothes, shoes, furniture, and drinks for local use, reducing the need for imports.

NEW VERSUS OLD

Brazil and Argentina both have vast plantations and ranches. Large-scale forest clearance has created environmental problems, as well as disturbing the traditional way of life of tribal people, who live by hunting and gathering. Offshore fishing is a major industry for both Chile and Peru.

EUROPEAN SETTLEMENT

During the 1400s, the Inca built up a great empire in the Andes. In the early 1500s, European settlers from Spain and Portugal—greedy for gold and silver—enslaved or killed many native people, and brought with them

▲ Paraguay's capital city Asunción was built by the Spanish, who arrived in the 1500s and ruled the country for 300 years.

diseases unknown to the continent, which wiped out millions of others. Missionaries introduced Christianity to replace traditional beliefs. The Napoleonic Wars in the early 1800s, however, weakened the hold of Spain and Portugal on their South American colonies.

TO INDEPENDENCE

Revolutions in the early 1800s brought independence. The leading revolutionary figures were Simón Bolívar and José de San Martín. The former Spanish colonies became republics, but Brazil was ruled by emperors until 1889. South American trade remained tied to Europe and, from the late 1800s onward, increasingly to the United States. Centuries of European influence are clearly shown in the Spanish-style architecture of many older cities.

STONE STATUES

Some 300 stone statues have been found in the hills near San Agustín in Colombia. They are at least 1,000 years old and appear to mark burial sites. Colombia was originally home to many groups of indigenous people, some living in rain-forest settlements, others wandering the open plains.

MILITARY RULE

Many South American countries have been ruled by dictators—usually backed by the military—and changes of government by revolution have been common. Since the 1980s, civilian rule has been restored in countries such as Argentina, Brazil, and Chile.

▲ *Ariane IV* is one of a number of rockets launched from the Kourou Space Center in French Guiana.

SEE ALSO
Argentina, Brazil, Continent

SOUTHEAST ASIA

The region of Southeast Asia consists of seven mainland countries and three island nations that lie east of India and south of China.

BRUNEI
Area: 2,000 sq. mi.
Population: 350,898
Capital: Bandar Seri Begawan
Language: Malay
Currency: Brunei dollar

Southeast Asia covers an area over 1,500,000 sq. mi. (4 million sq km). Its population of over 500 million is growing rapidly. The landscape is mainly mountainous uplands and tropical forests, with swampy coastland. Countries north of the equator, like Thailand, get heavy rain from May to October; Indonesia, south of the equator, has its rainy season from November to April. Temperatures are usually above 77°F (25°C) all year round.

VOLCANIC LAND
A chain of volcanoes runs through the Indonesian islands of Sumatra, Java, and the Lesser Sunda Islands. Over 70 have erupted in the last 200 years. The eruption on the island of Krakatoa which took place in 1883 was the loudest explosion in modern history.

OLD CULTURES
Early centers of civilization emerged in the valleys of rivers such as the Irrawaddy, Chao Praya, and Mekong, where annual flooding fertilized the soil. Rich harvests of rice supported ruling classes of warriors and priests. The harvests also fed the

CAMBODIA (KAMPUCHEA)
Area: 68,200 sq. mi.
Population: 12,775,324
Capital: Phnom Penh
Language: Khmer
Currency: Riel

INDONESIA
Area: 705,200 sq. mi.
Population: 232,073,071
Capital: Jakarta
Language: Bahasa Indonesian
Currency: Rupiah

▲ Thailand's capital city Bangkok is one of the region's modern cities. Tourism has been boosted by relatively low airfares.

▲ Most Cambodians live in farming villages and work in paddy fields. On Cambodia's Lake Tonle Sap, there are floating villages.

MODERN TIMES

Since regaining their independence after 1945, Southeast Asian countries have dramatically raised their standards of living, health, and education, despite the damage caused by the Vietnam War which lasted from 1965 to 1973. Malaysia, Singapore, and Thailand have developed modern industries, making cars and electronic goods. Farming, however, is still the main occupation, the chief crops being rice, maize, palm oil, sugar, tea, and coffee.

FUTURE CONCERNS

The rapid use of the region's resources is raising concern about pollution problems, the destruction of forests, and threats to wildlife. Most nations of the region belong to the Association of South East Asian Nations (ASEAN), which was founded in 1967 to help cooperation in trade, education, and development.

▲ Southeast Asia has a wealth of religions and cultures. In the mountains and forests, there are still many tribal peoples such as the Karen of Myanmar.

SINGAPORE
Area: 241 sq. mi.
Population: 4,452,732
Capital: Singapore City
Languages: English, Malay, Mandarin Chinese, Tamil
Currency: Singapore dollar

craftsworkers and laborers who made their luxuries and built their palaces, forts, and temples. Thailand and Myanmar (Burma) are famed for their historic pagodas. In Cambodia are the ruins of the temple-city of Angkor Wat, the capital of the great Khmer Empire (900 to 1500).

MATERIALS FOR TRADE

Southeast Asia is rich in raw materials such as oil, tin, and timber. Myanmar and Thailand produce most of the world's rubies and sapphires. Five hundred years ago, European merchants came trading for spices such as cloves, nutmeg, and cinnamon. Apart from Thailand, the whole region gradually came under European rule and plantation crops such as rubber and coffee were introduced. Many Chinese and Indians moved there as traders and laborers.

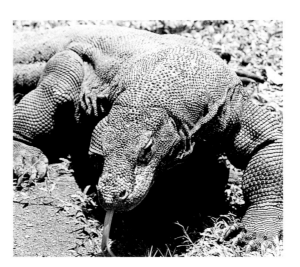

▲ The Komodo dragon, the largest living lizard, is named after the Indonesian island on which it is found.

THAILAND
Area: 197,600 sq. mi.
Population: 62,354,402
Capital: Bangkok
Language: Thai
Currency: Baht

VIETNAM
Area: 125,600 sq. mi.
Population: 81,098,416
Capital: Hanoi
Language: Vietnamese
Currency: Dong

LAOS
Area: 91,482 sq. mi.
Population: 5,777,180
Capital: Vientiane
Language: Lao
Currency: Kip

MALAYSIA
Area: 128,703 sq. mi.
Population: 22,662,365
Capital: Kuala Lumpur
Language: Malay
Currency: Ringgit (Malaysian dollar)

MYANMAR (BURMA)
Area: 254,000 sq. mi.
Population: 42,238,224
Capital: Rangoon (Yangon)
Language: Burmese
Currency: Kyat

PHILIPPINES
Area: 114,830 sq. mi.
Population: 84,525,639
Capital: Manila
Languages: Filipino, English
Currency: Peso

SEE ALSO

Asia, Indonesia, Malaysia, Philippines, Singapore

SPACECRAFT

There are three main types of spacecraft: artificial satellites, unmanned probes, and manned spacecraft. All require powerful rockets to lift them into space.

Satellites are spacecraft that orbit the Earth without a crew. They are used for surveying our planet, communication, forecasting the weather, or, as in the case of the Hubble Space Telescope, investigating the universe. They carry equipment, including radio receivers and transmitters, measuring instruments, cameras, and computers. The energy needed to run the onboard equipment comes from solar panels that convert sunlight into electricity.

GETTING THERE

A space shuttle takes off like a rocket, lands like a plane, and can reach speeds of 17,400 mph (28,000kph). The launch in 1981 of the first space shuttle, *Columbia*, by NASA meant that a reusable vehicle could launch craft into space instead of having to build a new rocket for each mission.

Main fuel tank contains liquid fuel. Tank burns up as it falls back to Earth

Nose cone protects against heat on reentry of 2,300°F (1,260°C)

Heat insulation felt and tiles are fixed to the outside of the orbiter

Two side, reusable rocket boosters of solid fuel provide a thrust of 3.3 million lb. at takeoff

Two engines either side of the tail move the orbiter into and during orbit

The shuttle has three main rocket engines

▼ Two minutes after launch, the booster rockets fall away; six minutes later, the main liquid-fueled tank drops away. The boosters splash down in the Atlantic Ocean and are retrieved by ships.

▲ The shuttle launches its cargo into orbit—here, a satellite. The shuttle's speed at the time of launch is crucial: if it's too fast, the satellite will fly off into space; too slow and it will drop to Earth.

Sputnik (U.S.S.R.), the first satellite, launched in 1957, orbited for six months.

Mir space station (U.S.S.R., 1986) was almost continuously occupied.

ROBOTS IN SPACE

Robotic spacecraft called probes have been sent to fly past, orbit, or land on other planets. They carry cameras and instruments to gather data that is sent back to Earth as a stream of radio signals. Space probes have small rocket engines that are fired to alter course or slow down before they enter orbit. Some probes send a lander to a planet's surface, where it soft-lands.

MANNED SPACEFLIGHT

Early manned spacecraft include the U.S.S.R.'s 1961 *Vostok I*, which carried the first human into space, and the U.S.'s 1969 *Apollo* craft, which carried the first astronauts to the Moon. Later came orbital space stations and the space shuttle. Manned spacecraft must carry enough air, food, and water to keep astronauts alive and working for what may be months in space. Fresh supplies can be brought from Earth in unmanned vehicles that dock with the manned spacecraft. In this way permanent space stations can be maintained in orbit.

ROCKETS

To gather enough speed to go into orbit around the Earth or to escape from Earth's gravity spacecraft need rocket-launch vehicles. These usually come in three parts, or stages. As one stage runs out of fuel it falls away, and the next stage fires.

Luna 9 was the first craft to land on the Moon and send back pictures, in 1966.

The European Space Agency's *Ariane* rocket was first launched in 1981.

SEE ALSO
Astronaut, Planet, Rocket, Satellite, Solar system, Space exploration

SPACE EXPLORATION

Space exploration began in 1957 with the launch of the first artificial satellite. By 1961, people were orbiting Earth. Most major planets have now been investigated.

▲ A dog named Laika was the first "astronaut," sent into orbit in *Sputnik 2* in 1957. It stayed up for two weeks.

The *Luna 2* (U.S.S.R.) was the first spacecraft to reach the Moon, in 1959.

Five *Surveyor* spacecraft (U.S.A.) landed on the Moon in the 1960s.

Radio-controlled *Lunokhods* (U.S.S.R.) traveled on the Moon's surface in 1970 and 1973.

The Moon was the first target for space probes. In 1959, Russia's *Luna 1* flew past the Moon at a distance of 3,700 mi. (5,955km). Later that year, *Luna 2* crash-landed on the Moon, and *Luna 3* went around it, to send back the first pictures of the far side, not visible from Earth. In the 1960s, several U.S. and Russian probes landed on the Moon and sent back pictures of its surface. These, and a series of manned orbital flights to practice docking the spacecraft, prepared the way for manned landings, beginning with *Apollo 11* in 1969. Altogether, the six successful Apollo missions brought back 840 lb. (381kg) of lunar rock and dust.

HOT VENUS

Venus is the planet closest to Earth (about 26 million mi. [41 million km] away), but its surface is hidden by thick clouds, so it's hard to get a clear picture of it by telescope or spacecraft. In 1967, the Russian probe *Venera 4* parachuted down through the gaseous clouds and sent back information about their makeup.

SEARCHING PROBES

During the 1970s, several Russian probes landed on Venus and took measurements of their surroundings. But in scorching temperatures of over 840°F (450°C), none of the spacecraft survived for more than about an hour. Maps of Venus have been made by probes using radar. ▶

APOLLO **COMMAND MODULE**

APOLLO **LUNAR MODULE**

A GIANT LEAP FOR MANKIND

In 1969, U.S. astronaut Neil Armstrong made history when he stepped from *Apollo 11*'s lunar module onto the Moon. Later missions, like this fourth U.S. landing in 1971, used lunar rovers to explore and collect soil samples. The lunar module took them back to the orbiting command module.

The Sun
Ulysses, 1994-95, examined the polar regions

Comets
Giotto met Halley's Comet, 1986, and Grigg-Skjellerup, 1992

Earth

Saturn
Pioneer 11, 1979
Voyager 1, 1980
Voyager 2, 1981
Cassini, launched 1997

Neptune
Voyager 2, 1989 (stunning photographs)

Uranus
Voyager 2, 1986

Mercury
Mariner 10 is the only spacecraft to have visited Mercury. It flew past three times in 1974 and 1975, taking photographs

Venus
Soviet *Venera* craft 1-13, first landed in 1970; *Mariner 10*, 1974; *Pioneer 1-2*, 1978, radar mapped surface; *Magellan* orbited three times—1990, 1991, 1994

Mars
Mariner 4, 1965, first photos
Mariner 9, 1971–72, discovered Mariner Valley
Viking 1, 1976, landed on Mars and took photographs
Pathfinder/Sojourner, 1997
Mars Global Surveyor, 1998
Mars Polar Lander going up in 1999

Jupiter
Pioneer 10 and *Pioneer 11*, 1973, 1974
Voyager 1, March 1979
Voyager 2, July 1979, took photos and discovered sulfur volcanoes on the orange moon, Io
Galileo, 1995, parachute probe
Galileo Europa Mission, studying Jupiter's moons Io and Europa, 1999

Mars 96 Penetrator (U.S.S.R.) has a 20-ft. (6-m) spike full of instruments to monitor composition of the ground.

Artist's impression of the *Magellan* radar-mapping spacecraft orbiting Venus in 1994.

Earth-controlled exploring robot designed to roam Mars or the Moon and send back images.

▲ Unmanned probes have now been sent to all of the major planets—only faraway Pluto has yet to be explored. Recent ventures include further deep-space missions and the 1999 *Mars Polar Lander*, which carried a CD-ROM full of children's names from around the world.

MAPS AND PHOTOS

The most accurate maps of Venus came from the *Magellan* probe, which went into orbit around Venus in August 1990. It discovered the longest canyon in the solar system and a landslide that happened while the craft was taking measurements. The probe *Mariner 10*, which skimmed past Venus in 1974, also flew past Mercury, sending back the first clear photos of this small world's heavily cratered surface.

LIFE ON MARS?

One of the most exciting moments in space exploration came in 1971 when the American probe *Mariner 9* photographed what looked like dried-up riverbeds on Mars. This suggested that millions of years ago, Mars had water and a thicker, warmer atmosphere, and therefore may have supported life. In 1976, the American spacecraft *Viking 1* and *Viking 2* went into orbit around Mars, known as the Red Planet from the color of its soil. Probes descended to the surface by parachute. Each lander collected samples of the Martian soil and ran tests to see if they contained any life. Results were uncertain.

Solar panels generating power from the Sun

Telescopes and solar observation unit

Apollo command module

Docking unit

Living quarters and orbital workshop

◀ *Skylab*, launched in 1973, was built by NASA as a laboratory in space. It lasted until 1979, when it broke up and fell back to Earth. Some astronauts have now lived and worked in orbit for a year at a time on the Russian space station, *Mir*.

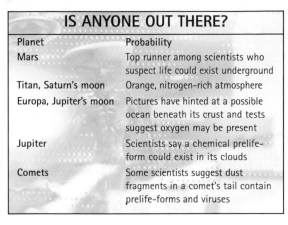

IS ANYONE OUT THERE?

Planet	Probability
Mars	Top runner among scientists who suspect life could exist underground
Titan, Saturn's moon	Orange, nitrogen-rich atmosphere
Europa, Jupiter's moon	Pictures have hinted at a possible ocean beneath its crust and tests suggest oxygen may be present
Jupiter	Scientists say a chemical prelife-form could exist in its clouds
Comets	Some scientists suggest dust fragments in a comet's tail contain prelife-forms and viruses

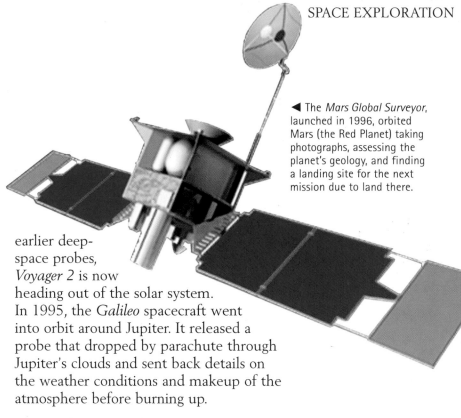

◄ The *Mars Global Surveyor*, launched in 1996, orbited Mars (the Red Planet) taking photographs, assessing the planet's geology, and finding a landing site for the next mission due to land there.

RETURN TO THE RED PLANET

In 1997, *Mars Pathfinder* made the most unusual landing of any spacecraft so far. Parachutes and small rocket engines helped to slow it down. It bounced along the Martian surface using big balloons until it finally came to rest. The probe released a roving vehicle, *Sojourner*, which analyzed rocks and returned 550 images.

DEEP SPACE

Beyond Mars lie the giant planets Jupiter, Saturn, Uranus, and Neptune. These are much more remote worlds, and it was only in 1973 that the first probe to Jupiter, *Pioneer 10*, flew past its target. Its sister craft, *Pioneer 11*, used the gravity pull of Jupiter to swing it on to an encounter with Saturn. This slingshot effect was also used by the later probes, *Voyager 1* and *Voyager 2*. In 1979, *Voyager 2* swung past Jupiter on its way to Saturn in 1981, Uranus in 1986, and Neptune in 1989. Like the three

earlier deep-space probes, *Voyager 2* is now heading out of the solar system. In 1995, the *Galileo* spacecraft went into orbit around Jupiter. It released a probe that dropped by parachute through Jupiter's clouds and sent back details on the weather conditions and makeup of the atmosphere before burning up.

MANNED EXPLORATION

More than 400 astronauts have flown in space, and 12 have set foot on the Moon. The next target for manned exploration is Mars. A craft to make this journey could be built in space by astronauts working at an international space station orbiting the Earth.

▼ *Huygens* will take two-and-a-half hours to parachute to Titan's surface, sending information back to *Cassini* about the moon's atmosphere, which will be relayed to Earth.

TO SATURN AND BEYOND

Launched in 1997, NASA's *Cassini* spacecraft will take seven years to reach Saturn, where it will orbit and circle the planet for four years. It will take around 30,000 color photos and carry scientific instruments to study Saturn's rings and moons. A robot probe, *Huygens*, will attempt to land on Saturn's moon, Titan. If the probe survives the landing and can still send a signal back to *Cassini*, it will send back measurements from the surface.

SEE ALSO

Astronaut, Planet, Satellite, Solar system, Spacecraft, Star, Sun

SPAIN AND PORTUGAL

Spain and Portugal lie in the most southwesterly part of Europe, in an area known as the Iberian Peninsula. The countries have a linked history.

▲ Traditional costumes, like those of these women and children from Seville, are still worn by many Spanish people for festivals and other celebrations.

SPAIN
Area: 192,800 sq. mi.
Population: 40,077,100
Capital: Madrid
Languages: Spanish, Catalan, Galician, Basque
Currency: Euro

PORTUGAL
Area: 35,400 sq. mi.
Population: 10,081,245
Capital: Lisbon
Language: Portuguese
Currency: Euro

Much of the Spanish mainland is a huge plateau called the Meseta. The country's high mountains include the Sierra Nevada and the Cantabrian ranges. The Pyrenees separate Spain from France. The Mediterranean coastline consists of fertile plains and, together with Spain's Balearic Islands, it attracts many tourists. The Canary Islands in the Atlantic are also popular; Spain's highest peak, Pico de Teide at 12,200 ft. (3,718m), lies on the island of Tenerife. Central Spain has hot summers, reaching 108°F (42°C), and cold winters; the coasts have a more moderate climate. Portugal is also mountainous, with high cliffs along its sandy Atlantic coastline. It has a milder climate than Spain. Its territory includes the islands of the Azores and Madeira in the Atlantic.

KEY CITIES
Spain's capital city, Madrid, is in the center of the country. Other major cities include the industrial ports of Barcelona, Valencia, Malaga, and Bilbao, as well as the historic fortress-cities of Granada, Cordoba, Seville, and Murcia. Portugal's capital city, Lisbon, stands on the Tagus River, which divides the country. Lisbon was rebuilt after being destroyed by an earthquake in 1755. Portugal's other major city, Porto, is the center of the port wine trade. Two thirds of the Portuguese people live in rural villages.

TOURISM AND TRADE
In Spain, tourism and industry have grown rapidly since the 1950s, alongside traditional activities such as crafts, winemaking, fishing, and growing fruit and vegetables. Portugal's main products are wine, fish, cork, and marble. Portugal also depends heavily on tourism. Many Portuguese work abroad, sending money back home. A fifth of the country's adults cannot read or write.

THE SPANISH LANGUAGE
Southern Spain was ruled by Moors— Muslims from North Africa—from A.D. 711 to 1492. Moorish civilization left its mark on language, architecture, food, and music. By 1516, Spain's several kingdoms

▲ Forests of cork oak trees in central and southern Portugal are stripped of their bark to provide large quantities of cork, a major product.

▶ Spain has about 1,400 castles and palaces. The fortified Alhambra Palace in Granada was built in the 1200s and 1300s.

Azores (Portugal)

miles
0   100

km
0   100

Corvo

Flores

Graciosa

Sao Jorge   Terceira

Fayal   Pico

Sao Miguel

Santa Maria

Madeira Islands (Portugal)

miles
0   100

km
0   100

Madeira

Porto
Santo

Canary Islands (Spain)

La Palma   Lanzarote

Pico de Teide   Fuerteventura

Gomera   Tenerife   Las Palmas

Hierro   Gran
Canaria

miles
0   100

km
0   100

AFRICA

ATLANTIC
OCEAN

Bay of Biscay

FRANCE

Miño

GALICIA

Cantabrian Mts.   Bilbao

Pico de Aneto

Porto

Valladolid

Duero

Saragossa

Pyrenees

ANDORRA

BASQUE
PROVINCES

Ebro

CATALONIA

Barcelona

Madrid

S P A I N

Estrela

Tagus

Guadiana

Valencia

Balearic Islands

Minorca

Majorca

Palma

Ibiza

Formentera

Lisbon

Cordoba   Guadalquivir

Murcia

ANDALUCIA

Seville   Granada

Malaga   Sierra Nevada

GIBRALTAR (U.K.)

Strait of Gibraltar

Ceuta
(Spain)

Melilla
(Spain)

MOROCCO

MEDITERRANEAN SEA

ALGERIA

ALGARVE

N

miles
0   100

km
0   100

▼ Antonio Gaudi was
Spain's most famous
architect. From 1884 until
1926, he worked on the
cathedral of La Sagrada
Familia (the Holy Family)
in Barcelona.

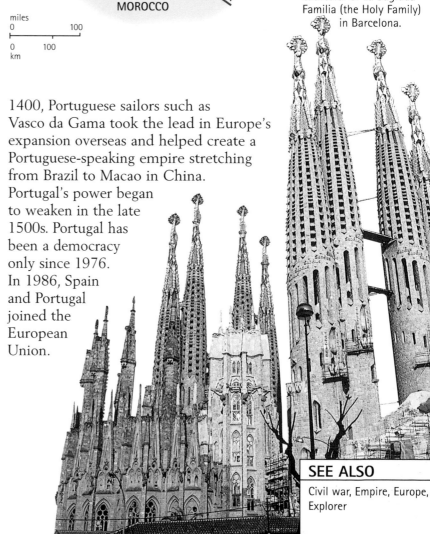

were united under one ruler and the
Roman Catholic Church. Wealth from
a newly conquered empire in South
America made Spain the greatest military
power in Europe, and colonization,
especially in the Americas, made
Spanish a world language.

SETBACKS TO PROGRESS

From 1800, Spain was weakened by wars,
revolutions, and poverty. After the Spanish
Civil War of 1936–39, General Francisco
Franco ruled as a dictator until his death
in 1975. The monarchy was then restored
with King Juan Carlos I, and a democratic
form of government was established.

PORTUGAL'S HISTORY

Although overshadowed by Spain,
Portugal has managed to keep its language,
identity, and independence. Like Spain,
Portugal has a Moorish heritage, is strongly
Roman Catholic, and has suffered from
wars, dictatorship, and poverty. From

1400, Portuguese sailors such as
Vasco da Gama took the lead in Europe's
expansion overseas and helped create a
Portuguese-speaking empire stretching
from Brazil to Macao in China.
Portugal's power began
to weaken in the late
1500s. Portugal has
been a democracy
only since 1976.
In 1986, Spain
and Portugal
joined the
European
Union.

SEE ALSO

Civil war, Empire, Europe,
Explorer

SPIDER AND SCORPION

Spiders and scorpions are invertebrates (animals with no backbone) belonging to a group called arachnids. They have four pairs of legs—insects have only three.

The wind scorpion (or sun spider) uses the wind to run and has huge jaws.

Mites, like this giant desert mite, are members of the arachnid family.

Unlike spiders, harvestmen have just one body section and eight slender legs.

A scorpion has large claws at the front to crush prey, and a sting in its tail.

All spiders and scorpions are predatory animals, feeding mainly on insects. Some of the big tropical spiders eat lizards and mice and even take baby birds from their nests.

WEB OF DEATH

Spiders are famous for the silk webs they spin to trap their prey. There are lots of different web designs, the best known being the circular orb webs. These have sticky spiral threads fixed to a set of radial threads that look like the spokes of a bicycle wheel. They are designed to catch flying insects. Other webs are designed to trap insects that scuttle over the ground.

HUNTING OR TRAPPING

The Australian dinopis spider spins a net, and holding this in its front legs, waits for an insect to pass by. Then it throws the net over the insect. But not all spiders make webs. Wolf spiders run after their prey, and crab spiders usually sit on plants, seizing insects that come within range.

POISONOUS FANGS

A spider kills its prey with poison, which is injected with a pair of needlelike fangs close to its mouth. The poison also starts to digest the prey, making it liquid, so the spider can suck the juices into its tiny mouth. It

◀ Crab spiders use their colors to hide in the center of flowers, ready to pounce on pollen-hunting bugs.

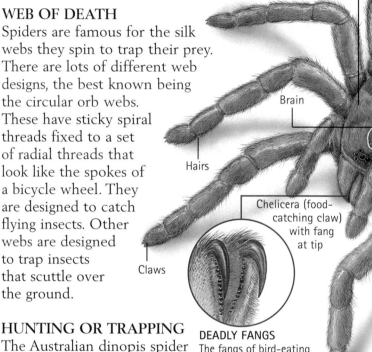

Spiders have two body parts—an abdomen (back end) and a cephalothorax (head and chest). The legs are joined to the cephalothorax

Sucking stomach

Heart

Ovaries

Brain

Hairs

Claws

Chelicera (food-catching claw) with fang at tip

Silk glands

DEADLY FANGS
The fangs of bird-eating spiders point straight down. In other species, they point sideways.

SILK SPINNERS
All spiders have spinnerets to make silk, even if, like the bird-eating spider, they don't make webs.

BIG, HAIRY BIRD EATER

Bird-eating spiders are among the largest spiders, with a leg span of up to 10 in. (25cm) and 2.5 in. (6cm)-wide bodies. Despite their eight eyes, they have poor eyesight and use their sense of touch and body hairs to detect vibrations. They leave trails of silk to help would-be mates find them, to help them climb, and to wrap their eggs.

cannot eat solid food. Some spider poisons are powerful enough to kill people, but only about 30 of the 30,000 or so species of spider are really dangerous. They include the black widow and the funnel-web spiders. The most venomous spider known to humans is the wandering spider from Brazil, and there is still no antidote for the bite of the recluse spider, also found in South America. The fangs of most spiders are too small or weak to pierce human skin.

▲ Scorpions are fluorescent. Their outer shell glows bright green when an ultraviolet light is shined at it. This helps scientists to spot them at night when they are most active.

SENSITIVE HAIRS

Each leg of a spider has seven segments. Most species have three claws at the tip of the leg and a pad of hairs that helps them stick to surfaces. The legs are covered with three kinds of sensory hairs. On most spiders, the hairs are irritants that can be rubbed off onto attackers. They are also used to taste (by detecting chemicals in the surroundings), to feel, and to "hear," picking up vibrations either on the ground or in the web. A male spider often drums on a female's web as a mating signal.

A DANGEROUS COURTSHIP

Mating can be dangerous for many arachnids. The male spiders are mostly smaller than the females and often risk being mistaken for prey and eaten when they approach a would-be mate. In fact, the female often eats the male after, or even during, mating. The male nursery web spider gives his partner a gift of an insect wrapped in silk. As she eats the insect, he can mate safely.

EGGS IN SILK BAGS

A female spider wraps her eggs in silk bags, or sacs. Wolf spiders carry these around with them, and even carry their babies on their backs for a while. Some spiders, such as the pink-haired bird-eating spider, lay 3,000 eggs in one batch—the hatched spiderlings are larger than many fully grown species.

▶ A scorpion's sting is at the end of a long flexible tail, which it can quickly flick over to inject venom into its prey. The poison comes from two glands at the base.

STICKY TRAPS

Spiders have a variety of ways to trap prey. The orb-web spider (like many common garden spiders) creates a circular web in which unsuspecting flies get stuck. Bolas spiders fish for prey using a sticky line of silk which they throw at nearby insects. Trap-door spiders lurk in tunnels with little trapdoors. They dart out to catch passing insects and drag them below.

SCORPIONS

There are about 1,200 species of scorpion, and all live in hot countries. Many of them live in deserts, where they can survive the high temperatures without ever needing a drink. Scorpions range from 0.8–8 in. (2–20cm) in length, the largest being the imperial scorpion of West Africa. All scorpions and spiders molt or shed their skin around 5 to 10 times as they grow.

A STING IN THE TAIL

Scorpions have large pincers—pedipalps— at the front and use them to catch lizards, insects, and other small animals. A scorpion also has a sting at the end of its slender tail. The sting is used mainly for defense, and some species are dangerous to people. The fat-tailed scorpion (found in parts of north Africa and the Middle East) is one of the most venomous scorpions. Its sting can kill a human in 6 to 7 hours.

Common garden spiders spin sticky, circular orb webs between branches.

Water spiders make a tent of silk under water, using air bubbles to breathe.

Trap-door spiders make a silk-lined tunnel in the ground with a lid on top.

SEE ALSO

Animal, Insect

391

SPORTS

A sport is a game or activity involving physical skills, often in competition. It is enjoyable as a form of exercise and also provides big-business entertainment.

Sports can be played either in teams or individually, on a professional or an amateur basis. Most sports are competitive and winning may be decided in a number of ways: by timing speeds (running or swimming events), measuring distances (jumping or throwing events), scoring points (most ball games), or judging performances (diving, boxing, and gymnastics).

Ice hockey players reach 30 mph (48kph) and drive a hard, disk-shaped puck at 100 mph (160kph).

In motorcross, strong, light bikes with chunky tires race across rough and hilly cross-country terrain.

A discus thrower spins around one and a half times before releasing the discus from his hand.

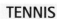

120 yards (110m)
100 yards (91.4m)
160 feet (49m)

KEY

1 Goalpost	4 Goal line
2 End line	5 Sideline
3 End zone	6 Inbounds lines

Goalpost

Helmet
Face mask
Shoulder pad
Chest pad
Arm guard
Rib and kidney guard
Elbow pad
Hip pad
Thigh pad
Knee pad
Athletic supporter

FOOTBALL

Football evolved from English soccer and rugby. Professional teams have squads of up to 45 players divided into three areas: one for offense, another for defense, and the third for kicking. The team in possession (offense) has four plays, or "downs," to advance the ball 10 yards (9.1m) by running with it or passing it. If successful, the team has another series of plays. If it fails, the opposition takes possession of the ball. All plays start on or between the inbounds lines. Six points are awarded for a touchdown, plus an extra point for converting the ball over the crossbar. Placekicking the ball over the crossbar from anywhere in the field gains three points. The defense can also score two points from a "safety" either by tackling the ball carrier in his own end zone, or if the carrier steps out of the back or side of his zone.

TENNIS

The modern game of lawn tennis was developed in Britain in the 1860s. The object of the game is to score points by hitting the ball with a racket over the net into the opponent's court so that it cannot be returned. The ball may be struck either before it has hit the ground or after one bounce. Tennis is played in sets, usually the best of three or five. A set is won when one side wins six games, with a lead of at least two games. A game's scoring goes from "love" (0) to 15, 30, 40, and "game." If the score reaches 40–40 ("deuce"), it continues until one side leads by two clear points.

◀ Success in men's tennis depends greatly on having a powerful serve, as Pete Sampras demonstrates.

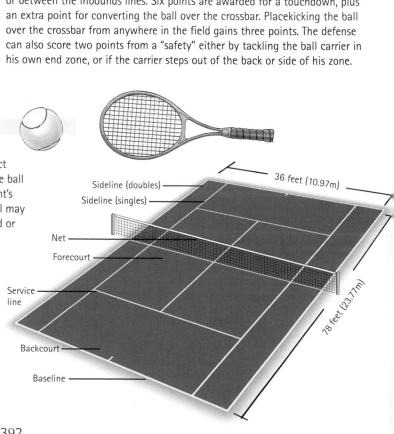

Sideline (doubles)
Sideline (singles)
Net
Forecourt
Service line
Backcourt
Baseline
36 feet (10.97m)
78 feet (23.77m)

SOCCER

Professional soccer is played 11 to a team, with three substitutes allowed, and consists of two 45-minute halves. The object of the game is to kick or head the ball into the opponents' net to score a goal. The team with the most goals at the end of play wins. Players can move the ball with their feet, head, or body, but not their hands or arms. Only the goalkeeper may handle the ball, and then only inside the penalty area. A free-kick is given if a player commits a foul or is offside. A player is offside when fewer than two defending players are positioned between him and the goal line as the ball is being passed forward to him.

▼ Brazilian defenders attempt to tackle Cobi Jones of the U.S.A. in the 1994 World Cup competition. Brazil went on to beat Italy in the final.

Goal
Dead ball line
Sideline
Centre circle
Halfway line
Penalty area
Six-yard box

295–393.7 ft. (90–120m)

147.6–295 ft. (45–90m)

TRACK AND FIELD EVENTS

Outdoor running events, except for the marathon, take place on the 400m track. They include the 100m, 200m, and 400m sprint. The longest middle-distance track race is 10,000m (25 laps), and other running events include the steeplechase and relay. Field events include: high, long, and triple jump; hammer, discus, and javelin throwing; pole vaulting; and shot putting. Combined track and field events include the ten-event decathlon and seven-event heptathlon.

HIGH JUMP

Run-up

Landing area

POLE VAULT

◄ Leading high jumpers use a technique called the "Fosbury flop." This involves clearing the bar head first, followed by the back, and, last of all, the legs. In pole vaulting, the pole may be of any length or width.

Staggered 400m start
Finish line
High jump
100m start
Steeplechase water jump

▲ Runners use adjustable starting blocks to keep them from slipping when they push off.

Staggered 200m start

Pole vault

Shot put
Javelin
Triple jump
Hammer and discus
Long jump

An old Scottish game, golf is now one of the most popular sports worldwide.

Horse racing can either be flat racing or racing over jumps, and is a major betting sport.

Skiing is a snow sport that includes downhill, slalom (obstacle course), ski-jumping, and cross-country.

BASKETBALL

Basketball was invented in Massachusetts in 1891, and is now one of the most popular sports worldwide. It is played by two teams of ten, although only five players may be on court at any one time. The object of the game is to score points by throwing the ball into the opposition's basket. Players move the ball around with their hands by passing, dribbling, and shooting. Running with the ball is not allowed. Baskets may be scored from any part of the court and are worth three points from outside the three-point arc, two from inside it, and one from a free throw.

▲ Michael Jordan slam dunks for the Chicago Bulls.

Backboard
Basket
Free-throw line
Sideline
End line
Center circle

FENCING

As a combat practice, fencing dates from the Middle Ages. Three weapons are now used—the épée, saber, and foil. The object of fencing is to touch your opponent on the target area with your sword to score a hit. The fencers are wired so that any hit can be registered electronically. Only the point of the weapon may be used in épée and foil, but with the saber the edge of the blade also counts.

Face mask
Target areas
SABER
Handle
Guard
Blade
ÉPÉE
FOIL
On-guard line
Center line
Electronic scorer
Rear limit

CRICKET

Organized cricket began in England in the late 1600s, but its origins probably go as far back as 1300. The modern game has 11 on each team. At each end of the pitch is a wicket, which is defended by a batsman. The object of the game is to get the opponents' side out with the least number of runs. A side's innings ends when ten batsmen have been dismissed, caught, or run out. Any member of the fielding side may bowl an "over" consisting of six balls. After each over, another bowler starts from the other end of the pitch. A run is scored when a batsman hits the ball with the bat and both batsmen run to the opposite end of the pitch without being dismissed. A hit over the boundary scores four runs, or six runs if it does not touch the ground first.

▲ The possible fielding positions for a right-handed batsman (only 11 fielders allowed): **1** Bowler; **2** Wicket-keeper; **3** First slip; **4** Second slip; **5** Gully; **6** Point; **7** Cover point; **8** Extra cover; **9** Silly point; **10** Silly mid-off; **11** Mid-off; **12** Deep mid-off; **13** Long-off; **14** Long-on; **15** Deep mid-on; **16** Mid-on; **17** Mid-wicket; **18** Silly mid-on; **19** Deep square-leg; **20** Square-leg; **21** Forward short-leg; **22** Backward short-leg; **23** Leg slip; **24** Short extra cover; **25** Backward point; **26** Short third man; **27** Third man; **28** Deep mid-wicket; **29** Deep extra cover.

Batting glove
Bails
Leg pad
Stumps

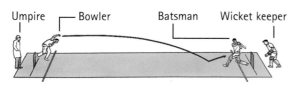

Umpire   Bowler   Batsman   Wicket keeper

BASEBALL

Baseball probably developed from games such as cricket and rounders. It was first played in 1846 in New Jersey. It is played nine to a team on a square field, the diamond, within a larger outfield. At one point of the diamond is home plate, where the batter stands, and at the other points are first, second, and third bases, each of which is defended by a baseman. The pitcher throws the ball from a mound in the center of the diamond. To score a run, the batter moves around the bases to reach home plate. He may do this with one hit or on hits of succeeding batters. Each side has nine turns at batting. The fielding side must get three batters out to close an inning and take its next turn at batting.

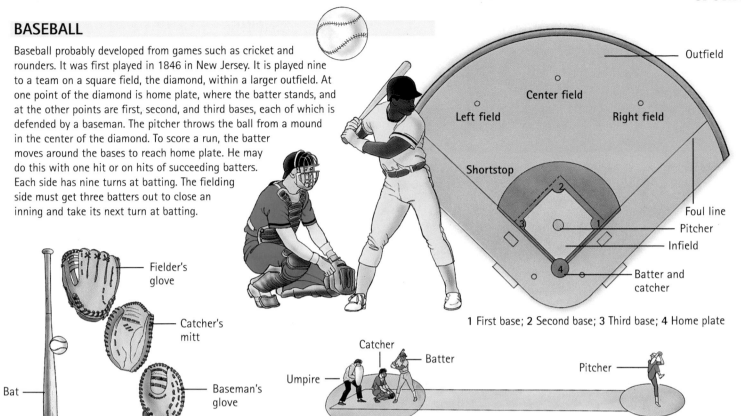

Fielder's glove

Catcher's mitt

Bat

Baseman's glove

Outfield

Center field

Left field

Right field

Shortstop

Foul line

Pitcher

Infield

Batter and catcher

1 First base; **2** Second base; **3** Third base; **4** Home plate

Umpire

Catcher

Batter

Pitcher

GYMNASTICS

Born in Ancient Greece, the idea of gymnastics was revived in the late 1700s and was held at the first modern Olympic Games in 1896. In competition, gymnasts are marked out of ten by a panel of judges. The classic events involve floor exercises, high bar, parallel bars, pommel horse, rings, and vault. Rhythmic gymnastics is performed to music and involves ballet steps and hand apparatus. Its individual exercises include twirling, throwing, catching, rolling, bouncing, or swinging the apparatus. Sports acrobatics, for individuals or teams, include somersaults and springs.

WOMEN'S VAULT

Handspring

Landing

Springboard

Horse

SWIMMING AND DIVING

The earliest swimming races took place 2,000 years ago in Japan. Today, they involve four main strokes—front crawl, backstroke, breaststroke, and butterfly—as well as freestyle. There are also separate diving events, either from a highboard or springboard, which involve specific somersaults, twists, and turns while in the air.

Dive

Recovery

Turn

SEE ALSO

Olympic Games

STAR

Stars are large balls of hot gas that produce light and heat through nuclear reactions. Our Sun is an average yellow star, but seems bright because it is so close.

THE BIRTH OF A STAR

A star begins its life by condensing out of material from a cloud of dust and gas. When the star's temperature is hot enough, nuclear reactions begin, and hydrogen converts to helium, creating a steady glow. Yellow stars, such as the Sun, may shine steadily for billions of years before expanding and cooling into red giants. Finally, they collapse into small, dense white dwarfs, and then die.

1 A nebula (cloud of dust and gas), the birthplace of a star.

2 The gas and dust condense, and the star begins to form.

3 Nuclear reaction takes place: hydrogen is converted to helium.

4 The new star generates light and heat.

5 The yellow star remains stable for billions of years.

▲ The constellation of Orion is a place where new stars are being born, in areas such as the Orion Nebula (M42).

Stars form from large clouds of gas and dust in space, called nebulae. These clouds shrink due to the inward pull of their own gravity. At the center of a shrinking cloud, the gas becomes hotter and denser. Eventually, nuclear reactions start, in which hydrogen is turned into helium by a process known ias nuclear fusion, and a new star is born.

STAR TEMPERATURES

At the center of a star, where nuclear fusion occurs, it is over 50 million°F (10 million°C). Stars may be classified according to their temperature. The temperature at the surface varies from star to star. A red dwarf may be 5,432°F (3,000°C), and a blue supergiant may be over 37,832°F (20,000°C). Stars also have different luminosities, or brightnesses, so a bright, distant star may look closer than a nearby star that is very dim.

STARS IN OLD AGE

When all the hydrogen at the center of a star is used up, the star begins to change. Its outer layers swell until the star is many times larger than before, and it becomes a red giant. After this, the fate of the star is decided by its mass. Stars such as the Sun end up as small, hot stars called white dwarfs. More massive stars, however, are

shorter-lived and blow up in huge explosions called supernovae. One of two final stages may follow: in the first, the remaining part of the star collapses until it becomes a neutron star, the densest type of star. A handful of its material weighs billions of tons. The second possibility is that a star of very great mass may collapse and become a black hole, a funnel-like shape that sucks all nearby material into it—even light cannot escape.

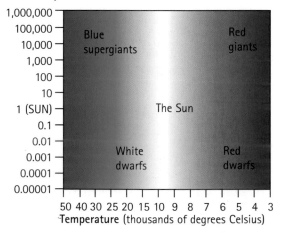

▲ The diagram plots the temperature and luminosity of stars. The more material a star has, the hotter it is. Blue supergiants are the hottest, and red dwarfs the coolest.

BRIGHTEST STARS

Name	Constellation
Sun	-
Sirius	Canis Major
Canopus	Carina
Rigil Kent	Centaurus
Arcturus	Bootes
Vega	Lyra
Capella	Auriga
Rigel	Orion
Procyon	Canis Minor
Achernar	Eridanus

SEE ALSO

Astronomy, Black hole, Color, Constellation, Galaxy, Sun, Universe

STARFISH AND OTHER ECHINODERMS

Starfish are star-shaped, marine invertebrates with between 5 and 40 arms. Other echinoderms include brittle stars, sea urchins, and sea cucumbers.

A sea cucumber can grow up to 20 in. (50cm). It has suckered feet for climbing.

A brittle star has no suckers. It uses its long arms to pull itself along.

A rock urchin grows up to 2.5 in. (6cm) and has sharp spines. It eats algae.

A violet heart urchin has furry spines on top. It burrows in sand and mud.

Echinoderm means "spiny-skinned," and all members of the group have a rough or spiny skin to protect them. All live in the sea. Brittle stars often live at great depths. Most starfish and sea urchins live in fairly shallow water. There are about 1,700 different kinds of starfish, ranging from about 0.4 in.–3.3 ft. (1cm–1m).

POWERFUL SUCKERS

Using its suckers, a starfish can move in any direction it chooses. It feeds on other small animals, including fish and worms, and can even open the shells of cockles and other bivalves with its powerful suckers. The starfish wraps its arms around a shell and grips with its suckers, which gradually pull the two halves of the shell apart. The starfish then pushes its stomach through the crack and digests the soft body inside.

DRIFTING YOUNGSTERS

Starfish do not mate. The males and females release clouds of sperm and eggs into the water, and fertilization takes place there. The young starfish (or larvae) are

▲ A starfish digests a mussel. It turns its stomach inside out and pushes it into the shell to eat the soft body.

bloblike with no arms and, instead of living on the seabed, they float near the surface of the sea so they spread to new areas. They alter shape as they grow, and metamorphose (change) into adults.

SLENDER RELATIVES

Brittle stars look like starfish, but their arms are more slender and are clearly separated from the central disk. Some brittle stars catch small animals with their arms, but most species shovel mud into their mouth and digest any tiny creatures living there. Sea cucumbers have feeding tentacles around their mouth to filter food from water. Some sea urchins also feed like this.

SOFT SUCKERS
Rows of circular tube-feet with suckers at the ends are spaced along the arms.

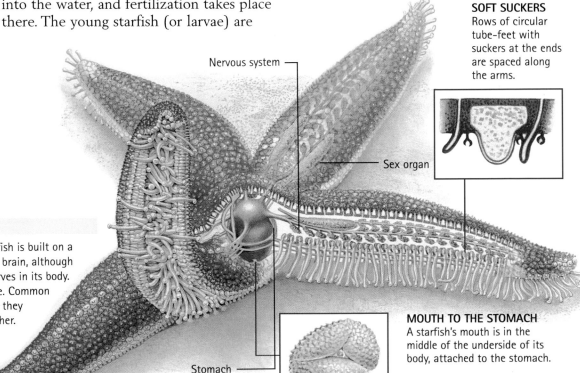

Nervous system

Sex organ

SYMMETRICAL STAR

Like all echinoderms, the starfish is built on a circular plan, with no head or brain, although it has a simple network of nerves in its body. The mouth is on the underside. Common starfish have five arms, and if they lose one, they may grow another.

Stomach

MOUTH TO THE STOMACH
A starfish's mouth is in the middle of the underside of its body, attached to the stomach.

SEE ALSO
Animal, Ocean and sea, Seashore

STOMACH AND DIGESTIVE SYSTEM

The food we eat is broken down into nutrients by the stomach and intestines, and then taken into the body for energy, growth, maintenance, and repair.

▲ A magnified view of human taste buds, which detect sweet, sour, bitter, and salt flavors.

The stomach is the widest part of the digestive system, a long passageway or tube within the body. This begins at the mouth and continues through the throat, gullet, stomach, small intestine, and large intestine, ending at the anus. The whole tube is about 30 ft. (9m) long.

CHEWED TO A PULP
Chewing mashes food into a pulp so that digestive juices can reach it more easily.

▲ Sugar and fat contain important nutrients. Too much, however, can damage health.

Three pairs of glands pour saliva into the mouth. The saliva contains enzymes to break down starches and sugars.

DIGESTING AND ABSORBING
In the stomach, the food is mixed with powerful acid and digestive enzymes. From there food passes to the small intestine, 1.6 in. (4cm) wide and 20 ft. (6m) long. Its lining is covered with thousands of villi (tiny projections), each about 0.04 in. (1mm) long. This provides a huge area for absorbing nutrients. The small intestine lining and nearby pancreas gland make more strong enzymes to digest chyme (semidigested food). Another digestive fluid, bile, is made in the liver and stored in the gallbladder. Bile is especially good at digesting fatty substances in food.

LARGE INTESTINE
Undigested food passes into the large intestine, about 2.4 in. (6cm) wide and 5 ft. (1.5m) long. The semisolid feces are stored near the end of the tract, in the rectum, until it is convenient to expel them through the anus.

LIVER
Blood from the intestines flows to the liver, which stores some nutrients from digestion, and converts sugars into starch for storage. It also breaks down possibly harmful substances, such as alcohol.

DIGESTIVE JOURNEY
Food takes 24 to 36 hours to pass through the human digestive system. It is digested, or broken down, by squeezing and mashing, and by strong chemical juices called digestive enzymes.

1 In the mouth, food is chewed into a pulp and mixed with watery saliva. This makes food slippery and easy to swallow. (Each mass of swallowed food is called a bolus.)

2 As food passes down the throat and the esophagus (gullet), it is squeezed and massaged along by wavelike contractions of the muscles in the wall.

3 Strong muscles in the stomach wall churn and squash the food. After 3 to 6 hours, the soupy, semidigested food, called chyme, trickles into the small intestine.

4 In the small intestine, the chyme is broken down into chemicals. The nutrients are taken into the bloodstream.

5 Undigested food and wastes pass into the large intestine. Water and body salts are absorbed by the bloodstream before the feces are expelled through the anus.

SEE ALSO
Food, Gland, Human body, Nutrition, Taste and smell

SUBMARINE

A submarine is a craft that can travel under the sea. It can be a deadly naval weapon, but can also explore the seabed and carry out repairs on underwater pipelines.

Periscope, radio and radar antennae

Navigation room

Dining room

Nuclear missile

Hydroplane

Crew's quarters

Engine control room

Rudder

Turbines

Heat exchanger

Nuclear reactor

Torpedo room

▲ David Bushnell's *Turtle* was the first submarine to be used in warfare, in the American Revolution, 1776. The craft was driven by hand- and foot-propellers and steered by a rudder.

KEY DATES

c.1620 First submarine is built by Dutchman Cornelius Drebbel

1864 USS *Hunley* becomes first submarine to sink an enemy ship, in American Civil War

1954 USS *Nautilus* is the first nuclear submarine

1960 *Trieste* submersible dives to a record 6.8 mi. (10.9km) in the Pacific

The earliest submarines were barrel-like vessels powered by hand-cranked propellers or oars during the 1600s and 1700s. American engineer Robert Fulton (1765–1815) tried in vain to interest the French navy in his submarine in 1800. Submarine warfare was tried during the American Civil War (1861–65), and it was the U.S. Navy that accepted the first practical submarine, built in 1898 by Irish-born inventor John P. Holland (1840–1914).

SUBMARINES IN WAR

Submarines armed with torpedoes sank ships in both world wars. They had electric motors for use under water, but moved faster on the surface, using diesel engines to recharge the electric motors' batteries. The United States launched the first nuclear-powered submarine in 1955. Modern naval submarines have nuclear reactors driving turbine engines and can travel around the world under water without refueling. They can fire guided missiles and, with the aid of computerized navigation systems, can go almost anywhere in the world's seas.

▲ Much of the space in a nuclear submarine is taken up by the turbines that drive it and the reactor. The crew's quarters and operating area take up a very small space.

HOW A SUBMARINE WORKS

A submarine's depth in the sea is controlled by ballast tanks. When the tanks are filled with water, the submarine sinks. When water in the tanks is forced out by compressed air, the submarine rises. Under water, the submarine is steered by rudders, while its depth is controlled by winglike hydroplanes at the front and rear. The submarine's whalelike shape helps it to slip through the water with the least resistance. The largest nuclear submarines are huge, weighing more than 20,000 tons, and have room for about 150 crew members and 16 nuclear missiles.

Hatch

Thruster

Thruster

Batteries

Ballast tank

Titanium cabin helps resist high water pressure

SUBMERSIBLES

Submarines used for scientific and industrial work are called submersibles. Some have no crew and are guided by remote control as they explore the oceans. Others, such as the U.S.'s *Alvin* (right), can seat up to three crew members. The *Alvin* can dive to 13,100 ft. (4,000m) and has been used to locate ocean mineral deposits and marine life. A remotely operated vehicle, *Jason Junior* (near right), can be operated from within the submersible to explore places too small or dangerous for the *Alvin*.

Video camera

Thruster

Strobe light

Cable for remote control

SEE ALSO

Engine, Nuclear power, Ship, World War I, World War II

SUDAN

Sudan is the largest country in Africa. It lies in the
northeast of the continent and borders nine other
African countries.

Area: 967,500 sq. mi.
Population: 37,090,298
Capital: Khartoum
Language: Arabic
Currency: Dinar

▲ The tomb of a religious
leader known as the
Mahdi stands in Sudan's
largest city, Omdurman.
The Mahdi led Sudanese
Muslims to victory over
the British in 1881-85.

Most of the population of Sudan
lives along the banks of the White
Nile and the Blue Nile, which join at the
capital, Khartoum, flowing north into
Egypt. Northern Sudan is desert, which
gives way to grassy plains in the central
region. In the south, where there is more
rainfall, there are forests and a swamp
called the Sudd which is about the size
of Alabama. The south is rich in wildlife,
including giraffes, lions, leopards, and
elephants, with hippos and crocodiles
along the Nile. It is hot, reaching 115°F
(46°C) in the north in the summer.

A DIVIDED LAND
For centuries, northern Sudan has been
the home of Arabs, who are Muslims and
make up 50 percent of the population.
The people of the south belong to several
different black African ethnic groups, and
are either Christians or followers of
traditional African religions. Over 100
different African languages are spoken.

FARMING AND INDUSTRY
Cotton is the major export crop, and
wheat and millet are the main food crops.
Mining produces chromium, gypsum, and
gold. Sudan is also the world's largest
supplier of gum arabic, which is used in
inks and medicines. Civil war between the

north and south broke out in the 1950s
and 1960s, and fighting has recurred
since 1983. War and drought together
have created a major refugee problem
and stopped the development of oil
fields found in the south. More irrigation
schemes could increase crop output and
employment, but finding money to pay
for machinery, fuel, and fertilizers remains
a major problem. Many skilled Sudanese
work abroad, sending money home.

ANCIENT LAND
People first settled in Sudan around 9,000
years ago, and farming began 6,000 years
ago. Missionaries brought Christianity from
A.D. 500, but Muslims later conquered the
area. Britain and Egypt controlled Sudan
together from 1899, until Sudan became
independent in 1956. Since then, it has
been ruled mostly by the military.

◀ Most people in Sudan,
including the Dinka, still
live by farming or herding.
The Dinka people make up
the country's largest
black African group.

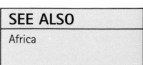

SEE ALSO

Africa

SUN

The Sun is the nearest star to Earth. It is a globe of hot gas, mostly hydrogen, and lies at the center of our solar system. It contains no solid material.

▼ Solar flares occur over sunspots. They can disturb Earth's magnetic field and interfere with radio transmissions on Earth.

The Sun is so large that more than a million Earths would fit inside it. It looks different from other stars because it is so much nearer to Earth. At the Sun's core, high temperatures and pressures cause nuclear reactions to take place in which hydrogen is turned into helium. This process releases huge amounts of energy, which eventually finds its way to the Sun's surface, called the photosphere. From there, it escapes into space as light, heat, and other radiations.

EVER-CHANGING

Cooler areas of the Sun form dark patches on the Sun's surface known as sunspots. From these, releases of energy, called solar flares, send bursts of radiation into space. Other eruptions, known as prominences, reach into the Sun's inner atmosphere, the chromosphere, and into its outer atmosphere, the corona. From the corona, there is a constant stream of particles into space, called the solar wind.

GOOD AND BAD RAYS

Without the warmth and light of the Sun, life on Earth would be impossible. But the Sun also gives off other kinds of radiation, including ultraviolet rays and X rays, that can be harmful. We are shielded from most of this damaging radiation by the ozone layer of Earth's atmosphere, but enough ultraviolet radiation penetrates to the surface to be able to cause sunburn.

LIFE STORY OF THE SUN

The Sun was formed about five billion years ago from a cloud of gas and dust. In another four or five billion years, its supply of hydrogen will run out and the core will collapse. The outer layers will swell as it becomes a red giant, then it will end its life as a slowly cooling white dwarf star.

THE SUN'S ENERGY

The Sun's energy is produced in the core. It flows out as radiation, through the radiative zone to the convective zone. The energy reaches the visible surface of the Sun (the photosphere) by a churning motion called convection. Hot gas rises to the surface, gives off its energy and cools, then sinks back. The surface gives off the energy as light and heat.

Corona

Solar flare

Chromosphere

Sunspot

Prominences erupt from the Sun's surface and can stretch for many thousands of miles

Sunspot

The shining surface of the Sun is called the photosphere

Sun's core

Radiative zone

Convective zone

SEE ALSO

Astronomy, Atmosphere, Gravity, Nuclear power, Solar power, Solar system, Star, Wavelength, X ray

SURGERY

Surgery is a branch of medicine that involves cutting into the body to remove or repair a body part that is damaged or diseased.

Artificial limbs were made over 2,000 years ago. In the 1500s, they were made of metal or wood.

Military surgeons in the 1700s carried their surgical instruments with them in a wooden case.

The surgeon Joseph Lister (1827–1912) used carbolic acid to disinfect the air during operations.

An early surgical knife is the forerunner of the modern-day scalpel, used to cut into the body.

Anesthetics can be given as gases inhaled through a mask, but they are now more likely to be injected.

A surgical procedure is called an operation and is usually done in the hospital. Operations are performed in an operating room—a room designed to protect the patient from infection.

THE SURGICAL TEAM
Operations are carried out by a specially qualified doctor called a surgeon. He or she works with an assistant, a surgical (or OR) nurse, and an anesthesiologist (a doctor who administers an anesthetic). The surgical team all wear sterile gowns, gloves, and masks to make sure that they neither receive nor transmit germs.

SURGICAL INSTRUMENTS
The surgeon uses various instruments during an operation. A scalpel is a knife that cuts into the body. Retractors hold the incision (cut) open. Forceps are used to handle tissue, which may be cut with surgical scissors. After the operation, the surgeon stitches the incision closed or seals it with special tape.

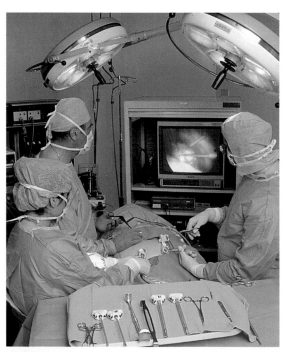

▲ Cameras are often used in the operating room, so that the surgical team can see the area they are operating on in greater detail on a video screen.

▲ Until the 1600s, the Church did not allow people to cut open human bodies for scientific purposes. The study of anatomy, shown here in Rembrandt's 1632 painting, enabled surgeons to perform more complex operations.

TYPES OF SURGERY
There are several types of surgery. In transplant operations, diseased organs such as the liver or heart are removed and replaced by healthy organs from human donors. Plastic surgery involves repairing skin that has been damaged by burns or injury. It is also done to improve a person's appearance. Today, many operations are done using keyhole surgery, which helps the patient recover more quickly. Here, the surgeon makes a tiny incision and uses miniature instruments to do the surgery.

DULLING THE PAIN
Without anesthetics, most of the surgery done today would be impossible. An American dentist, William Clarke, was the first to use anesthesia in 1847. He used ether to make a patient unconscious while he pulled out a tooth. Nitrous oxide, which is still used today, was another early anesthetic.

Biopsy forceps for taking samples
Viewer
Steering mechanism
Light supply
Optic viewer
Flexible tube

▲ The endoscope is a long, flexible tube with its own fiber-optic light source. This allows doctors to see inside the body before making an incision.

SEE ALSO

Drug, Medicine

SWAMP AND MARSH

Swamps, marshes, bogs, and fens are all varieties of wetlands, in which the soil is permanently waterlogged or even completely covered with water.

A swamp is a wetland area dominated by trees and shrubs—a kind of permanently flooded forest. Waterlogged areas without trees are called marshes.

UNDERWATER ROOTS

The species found growing in swamps are those that can withstand having their roots permanently under water. Some of the world's largest swamps are found in southern Asia. Here, mangrove swamps form a tangle of tall, stiltlike roots along thousands of miles of coast. Strange fish called mudskippers scurry around on exposed areas of mud, and archerfish spit water to knock insects off overhanging branches. Other creatures include crab-eating frogs and monkeys, and some of the world's most poisonous water snakes.

MARSHLAND

Marsh vegetation consists mainly of grasses and sedges. Dense patches of reeds and rushes surround patches of open water, which may contain water lilies, rooted to the bottom but with their leaves floating on the surface, or true floaters, such as the water hyacinth and duckweed. Many of Europe's large rivers have marshlands alongside them, providing homes for a huge variety of birdlife—from herons, egrets, and avocets to tiny reed warblers and bearded tits. Salt marshes are common around the coasts in temperate regions. They contain a variety of grasses, depending on how saline (salty) they are and whether they are permanently flooded. Like freshwater marshes, they contain huge numbers of insects, snails, and frogs and are vital breeding and feeding areas for waterbirds.

BOGS AND FENS

The term "bog" is usually used for a waterlogged area consisting of thick layers of peat. There is often no water on the surface, but the ground is soggy, and the surface is usually covered with spongy sphagnum moss. The peat is so acidic and contains so little oxygen that 2,000-year-old bodies have been found in it, perfectly preserved. Less acidic wetland areas are often called fens.

THE EVERGLADES

The Florida Everglades are the best-known Northern Hemisphere swamps, extending over 7,000 acres. The region is essentially a river filled with coarse grasses and rushes, and scattered with dense stands of cypress, red maple, and gum trees, draped with Spanish moss.

Rough green snake

Pileated woodpecker

Zebra butterfly

Raccoon

Roseate spoonbill

Green tree frog

Mississippi alligator

Mangrove roots

Terrapin

Oxeye tarpon

SEE ALSO

Alligator and crocodile, Bird, Fish, Habitat, Insect, Snake, United States of America

SWITZERLAND AND AUSTRIA

Switzerland and Austria lie north of Italy, in Europe, with Liechtenstein sandwiched between them. The Alps cover a large area of the two countries.

AUSTRIA
Area: 32,375 sq. mi.
Population: 8,169,929
Capital: Vienna
Language: German
Currency: Euro

SWITZERLAND
Area: 15,400 sq. mi.
Population: 7,301,994
Capital: Bern
Languages: German, French, Italian, Romansh
Currency: Swiss franc

▲ Switzerland is famous for its beautiful lakes, including Lake Geneva.

▲ Swiss banks are probably the most secure in the world. Gold bars are stored in their vaults.

Two great rivers, the Rhine and the Rhône, start in the Swiss Alps within 15.5 mi. (25km) of each other, and the mighty Danube flows through Austria. The mountainous landscape of both countries attracts many tourists.

ALPINE INDUSTRY
Switzerland is one of the richest countries in Europe, despite its lack of natural resources and flat farmland. Its wealth has come from banking, tourism, and industry —it produces cheese, chocolate, medicines, machinery, and watches. Over a third of Austria is wooded, supplying timber and paper. Austria's mountain waters feed hydroelectric plants that provide two thirds of the nation's power.

SWISS GOVERNMENT
Switzerland is divided into 26 regions, or cantons, but the central government controls the army, railroads, and mail, and links with foreign countries. Over 150 international organizations have their headquarters in Switzerland, including the Red Cross, founded there in 1864. Through all the wars of modern history, Switzerland has remained neutral, but all Swiss men must train as soldiers. About one sixth of the population was born outside Switzerland, nearly a third of them in Italy.

AUSTRIA'S PEOPLE
Until 1918, Austria ruled Europe's sprawling Austro-Hungarian Empire from Vienna. Vienna is Austria's capital city today, and almost a fifth of the population lives there. The majority of Austrians are Roman Catholics and keep up old customs and festivals. Many country people wear traditional dress, like lederhosen.

POPULAR PASTIMES
Austria has a rich musical history as the home of the waltz and of the composers Mozart, Schubert, and Strauss. Favorite Swiss and Austrian pastimes include folk dancing, yodeling, shooting, and cycling.

▲ Skiing is a popular pastime in both countries and attracts many tourists. In Austria alone, there are more than 50 resorts.

SEE ALSO
Europe

TASTE AND SMELL

Taste and smell are two of our five main senses. They warn us of harmful fumes or rotten food—and also allow us to enjoy a delicious meal.

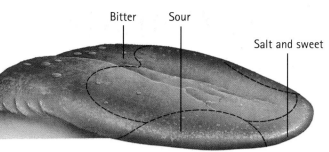

▲ Taste has only four main kinds of flavors: sweet, salty, sour, and bitter. Each is detected by a certain part of the tongue, with the tip most sensitive to sweetness.

FAST FACTS

• We can identify 10,000 or more smells

• There are only four kinds of flavors—other "flavors" are really the same four, combined in different proportions

• When we have a cold, food seems bland because we cannot smell it

• The middle of the tongue has hardly any taste buds

▲ A snake uses its tongue to pick up scents in the air, so it can tell whether a mate, a meal, or an enemy is near.

Smell and taste are called chemosenses because they work by detecting tiny particles of chemicals. In the case of smell, these particles, called odorants, float in the air that we breathe. In the case of taste, they are flavor particles in food and drinks.

DETECTING SMELLS
When odorant particles land on the sticky liquid, or mucus, at the top of the nose, they touch the hairs of the smell cells. Different smells have differently shaped particles and the hairs have differently shaped pits or holes, called receptors. If an odorant particle fits exactly into a receptor, this triggers the smell cell to generate a nerve signal. This passes along the olfactory nerve to the brain, where it is analyzed and identified. Unlike other senses, smell has direct nerve connections with the parts of the brain that deal with memory and emotion. This is why certain aromas can arouse strong memories and feelings.

DOWN IN THE MOUTH
The tongue's upper surface has pimple-like protrusions called papillae, which help to grip and move food during chewing. It also has 10,000 microscopic taste buds, scattered mainly between and on the sides of the papillae. A taste bud is a tiny pit containing a ball-shaped cluster of 20 to 30 gustatory (taste) cells, which are arranged like segments of an orange. Flavor particles dissolve in saliva, and, as in the nose, probably fit into receptors on the hairs of the gustatory cells. This triggers nerve signals that travel along two main nerves to the taste center of the brain for analysis and identification.

TASTING SMELLS
When we eat, the mouth mainly tastes the food, but we also smell it. This is because some odorant particles in the mouth float around the back of the roof of the mouth up into the nasal cavity. There, they are smelled in the same way as odorant particles breathed in through the nose.

Olfactory nerve

Olfactory bulb

Olfactory cells

Nasal cavity

Nerve to brain

Nerve fibers

Tongue

NOSE AND MOUTH CELLS

Inside the nose is a two-part chamber called the nasal cavity. The roof of each part has a thumbnail-size patch of lining which contains about 12 million microscopic olfactory (smell) cells. The tip of each of these cells is covered with 10 to 20 tiny hairs, called cilia. These stick in the thin, sticky mucus that coats the nasal cavity lining. The gustatory (taste) cells of the tongue's taste buds also have tiny hairs, projecting into the saliva that coats the tongue.

SEE ALSO
Brain and nervous system, Cell, Food, Human body

TECHNOLOGY

Technology is the practical use of knowledge to construct things, to make work easier, and to make our lives more comfortable. It is also used to cure diseases.

▶ The Romans developed expert engineering skills to construct viaducts and aquaducts across valleys.

The invention of the wheel meant easier travel—now chariots and carts could carry goods and people.

The abacus—a type of early calculator—has been used in China from around 5000 B.C.

No one knows when technology began. The earliest examples—hand-ax flints—are about 250,000 years old. Technology is now advancing very quickly, dramatically changing the way we live.

MATERIALS

Before 6000 B.C., wood, bone, hide, stone, and shell were used to make things. By controlling fire, ancient peoples could heat ores, such as iron and bronze, to make tools, weapons, and jewelry. In India and Egypt people became skilled at making pottery and glass. Eventually, processed natural materials such as leather, rubber, and bricks were developed. Synthetic materials, such as plastics, have been made only since the mid-1800s.

POWER AND PRODUCTION

The invention of the wheel (c.2000 B.C.) eventually led to the watermill and the windmill, which provided power for manufacturing. The steam engine paved the way for the Industrial Revolution, aided by the harnessing of electrical power in the 1830s. The internal combustion engine of 1876 led to the widespread use of automobiles. Machines using systems of wheels, gears, cranks, and cams were developed to carry out repetitive processes like weaving.

MODERN TECHNOLOGY

Nano-technology, which uses miniature, computerized robots, is revolutionizing the production of ever more sophisticated devices. Biotechnology (manipulating cells) and genetic engineering (manipulating genes) have far-reaching effects on society. Medical technology is used to help people live longer and healthier lives. Today, technologists must find ways to enrich our lives in ways that respect the Earth's environment, and sources of power that do not use fossil fuels and cause pollution.

VIRTUAL REALITY

Sophisticated computer graphics make it possible for people to experience things in virtual reality (VR) that would not normally be possible. A VR headset and gloves are worn by an engineer (left). These are connected to a computer that sends sensory impulses to his eyes, ears, and hands, enabling him to see and trace the path of a spacecraft in a wind tunnel. Doctors use VR to practice surgery.

SEE ALSO

Architecture, Construction, Engine, Genetics, Machine, Materials, Medicine, Telecommunication

TEETH

Teeth are hard, bonelike, enamel-coated structures embedded in the jawbones of animals, including humans. They are used mainly for biting and chewing.

Meat eaters such as the hyena have sharp teeth for tearing and crushing.

The male African elephant's tusk is the largest incisor tooth of any animal.

Snakes have teeth that curve backward to help pull prey into the throat.

A spider's fangs are hollow and filled with poison for paralyzing its victims.

A shark's teeth are serrated and are regularly replaced as they fall out.

Teeth are extremely strong and hard-wearing, and are covered with the body's hardest substance—enamel. But to prevent toothache, tooth decay, and gum disease, they need regular cleaning.

TYPES OF TEETH

Our four main kinds of teeth do different jobs. Incisors at the front are thin and square-tipped, like a chisel or spade, to slice and bite off food. Next are canines, or eye teeth, which are longer and more pointed in order to tear and rip. Premolars and molars, or cheek teeth, at the back of the mouth, are broad and wide-topped for powerful grinding and chewing.

FIRST SET OF TEETH

Humans grow two sets of teeth. The first set—baby, milk, or deciduous teeth—numbers 20. It begins to appear about six months after birth, and is complete by the age of three. Baby teeth consist of two incisors, one canine, and two premolars in both the left and right halves of the upper jaw, and the same in the lower jaw.

▲ A dentist looks after his patient by diagnosing and treating diseases of the teeth and gums. Regular visits to the dentist help to detect problems early.

SECOND SET OF TEETH

From the age of about seven, a child's first teeth loosen and fall out naturally, to be replaced by 32 permanent, or adult, teeth. In each half of each jaw there are two incisors, one canine, two premolars, and three molars. The rear molars, or wisdom teeth, are usually the last to erupt, or grow, above the gum, which happens at around the age of 20. In some people they never erupt, staying small and hidden in the jawbone.

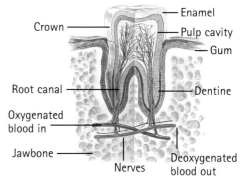

Crown — Enamel
— Pulp cavity
— Gum
Root canal — Dentine
Oxygenated blood in
Jawbone — Deoxygenated blood out
Nerves

INSIDE THE TOOTH

All teeth have the same basic structure. The upper part, or crown, of the tooth shows above the gum, and the root is in the jawbone. At the base of the crown, soft gum tissue (gingiva) joins to the neck of the tooth. In between the crown and root is the pulp cavity. This contains tiny blood vessels to nourish the tooth, and nerves to detect pressure, temperature, and pain. The vessels and nerves pass into the jawbone through a tiny hole, the root canal, at the root's base.

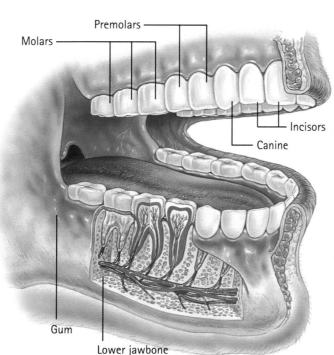

Molars
Premolars
Incisors
Canine
Gum
Lower jawbone

SEE ALSO

Elephant, Horse, Human body, Shark, Spider and scorpion

TELECOMMUNICATION

Telecommunication is the transmission of words, sounds, images, or data over long distances as electronic or electromagnetic signals.

Simple communication systems were already in use in the early 1800s. A code, known as semaphore, that used two movable arms for each letter and a mirror called a heliograph to flash sunlight, allowed people within sight of each other to send messages.

▲ Semaphore telegraphy became the fastest way to send messages across long distances in the early 1800s.

▲ The first submarine cables were laid between Dover in southern England and Cap Grisnez in northern France in 1850.

▲ Advances in telecommunication have changed the way we work. Automated teller machines, or ATMs, have widely replaced bank tellers for cash withdrawals.

ELECTRIC PULSES

The electric telegraph allowed coded messages to be sent much farther, as pulses of electric current along copper wires. It was invented in Britain in 1837 by William Cooke and Charles Wheatstone and was soon used by railroad companies. Developed at the same time, Samuel Morse's American telegraph system used coded pulses to transmit messages from place to place. The dots and dashes of the Morse code were internationally authorized until 1997.

MESSAGES WITHOUT WIRES

In 1876, Alexander Graham Bell discovered how to send the human voice along wires. In doing so, he invented the telephone. Then, using the discoveries about electromagnetic waves made by German physicist Heinrich Hertz in 1894, the Italian inventor Guglielmo Marconi made a "wireless" telegraph. Sending messages as radio waves, Marconi linked telegraph operators on opposite sides of the Atlantic Ocean in 1901. As the use of radio developed, speech, and later pictures, could be transmitted. High-frequency microwave radio signals can now carry tens of thousands of telephone conversations, telex, and fax messages all at the same time, together with television and data signals.

AROUND THE WORLD IN SECONDS

Microwave radio signals travel in straight lines, so they need to be passed along by relay stations in order for them to carry smoothly around the curve of the Earth's surface. The British science fiction writer

▲ The invention of radio in 1901 helped police and armed forces keep in contact with those working outside.

Arthur C. Clarke came up with an ingenious solution to the problem in 1945. He suggested putting the relay equipment on satellites which could orbit the Earth every 24 hours, staying fixed in one point in the sky 22,370 mi. (36,000km) above the ground. His dream become a reality in 1964, when the first geostationary satellite *Syncom 3* was successfully launched and put into orbit. Complete networks of satellites and ground stations can now link any two places on the Earth almost instantly.

TOO MUCH INFORMATION?

The kinds and amount of information being carried by telecommunication systems is increasing all the time. Converting voice, sound, and pictures into digital code allows increasingly more

▲ Fax (facsimile) machines send messages and images down telephone lines. They were demonstrated in 1902 by the German Arthur Korn, and were in use by the 1920s.

THROUGH THE CABLES
Multimode fibers have glass cores which can carry several light messages at once over short distances.

Outer sheath
Filter
Fiber
Cushion

Satellite

▲ Using the World Wide Web, children on two continents can send messages directly to each other within minutes.

CHATTING ELECTRONICALLY

The rapid growth of the Internet has revolutionized the telecommunication industry. An electronic mail (E-mail) message sent from one country to another can travel by a variety of routes. Here, it travels from the computer by fiber-optic cable, then by microwaves relayed by a satellite. It finishes its journey by cable.

Ground station transmits and receives signals

information to be carried across continents and seas, and this information travels almost instantaneously. Today, fiber-optic cables made of bundles of fine glass fibers are used to transmit telephone calls. A caller's voice is changed into digital signals that are carried as rapidly flashing pulses of laser light. Fiber-optic cables channel light around corners and can carry far more digital information than the copper wires that carry analog signals.

INFORMATION SQUEEZE

It is now possible to squeeze more information through existing networks by compression. The capacity, or bandwidth, of the networks is increased, and this helps to ease the flow of data while new networks are designed and built. A purely digital system called ISDN (Integrated-Services Digital Network) began operating in Japan in 1988 and has since been adopted by many countries.

FAST FACTS

• Two optical fibers can carry 6,000 telephone conversations at the same time

• People in the U.S.A. make the most telephone calls—around 1 million calls per minute

• Despite the success of ICT (Information Communications Technology), most people on Earth have still never made a telephone call

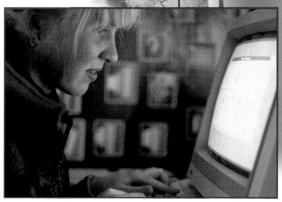

▲ By checking her electronic mailbox, this user can receive mail and reply immediately. She doesn't have to rush out to mail a letter.

SEE ALSO

Communication, Computer, Internet, Laser, Satellite, Telephone

TELEPHONE

Telephones are instruments for communicating over long distances. They send speech to another location as electric currents, laser light, or radio waves.

Alexander Graham Bell's prototype telephone (1876) had an exposed coil, electromagnet, and wires.

The telephone was invented in 1876 by the Scottish engineer Alexander Graham Bell (1847–1922). He had been working in the United States on improvements to the telegraph, which could only send Morse code dots and dashes. By 1880, the first public telephone systems were in use, although at first they had very few customers.

GETTING CONNECTED

Early telephones were connected by wires to a telephone exchange, where operators connected one line to another by hand. The invention of automatic switches in the 1890s allowed exchanges to connect calls without going through an operator. Modern telephone systems change the varying electrical signal of older telephones into a digital signal made up of pulses that are handled by computerized exchanges, removing the need for mechanical switches.

The telephone of 1919 had a body with a mouthpiece, a rotary number dial, and a separate earpiece.

▲ Until the early 1900s, telephone operators connected phone calls manually through a switchboard. A caller gave the operator the number; the operator then connected the caller's line to the line of the person being called.

SENDING THE SIGNAL

Calls can be sent around the world as radio signals relayed by satellites, or digital signals can be sent as pulses of laser light along fiber-optic cables under the oceans. The fiber-optic cables can carry thousands of calls at once. Cellular phones use microwave radio frequencies to connect to nearby transceivers, which transmit and receive calls in a network.

NEW TECHNOLOGY

Phones are becoming even more useful as the technologies of telephones and computers mix. Internet access, E-mail, and video telephones, which display images of the caller, are all possible from a small, mobile handset using digital technology.

HOW DOES A TELEPHONE WORK?

A telephone handset has a mouthpiece and an earpiece. When a caller speaks, sound waves made by their voice hit a diaphragm (thin metal disk) in the mouthpiece, making it vibrate. This pushes against carbon grains, making their resistance to an electric current flowing through them vary in a pattern that copies the sound wave pattern. At the receiver's end, this current causes an electromagnet to make the diaphragm in their earpiece vibrate. This makes sound waves that reproduce the sound of the caller talking.

Cellular phones are small and portable. They allow people to communicate while on the move.

Earpiece

Electromagnet

Diaphragm

Mouthpiece

Cable

Number pad sensors

Electronic circuit board

Diaphragm

Carbon granules

Electric current

◄ Sound waves vibrate the diaphragm, compressing carbon granules to alter the flow of electricity and send the caller's voice.

SEE ALSO

Communication, Internet, Laser, Light, Sound, Telecommunication

410

TELESCOPE

Telescopes are instruments for studying objects that are far away. Astronomers use various kinds of telescopes to find out more about stars and planets.

REFRACTING TELESCOPE

Viewfinder
Eyepiece
Telescope tube
Object lens
Eyepiece lens
Object lens
Focus
Light rays

Sir Isaac Newton (1642–1727) invented a reflecting telescope that used curved mirrors to reflect light.

Galileo (1564–1642) used this telescope to view the phases of Venus and the moons of Jupiter.

William Herschel (1738–1822) built a reflector with a 47-in. (120-cm) aperture to study faint objects.

Edwin Hubble (1889–1953) used this 8-ft. (2.4-m) reflector to discover the expansion of the universe.

The Hubble Space Telescope orbits Earth and sends back pictures from the farthest parts of the universe.

OPTICAL TELESCOPES

The two main types of optical telescope are refractors and reflectors. Refractors, such as the Simmons 100X magnification telescope, use a lens to form an upside-down image. Reflectors have a large, curved mirror instead of a lens. The mirror gathers light, which is reflected off a second mirror into the eyepiece. The image seen is right-side up.

Eyepiece lens
Focus
REFLECTING TELESCOPE
Object mirror
Flat mirror
Light rays

The first telescope was built by a Dutch scientist called Hans Lippershey (c.1570–1619) in 1608. It was an optical telescope, with glass lenses that made distant objects appear larger.

REFRACTING TELESCOPES
Refractors have two lenses. A large lens at the front of the telescope, called the objective, collects light. A small eyepiece lens focuses the light into the observer's eye. Galileo used this kind of telescope in 1609 to look at the Moon, which he could see 30 times more clearly than before.

REFLECTING TELESCOPES
Modern astronomers mainly use reflectors with a big, curved mirror to collect light, and a small, flat mirror to shine the light through an eyepiece lens. The first reflector, built by Isaac Newton in 1668, used a primary mirror only 3 in. (7.5cm) wide. Modern reflectors use larger ones. The Keck telescope in Hawaii has 36 six-sided mirrors joined to make a mirror 33 ft. (10m) across. Images are viewed on a computer screen or camera film.

SEEING THE UNSEEN
Light reaching us from distant parts of the universe is very faint, and the Earth's atmosphere blurs what we can see through optical telescopes. To record faint images, astronomers use electronic detectors called charged-coupled devices (CCDs) instead of their eyes. The Hubble Space Telescope (HST) orbits high above the Earth's atmosphere, so the light it collects is not distorted. Radio, X-ray, infrared, gamma-ray, and microwave telescopes collect other kinds of energy radiating from stars and galaxies that we cannot see with our eyes.

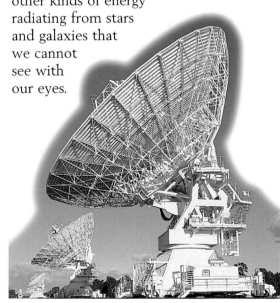

▲ The Hanbury Brown radio telescope in New South Wales, Australia, picks up long-wavelength radio waves from space.

SEE ALSO
Astronomy, Lens, Radio, Satellite, Wavelength, X ray

411

TELEVISION

Television (TV) is the transmission of pictures and sounds from one place to another. It is one of the most important means of mass communication in the world.

▲ A Serb army officer stops a TV news crew from filming during the Bosnian crisis of 1995. Television is a powerful media tool which many governments try to control.

Television began in 1937 when public broadcasts were made from Alexandra Palace in London. Several scientists had worked on developing television, including the Scot John Logie Baird and Americans Vladimir Zworykin and Philo Farnsworth.

John Logie Baird's 1926 television system used lenses set in revolving disks to scan a picture.

Large-screen televisions use a back projection system with mirrors to enlarge the image.

IN THE PICTURE
Television pictures and sounds are made up of electronic signals produced by a camera and recreated by a television set. A TV camera has lenses which focus the picture onto a surface that converts light to electronic signals, which can be recorded on videotape. The signals can be turned into radio waves, to be broadcast from radio transmitters, beamed via satellite, or sent along cable networks directly to the TV sets in homes.

MAKING A TV PROGRAM
Producing a TV show is a team effort. Camera operators take the pictures, while mike boom operators keep microphones in position. The director in a control room cuts from one camera to another. There are also scriptwriters, makeup artists, costume designers, caterers, lighting crews, postproduction teams, and technical staff.

INTO THE FUTURE
Liquid crystal displays (LCDs) are used for camcorder screens. High-definition TV has twice the number of lines on the screen, producing very detailed images. TVs using digitized signals to give sharper sounds and pictures are being developed. In the future, 3-D television may be possible.

HOW TELEVISION WORKS

A TV camera has a lens which focuses the picture onto light detectors, which convert light to electronic signals for broadcasting. The main part of a TV is a large, funnel-shaped glass tube with a screen at one end. The inside of the screen is coated with strips of a chemical called phosphor, which light up when electrons hit them. A beam of electrons is fired at the screen from electron guns in the back of the tube. Focusing plates, controlled by the TV signal, target the beam on the screen, creating the picture. A mask blocks any stray electrons. Color TV sets have three electron beams—one each for red, green, and blue.

TELEVISION CAMERA

Microphone

Lens

Light detectors

Viewfinder

Movable base

Cable carries signal from camera

Electron guns

Focusing plates

TELEVISION SCREEN

Electron beams

Mask

Phosphor strips

Picture on glass screen

SEE ALSO
Electricity, Invention, Media, Radio, Telecommunication, Video

TEXTILE

The word textile means "to weave," and the first textiles were all woven. Now they can be created from natural fibers or manufactured using chemical processes.

Originally, textiles were fabrics made by spinning natural fibers into threads and then weaving them together on a loom. Modern textiles are also produced by other methods such as knitting (using a single yarn or set of loops) or felting (matting fibers together by heat and pressure), and include such materials as lace, braid, and net.

▲ A Chinese woman weaves silk on a hand loom. Woven fabrics use two sets of yarns: one lengthwise (the warp) and one crosswise (the weft).

GROWING MATERIALS
The five most important natural fibers are wool, cotton, silk, linen, and jute. Wool comes from sheep, goats, or llamas; cotton has been grown in Egypt and India since ancient times, and silk was first made in Ancient China. Linen, made from the flax plant, is used for shirts, sheets and pillowcases, tablecloths and napkins; jute, which grows best in India and Bangladesh, is used for sacks, matting, and ropes.

▲ Cotton machines in a Ugandan factory. The raw cotton has been arranged into long fibers and coiled. The fibers are twisted into yarn and woven.

WEARING CHEMICALS
The chemical industry produces synthetic (artificial) fibers such as nylon and acrylic, which can be made stronger, cheaper, more elastic, and easier to wash than natural fibers. These include neoprene, a synthetic rubber used in wetsuits, Gore-Tex, a waterproof fabric used in climbing and outdoor clothing, and stretchy nylon Lycra, used in everyday casual wear.

▲ Tapestries are textile art. They are woven in different color threads to create a picture. Some tell a story. The Bayeux Tapestry recounts the Battle of Hastings in 1066.

FROM HOME TO FACTORY
Textile-making has often made great use of women's labor. Weaving was traditionally practiced at home and still is in many parts of the world. Textile-making was the first industry to be completely mechanized, starting with cotton in Britain in the 1700s. Modern textile machinery is often computer-controlled to produce intricate designs.

A WAY OF LIFE
Many areas of the world have depended on textiles for employment. Special types of cloth, such as denim, duffel, muslin, and chantilly, take their names from the towns which specialized in making them. Making rugs and carpets is still a major industry in countries such as Turkey, Iran, Afghanistan, and Pakistan. Indonesia is famous for a resist-dyeing process called batik.

TEXTILE USE
The largest demand for textiles comes from the clothing industry, but they are also used for upholstery, sports, and car accessories.

▶ A young child makes a traditional Jaipur carpet in India. He pulls threads through using a hand tool.

◀ In a factory, textile patterns are printed using rollers on a rotary printer—each prints a single color. Some textiles are still hand-printed by batik or screen printing.

SEE ALSO
Central America, Clothing, Design, Paint and dye, Printing, Technology

THEATER

Theater is the production of a drama, comedy, music, or other artistic performance in front of an audience. It usually takes place in a specially designed building.

Sophocles (c. 496–406 B.C.) wrote 123 tragedies in Ancient Greece.

William Shakespeare (1564–1616) was England's finest playwright.

Okuni (c.1620) established the Japanese style of theater called Kabuki.

Molière (1622–73) created a new kind of comedy in the French theater.

Irishman Samuel Beckett (1906–89) wrote abstract, philosophical plays.

Tennessee Williams (1911–83) wrote tense plays about the southern U.S.A.

THE GLOBE THEATER

The Globe Theater was built in London in 1614 after a fire destroyed an earlier theater. The audience sat in galleries or stood around the stage. Most of Shakespeare's plays first appeared here.

Modern theater can be traced back to dramatic performances in the theaters of Ancient Greece. Theater may mix design, music, dance, poetry, and prose to create drama in front of an audience.

ANCIENT PLAYS

The Ancient Greeks established both tragedy and comedy. In Greek theater, the chorus (a group of singers) chanted the story, while the actors mimed their roles. At first, the audience sat on hillsides, and the action took place on a level space—known as the orchestra. By 450 B.C., theaters with banks of stone benches for the audience, like the one at Epidaurus, had been constructed. The Romans added an elaborate "scene house," which provided backdrop scenery for the action. In front of this, there was a raised stage above the orchestra, as in modern theaters.

REVIVAL IN EUROPE

During the Middle Ages, theater in Europe almost ceased to exist. In the 1500s, William Shakespeare and others led a revival. All the roles were played by men and boys, not women. Actresses first appeared in Europe with the Italian traveling players performing *commedia dell'arte*—plays with themes of love and intrigue. In Japan, actors developed the formal No and popular, stylized Kabuki dramas.

ARCHES AND STAGES

In the 1590s, English theaters were circular wooden buildings with an open stage. In the 1600s, the proscenium arch—a frame around the front of the stage—was introduced. This masked the areas where actors or sceneshifters waited. One of the most important figures of European theater in the 1700s was David Garrick (1717–79), an actor-manager who put on new plays, as well as works by Shakespeare.

MUSIC HALL AND DRAMA

Increasingly popular during the 1800s was music hall, known as vaudeville in North America. These shows had actors, singers, and comedians performing to enthusiastic and noisy audiences. Opera (drama in which the actors sing) and ballet (dance drama) also flourished in the 1800s. At the same time, electric lighting, larger sets, revolving stages, and exciting special effects with water, smoke, and illusions developed. Productions became so elaborate that, by 1910, some directors preferred a simple approach with little scenery. New ideas included the open-thrust stage, which projected forward, theater-in-the-round (with the audience all around the stage), and open-air theater.

THEATER TODAY

Modern theater productions involve a team of backstage people—designers, set-builders, technicians, and wardrobe and make-up artists, as well as the actors and director. Professional theaters offer the latest electronic gadgetry, lighting, and sound systems, although plays are still performed very successfully by amateurs in small halls and schools. The Ancient Greek theater of Epidaurus continues to stage classic Greek dramas. In London, the reconstructed Globe Theater offers modern audiences the opportunity to experience Shakespeare's plays as they were originally performed.

"THE MET"

There has been a Metropolitan Opera House, known as "the Met," in New York City since 1833. The new house at Lincoln Center opened in 1966 and both opera and ballet are presented there. Each time a performance is put on, the theater employs a team of about 1,000 people.

▲ These Indian puppets are ten feet high. They are used in dramatic performances to tell tales of love and bravery.

Stage

3,800 seats in auditorium

Backdrops waiting to be lowered

Lighting system

ffices for dministration

Ballet rehearsal room

Slip stage with scenery for next act

Wardrobe department

SEE ALSO

Dance, Greece (Ancient), Literature

TIGER AND OTHER BIG CATS

Tigers, lions, and leopards belong to a group of the cat family known as "big cats." The cat family also includes many smaller wildcats, as well as the domesticated cat.

The cheetah is the only cat to outrun its prey rather than stalk it.

The black panther is a natural variation of the leopard with very dark fur.

The lynx is a wildcat that lives in the forests of Asia, Europe, and North America.

Tigers belong to the cat family (*Felidae*). So do six other kinds of big cat—lions, cheetahs, jaguars, leopards, snow leopards, and clouded leopards. The cat family also includes about 28 kinds of smaller wildcat, from the puma, bobcat, and lynx down to the smaller margay, kodkod, and sandcat. The black-footed cat of southern Africa is even smaller than a domesticated cat.

CAT FEATURES

All cats are meat-eaters, members of the carnivore group. They live by hunting, although a few scavenge dead meat. They have sharp senses, with excellent sight even at nighttime, and amazing balance for climbing. Long whiskers feel the way in

NIGHT HUNTER

Like other cats, the tiger hunts mainly at twilight or night. It prefers dense, swampy forest and ambushes deer, wild pigs, wild cattle, and the occasional baby elephant or rhino. Very rarely, a tiger preys on people. The record-holding man-eater killed over 400 people.

▲ Although not classed as a big cat, the puma is as big as a leopard. Also known as the cougar, mountain lion, or panther, it ranges through the Americas and eats a varied menu, from deer to birds.

darkness. The cat's body is lithe and agile, with stealthy movements. The fur is striped, spotted, or patterned for camouflage, so the cat can creep silently and unseen. Long claws grip, scratch, and slash, and can be pulled or retracted into the toe tips, keeping them sharp. Long, sharp teeth bite and tear apart prey.

BIGGEST OF THE BIG CATS

Tigers live across India, on some islands of Indonesia, and in South China and Manchuria. Siberian tigers of Manchuria are huge and powerful predators, up to 13 ft. (4m) from nose to tail and over 660 lb. (300kg). Like most cats, tigers live alone. They are only together when mating, or when a mother is with her cubs.

▲ Lions are the only cats that live and hunt in groups (or prides). The lionesses do the hunting, usually at night. One lioness stalks the prey, driving it toward the other lionesses who lie in wait. The adult male does not join in, but claims a share of the kill. Lions sleep during the day.

Cat family (Felidae)

Cheetah (Acinonyx)

Cheetah

Small cats (Felis)

Lynx African wildcat Domestic cat

Big cats (Panthera)

Leopard Tiger Lion Jaguar Snow leopard

THE LEOPARD

The leopard is the most widespread big cat, ranging across Africa and Southern Asia, into China and Indonesia. It is adaptable, too, living in high hills, deserts, scrub, rain forests, and even near towns and villages. Leopards eat a wide variety of prey and will drag a carcass into a tree to store it away from scavengers. The rare snow leopard, or ounce, lives in the Himalayas and nearby mountains. It has long, thick, pale fur for warmth and camouflage in the snow. The clouded leopard is the smallest big cat, weighing just 45–65 lb. (20–30kg). It lives in India and Southeast Asia.

THE CHEETAH

This lean, long-legged big cat is the fastest land animal. It sprints at almost 62 mph (100kph) after swift prey such as antelope, hares, and even young ostriches. It has spotted fur and a long tail to help it balance and turn at speed. The cheetah is the only cat that cannot retract its claws. For this reason,it is classed on its own in the cat family.

THE LION

Prides of lions were once common in Europe, Africa, and Asia, but now can be found only in protected areas south of the Sahara Desert in Africa and in the Gir Forest, a wildlife sanctuary in India. They live in open, grassy plains where water is

THE CAT FAMILY

The cat family is divided into three groups, with the cheetah forming a group of its own. The group known as *Felis* includes the domestic cat, as well as about another 27 types of small cat. The big cats belong to the *Panthera* group, which includes six big cats—the five shown here and the clouded leopard.

available and are territorial, fiercely protecting their hunting ground, where they stalk zebras, wildebeest, and antelope.

THE JAGUAR

The only American big cat, the muscular jaguar is found in the southern U.S.A. and in Central and South America. With its spotted coat, it resembles a leopard, but is larger and more powerful, weighing about 220 lb. (100kg). Jaguars like thick forests with swamps, lakes, and rivers. They swim well.

▼ The leopard has a full body length of about 60 in. (150cm). As with most cats, the males are larger than the females, at 130–155 lb. (60–70kg). The leopard's larger spots are not single black patches, but circular groups, or rosettes.

SEE ALSO
Animal, Cat, Mammal

TIME

We use time to track the passing of days, in hours, minutes, and seconds. In addition to natural units of time, people have invented other ways to measure it.

One day

One day is exactly the time it takes for the Earth to revolve on its axis once.

One year

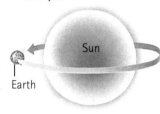

One year is approximately the time it takes for the Earth to orbit the Sun.

One lunar month

A month is based roughly on the time it takes the Moon to orbit the Earth.

When you need to know the time, you look at a watch or clock. This tells you how many hours and minutes it is since noon (midday) or midnight. For example, if your watch says the time is exactly 3:30 ("half past three") in the afternoon, you know that three hours and thirty minutes have passed since noon. If your watch is very precise, it may also tell you how many seconds have passed.

DAYS

The measurement of time is based on the position of the Sun in the sky. Every day, the Sun seems to rise at dawn, move across the sky, then set at dusk. This happens because the Earth is continually spinning around. Each place on Earth can only see the Sun for part of the day; when the Sun is out of view, it is nighttime in that part of the world. The Sun appears to rise as it comes into view and set as it disappears again. At one moment in the day, each place faces the Sun directly. When this happens, the Sun is highest in the sky and the daylight is brightest (on a sunny day).

▲ The Greenwich Observatory in England is the place where astronomers first devised the Greenwich meridian in 1866. This is the line at zero longitude that divides east from west; time zones are still calculated from it.

HOURS

As early as 2400 B.C., the Babylonians divided the day into 24 equal parts, called hours. The modern day starts at midnight, a time when the sky is dark in most areas. A few hours later, the Sun rises. Twelve hours after midnight it is noon, the time when the Sun is highest. In another 12 hours, it is midnight again.

CALENDARS

Every civilization has used some kind of calendar to keep track of years, months, weeks, and days. Calendars are used to plan planting and harvesting, and also to mark special holidays and festivals. The Julian calendar was instituted by Julius Caesar in 46 B.C. Pope Gregory XIII (1502–85) adjusted it in 1582, and his Gregorian calendar is still used in Western countries today. The Chinese calendar is lunar, with a 60-year cycle, but the Chinese use the Western calendar, too. The Jewish calendar is a complex combination of solar and lunar cycles, with 12 or 13 months.

THE AZTEC CALENDAR

CALENDARS OF THE AMERICAS

The Aztecs of Central America made a calendar in the ground from a huge stone shaped liked the Sun. The face of the Sun god, Tezcatlipoca, was carved in the middle, and signs for the days were carved around the edges. The Maya—also of Central America—used a calendar with two interlocking cog wheels to represent circular time. Native American tribes kept track of time by watching the seasons and phases of the Moon.

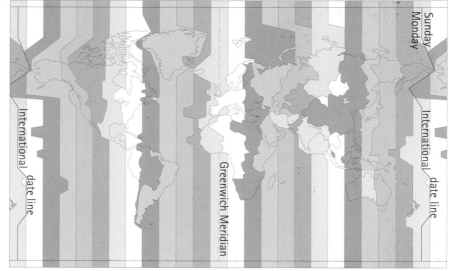

Hours -12 -11 -10 -9 -8 -7 -6 -5 -4 -3 -2 -1 0 +1 +2 +3 +4 +5 +6 +7 +8 +9 +10 +11 +12

TIME ZONES

Because the Earth is spinning, different places on Earth face the Sun at different times of day. When it is midday in London, it is dawn in New York, and in Adelaide, Australia, it is still night. If people read the time directly from the Sun's position, watches worldwide would be set to thousands of different times. Chaos would result; for example, it would be impossible to write accurate train timetables.

GREENWICH MEAN TIME

To get around this timing problem, governments approximate time by dividing the world into 24 time zones. These zones follow the Earth's longitude lines, and are based on Greenwich Mean Time (GMT), the time at Greenwich, England. Tokyo, Japan, is nine hours ahead of GMT, so when it is 2:00 A.M. in Greenwich, it is 11:00 A.M. in Tokyo.

▲ The world is divided into 23 full, and 2 half, time zones, starting at the prime meridian at Greenwich. Each zone west of the meridian is an hour earlier than the last. Each zone to the east is one hour ahead.

THE FOURTH DIMENSION

All objects have three dimensions: width, height, and depth (the dimensions of space). Scientists believe that objects also have a fourth dimension: time. Every day, we move through the four dimensions (called space-time). We can move in all directions through space (up and down, or from side to side); however, it is believed that we can only move forward through time. Many science-fiction writers have played with the idea that time travel into the future (or into the past) is possible.

▲ H. G. Wells's (1866–1946) remarkable science-fiction novel, *The Time Machine* (1895), tells the story of a man who builds a machine that carries him into the future. In the 1960 film, above, the machine vanishes forward in time.

▲ The giant Sun clock in New Delhi, India, tells the time as the Sun casts shadows on graduated markings.

▼ Stonehenge in England (begun c. 2700 B.C.) is a stone circle thought to have been used as an astronomical observatory and calendar. Its axis was aligned with midsummer sunrise (June 21), which suggests it was used to track the movements of the Sun, Moon, and planets.

SEE ALSO
Astronomy, Clock, Earth, Moon, Navigation, Season, Star, Sun

TOUCH

Touch is one of the body's five main senses. It allows us to detect not only physical contact, but also temperature, pressure, heat, cold, and pain.

▲ Touch sensors are packed closer together in places such as the lips and fingertips, with hundreds in a pinhead-size area. These body parts are most sensitive to touch.

Touch can distinguish between light and heavy pressure, and between things that are soft and hard, cold and hot, dry and wet, rough and smooth, still and moving. From this variety of information, we build up an impression of what our skin comes into contact with—from a cold, slippery ice cube to a warm, furry kitten.

TOUCH SENSORS

There are millions of microscopic sensors in the skin. Each is the specialized ending of a nerve fiber. When stimulated, the sensor sends bursts of nerve signals along its fiber to the brain. Touch sensors are all over the body in the skin. Hairs are mostly dead, so they cannot feel. But touch sensors are

▲ Braille is a special raised-dot type system that enables blind people to read with their fingertips. The system was invented by Louis Braille (1809–52).

wrapped around each hair root. When the hair is rocked or tilted, the sensors send out nerve signals. Similarly, nails are dead but have touch sensors in the skin underneath.

TYPES OF SENSOR

There are different types of touch sensor. Merkel sensors are tiny disks in the base of the skin's upper layer, or epidermis. Meissner sensors are slightly larger and egg-shaped, in the upper part of the skin's lower layer, or dermis. Krause sensors, also egg-shaped, and Ruffini sensors, larger and sausagelike, are in the middle of the dermis. Pacini sensors are multilayered, like onions. At up to 0.04 in. (1mm) long, they are the largest sensors and are just visible to the naked eye. The most numerous sensors are free nerve endings, each one resembling a tiny, many-branched tree.

WHAT DO THEY DETECT?

Some types of sensor respond better to certain kinds of touch. Meissner and Merkel sensors detect light touch, and Pacini sensors respond better to heavier pressure. Ruffini sensors pick up vibrations well. But in daily life, most types of sensor respond to most kinds of touch. Free nerve endings, which are the most widespread, respond to almost any kind of touch, including heat and cold, as well as the great pressure and damage that cause pain.

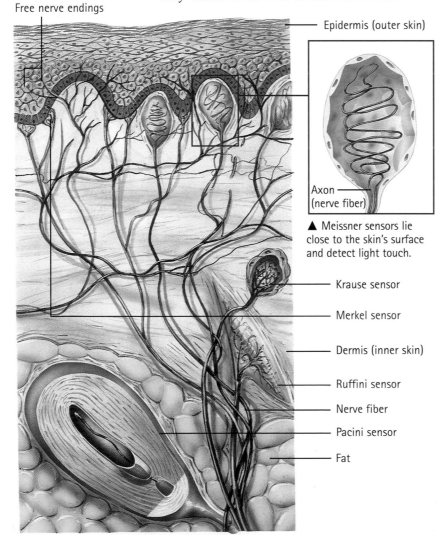

Free nerve endings

Epidermis (outer skin)

Axon (nerve fiber)

▲ Meissner sensors lie close to the skin's surface and detect light touch.

Krause sensor

Merkel sensor

Dermis (inner skin)

Ruffini sensor

Nerve fiber

Pacini sensor

Fat

SEE ALSO

Brain and nervous system, Skin and hair

TRADE

Trade is the buying and selling of goods. It takes place between individuals or companies, but the largest exchanges take place between different countries.

▲ During the Renaissance (1400–1600), trade in Europe increased greatly until it overtook farming as a source of wealth.

International trade allows countries to exchange what they have for what they need. A country with plenty of farmland but no coal mines can export (sell abroad) food and import (buy in) coal. Some countries specialize in one product, others produce a variety of goods and services.

VISIBLES AND INVISIBLES
International trade is divided into visible and invisible trade. Most goods, such as food, computers, and washing machines, which are moved from one country to another are visibles. Invisibles include banking charges, insurance policies, and people spending money on vacation. Some countries, such as Switzerland and Britain, rely heavily on invisible trade.

PROTECTION
Some countries limit import trade to try to protect jobs and industries at home.

▲ A customs officer uses a dog to sniff out smuggled goods. People sometimes try to smuggle goods that are illegal or will be heavily taxed.

A special tax, called a tariff, may be placed on imported goods, or a limit set on imports. This is known as protection.

LAISSEZ FAIRE
Free trade, also known as laissez faire, means that people are free to import or export without restrictions or tariffs. A laissez-faire policy encourages trade and is believed to increase employment and wealth. International trading organizations, such as the European Union (EU) and the North American Free Trade Agreement (NAFTA), establish free trade between members. The World Trade Organization, sometimes called GATT—the General Agreement on Tariffs and Trade—works to reduce trade barriers with all countries.

BALANCE OF PAYMENTS
The difference between the money coming into and going out of a country (both for visible and invisible items) is called the balance of payments. Large amounts of money or goods continually flowing in one direction may damage the economy of the country. If the value of the nation's currency is allowed to fall or rise, it affects the price of imports and exports and helps to bring the balance of payments back to zero.

◄ Most visible trade is carried out by sea. Ships transport goods relatively cheaply, using large, packed containers. Goods that need to be moved quickly are carried by aircraft.

SEE ALSO
Explorer, Great Depression, Industry, Money, Slavery, Transportation

TRAIN

Trains are simply lines of passenger or freight cars pulled along a steel track by an engine. They provide fast transportation either above or below ground.

▲ On February 21, 1804, Cornish engineer Richard Trevithick won a bet when he built the first steam locomotive able to haul 10 tons of freight over 10 miles (16km).

The fastest steam train was the *Mallard* at 125 mph (201kph).

The first diesel train was built in Germany in 1912.

Diesel locomotives haul heavy goods trains.

Subway trains carry people under city streets.

Rack and pinion trains climb steep slopes up hills.

Trains were developed during the Industrial Revolution in the 1700s. At first, horses were used to pull trucks carrying heavy loads along simple metal tracks at mines and factories. Later, steam engines mounted on wheels were developed, which were used to link cities with one another and achieved much higher speeds.

GETTING GOING
In 1802, the British engineer Richard Trevithick patented a high-pressure steam engine mounted on wheels. In 1825, British engineer George Stephenson overcame problems with engine power and tracklaying to build the Stockton and Darlington Railway. He went on to build the Liverpool–Manchester line in 1829.

STEAM TRAINS
After the success of George Stephenson's Liverpool–Manchester Railway, trains quickly became extremely successful and popular for moving both freight and passengers.. At the time, there were few good roads and no powered vehicles to run on them. By 1900, most of the developed countries of the world had built extensive networks of railroad lines that were able to carry millions of passengers and a great deal of freight.

STEEL ON STEEL
Most modern trains have steel wheels which run on twin steel rails. This arrangement means that resistance to motion is small, so that a heavy train can be propelled using relatively little power. It also means that there is no need to worry about steering, since the train will always follow the rails. A railroad line therefore needs to be only slightly wider than the widest train intended to pass along it.

UNDERGROUND RAILWAYS
Many cities have railways running in tunnels under their streets. These ease congestion and move people quickly. The first underground railroad was the Metropolitan, in London, England, which opened in 1863. The smoke from the steam engines caused problems, so later lines used electric trains. Other cities began building underground railroads— Boston in 1895, Budapest in 1896, Paris in 1898, and New York in 1904.

▼ In 1981, the French national railroads introduced the TGV, or *Train à Grande Vitesse*—a high-speed service between major cities. The fastest scheduled route is Paris–Lyons with an average speed of 132 mph (212.5kph). One train made a special run, reaching 320 mph (515kph) on the stretch between Tours and Courtalain.

RAIL SYSTEMS

Trains run on a number of tracks, switching from one track to another at points. The points and signals are controlled from a tower with the aid of computers. The signal controllers keep the lines free for high-speed passenger trains, or express trains, by moving local and freight trains onto side tracks called sidings. Modern trains are either electric or diesel, although steam trains are still used in some countries.

High-speed passenger train

Signals protecting junction

Signal box

Local passenger (commuter) train

Sidings

Overhead electric cables

Diesel freight train

Diesel shunting engine

Level crossing

Experimental maglev trains run at 250 mph (400kph).

Car drivers can relax while they travel on car trains.

Monorails have been built above crowded streets.

RAILROADS DECLINE

In the second half of the 1900s, railroads began to lose both passenger and freight traffic to the roads and to the airlines. Railroads were not "flexible"—they could not deliver to everyone's front door as the roads could—and they were very expensive to maintain to the high standard that safety demanded. Trains need long distances for acceleration and braking. This meant that they had to be a long way apart, limiting the number that could use a line. Railroads began to lose money. During the 1970s, several U.S. railroad companies declared bankruptcy.

FUTURISTIC DESIGNS

Railroad engineers are now seeking ways to attract passengers and freight back to trains. After many years when train speeds remained almost the same, most systems now operate some kind of high-speed train running at 125 mph (200kph) or more, for example the French TGV. More adventurous designers are looking at ways to eliminate the steel rails altogether. They suggest using magnets to lift the train above a track. This "maglev" system, being developed in Germany and Japan, would allow even higher speeds while at the same time reducing noise.

SEE ALSO

City, Engine, Industrial Revolution, Transportation

TRANSPORTATION

Transportation is a means of carrying people, animals, or goods from one place to another. This can be by land, water, or air, or through space.

Britain's *Flying Scotsman* made the world's longest nonstop run in 1928, from London to Edinburgh.

The Japanese intercity Bullet train can travel over 130 mph (210kph) and provides smooth and noiseless transportation for thousands of commuters daily.

Humans have always needed to move from place to place and to carry their goods. This is why the earliest civilizations were built along rivers. Eventually, people began to ride on horseback to cover long distances more quickly. They also used pack animals and carts to carry goods.

TRADE BY WATER

As civilizations developed, the need for transportation grew. Any trading center close to water built a harbor and began to send heavy goods to other centers by boat. At the same time, vehicles with wheels also became important. But few roads were strong enough to support heavily laden carts. So, up until the 1800s, water transportation, in the form of ships and barges, developed more quickly than land transportation, and most of the world's trade went by sea.

STEAM ENGINES

At the end of the 1700s, the first practical steam engine was invented. This gave birth to the steamship and, in the 1820s, railroad transportation. Railways became so successful that they soon put inland canals

ON THE ROAD

The first travelers had to carry or drag their belongings. Then they trained animals to carry loads and drag sleds. Around 3500 B.C., the Sumerians began to use wheeled carts. From that time and for hundreds of years, people travelled in various types of carriages pulled by animals. However, for many years there were no roads. Since the invention of the automobile, a vast network of roads and expressways has run across countries.

300 B.C.: logs pulled by oxen

c.1500 B.C.: Ancient Egyptian chariot

A.D. 1100: heavy wagon

1300: pack horse

1908: Model T Ford was the first car to be mass-produced

1880s: the first automobiles

1880s: horse-drawn omnibus

1760s: mail coach

1880s: penny-farthing bicycle

1500: horse and carriage

1960s: semitrailer truck

1990s: minivan capable of seating up to eight adults

1930s: automobile

1940s: Formula 1 race car

1950s: motorcycle

1960s: economy hatchback

1970s: sports car

▲ In the early 1900s, the German Zeppelin, up to 790 ft. (240m) long and with a speed of 80 mph (130kph), was a useful means of transportation.

out of business. At the same time, larger, faster steamships were carrying more and more passengers and goods across the oceans.

TRADE BOOM

This progress had the effect of further boosting trade. By the end of the 1800s, the world's major ports were huge places employing thousands of people, and the railroads in most countries had been fully extended. Also, networks of blacktopped roads were being built. This meant that goods could be delivered from the ports and railroad yards directly to the front doors of stores and houses, and people could travel to work. The development of the roads was aided by two inventions: the pneumatic (air-filled) tire and the internal combustion engine, which, between them, led to modern automobiles and trucks.

▲ Modern jet airliners can carry up to 500 passengers and fly around the globe in under three days.

THE AGE OF THE CAR

Roads quickly became the most useful form of transportation. Anyone with a car could travel almost anywhere, for business or pleasure. At first, few people could afford a car of their own. During the 1920s, however, cheap motor cars began to be mass-produced, and heavy trucks became much more efficient. By about 1950, road transportation had taken a lot of business away from the railroads. In addition, by this time, air transportation, with the development of larger planes and jet engines, was attracting passengers away from oceangoing liners, which had become too expensive to run.

Great ocean liners have six or more decks with luxuries for passengers such as elevators, suites, ballrooms, and swimming pools.

MERCHANT SHIPPING

Today, most short-distance transportation—of people or goods—is by road, while almost all long-distance transportation is by air and sea. Heavy cargo is transported mostly by merchant shipping, which consists of specially built cargo carriers, such as oil tankers, bulk carriers, and container ships.

DEATH OF THE RAILROADS

An increase in air traffic has meant that the role of the train in many countries has been reduced to carrying people to and from work in city centers. However, the growth of electric underground train systems in many large cities has helped take the strain off buses and trams, as well as cut down on city pollution.

▲ Road traffic in cities such as Los Angeles has become a real global problem because of the pollution it creates and the damage this does to the ozone layer.

The bicycle remains an efficient means of short-distance transportation and causes no pollution.

SEE ALSO

Aircraft, Balloon and airship, Bicycle and motorcycle, Boat, Car, Horse, Hovercraft, Road, Ship, Train, Truck and bus

TREE

A tree is a large, upright plant with a single, woody main stem. The biggest trees are among the largest, heaviest, and longest-living organisms on Earth.

Trees come in all shapes, with most over 20 ft. (6m). Some, like oaks, have a short trunk dividing into huge, spreading branches. Others, like redwoods, are tall and conical; trunks are 330 ft. (100m) tall, 30 ft. (9m) thick at the base.

CLASSIFYING TREES

The two main tree families are the conifers, or softwood trees, and the deciduous trees, or hardwoods. Scientists refer to conifers as gymnosperms (meaning "naked seeds"), because their seeds form on the woody scales that make up their cones. Deciduous trees are called angiosperms ("enclosed seeds"), because their seeds are enclosed inside fruits. Pines, firs, spruces, larches, and hemlocks are all conifers—also called evergreens because most keep their thin, needle-shaped leaves throughout the year. Deciduous trees, such as the oak, ash, maple, beech, elm, and horse chestnut, shed their leaves in the autumn.

TREE PARTS

The three main parts of a tree are its roots, trunk, and leaves. The roots take in water and nutrients from the soil. The trunk supports the tree and carries water and nutrients to the leaves through tubes, and food from the leaves back down to the rest of the tree.

The silver birch has pure white bark, often pocked with black marks. It has a tall and elegant shape.

Like the sugar maple, the silver maple is tapped for its syrup. Its five-lobed leaves are deeply toothed.

▶ Acorns are the fruit of the oak tree. On the English oak, they are attached to stalks.

Oak leaf

Acorn

The bark of the oak tree is fissured (ridged) and brownish-gray in color.

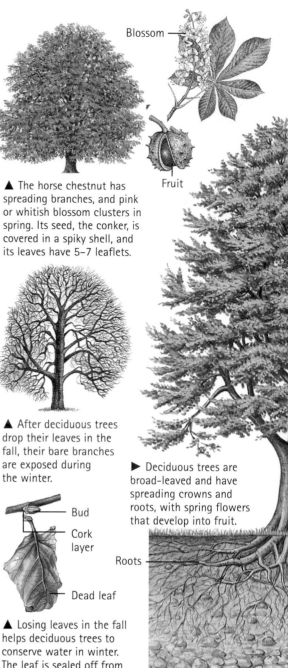

Blossom

Fruit

▲ The horse chestnut has spreading branches, and pink or whitish blossom clusters in spring. Its seed, the conker, is covered in a spiky shell, and its leaves have 5–7 leaflets.

▲ After deciduous trees drop their leaves in the fall, their bare branches are exposed during the winter.

Bud

Cork layer

Dead leaf

▲ Losing leaves in the fall helps deciduous trees to conserve water in winter. The leaf is sealed off from the stem's food supply near the bud; it dies and falls.

▶ Deciduous trees are broad-leaved and have spreading crowns and roots, with spring flowers that develop into fruit.

Roots

▲ Many species of oak grow in the Americas and Europe. Most are deciduous, such as the English oak, which can survive for 1,000 years. Its trunk is stout and burred.

▲ The banyan tree, native to India, has branches that hang down to the ground and root themselves. On one banyan in Sri Lanka, over 3,300 trunks have been counted.

Monkey puzzle female pine cone

Monkey puzzle bark

▲ The monkey puzzle is an unusual conifer with sharp, leathery leaves. Male and female cones grow on separate trees; the bark is ringed.

Chinese windmill palm leaf

Stem

▲ The spiky, fanned fronds of the Chinese windmill palm leaf can spread to a width of 3 ft. (1m).

▲ Deciduous trees produce vivid and beautiful fall colors in North American woodlands. Leaves may change from green to shades of red, orange, purple, and gold.

◄ Most coniferous trees are evergreen and rarely drop their leaves (needles). They have shallow roots and produce seeds in cones.

PHOTOSYNTHESIS

The leaves are the tree's chemical factory. Through a process called photosynthesis, sunlight acts with the chemical chlorophyll (which also gives the leaves their green color) to break down molecules of water and carbon dioxide, rearranging their atoms to make the starch and sugars the tree needs to grow. Oxygen is the waste product of this process, and whatever is not needed for respiration passes back into the air.

Outer bark

Inner bark

Sapwood

Heartwood

▲ The heartwood of a tree trunk section is surrounded by lighter sapwood. A fresh growth ring is added every year; the number of rings shows the tree's age.

USES OF TREES

Trees were among the first natural resources used by people. They provided fuel for fires; wood for shelters, tools, and weapons; and fruits and nuts for food. Today, two billion people in developing countries still rely on wood for fuel. The industrial world also uses huge amounts of lumber, plywood, and hardboard. Wood pulp is used to make paper and fibers.

TREES AND THE ENVIRONMENT

Trees help to keep the atmosphere healthy, because they remove carbon dioxide from the air and give off oxygen not used during photosynthesis. Trees also protect the land from erosion. Their giant canopies of leaves and branches absorb heavy rainfall; their roots bind the soil and prevent it from being washed away. This is why it is important to preserve rain forests in Brazil and Indonesia. In parts of Africa, where natural forests have been cut down, fast-growing trees are being planted to help prevent the desert taking over.

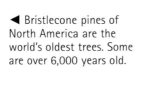

◄ Bristlecone pines of North America are the world's oldest trees. Some are over 6,000 years old.

► The baobab tree is native to Africa and Australia. It has a wide, bulbous trunk with short, thick branches.

▲ Bonsai is the art of growing miniature trees. Almost any tree seedling can be grown as a bonsai by pruning its roots and branches, but evergreens are the most popular.

Fan-shaped leaf

Stalked fruit

Leaf clusters

▲ The *ginkgo biloba*, or maidenhair tree, has remained unchanged for 160 million years. The tree was cultivated for centuries in Chinese temple gardens.

SEE ALSO

Conservation, Ecology, Forest, Fruit, Habitat, Leaf, Plant, Rain forest, Seed and pollination

TRUCK AND BUS

Trucks and buses are commercial road vehicles. Trucks are used to carry goods and products, and buses provide public transportation for people.

Commercial trucks and buses have many features in common and are often built by the same companies.

A Foden C-type steam truck of 1922. Steam trucks were popular until the 1930s.

A 1914 Hallford 3-ton truck used by the British army in World War I.

A London double-decker bus. The second deck boosts passenger capacity.

Modern trucks carry pre-packed containers of goods for easy loading.

RANGE OF SIZES

Unlike cars, most trucks and buses have a separate chassis, or wheeled frame, on which is mounted a body designed for a particular purpose. A truck may be a light, local delivery vehicle, a middle-range goods transporter, or a heavy-load carrier weighing up to 44 tons. A public bus may carry anything from 20 to 100 passengers.

ROAD TRAINS

There are two main types of truck: rigid and articulated. Rigid trucks are built as a single unit, with all the wheels attached to one chassis. The articulated truck consists of a "tractor" unit, which contains the engine and cab, and a trailer, which carries the goods. It is easier to handle and more flexible in operation. Truck chassis may be adapted for special purposes, for example, tankers (which carry liquids such as milk, fuel, or chemicals), cement mixers, and fire engines. In some countries, such as Australia, heavy trucks may tow many trailers as a "road train."

▲ Long-distance bus routes were established in the United States in 1925 by the Greyhound Corporation, and are now found in most countries with a good road system.

CARRYING PASSENGERS

Buses may be single-decked or double-decked. A double-decker can carry more passengers in the same road space. Very long single-deck buses are hinged near the center so they can turn tightly. Most buses operate in cities, but others run long-distance routes, usually offering much lower fares than the railroad. The tram, a streetcar on rails, follows a fixed route through a city. Many cities use streetcar lines to solve traffic jams.

▲ Road trains (articulated trucks pulling several trailers) are used for long-haul transportation in remote areas.

ARTICULATED TRUCKS

An articulated truck is made up of a tractor and a semitrailer. The tractor contains the engine, cab, fuel tanks, brakes, and other equipment. The semitrailer carries the main load. It has wheels at the rear, and rests on the tractor at the front by means of a device called the fifth wheel.

SEE ALSO

Car, Engine, Road, Transportation

TUNNEL

Tunnels are natural or artificial passageways built underground. They can be built through hills or mountains, or under land or water.

Tunnels are constructed to carry roads, railroads, water, sewage, or cables. They are also built to reach mineral deposits, or to create underground shelters or storage areas. Tunnels that carry traffic or people need ventilation systems to remove fumes and circulate fresh air.

ANCIENT TUNNELS

Tunneling began in prehistoric times when cave dwellers began to extend natural caves and dig for useful flints to make into tools. Ancient empires had tunnels built to house royal tombs and temples and to carry water to irrigate fields. The Romans built tunnels to connect the aqueducts that carried their water supply.

EXPLOSIVES AND SHIELDS

The first major traffic-carrying tunnel was built in the 1670s, when a 518-ft. (158-m) tunnel was blasted through a hill near Béziers in France. Tunnel-builders today still use explosives to blast through solid rock. Building through less dense materials

▲ The tunnel under the English Channel is 30.8 mi. (49.2km) long. Opened in 1994, it links England with France.

The soil is lifted on to a conveyor belt by a long, rotating Archimedes screw

Concrete lining segment erector

Powerful rams force the cutting head forward

An operator sits in a control cab behind the cutting head

Spoil (muck) conveyor

The cutter head has tough cutting rollers and teeth

TUNNEL–BORING MACHINE (TBM)

Modern tunneling machines use very tough, tungsten carbide cutting teeth. These can bore through soft rock, like chalk, at a rate of up to 3,280 ft. (1,000m) a month. A segment erector follows the cutting machine and places the lining sections in position.

requires a tunneling shield. Invented in Britain by the French-born engineer Marc Isambard Brunel (1769–1849), the shield protects laborers as they dig. As the shield is gradually moved forward in sections, the walls of the tunnel are shored up with brickwork or concrete to stabilize them. Brunel used this method to build the first tunnel under the Thames River, London, completed in 1843.

UNDERWATER TUNNELS

A cheaper method of building tunnels under water is to dig a trench, drop in preformed sections of metal or concrete, and then, after divers have fitted them together, pump out the water and fill in the trench. The Hong Kong Cross Harbor Tunnel was built this way.

◀ The Thames Tunnel, built by Marc Brunel in the early 1840s, was the first underwater tunnel. It is still used as part of London's Underground train system.

▲ A mole can dig five times faster than a TBM using just its two front paws. Its tunnels are, of course, on a smaller scale.

SEE ALSO

Hibernation, Mining, Oil

UNITED KINGDOM

England, Scotland, and Wales lie on the island of Great Britain in northwest Europe. Together with Northern Ireland, they form the United Kingdom (U.K.).

UNITED KINGDOM
Area: 93,300 sq. mi.
Population: 59,778,002
Capital: London
Languages: English, Welsh
Currency: Pound sterling

Much of England is lowland, with the flattest areas in the east. Upland regions include the Lake District and the Pennines. Scotland, Wales, and Northern Ireland are more mountainous than England. Scotland's Ben Nevis (4,406 ft./ 1,343m) is the United Kingdom's highest peak. Loch Neagh, in Northern Ireland, is its largest lake. The Severn (210 mi./ 338km), which runs through Wales and England, is the longest river. In most parts, summers are generally cool and winters mild, with rainfall all year round.

TOWN AND COUNTRY

The U.K. is a crowded nation. Four out of every five British people live in cities and towns. England—especially the southeast around London—is the most densely populated part of the U.K. London is one of the world's great cultural centers. The U.K. has an extensive road system with many expressways, and London's Heathrow is the world's busiest airport for international traffic. Since 1994, the Channel Tunnel, under the English Channel, has linked Great Britain with France.

▲ Many commuters use London Bridge, over the Thames River, to reach the City, the heart of London's business community—like Wall Street in New York.

INDUSTRY AND FARMING

Resources include oil and natural gas deposits in the North Sea. The nation's many rivers provide drinking water, as well as water for crops. Much of the countryside is farmed and the crops include wheat, sugar beet, potatoes, and oilseed rape. Dairy cattle and sheep are raised as well as pigs and poultry. Manufacturing industries include aerospace, chemicals, telecommunication, and electronics. Scotland also produces fine woolens and Northern Ireland is famous for its pure white linen. Industries such as banking, publishing, and tourism are also important.

▲ Northern Ireland has been the scene of violent conflict between Catholics and Protestants. Here, the Protestant Orange Order celebrates the anniversary of the victory of William of Orange over Catholic King James II in the Battle of the Boyne in 1690.

▶ Wales is a land of green valleys, grassy plains, hill farms, and mountains. Its castles include Carreg Cennen in the southwest, shown here.

430

◀ Loch Tulla is a small lake in Scotland's Grampian Hills, between the Lowlands and the Highlands.

FROM CONQUEST TO KINGDOM

The Romans conquered lowland Britain from A.D. 43. After the Romans came Anglo-Saxons, Vikings, and Normans. The United Kingdom of Great Britain and Ireland was formed in 1801. It became the United Kingdom of Great Britain and Northern Ireland in 1922, after the southern part of the island of Ireland became independent.

WORLD POWER

During the 1700s, Britain colonized large parts of North America, Africa, and Asia. Wealth from the colonies supplied money for the Industrial Revolution to begin at home, and factories and machinery were built. By 1900, the British Empire had become the world's largest empire, defended by the greatest navy.

DECLINE OF THE EMPIRE

In the first half of the 1900s, two world wars caused loss of life and economic strain. From the 1950s, the U.K.'s wealth and power declined as many of the colonies became independent and Britain's

▲ England's south coast, including Dartmouth Quay in Devon, is popular with tourists for its scenery and climate.

traditional manufacturing industries such as coal, iron, steel, and shipbuilding declined.

THE U.K. TODAY

Today, the U.K. is still a major player in finance and in the service industries, and plays a leading part in world affairs through the United Nations, the Commonwealth, and the European Union. The U.K. is a constitutional monarchy, which means the king or queen is head of state but political power is controlled by Parliament. The Isle of Man and the Channel Islands are largely self-governing, but some of their laws are made by Parliament. In 1997, a degree of power was devolved to a regional parliament in Scotland and an assembly in Wales.

▲ London's Tower Bridge, opened in 1894, is a symbol of the city and a magnet for tourists.

SEE ALSO

Civil war, Empire, Europe, Government, Industrial Revolution, Ireland (Republic of), United Nations, Viking, World War I, World War II

UNITED NATIONS

The United Nations is an international organization based in New York. Governments send representatives there to discuss problems and to try and find solutions.

The United Nations flag features the world surrounded by the olive branch, a symbol of peace.

Founded in 1945 by the winners of World War II, the United Nations (UN) has grown to include 191 of the nearly 200 independent states on Earth. The UN sponsors negotiations between countries that have disputes, and has many agencies that carry out humanitarian work.

GENERAL ASSEMBLY

Each UN member country has one vote in the General Assembly, which meets in New York City. The General Assembly approves UN work, debates important issues, and decides how to spend money. The 15-member Security Council is responsible for peace and security. It can send a peacekeeping force to any country, and may condemn aggressive action. Five countries are permanent members: the U.S., Russia, the U.K., France, and China.

HUMANITARIAN WORK

The UN works to promote trade, health education, and cultural understanding. This work is carried out by the bodies of the Economic and Social Council (ESC), which pays for aid projects in poor countries, encourages healthcare, and promotes the rights of minorities. UNICEF (UN Children's Fund) promotes the welfare of children in poor countries. In 1991, the UN held an Earth Summit in Rio de Janeiro so that world leaders could agree on solutions to environmental problems.

PROBLEMS IN THE UN

Problems have beset the UN in recent years. In the 1990s, civil wars in Rwanda and Bosnia continued despite UN efforts. The U.S. has accused the UN of bias against developed countries and refused to pay its share until reforms are made. In 2003, the Security Council disagreed about military action against Iraq. A U.S.-led coalition attacked Iraq without UN backing.

UN AGENCIES
• World Health Organization (WHO)
• Food and Agriculture Organization (FAO)
• International Monetary Fund (IMF)
• UN Educational, Scientific, and Cultural Organization (UNESCO)
• International Civil Aviation Organization (ICAO)
• World Bank
• United Nations Children's Fund (UNICEF)

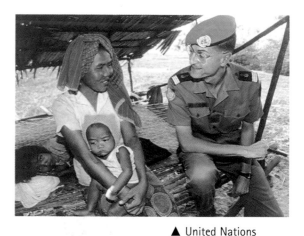

▲ United Nations forces are stationed in many parts of the world, such as Cambodia, to help keep the peace. Here, a UN soldier talks to a Cambodian woman and her child.

◀ The United Nations General Assembly meets for three months every autumn to decide on important issues. It can hold a special session during an emergency, such as the Soviet invasion of Hungary in 1956.

SEE ALSO

Civil war, Education, Government, Politics, World War II

432

UNITED STATES OF AMERICA

The United States is the world's third largest country in population and fourth in area. It is rich in natural resources and highly advanced in technology.

Area: 3,539,200 sq. mi.
Population: 280,562,489
Capital: Washington, D.C. (District of Columbia)
Language: English
Currency: U.S. dollar

▼ The Statue of Liberty stands at the entrance to New York Harbor. It was a gift from France in 1884 and represents freedom for the people of the United States.

The United States (U.S.) consists of 50 states, 48 contiguous (touching) and two apart from the rest. Alaska lies west of Canada and includes Mount McKinley (20,320 ft./6,194m), North America's highest peak. Hawaii is a group of islands in the Pacific Ocean, 2,400 mi. (3,900km) from the U.S. mainland.

THE 48 STATES

Climate and geography divide the 48 states below Canada into groups from east to west and north to south. Those on the Atlantic coast consist of the New England, Middle Atlantic, and Southern states. The Midwest and Southwest form the center of the country. To the west are the Rocky Mountain states, and west of these are the Pacific Coast states, running south to Mexico.

VIGOR AND VARIETY

The United States is a country of vast plains and bustling cities, everglades and deserts, spectacular seacoasts, and majestic mountains. Southern plantations grow cotton and tobacco. Midwestern prairies run gold with grain crops. The West Coast has rugged mountains and endless Pacific beaches. Business booms from coast to coast: New

▲ New York is the largest city in the U.S. One of its key symbols is the yellow cab, a common sight on the streets of Manhattan and the other four boroughs.

York and Chicago are major financial centers; Detroit and Cleveland are industrial bases; Atlanta, Dallas, and Houston have become hubs of commerce; Los Angeles and San Francisco dominate the West Coast. The country's historical roots still live in Boston and Philadelphia. Images of Washington, D.C. symbolize the country around the world. New Orleans, Miami, Seattle, St. Louis—all make their unique contribution to the mosaic that is the modern United States. ▶

▲ The Grand Canyon lies in northwestern Arizona. It is one of the most spectacular river gorges in the world, carved from the desert rock by the Colorado River over six million years.

▲ The 800 mi. (1,300km) Trans-Alaska pipeline carries oil from the frozen north of the state to the Gulf of Alaska in the south.

▲ The brilliant lights of Las Vegas, Nevada, invite thousands of tourists to enjoy the luxury hotels or try their luck at the world-famous casinos.

THE PEOPLE

Since 1940, the population of the United States has more than doubled. Native Americans, who lived in North America for thousands of years before Europeans began arriving, now make up just under one percent of the population. About half of all U.S. citizens are Protestants; nearly a third are Roman Catholics. Jewish people make up two percent of the population; followers of Islam about the same.

SETTLEMENT AND REVOLUTION

Permanent European settlement of what was to become the U.S. began with a British colony founded in 1607 at Jamestown, Virginia. British colonists spread along America's eastern coast. In the South, they grew tobacco, cotton, and indigo on plantations worked by slaves shipped from Africa. In the North, timber and furs were key products, and fishing was a major industry. French and Spanish explorers and colonists began to settle other territories to the

west. Disputes between Britain and its 13 colonies over trade, taxes, and defense led to the Revolutionary War (1775–83), and on July 4, 1776, a group of colonial leaders signed the Declaration of Independence. The war ended in victory for the colonists, led by General George Washington.

NEW LAWS

In 1787, the Constitution was drawn up and sent to the states for approval. In it, power was divided between the federal government and the individual states. In 1789, a number of amendments that guaranteed specific rights were proposed. Ten were approved by the states and are known as the Bill of Rights. There are now 27 amendments.

▶ About 80 percent of Americans are white or Hispanic. African-Americans form about 12 percent of the population, and Asians, Native Americans, and other groups make up the remaining 8 percent. This classroom reflects the multicultural makeup of the United States.

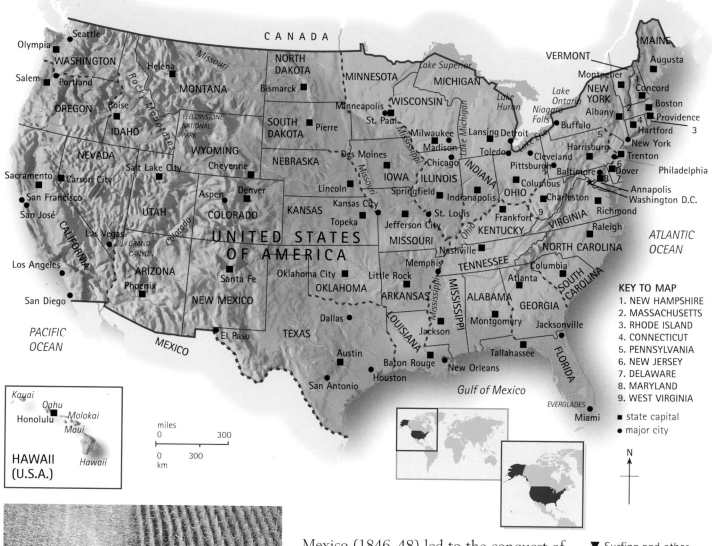

CANADA

Seattle
Olympia
WASHINGTON
Helena
Salem
Portland
OREGON
Boise
IDAHO
Sacramento
Carson City
NEVADA
San Francisco
San José
CALIFORNIA
Las Vegas
Los Angeles
San Diego
PACIFIC
OCEAN

Missouri
MONTANA
Rocky Mountains
YELLOWSTONE
NATIONAL
PARK
WYOMING
Salt Lake City
Cheyenne
UTAH
Aspen
Denver
COLORADO
Colorado
GRAND
CANYON
ARIZONA
Phoenix
Santa Fe
NEW MEXICO
El Paso
MEXICO

NORTH
DAKOTA
Bismarck
SOUTH
DAKOTA
Pierre
NEBRASKA
Lincoln
KANSAS
Topeka
UNITED STATES
OF AMERICA
Oklahoma City
OKLAHOMA
Dallas
TEXAS
Austin
San Antonio

MINNESOTA
Minneapolis
St. Paul
Des Moines
IOWA
Kansas City
Jefferson City
MISSOURI
Memphis
ARKANSAS
Little Rock
Mississippi
LOUISIANA
Jackson
Baton Rouge
New Orleans
Houston

Lake Superior
WISCONSIN
Milwaukee
Madison
Chicago
ILLINOIS
Springfield
St. Louis
Nashville
TENNESSEE
MISSISSIPPI
ALABAMA
Montgomery

MICHIGAN
Lansing Detroit
Lake Michigan
Mississippi
INDIANA
Indianapolis
Frankfort
KENTUCKY
Columbia
Atlanta
GEORGIA
Jacksonville
Tallahassee
Gulf of Mexico

Lake Huron
Niagara Falls
Toledo
Cleveland
Pittsburgh
OHIO
Columbus
Charleston
9
VIRGINIA
NORTH CAROLINA
SOUTH CAROLINA
FLORIDA
EVERGLADES
Miami

MAINE
Augusta
VERMONT
Montpelier
NEW YORK
Concord
Albany
Buffalo
Boston
Providence
Hartford
New York
Trenton
Harrisburg
Baltimore
Dover
Philadelphia
Annapolis
Washington D.C.
Richmond
Raleigh
ATLANTIC
OCEAN

Lake Erie
Lake Ontario

1
2
4
5
6
8 7
3

KEY TO MAP
1. NEW HAMPSHIRE
2. MASSACHUSETTS
3. RHODE ISLAND
4. CONNECTICUT
5. PENNSYLVANIA
6. NEW JERSEY
7. DELAWARE
8. MARYLAND
9. WEST VIRGINIA

■ state capital
● major city

N

Kauai
Oahu
Honolulu
Molokai
Maui
HAWAII
(U.S.A.)
Hawaii

miles
0   300
0   300
km

▲ The Midwestern states of North Dakota and Kansas are the country's largest producers of wheat.

GROWTH OF A NATION

George Washington was the first president, and a new national capital was founded and named in his honor. In 1791, a Bill of Rights was added to the Constitution, guaranteeing the rights of all citizens. In 1802, President Thomas Jefferson bought vast western territories claimed by France, doubling the size of the new nation. In 1804, he sent an expedition to explore the continent from east to west. War against Mexico (1846–48) led to the conquest of the southwest and Pacific coast. Lured by the discovery of gold in California in 1849 and by the prospect of free land on the prairies, Americans headed west. Washington Irving and other writers helped create a new national identity, and Noah Webster compiled the first dictionary of American English.

WAR AND PEACE

From 1861 to 1865, America was torn by a civil war which made the South poor, but boosted industry in the North. Peace brought a boom in railroad building. By 1869, railroads joined the East and West coasts. San Francisco, Chicago, and St. Louis grew from frontier posts into great cities. ▶

▼ Surfing and other water sports are popular in the Hawaiian islands, including Oahu, where 80 percent of Hawaii's population lives.

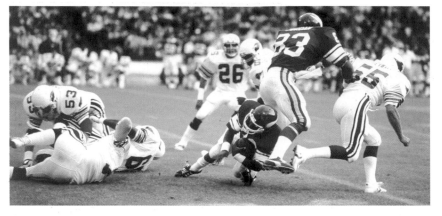

▲ Football, a popular professional and college sport, developed in the 1800s.

▲ The White House had to be rebuilt after it was damaged by fire in the War of 1812.

INDUSTRY AND IMMIGRATION

Millions of Europeans moved to the U.S., and Native Americans were driven from their traditional lands. America grew rich from its farms and factories. By 1900, the average American was better off than the average European. Half of all Americans still lived on farms, but cities were booming. American inventions, such as the lightbulb, elevator, skyscraper, and airplane, were to change the world.

A WORLD POWER

In 1867, the United States bought Alaska from Russia. In 1898, it took over the Pacific islands of Hawaii and also went to war with Spain. This led to independence for Cuba and American rule over the Philippines. The U.S. developed a great navy. In 1917, the country joined in World War I to help Britain and France defeat Germany and its allies.

BOOM, BUST, AND WAR

In the 1920s, the United States was the first country in which millions of people drove cars, listened to the radio, and enjoyed the movies. But the "roaring twenties" ended in a business collapse in 1929, with millions out of work. President Franklin D. Roosevelt used government money from taxes to create new jobs. Following Japan's attack on the naval base at Pearl Harbor (Hawaii) in 1940, Roosevelt led the country during World War II, but died just before the German surrender.

SUPERPOWER

War boosted industry in the United States and left the country as a superpower, armed with atomic bombs and with a new role as leader of the democratic world. U.S. wealth helped Europe recover from war damage. Today, the United States is the world's most powerful nation, and its culture has spread across the world.

▲ In 1620, a group of English Puritans who called themselves Pilgrims founded a colony at Plymouth, Massachusetts. A recreation of their settlement now stands on the site of the original colony.

◄ In the early 1900s, jazz emerged in New Orleans and developed as a new and distinctly American style of music. Today, the New Orleans jazz festival is world famous.

SEE ALSO

Bridge, Civil rights, Civil War (American), Cold War, Habitat, Native American, North America, Slavery, World War I, World War II

UNIVERSE

The universe is made up of stars, planets, and other matter scattered throughout space. It may contain up to 100 billion galaxies with 100 billion stars in each.

▲ NASA put a diagram of humans on a spacecraft, so that it could be found by intelligent life elsewhere in the universe. The dumb-bell represents a hydrogen atom; the symbols below it represent the solar system.

Most scientists believe that the universe began with an enormous explosion called the Big Bang, which happened about 15 billion years ago. During this event, all the matter and energy that would ever exist was created in a fraction of a second, in an area smaller than the size of a grape. Ever since the Big Bang, the universe has been expanding outward into space.

SEEING INTO THE PAST

A galaxy that is five billion light-years away is seen by astronomers as it was five billion years ago. Therefore, looking at very remote objects gives us a way of seeing the universe when it was much younger than it is today. The most distant objects ever seen are newborn galaxies or galaxies that are still being formed. At even greater distances and earlier times, astronomers can detect only faint radio waves, which come from all parts of space. These are the cooled down remains of the fireball that erupted out of the Big Bang.

MYSTERIES OF THE UNIVERSE

Scientists ask: will the universe go on expanding forever, or will it eventually begin to shrink and end in a Big Crunch? At present, the answer is unknown, but it seems that the universe may be delicately balanced between the two options. Another question is: does life exist elsewhere in the universe? Again, the answer is not yet known, but the evidence suggests that life may be common throughout space. Space probes sent to other planets search for water, the main ingredient that supports life as we know it. Over 90 percent of the universe consists of dark matter, which cannot be seen. The composition of this remains another great mystery.

SEE ALSO

Astronomy, Big Bang theory, Galaxy, Planet, Solar system, Star, Time

VEGETABLE

Vegetables are plants grown to provide food. Most are grown from seeds, bulbs, or tubers, then harvested within a year. A few grow on long-lived plants.

EDIBLE VEGETABLE PARTS

Eight different parts of vegetable plants are eaten: the bulbs of onion and garlic; the flowers of broccoli and cauliflower; the leaves of lettuce and kale; the roots of carrots and turnips; the seeds and pods of peas and beans; the stems of celery and rhubarb; and the tubers of potatoes and yams. Tomatoes, peppers, eggplants, and squashes such as pumpkins are really fruits, since they contain seeds, but are grown as vegetables.

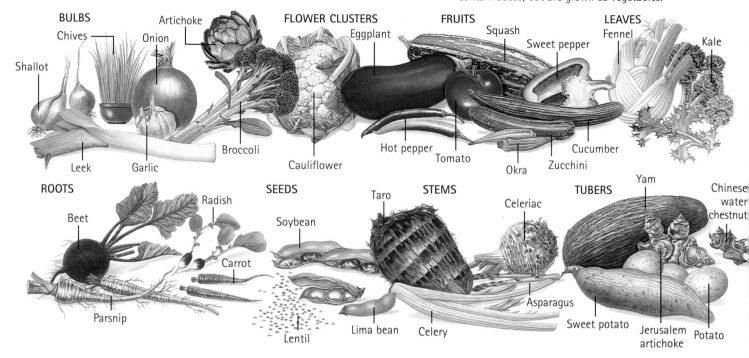

BULBS — Chives, Artichoke, Onion, Shallot, Leek, Garlic, Broccoli
FLOWER CLUSTERS — Eggplant, Cauliflower
FRUITS — Squash, Sweet pepper, Hot pepper, Tomato, Okra, Zucchini, Cucumber
LEAVES — Fennel, Kale
ROOTS — Beet, Radish, Carrot, Parsnip
SEEDS — Soybean, Lentil, Lima bean
STEMS — Taro, Celeriac, Asparagus, Celery
TUBERS — Yam, Chinese water chestnut, Sweet potato, Jerusalem artichoke, Potato

VEGETABLE FACTS

- Potatoes, tomatoes, peppers, and corn are native to the Americas and were unknown in Europe before A.D. 1500
- Some types of beans are poisonous if they are eaten raw
- Organic vegetables are grown without pesticides

Vegetables are very important to a healthy diet: they are low in fat, and different types provide protein, carbohydrates in the form of starches and sugars, vitamins, minerals, and fiber. Some vegetables, such as potatoes, must be cooked before being eaten; others are best eaten raw, and many vegetables may be eaten either way. Cooking vegetables for too long destroys some of their vitamins.

SEASONAL VEGETABLES

Vegetables are harvested at different times of the year. Some, like lettuce, are usually eaten fresh, but others, such as peas and beans, can be dried or frozen and cooked later. Root vegetables last for a long time when stored in cool, dry conditions—they can even be left in the soil. Freezing and canning make it possible to eat from a wide selection throughout the year, although fresh vegetables have the highest nutritional value.

CROPS AND BREEDING

All vegetables contain nutrients. Cultivated crops have more nutrients than their wild ancestors. Many people, particularly in developing countries, have to rely on their own crops for food. If crops fail, they face starvation, so over thousands of years, farmers have selected and bred edible plants that give the best yield for the climate in their area. Through plant-breeding techniques, scientists have developed new varieties of vegetables that are resistant to attack by pests and diseases.

◀ Giant vegetables, such as green beans, are grown for contests, but they are too tough to eat.

SEE ALSO

Crop, Farming, Nutrition, Plant, Seed and pollination

VIDEO

Video technology turns moving pictures and sounds into electronic form, stores them on a magnetic tape or disc, then plays them back on a screen.

▲ Modern DV (digital video) camcorders store images in digital form. These give high-quality recordings, which can be edited on a multimedia PC.

The first videocassette recorder (VCR) was made by Sony in 1969. VCRs record the signal from a TV antenna, satellite dish, cable, or video camera onto magnetic tape. Some video players play videodiscs instead of videotape.

GET THE PICTURE
Before video, silent home movies were made using cartridges containing reels of photographic film. These had to be sent off for developing before they could be played back with a projector. Early video systems used a big TV camera connected to a separate, heavy VCR. All this changed in the mid-1980s with the invention of the camcorder (*cam*era-re*corder*)—a portable video camera with a built-in recorder.

VIDEO CAMERAS
In a camcorder, a lens bends the incoming light to form a sharp image on a flat light sensor called a charge-coupled device (CCD). This turns the image into an electrical signal, which is recorded on tape together with a sound track. The user looks at a viewfinder, which has a small TV or liquid-crystal display (LCD). There are several kinds of tape which can be

▲ Closed-circuit television (CCTV), with small video cameras, is being used increasingly for security surveillance in buildings and public places.

▲ Computer-controlled video-editing setups, using two or more professional VCRs, are used to assemble images and add special effects.

played back through a TV or copied using a VCR. Camcorders are continually getting smaller and lighter, and their quality is improving all the time.

VIDEOCONFERENCING
The use of video has become increasingly widespread. For instance, video-equipped police cars and traffic cameras help to monitor roads and enforce speed limits. Video telephones never caught on, but videoconferencing over the Internet may become common. This is when tiny video cameras next to computer monitors enable people to see each other as they talk.

HOW THE VCR WORKS

When recording with a VCR, changes in the incoming signal, which match the changing brightness and colors of the picture, are turned into fluctuating magnetic fields on a recording head. This head spins on a drum and records the magnetic changes on the tape as it moves past. The head crosses the tape diagonally so that the maximum amount of tape is used. During playback, the VCR translates the magnetic changes recorded on the tape back into a picture on a television screen.

Remote control unit

Take-up spool
Video recording head
Audio head
Erase head
Guide rollers
Videotape
Sound track
Video track
Control track

SEE ALSO

Computer, Film, Internet, Lens, Photography, Television

VIKING

The Vikings were a seafaring, warrior people from Norway, Sweden, and Denmark. They invaded northern Europe and explored as far away as North America.

▲ Viking trade and expansion routes in the 800s and 900s ran east through Russia, as far south as Seville and Pisa, and, by A.D. 1000, west to North America.

During the 700s, the population of Scandinavia rose dramatically, but there was not enough land there for farming. At about the same time, the Vikings developed the longship, which gave them the means to reach other lands.

Thor was the Viking god of thunder and war. Thursday is named after him.

EARLY RAIDS
The first Viking raids were small; one or two longships would raid a few coastal villages and escape with the loot. Around 800, they began to attack in force. They destroyed the monastery on Holy Island (Lindisfarne) and created fear with a series of ferocious attacks from northern France to the coast of Ireland.

In battle, Vikings often used a spear made of ash wood with an iron head.

FIERCE RELIGION
Viking gods were fierce and warlike. The Vikings told stories of the gods and heroes in long poems called sagas. They believed the world would end in a war between the gods and giants at Ragnarok ("twilight of the gods"). Odin was their chief god. Men who died bravely in battle were thought to be taken by the Valkyries, 12 handmaidens from Odin's court, to Valhalla, a great hall, to spend eternity feasting and fighting.

A Viking silver amulet in the shape of Thor's hammer and decorated with a face.

INVASION OF ENGLAND
In 851, Vikings arrived in England with a great army and 350 ships. They invaded Kent, destroying Canterbury. In 866, an even larger Viking army, led by Halfdane and Basecg, invaded Kent. Within five years nearly all of England had been defeated and conquered. The victory of King Alfred the Great (849–99) over Guthrum's Viking army at Edington in 878 saved southern and western England.

VIKING SETTLEMENTS
Large numbers of Vikings sailed to England and settled in the conquered lands as farmers and traders. York, Lincoln, and Derby became Viking towns. In Ireland, the Vikings founded Dublin and Waterford as trading cities. A large section of northern France—later known as Normandy (from Norsemen)—was captured by Earl Rollo and settled by Vikings. Some Vikings sailed east to travel up the rivers of eastern Europe. At Kiev, they founded a kingdom called the Russ, or Russia.

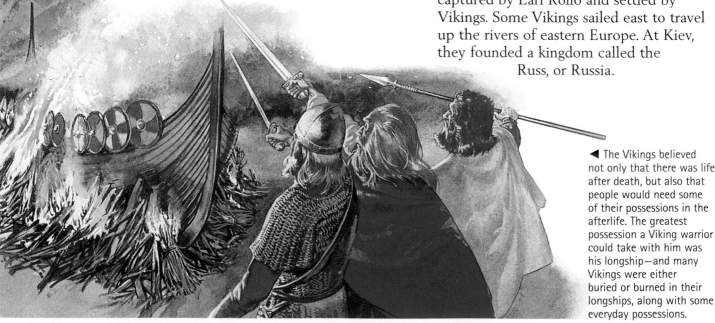

◄ The Vikings believed not only that there was life after death, but also that people would need some of their possessions in the afterlife. The greatest possession a Viking warrior could take with him was his longship—and many Vikings were either buried or burned in their longships, along with some everyday possessions.

440

▲ Swords were highly valued by the Vikings and were often richly decorated with gold and silver.

FEARLESS RAIDERS FROM THE SEA

From the late 700s to about 1100, fearless Viking warriors from the Scandinavian countries of Norway, Sweden, and Denmark made several raids on the coasts of Christian countries, inflicting terror on the local inhabitants. They plundered monasteries and churches, killing, burning houses, and driving away the cattle.

OCEAN VOYAGES

The Vikings were skilled navigators. By studying the stars and the Sun they could travel accurately across vast distances of open sea. In about 825, they reached and settled the Faeroe Islands. Fifty years later, they reached Iceland. There, they founded an assembly—the Althing—to discuss and decide communal matters. The Althing still meets and is the world's oldest governing assembly. In 982, the first Viking settlements on Greenland were established. About the year 1000, a Viking named Leif Ericsson traveled to Newfoundland in search of timber, which was scarce in Greenland. They continued to visit North America for many years, but the Vikings never settled there.

VIKING TWILIGHT

By 900, the great Viking raids were over. Wars between Viking settlements and surrounding kingdoms remained common, but most Vikings settled down to a more peaceful existence. The Viking kingdoms in England and Ireland were taken over by the native kingdoms by 970.

CHRISTIAN CONVERTS

The Vikings and English lived side by side and, for a time, England became part of the Scandinavian Empire, under Canute (1016–35). A last attempt at conquest was made by the Norwegian Viking Harald Hardrada when he invaded England in 1066, but he was defeated and killed. From then on, most of the Vikings adopted Christianity and turned to farming and trading, abandoning raiding and conquest.

▲ A Viking man and woman dressed in everyday clothes.

SEE ALSO
Myth and legend, Religion, Ship, Warfare

VOLCANO

When lava bursts through an opening in the Earth's crust, a volcano forms. The word "volcano" comes from Vulcan, the Roman god of fire and metalworking.

The Earth's surface is continuously moving through the action of plate tectonics, as sections of the Earth's crust are moved by currents in the molten rock below. There are two types of volcano: basaltic volcanoes found where new plate material is being created, and andesitic volcanoes in areas where plates are being destroyed.

BASALTIC VOLCANOES

Where new crust forms along oceanic ridges, the molten material from the Earth's mantle wells up and spreads out, pushing the plates apart. This usually happens at the bottom of the sea, but in Iceland it has risen above the sea and produced a whole island. The molten material, or lava, that erupts from these basaltic volcanoes is very runny and flows a long distance before becoming solid. Basaltic volcanoes are also found a long way from the edges of the plates. The Hawaiian islands were formed as basaltic material pushed its way up through the plate from the Earth's mantle. These "hot-spot" volcanoes have produced many other islands of the Pacific, including the Galapagos Islands and Fiji.

▲ Volcanic activity has formed the whole landscape of Iceland. The terrain is littered with jets of boiling water, called geysers.

Ash and smoke

Layers of ash and lava

Volcanic cone

Caldera

Geyser

Fumarole

Lava flow

Side vent

Central vent

Magma chamber

INSIDE A VOLCANO

A typical volcano has a crater and a cone of solidified lava and ash. Eruptions take place through a chimney-like vent. Far below the surface is a chamber of magma (molten rock), containing bubbling gases that make some volcanic rock frothy. A caldera forms when a violent eruption empties the magma chamber that feeds it. The roof then collapses, leaving a hole. Fumaroles are openings that let out only gas and steam, and geysers sometimes shoot fountains of boiling water high into the air.

VIOLENT ERUPTIONS

Andesitic volcanoes are found where plates are being drawn beneath one another and destroyed. Molten plate material rises through the overriding plate and bursts through at the surface. These andesitic volcanoes occur in the great mountain chains, and in island arcs around the edges of oceans, close to deep ocean trenches. The lava of an andesitic volcano is stiff and sticky, and when it erupts, it does so explosively. Mount St. Helens, in Washington, and the island of Montserrat are recent examples of such violent and destructive eruptions. Because of accurate forecasting, few were killed, but the hot ash from Mount St. Helens destroyed trees up to 19 mi. (30km) away.

Vulcanian eruption

Plinian eruption

Hawaiian eruption

Volcano cones created by Hawaiian eruptions slope gently, because the lava flow is quite runny

A vulcanian eruption, after Vulcano, in Italy, throws almost solid magma during an explosion

Plinian eruptions, such as the one that destroyed Pompeii in A.D. 79, explode with great clouds of ash and pumice

SEE ALSO

Earth, Earthquake, Mountain and valley, Ocean and sea, Rock

WARFARE

Warfare is armed conflict between the military forces of two nations or states, or between organized groups within a state.

Much of recorded history is a recounting of war and conflict. This is often because one group seeks to impose its will on another for some form of gain, such as territory, food, or natural resources.

TURNING TO ARMS

Wars start for different reasons. The Crusades and the Thirty Years' War, in the 1600s, started for religious reasons. In 1701, the Ashanti fought for freedom from another African people and created a great trading nation. The Indian Wars of the late 1800s saw Native Americans defending their way of life against those who wanted their land. Involvement in Korea and Vietnam stemmed from opposition to communism in the Cold War.

OUTBREAK OF WAR

Countries going to war want to appear to be in the right. This encourages citizens to support the war, and deters other countries from helping the enemy. Often a relatively minor incident will trigger a war.

▲ Samurai warriors used their discipline and skill with weapons to control Japan from 1200 to 1871.

In 1914, the Hapsburg Empire declared war on Serbia after a Serb killed the Austrian archduke. But the Hapsburgs really wanted to stop Serbia encouraging unrest within the empire.

INTELLIGENCE

Once at war, commanders need to know about the strengths and plans of the enemy. The lack of such knowledge left France vulnerable to the German attack of 1940. Information may be gathered by watching the enemy from satellites and aircraft, by capturing or decoding messages, or by using spies. Information would then be given to commanders to help make battlefield decisions. ▶

Ancient Egyptians used stone for maceheads, knives, and arrowheads and spearheads.

Medieval crossbows shot bolts accurately, but were slow to load and use.

OARS AND RAMS

The Battle of Salamis in 480 B.C. was fought between the oared galleys of Greece and the Persian Empire. The Greeks defeated the larger Persian fleet because their *triremes* (ships with three banks of oars) were faster and easier to handle than the Persian ships.

▲ Hand weapons of the Middle Ages included:
1 Daggers for stabbing; 2 Maces to crack metal armor; 3 War hammers, used as maces; 4 Spiked staffs; 5 Pikes with handles up to 6.5 ft. (2m) long to keep horsemen at a distance.

▲ In Europe in the 1400s, armor covered the body with carefully shaped metal plates, each curved and ribbed to deflect blows.

▲ Helmets fringed with chain mail gave protection while allowing movement.

TOTAL WAR

In a total war, an entire country is organized for fighting. In the Zulu Empire, during the 1800s, every young man had to serve in the army and boys, older men, and women provided supplies. Both world wars of the 1900s were total wars. Men were conscripted into the armed forces, and many industries switched to producing weapons. It was considered fair to bomb cities in which factories were located, even though this might mean killing civilians.

THE FATE OF PRISONERS

Prisoners are taken in all wars, but their treatment has differed. The Romans sold prisoners as slaves. The Aztecs sacrificed prisoners to their gods. During the 1800s, in wars with the British, the Afghans tortured all prisoners to death—the British often shot their men if they could not rescue them. World War II prisoner of war camps in Japan were notorious for

▲ Early cannons, called bombards, of about 1360 were slow to load and difficult to move and aim. They were made from iron rods bound together by iron hoops, which occasionally burst when firing. By about 1450, cannons were cast in one piece from bronze or iron.

bad conditions. The Geneva Convention of 1864, and its later revisions in 1906, 1929, 1949, and 1977, lays down strict rules about prisoners of war. They cannot be tortured. They must be given the same food and shelter as their captors, and they cannot be forced to do work to help the war effort. Prisoners are usually released at the end of a war.

LIMITED BLOODSHED

War by its nature is violent. Soldiers may kill civilians, steal goods, and burn houses, so attempts have been made to reduce the violence. During the 1100s, the idea of chivalry encouraged knights to avoid hurting women or children and to take prisoners rather than killing captives. In 1631, the German city of Magdeburg was captured by an army of Croats and Walloons. The soldiers looted the city and slaughtered thousands. European monarchs were appalled and developed

KEY DATES

c.5000 B.C. Cities in Mesopotamia form first armies

c.90 B.C. Marius reforms the Roman armies into professional and full-time forces

c.800 Feudal armies made up of semiprofessional knights form in Europe

c.1350 Gunpowder is invented

1916 Tanks are used for the first time

1945 Nuclear weapons are used for the first time

1991 The first major use of cruise missiles in the Gulf War by the United States

THE BATTLE OF WATERLOO

The Battle of Waterloo was fought in 1815 between the French, led by Napoleon Bonaparte, and a joint British, Dutch, and German army. The muskets and cannons of the time had only a limited range. The colorful uniforms helped soldiers tell friend from foe in the smoke of the battlefield.

the idea of limited war, which meant that civilians were to be unharmed and armies could surrender peacefully.

OBEYING THE RULES

Many wars have been fought according to a set of rules. In Ancient Greece, most cities depended on olive oil for food, so olive trees were usually not destroyed when an enemy city was captured. The people of each city knew that they might be defeated at some time, and wanted to have enough food to survive. During the Middle Ages, prisoners were given a chance to buy their freedom immediately by paying a ransom.

WAR CRIMES

Before 1945, any enemy soldier or leader who broke the rules of war was hanged or put in prison. At the end of World War II, the Allies set up special courts to try

▲ In 1906, HMS *Dreadnought* was a new type of battleship, armed with 12-in. guns and able to steam at over 20 knots (30 mph). Battleships remained the most powerful ships afloat until aircraft carriers in the 1940s.

people as war criminals for breaking the Geneva Convention and for the mass murder of Jews and others in the Holocaust. In the 1990s, new war crimes courts were set up to try people who had killed civilians during the Bosnian civil war.

GUERRILLAS

Some wars are fought by irregular troops called guerrillas. Such wars are usually fought when the enemy is too strong to be faced in battle. Using any weapons at hand and operating in small groups, ▶

A handgun of 1400.

A 1500s' wheel lock.

A 1600s' flintlock.

The Colt revolver of 1851.

A matchlock musket.

A breechloading rifle of the 1800s.

The German Mauser pistol of 1896.

The Gatling gun of 1862 was an early machine gun.

A German 50-ton siege cannon of 1867.

▲ The British Mark IV tank of World War I was designed to crush barbed wire and cross trenches while protecting its crew from machine-gun fire.

Commander's hatch and periscopes — Ammunition store — Engine

Machine gun

105-mm cannon

Sloped armor

Driver's seat

Tracks

THE MAIN BATTLE TANK

The Abrams M1 is the main battle tank (MBT) of the United States. MBTs are any army's most important weapon. They have guns up to 120mm caliber that are able to destroy strongholds and enemy tanks; armor protects the crew from all but the heaviest guns; mobility allows them to move through enemy territory to reach targets.

Modern warships have guns, missiles, and complex electronics.

The Mustang was the fastest American fighter of World War II.

The German V1 could fly 150 mi. (240km) with a 2,000 lb. (900kg) warhead.

The American Honest John missile can reach a range of 12.4 mi. (20km).

Modern Intercontinental Ballistic Missiles (ICBMs) carry nuclear warheads.

U.S. NAVY TOMCAT

The Grumman F14-A Tomcat is a twin-engined, two-seater fighter designed to fly from aircraft carriers to protect the U.S. fleet from enemy bombers.

Wing pivot mounting

Retracting undercarriage

Armored glass screen

Retractable air-refueling probe

Fuel tanks

Ejector seat

guerrillas cut enemy supply lines and ambush patrols. The aim is to wear down the enemy forces, so that they give in.

PSYCHOLOGICAL WEAPONS

Many commanders try to persuade the enemy to surrender or to retreat by tricking them. In the 1740s, Frederick the Great of Prussia had a special regiment of men over 7 ft. (2.2m) tall. Because he only used his "giants" when he thought he would win, enemies seeing them advancing would think they were beaten. In World War II, British aircraft dropped leaflets on Germany urging troops to surrender. They failed because the leaflets contained obvious lies.

RADIO TRICKS

During World War II, a British radio station aimed at German troops claimed to be broadcast by a German army officer. Because the "officer" used army slang, many Germans believed the stories of German defeats. Tokyo Rose, a Japanese radio show, mixed stories of American defeats with popular music during World War II.

PEACEFUL SOLUTIONS

At the end of every war is a period of peace. This is often agreed between the two sides in a document called a treaty. Treaties set out conditions, such as the handing over of territory and the return of prisoners, which are signed by all parties. The Treaty of Amiens ended a war between Britain and France in 1802, but it left so many issues unresolved that the two were at war again just one year later. Other treaties have been more successful. The Treaty of Vienna in 1815 was signed by every nation in Europe and meant that peace lasted for decades. After World War II, the United Nations was set up to solve international disputes with the aim of preventing war from breaking out.

▶ Soldiers of the U.S. 82nd Airborne Division wear gas masks during the Gulf War of 1991. Chemical and biological weapons can cause massive casualties.

SEE ALSO

Castle, Celt, Civil war, Crusades, Greece (Ancient), Mongol Empire, Napoleonic Wars, Rocket, Roman Empire, United Nations, World War I, World War II

WATER

Water is the most common substance on Earth. It is the main ingredient in all living organisms—without water, life on the planet could not exist.

WATER FACTS

- A person drinks over 15,800 gal. (60,000 l) of water in a lifetime

- Human beings will die if they lose more than 20 percent of the body's normal water content

- It takes about 21 pt. (10 l) of water to flush a toilet; 37 gal. (140 l) to fill a bathtub; nearly 11 gal. (40 l) to wash the dishes; and up to 32 gal. (120 l) for a washing machine

- The wettest place on Earth is Cherrapunji in India, with an average annual rainfall of 426 in. (10,820mm)

▲ Three fourths of the world's fresh water is frozen in glaciers and polar ice caps.

Water vapor condenses and forms clouds

Rain and snow

Transpiration from plants

Water vapor in atmosphere

River flows back to oceans

Evaporation from seas and lakes

Water vapor cools and forms rain

Groundwater runs off

THE WATER CYCLE

Water is constantly being recycled. When the Sun heats the Earth's surface, water evaporates into the atmosphere. Over 80 percent of this comes from seas, but some comes from plants giving off water vapor (transpiration). As water in the atmosphere cools, it condenses to form clouds. Some of this water falls again as rain.

Water vapor   0.05 percent
Moisture in soil   0.2 percent
Rivers and lakes   0.35 percent
Saltwater lakes
and inland seas   0.4 percent

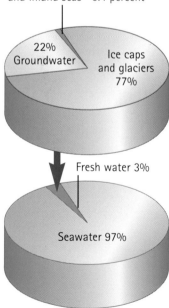

22% Groundwater
Ice caps and glaciers 77%

Fresh water 3%

Seawater 97%

▲ Of the 3 percent of the world's water that is not in the seas, 77 percent is locked in ice and glaciers.

Water exists naturally in three different forms: solid (frozen as ice), liquid (water), and gas (water vapor in the air). It can dissolve more substances than any other liquid. The force of natural water power has shaped the world's mountains, valleys, coastlines, and plains.

UNIVERSAL SUBSTANCE

Water covers 70 percent of the Earth's surface—over 5.6 billion cu. mi. (1.4 billion cu km)—but only a tiny fraction is of use to humans. Almost 97 percent of all water is seawater, with up to about 77 lb. (35kg) of dissolved salts in every ton—eight times too salty to drink or to use for crops. Only about three percent of all water is fresh—and three fourths of that is in polar ice caps and mountain glaciers. Every living thing depends on the small amount of fresh water (under one percent of the total) that falls as rain and fills rivers and lakes.

WATER FOR LIVING

Life began in the sea 3.5 billion years ago, and water is still essential for all life-forms. The human body consists of about two-thirds water. People need 5 pt. (2.5 l) of water a day to stay alive, but in the West, we use about 66 gal. (250 l) each per day for bathing, toilets, and washing machines. We also use vast amounts of water in industry and agriculture. It takes 105 gal. (400 l) of water to grow enough wheat for one loaf of bread, and 270 tons of water to produce a ton of steel.

SHAPING THE LAND

Water is the most important force in shaping the land. Rivers and glaciers carve valleys, wear down mountain ranges, and carry gravel, sand, silt, and clay onto lowland plains and eventually out into the sea. Even spectacular desert scenery is carved mainly by water from flash floods.

SEE ALSO

Lake, Mountain and valley, Ocean and sea, River, Waterpower, Weather

WATERPOWER

Waterpower uses the movement of water to turn machinery or to generate electricity. It is a renewable, nonpolluting source of energy.

Waterwheels have been used to grind grain into flour since the time of Ancient Greece. In Britain in the 1800s, they provided the power for big textile mills during the Industrial Revolution. Electric generators that could convert the turning motion of a waterwheel into electricity led to the rapid development of hydroelectric power in the early 1900s.

HYDROELECTRIC POWER

Water is first stored in a reservoir, often made by damming a river and flooding its valley. The water flows down pipes through turbines, propellerlike blades that are spun around by the flow of the water. In turn, these spin the electric generators. Pumped storage plants can push the water back up into the reservoir using off-peak electricity, then generate electricity again when demand is high, like charging up a giant battery. About 20 percent of the world's electricity comes from hydroelectric power, but it is available mainly in mountainous areas, far away from large cities, where most of the power is needed.

▲ A huge wave crashing against the shore shows the awesome force of natural waterpower. The sea can be harnessed to generate electricity in tidal power plants and wave-power generators.

▲ In the Middle Ages, waterwheels were used to power hammers for ironworking. They saved time and labor.

TIDAL POWER

Dams built across river estuaries trap the rise and fall of ocean tides. The trapped water turns turbines as it flows through holes in the dam. These use the "head" of water made by the rise and fall of ocean tides to spin turbines. The largest tidal power plant, on the Rance River in Brittany, France, has been generating 240 megawatts of electricity since 1966.

WAVE POWER

The up-and-down movement of sea waves can be used to make electricity, but this is more difficult than using flowing water to turn a turbine. Wave-powered electric generators began operating in the 1980s. One plant, built on the Clyde River in Scotland, generates only two megawatts of electricity, but larger plants are planned.

TURBOGENERATOR

Water flows past turbogenerators inside the dam wall of a hydroelectric power plant. A turbogenerator converts the energy of flowing water into electrical energy. The shaft is turned by the pressure of water against its curved blades, and this moves the generator rotor, which generates (produces) an electric current.

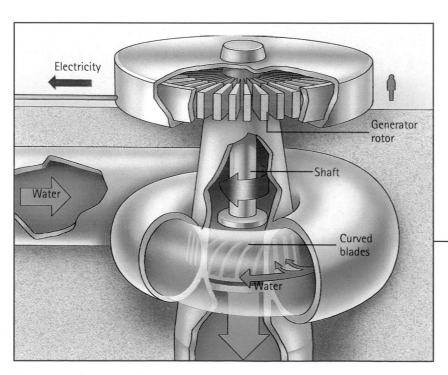

Electricity

Generator rotor

Shaft

Water

Water

Curved blades

Water

SEE ALSO

Dam, Electricity, Energy, Engine, Water

WAVELENGTH

Wavelength is the distance between two identical points on a wave. This is usually measured from one peak of the wave to the next.

Most of us have seen waves on the sea. Before they reach the coast, these waves make the seawater ripple. The highest points of these ripples are called peaks, the lowest points are called troughs. The distance between one peak and the next is called the wavelength of the waves.

SOUND WAVES

All forms of moving energy, including sound, light, and heat, travel in waves. All of them have a wavelength just like waves on the sea. When sound waves travel through air, for example, they create tiny changes in the air pressure. The peaks of a sound wave are where the air pressure is greatest. Our ears pick up the changes in air pressure and send signals to the brain.

DIFFERENT WAVELENGTHS

Just like frequency (the rate at which a wave moves up and down), wavelength affects a wave's properties because wavelength and frequency are closely related. For instance, low-frequency sound waves have a longer wavelength than high-frequency ones. Similarly, red light waves have a longer wavelength than blue ones. Light is one of a range of energy waves, including radio waves, micro-waves, infrared rays, ultraviolet rays, X rays, and

gamma rays, all of which travel at 483,000 mi./sec. (300,000km/sec). Together, these form the electromagnetic spectrum.

▲ Police often use radar to catch speeding motorists. Radar waves from a gun bounce off a moving vehicle. The frequency at which they return gives its speed.

WAVELENGTH AND FREQUENCY

If you divide the speed of a wave (measured in meters per second) by its frequency (measured in Hertz), you can work out its wavelength (in meters). For example, a sound wave that travels at 344m/sec and has a frequency of 688 Hz has a wavelength of 0.5m (because 344 ÷ 688 = 0.5).

Wavelength

Peak

Trough

Gamma rays, used to detect cracks in metal

X rays, used to look inside bodies

Ultraviolet rays, used in a sunbed

Visible light, from red to violet

Infrared rays, as in a heat-sensitive camera

Shorter microwaves, used in a microwave oven

Longer microwaves, used in radar

Ultrahigh Frequency (UHF) radio waves for TV transmissions

Radio waves used in radio broadcasts

ELECTROMAGNETIC SPECTRUM

The electromagnetic spectrum covers a huge range of energy waves, all of which travel in the same way. As different parts of the spectrum have different wavelengths, they have different properties. A light wave, for example, is one that we can see. An X ray is a part of the spectrum that can pass through some solid objects, such as skin.

SEE ALSO

Energy, Light, Musical instrument, Radar and sonar, Radio, Sound, X ray

WEATHER

Atmospheric conditions, such as rain, wind, and sunshine, make up the weather at a particular place and time. Weather may change slowly or rapidly.

An anemometer is used to measure the speed of the wind. Its sensitive shells move in the wind's path.

A barograph records changes in air pressure on a rotating drum, using an inked pen to draw a graph.

The psychrometer uses a dry bulb and a wet bulb to measure the humidity in the air.

Thermometers measure air temperature. They are used either inside or outside buildings.

The weather depends on the way air masses move around the globe. The climate of a place is the average of these weather conditions over a long period of time. Though weather may change within hours, climates change over years.

CAUSES OF WEATHER
The way that air masses are driven depends on factors such as distance from the equator and the presence of mountains or seas. When an air mass moves from the sea over high ground, it cools, and the water it contains falls as rain. If an air mass moves from the center of a continent, it contains no water and brings dry weather. If a mass of air rests over tropical waters for a long time, it becomes extremely moist and warm, leading to severe storms.

REGULAR CYCLES
The weather follows regular cycles. In many areas, the summer means warmer weather than the winter because more solar (sun) energy is received during long, hot days. In Southeast Asia, the monsoon period is dominated by warm, wet winds from the Indian Ocean, causing heavy rains. Every ten years or so, a phenomenon called El Niño occurs: the temperature of the southeast Pacific Ocean rises slightly, which alters the movements of air masses.

This can lead to drought, severe rainstorms, and economic disaster.

Stratus cloud

When water freezes, its molecules bind together into a flat, six-sided crystal, with four long sides and two short ones. The crystal grows as other water molecules attach themselves to its sides. Each snowflake is unique.

Temperature

Wet snow

Dry snow

Sleet

Rain

Drizzle

▲ When rain clears quickly after a shower, a colorful rainbow may stretch across the sky. Sunlight shines on water droplets, and light is bent, or refracted, until it is split into spectrum colors.

▲ Inside a storm cloud, raindrops may be carried up by air currents and frozen in the clouds. Layers of ice build up as water vapor freezes onto these icy crystals. The growing hailstones fall to warmer levels, then rise again until they are heavy enough to fall from the clouds.

RAIN AND SNOW

Two main types of rain occur. In the tropics, rain forms when tiny droplets come into contact in a cloud, join together, and fall. Rain outside the tropics is caused by melting snowflakes. If the base of a stratus cloud is low enough, rain falls as drizzle. Dry snow falls when the ground temperature is cold, but if snow falls into air that is above freezing, sleet (a mixture of rain and snow) occurs.

1 The Sun heats one area of ground, such as bare soil, more than others. On warm days, bubbles of hot air form over these areas, and rise up through the cooler air around them.

2 Warm air rises into low-pressure air, then expands and cools. The air cools so much that water vapor condenses into droplets, and a small cumulus cloud is formed.

3 As it is fed by a series of air bubbles, the cloud grows, and the wind detaches it. Fair-weather cumulus clouds look like cotton balls. They do not carry enough water to cause rain.

▲ Radiosondes are balloons that carry instruments to measure temperature, air pressure, and humidity in the upper atmosphere.

HIGH AND LOW PRESSURE

In most parts of the world, weather is determined by areas of low air pressure (cyclones) or areas of high pressure (anticyclones). Some last for months; the Bermuda High is an anticyclone that appears in the North Atlantic during the summer. Others last only a few days or weeks. In tropical areas, belts of low pressure can be massive and move slowly westward. As they suck in warm air, heavy rain and storms are created.

FRONTS

When a mass of cold air meets a mass of warm air, a front develops. If cold air cuts sharply under warm air, a cold front forms. The warm air rises rapidly, cools, and produces heavy rains. If warm air rises slowly, it produces a warm front marked by long periods of gentle rain and drizzle.

DESTRUCTIVE WEATHER

Although most thunderstorms are harmless, a large storm can produce strong winds, heavy rain, lightning, and hail. In 1986, a storm in Gopalganj, India, created a downpour of hailstones weighing 2.2 lb (1kg) each, killing 100 people in a few seconds. Lightning kills around 200 people a year and starts over 20,000 fires. Tornadoes form when thunderstorms create strong updrafts. The spinning air can reach 310 mph (500kph) and wreak destruction along a path 0.6 mi. (1km) wide and 62 mi. (100km) long.

FORECASTING

Traditionally, people have forecast weather either by watching the sky or noticing the behavior of animals, which is affected by basic weather changes. Modern weather forecasting is based on the global movement of areas of low and high pressure and fronts, which is tracked using satellite photographs.

▲ Weather maps, such as this synoptic chart, use standard symbols. Isobars are lines that connect places where air pressure is the same. Winds flow parallel to isobars; the closer together they are, the stronger the wind. Air pressure (in millibars) is shown at centers of low and high pressure. Wind speed, and warm and cold front symbols, are also shown.

◄ ▲ As water droplets collide in a large cloud, water becomes electrically charged. Positive charges collect at the cloud's top, and negative charges at the bottom. As a negative charge meets a positive charge on the ground, forked lightning flashes; sheet lightning flashes between clouds. Thunder is the sound of hot air expanding.

Warm front   Cold front

Wind speed and cloud cover

Isobar

SEE ALSO

Climate, Ecology, Electricity, Light, Satellite, Season, Water

WEIGHTS AND MEASURES

Weights and measures are the standard units that we use to work out how much we have of things. Each form of measurement needs its own kind of "ruler."

A yard was the length of a man's arm from nose to tip

A cubit was the length from the fingers to the elbow

A fathom was a man's arm span

A pace was about the same as a yard or three feet

One foot

ANCIENT MEASUREMENTS

In the ancient world, different parts of the human body were used as measuring units. Ancient Egyptian units included the cubit, which was the length of the lower arm. Units were also mixed together—four palms were equal to one cubit. The Romans divided their foot unit into 12 parts.

▲ Units based on the hand included the digit, which was the width of a finger. This later became the inch. A span was the length from thumb to little finger, and there was also the palm unit.

Ever since people started making things, trading goods, or carrying out experiments, they have needed to measure amounts. Ancient civilizations based their measurements on parts of the body. These were standard (the same) only within each civilization. An Egyptian cubit, for example, was different from a Greek or Roman cubit. This caused many problems, especially when people needed to trade with one another. That's why, over time, standard measurement systems have come into use.

TRADITIONAL MEASUREMENTS

Until about 30 years ago, most people used the imperial system of measurement. This measured length in inches, feet, yards, and miles; and weight in ounces, pounds, and tons. The use of the foot as a unit of measurement dates back to Anglo-Saxon times. The inch (3 grains of barley, lengthwise) dates to the 1300s, when it

was established as one twelfth of a foot. The mile has its origins in measuring thousands of paces. Ounces and pounds are units of the *avoirdupois* ("goods sold by weight") system, in use since at least the 1400s. The imperial system isn't always easy to use, however, and people who took complex measurements realized they needed a simpler system. In the 1790s, the metric system was created in France.

METRIC SYSTEM

Many countries use the metric system, or SI (Système International). The basic units are the meter (length) and the kilogram (weight). There are many other units with their own special names such as the joule, the newton, and the volt. However, scientists can relate most of them to the basic set: one newton (1N), for example, the unit of force, can also be written as one kilogram meter per second per second (1kg m/sec^2).

SETTING STANDARDS

A laboratory near Paris holds examples of the SI units—the Standard Meter is the length of a certain number of wavelengths of a specially made laser beam. The Standard Kilogram is the weight of a special ingot of platinum-iridium metal, stored at a controlled temperature.

▲ Scales have been used to weigh objects for sale for thousands of years. Here, they are used to weigh dried flower and plant remedies for sale at an herbalist dispensary.

WEIGHT

Metric

1,000 milligrams (mg)	=	1 gram (g)
1,000 grams	=	1 kilogram (kg)
100kg	=	1 quintal (q)
1,000kg	=	1 metric ton or tonne (t)

Standard

16 ounces (oz.)	=	1 pound (lb.)
112 lb.	=	1 hundredweight (cwt.)
20 cwt.	=	1 (long) ton (= 2,240lb.)
2,000 lb.	=	1 short ton

Conversions

1 gram	=	0.035oz.
1kg	=	2.205 lb.
1 metric ton or tonne (t)	=	2,200 lb.
1t	=	0.984 (long) tons
1 oz.	=	28.35g
1 lb.	=	454g
1 (long) ton	=	1.02t

AREA

Metric

100 square mm (mm^2)	=	1 square cm (cm^2)
10,000cm^2	=	1 square metre (m^2)
100m^2	=	1 are (a)
100a	=	1 hectare (ha)
100ha	=	1 square kilometre (km^2)

Standard

144 square inches (in.^{2})	=	1 square foot (ft.^{2})
9 ft.^{2}	=	1 square yard (yd.^{2})
4,840 yd.^{2}	=	1 acre
640 acres	=	1 square mile (mi.^{2})

Conversions

1cm^2	=	0.155 in.^{2}
1m^2	=	10.76 ft.^{2}
1 hectare	=	2.47 acres
1km^2	=	0.386 square miles
1 in.^{2}	=	6.45cm^2
1 ft.^{2}	=	0.093m^2
1 acre	=	0.405 hectares
1 sq. mi.	=	2.59km^2

LENGTH

Metric

10 millimeters (mm)	=	1 centimeter (cm)
100cm	=	1 meter (m)
1,000m	=	1 kilometer (km)

Standard

12 inches (in.)	=	1 foot (ft.)
3 ft.	=	1 yard (yd.)
1,760 yd.	=	1 mile (mi.)

Conversions

1mm	=	0.0394 in.
1cm	=	0.394 in.
1m	=	1.094 yd.
1km	=	0.621 mi.
1 in.	=	2.54cm
1 ft.	=	30.48cm
1 yd.	=	0.914m
1 mi.	=	1.609km

VOLUME

Metric

1,000mm^3	=	1 cubic centimeter (cm^3)
1,000cm^3	=	1 cubic decimeter (dm^3)
1,000dm^3	=	1 cubic meter (m^3)

Standard

1,728 cubic inches (in.^{3})	=	1 cubic foot (ft.^{3})
27 ft.^{3}	=	1 cubic yard (yd.^{3})

Conversions

1cm^3 = 0.06 1 in.^{3}	1m^3 = 35.3 ft.^{3}
1 in.^{3} = 16.4cm^3	1 ft.^{3} = 0.028m^3

CAPACITY

Metric

1,000 milliliters (ml)	=	1 liter (l)
100 liters	=	1 hectoliter (hl)

Standard

4 gills	=	1 pint (= 16 fluid ounces)
2 pints	=	1 quart
4 quarts	=	1 gallon

Conversions

1 liter = 0.908 quart	1 pint = 0.473 liters
1 deciliter = 0.21 pint	

The Egyptians used delicate balancing scales to weigh gold and precious stones. Later, the Babylonians (who lived in what is now Iraq) made standard weights from metal to use at markets.

The builders of the pyramids in Egypt had to measure length so that they knew how many stones they needed, as well as how to drive shafts accurately through the huge structures.

The measuring cup is used to measure liquids in fluid ounces (imperial units) and milliliters (metric units). Wine bottles usually hold 700 or 750 milliliters (ml) of wine when they are full.

SEE ALSO

Babylon, Clock, Gravity, Time

WHALE AND DOLPHIN

Whales, dolphins, and porpoises are collectively known as cetaceans, which means "large sea animal." They are divided into two groups: toothed and baleen whales.

There are about 37 species of dolphin; 23 species of large-toothed whale; ten species of baleen whale; and six types of porpoise. They may look like fish, but whales and dolphins are warm-blooded, air-breathing mammals.

FROM EARTH TO SEA

Whales first appeared on the Earth over 50 million years ago. Their ancestors once lived on land, but then moved into the water and gradually lost their back legs; their front legs became flippers. The flippers are used for steering and balance, but the power comes from the big tail with its horizontal fins or flukes. The tail is waved up and down to drive the whale forward. (Fish have vertical tail fins, waved from side to side.)

A white-sided dolphin eats fish and has 92–128 teeth. It is found in large schools of up to 1,000 dolphins.

A rough-toothed dolphin is a small (up to 8 ft./2.5m), tropical species known to follow ships.

Common porpoises are one of the smallest cetaceans (up to 6.5 ft./2m). There are six species.

The adult beluga, or white whale, is pure white, but the young are gray. Belugas have no dorsal fin.

True's beaked whale has a single pair of teeth, in the lower jaw. It is found in the North Atlantic.

A male bottle-nosed dolphin grows up to 13 ft. (4m). It eats squid, cuttlefish, and herring.

▶ Black right whales belong to the right whale family of three species. They reach 60 ft. (18m) in length and are rare.

◀ Fin whales belong to the rorqual and humpback family that have grooved throats. They grow to 66 ft. (20m).

▶ Bowhead whales grow up to 60 ft. (18m) and their baleen plates can be 9 ft. (3m) long. They belong to the right whale family.

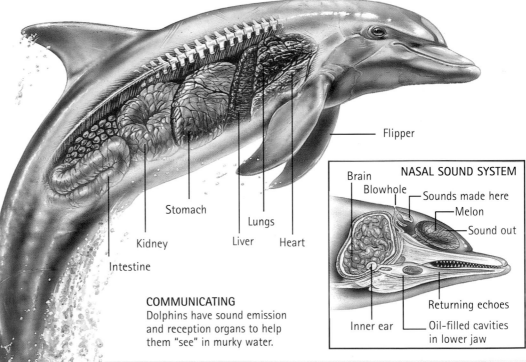

Flipper

Stomach

Kidney

Lungs

Liver

Heart

Intestine

NASAL SOUND SYSTEM

Brain
Blowhole
Sounds made here
Melon
Sound out
Returning echoes
Inner ear
Oil-filled cavities in lower jaw

COMMUNICATING

Dolphins have sound emission and reception organs to help them "see" in murky water.

SEEING WITH SOUND

Dolphins communicate, find food, and navigate using a kind of radar sound system under water. They make high-frequency clicking noises by blowing air through their nasal passages. Then the melon (a waxy cavity in the dolphin's head) focuses the sound into a beam. Sound vibrations travel through the water and bounce off objects. A dolphin receives the sound echoes through an area in its jaw where the bones are thinner. The echoes then travel to the inner ear.

STRAIN OR BITE

There are two types of whale: baleen whales and toothed whales. Baleen whales are filter feeders that strain tiny creatures from the water through fringed curtains of a horny material called baleen or whalebone.

◄ Blue whale.

▲ The number and size of teeth varies with species. Dolphins (above) have conical, interlocking teeth, porpoises have spade-shaped teeth, and most beaked whales only have two visible pairs.

THERE SHE BLOWS

Whales come to the surface to breathe. As they breathe out, warm moist air rushes out through nostrils on the top of the head—the blowhole. This "blow" may reach 33 ft. (10m) into the air. They then take a few breaths through the blowhole and dive down for several minutes. Toothed whales have just one blowhole, baleen whales have two.

FRIENDLY GIANT

The blue whale is the largest animal that has ever lived on Earth. It can reach a length of 100 ft. (30m) and a weight of 150 tons—as heavy as 20 full-grown elephants. Like most of the other large whales, the blue whale has no teeth. It is a baleen whale that feeds on tiny plankton and krill living near the surface of the sea. Other whales and dolphins have many teeth and feed on fish, squid, seals, and penguins.

SMILING DOLPHINS

Dolphins are small whales with a pointed snout and appear to have a permanent smile. They are playful and intelligent animals. They live in groups called schools and communicate with clicks and whistles. They use sound location to navigate and find fish to eat. An injured dolphin will usually be helped by other members of the school. There are even reports of dolphins helping drowning people. Like all whales, dolphins never come ashore. They mate and give birth to their young in the sea. A mother dolphin feeds her baby on her milk for a year and they often stay together for several years.

▲ Narwhals grow up to 18 ft. (5.5m) with no dorsal fin and two teeth. In males, one tooth develops into a spiral tusk up to 9 ft. (2.7m) long.

◄ Sperm whales are a family of three species. They are the largest toothed whales (growing to 66 ft./20m) and the deepest divers. They eat mostly squid.

◄ Orcas, or killer whales, are dolphins with a tall (6 ft./2m) sharklike fin. They have long, sharp teeth and eat young whales, seals, squid, or fish.

SEE ALSO

Animal, Conservation, Mammal, Migration

455

WIND

Wind is the movement of air over the Earth's surface. It can range from a gentle summer breeze to the destructive power of a hurricane or tornado.

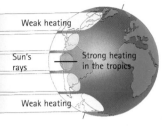

Weak heating

Sun's rays

Strong heating in the tropics

Weak heating

▲ The sun is strongest in the tropics, where it is almost overhead. Closer to the poles, the sun's rays are more spread out and therefore weaker.

North Pole (high pressure)

Sun's rays

South Pole (high pressure)

▲ Wind is the flow of air from high- (H) to low-pressure areas (L). This creates six main bands of air across the globe.

Wind is the movement of air from an area of high pressure to an area of low pressure. A wind is named after the direction from which it is blowing. So a north wind is one blowing from the north.

BLOWING HOT AND COLD

Big global wind systems such as the trade winds and easterlies are caused by the heating effect of the sun. Near the equator, the sun is almost overhead, and so the land, sea, and air receive the maximum amount of heat. Warm air tends to rise (just as a hot-air balloon rises), and because it is rising, it does not press down so much on the Earth's surface. This creates a low-pressure area. Colder, heavier air sinks down toward the Earth's surface in cooler regions, farther from the equator, and this creates high-pressure areas. The cooler, heavier air flows over the Earth's surface from high-pressure areas to low-pressure areas, creating winds.

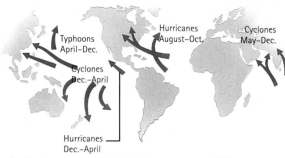

Typhoons April–Dec.

Hurricanes August–Oct.

Cyclones May–Dec.

Cyclones Dec.–April

Hurricanes Dec.–April

▲ Hurricanes form in the late summer and fall over warm areas in the Atlantic, Pacific, and Indian oceans. They then move westward, along the coasts.

LOCAL WINDS

Local winds arise from a combination of weather patterns and the shape of the land. Land heats up and cools down quicker than water, and this produces the gentle breezes you often feel at the coast. During the day, the land heats up, the air above it warms up and rises, and moist air flows in from the sea to replace it, creating a cool sea breeze. At night, the land cools quickly, the air above it descends and spreads out, and this produces a light offshore breeze. Other local winds form around mountains, especially where there are glaciers. At night, cold, heavy air pours down the hillsides and valleys, and out over the surrounding lowlands.

Direction of storm

Eye

Dry air sinks

Strong spiral winds

Strong upcurrents

Clouds

Rising warm, moist air

Low pressure at center

Rain

Warm sea

Inward-flowing winds

INSIDE A HURRICANE

Hurricanes are huge rotating storm systems that form over warm tropical seas. They can be 600 mi. (1,000km) across, with circular walls of storm clouds rising 10 mi. (16km) into the air. Winds inside the cloud bands can top 200 mph (320kph), and the whole storm usually moves across the ocean at about 16 mph (25kph). When a hurricane reaches land it can do enormous damage.

SEE ALSO

Climate, Season, Sun, Weather, Wind power

WIND POWER

Wind power uses the power of the wind to turn machinery or generate electricity. It is a renewable, nonpolluting source of energy.

Windmills have been used to grind corn or pump water from the ground for hundreds of years. Simple windmills may have been used in Ancient Persia (now Iran) in the A.D. 600s. Modern windmills, called wind turbines, use the turning motion of the blades to spin a turbine, which generates electricity.

Fantail

▲ Although often only 1,600 ft. (500m) across, tornadoes unleash a devastating force. They form over land, like dark funnels of cloud, and can contain winds of over 250 mph (400kph)—strong enough to demolish buildings and throw cars around like toys.

▲ The addition of a fantail, invented in 1745, automatically turned the top of the mill so that the sails caught the wind.

SPINNING SAILS

In a windmill, four to eight wind sails, each 10–30 ft. (3–9m) long, catch the wind. As they spin, a shaft turns. Gears transfer the power to turn a heavy grinding stone at the bottom of the building. Spring sails made of wooden shutters, invented in 1772, could be adjusted to turn steadily in varying winds.

WIND TURBINES

Windmills were largely replaced in the 1900s by engine power. But wind turbines are a growing energy source. Pioneered in Denmark in the 1890s, they use airfoils like airplane propellers to turn a turbine and make electricity. Used to supply electricity in remote areas, wind farms may have hundreds of wind turbines, with blades 50–100 ft. (15–30m) in diameter. The largest wind farms can generate up to 1,120 megawatts, as much electricity as produced by a nuclear power plant. Although nonpolluting, wind farms use great areas of land.

WIND FARMS

Wind turbines need to be made so that they turn, even in gentle wind, and also cope with gales. They also need to be built where there is plenty of wind, such as along the coast or on flat plains. These places are usually a long way from where the electricity is needed, and much energy is lost sending it along power lines.

FAST FACTS

• The sailboat is one of the most common users of wind power

• The largest wind farms are in California, and can generate over 1,000 megawatts of power on a windy day

• By 2050, 10 percent of the world's electricity may be generated using wind power

SEE ALSO

Boat, Electricity, Wind

WOLF AND OTHER WILD DOGS

Wolves, coyotes, jackals, and foxes are all kinds of wild dog. They are strong, quick, alert carnivores, many of which hunt in packs.

A skillful hunter, the red fox lives in Asia, Europe, and North America.

In winter, the long fur of the Arctic fox turns from brown or gray to white.

Known for its eerie howl, the coyote is found in Canada, the U.S., and Mexico.

Wolves belong to the group known as *Canidae*, or the dog family. This group also includes the gray, red, and maned wolf, coyote, and dingo, African and Asian (dhole) wild dogs, raccoon and bush dogs, 4 kinds of jackal, about 20 kinds of fox—as well as the hundreds of breeds and varieties of domestic dog. These were probably tamed and bred from wolf ancestors at least 10,000 years ago.

FEATURES OF THE HUNTER
All members of the dog family are meat-eaters, or carnivores. They live by hunting or scavenging. But they eat almost anything if they are hungry, even fruits and berries. They have acute senses, including sharp eyesight and hearing, and an excellent sense of smell. Their long, strong legs, which they use for fast running and relentless pursuit, have clawed toes for good grip and scratching. Their long, sharp teeth bite and tear flesh.

WHERE WOLVES LIVE
The gray, or timber, wolf, usually just known as the wolf, is widespread across North America, parts of Europe, the Middle East, and northern Asia. It prefers forests but can live in mountains, grasslands, and even deserts. The red wolf is extremely rare, limited to a small area of

◄ When gathering to begin a hunt, wolves greet each other with loud howls. This warns wolves from other packs to stay out of their territory.

▲ In each pack, some wolves are more dominant than others. Here, a dominant wolf stands with its tail and ears held up, while a subordinate wolf approaches it in a crouched position, tail between legs and ears flattened.

southeast North America. The maned wolf, which is really more like a long-legged fox, dwells in grassy scrubland in central South America.

WILD DOGS AROUND THE WORLD
The coyote, with its mournful howl, is a wolflike wild dog that has extended its territory from the southwestern United States and Mexico. In Australia, the dingo is probably descended from the part-tamed dogs of Aboriginal people, brought to the continent more than 7,000 years ago. Jackals live across Africa, the Middle East, and southern Asia. Different kinds of bushy-tailed fox dwell in almost every habitat, from the Arctic fox of the snowy far north, to the Cape fox of southern Africa's deserts, and the well-known, widespread, and adaptable red fox, which scavenges trash in towns and cities.

KEY FACTS
• Various members of the dog family can breed with each other. For example, a domestic dog and a coyote produce coydog puppies. This interbreeding makes it difficult to know exactly how many true species are in the dog family

• The main difference between wolves and dogs that look like them is that wolves carry their tail hanging down while dogs carry it curled up

• The crab-eating fox of South America really does eat crabs, and tortoises, too, but it prefers easier meat, such as mice, birds, lizards, insects, and eggs

HUNTING IN PACKS

Many wild dogs, especially wolves and African and Asian wild dogs, hunt with others of their kind. The group is called a pack. It can catch much larger prey than one dog hunting alone. A pack of wolves can bring down a full-grown moose over 6.5 ft. (2m) high. Each pack has dominant males, or leaders, who get the best food and mate with females at breeding time.

A VARIETY OF PREY

Other wild dogs, especially foxes, live and hunt alone, or with a mate. Jackals have a reputation as scavengers. In fact, they usually hunt live prey—from frogs, lizards, and mice to small gazelles and young zebras. Smaller wild dogs usually eat smaller meals. Most foxes have a diet of mice, voles, fish, frogs, birds, eggs, and insects. The smallest kind, the fennec fox, with huge ears, survives in the Sahara and Middle Eastern deserts by consuming small beetles, spiders, locusts, and worms.

▲ The dingo, which can be bred with the domestic dog, howls, but rarely barks. Dingoes come together to run down and kill large prey, such as kangaroos.

A DOG'S LIFE

Wolves have long been feared in legend and have therefore been persecuted. In fact, wolves attack people only when threatened or if they are extremely hungry. Many other wild dogs are also hunted, and some are endangered. People shoot, poison, or trap them in case they raid farm animals. Also some kinds, especially foxes, are still killed for their handsome fur pelts.

The jackal is up to 30 in. (75cm) in length. It has a strong body smell.

The raccoon dog lives throughout eastern Asia and is mainly nocturnal.

The African wild dog lives in large parts of Africa, and hunts its prey in packs.

PACK HUNTERS

Wolves hunt in packs, feeding on almost any animal that they can catch. In order to kill prey such as reindeer and elk, which are faster and stronger than they are, wolves must be quick and skillful. Wolves hunt by day and by night, roaming through territory until they find prey. They stalk it by moving toward it against the wind to prevent it from picking up their scent. Once close enough, the wolves break into a run and the chase begins. If they succeed in catching their victim, they weaken it through injury, then grab it by the throat.

SEE ALSO

Animal, Desert, Dog, Mammal

WOMEN'S RIGHTS

Women's rights are those civil rights that have
traditionally been denied to women in many societies.
Women have had to struggle to gain these rights.

▲ Imprisoned women's rights campaigners in the U.K.
went on hunger strikes and were brutally force-fed.

MARY WOLLSTONECRAFT
(1759–97), Irish–English
writer of one of the first
feminist books, *Vindication
of the Rights of Women*
(1792). A later pamphlet,
*Thoughts on the Education
of Daughters* (1797),
criticized girls' schooling.

**ELIZABETH CADY
STANTON** (1815–1902),
organized the first women's
rights assembly in the U.S.
in 1848. She fought for
fair property and divorce
laws for married women,
coeducation, and the right
to vote (suffrage).

EMMELINE PANKHURST
(1858–1928), a women's
rights leader in the U.K.,
founded the Women's
Social and Political Union
(1902) campaigning for the
right to vote. She and her
daughter, Christabel, were
imprisoned many times.

In different societies the status of men
and women has varied greatly. Today it
is generally thought that men and women
should have equal rights, and some
countries have laws to make forms of
discrimination (unfair treatment) illegal.

ANCIENT RIGHTS

The role of women within society has
varied greatly. In Ancient Greece, women
had few rights. They were expected to stay
at home and to take no part in social life.
Some Greek teachers believed it was wrong
to teach women to read in case they
learned too much and disagreed with the
men. In Egypt, however, women played a
full part in society. They could take jobs,
own property, and divorce their husbands.
Some became rulers, but usually after the
death of a husband.

DIVISION OF LABOR

In traditional farming communities,
the work of a family was divided.
Men mainly carried out heavy physical
work. Women took on household
tasks and childcare. Other jobs
in society were also divided.

▶ The U.S. Army 24th Infantry
in Saudi Arabia. The Gulf
War, in 1990–91, was
the first conflict that
saw women soldiers of
the U.S. Army fighting
alongside men.

Traditionally, men fought in the army,
while women often cared for the sick.

CHANGING RIGHTS

Industrial revolution in the 1800s brought
changes. The work in many new industries
did not need strength, but skill. Women
were able to do many factory jobs just as
well as men. A family could be supported
by a woman instead of a man. By the late
1800s, most industrialized nations had

SEE ALSO
Civil rights, Democracy, Education, Industrial Revolution, Israel, Textile, World War II

KEY U.S. DATES

1848 Convention on women's rights, Seneca Falls, N.Y.

1860 Married Woman's Property Act gives the right to hold property and earn and keep money

1869 Wyoming Territory gives vote to women

1916 Jeanette Rankin elected to Congress

1920 19th Amendment gives vote to women

1963 U.S. Equal Pay Act rules that men and women should receive equal pay; Betty Friedan's sparks women's movements

1966 National Organization for Women founded

1972 Equal Rights Amendment goes to states for ratification (it fails to receive it)

1981 Sandra Day O'Connor becomes Supreme Court Justice

civil rights for women. Women were allowed to keep their own property when they married, instead of giving control to their husbands. They could enter into contracts and sign legal papers, teach, and become nurses and doctors, although education for girls was still less formal than for males and ended at an earlier age.

THE VOTE

For a long time only those who owned property could vote. During the 1800s, this was challenged. The right to vote (suffrage) was extended to poor men, but not to women. In 1869, Elizabeth Cady Stanton and Susan B. Anthony founded the National Woman Suffrage Association; in the same year Lucy Stone set up the rival National American Woman Suffrage Association. Activists were called suffragists. In the U.K., Emmeline Pankhurst organized the Women's Social and Political Union; U.K. activists were called suffragettes.

SLOW PROGRESS

Women in New Zealand were the first to get the vote, in 1893—but Maori women had to wait until 1967. By the 1920s, most democracies had given women the vote, although Swiss women won it only in the 1970s. Women in some Muslim countries are still not equal to men and cannot vote or stand for election.

SHIFTING HORIZONS

During the 1960s, a movement called Women's Liberation sought to make women equal to men in social and economic terms. Gradually women's choices have widened. Today there are women doctors, lawyers, and judges. The number of women running companies is slowly rising. It is not unusual to see women as bus drivers, firefighters, or construction workers. Women have taken frontline roles in some Western armies. Even so, balancing a career and motherhood is still a dilemma for many women.

▲ During the two world wars, many Western women took jobs making weapons in factories. It was their war efforts that led to greater recognition of women's value.

▲ Israel's Golda Meir was deputy foreign minister in 1948, and later foreign minister. She became the Israeli prime minister in 1969.

◄ In 1996, the Taliban (fundamentalist Muslims) took over the government in Afghanistan. They banned girls from schools, women from working, and made women cover themselves. In 2001, the Taliban government was overthrown.

WORLD WAR I

World War I was a terrible war fought between 1914 and 1918 in which millions of people died. It began in Europe, but spread to many parts of the globe.

Kaiser Wilhelm II (1859–1941) of Germany led an aggressive foreign policy against other nations.

Lloyd George (1863–1945), British prime minister from 1916, reorganized the war effort for victory.

Russia's Tsar Nicholas II (1868–1918) backed Serbia against Austria, bringing Russia into the war.

People living at the time called World War I "the Great War" because no other war had been so widespread nor so destructive. Millions of soldiers were killed and the world economy changed for ever.

OUTBREAK OF WAR
In 1914, Europe was divided into two major alliances. The Hapsburg Empire was allied to Germany to block Russian moves in the Balkans, while France sided with Russia against the growing might of Germany. On June 28, 1914, the Hapsburg archduke Franz Ferdinand was shot dead by a Serb terrorist, prompting the Hapsburgs to declare war on Serbia. Serbia, in turn, asked for help from the Russians, who then declared war on the Hapsburgs. This brought Germany and France into the war. Britain joined the war when Germany invaded Belgium.

EARLY BATTLES
In the east, Russian armies were smashed by the Germans at Tannenberg, while Hapsburg armies were defeated by the Russians in several encounters during the month of September. In the west, the Germans intended to capture Paris and defeat France, but were stopped on the Marne River on September 8, 1914, while the British army blocked outflanking moves to the North. By October, the armies had settled into trenches for the winter.

NEW WEAPONS
Barbed wire barriers, machine guns, and artillery made defense so strong that attacks were almost useless. Troops experimented with poison gas to help attackers, but it rarely had much effect. Tanks, first used by the British in 1916,

▲ World War I began after Serb terrorist Gavrilo Princip killed the Hapsburg archduke Franz Ferdinand. Princip was sentenced to 20 years in prison, but got sick and died in 1918.

could defeat barbed wire or machine guns, but they often broke down. Aircraft were more successful, and were used to spy on enemy troops, target artillery shells, and drop bombs. The German pilot Manfred von Richthofen, nicknamed the "Red Baron," successfully shot 80 enemy aircraft down in flames.

WORLD WAR
In Africa, British and French troops attacked German colonies. In 1915, Australian and New Zealand troops attacked Turkey at Gallipoli, but were badly defeated and sustained heavy losses. At sea, German ships and submarines sank Allied ships, and in 1917 began attacking any ships heading for Allied ports. The United States first protested about these attacks on its ships, and then joined the Allies, declaring war on Germany.

◀ Russian Cossacks and other cavalry were used for scouting, but were useless in the trenches.

Britain
Germany
Eastern Front
Russia
Western Front
France
Habsburg Empire
Italian Front
Romania
Italy
Serbia
Bulgaria
Greece
Ottoman Empire

☐ Allies
☐ Central Powers
☐ Neutral countries
☐ Major battle fronts

▲ Trench warfare led to small battlefronts. Only on the Eastern Front were sweeping movements made.

Aircraft were a new weapon, used for scouting and fighting.

KEY DATES

August 1914 War breaks out between the Allies (France, Britain, Russia, Belgium, Serbia, and Montenegro) and the Central Powers (Germany and the Hapsburg Empire)

November 1914 Turkey joins the Central Powers

May 1915 Italy joins the Allies

October 1915 Bulgaria joins the Central Powers

August 1916 Romania joins the Allies

April 1917 The United States joins the Allies

December 1917 Russia makes peace with Germany

November 1918 Fighting ceases

1919 Peace Treaties signed at Versailles in France

The small Serb army was driven out of Serbia into Greece in December 1915.

FINAL MOVES

In 1917, the Communists took over Russia and made peace. The German troops, freed from Russia, launched a massive attack in March 1918 in France. American troops helped to stop the attack. But Bulgaria, Turkey, and the Hapsburgs were close to collapse and Germany asked for peace. A ceasefire was finally agreed on November 11, 1918.

THE WAR ENDS

The cost of World War I was immense. Germany lost 1.9 million men, Russia 1.7 million, France 1.5 million, and Britain and the Hapsburgs 1 million each, as well as vast amounts of money. The Hapsburg Empire was split into Austria, Hungary, Czechoslovakia, and Yugoslavia. Poland, Estonia, Latvia, and Lithuania became independent. European countries lost economic power as others built up their industries. The world was changed for ever.

Britain had the smallest army in 1914, but it was made up of professionals.

TRENCH WARFARE

The war in the West was fought from trenches guarded by barbed wire and machine guns. Conditions were appalling, with knee-deep mud, constant shelling, sniping, and raids. The battles of the Somme and Verdun in France in 1916 cost over two million casualties, although neither side managed to advance more than a few hundred yards.

Machine gun post in the French trenches

German troops

In 1914, the German army was the largest and best trained in the world.

SEE ALSO

Communism, Empire, Warfare, World War II

WORLD WAR II

World War II was fought between 1939 and 1945. It involved more countries, cost more lives, and caused more destruction than any other war.

The American B17 Flying Fortress

Erwin Rommel (1891–1944) was a daring leader of German armored units.

Yamamoto Isoroku (1884–1943) planned Japan's attack on Pearl Harbor.

Bernard Montgomery (1887–1976) led the British in North Africa and Europe.

Georgy Zhukov (1896–1974) commanded the Soviet Red Army.

Dwight D. Eisenhower (1890–1969) led the D-Day invasion of 1944.

Adolf Hitler in Germany, Benito Mussolini in Italy, and General Tojo Hideki in Japan wanted to extend the power and territories of their countries. They formed a pact, called the Axis, to gain what they wanted.

BLITZKRIEG

In September 1939, Germany invaded Poland to regain land it had lost in World War I. Britain and France supported Poland. The Germans used a tactic called *blitzkrieg*—lightning war. Bomber aircraft began the attack, then tanks, or panzers, plunged deep behind enemy lines, followed by infantry and artillery. Poland was defeated in just five weeks. In April 1940, Hitler invaded Denmark, Belgium, Holland, Norway, and France. By July, only Britain had not surrendered. In the Battle of Britain, the determined Royal Air Force beat off German air attacks.

INTO RUSSIA

Hitler wanted to expand Germany and create *lebensraum* ("living space") for the German nation. In June 1941, 3.5 million German, Italian, Romanian, and Hungarian troops stormed into Russia, capturing vast territories. In December, a reinforced Red Army finally stopped the invaders just outside Moscow.

The Japanese Mitsubishi Ki-67, codenamed "Peggy"

The German Dornier Do217

The British Lancaster

▲ Small bombers, such as the Dornier and Mitsubishi, were used to destroy battlefield targets, such as tanks and artillery. The Lancaster, Flying Fortress, and other heavy bombers pounded cities and factories.

PEARL HARBOR

Japan wanted to capture large areas of Southeast Asia to secure industrial raw materials. The Japanese hoped that a quick defeat would persuade the United States to allow Japanese expansion, so they launched a surprise attack on Pearl Harbor. The U.S. did not give way, but declared war. The same day, Japan invaded Southeast Asia. By May 1942, Japan had conquered Burma, Malaya, the Philippines, and the East Indies.

THE TIDE TURNS

After three years of war, the Allies had built up their armed forces. In North Africa, German and Italian troops were defeated at El Alamein in October 1942, and in December 1942, the German 6th Army was

◀ On December 7, 1941, 360 Japanese aircraft attacked Pearl Harbor, Hawaii, the base of the U.S. Pacific Fleet. The attack opened the way for Japanese conquests and brought the U.S. into the war.

▶ Germany, Japan, and their allies made large conquests in 1939–42. But the greater resources of the Allies were brought into action after 1942.

wiped out at Stalingrad. The Japanese were halted in February 1943. The Allies then organized strike forces to retake Burma, and to use island-hopping tactics in the Pacific.

GERMANY COLLAPSES

In June 1944, Germany was caught between the Normandy landings and the Russian advance. On April 30, 1945, Hitler killed himself; two days later Germany surrendered. The Allies found that the Nazis had murdered millions, six million of them Jews, in the worst case of mass human extinction in history. It has come to be called the Holocaust. Jewish people refer to it as the Shoah, meaning "chaos" or "annihilation."

THE ATOMIC BOMB

With the war over in Europe, President Truman wanted to bring U.S. troops home from the Pacific—Japanese forces were determined to fight on. To end the war and cut casualties, the U.S. decided to use the atomic bomb. It obliterated the cities of Hiroshima and Nagasaki; 200,000 people died. Japan surrendered on September 2, 1945.

PEACE AND COLD WAR

The war had cost the lives of some 15 million troops and 35 million civilians. After the war, the world divided into two powerful blocs: the communist countries, led by the Soviet Union and China, and the democratic world, led by the United States. The Cold War had begun.

▲ The Allied leaders, Winston Churchill (left), Franklin D. Roosevelt (center), and Joseph Stalin, met at Yalta in 1945 to decide the postwar arrangements for Europe.

D-DAY

At dawn on June 6, 1944, the largest invasion fleet in history landed Allied forces on the coast of Normandy. In all, 1,200 warships and 4,100 landing craft put 132,500 soldiers ashore, while 10,000 aircraft attacked German positions inland. The success of the D-Day invasion allowed American, British, and French troops to drive the Germans out of France.

SEE ALSO

Cold War, Fascism, Great Depression, Warfare, World War I

WORM

Worms are legless invertebrates (animals with no backbone). There are four major groups: ribbon worms, flatworms, roundworms, and segmented worms.

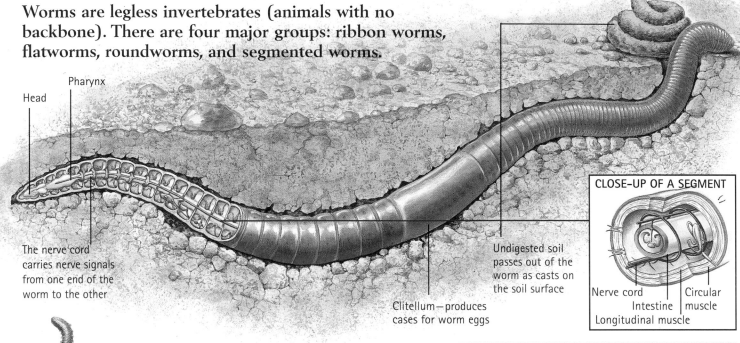

Head

Pharynx

The nerve cord carries nerve signals from one end of the worm to the other

Clitellum—produces cases for worm eggs

Undigested soil passes out of the worm as casts on the soil surface

CLOSE–UP OF A SEGMENT

Nerve cord

Intestine

Longitudinal muscle

Circular muscle

A lugworm (segmented) has feathery gills.

A horse leech (segmented) can grow to 1 ft. (30cm).

Flatworms can cause serious illnesses in humans.

Roundworms make up the largest group of worms.

Ribbon worms live in the sea and can be 6.5 ft. (2m).

A ragworm (segmented) has strong jaws to eat prey.

There are thousands of kinds of worm. The simplest, such as flatworms, are found mostly in the sea or are parasites that live inside animals and humans. Ribbon worms are like long flatworms—the bootlace worm grows to 85 ft. (25m).

EARTHWORMS

The earthworms that tunnel in gardens belong to a group called annelids, or segmented worms. Their bodies are made of many ringlike sections. There are hundreds of species of earthworm and all feed by swallowing soil and digesting any decaying matter in it. They also pull dead leaves into their tunnels and eat them. Earthworms are important for farmers and gardeners because their tunnels drain and bring air into the soil and allow plant roots to grow. There are no separate male and female worms: each one has both male and female parts. After mating, which usually takes place above ground at night, each worm lays its own eggs.

BLOOD-SUCKING LEECHES

Leeches are related to earthworms, but instead of having bristles for moving they have a large sucker at each end. Most of them live in water or damp soil and feed on other animals. Some of the bigger ones are bloodsuckers and may attack people.

SLITHERING SEGMENTS

Each segment of an earthworm's body has several little bristles on the underside and these enable the worms to move through their tunnels. The bristles of one group of segments dig into the walls like anchors while powerful muscles push or pull the others forward. There are no lungs; respiration takes place through the body surface.

PARASITIC WORMS

Many flatworms and roundworms (also called nematodes) live inside other animals as parasites. Hooks or suckers on their head cling to the lining of the host's intestines and the worms soak up digested food. Tapeworms, which can reach 98 ft. (30m), produce many eggs, which pass out with the host's droppings. Some eggs find their way into new host animals.

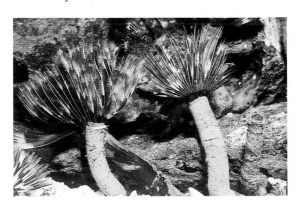

▲ Peacock worms live in the sea. They catch food with bristles and live in a tube made from secretions.

SEE ALSO

Animal, Blood, Earth, Sight, Zoology

466

X RAY

X rays are a form of energy that can pass straight through many solid materials. We use X rays to look inside bodies and machines and to kill some cancers.

▲ X-ray radiation was discovered by the German physicist Wilhelm Roentgen (1845–1923), who was awarded the first Nobel Prize for Physics in 1901.

▼ High doses of X rays can damage body cells. The harmful effects of X rays are often used to help cure cancers. Powerful beams of X rays are directed at cells in a tumor, killing them off.

If you break a bone, you will probably go to the hospital for an X ray. An X-ray image lets the doctor see where your bone is fractured or damaged. A special machine directs a narrow beam of X rays at the part of your body that needs examining. Unlike light waves, these X rays can pass right through the soft parts of your body, the skin and muscles.

X-RAY IMAGE

When X rays come through your body, they hit a photographic plate, where they form an image. Because your bones and teeth are heavy and dense, they block the path of the X rays. This is why they leave blank areas on the X-ray image. Trained people can look at these blank areas and work out the exact shape of your skeleton.

▲ This X-ray image of a human skull found at a Roman burial site reveals a missing top molar tooth.

SOFT TISSUE

Sometimes, doctors use X rays to look at softer, lighter parts of your body, such as the liver or bladder. To do this, they inject you with a special chemical called barium sulfate. This makes these tissues block the path of X rays. The body gets rid of this chemical naturally after a few hours.

MACHINES AND CRYSTALS

X rays are not only used to look inside people. They are also used to examine the insides of certain machines. Aircraft makers, for example, take X-ray images of various machine parts to make sure they have no inner cracks. Chemists take X-ray images of crystals. They use these to study how the X rays bounce off a crystal's inner structure. This can help them work out how the atoms in the crystal are arranged.

▲ In an X-ray machine, a hot wire produces a stream of electrons. These are fired at a tungsten metal target, giving out X rays. Some pass through the patient's body, making an image on film or a fluorescent screen.

Power supply · Heated wire · Electron beam · Target · Window · X-ray beam

SEE ALSO
Astronomy, Atom and molecule, Light, Medicine, Wavelength

ZOOLOGY

Zoology is the scientific study of all animals—their body structure, how they live, feed, breed, move, and behave—in nature or captivity.

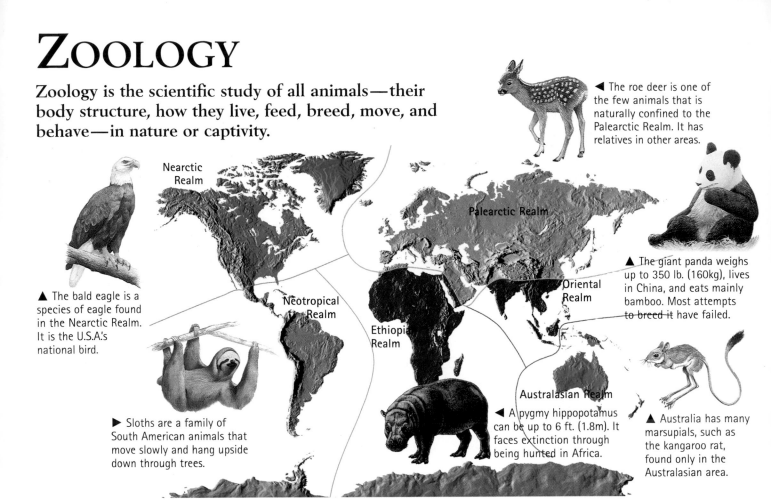

◄ The roe deer is one of the few animals that is naturally confined to the Palearctic Realm. It has relatives in other areas.

Nearctic Realm

Palearctic Realm

▲ The bald eagle is a species of eagle found in the Nearctic Realm. It is the U.S.A.'s national bird.

Neotropical Realm

Oriental Realm

▲ The giant panda weighs up to 350 lb. (160kg), lives in China, and eats mainly bamboo. Most attempts to breed it have failed.

Ethiopian Realm

▶ Sloths are a family of South American animals that move slowly and hang upside down through trees.

Australasian Realm

◄ A pygmy hippopotamus can be up to 6 ft. (1.8m). It faces extinction through being hunted in Africa.

▲ Australia has many marsupials, such as the kangaroo rat, found only in the Australasian area.

GROUPING ANIMALS

Zoologists divide the Earth into six distinct regions, or realms, following the work, in the 1800s, of British wildlife expert, Alfred Russel Wallace. He first noticed that whole orders or families of animals, birds, and freshwater fish may be confined to one region. This map shows the six realms and an example of the animals found only in each area.

The animal kingdom is vast, varied, and complicated. Zoology has many specialist branches. These often overlap. Some branches deal with particular groups of animals. For example, entomology is the detailed study of insects. Ichthyology specializes in fish. Herpetology is the study of amphibians and reptiles.

LEARNING ABOUT ANIMALS

Other branches of zoology deal with the features that animals share. Anatomists study the structure of an animal's body and the parts inside, such as the heart, nerves, intestines, and kidneys. Physiologists look at how these parts work, for example how worms take food from soil or how fish take in oxygen through gills. Embryologists deal with development of animals before birth.

THE LIVING AND THE DEAD

Some areas of zoology are very wide-ranging. Ethologists watch animal behavior—their actions and instincts. Ecologists study how a creature fits into its surroundings or habitat. They observe its needs, such as food and shelter, and its predators. Paleontologists study fossil remains that tell us about prehistoric life, such as dinosaurs. They deal with dead remains, but still need a good knowledge of living animals to reconstruct finds and compare them with other creatures.

WHAT ZOOLOGISTS DO

Some zoologists are desk-based, writing reports or books. Others work in laboratories, carrying out tests and experiments. Some are based in museums, zoos, or wildlife parks, and others are in the field—watching, taking notes on, and photographing animals in the wild. Many deal with the media: for example, campaigning to save endangered creatures or giving pet advice.

▼ A keeper at Marwell Zoo (U.K.) bottle-feeds a baby okapi, a very rare African animal. Breeding threatened species such as this is one invaluable role of a zoo. Many breed animals in captivity to help boost their dwindling numbers in the wild.

SEE ALSO

Animal, Conservation, Evolution, Mammal, Prehistoric animal

Propelled by rocket engines, the supersonic X-15 holds the world air-speed record at 4,520 mph set in 1967.

The funeral mask of the pharaoh Tutankhamen was found in his tomb, discovered in 1922.

The first washing machine (invented by Hamilton Smith, U.S.A., 1858) still relied on muscle power.

On April 12, 1961, Yuri Gagarin of the U.S.S.R. became the first person in space onboard *Vostok 1*.

The steam gun carriage of 1769, invented by French engineer Cugnot, was the first motorized vehicle.

FACTFINDER

Whether for school projects, or just for fun, this section provides facts, figures, and other essential information—from a world map to presidents and states, and on to biographies of famous figures, finishing with the highlights of the last 100 years. Timelines present key international (top) and U.S. (bottom) developments.

The *chanoyu*, a Japanese tea ceremony which can last four hours, actually originated in China.

In 1834, Charles Babbage (1792-1871) designed the first mechanical computer, but he never saw it built.

The Venus flytrap is a carnivorous plant that feeds on the insects it traps in its leaves.

U.S. astronauts use a Manned Maneuvering Unit (MMU) to guide themselves when floating free in space. This contains several small rocket thrusters pointing in different directions. When one is fired, the astronaut moves in the opposite direction.

The Arctic tern is a long-distance flyer, making an annual round trip of up to 25,000 miles.

Camptosaurus was an ornithopod ("bird-footed") dinosaur that lived about 150 million years ago.

Edgar Allan Poe (1809-49) was one of America's greatest poets and an early writer of horror stories.

COUNTRIES OF THE WORLD

Arctic Circle

ALASKA
(U.S.A.)

GREENLAND
(Denmark)

ICELAND

CANADA

KI

IRELAND

NORTH PACIFIC
OCEAN

UNITED STATES
OF AMERICA

NORTH ATLANTIC
OCEAN

PORTUGAL S

MOROCC

Tropic of Cancer

BAHAMAS

WESTERN
SAHARA

HAWAII
(U.S.A.)

MEXICO

CUBA

DOMINICAN
REPUBLIC

CAPE
VERDE IS.

MAURITANIA

HAITI
JAMAICA

PUERTO RICO
28

SENEGAL

GUATEMALA
BELIZE
HONDURAS

29 30
31

GAMBIA
GUINEA-BISSAU

GUINEA

EL SALVADOR NICARAGUA

32 33
34

SIERRA LEONE

IVOR
COAS

COSTA RICA
PANAMA

35

LIBERIA

VENEZUELA GUYANA

SURINAME
FRENCH GUIANA

COLOMBIA

Equator

GALAPAGOS
IS. (Ecuador)

ECUADOR

BRAZIL

PERU

BOLIVIA

KEY TO MAP

1	NETHERLANDS	19	HUNGARY
2	BELGIUM	20	MOLDOVA
3	LUXEMBOURG	21	ESTONIA
4	SWITZERLAND	22	LATVIA
5	LIECHTENSTEIN	23	LITHUANIA
6	AUSTRIA	24	KALININGRAD (RUSSIA)
7	ANDORRA	25	GEORGIA
8	MONACO	26	AZERBAIJAN
9	SAN MARINO	27	ARMENIA
10	VATICAN CITY	28	ANTIGUA AND BARBUDA
11	CZECH REPUBLIC	29	ST. KITTS AND NEVIS
12	SLOVAK REPUBLIC	30	DOMINICA
13	SLOVENIA	31	ST. LUCIA
14	CROATIA	32	ST. VINCENT AND THE
15	BOSNIA–HERZEGOVINA		GRENADINES
16	SERBIA AND	33	BARBADOS
	MONTENEGRO	34	GRENADA
17	MACEDONIA	35	TRINIDAD AND TOBAGO
18	ALBANIA	36	EQUATORIAL GUINEA
		37	SÃO TOMÉ AND
			PRÍNCIPE

Tropic of Capricorn

CHILE

PARAGUAY

SOUTH ATLANTIC
OCEAN

URUGUAY

SOUTH PACIFIC
OCEAN

ARGENTINA

FALKLAND/MALVINAS
IS. (U.K.)

SOUTH GEORGIA
(U.K.)

Antarctic Circle

miles
0   3,000
0   3,000
km

ARCTIC
OCEAN

SWEDEN
FINLAND

RUSSIA

RK
21
22
24 23
BELARUS
POLAND
11   UKRAINE
12
6   19   20
3 14   ROMANIA
15 16   BULGARIA
9   18 17
GREECE   TURKEY

KAZAKHSTAN

MONGOLIA

NORTH PACIFIC
OCEAN

25
26 27
UZBEKISTAN   KYRGYZSTAN
TURKMENISTAN
TAJIKISTAN

CHINA

NORTH
KOREA
SOUTH
KOREA
JAPAN

MALTA
CYPRUS SYRIA
LEBANON
ISRAEL JORDAN
IRAQ
IRAN

AFGHANISTAN

PAKISTAN

BHUTAN
NEPAL
BANGLADESH

TAIWAN

LIBYA
EGYPT
KUWAIT
BAHRAIN
QATAR
UNITED ARAB
EMIRATES
SAUDI
ARABIA
OMAN

INDIA

MYANMAR
(BURMA)
LAOS VIETNAM
THAILAND
CAMBODIA

PHILIPPINES

CHAD
ERITREA
YEMEN

SUDAN
DJIBOUTI

SRI LANKA

MALDIVES

PALAU

FED. STATES OF
MICRONESIA

MARSHALL IS.

KIRIBATI

CENTRAL
AFRICAN REP.
ETHIOPIA
SOMALI REPUBLIC

DEM. REP. OF
CONGO
UGANDA
KENYA
RWANDA
BURUNDI
CONGO

MALAYSIA

SINGAPORE

INDONESIA

NAURU

PAPUA
NEW
GUINEA

SOLOMON IS.

TUVALU

ANGOLA
TANZANIA
SEYCHELLES

COMOROS
ZAMBIA MALAWI
AMIBIA
ZIMBABWE
MOZAMBIQUE
BOTSWANA
MADAGASCAR
MAURITIUS
REUNION (Fr.)

INDIAN
OCEAN

VANUATU

FIJI

NEW CALEDONIA (Fr.)

WESTERN
SAMOA

SWAZILAND
SOUTH
AFRICA LESOTHO

AUSTRALIA

NEW ZEALAND

ANTARCTICA

STATES OF THE UNITED STATES

STATE	CAPITAL	POPULATION (2001 ESTIMATE)	(RANK)	AREA (IN SQ. MI.)	(RANK)	ENTRY INTO UNION	(ORDER)
Alabama	Montgomery	4,464,356	(23)	52,419	(30)	December 14, 1819	(22)
Alaska	Juneau	634,892	(47)	663,267	(1)	January 3, 1959	(49)
Arizona	Phoenix	5,307,331	(20)	113,998	(6)	February 14, 1912	(48)
Arkansas	Little Rock	2,692,090	(33)	53,179	(29)	June 15, 1836	(25)
California	Sacramento	34,501,130	(1)	163,696	(3)	September 9, 1850	(31)
Colorado	Denver	4,417,714	(24)	104,094	(8)	August 1, 1876	(38)
Connecticut	Hartford	3,425,074	(29)	5,543	(48)	January 9, 1788	(5)
Delaware	Dover	796,165	(45)	2,489	(49)	December 7, 1787	(1)
Florida	Tallahassee	16,396,515	(4)	65,755	(22)	March 3, 1845	(27)
Georgia	Atlanta	8,393,915	(10)	59,425	(24)	January 2, 1788	(4)
Hawaii	Honolulu	1,224,398	(42)	10,931	(43)	August 21, 1959	(50)
Idaho	Boise	1,321,006	(39)	83,570	(14)	July 3, 1890	(43)
Illinois	Springfield	12,482,301	(5)	57,914	(25)	December 3, 1818	(21)
Indiana	Indianapolis	6,114,745	(14)	36,418	(38)	December 11, 1816	(19)
Iowa	Des Moines	2,923,179	(30)	56,272	(26)	December 28, 1846	(29)
Kansas	Topeka	2,694,641	(32)	82,277	(15)	January 29, 1861	(34)
Kentucky	Frankfort	4,065,556	(25)	40,409	(37)	June 1, 1792	(15)
Louisiana	Baton Rouge	4,465,430	(22)	51,840	(31)	April 30, 1812	(18)
Maine	Augusta	1,286,670	(40)	35,385	(39)	March 15, 1820	(23)
Maryland	Annapolis	5,375,156	(19)	12,407	(42)	April 28, 1788	(7)
Massachusetts	Boston	6,379,304	(13)	10,555	(44)	February 6, 1788	(6)
Michigan	Lansing	9,990,817	(8)	96,716	(11)	January 26, 1837	(26)
Minnesota	St. Paul	4,972,294	(21)	86,939	(12)	May 11, 1858	(32)
Mississippi	Jackson	2,828,029	(31)	48,430	(32)	December 10, 1817	(20)
Missouri	Jefferson City	5,629,707	(17)	69,704	(21)	August 10, 1821	(24)
Montana	Helena	904,433	(44)	147,042	(4)	November 8, 1889	(41)
Nebraska	Lincoln	1,713,235	(38)	77,354	(16)	March 1, 1867	(37)
Nevada	Carson City	2,106,074	(35)	110,561	(7)	October 31, 1864	(36)
New Hampshire	Concord	1,259,181	(41)	9,350	(46)	June 21, 1788	(9)
New Jersey	Trenton	8,484,431	(9)	8,721	(47)	December 18, 1787	(3)
New Mexico	Santa Fe	1,829,146	(36)	121,589	(5)	January 6, 1912	(47)
New York	Albany	19,011,378	(3)	54,556	(27)	July 26, 1788	(11)
North Carolina	Raleigh	8,816,268	(11)	53,819	(28)	November 21, 1789	(12)
North Dakota	Bismarck	634,448	(48)	70,700	(19)	November 2, 1889	(39)
Ohio	Columbus	11,373,541	(7)	44,825	(34)	March 1, 1803	(17)
Oklahoma	Oklahoma City	3,460,097	(28)	69,898	(20)	November 16, 1907	(46)
Oregon	Salem	3,472,867	(27)	98,381	(9)	February 14, 1859	(33)
Pennsylvania	Harrisburg	12,287,150	(6)	46,055	(33)	December 12, 1787	(2)
Rhode Island	Providence	1,058,920	(43)	1,545	(50)	May 29, 1790	(13)
South Carolina	Columbia	4,063,111	(26)	32,020	(40)	May 23, 1788	(8)
South Dakota	Pierre	756,600	(46)	77,116	(17)	November 2, 1889	(40)
Tennessee	Nashville	5,740,021	(16)	42,143	(36)	June 1, 1796	(16)
Texas	Austin	21,325,018	(2)	268,581	(2)	December 29, 1845	(28)
Utah	Salt Lake City	2,269,789	(34)	84,899	(13)	January 4, 1896	(45)
Vermont	Montpelier	613,090	(49)	9,614	(45)	March 4, 1791	(14)
Virginia	Richmond	7,178,734	(12)	42,774	(35)	June 25, 1788	(10)
Washington	Olympia	5,987,973	(15)	71,300	(18)	November 11, 1889	(42)
West Virginia	Charleston	1,801,916	(37)	24,230	(41)	June 20, 1863	(35)
Wisconsin	Madison	5,401,906	(18)	65,498	(23)	May 29, 1848	(30)
Wyoming	Cheyenne	494,423	(50)	97,814	(10)	July 10, 1890	(44)

PRESENTS OF THE UNITED STATES

NAME (PARTY)*	BIRTH-DEATH DATES	TERM IN OFFICE	VICE PRESIDENT(S)
1. George Washington (F)	1732 – 1799	Apr. 30, 1789 – Mar. 4, 1797	John Adams
2. John Adams (F)	1735 – 1826	Mar. 4, 1797 – Mar. 4, 1801	Thomas Jefferson
3. Thomas Jefferson (D–R)	1743 – 1826	Mar. 4, 1801 – Mar. 4, 1809	Aaron Burr George Clinton
4. James Madison (D–R)	1751 – 1836	Mar. 4, 1809 – Mar. 4, 1817	George Clinton Elbridge Gerry
5. James Monroe (D–R)	1758 – 1831	Mar. 4, 1817 – Mar. 4, 1825	Daniel D. Tompkins
6. John Quincy Adams (D–R)	1767 – 1848	Mar. 4, 1825 – Mar. 4, 1829	John C. Calhoun
7. Andrew Jackson (D)	1767 – 1845	Mar. 4, 1829 – Mar. 4, 1837	John C. Calhoun, Martin Van Buren
8. Martin Van Buren (D)	1782 – 1862	Mar. 4, 1837 – Mar. 4, 1841	Richard M. Johnson
9. William Henry Harrison (W)	1773 – 1841	Mar. 4, 1841 – Apr. 4, 1841	John Tyler
10. John Tyler (W)	1790 – 1862	Apr. 4, 1841 – Mar. 4, 1845	—
11. James K. Polk (D)	1795 – 1849	Mar. 4, 1845 – Mar. 4, 1849	George M. Dallas
12. Zachary Taylor (W)	1784 – 1850	Mar. 4, 1849 – July 9, 1850	Millard Fillmore
13 Millard Fillmore (W)	1800 – 1874	July 9, 1850 – Mar. 4, 1853	—
14. Franklin Pierce (D)	1804 – 1869	Mar. 4, 1853 – Mar. 4, 1857	William R. King
15. James Buchanan (D)	1791 – 1868	Mar. 4, 1857 – Mar. 4, 1861	John C. Breckinridge
16. Abraham Lincoln (R)	1809 – 1865	Mar. 4, 1861 – Apr. 15, 1865	Hannibal Hamlin, Andrew Johnson
17. Andrew Johnson (R)	1808 – 1875	Apr. 15, 1865 – Mar. 4, 1869	
18. Ulysses S. Grant (R)	1822 – 1885	Mar. 4, 1869 – Mar. 4, 1877	Schuyler Colfax Henry Wilson
19. Rutherford B. Hayes (R)	1822 – 1893	Mar. 4, 1877 – Mar. 4, 1881	William A. Wheeler
20. James A. Garfield (R)	1831 – 1881	Mar. 4, 1881 – Sept.19, 1881	Chester A. Arthur
21. Chester A. Arthur (R)	1829 – 1886	Sept. 19, 1881 – Mar. 4, 1885	—
22. Grover Cleveland (D)	1837 – 1908	Mar. 4, 1885 – Mar. 4, 1889	Thomas A. Hendricks
23. Benjamin Harrison (R)	1833 – 1901	Mar. 4, 1889 – Mar. 4, 1893	Levi P. Morton
24. Grover Cleveland (D)	1837 – 1908	Mar. 4, 1893 – Mar. 4, 1897	Adlai E. Stevenson
25. William McKinley (R)	1843 – 1901	Mar. 4, 1897 – Sept.14, 1901	Garret A. Hobart Theodore Roosevelt
26. Theodore Roosevelt (R)	1858 – 1919	Sept.14, 1901 – Mar. 4, 1909	Charles W. Fairbanks
27. William H. Taft (R)	1857 – 1930	Mar. 4, 1909 – Mar. 4, 1913	James S. Sherman
28. Woodrow Wilson (D)	1856 – 1924	Mar. 4, 1913 – Mar. 4, 1921	Thomas R. Marshall
29. Warren G. Harding (R)	1865 – 1923	Mar. 4, 1921 – Aug. 2, 1923	Calvin Coolidge
30. Calvin Coolidge (R)	1872 – 1933	Aug. 3, 1923 – Mar. 4, 1929	Charles G. Dawes
31. Herbert Hoover (R)	1874 – 1964	Mar. 4, 1929 – Mar. 4, 1933	Charles Curtis
32. Franklin D. Roosevelt (D)	1882 – 1945	Mar. 4, 1933 – Apr. 12, 1945	John N. Garner Henry A. Wallace Harry S. Truman
33. Harry S. Truman (D)	1884 – 1972	Apr. 12, 1945 – Jan. 20, 1953	Alben W. Barkley
34. Dwight D. Eisenhower (R)	1890 – 1969	Jan. 20, 1953 – Jan. 20, 1961	Richard M. Nixon
35. John F. Kennedy (D)	1917 – 1963	Jan. 20, 1961 – Nov. 22, 1963	Lyndon B. Johnson
36. Lyndon B. Johnson (D)	1908 – 1973	Nov. 22, 1963 – Jan. 20, 1969	Hubert H. Humphrey
37. Richard M. Nixon (R)	1913 – 1994	Jan. 20, 1969 – Aug. 9, 1974	Spiro T. Agnew Gerald R. Ford
38. Gerald R. Ford (R)	1913 –	Aug. 9, 1974 – Jan. 20, 1977	Nelson A. Rockefeller
39. Jimmy Carter (D)	1924 –	Jan. 20, 1977 – Jan. 20, 1981	Walter F. Mondale
40. Ronald Reagan (R)	1911 –	Jan. 20, 1981 – Jan. 20, 1989	George Bush
41. George Bush (R)	1924 –	Jan. 20, 1989 – Jan. 20, 1993	Dan Quayle
42. Bill Clinton (D)	1946 –	Jan. 20, 1993 – Jan. 20, 2001	Al Gore
43. George W. Bush (R)	1946 –	Jan. 20, 2001 –	Richard Cheney

*Federalist (F), Whig (W), Democratic–Republican (D–R), Republican (R), Democrat (D)

George Washington refused a third term as the first U.S. President.

Abraham Lincoln was the first president assassinated in office.

Franklin D. Roosevelt led the U.S. during the Depression and WWII.

John F. Kennedy symbolized the young spirit of the 1960s.

The Statue of Liberty welcomes all who enter New York Harbor.

Sir John A. MacDonald led the first government of Canada as a Dominion.

POPULATION OF LARGEST AMERICAN CITIES (2000 estimate)

RANK	CITY	POPULATION	RANK	CITY	POPULATION	RANK	CITY	POPULATION
1.	New York City, NY	8,008,278	26.	Charlotte, NC	540,828	51.	Santa Ana, CA	337,977
2.	Los Angeles, CA	3,694,820	27.	Fort Worth, TX	534,594	52.	Pittsburgh, PA	334,563
3.	Chicago, IL	2,896,016	28.	Portland, OR	529,121	53.	Arlington, TX	332,969
4.	Houston, TX	1,953,631	29.	Oklahoma City, OK	506,132	54.	Cincinnati, OH	331,285
5.	Philadelphia, PA	1,517,550	30.	Tucson, AZ	486,699	55.	Anaheim, CA	328,014
6.	Phoenix, AZ	1,321,045	31.	New Orleans, LA	484,674	56.	Toledo, OH	313,619
7.	San Diego, CA	1,223,400	32.	Las Vegas, NV	478,434	57.	Tampa, FL	303,447
8.	Dallas, TX	1,188,580	33.	Cleveland, OH	478,403	58.	Buffalo, NY	292,648
9.	San Antonio, TX	1,144,646	34.	Long Beach, CA	461,522	59.	St. Paul, MN	287,151
10.	Detroit, MI	951,270	35.	Albuquerque, NM	448,607	60.	Corpus Christi, TX	277,454
11.	San Jose, CA	894,943	36.	Kansas City, MO	441,545	61.	Aurora, CO	276,393
12.	Indianapolis, IN	791,926	37.	Fresno, CA	427,652	62.	Raleigh, NC	276,093
13.	San Francisco, CA	776,733	38.	Virginia Beach, VA	425,257	63.	Newark, NJ	273,546
14.	Jacksonville, FL	735,617	39.	Atlanta, GA	416,474	64.	Lexington, KY	260,512
15.	Columbus, OH	711,470	40.	Sacramento, CA	407,018	65.	Anchorage, AK	260,283
16.	Austin, TX	656,562	41.	Oakland, CA	399,484	66.	Louisville, KY	256,231
17.	Baltimore, MD	651,154	42.	Mesa, AZ	396,375	67.	Riverside, CA	255,166
18.	Memphis, TN	650,100	43.	Tulsa, OK	393,049	68.	St. Petersburg, FL	248,232
19.	Milwaukee, WI	596,974	44.	Omaha, NE	390,007	69.	Bakersfield, CA	247,057
20.	Boston, MA	589,141	45.	Minneapolis, MN	382,618	70.	Stockton, CA	243,771
21.	Washington, DC	572,059	46.	Honolulu, HI	371,657	71.	Birmingham, AL	242,820
22.	Nashville, TN	569,891	47.	Miami, FL	362,470	72.	Jersey City, NJ	240,055
23.	El Paso, TX	563,662	48.	Colorado Springs, CO	360,890	73.	Norfolk, VA	234,403
24.	Seattle, WA	563,374	49.	St. Louis, MO	348,189	74.	Baton Rouge, LA	227,818
25.	Denver, CO	554,636	50.	Wichita, KS	344,284	75.	Hialeah, FL	226,419

THE PROVINCES AND TERRITORIES OF CANADA

PROVINCES	CAPITAL	POPULATION (2001 CENSUS)	(RANK)	AREA IN SQ. MI.	(RANK)	DATE BECAME PROVINCE
Alberta	Edmonton	2,974,807	(4)	255,287	(4)	1905
British Columbia	Victoria	3,907,738	(3)	365,948	(3)	1871
Manitoba	Winnipeg	1,119,583	(5)	250,947	(6)	1870
New Brunswick	Fredericton	729,498	(8)	28,355	(8)	1867
Newfoundland	St. John's	512,930	(9)	156,649	(7)	1949
Nova Scotia	Halifax	908,007	(7)	21,425	(9)	1867
Ontario	Toronto	11,410,046	(1)	412,581	(2)	1867
Prince Edward Island	Charlottetown	135,294	(10)	2,185	(10)	1873
Quebec	Quebec City	7,237,479	(2)	594,860	(1)	1867
Saskatchewan	Regina	978,933	(6)	251,866	(5)	1905

TERRITORIES	CAPITAL	POPULATION (2001 CENSUS)	AREA IN SQ. MI.
Northwest Territories	Yellowknife	37,360	503,951
Nunavut	Iqaluit	26,745	818,959
Yukon Territory	Whitehorse	28,674	186,661

PRIME MINISTERS OF CANADA

NAME	SERVED	POLITCAL PARTY
Sir John A. Macdonald	1867–1873	Conservative
Alexander Mackenzie	1873–1878	Liberal
Sir John A. Macdonald	1878–1891	Convervative
Sir John Abbott	1891–1892	Conservative
Sir John Thompson	1892–1894	Conservative
Sir Mackenzie Bowell	1894–1896	Conservative
Sir Charles Tupper	1896	Conservative
Sir Wilfrid Laurier	1896–1911	Liberal
Sir Robert Borden	1911–1917	Conservative
Sir Robert Borden	1917–1920	Unionist
Arthur Meighen	1920–1921	Unionist
W.L. Mackenzie King	1921–1926	Liberal
Arthur Meighen	1926	Conservative
W.L. Mackenzie King	1926–1930	Liberal
Richard Bennett	1930–1935	Conservative
W.L. Mackenzie King	1935–1948	Liberal
Louis St. Laurent	1948–1957	Liberal
John Diefenbaker	1957–1963	Progressive Conservative
Lester B. Pearson	1963–1968	Liberal
Pierre E. Trudeau	1968–1979	Liberal
Charles Joseph Clark	1979–1980	Progressive Conservative
Pierre E. Trudeau	1980–1984	Liberal
John Turner	1984	Liberal
Brian Mulroney	1984–1993	Progressive Conservative
Kim Campbell	1993	Progressive Conservative
Jean Chrétien	1993–	Liberal

INTERNATIONAL ORGANIZATIONS

United Nations (UN)

was founded in 1945. Its goals are to maintain international peace and security, and solve cultural, social, and humanitarian problems. By 2003, it had 191 member nations. Its headquarters are in New York City. The UN's main organs include: the General Assembly, with representatives of all members; the Security Council, with 15 members, 5 of whom (China, France, Russia, U.K., and U.S.) have permanent seats and 10 of whom are elected for 2 years; and the International Court of Justice, or World Court, which sits in The Hague, Netherlands.

Following are eight of the UN's specialized and related agencies:

Food and Agriculture Organization (FAO)

helps improve production and distribution of food and world dietary standards. Headquarters: Rome, Italy.

International Bank for Reconstruction and Development (IBRD),

or World Bank, provides loans and technical help for economic projects in developing countries. Headquarters: Washington, D.C.

International Monetary Fund (IMF)

promotes monetary cooperation and the expansion of world trade. Headquarters: Washington, D.C.

United Nations Children's Fund (UNICEF)

helps children in developing nations. Headquarters: New York City.

United Nations Educational, Scientific, and Cultural Organization (UNESCO)

promotes exchange of information, ideas, and culture. Headquarters: Paris, France.

United Nations High Commissioner for Refugees (UNHCR)

provides assistance to refugees worldwide. It is based in Geneva, Switzerland.

World Health Organization (WHO)

fights disease and helps improve health standards. Headquarters: Geneva, Switzerland.

World Trade Organization (WTO)

administers trade agreements and attempts to settle disputes. Headquarters: Geneva, Switzerland.

Other international organizations include:

Caribbean Community and Common Market (CARICOM)

was founded in 1973. Members are Antigua and Barbuda, Bahamas, Barbados, Belize, British Virgin Islands, Dominica, Grenada, Guyana, Jamaica, Montserrat, St. Kitts-Nevis, St. Lucia, St. Vincent and the Grenadines, Suriname, Trinidad and Tobago, and Turks and Caicos. Headquarters: Georgetown, Guyana.

The Commonwealth,

founded in 1949, is a loose association of Great Britain and more than 50 other nations that were once part of the British Empire. Mozambique, the most recent member, had not been part of the British Empire. Headquarters: London, England.

Commonwealth of Independent States (CIS),

founded in 1991, is made up of 12 of the 15 former Soviet republics. Members are Armenia, Azerbaijan, Belarus, Georgia, Kazakhstan, Kyrgyzstan, Moldova, Russia, Tajikistan, Turkmenistan, Ukraine, and Uzbekistan. Headquarters: Minsk, Belarus.

European Union (EU),

founded in 1952 with 6 members, was originally a free-trade and customs union. It is now a closer political and economic union. By 2003 the EU had 25 members.

Group of Eight (G-8),

is a group of eight leading industrialized nations that meet to discuss economic issues. Until Russia was admitted in 1997, it was known as the Group of Seven (G-7). The original members are Canada, France, Germany, Japan, Italy, the U.K., and the U.S.

International Criminal Police Organization (Interpol),

founded in 1956, promotes cooperation between police authorities in 179 countries. Headquarters: Lyon, France.

League of Arab States,

also known as the Arab League; promotes economic, social, political, and military cooperation among members. Founded in 1945, it has 21 members, including Palestine, which it considers an independent nation. Headquarters: Cairo, Egypt.

North Atlantic Treaty Organization (NATO)

is a military alliance of Western nations. It was founded in 1949 to defend Western Europe, the U.S., and Canada from military aggression. Members are Belgium, Canada, Czech Republic, Denmark, France, Germany, Greece, Hungary, Iceland, Italy, Luxembourg, the Netherlands, Norway, Poland, Portugal, Spain, Turkey, the U.K., and the U.S. Beginning in 1997, plans were made to admit some former Eastern European communist nations into NATO. Headquarters: Brussels, Belgium.

Organization for Economic Cooperation and Development (OECD)

was founded in 1961. Its goals are to promote economic growth, financial stability, and social welfare in its 30 member nations and to assist developing nations. Headquarters: Paris, France.

Organization of African Unity (OAU)

was founded in 1963 to promote unity and cooperation among African nations. It has 53 members. Headquarters: Addis Ababa, Ethiopia.

Organization of American States (OAS)

was founded in 1948. Its major goal is the peaceful settlement of disputes between nations. It has 35 members. Cuba has been suspended from OAS activities since 1962 but not from membership. Headquarters: Washington, D.C.

Organization of Petroleum Exporting Countries (OPEC)

was founded in 1960 to coordinate oil production and prices. Members are Algeria, Indonesia, Iran, Iraq, Kuwait, Libya, Nigeria, Qatar, Saudi Arabia, United Arab Emirates, and Venezuela. Headquarters: Vienna, Austria.

Logo for the League of Arab States, which mediates disputes among its member nations.

Logo for the European Union. This was known as the European Community (EC) until 1994.

The Commonwealth of Independent States is not in itself a state but an alliance of fully independent states.

Since the end of the Cold War in the 1990s, NATO has had to reassess its military role.

BIOGRAPHIES

Leonardo was not only an artist, but also an inventor, mathematician, engineer, and anatomist.

Picasso was the most famous artist of the 20th century. His work changed the course of modern art.

Chaucer's *Canterbury Tales* is a collection of stories told by pilgrims on their journey to Canterbury.

Brought up in poverty himself, Dickens wrote knowledgeably about the lives of the poor.

ARTISTS

Audubon, John James (1785–1851), a U.S. artist and naturalist, was noted for his paintings of birds.

Botticelli, Sandro (c.1445–1510) was an Italian painter. Works such as *Primavera* (Spring) and the *Birth of Venus* reflect the humanist and classical interests of his time.

Copley, John Singleton (1738–1815) is considered the greatest painter of colonial America. He painted portraits of people such as Paul Revere in natural poses.

Cézanne, Paul (1839–1906), a French painter, started out as an impressionist. His paintings showed the effects of light on objects rather than the objects themselves. He later painted colorful, more solid forms.

Degas, Edgar (1834–1917), a French painter and sculptor, was influenced by impressionism and Japanese woodcuts. He was interested in the human form, and many of his subjects were ballet dancers. His paintings include *The Rehearsal* and *Dance Class.*

Giotto (c.1266–1337), an Italian painter, revived the art of painting in the early Renaissance period. He was especially known for his religious frescoes, including *Life of Christ* and the *Last Judgment.*

Goya y Lucientes, Francisco José de (1746–1828), a Spaniard, painted realistic portraits and scenes from everyday life, including *The Disasters of War.*

Hopper, Edward (1882–1967) painted ordinary American scenes. The people in many of his paintings are often shown as lonely or sad.

Homer, Winslow (1836–1910) is considered one of the greatest U.S. artists. His paintings, including *Breezing Up* and *Gulf Stream,* captured the power and beauty of the sea.

Leonardo da Vinci (1452–1519), an Italian painter and scientist, was a genius. His greatest works include the *Last Supper* and the *Mona Lisa.*

Michelangelo (1475–1564), an Italian painter, sculptor, and architect, created the frescoes on the ceiling of the Sistine Chapel and sculptures of the *Pietà* and *David.*

Monet, Claude (1840–1926), a French painter, was one of the creators of the impressionist movement. Among his most famous works are *Impression: Sunrise,* the Rouen Cathedral series, and the Water Lily series.

Picasso, Pablo (1881–1973), a Spaniard, is thought by many to be the greatest artist of the 20th century. With Georges Braque, he developed cubism, a style in which forms are broken down into geometric shapes.

Pollock, Jackson (1912–56), an American, one of the most influential artists of the 20th century, was an abstract expressionist who made the colors and shapes of his paintings reflect his feelings. Among his works are *Autumn Rhythm.*

Rembrandt (Harmenszoon van Rijn) (1606–69) was the greatest of the Dutch old master painters. He did many group portraits and self-portraits. Among his works are *The Night Watch* and *Syndics of the Cloth Guild.*

Rubens, Peter Paul (1577–1640), a Flemish painter, master of the baroque style. He painted portraits, landscapes, and religious and historical subjects.

Turner, Joseph M. W. (1775–1851) was a British landscape painter. He painted in both watercolors and oils. His atmospheric paintings include *The Fighting Téméraire* and *Old Chain Pier at Brighton.*

Van Gogh, Vincent (1853–90), a Dutch painter, was famous for his use of color. His paintings include *Sunflowers* and *Starry Night.*

Warhol, Andy (1926–87) was a U.S. pioneer in "pop art." He painted pop culture objects, such as Campbell's soup cans, and comic-strip characters.

Wren, Sir Christopher (1632–1723) is considered the greatest English architect. His best-known creation was St. Paul's Cathedral in London.

Wright, Frank Lloyd (1869–1959), the greatest U.S. architect of the 20th century, designed such masterpieces as the Falling Water House and the Guggenheim Museum.

WRITERS

Alcott, Louisa May (1832–88), a U.S. author, is best known for the novel *Little Women,* a story about the four March sisters and their family during the Civil War.

Andersen, Hans Christian (1805–75), a Danish writer, was one of the world's greatest storytellers. He is best known for his fairy tales, such as "The Emperor's New Clothes," "The Snow Queen," "The Little Mermaid," and "The Ugly Duckling."

Austen, Jane (1775–1817), an English novelist, wrote about the middle class of English country life in such novels as *Emma, Pride and Prejudice,* and *Sense and Sensibility.*

Cervantes, Miguel (1547–1616) was a Spanish novelist and dramatist. His greatest work, *Don Quixote,* details the life of a poor gentleman who wants to be a knight and do knightly deeds.

Chaucer, Geoffrey (c.1345–1400) was an English poet whose most famous work was a group of stories called the *Canterbury Tales.*

Cooper, James Fenimore (1789–1851) wrote novels about the American frontier in the 1700s. His most famous book was *The Last of the Mohicans.*

Dante Alighieri (1265–1321) was Italy's greatest poet. His most famous work was the *Divine Comedy.*

Dickens, Charles (1812–70) was one of England's greatest novelists. Some of his novels, including *Oliver Twist* and *David Copperfield,* drew attention to the plight of the poor and underprivileged.

1854		1859	1869		1870	1870–1914	1894–95

1854 Japan opens its doors to trade with the West
1859 Darwin writes *Origin of Species*
1869 Suez Canal opens
1870 France defeated in Franco-Prussian War
1870–1914 European colonization of Africa and Asia
1894–95 China defeated in Sino-Japanese War

Dickinson, Emily (1830–86)
was one of the most important U.S. poets of the 1800s. She wrote 1,775 poems, but only a few were published when she was alive.

Frost, Robert (1874–1963)
was one of the most important U.S. poets of the 20th century. He wrote about the people and the land of New England. Among his books of poetry are *New Hampshire* and *In the Clearing*.

Goethe, Johann Wolfgang von (1749–1832)
was a poet, novelist, and playwright of unequaled importance in German literature. His greatest work was *Faust*.

Hawthorne, Nathaniel (1804–64),
born in Massachusetts, was one of the most important American writers of the 1800s. His greatest novel was *The Scarlet Letter*.

Henry, O. (1862–1910)
was one of America's foremost short-story writers. His real name was William Sydney Porter. He wrote more than 300 stories, many with surprise endings. One of his most popular stories is "The Gift of the Magi."

Keats, John (1795–1821),
an English poet, wrote beautiful odes, including "To a Nightingale," "On a Grecian Urn," and "To Autumn."

Longfellow, Henry Wadsworth (1807–82)
was a modern language professor and popular poet who wrote poems about American history including such long poems as *The Song of Hiawatha*.

Melville, Herman (1819–91)
was one of the great U.S. writers. He used his experiences as a sailor when writing his most popular books, *Moby Dick* and *Typee*.

Poe, Edgar Allan (1809–49),
a U.S. author, has been called the father of modern mystery and horror stories. His short stories include, "The Fall of the House of Usher," and "The Pit and the Pendulum." Poems include "The Raven" and "The Bells."

Sandburg, Carl (1878–1967)
was one of the most beloved U.S poets, as well as a biographer. His biography of Abraham Lincoln won the 1940 Pulitzer Prize for history.

Shakespeare, William (1564–1616),
an English dramatist and poet, is considered by many to be the world's greatest writer. His plays include *A Midsummer Night's Dream*, *Hamlet*, and *Macbeth*.

Stevenson, Robert Louis (1850–94)
was a versatile Scottish author. He wrote *A Child's Garden of Verses*, and such adventure stories as *Treasure Island* and *Kidnapped*.

Stowe, Harriet Beecher (1811–96),
a U.S. author, was famous for her novel *Uncle Tom's Cabin*. It made a powerful case against slavery.

Swift, Jonathan (1667–1745)
was an English writer whose books poked fun at the silly, cruel behavior of people and governments. His most famous book is *Gulliver's Travels*.

Tolstoy, Count Leo (1828–1910)
was a Russian novelist. Two of his greatest books were *War and Peace* and *Anna Karenina*.

Twain, Mark (1835–1910)
was a popular U.S. novelist and journalist. His real name was Samuel Clemens. Among his bestselling books were *The Adventures of Tom Sawyer* and *The Adventures of Huckleberry Finn*.

Wordsworth, William (1770–1850)
was one of England's greatest poets. His poetry explores the lives of ordinary people in contact with nature. Together with his friend Samuel Taylor Coleridge, he wrote the *Lyrical Ballads*, which included his poem "Tintern Abbey."

COMPOSERS AND MUSICIANS

Bach, Johann Sebastian (1685–1750),
a German, was one of the world's greatest composers. He wrote concertos and sacred cantatas. His masterpieces include the six *Brandenburg Concertos*, *St. Matthew Passion*, and *B Minor Mass*.

Beethoven, Ludwig van (1770–1827),
a German, wrote sonatas, symphonies, choral and chamber music, and concertos. Major works include his Ninth Symphony, the Piano Concerto no. 5, and the opera *Fidelio*.

Berlin, Irving (1888–1989)
was one of the greatest U.S. writers of popular music. He wrote nearly 1,000 songs, including "*Alexander's Ragtime Band*," "*This Is the Army*," and "*God Bless America*."

Bizet, Georges (1838–75),
a French composer, is most famous for his opera *Carmen*.

Brahms, Johannes (1833–97),
a German Romantic composer and gifted pianist, wrote piano sonatas, symphonies, and choral works.

Britten, Benjamin (1913–76),
a British composer, wrote such operas as *Billy Budd* and *Death in Venice*. He also wrote large-scale instrumental works, including *The Young Person's Guide to the Orchestra*.

Copland, Aaron (1900–90),
U.S. composer best known for using jazz and American folk tunes in his classical compositions. His works include the music for such ballets as *Billy the Kid*, *Rodeo*, and *Appalachian Spring*.

Ellington, Duke (1899–1974)
was the greatest U.S. jazz composer. He wrote more than 2,000 jazz compositions, plus concert works, religious music, and scores for theater, ballet, and film.

Gershwin, George (1898–1937)
was one of the most important U.S. songwriters of the 20th century. He produced many concert works and Broadway musicals. Gershwin's best-known works include *Porgy and Bess*, an opera, and *Rhapsody in Blue*, an orchestral work.

Handel, Georg Frideric (1685–1759),
a German-born British composer, was famous for the oratorio *Messiah*. His orchestral works include *Water Music* and *Music for the Royal Fireworks*.

Haydn, Franz Joseph (1732–1809),
an Austrian composer, was the most famous composer of his day, and he is known as the "father of the symphony." His output included 104 symphonies, about 50 concertos, and 84 string quartets, among other works.

Ives, Charles (1874–1954)
was one of the most important U.S. composers of the 20th century. His works

Tolstoy introduced a new form of Christianity into Russia, writing religious works as well as novels.

Tom Sawyer's adventures on the Mississippi River were based on Twain's own boyhood experiences.

Beethoven's music is among the greatest in the world and still influences composers today.

Duke Ellington was one of America's best-known jazz band leaders of the 1930s. He wrote over 50 hits.

1904–5	1912	1914–18	1917	1929	1933	1936–39
Russia defeated in Russo–Japanese War	Chinese overthrow Manchu Dynasty; establish republic	World War I	Communists seize power in Russia	Wall Street Crash starts worldwide depression	Hitler comes to power in Germany	Civil war in Spain

Mozart began writing music at the age of five. Two years later, he was playing in concerts.

Marie and Pierre Curie devoted their lives to research, spending their own money on equipment.

Edison's first phonograph, a recording machine, led to the development of the record player.

Aristotle studied under Plato for 20 years before becoming tutor to Alexander the Great.

included symphonies, sonatas, and orchestral, choral, and chamber music. He also wrote some 150 songs. Many of his compositions used themes from American folk music.

Monteverdi, Claudio (1567–1643), an Italian composer, wrote *Orfeo*, which is considered to be the first opera.

Mozart, Wolfgang Amadeus (1756–91), an Austrian, was one of the world's greatest composers. He began composing at the age of five and eventually wrote more than 600 pieces of music, including symphonies, piano concertos, and operas such as *Don Giovanni* and *The Marriage of Figaro*.

Rodgers, Richard (1902–79) was one of the most successful U.S. composers in the history of entertainment. He wrote the music for such Broadway musicals as *Oklahoma!*, *Pal Joey*, *The King and I*, *South Pacific*, and *The Sound of Music*.

Sousa, John Philip (1854–1932) wrote so many U.S. marches he was known as the "March King." His most famous works include "The Stars and Stripes Forever," The Washington Post March," and "Semper Fidelis."

Stravinsky, Igor (1882–1971), a Russian-born U.S. composer, wrote symphonies and operas, as well as the music for such ballets as *The Firebird* and *The Rite of Spring*.

Tchaikovsky, Peter Ilyich (1840–93) was a Russian composer. He wrote ballet music, symphonies, piano concertos, and operas. Among his best-known works are the ballet *Swan Lake* and his First Piano Concerto.

Verdi, Giuseppe (1813–1901) was the leading Italian operatic composer of his day. *Rigoletto*, *La Traviata*, and *Aida* are among his best-known works.

Vivaldi, Antonio (c.1675–1741) was a Venetian violinist and composer. He wrote operas, sacred music, and concertos such as *The Four Seasons*.

Wagner, Richard (1813–83), a German composer, is best known for his opera cycle *The Ring of the Nibelung*, which consists of four works based on old Germanic mystical legends.

SCIENTISTS AND INVENTORS

Bell, Alexander Graham (1847–1922), a Scottish-born American, invented the telephone.

Benz, Karl (1844–19129), a German engineer, built the first practical gasoline-powered automobile.

Copernicus, Nicolaus (1473–1543), a Polish astronomer, proved that the Earth moves in orbit around the Sun.

Curie, Marie (1867–1934), a Polish physicist, discovered radium, a radioactive substance. She worked with her husband Pierre.

Daguerre, Louis (1789–1851), a French painter, invented the first practical photographic process.

Darwin, Charles (1809–82), a British naturalist, formulated the theory of evolution by natural selection.

Edison, Thomas Alva (1847–1931), a U.S. inventor, patented more than a thousand inventions, including the telegraph and electric lightbulb.

Einstein, Albert (1879–1955), a German-born American physicist, changed our view of the universe with his General Theory of Relativity (1915).

Faraday, Michael (1791–1867), a British physicist and chemist, was a pioneer in the field of electricity. His work made the dynamo and the electric motor possible.

Fermi, Enrico (1901–54), an Italian nuclear physicist, built the first nuclear reactor.

Fleming, Alexander (1881–1955), a British bacteriologist, discovered penicillin, the first antibiotic.

Franklin, Benjamin (1706–90), a U.S. scientist, publisher, and statesman, proved that lightning is a form of electricity.

Galilei, Galileo (1564–1642), an Italian astronomer and physicist, was the first to use the telescope. He also showed that light objects fall as fast as heavy ones when they are pulled toward the Earth by gravity.

Gutenberg, Johann (c.1400–68), a German printer, was the first to develop a way to print books with speed and accuracy.

Harvey, William (1578–1657), a British physician, discovered that the heart acted as a pump to circulate blood through the body.

Kepler, Johannes (1571–1630), a German astronomer, showed that the planets went around the Sun in elliptical paths.

Marconi, Guglielmo (1874–1937), an Italian-born British engineer, was the first person to transmit long-distance radio signals.

Mendel, Gregor (1822–84), an Austrian priest, biologist, and botanist, researched the laws of heredity using pea plants.

Morse, Samuel F.B. (1791–1872), a U.S. inventor, invented the first successful electric telegraph (1837).

Newton, Isaac (1642–1727), an English mathematician, devised laws of motion, theorized about gravity, and showed the nature of light and color.

Pasteur, Louis (1822–95), a French scientist, proved that disease is spread by bacteria, or germs.

Rutherford, Sir Ernest (1871–1937), a New Zealand-born British physicist, was a pioneer in the study of the atom's structure. His work led to the development of nuclear energy.

Watt, James (1736–1819), British engineer who improved the steam engine to make it a suitable power plant for all kinds of machinery.

Wright, Orville (1871–1948) and Wilbur (1867–1912), two U.S. aeronautical engineers, built and flew (1903) the first successful heavier-than-air aircraft.

PHILOSOPHERS AND REFORMERS

Aristotle (384–322 B.C.), a Greek philosopher, studied under Plato. He opened a school of philosophy in Athens. His work gave rise to the science of logical reasoning.

| 1939-45; 1945 | 1949 | 1952 | 1957-75 | 1979 | 1989-90 | 1994 | 1994 |

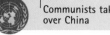

World War II; United Nations founded | Communists take over China | EU founded | Vietnam War | Islamic Revolution in Iran | Democracy sweeps Eastern Europe | Black rule in South Africa | Terrorist attacks on U.S.

Calvin, John (1509-64)
was a French religious reformer and leader of the Protestant Reformation. He believed that all people, not just bishops and kings, should share in religious and political policy making.

Confucius (c. 551-c. 480 B.C.)
was a Chinese philosopher whose teachings on moral responsibility have been a strong influence on Chinese thinking for over 2,000 years.

Gandhi, Mohandas Karamchand (1869-1948),
Indian spiritual and political leader, helped free India from British control through nonviolent resistance. He was known as Mahatma, or "Great Soul."

Gautama, Siddhartha (Buddha) (c. 563-483 B.C.),
Indian religious teacher, founder of Buddhism, one of the world's great religions. He gave up his life as a prince to become a wandering monk in search of enlightenment.

Jesus Christ (c. 4 B.C.-c. A.D. 33)
was the great religious leader on whose teachings the Christian religion was founded.

Joan of Arc, Saint (c. 1412-1431),
French national leader and heroine, believed God had chosen her to free France from English rule and led French armies to many victories.

King, Martin Luther (1929-68)
was a black American minister and leader of the U.S. civil rights movement. King won the 1964 Nobel Peace Prize, but was assassinated four years later.

Luther, Martin (1483-1546)
was a German religious reformer and leader of the Reformation— the religious movement that led to the birth of Protestantism.

Marx, Karl (1818-83)
was a German political philosopher and main founder of the socialist and communist movements. Wrote *The Communist Manifesto*, with Friedrich Engels, and *Das Kapital*.

Montessori, Maria (1870-1952),
Italian educator and doctor, she designed an educational system to help children develop their intelligence and independence. This system is used throughout the world.

Mother Teresa of Calcutta (1910-1997)
was a Roman Catholic nun born in Yugoslavia. She founded a religious order in Calcutta in 1950 called Missionaries of Charity, which has branches in about 30 other countries.

Muhammad (A.D. 570-632)
was an Arabian prophet and founder of the Islamic religion. He felt himself called as God's prophet and preached that there is only one God (Allah).

Nightingale, Florence (1820-1910),
English nursing pioneer, reformed the nursing profession.

Pankhurst, Emmeline (1858-1928)
was an English political reformer. She led the fight for women's right to vote in England.

Plato (c. 427-c.347BC),
a Greek philosopher, founded what is probably the first-ever university, known as the Academy. He wrote *The Republic*, in which he outlined the ideal state or society.

Sanger, Margaret (1883-1966)
was the American leader of the birth control movement.

Socrates (c. 469-399 B.C.),
a Greek philosopher and teacher, devoted himself to seeking truth and goodness.

Stanton, Elizabeth Cady (1815-1902)
was a leader of the U.S. women's rights movement. She also worked for the abolition of slavery.

Wesley, John (1703-91),
English clergyman, founder of Methodism. He traveled over 5,000 miles a year, preaching.

Wilberforce, William (1759-1833)
was an English politician and reformer. He led the fight to abolish slavery in the British Empire.

Wollstonecraft, Mary (1759-97)
was an English author who argued that women should have equal rights to men in her book, *A Vindication of the Rights of Women*.

EXPLORERS

Amundsen, Roald (1872-1928),
a Norwegian, discovered the Northwest Passage and was the first man to reach the South Pole (1911).

Balboa, Vasco Núñez de (1475-1519),
a Spaniard, was the first European to sight the east coast of the Pacific Ocean (1513).

Bird, Richard E. (1888-1957),
a U.S. polar explorer, was the first to fly over the North Pole (1926) and the South Pole (1929).

Cabot, John (c.1461-98),
an Italian-born English explorer, claimed North American territory for England.

Champlain, Samuel de (1567-1635),
a French explorer, explored the Atlantic coast of Canada and founded Quebec (1608).

Columbus, Christopher (1451-1506),
an Italian explorer, discovered the New World while seeking a route to Asia.

Cook, James (1728-79),
an English sea captain, was the first to sight Antarctica and explore the Pacific Ocean.

Cortés, Hernán (1485-1547),
a Spanish explorer, conquered the Aztec Empire of Mexico (1521).

Da Gama, Vasco (c.1469-1524),
Portuguese navigator and explorer, sailed around Africa to India and back to Europe.

Ericsson, Leif (fl. 900-1000),
a Viking sailor, was the first European to land in North America (c.1000).

Livingstone, David (1813-73),
a Scottish explorer, traveled through much of Africa's interior.

Magellan, Ferdinand (c.1480-1521),
a Portuguese explorer, led the first expedition to sail around the world (1519-22). He was killed by natives in the Philippines before the journey was completed.

Peary, Robert E. (1856-1920),
a U.S. explorer, claimed to be the first person to reach the North Pole (1909).

Pizarro, Francisco (c.1475-1541),
a Spanish explorer, conquered the Inca Empire of Peru (1533).

Polo, Marco (c.1254-1324),
a Venetian (Italian) explorer, traveled through Asia and met Kublai Khan, the Mongol emperor.

Elizabeth Cady Stanton began the U.S. women's suffrage movement in 1848.

Gandhi is often called the "father of modern India" for his work in freeing India from British rule.

Vasco da Gama reached India in 1498 by sailing around the Cape of Good Hope in southern Africa.

Henry Morton Stanley, a reporter, found Livingstone (feared dead in Africa) at Lake Tanganyika in 1871.

| Vietnam War ends | U.S. invades Panama | U.S. and Allies defeat Iraq in Persian Gulf War | Truck bomb kills 168 in Oklahoma City | U.S. peacekeeping troops arrive in Bosnia | Timothy McVeigh sentenced to death for Oklahoma City bombing |

| 1975 | 1989 | 1991 | 1995 | 1995 | 1997 |

HIGHLIGHTS OF THE LAST 100 YEARS

In Germany, Adolf Hitler's aggressive policies led to the outbreak of WW II.

DNA determines which traits children inherit from their parents.

Personal computers became commonly available in the early 1980s.

U.S. spacecraft Viking I and 2 landed probes on Mars by parachute.

Half of the world's robots, such as this automated arm, are used in Japan.

In 1953 Hillary and Tenzing were the first to scale Mt. Everest.

SPACE EXPLORATION

1957: The Soviet Union launches *Sputnik 1*, the first artificial satellite to orbit Earth.
1961: Soviet cosmonaut Yuri Gagarin, aboard the *Vostok 1* spacecraft, becomes the first man to orbit Earth.
1962: Astronaut John H. Glenn, Jr., aboard the *Mercury 6* spacecraft, becomes the first American to orbit Earth.
1963: Soviet cosmonaut Valentina Tereshkova orbits Earth in the *Vostok 6* spacecraft, becoming the first woman in space.
1965: Soviet cosmonaut Aleksei Leonov takes the first space walk.
1968: *Apollo 8* becomes the first spacecraft to orbit the Moon.
1969: *Apollo 11* astronauts Neil Armstrong and Edwin Aldrin become the first men to land on the Moon.
1970: *Venera 7*, a Soviet spacecraft, lands on Venus and transmits data back to Earth.
1975: The Soviet Union's *Venera 7* takes the first photographs of the surface of Venus.
1976: *Viking 1* and *Viking 2*, U.S. spacecraft, land on Mars and send photos and data back to Earth.
1977: The U.S. launches *Voyager 2*, which will later photograph Jupiter (1979), Saturn (1981), Uranus (1986), and Neptune (1989).
1981: The U.S. launches the space shuttle *Columbia*, the first reusable manned spacecraft.
1986: The U.S. space shuttle *Challenger* blows up shortly after launch, killing all seven astronauts.
1990: The U.S. space probe *Magellan* orbits Venus and sends radar images of the planet back to Earth. The Hubble Space Telescope is launched.
1997: The U.S. Mars *Pathfinder* spacecraft lands on Mars and deploys *Sojourner*, a roving vehicle to analyze Martian rocks and soil.
1998: Water is discovered frozen in rocks on the Moon.
2003: Space shuttle Columbia explodes on reentry, killing seven astronauts.

POLITICAL EVENTS

1914: World War I starts when Archduke Francis Ferdinand of Austria is assassinated. The war ends in 1918.
1917: The Communists seize power in Russia during the Russian Revolution.
1929: The Wall Street Crash sets off the Great Depression.
1933: Adolf Hitler becomes the dictator of Germany.
1939: The German invasion of Poland starts World War II.
1941: The U.S. enters World War II after Japan attacks Pearl Harbor.
1945: World War II ends after the U.S. drops two atomic bombs on Japan. Tens of millions of people were killed during the war, including six million Jews killed in the Holocaust. The United Nations is founded.
1948: The state of Israel is founded.
1949: The Communists take control of China.
1950: Communist North Korea invades South Korea, starting the Korean War. The fighting ended three years later.
1952: European Community (now European Union), is founded.
1965: U.S. combat troops enter the Vietnam War. The war ends with the defeat of the U.S. in 1973.
1989: Communism begins to collapse in Eastern Europe, with democratic governments replacing communist dictatorships.
1990: Apartheid ends and black rule begins in South Africa.
1991: The Soviet Union ceases to exist and breaks up into 15 independent states.
2001: Terrorist attacks on U.S.

SCIENCE AND MEDICINE

1905: German-born U.S. physicist Albert Einstein publishes his special theory of relativity.
1913: Hungarian-born pediatrician Bela Schick discovers an immunity test for diphtheria.
1915: Physicist Albert Einstein publishes his general theory of relativity.
1921: Canadian physicians Frederick Banting and Charles Best discover the hormone insulin, a treatment for diabetes.
1928: Scottish bacteriologist Alexander Fleming discovers penicillin, the first antibiotic.
1942: U.S. physicist Enrico Fermi directs the first controlled nuclear reaction.
1945: The first atomic bomb is detonated in New Mexico.
1953: Biologists Francis Crick (U.K.) and James Watson (U.S.) discover the structure of deoxyribonucleic acid (DNA), the actual material that chromosomes are made of.
1954: Harvard University physicians perform the first successful organ (kidney) transplant.
1955: U.S. microbiologist Jonas Salk develops the first vaccine against polio, a crippling disease.
1967: South African surgeon Christiaan Barnard performs the first heart transplant.
1982: U.S. surgeons working at the Utah Medical Center implant the first artificial heart.
1997: Scottish scientists are the first to clone a sheep.

TELECOMMUNICATIONS

1901: Italian-born inventor Guglielmo Marconi, using Morse code-like dot-and-dash signals, sends the first radio message across the Atlantic Ocean.
1906: U.S. engineer Reginald A. Fessendon broadcasts the first radio program of voice and music.
1915: First transcontinental telephone call between inventor Alexander Graham Bell in New York and his assistant Thomas Watson in San Francisco, over 3,000 miles away.
1929: Russian-born American electronic engineer Vladimir Zworykin demonstrates the first electronic television system.
1936: The British Broadcasting Corporation makes the first television broadcasts.
1946: U.S. engineers J. Presper Eckert, Jr. and John W. Mauchly build ENIAC, the first electronic digital computer.
1947: Bell Telephone Laboratories develops the first transistor.
1951: Eckert and Mauchly build UNIVAC I, the first commercially available computer.
1953: Color television broadcast begins in the U.S.
1960s: Internet begins as a military security network.
Early 1960s: The integrated circuit is developed.
1961: Bell Telephone Laboratories builds the first practical laser.
1965: Early Bird, the first commercial communications satellite, is launched.
1977: The Apple Computer Company introduces the first personal computer.
1983: Cellular phone service begins.
1992: Introduction of worldwide web.
2001: Broadband technology enters mainstream usage.

INDEX

Page numbers shown in **bold** indicate where the main reference to the subject can be found. Numbers in *italic* refer to pages where illustrations can be found.

ACKNOWLEDGMENTS

The publishers wish to thank the following for supplying photographs for this book:

ABBREVIATIONS (t = top; b = bottom; c = center; l = left; r = right)

PICTURE LIBRARY ABBREVIATIONS: AAA: The Ancient Art & Architecture Collection; AKG: AKG London; BAL: The Bridgeman Art Library; B&C Alexander: Bryan & Cherry Alexander; BC: Bruce Coleman Collection; EB/JD: Eye Ubiquitous/James Davis Travel Photography; ET: E.T. Archive; FLPA: Frank Lane Picture Agency; FS: Frank Spooner Pictures; GI: Getty Images; HL: The Hutchison Library; NHPA: Natural History Photographic Agency; OSF: Oxford Scientific Films; Panos: Panos Pictures; PE: Planet Earth Pictures; Popper: Popperfoto; RGA: The Ronald Grant Archive; RHPL: Robert Harding Picture Library; SP: Still Pictures; SPL: Science Photo Library

Front Cover: Satellite Dish/SPL, London; Violin/Corbis, London; Footballer/Empics; Samburu Warrior/Getty Stone. Pages: viii: Colorific 1: NHPA (tl, br), GI (tr), Panos (bl) 2: RHPL (tr), NHPA (b) 3: SP (b) 4: BAL (tr), SP (tl), RHPL (bl) 5: RHPL (tl), Empics (cr), Panos (bl) 8: Telegraph Colour Library (tr) 9: OSF (tr) 10: PE (tr) 12: NHPA (tl), PE (tr) 16: Popper (tl), BC (cr), NHPA (bl) 17: The British Museum, EA24957 (bl), AAA (br) 18: RHPL (tr) 20: NHPA (cr), B&C Alexander (bc) 21: RHPL (cl), GI (cr), HL (bl) 22: AKG (clt), AKG/©ADAGP, Paris and DACS, London 1998 (tr), BAL (tl, clb, cr, bl, br) 23: AKG/©Estate of Roy Lichtenstein/DACS, 1998 (tl), AKG/©Man Ray Trust/ADAGP, Paris and DACS, London 1998 (cr), ET/©Succession Picasso/DACS, 1998 (tr), BAL (br), ©Duane Hanson/Saatchi Collection, London (bl) 24: SP (tr), NHPA (bl), RHPL (tl) 25: Panos 26: HL (tl, b), FS (tr) 27: Panos (cr, tl), BAL (tr) 28: Popper (tl), SPL (tr), Portfolio Pictures/NASA (br, clb, clt), Genesis Space Photo Library (bc) 30: SPL (trt, trb) 32: SPL (tl, tr) 34: PE (tr), OSF (bc) 35: PE (bc), NHPA (br) 36: Colorific (tl), SP (bc) 37: RHPL (tl), Colorific (tr), NHPA (c) 40: Virgin (cl), Images Colour Library (tr) 43: GI (tr) 44: SPL (tr) 46: NHPA (br) 49: SPL (br) 50: Corbis (tl), SPL (tr) 51: Zefa (br) 54: EB/JD (tr), RHPL (cl), GI (b) 55: GI (tr), EB/JD (bl) 57: Graham Harrison (tr, cl), GI (tr) 58: BC (c, bc), GI (tr), Robert Estall Photo Library (cr), FS (cl) 61: Robert Estall Photo Library (cl), RHPL (br) 62: Allsport (bl) 63: ©Aerospace Publishing (tr), Ford Motor Company (br) 64: Panos (tr), HL (b) 65: SuperStock (br), HL (cl) 66: Portfolio Pictures (tl), ©Uli Meyer Studios (tr) 70: SPL (tl, clt, cl, cb, bl) 71: The National Museum of Ireland (tl), AAA (cl), BAL (bl) 72: RHPL (tr), Panos (b) 73: GI (tr, b), Panos 75: BC (tl), SP (cl), Image Bank (b) 76: BC (b) 77: GI (tr, bl), RHPL (br) 78: Panos (tr, bl, br) 79: GI (c, bcl), Zefa (bl), FS (bcr), Rex Features (br) 80: ©Amnesty International (tl), Popper (tr), Corbis (b) 81: Corbis (tl), Popper (bl), Camera Press (br) 82: Peter Newark's Military Pictures (tl) 86: RHPL (tr), Camera Press (cl) 87: Zefa (tc), FS (tr), GI (c), RHPL (br) 88: RHPL (cr) 89: Corbis (b) 90: AKG (tr) 91: SPL (tl, clt, clb, bl) 92: GI (tr) 93: Camera Press (bl, clb), AKG (br) 94: GI (bc) 95: Corbis (tr) 96: SPL (tl), AKG (tr) 98: Travel Ink (tr) 104: RHPL (br) 106: Allsport (tr), Performing Arts Library (br) 107: EB/JD (tl), Rex Features (cr), Performing Arts Library (br) 108: Popper (b) 109: GI (tl) 110: ©Salvador Dali – Fundacion Gala-Salvador Dali, DACS, London 1998 (tl), RHPL (clt), Steve Shott (bl) 112: The Natural History Museum, London (cl) 114: FS (tl), SPL (bl) 115: Farmers Weekly Picture Library (br) 120: Rex Features (b) 121: Panos (tr), GI (b) 122: Panos (b) 123: Panos (tl), GI (tr), Rex Features (b) 124: Panos (tr) 125: Panos (tr), EB/JD (cl), GI (cr, b) 126: GI (tl, bl, br) 127: Simon Farrell (tr) 133: GI (cr) 134: RHPL (bc) 136: Popper (tl, cl), Colorsport (tr) 138: FLPA (tr), GI (b) 139: FLPA (br) 140: Zefa (tl), GI (tr), Rex Features (bl) 141: GI (tr), RHPL (cl), Rex Features (b) 145: W.J. Hatt Ltd, The Institute of Explosives (tl, clt, clb, bl, br) 146: Topham (tr) 147: Popper (tl, bl), Camera Press (clb), Corbis (br) 149: Photofest (tr, cr), Kobal Collection (br), RGA/© Disney Enterprises, Inc. (bl) 150: NHPA (tl) 152: FLPA (tr) 156: NHPA (bc) 158: GI (c) 159: RHPL (cl), GI (tr) 160: Telegraph Colour Library (tr) 161: Robin Keeley/The Forensic Science Service, London (tl), Topham (cl) 162: GI (tl) 164: GI (tr, br, cl) 165: FS (tl), Popper (bl), RHPL (br) 168: SPL (tl, clb) 169: SPL (tl, clt, clb) 170: SP (bl), Telegraph Colour Library (bcl, bl) 171: SPL (bl), Rex Features (cr), Performing Arts Library (bcr) 172: Zefa (tr), FS (cl), RHPL (b) 173: Popper (cl), BAL (b) 176: Sonia Halliday Photographs (cl) 177: SPL (tr, bc), The Wallace Collection, London (cl) 178: RHPL (cr), Topham (bl) 179: NHPA (tl) 180: Corbis (tl), GI (b) 181: Corbis (tr, cr) 182: GI (tr, b) 183: Popper (tl), RHPL (cl), Panos (br) 185: RHPL (tr) 186: NHPA (tr), PE (tl, bl, bc, br), GI (cr) 189: RHPL (tr) 192: FS (tr), GI (b) 193: BC (tr) 194: Image Bank (tr), GI (br) 196: Neff (UK) Ltd (tr) 197: GI (tr), Panos (bl), Zefa (br) 198: OSF (tr) 199: FS (tr), GI (b), Panos (bl, clt), EB/JD (clb, cl, br) 201: Image Bank (tr) 204: Panos (b) 205: Panos (tr), Image Bank (bl) 206: Colorific (tl), GI (b) 207: OSF (tr), Panos (b) 208: GI (cl, bl), Panos (cr) 210: GI (tr) 212: RHPL (tr), Panos (b) 213: OSF (tr), GI (b) 214: OSF (tl, clt, clb, bl), BC (tr) 216: FS (tr) 217: BAL (tr) 218: GI (cl, bl), Houghton's Horses Picture Library (br) 219: GI (tr) 220: RHPL (cl), GI (b) 221: FLPA (tr), GI (cl), Network/Mike Abrahams (bl) 222: GI (tr, b, cl) 223: FS (cr), John Ferro Sims (bl) 224: GI (tr, b), Panos (cl) 225: RHPL (cr), Zefa 226: Zefa (tr) 227: GI (tr, cl), Image Bank (bl), Colorific (bc) 229: Panos (cl), PE (bl), GI (br) 230: SPL (tr) 232: EB/JD (tl), BAL 233: RHPL (tl), Zefa (tr, bl), TRH Pictures (cl) 234: Image Bank (tl) 237: Zefa (tr, cr), Corbis (tl), Image Bank (cl), OSF (bc) 238: Image Bank (tl) 244: RHPL (cl), Panos (bl), RHPL (br) 249: Image Bank (tr) 250: Panos (tr) 251: Alpha (tr), GI (b), A.C. Edwards (tl) 252: Glaxo Group Research (tr) 253: SPL (tr, bc) 255: AAA (cr, bc) 256: Telegraph Colour Library 257: South American Pictures (tr), Spectrum Colour Library (tl), Panos (b) 258: SPL (tl, clt, cl, clb, bl) 259: LEO Electron Microscopy Ltd (tr), Leica Microsystems (UK) Ltd (bc), SPL (tl, clt, clb, bl) 261: RHPL (tr), Panos (b) 262: HL (c) 263: Spectrum Colour Library (tl), FS (tr), HL (bc) 264: PE (bl) 265: OSF (tr) 267: SP (tl) 271: OSF (cr) 276: Zefa (tl), Redferns (cl, bl, br) 277: RHPL (b) 278: Edinburgh University (cr), Keith Saunders/LSO with Michael Tilson Thomas (b) 283: Corbis (tr) 285: FS (bl) 287: Spectrum Colour Library (tc, cl), FS (bl) 288: Panos (cl, b) 289: Panos (tr), HL (br) 290: NHPA (tr) 291: Panos (tl), HL (tr), Zefa (b) 292: Popper (tr) 293: SP (tr) 296: SPL (tr) 297: Allsport (cr), Topham (bl) 298: Topham (tl) 299: Allsport (tr, cr) 301: SPL (tl) 303: HL (cl), Panos (bl, bc) 304: Polaroid (clb), Canon (bl), BAL (tr) 305: Science & Society Picture Library (tr), Nikon UK (b) 306: HL (cl) 309: Universal/courtesy Kobal Collection (tr) 312: ICI (tr) 313: NHPA (tl, tr) 314: Corbis (t) 315: HL (tr) 317: AAA (c) 319: Popper (bl) 323: NHPA (cl) 324: PE (tr) 326: SP (tl), Jean-Loup Charmet (tr), Popper (br) 327: HL (b) 328: BAL (tr) 329: BAL (tr) 330: GI (cr) 336: Rex Features (tl), Popper (tr), GI (cl) 337: PE 338: NHPA (bl), HL (bc) 340: GI (tl), HL (bc) 341: SPL (tl, cl), UFA/courtesy Kobal Collection (tc), Honda Motor Company (tr) 342: NHPA (tr) 343: Sophie Mortimer/NASA (tr) 345: Zefa (crt), GI (crb) 346: SCR Photo Library/Novosti (tr), RHPL (b) 347: HL (br) 348: Rex Features (tl), Novosti, London (cl), HL (bl, br) 350: GI (tr, b) 351: RHPL (bl), FLPA (b) 352: AKG (tl), Rex Features (tr), ©Andy Goldsworthy (cl), GI (b) 353: GI (tr), HL (br) 354: HL (cr), Spectrum Colour Library (br) 359: Zefa (tr) 361: RHPL (tr), AAA (c), Christie's Images (cr) 362: GI (tr) 365: Travel Ink (tl) 366: BAL (tr), Mary Evans Picture Library/Explorer 367: SPL (tl), AKG/©Salvador Dali – Fundacion Gala-Salvador Dali, DACS, London 1998 (cr) 368: OSF (bl) 369: NHPA (tr) 370: Zefa (tr) 371: Topham (tr) 375: Popper (b) 376: RHPL (cl, tr), GI 377: FS (bl), RHPL (cr) 378: South American Pictures (tr, cl, b) 379: HL (tl), South American Pictures (bl), Panos (b) 380: Panos (tl, b), South American Pictures (tr) 381: South American Pictures (tr, cr), HL (tr) 382: Panos (cr) 383: Panos (tl, c), HL (tr) 385: SPL (tr), Portfolio Pictures/NASA (bl) 386: SPL (cl, clb, bl) 388: GI (tr), HL (cl), RHPL 389: HL (b) 391: NHPA (tr) 392: Allsport (b) 393: Sporting Pictures (b) 394: SPL (cr) 396: SPL (tl), NHPA (b) 397: NHPA (tr) 398: SPL (tl), GI (tr) 400: HL (cl), Panos (bl) 402: AKG (tr), RHPL (b) 404: RHPL (cl, bl, br) 406: SPL (tr) 407: Zefa (tr) 408: Mary Evans Picture Library (tl), British Telecommunications plc (cr), Corbis (bl), Philips UK (br) 409: Corbis (br), GI (tr) 410: Panasonic UK Ltd (clb) 411: Simmons Ltd (tc), SPL (br) 412: Popper (tr) 413: AKG (tr), SPL (bl), RHPL (br) 418: Topham 419: Panos (cl), RGA (cr), RHPL (b) 420: GI (tr) 421: Panos (b), Corbis (cl) 424: SPL (tr) 425: FS (bl) 427: Telegraph Colour Library (tr) 428: Greyhound Ltd (tr) 429: GI (bl) 430: Popper (cl), RHPL (tr), BTA/Britain On View (b) 431: BTA/Britain On View (tl), HL (bl), RHPL 432: FS (cr), Popper (b) 433: Panos (tr), RHPL (bl, br) 434: RHPL (tl, cl), Zefa (br) 435: RHPL (cl, br) 436: RHPL (tl, cl), Corbis (cr), Redferns (b) 437: SPL (tl) 438: Popper (b) 439: Sanyo UK (tl), SPL (tr, cl), Sony (bl) 442: HL (tl) 446: Topham (br) 447: HL (tc) 448: Corbis (tl) 449: SPL (tr) 451: SPL (c) 452: SPL (br) 457: RHPL (tr), SPL (b) 459: NHPA (tc) 460: Corbis (b) 461: Corbis (cr), Popper (bl) 466: PE (br) 467: SPL (tr, bl) 468: Gaynor Worman/Marwell Zoo (br)

The publishers would also like to thank the following for their help in supplying information used as visual reference: 6–7: Boeing Aircraft Corporation (Boeing 747); 11: Zoological Society of London (fire salamander cutaway); 17: Geoscan Research (scanner); 19: Ove Arup & Partners (Sydney Opera House); 30–31: W.M. Keck Observatory (Keck observatory); 62–63: John Willoughby, The Mustang Owners Club of Great Britain, Selby (Mustang); 146: Fullwood Ltd (milking shed); 190: Bell Helicopter Textron (helicopter cutaway); 196: Dyson Appliances Ltd (Dyson vacuum cleaner cutaway); 198: The Hovercraft Museum Trust; 242–243: Otis plc, Ove Arup & Partners (lift); 252–253: Picker International Ltd, Siemens Medical Engineering (CAT scanner); 292: Nuclear Electric (nuclear reactor); 296: British Petroleum (platform); 297–299: Olympic Museum; 361: Balco Ltd (electroplating system); 410: British Telecom (telephone); 425: Ford Motor Company (people carrier).

Every effort has been made to trace the copyright holders of the photographs. The publishers apologize for any unavoidable omissions.

INTERNET LINKS

There are countless web sites that can help you research your area of interest. Below are some useful web sites

General
www.enchantedlearning.com
www.gridclub.com/info/index.html
www.infoplease.com/encyclopedia.html
http://about.com/homework

Earth
www.kids.earth.nasa.gov/site.htm

Continents and countries
www.cia.gov/cia/publications/factbook
www.cyberschoolbus.un.org/
    infonation/index.asp

Plant life
www.stemnet.nf.ca/CITE/rforest.htm

Animal life
www.worldwildlife.org/fun/kids.cfm
www.kidsplanet.org/factsheets/map.html

Human body
www.kidshealth.org/kid

Science and technology
www.bbc.co.uk/science
howstuffworks.lycoszone.com

Transportation
www.ltmuseum.co.uk

Construction and buildings
www.greatbuildings.com

History
www.historyforkids.org

Politics
www.whitehouse.gov/kids/news

Sport
www.library.thinkquest.org/10480

Religion
www.bbc.co.uk/religion

The arts and media
www.louvre.fr/anglais/fr_g.htm

People and cultures
www.library.thinkquest.org/J0111929

Space
www.starchild.gsfc.nasa.gov